DATE DUE

MY 29 '97			
DE 19 '97			
JL 1 '0			

Demco, Inc. 38-293

D

ORGANIZATION DEVELOPMENT AND TRANSFORMATION

Managing Effective Change

Edited by

Wendell L. French
Graduate School of Business Administration
University of Washington

Cecil H. Bell, Jr.
Graduate School of Business Administration
University of Washington

Robert A. Zawacki
Graduate School of Business Administration
University of Colorado
and
KPMG Peat Marwick

IRWIN

Burr Ridge, Illinois
Boston, Massachusetts
Sydney, Australia

Senior sponsoring editor: Kurt L. Strand
Editorial assistant: Michele Dooley
Marketing manager: Kurt Messersmith
Project editor: Susan Trentacosti
Production manager: Diane Palmer
Cover design: Laura L. Zawacki/Crispin Prebys
Art studio: Wm. C. Brown Publishing
Compositor: Graphic Sciences Corporation
Typeface: 10/12 Bembo
Printer: Malloy Lithographing, Inc.

Library of Congress Cataloging-in-Publication Data

Organization development and transformation : managing effective
    change / edited by Wendell L. French, Cecil H. Bell, Jr., Robert A.
    Zawacki. — 4th ed.
        p.   cm.
    3rd ed. published under title: Organization development.
    Includes bibliographical references.
    ISBN 0-256-10339-9
    1. Organizational change.   I. French, Wendell L., 1923-
    II. Bell, Cecil H., 1935-   III. Zawacki, Robert A.   IV. Title:
    Organization development.
    HD58.8.O724   1994
    658.4'06—dc20   93-38865

Printed in the United States of America
    3 4 5 6 7 8 9 0 ML 0 9 8 7 6 5

From Wendell to
Marjorie,

From Cecil to
Dianne,

From Bob to two
people who teach
a post graduate
course in change
to me every time
we revise this
book: Wendell
and Cecil.

The field of organization development continues to gain practitioners, clients, theorists, researchers, and new technologies. It has been applied in a wide range of settings and has become a preferred strategy for facilitating change in organizations. What began as isolated experiments for improving organizational dynamics and managerial practices in the 1950s has now become a coherent discipline of applied behavioral science practices to promote increased individual and organizational effectiveness. Organization development (or OD as it is called) provides a highly useful view of how people *and* organizations and people *in* organizations function, and what is required to make them function better.

This new edition adds two important new dimensions. One is the dimension of "organizational transformation," or large-scale, systemwide development, usually involving a paradigm shift. The paradigm shift might be a major redirection of the organization and/or a major reconceptualization of management philosophy and the leadership required for a high-performance empowering organization. The second added dimension is the application of OD approaches to total quality management (TQM) programs. We believe that OD approaches have a vital role to play in successful TQM efforts.

Organization development offers a prescription for improving the goodness of fit between an individual and the organization and between the organization and its environment. Ingredients of that prescription include a focus on the culture and processes of the organization; guidelines for designing and implementing action programs; conceptualizing the organization and its environment in system theory terms; and creating change processes that empower individuals through involvement, participation, and commitment.

OD is the applied domain of organizational psychology and sociology. It is the engineering side of the organizational sciences. Planned change involves common sense; hard work applied diligently over time; a systemic, goal-oriented approach; and valid knowledge about organizational dynamics and how to change them. The valid knowledge comes from basic and applied behavioral science. The total prescription comes from almost four decades of practice in discovering what works in organizations and why.

We think it is important to know how to help individuals and organizations function better in today's increasingly interdependent, complex, and competitive world. But a good road map is needed to get one to the destination of improved effectiveness. We have assembled this book of readings on theory, practice, and research in organization development and transformation to serve as a road map for you.

We wish to acknowledge our debt to the authors whose writings we have included. In addition, we wish to thank Anamarie Bourgeois for her outstanding work as our research assistant. A special "thank you" to Dean James T. Rothe for his financial support throughout this project.

Wendell L. French
Cecil H. Bell, Jr.
Robert A. Zawacki

CONTENTS

PART II

THE FOUNDATIONS OF OD: THEORY AND PRACTICE ON CHANGE IN ORGANIZATIONS

PART III

BASIC OD INTERVENTIONS

PART IV

CUTTING EDGE CHANGE STRATEGIES

Organization development (OD) is a powerful set of concepts and techniques for improving organizational effectiveness and individual well-being that had its genesis in the behavioral sciences and was tested in the laboratory of real-world organizations. OD addresses the opportunities and problems involved in managing human dynamics in organizations. It offers solutions that have been shown to work. Organization development consists of intervention techniques, theories, principles, and values that show how to take charge of planned change efforts and achieve success.

Organization transformation (OT) is a recent extension of organization development that seeks to create massive changes in an organization's structures, processes, culture, and orientation to its environment. Organization transformation is the application of behavioral science theory and practice to effect large-scale, paradigm-shifting organizational change. An organizational transformation usually results in totally new paradigms or models for organizing and performing work. Organization transformation has been referred to as "second-generation organization development." The demands on today's organizations for constant change and adaptation are so great that new behavioral science responses were required. OT represents one of those responses. But simultaneously improving organizational effectiveness and individual well-being is still the goal. Both OD and OT are means to accomplish that goal.

Understanding what OD is and how it is practiced is important for several reasons. First, it works. Organization development programs can improve individual performance, create better morale, and increase organizational profitability. Many chronic problems of organizations can be cured by OD techniques.

Second, the use of organization development is growing. The approach and methods of OD are applied throughout the gamut of today's organizations and industries. Manufacturing and service companies, high-technology and low-technology organizations, and public-and private-sector institutions all have sponsored successful OD programs.

Third, it is now recognized that the most important assets of organizations are human assets—the men and women who produce the goods and make the decisions. Finding ways to protect, enhance, and mobilize human assets doesn't just make good human-relations sense, it makes good economic sense. OD offers a variety of methods to strengthen the human side of organizations to the benefit of both the individual and the organization.

Fourth, OD is a critical managerial tool. We believe that the concepts and techniques of organization development will soon be as much a part of the well-trained manager's repertoire as knowledge of accounting, marketing, and finance. We predict that a significant period of transition lies just ahead in which the charter and boundaries of organization development will be expanded; specifically, the practice of OD will be incorporated within the art and science of management. Organization development offers a set of generic tools available to any managers and members of organizations who want to improve goal achievement. Today's managers manage change, and OD is a prescription for managing change. Managers need to know what OD is and how to use it. A good understanding of organization development has great practical value for present and future managers and leaders.

This collection of readings tells the story of OD's and OT's theory, practice, and research foundations. Articles by prominent authors in the field present a comprehensive portrait that we hope will be useful to managers, students of organizational dynamics, and professionals in the fields of human resource management and organization development and transformation.

The field of organization development is fun and exciting. We hope this anthology will convey some of that sense of excitement.

An Overview of the Book

This fourth edition is substantially different from its predecessors. The first edition contained 53 articles. The second edition contained 70 articles, including 44 new ones. The third edition contained 66 articles, with 24 new ones. The present edition contains 54 articles, with 28 new ones. This edition adds articles on large-scale system change, "visioning" interventions and models, Total Quality Management, self-directed teams, organization transformation, examples of change programs, and the underlying theory of organizational change. The field of organization development and transformation is evolving, and this anthology evolves with it.

Part I, Mapping the Territory, provides a foundation and an overview of the field. Early definitions and descriptions of organization development and a historical look at the origins of OD begin the story. Next, contemporary trends are identified. Finally, new ideas and directions are presented to complete the introductory picture. Part II, Foundations of OD: Theory and Practice on Change in Organizations, contains classic articles on change and changing. These readings emphasize the theoretical roots of planned change and human dynamics in organizations. The articles blend theory and practice—a hallmark of organization development practitioners. This section will help to "map the territory" for readers new to the field.

Most of the actual work in organization development consists of structuring sets of activities, called "interventions," so that learning or change takes place. OD interventions have been developed for diagnosis, role clarification, team building, conflict resolution, guiding the overall change program, and the like. Selected interventions are described in Part III, Basic OD Interventions. Part IV, Cutting Edge Change Strategies, presents some of the newest behavioral science approaches for improving individual and organizational effectiveness. All these articles are new to this edition. Exciting and efficacious change programs in organization development and transformation are being tested in organizations today. Self-directed teams, Total Quality Management, gainsharing, "learning organizations," and large-scale system change interventions all demonstrate the vitality of this ever-evolving field of applied behavioral science.

Part V, Effective Implementation of OD and OT, offers suggestions for increasing the chances that consultants and clients will be successful in their change programs. What are some of the ingredients of successful OD consulting? What are some of the critical success factors in managing a long-term change program? These questions are answered in this section.

Part VI contains Examples, Issues, and Challenges of OD and OT. Descriptions of organization development and organization transformation programs are presented, with the authors reflecting on what they did and why they did it. Next, such issues as ethics, values, and research are discussed. Finally, such challenges as diversity programs, competitiveness, and maintaining organizational effectiveness are examined.

The need for organization development and transformation has never been greater. We believe organization development offers a way to achieve organizational and individual effectiveness in a turbulent world. Again we express our thanks to the authors of these articles for their insights. The "present" is an exciting time, and organization development is an exciting field.

I Mapping the Territory

The subject matter of this book is organization development and transformation, a relatively specific kind of planned change effort aimed at helping members of organizations do the things they want to do—better. We have attempted to fashion a systematic examination of organization development to help the reader determine the applicability, utility, and viability of this particular approach as a means of organization improvement.

Organization development (OD) focuses primarily on the human and social aspects of organizations; it views organizational behavior as consisting essentially of the coordinated goal-directed activities of a number of people. Other possible approaches to understanding and intervening in organizations exist—one can focus exclusively on organization structure and design, technology and task design, or organization-environment congruence, for example. Organization development programs attend to these issues, but the principal emphasis is on *all* the human aspects of the organization conceived as a social system.

In Part I we begin at the beginning—mapping the territory of organization development and transformation. What is OD? What characteristics differentiate OD from other improvement programs? What are some of the varieties of OD and organization transformation (OT)?

Toward a Definition of Organization Development

The words *organization development* refer to something about organizations and developing them. According to Edgar Schein, "An organization is the planned coordination of the activities of a number of people for the achievement of some common explicit purpose or goal, through division of labor and function, and through a hierarchy of authority and responsibility."[1] Organizations are social

---

[1] Edgar H. Schein, *Organizational Psychology,* 3rd ed. (Englewood Cliffs, N.J.: Prentice Hall, 1980), p. 15.

systems possessing characteristics described by Schein, and OD efforts are directed toward organizations or major subparts of them.

Development is the act, process, result, or state of being developed—which, in turn, means to advance, to promote the growth of, to evolve the possibilities of, to further, to improve, or to enhance *something*. Two elements of this definition seem important: first, development may be an act, process, or end state; second, development refers to "bettering" something.

Combining these words suggests that organization development is the act, process, or result of furthering, advancing, or promoting the growth of an organization. According to these definitions, organization development is anything done to "better" an organization. But this definition is too broad and all-inclusive. It can refer to almost anything done in an organizational context that enhances the organization—hiring a person with needed skills, firing an incompetent, merging with another organization, installing a computer, removing a computer, buying a new plant, and so on. This definition serves neither to identify and specify nor to delimit (perhaps something done to "worsen" an organization would be ruled out). The term *organization development* must be given added meaning, must refer to something more specific, if productive discourse on the subject is desired.

Another way of defining organization development is to examine the following definitions, which have been suggested in the early OD literature:

> Organization development is an effort (1) *planned,* (2) *organizationwide,* and (3) *managed* from the *top,* to (4) *increase organization effectiveness* and *health* through (5) *planned interventions* in the organization's "processes," using *behavioral-science* knowledge.[2]

> *Organization development* (OD) is a response to change, a complex educational strategy intended to change the beliefs, attitudes, values, and structure of organizations so that they can better adapt to new technologies, markets, and challenges, and the dizzying rate of change itself.[3]

> *Organization development* is the strengthening of those human processes in organizations which improve the functioning of the organic system so as to achieve its objectives.[4]

> *Organization renewal* is the process of initiating, creating, and confronting needed changes so as to make it possible for organizations to become or remain viable, to adapt to new conditions, to solve problems, to learn from experiences, and to move toward greater organizational maturity.[5]

> OD can be defined as a planned and sustained effort to apply behavioral science for system improvement, using reflexive, self-analytic methods.[6]

> Organization development is a process of planned change—change of an organi-

---

[2] Richard Beckhard, *Organization Development: Strategies and Models* (Reading, Mass.: Addison-Wesley Publishing, 1969), p. 9.

[3] Warren G. Bennis, *Organization Development: Its Nature, Origins, and Prospects* (Reading, Mass.: Addison-Wesley Publishing, 1969), p. 2.

[4] Gordon L. Lippitt, *Organization Renewal* (New York: Appleton-Century-Crofts, 1969), p. 1.

[5] Ibid., p. 4.

[6] Richard Schmuck and Matthew Miles, *Organization Development in Schools* (Palo Alto, Calif.: National Press Books, 1971), p. 2.

zation's culture from one which avoids an examination of social processes (especially decision making, planning, and communication) to one which institutionalizes and legitimizes this examination.[7]

In the behavioral science, and perhaps ideal, sense of the term, *organization development is a long-range effort to improve an organization's problem-solving and renewal processes, particularly through a more effective and collaborative management of organization culture—with special emphasis on the culture of formal work teams—with the assistance of a change agent, or catalyst, and the use of the theory and technology of applied behavioral science, including action research.*[8] [Italics in the original.]

Analysis of these definitions suggests that organization development is *not* just "anything done to better an organization"; it is a particular kind of change process designed to bring about a particular kind of end result. In Figure 1 the definitions are dissected and put into an analytic framework to discover the particular kind of change processes and the particular kind of end results desired.

Examination of Figure 1 suggests the following conclusion. Organization development (OD) is a prescription for a process of planned change in organizations in which the key prescriptive elements relate to (1) the nature of the effort or program (it is a long-range, planned, systemwide process); (2) the nature of the change activities (they utilize behavioral science interventions of an educational, reflexive, self-examining, learn-to-do-it-yourself nature); (3) the targets of the change activities (it is directed toward the human and social processes of organizations, specifically individuals' beliefs, attitudes, and values, the culture and processes of work groups—viewed as basic building blocks of the organization—and the processes and culture of the total organization); and (4) the desired outcomes of the change activities (the goals are *needed changes* in the targets of the interventions that cause the organization to be better able to adapt, cope, solve its problems, and renew itself). Organization development thus represents a unique strategy for system change, a strategy largely based in the theory and research of the behavioral sciences, and a strategy having a substantial prescriptive character. Organization development is thus a normative discipline; it prescribes how planned change in organizations should be approached and carried out if organization improvement is to be obtained.

In summary, organization development is a process of planned system change that attempts to make organizations (viewed as social-technical systems) better able to attain their short-and long-term objectives. This is achieved by teaching the organization members to manage their organization processes, structures, and culture more effectively. Facts, concepts, and theory from the behavioral sciences are utilized to fashion both the process and the content of interventions. A basic belief of OD theorists and practitioners is that for effective, lasting change to take place, the system members must grow in the competence to master their own fates.

Let us examine in detail some of the distinguishing characteristics of OD.

---

[7] Warner Burke and Harvey A. Hornstein, *The Social Technology of Organization Development* (Fairfax, Va.: Learning Resources Corp., 1972), p. xi.

[8] Wendell L. French and Cecil H. Bell, Jr., *Organization Development*, 2nd ed. (Englewood Cliffs, N.J.: Prentice Hall, 1978), p. 14.

FIGURE 1

An analysis of selected definitions of organization development

Components of the Organization Development Process

Author	Nature and Scope of the Effort	Nature of Activities/Interventions	Targets of Interaction/Activities	Knowledge Base	Desired Goals, Outcomes, or End States of Organization Development Effort
Beckard	Planned. Organizationwide. Managed from the top.	Planned interventions in the organization's "processes."	Total organization. Organization's "processes."	Behavioral science knowledge.	Increased organization effectiveness and health.
Bennis	Complex educational strategy. A response to change.	Educational. Change-oriented.	Beliefs, attitudes, values, and structures of organizations.		Better ability to adapt to new technologies, markets, and challenges, and the dizzying rate of change itself.
Gordon Lippitt (on OD)		Designed to strengthen human processes in organizations.	Those human processes in organizations that improve the organic system.		Enable the organization to achieve its objectives (through improved functioning of the organic system).
Gordon Lippitt (on organization renewal)	A process.	A process of initiating, creating and confronting needed changes.	[Implied] total organization.		Enhance the ability of the organization to: Become or remain viable. Adapt to new conditions. Solve problems. Learn from experience. Move toward greater organizational maturity.

Schmuck and Miles	A planned and sustained effort.	Apply behavioral science for system improvement. Using reflexive, self-analytic methods.	Total system (organization).	Behavioral science.	System improvement. [implied] continued self-analysis and reflection.
Burke and Hornstein	A process of planned change.	Change-oriented and self-examining oriented; specifically change of an organization's culture from one which avoids an examination of social processes in organization . . . to one which institutionalizes and legitimizes this examination.	The organization's culture and the social processes in organization, especially decision making, planning, and communication.		[Self-examination] of social processes in organization, especially decision making, planning, and communication.
French and Bell	A long-range effort.	Designed to bring about a more effective and collaborative management of organization culture; using assistance of change agent, or catalyst.	Organization culture. Culture of formal work teams. Organization's problem-solving and renewal processes.	The theory and technology of applied behavioral science, including action research.	Improve an organization's problem-solving and renewal processes.

Distinguishing Characteristics of Organization Development

Perusal of the many descriptions and definitions of organization development in the literature leads to the conclusion that most authors believe OD is a unique change strategy possessing the characteristics described in this section. Two of us (Wendell and Cecil) have been concerned with the issue of identifying and specifying the nature of organization development for some time now. In an earlier publication we stated:

> We see eight characteristics that we think differentiate organization development interventions from more traditional interventions:
>
> 1. An emphasis, although not exclusively so, on group and organizational processes in contrast to substantive content.
> 2. An emphasis on the work team as the key unit for learning more effective modes of organizational behavior.
> 3. An emphasis on the collaborative management of work-team culture.
> 4. An emphasis on the management of the culture of the total system.
> 5. Attention to the management of system ramifications.
> 6. The use of the action research model.
> 7. The use of a behavioral scientist-change agent, sometimes referred to as a "catalyst" or "facilitator."
> 8. A view of the change effort as an ongoing process.
>
> Another characteristic, number 9, a primary emphasis on human and social relationships, does not necessarily differentiate OD from other change efforts, but it is nevertheless an important feature.[9]

While we still believe these characteristics describe organization development efforts, let us add another means of identifying OD.

An Organization Development Program Is a Long-Range, Planned, and Sustained Effort that Unfolds According to a Strategy

The key elements here are long range, planned and sustained, and strategy. There is a long-range time perspective on the part of both the client system and the consultant in OD programs. Both parties envision an ongoing relationship of one, two, or more years together if things go well in the program. A one-shot intervention into the system is thus not organization development according to this criterion, even though the intervention may be one that is used in OD efforts. Thus the dozens of case studies reporting a three-day or week-long T-group (T for training) experience for system members do not constitute OD as we see it, if the T-group experience was the only intervention of the program.

The reasons for OD practitioners and theorists conceptualizing OD pro-

---

[9] Ibid., p. 18.

grams in long-range terms are several. First, changing a system's culture and processes is a difficult, complicated, and long-term matter if lasting change is to be effected. OD programs envision that the system members become better able to manage their culture and processes in problem-solving and self-renewing ways. Such complex new learning takes time. Second, the assumption is made that organizational problems are multifaceted and complex. One-shot interventions probably cannot solve such problems, and they most assuredly cannot teach the client system to solve them in such a short time period.

OD programs are planned and sustained efforts. They are planned, not accidental—they represent a deliberate entry of either an OD consultant or OD activities into the client system. And they are sustained. The assumption is made that follow-up and sustained effort and energy are needed in order to solve organization problems. These points are fairly straightforward. There is, however, a related point that is a source of some confusion. When some good management practices are taking place in an organization without an OD program—for example, a manager has worked out effective ways to manage team and intergroup culture and processes—is that organization development? We do not think so. OD practitioners try to inculcate good management practices in organizations; that is, they try to help organization members learn to manage themselves and others better. But many managers and many organizations are competently managing their affairs without help from organization development consultants and OD programs; what they are doing would not be called OD even though they may be using some techniques found in the OD technology. OD practitioners did not invent good management practices; OD practitioners are not the sole source for learning good management practices; and finally, the term *organization development* is not synonymous with the term *good management*.

Organization development programs unfold according to a strategy. A part of the planned nature of OD programs almost always involves an overall strategy even though the strategy may be only dimly obvious and articulable, and even though the strategy may emerge and change shape over time. (From our experience, the more viable OD efforts have a fairly clear and openly articulated strategy.) Consultants and clients develop overall goals and paths to goals in organization development programs, and these guide the programmatic activities. It is preferable and usual for the strategy to be developed out of the diagnosed problems and opportunities of the client system, the client system's desires and capabilities, and the consultant's capabilities and insights into client system needs.

The Organization Development Consultant Establishes a Unique Relationship with Client System Members

Probably the most fundamental differences between organization development programs and other organization improvement programs are found in the role and behavior of the consultant vis-à-vis the client system. In OD the consultant seeks and maintains a collaborative relationship of relative equality with the organization members. Collaboration means "to labor together"—essentially it implies that the consultant does not do all the work while the client system passively waits for solutions to its problems; and it means that the client system does not do all the work while the consultant is a disinterested observer. In organization development, consultant and client co-labor.

A second distinguishing feature of the consultant-client relationship is that it is one of relative equality—the two parties come together as relative equals, each possessing knowledge and skills different from but needed by the other. The client group is encouraged to critique the consultant's program and his or her effectiveness in terms of meeting client system needs and wants. In OD the consultant's role is generally that of a facilitator, not an expert on matters of content; the consultant acts primarily as a question-asker, and secondarily as an answer-giver.

The consultant's role is often described as nondirective and that is partially true, but the rationale behind this nondirective posture is less well understood. The OD consultant role rests on three beliefs. The first belief is simply an affirmation of the efficacy of division of labor and responsibility: let the consultant be responsible for doing what he or she does best (structuring activities designed to solve certain problems); and let the client system do what it does best (bring to bear its special knowledge and expertise on the problem and alternative solutions). The second belief is derived from the question: Where is the best solution to this problem likely to be found? In situations where the consultant is in an expert role, the answer to the question is that the best solution is in the consultant's head due to that person's education, experience, and expertise. Both clients and consultant believe this. In organization development situations where the consultant is playing an enabling and facilitating role, the answer is that the best solution is in the heads of the client members and the challenge is to structure situations to allow it to become known. The third belief is that the responsibility for changing something rests ultimately in the client system members, not in the consultant. Therefore the members of the client system must "own" the problem and the solution, and that is best done when they generate both the problems and the solutions. This belief no doubt rests on Lewin's conceptualization of "own" and "induced" forces. Lewin believed, and demonstrated, that an individual's own forces toward a particular behavior were more powerful in determining the behavior than forces/motives/pushes induced by some outside agent.

The consultant is both expert and directive on matters relating to the best ways to facilitate/enable the client group to approach, diagnose, and solve its problems. In organization development, it is this expertise that the clients expect from the consultant—the expertise to offer the clients effective *ways* to work on problems, not *answers* to problems.

The Nature of the Intervention Activities Differentiates OD from Other Improvement Strategies

OD consultants fashion, conduct, or cause to happen, interventions—structured sets of activities and events in the life of the organization designed to achieve certain outcomes. As indicated in Figure 1, the nature of these interventions is that they are reflective, self-analytical, self-examining, proactive, diagnostically oriented, and action oriented. Further, they focus on the organization culture and its human processes. OD consultants try to inculcate diagnostic skills, self-analytical skills, and reflexive skills in organization members, based on the belief that the organization's members must be able to diagnose situations accurately in order to arrive at successful solutions. But there are several additional beliefs hidden in this statement. Diagnosis and self-reflection are necessary skills to have for problem solution—that is a belief of OD consultants. But *who* should possess those skills? "The client system members," answer OD consultants; "me," answer expert consultants. This is a key difference in the OD prescription. Another belief involved here is the belief that both the problems and the solutions to the problems abound in the client system members. Teaching the client system to diagnose and solve problems and take corrective actions is the goal of the OD consultant. The overriding goal is that the client system members learn to do it themselves. This tenet derives from nondirective therapy notions suggesting that responsibility for improvement and change rests in the individual (organization) that needs to change, not some outside agent. This is supported by most discussions of normalcy and maturity in psychotherapy that include the patient's ability to solve problems, adapt effectively, and cope effectively as criteria for a healthy organism. Many authors, including Gordon Lippitt, speak of the organization "learning from experience," and the OD literature suggests that "learning how to learn" is a desired outcome of OD interventions. This is what is being discussed: that the client system become expert in self-examination, diagnosis, and corrective action taking.

Planning, problem solving, and self-renewal are also mentioned as important processes for the client system to be reflexive about. The same overriding goal applies here: the client system members must learn to manage these processes effectively by themselves. There is thus a unique character to the nature of OD interventions: the intent that the client system becomes proficient in solving its own problems—present and future—*by itself.* The ancient Chinese proverb seems to describe the underlying rationale: "Give a man a fish, and you have given him a meal; teach a man to fish, and you have given him a livelihood."

The Targets of OD Interventions Differentiate OD from Other Improvement Strategies

The OD prescription calls for certain configurations of people as targets of OD interventions—intact work groups, two or more work-related groups, subsystems of organizations, and total organizations. Katz and Kahn speak of "role sets," the offices (positions) and people an individual interacts with while performing role-relevant behavior in an organization. They state:

> Each member of an organization is directly associated with a relatively small number of others, usually the occupants of offices adjacent to his in the work-flow structure

or in the hierarchy of authority. They constitute his role set and typically include his immediate supervisor (and perhaps his supervisor's immediate superior), his subordinates, and certain members of his own or other departments with whom he must work closely. These offices are defined into his role set by virtue of the work-flow, technology, and authority structure of the organization.[10]

Many of an individual's values, norms, and perceptions of organization reality are derived from contact with role-set members. Role-enactment problems derive from interaction with role-set members. A person's immediate work group, immediate superior, and immediate subordinates are immensely important factors for an individual's effectiveness in an organization. OD interventions concentrate on work-relevant constellations of people in the belief that these groups have inherent in them considerable power to determine individual and group behavior and also contain many of the sources of organizational problems and opportunities.

What goes on *between* units is also of vital importance in organizational effectiveness. OD goes beyond intact work teams and also focuses on enhancing key interdependencies across units and levels. For example, data are typically collected about the degree of cooperation versus dysfunctional competition between the various units, and identified problems are then worked on with members of the relevant groups present. Thus intergroup configurations are a second major target of OD interventions.

A third target of OD interventions is the organization's processes and culture. In a sense, OD is a comprehensive long-term effort to collaboratively manage the culture of an organization (since processes can be considered part of organization culture). As shown in Figure 1, some of the authors mention culture and some of the authors mention human and social processes as the targets of OD interventions. Problem-solving, planning, self-renewal, decision-making, and communications processes are identified as important processes. This focus on culture and processes is simply a part of the bet/hypothesis/belief system that OD consultants have: culture and processes are important strategic leverage points in an organization for bringing about organization improvement and change. Other consultants and practitioners make different bets on the best strategic leverage points—the technology of the organization, the strategy of the organization, its design, and so forth. OD consultants, because they are working with a behavioral science knowledge base, focus on culture, structure and processes. And the OD prescription suggests that these targets are important ingredients in the process of planned organizational change.

OD Consultants Utilize a Behavioral Science Base

This is a characteristic of the practice of OD, but it is shared by many different improvement strategies. We will not discuss this point extensively. Perhaps it is

---

[10] Daniel Katz and Robert L. Kahn, *The Social Psychology of Organizations* (New York: John Wiley & Sons, 1966), p. 174.

sufficient to say that the behavioral science knowledge base of the practice of OD contributes to its distinctive gestalt. OD is an applied field in which theories, concepts, and practices from sociology, psychology, social psychology, education, economics, psychiatry, and management are brought to bear on real organizational problems.

The Desired Outcomes of OD Are Distinctive in Nature

The desired outcomes of OD efforts are both similar to other improvement strategies, and different from other improvement strategies. OD programs and efforts are designed to produce organizational effectiveness and health, better system functioning, greater ability to achieve objectives, and so forth, as shown in some of the definitions in Figure 1. But some of the definitions point to additional desired outcomes: outcomes relating to a changed organization culture, to changed processes (especially renewal and adaptation processes) and to the establishing of norms of continual self-study and proaction.

Michael Beer lists the aims of OD as: "(1) enhancing congruence between organizational structure, processes, strategy, people, and culture; (2) developing new and creative organizational solutions; and (3) developing the organization's self-renewing capacity."[11] It is these self-renewal outcomes that seem particularly distinctive in the OD process.

Summary of the Distinctive Features of Organization Development

We believe that organization development is a particular kind of organization improvement strategy possessing distinguishing characteristics as follows:

1. An OD program is a long-range, planned, and sustained effort that is based on an overall strategy.
2. A consultant (one or more) is used, and that consultant establishes a unique relationship with the client system: the consultant seeks and maintains a collaborative relationship of relative equality with the organization members.
3. OD interventions are distinctive in their nature: they are reflexive, self-analytical, self-skill-building in nature. Another way of saying this is that a pervasive use of a collaborative action-research model underlies most OD interventions.
4. OD interventions assume that work-related groups of individuals and work-related intergroup configurations are more important leverage

---

[11] Michael Beer, *Organization Change and Development* (Santa Monica, Calif.: Goodyear Publishing, 1980), p. 10.

points for change than are other configurations, and also assume that organization culture and organizational processes are strategic leverage points for effecting organizational change.

5. OD utilizes a behavioral science base.

6. The desired outcomes of organizational effectiveness and health are supplemented in OD with the goal that organization culture and processes be changed in order that the organization continue to be reflexive and self-examining.

This overview provides a broad outline of the field. The rest of the book will expand on these themes, will add details and implications, and will make clearer what organization development is and what it can do.

The Emergence of Organization Transformation (OT)

The preceding discussion describes "classical" organization development, which began in the mid-1950s and continues to the present. Over the years the practice of OD has evolved and matured, clarifying its values, theories, methods, and interventions, as well as adding new values, theories, and so forth. Beginning in the 1980s, articles and books appeared that described change programs designed to cause large-scale, radical, and fundamental changes in organizations. These paradigm-shifting changes were referred to as "organization transformation" or "organizational transformation." Some authors believe OT is an extension of OD; others believe OT represents a new discipline in its own right. It is too early to categorize organization transformation; for now, we see it as an extension of OD. Some forces leading to the emergence of OT can be identified, however.

In the 1960s and 1970s OD focused on improving the internal workings of organizations through the use of role clarification, improved communication, team building, intergroup team building, and the like. The organization was conceptualized as an open system in interaction with its environment, but primary attention was directed toward making the parts and the whole function better. In the 1970s new work arrangements were tested in the form of sociotechnical systems theory experiments and Quality of Work Life experiments. Sociotechnical systems theory (STS) postulates that an organization is comprised of both a social system and a technical system, and that these two systems must be jointly optimized for best results.[12] One result of STS experimentation was the discovery that "autonomous work groups" (similar to today's self-managed teams and self-directed teams) constituted a better working arrangement than the usual isolated individuals with a boss to tell them what to do. This was an important

---

[12] E. Trist and K. Bamforth, "Some Social and Psychological Consequences of the Longwall Method of Coal-Getting," *Human Relations* 4 (January 1951), pp. 1–38.

discovery, and autonomous work groups and self-managed teams proliferated in a variety of settings. Quality of Work Life experiments led to similar discoveries about the value of self-directed teams, and they additionally produced new ways for labor and management to work together to lessen adversarial relations.[13] These experiments and others in work redesign and reorganization called into question old paradigms (beliefs and assumptions) about working arrangements and authority relations in organizations.

In the 1980s Strategic Management achieved prominence in managerial thinking, and attention was directed toward the fit between the environment with its "threats" and "opportunities" and the organization with its "strengths" and "weaknesses." Considerable effort was directed toward defining the mission, purpose, vision, and strategy of organizations. OD practitioners developed interventions to facilitate Strategic Management by the organization's executives. It was soon realized that a clear, articulated vision was a powerful component of organizational effectiveness.

Also in the 1980s the demands on organizations intensified: competition increased; customers demanded better products and services; the Total Quality movement created winners and losers; information technology exploded; economic and political changes occurred. Organizations had to change—fast—to survive. The old ways of doing things were no longer good enough; the old belief systems were no longer adequate. Organizations had to be transformed, not just "tweaked." Paradigms had to be changed, not just adjusted. All these conditions and more gave rise to explorations in the theory and practice of organization transformation.

Porras and Silvers state in Reading 6: "Planned change interventions can be divided into two general types. The first comprises the more traditional approach, Organization Development (OD), which until recently was synonymous with the term *planned change.* The second, Organization Transformation (OT), is the cutting edge of planned change and may be called 'second generation OD.'" These authors emphasize the importance of "vision," "guiding beliefs and principles," "purpose," and "mission" as major features of OT interventions.

Cummings and Worley describe OT as follows:

> Organization transformations can occur in response to or in anticipation of major changes in the organization's environment or technology. In addition, these changes are often associated with significant alterations in the firm's business strategy, which, in turn, may require modifying corporate culture as well as internal structures and processes to support the new direction. Such fundamental change entails a new paradigm for organizing and managing organizations. It involves qualitatively different ways of perceiving, thinking, and behaving in organizations.[14]

---

[13] R. E. Walton, "Quality of Working Life: What Is It?" *Sloan Management Review,* Fall 1973, pp. 11–21.

[14] T. G. Cummings and C. G. Worley, *Organization Development and Change,* 5th ed. (Minneapolis, Minn.: West Publishing Co., 1993), p. 520.

They suggest three interventions to facilitate organization transformations: culture change, strategic change, and self-designing organizations.

Clearly the phenomenon of organization transformation is important, real, and here to stay. The task for OD and OT practitioners is to develop behavioral science theories, models, practices, and interventions to facilitate the transformations.

Readings in Part I

The readings in this section range from early statements about the nature and characteristics of organization development to recent articles describing both OD and organization transformation.

The first selection is by Richard Beckhard, an early OD practitioner and theorist. Beckhard asks and answers the question: What is Organization Development? His operational definition, operational goals of OD, and characteristics of OD efforts combine to make this one of the best statements available on what OD is all about. He is pithy, to the point, and right on target. He identifies several distinguishing features about OD that are not found in other organizational change approaches. This selection is taken from his little book titled *Organization Development: Strategies and Models* that appeared in 1969. In that year Addison-Wesley Publishing Company published six little paperback books on OD, all packaged together. These came to be known as "The Addison-Wesley OD Six Pack" among practitioners. Collectively these books defined the field of OD at that time. Other authors and titles in the "Six Pack" were Warren Bennis, *Organization Development: Its Nature, Origins, and Prospects;* Paul Lawrence and Jay Lorsch, *Developing Organizations: Diagnosis and Action;* Edgar Schein, *Process Consultation: Its Role in Organization Development;* Richard Walton, *Interpersonal Peacemaking: Confrontations and Third-Party Consultation;* and Robert Blake and Jane Srygley Mouton, *Building a Dynamic Corporation through Grid Organization Development.*

The roots, birth, and major milestones in the development of the field of organization development are described in the next article. Wendell French has been intrigued with tracing the history of OD for many years. The selection was written by him; it appears in a book on organization development by Wendell French and Cecil Bell.[15] French points to the importance of Kurt Lewin as a prime contributor to events leading up to the emergence of OD, and to three mainstreams of activities as precursors of OD—laboratory training, survey research and feedback, and action research. Early projects and the people involved in them are described, using as source materials both published accounts and extensive correspondence with the individuals who were in the forefront of the new applied behavioral science developments at that time—Robert Blake, Herbert Shepard, Ronald Lippitt, Richard Beckhard, and others.

---

[15] Wendell L. French and Cecil H. Bell, Jr., *Organization Development: Behavioral Science Interventions for Organizational Improvement,* 4th ed. (Englewood Cliffs, N.J.: Prentice Hall, 1990).

An article on the history of OD by Michael McGill, not included in this reader, gives a somewhat different view of early events.[16] McGill goes back to just after World War II to search for the beginnings of OD and, in so doing, finds reason to include the activities, writings, and conceptualizations of Leland Bradford and Neely Gardner as important foundations. Both Leland Bradford and Neely Gardner were engaged in training and development activities in large organizations and conceived the necessity to develop *both* the individual and the organization. Bradford has been intimately involved with most of the applied behavioral science developments in the United States because he was the director of the National Training Laboratory in Group Development (NTL) from its inception in 1947 to his retirement in 1970. NTL (now the NTL—Institute for Applied Behavioral Science) was both a source of support for the fledgling organization development movement and also a source of most of the OD practitioners.[17]

Marshall Sashkin and Warner Burke survey the trends in organization development in the 1980s in the third and fourth articles in this section. They note the increased importance of structural interventions and the rising importance of organizational culture as targets of OD theory and practice. Structural interventions relate to both redesigning work arrangements (work tasks) and redesigning total organizational forms. Advances in these areas have come from Quality of Work Life practitioners and from sociotechnical systems theory practitioners. Organizational culture is receiving increased attention because it is such a powerful determiner of individual behavior. The authors make some predictions about the future—or at least present some possible scenarios. These are excellent summaries of what was happening in the field of OD in the mid and late 1980s. These authors believe that "OD is entering an exciting and productive new area of maturity and achievement." Stay tuned for late-breaking developments!

The selection by Marvin Weisbord sets the stage for thinking about organization transformations and how a consultant can help. Weisbord is pondering the differences between traditional organization development thinking and practice and the thinking and practice required in a "third-wave" world as described by futurist Alvin Toffler. New times require new paradigms. Weisbord supplies some. His "four useful practices" suggest new ways consultants can facilitate organization transformation. His discussion of the "four-room apartment" provides great insights. These are important issues for leaders, managers, and OD consultants.

The final selection in this section, by Porras and Silvers, is taken from the *Annual Review of Psychology.* About every four years the latest developments in the field of OD (and now, OT) are summarized by prominent theorists/practitioners in this publication. This article represents the first time that organization trans-

---

[16] Michael E. McGill, "The Evolution of Organization Development: 1947–1960," *Public Administration Review,* March–April 1974, pp. 98–105.

[17] Leland P. Bradford, *National Training Laboratories—Its History: 1947–1970.* Copyright 1974 by Leland P. Bradford, Bethel, Maine.

formation has been featured. An especially important contribution of this reading is its model of planned change. Organization development and transformation need better theoretical underpinnings, and this article begins to address that deficiency. The Porras and Silvers selection presents the latest research and thinking in the field of organization development and transformation.

These selections should give the reader a good foundation for understanding what organization development and transformation are all about. Future sections of the book elaborate on these foundations.

READING 1
WHAT IS ORGANIZATION DEVELOPMENT?

Richard Beckhard

Definition. Organization development is an effort (1) *planned,* (2) *organizationwide,* and (3) *managed* from the *top,* to (4) increase *organization effectiveness* and *health* through (5) *planned interventions in* the organization's "processes," using *behavioral-science* knowledge.

1. It is a *planned change* effort.

An OD program involves a systematic diagnosis of the organization, the development of a strategic plan for improvement, and the mobilization of resources to carry out the effort.

2. It involves the total "*system.*"

An organization development effort is related to a total organization change such as a change in the culture or the reward systems or the total managerial strategy. There may be tactical efforts which work with subparts of the organization but the "system" to be changed is a total, relatively autonomous organization. This is not necessarily a total corporation, or an entire government, but refers to a system which is relatively free to determine its own plans and future within very *general* constraints from the environment.

3. *It is managed from the top.*

In an organization development effort, the top management of the system has a personal investment in the program and its outcomes. They actively participate in the *management* of the effort. This does not mean they must participate in the same *activities* as others, but it does mean that they must have both knowledge and *commitment*

Source: Richard Beckhard, *Organization Development: Strategies and Models* (Reading, Mass.: Addison-Wesley Publishing, 1969), pp. 9, 10, 14. Reprinted with permission.

to the goals of the program and must actively support the methods used to achieve the goals.

4. It is designed to *increase organization effectiveness* and *health.*

To understand the goals of organization development, it is necessary to have some picture of what an "ideal" effective, healthy organization would look like. What would be its characteristics? Numbers of writers and practitioners in the field have proposed definitions which, although they differ in detail, indicate a strong consensus of what a healthy operating organization is. Let me start with my own definition. An effective organization is one in which:

a. The total organization, the significant subparts, and individuals, manage their work against *goals* and *plans* for achievement of these goals.

b. Forms follows function (the problem, or task, or project, determines how the human resources are organized).

c. Decisions are made by and near the sources of information regardless of where these sources are located on the organization chart.

d. The reward system is such that managers and supervisors are rewarded (and punished) comparably for:
   Short-term profit or production performance.
   Growth and development of their subordinates.
   Creating a viable working group.

e. Communication laterally and vertically is *relatively* undistorted. People are generally open and confronting. They share all the relevant facts including feelings.

f. There is a minimum amount of inappropriate win/lose activities between individuals and groups. Constant effort exists at all levels to treat conflict, and conflict situations, as *problems* subject to problem-solving methods.

g. There is high "conflict" (clash of ideas) about tasks and projects, and relatively little energy spent in clashing over *interpersonal* difficulties because they have been generally worked through.

h. The organization and its parts see themselves as interacting with each other *and* with a *larger* environment. The organization is an "open system."

i. There is a shared value, and management strategy to support it, of trying to help each person (or unit) in the organization maintain his (or its) integrity and uniqueness in an interdependent environment.

j. The organization and its members operate in an "action-research" way. General practice is to build in *feedback mechanisms* so that individuals and groups can learn from their own experience.

Another definition is found in John Gardner's set of rules for an effective organization. He describes an effective organization as one which is *self-renewing* and then lists the rules:

The *first rule* is that the organization must have an effective program for the recruitment and development of talent.

The *second rule* for the organization capable of continuous renewal is that it must be a hospitable environment for the individual.

The *third rule* is that the organization must have built-in provisions for self-criticism.

The *fourth rule* is that there must be fluidity in the internal structure.

The *fifth rule* is that the organization must

have some means of combating the process by which men become prisoners of their procedures.[1]

Edgar Schein defines organization effectiveness in relation to what he calls "the adaptive coping cycle," that is, an organization that can effectively adapt and cope with the changes in its environment. Specifically, he says:

The sequence of activities or processes which begins with some change in the internal or external environment and ends with a more adaptive, dynamic equilibrium for dealing with the change, is the organization's "adaptive coping cycle." If we identify the various stages or processes of this cycle, we shall also be able to identify the points where organizations typically may fail to cope adequately and where, therefore, consultants and researchers have been able in a variety of ways to help increase organization effectiveness.[2]

The organization conditions necessary for effective coping, according to Schein, are:

The ability to take in and communicate information reliably and validly.

Internal flexibility and creativity to make the changes which are demanded by the information obtained (including structural flexibility).

Integration and commitment to the goals of the organization from which comes the willingness to change.

An internal climate of support and freedom from threat, since being threatened undermines good communication, reduces flexibility, and stimulates self-protection rather than concern for the total system.

Miles et al. (1966) define the healthy organization in three broad areas—those concerned

[1] J. W. Gardner, "How to Prevent Organizational Dry Rot," *Harper's Magazine,* October 1965.

[2] E. H. Schein, *Organizational Psychology* (Englewood Cliffs, NJ: Prentice Hall, 1965.

with task accomplishment, those concerned with internal integration, and those involving mutual adaptation of the organization and its environment. The following dimensional conditions are listed for each area:

> In the task-accomplishment area, a healthy organization would be one with (1) reasonably clear, accepted, achievable and appropriate goals; (2) relatively understood communications flow; (3) optimal power equalization.

> In the area of internal integration, a healthy organization would be one with (4) resource utilization and individuals' *good fit* between personal disposition and role demands; (5) a reasonable degree of cohesiveness and "organization identity," clear and attractive enough so that persons feel actively connected to it; (6) high morale. In order to have growth and active changefulness, a healthy organization would be one with innovativeness, autonomy, adaptation, and problem-solving adequacy.[3]

Lou Morse, in his recent thesis on organization development, writes that:

> The commonality of goals are cooperative group relations, consensus, integration, and commitment to the goals of the organization (task accomplishment), creativity, authentic behavior, freedom from threat, full utilization of a person's capabilities, and organizational flexibility.[4]

5. Organization development achieves its goals through *planned interventions* using behavioral science knowledge.

A strategy is developed of intervening or moving into the existing organization and help-

---

[3] M. B. Miles et al., "Data Feedback and Organization Change in a School System." (Paper given at a meeting of the American Sociological Association, August 27, 1966.)

[4] L. H. Morse, "Task-Centered Organization Development." (Master's thesis, Sloan School of Management, MIT, June 1968.)

ing it, in effect, "stop the music," examine its present ways of work, norms, and values, and look at alternative ways of working, or relating, or rewarding. . . . The interventions used draw on the knowledge and technology of the behavioral sciences about such processes as individual motivation, power, communications, perception, cultural norms, problem solving, goal setting, interpersonal relationships, intergroup relationships, and conflict management.

Some Operational Goals in an Organization-Development Effort

To move toward the kind of organization conditions described in the above definitions, OD efforts usually have some of the following operational goals:

1. To develop a self-renewing, *viable system* that can organize in a variety of ways depending on tasks. This means systematic efforts to change and loosen up the way the organization operates, so that it organizes differently depending on the nature of the task. There is movement toward a concept of "form follows function," rather than that *tasks* must *fit* into existing structures.

2. To optimize the effectiveness of both the stable (the basic organization chart) and the temporary systems (the many projects, committees, et cetera, through which much of the organization's work is accomplished) by built-in, *continuous improvement mechanisms*. This means the introduction of procedures for analyzing work tasks and resource distribution, and for building in continuous "feedback" regarding the way a system or subsystem is operating.

3. To move toward *high collaboration* and *low competition* between interdependent units. One of the major obstacles to effective organizations is the amount of dysfunctional energy spent in inappropriate competition—energy that is not, therefore, available for the accomplishment of tasks. If all of the energy that is used by, let's say, manufacturing people disliking or wanting to "get those sales people," or vice versa, were

available to improve organization output, productivity would increase tremendously.

4. To create conditions where conflict is brought out and managed. One of the fundamental problems in unhealthy (or less than healthy) organizations is the amount of energy that is dysfunctionally used trying to work around, or avoid, or cover up, conflicts which are inevitable in a complex organization. The goal is to move the organization towards seeing conflict as an inevitable condition and as problems that need to be *worked* before adequate decisions can be made.

5. To reach the point where decisions are made on the basis of information source rather than organizational role. This means the need to move toward a *norm* of the *authority of knowledge* as well as the authority of role. It does not only mean that decisions should be moved down in the organization; it means that the organization manager should determine which is the best source of information (or combination of sources of information) to work a particular problem, and it is there that the decision making should be located.

READING 2
A HISTORY OF ORGANIZATION DEVELOPMENT

Wendell L. French and Cecil H. Bell, Jr.

The history of organization development is rich with the contributions of behavioral scientists and practitioners, many of whom are well known, and the contributions of many people in client organizations. Even if we were aware of all the significant contributors, which we are not, we could not do justice to the richness of this history in a short essay. Therefore, all we can do is write about what we believe to be the central thrusts of that history based on our research to date and hope that the many people who are not mentioned will not be offended by our incompleteness.

Systematic organization development activities have a recent history and, to use the analogy of a mangrove tree, have at least three important trunk stems. One trunk stem of OD consists of innovations in the application of laboratory training insights to complex organizations. A second major stem is survey research and feedback methodology. Both stems are intertwined with a third stem, the emergence of action research. Paralleling these stems, and to some extent linked, was the emergence of the Tavistock sociotechnical and socioclinical approaches. The key actors focused upon in this account interacted with each other and were influenced by experiences and concepts from many fields, as we will see.

The Laboratory Training Stem

The T-Group.   One stem of OD, laboratory training, essentially unstructured small-group sit-

Source: Wendell L. French and Cecil H. Bell, Jr., *Organization Development: Behavioral Science Interventions for Organization Improvement,* 3rd ed. (Englewood Cliffs, NJ: Prentice Hall), pp. 24–44. Copyright © 1984. Reprinted by permission of Prentice Hall.

uations in which participants learn from their own interactions and the evolving dynamics of the group, began to develop in about 1946 from various experiments in the use of discussion groups to achieve changes in behavior in back-home situations. In particular, an Inter-Group Relations workshop held at the State Teachers College in New Britain, Connecticut, in the summer of 1946 was important in the emergence of laboratory training. This workshop was sponsored by the Connecticut Interracial Commission and the Research Center for Group Dynamics, then at MIT.

The Research Center for Group Dynamics (RCGD) had been founded in 1945 under the direction of Kurt Lewin, a prolific theorist, researcher, and practitioner in interpersonal, group, intergroup, and community relationships.[1] Lewin had been recruited to MIT largely through the efforts of Douglas McGregor of the Sloan School of Management who had convinced MIT President Carl Compton of the wisdom of establishing a center for group dynamics. Lewin's original staff included Marian Radke, Leon Festinger, Ronald Lippitt, and Dorwin Cartwright.[2] Lewin's field theory and his conceptualizing about group dynamics, change processes, and action research were of profound influence on the people who were associated with the various stems of OD.

The staff for the New Britain Workshop of 1946 consisted of Kurt Lewin, Kenneth Benne, Leland Bradford, and Ronald Lippitt. Feedback at the end of each day to groups, and to group leaders and members about their individual and group behavior, stimulated great interest and appeared to produce more insight and learning than did lectures and seminars. From this experience emerged the National Training Laboratory in Group Development, which was organized by Benne, Bradford, and Lippitt (Lewin died in early 1947) and which held a three-week session during the summer of 1947 at the Gould Academy in Bethel, Maine. Participants met with a trainer and an observer in Basic Skill Training Groups (later called T-groups) for a major part of each day. The 1947 laboratory was sponsored by the Research Center for Group Dynamics (MIT), the National Education Association (NEA), Teachers College of Columbia University, University of California at Los Angeles (UCLA), Springfield College, and Cornell University. The work of that summer was to evolve into the National Training Laboratory, later called NTL Institute for Applied Behavioral Science, and into contemporary T-group training. Out of the Bethel experiences and NTL grew a significant number of laboratory training centers sponsored by universities. One of the first was the Western Training Laboratory, headed by Paul Sheats and sponsored by UCLA. The Western Training Laboratory offered its first program in 1952.

In addition to Lewin and his work, influences on Bradford, Lippitt, and Benne relative to the invention of the T-group and the subsequent emergence of OD included extensive experience with role playing and Moreno's psychodrama.[3] Further, Bradford and Benne had been influenced by John Dewey's philosophy of education, including concepts about learning and change and about the transactional nature of humans and their environment.[4] In addition, Benne had been influenced by the works of Mary Follett, an early management theorist, including her ideas about integrative solutions to problems in organizations.[5]

As a footnote to the emergence of the T-group, the widespread use of flip-chart paper as a convenient way to record, retrieve, and display data in OD activities and in training sessions was invented by Ronald Lippitt and Lee Bradford during the 1946 New Britain sessions. As Lippitt reports,

> The blackboards were very inadequate, and we needed to preserve a lot of the material we produced. So I went down to the local newspaper and got a donation of the end of press runs. The paper was still on the rollers. We had a "cutting bee" of Lee, Ken, myself and several others to roll the sheets out and cut them into standard sizes that we could put up in quantity with masking tape on the blackboards and walls of the classrooms. We took the practice back to MIT and I had the shop make some boards with clamps across the top. We hung them in our offices and the seminar room, and Lee did the same thing at the NEA in Washington.... The next summer at Bethel we had a large supply of cut newsprint and used some of the boards on easels, as well as using the walls.[6]

Bradford also reports that he and Ronald Lippitt used "strips of butcher paper" in their early work with organizations.[7]

Over the next decade, as trainers began to work with social systems of more permanency and complexity than T-groups, they began to experience considerable frustration in the transfer of laboratory behavioral skills and insights of individuals into the solution of problems in organizations. Personal skills learned in the "stranger" T-groups setting were very difficult to transfer to complex organizations. However, the training of "teams" from the same organization had emerged early at Bethel and undoubtedly was a link to the total organizational focus of Douglas McGregor, Herbert Shepard, and Robert Blake, and subsequently the focus of Richard Beckhard, Chris Argyris, Jack Gibb, Warren Bennis, and others.[8] All had been T-group trainers in NTL programs.

Robert Tannenbaum. Within our present awareness, some of the earliest sessions of what would now be called "team building" were conducted by Robert Tannenbaum in 1952 and 1953 at the U.S. Naval Ordnance Test Station at China Lake, California.[9] According to Tannenbaum, the term *vertically structured groups* was used, with groups dealing with "personal topics (such as departmental sociometrics, interpersonal relationships, communication, and self-analysis), and with organizational topics (such as deadlines, duties and responsibilities, policies and procedures, and—quite extensively—with interorganizational-group relations)."[10] These sessions, which stimulated a 1954 *Personnel* article by Tannenbaum, Kallejian, and Weschler, were conducted "with all managers of a given organizational unit present."[11] The more personally oriented dynamics of such sessions were described in a 1955 *Harvard Business Review* article by the same authors.[12]

Tannenbaum, along with Art Shedlin, also was the leader of what appears to be the first nondegree training program in OD, the Learning Community in Organizational Development at UCLA. This annual program was first offered as a full-time, 10-week, residential program, January–March 1967.[13]

Tannenbaum, who held a PhD in industrial relations from the School of Business at the University of Chicago, had early been influenced by such authors as Mary Parker Follett in management theory, V. V. Anderson's *Psychiatry in Industry,* Roethlisberger and Dickson's *Management and the Worker,* and Burleigh Gardner's *Human Relations in Industry.* He was on the planning committee for the Western Training Laboratory (WTL) and a staff member for the first session (1952). During that first session he co-trained with a psychiatric social worker who had attended a Bethel program, and in subsequent sessions, in his words, "co-trained with a psychiatrist, an educator, a clinical psychologist . . . and I learned much from them."[14]

Douglas McGregor.   Douglas McGregor, as a professor-consultant, working with Union Carbide, beginning about 1957, was also one of the first behavioral scientists to begin to solve the transfer problem and to talk systematically about and to help implement the application of

T-group skills to complex organizations.[15] John Paul Jones, who had come up through industrial relations at Union Carbide, in collaboration with McGregor and with the support of a corporate executive vice president and director, Birny Mason, Jr. (later president of the corporation), established a small internal consulting group that in large part used behavioral science knowledge in assisting line managers and their subordinates to learn how to be more effective in groups. McGregor's ideas were a dominant force in this consulting group; other behavioral scientists who had had an influence on Jones's thinking were Rensis Likert and Mason Haire. Jones's organization was later called an "organization development group."[16]

Herbert Shepard.   During the same year, 1957, Herbert Shepard, through introductions by Douglas McGregor, joined the employee relations department of Esso Standard Oil (now Exxon) as a research associate. Shepard was to have a major impact on the emergence of OD. While we will focus mainly on Shepard's work at Esso, it should also be noted that Shepard was later involved in community development activities and, in 1960, at the Case Institute of Technology, founded the first doctoral program devoted to training OD specialists.

Before joining Esso, Shepard had completed his doctorate at MIT and had stayed for a time as a faculty member in the Industrial Relations Section. Among influences on Shepard were Roethlisberger and Dickson's *Management and the Worker* (1939) and a biography of Clarence Hicks. (As a consultant to Standard Oil, Hicks had helped to develop participative approaches to personnel management and labor relations.) Shepard was also influenced by Farrell Toombs, who had been a counselor at the Hawthorne plant and had trained under Carl Rogers, a leading theorist and practitioner in nondirective counseling. In addition, Shepard had been heavily influenced by the writings of Kurt Lewin. NTL influence was also an important part of

Shepard's background; he attended an NTL lab in 1950 and subsequently was a staff member in many of its programs.[17]

In 1958 and 1959 Shepard launched three experiments in organization development at major Esso refineries: Bayonne, New Jersey; Baton Rouge, Louisiana; and Bayway, Texas. At Bayonne an interview survey and diagnosis were made and discussed with top management, followed by a series of three-day laboratories for all members of management.[18] Paul Buchanan, who had worked earlier at the Naval Ordnance Test Station and more recently had been using a somewhat similar approach in Republic Aviation, collaborated with Shepard at Bayonne and subsequently joined the Esso staff.

Blake and Shepard.   At Baton Rouge, Robert Blake joined Shepard, and the two initiated a series of two-week laboratories attended by all members of "middle" management. At first, an effort was made to combine the case method with the laboratory method, but the designs soon emphasized T-groups, organizational exercises, and lectures. One innovation in this training program was an emphasis on intergroup as well as interpersonal relations. Although working on interpersonal problems affecting work performance was clearly an organizational effort, between-group problem solving had even greater organization development implications in that a broader and more complex segment of the organization was involved.

At Baton Rouge, efforts to involve top management failed, and as a result follow-up resources for implementing organization development were not made available. By the time the Bayway program started, two fundamental OD lessons had been learned: the requirement for active involvement in and leadership of the program by top management and the need for on-the-job application.

At Bayway, there were two significant innovations. First, Shepard, Blake, and Murray Horwitz utilized the instrumented laboratory, which Blake and Jane Mouton had been developing in social psychology classes at the University of Texas and which they later developed into the Managerial Grid approach to organization development.[19] (An essential dimension of the instrumented lab is the use of feedback based on scales and measurements of group and individual behavior during sessions.)[20] Second, at Bayway more resources were devoted to team development, consultation, intergroup conflict resolution, and so forth than were devoted to laboratory training of "cousins," that is, organization members from different departments. As Robert Blake stated, "It was learning to *reject* T-group stranger-type labs that permitted OD to come into focus," and it was intergroup projects, in particular, that "triggered real OD."[21]

Robert Blake.   As in the case of Shepard and others, influences on Robert Blake up to that point were important in the emergence of OD. While at Berea College majoring in psychology and philosophy (later an MA, University of Virginia, and a PhD, University of Texas), Blake had been strongly influenced by the works of Korzybski and the general semanticists and found that "seeing discrete things as representative of a continuous series was much more stimulating and rewarding than just seeing two things as 'opposites.'" This thinking contributed in later years to Blake's conceptualization of the Managerial Grid with Jane Mouton and to their intergroup research on win-lose dynamics. This intergroup research and the subsequent design of their intergroup conflict management workshops were also heavily influenced by Muzafer Sherif's fundamental research on intergroup dynamics.[22] Jane Mouton's influence on Blake's thinking and on the development of the Grid stemmed partly, in her words, "from my undergraduate work (at Texas) in pure mathematics and physics which emphasized the significance of measurement, experimental design, and a scientific approach to phenomena."[23] (Mouton later attained an MA from the University of Virginia and a PhD from the University of Texas).

During World War II, Blake served in the Psychological Research Unit of the Army Air Force where he interacted with a large number of behavioral scientists, including sociologists. This contributed to his interest in "looking at the system rather the individuals within the system on an isolated one-by-one basis."[24] (This is probably one of many links between systems concepts or systems theory and OD.)

Another major influence on Blake had been the work of John Bowlby, a medical member of the Tavistock Clinic in London, who was working in family group therapy. Blake, after completing his PhD work in clinical psychology, went to England for 16 months in 1948 and 1949 to study, observe, and do research at Tavistock. As Blake states it,

> Bowlby had the clear notion that treating mental illness of an individual out of context was an ... ineffective way of aiding a person.... As a result, John was unprepared to see patients, particularly children, in isolation from their family settings. He would see the intact family: mother, father, siblings.... I am sure you can see from what I have said that if you substitute the word organization for family and substitute the concept of development for therapy, the natural next step in my mind was organization development.

Among others at Tavistock who influenced Blake were Wilfred Bion, Henry Ezriel, Eric Trist, and Elliott Jaques.[25]

After returning from Tavistock and taking an appointment at Harvard, Blake joined the staff for the summer NTL programs at Bethel. His first assignment was co-responsibility for a T-group with John R. P. French. Blake was a member of the Bethel staff from 1951 to 1957 and continued after that with NTL labs for managers at Harriman House, Harriman, New York. Among other influences on Blake were Jacob Moreno's action orientation to training through

the use of psychodrama and sociodrama and E. C. Tolman's notions of purposive behavior in humans.[26]

Richard Beckhard.   Richard Beckhard, another major figure in the emergence and extension of the OD field, came from a career in the theater. In his words,

> I came out of a whole different world—the theatre—and went to NTL in 1950 as a result of some discussions with Lee Bradford and Ron Lippitt. At that time they were interested in improving the effectiveness of the communications in large meetings and I became involved as head of the general sessions program. But I also got hooked on the whole movement. I made a career change and set up the meetings organization, "Conference Counselors." My first major contact was the staging of the 1950 White House conference on children and youth.... I was brought in to stage the large general sessions with six thousand people.... I had been doing a lot of large convention participative discussion type things and had written on the subject.... At the same time I joined the NTL summer staff.... My mentors in the field were Lee Bradford, in the early days, and Ron Lippitt and later, Ren Likert, and very particularly, Doug McGregor, who became both mentor, friend, father figure ... and in the later years, brother. Doug had left MIT and was at Antioch as president.... Doug and I began appearing on similar programs. One day coming back on the train from Cincinnati to Boston, Doug asked if I was interested in joining MIT....
>
> In the period 1958–63, I had worked with him [McGregor] on two or three projects. He brought me to Union Carbide, where I replaced him in working with John Paul Jones, and later, George Murray and the group. We [also] worked together at ... Pennsylvania Bell and ... at General Mills.[27]

Beckhard worked with McGregor at General Mills in 1959 or 1960, where McGregor was working with Dewey Balsch, vice president of personnel and industrial relations, in an attempt to facilitate "a total organizational culture change program which today might be called quality of work life or OD." Beckhard goes on to say, "The issues that were being worked were relationships between workers and supervision; roles of supervision and management at various levels; participative management for real. . . . This experience was one of the influences on Doug's original paper, 'The Human Side of Enterprise' . . . and from which the book emerged a year or so later."[28]

Beckhard developed one of the first major nondegree training programs in OD, NTL's Program for Specialists in Organizational Training and Development (PSOTD). The first session was an intensive four-week session held in the summer of 1967 at Bethel, Maine, the same year as UCLA launched its Learning Community in OD. Core staff members the first year in the NTL program were Beckhard as dean, Warner Burke, and Fritz Steele. Additional resource persons the first year were Herbert Shepard, Sheldon Davis, and Chris Argyris. In addition, along with McGregor, Rensis Likert, Chris Argyris, Robert Blake, Lee Bradford, and Jack Gibb, Beckhard was a founder of NTL's Management Work Conferences that are essentially laboratory training experiences for middle managers. As an extension of this program, Beckhard was also active in the development and conducting of NTL's senior executive conferences and presidents' labs.[29]

The Term *Organization Development.*   It is not entirely clear who coined the term *organization development,* but it is likely that the term emerged more or less simultaneously in two or three places through the conceptualization of Robert Blake, Herbert Shepard, Jane Mouton, Douglas McGregor, and Richard Beckhard.[30] The phrase *development group* had earlier been used by Blake and Mouton in connection with human relations training at the University of Texas and appeared in their 1956 document that was distributed for use in the Baton Rouge experiment.[31] (The same phrase appeared in a Mouton and Blake article first published in the

journal *Group Psychotherapy* in 1957.)[32] The Baton Rouge T-groups run by Shepard and Blake were called *development groups,*[33] and this program of T-groups was called "organization development" to distinguish it from the complementary management development programs already underway.[34]

Referring to his consulting with McGregor at General Mills, Beckhard gives this account of the term emerging there:

> At that time we wanted to put a label on the program at General Mills. . . . We clearly didn't want to call it management development because it was total organization-wide, nor was it human relations training although there was a component of that in it. We didn't want to call it organization improvement because that's a static term, so we labelled the program "Organization Development," meaning system-wide change effort.[35]

Thus the term emerged as a way of distinguishing a different mode of working with organizations and as a way of highlighting its developmental, systemwide, dynamic thrust.

The Role of Personnel and Industrial Relations Executives.   It is of considerable significance that the emergence of organization development efforts in three of the first corporations to be extensively involved, Union Carbide, Esso, and General Mills, included personnel and industrial relations people seeing themselves in new roles. At Union Carbide, John Paul Jones, in industrial relations, now saw himself in the role of a behavioral science consultant to other managers.[36] At Esso, the headquarters human relations research division began to view itself as an internal consulting group offering services to field managers, rather than as a research group developing reports for top management.[37] At General Mills, the vice president of personnel and industrial relations, Dewey Balsch, saw his role as including leadership in conceptualizing and coordinating changes in the culture of the total organization.[38] Thus, in the history of OD, we see both external consultants and internal staff departments departing from their traditional roles and collaborating in a new approach to organization improvement.

The Survey Research and Feedback Stem

Survey research and feedback,[39] a specialized form of action research ... constitutes the second major stem in the history of organization development. The history of this stem, in particular, revolves around the techniques and approach developed by staff members at the Survey Research Center of the University of Michigan over a period of years.

Rensis Likert.   The SRC was founded in 1946 after Rensis Likert, director of the Division of Program Surveys of the Federal Bureau of Agricultural Economics, and other key members of the division, moved to Michigan. Likert held a PhD in psychology from Columbia, and his dissertation, *A Technique for the Measurement of Attitudes,* was the classic study in which the widely used five-point "Likert scale" was developed. After a period of university teaching, Likert had been employed by the Life Insurance Agency Management Association where he conducted research on leadership, motivation, morale, and productivity. He had then moved to the U.S. Department of Agriculture, where his Division of Program Surveys furthered a more scientific approach to survey research in its work with various federal departments, including the Office of War Information.[40] After helping to develop and direct the Survey Research Center, following World War II, in 1948 Likert then became the director of a new Institute for Social Research, which included both the SRC and the Research Center for Group Dynamics, the latter moving to Michigan from MIT after Lewin's death.

Floyd Mann, Rensis Likert, and Others. Part of the emergence of survey research and feedback was based on the refinements made by SRC staff members in survey methodology. Another part was the evolution of the feedback methodology. As related by Rensis Likert,

> In 1947, I was able to interest the Detroit Edison Company in a company-wide study of employee perceptions, behavior, reactions and attitudes which was conducted in 1948. Floyd Mann, who had joined the SRC staff in 1947, was the study director on the project. I provided general direction. Three persons from D.E.: Blair Swartz, Sylvanus Leahy and Robert Schwab with Mann and me worked on the problem of how the company could best use the data from the survey to bring improvement in management and performance. This led to the development and use of the survey-feedback method. Floyd particularly played a key role in this development. He found that when the survey data were reported to a manager (or supervisor) and he or she failed to discuss the results with subordinates and failed to plan with them what the manager and others should do to bring improvement, little change occurred. On the other hand, when the manager discussed the results with subordinates and planned with them what to do to bring improvement, substantial favorable changes occurred.[41]

Another aspect of the Detroit Edison study was the process of feeding back data from an attitude survey to the participating departments in what Mann calls an "interlocking chain of conferences."[42] Additional insights are provided by Baumgartel, who participated in the project and who drew the following conclusions from the Detroit Edison study:

> The results of this experimental study lend support to the idea that an intensive, group discussion procedure for utilizing the results of an employee questionnaire survey can be an effective tool for introducing positive change in a business organization. It may be that the effectiveness of this method, in comparison to traditional training courses, is that it deals with the system of human relationships as a whole (superior and subordinate can change together) and it deals with each manager, supervisor, and employee in the context of his own job, his own problems, and his own work relationships.[43]

Links between the Laboratory Training Stem and the Survey Feedback Stem. Links between people who were later to be key figures in the laboratory training stem of OD and people who were to be key figures in the survey feedback stem occurred as early as 1940 and continued over the years. These links were undoubtedly of significance in the evolution of both stems. Of particular interest are the links between Likert and Lewin and between Likert and key figures in the laboratory training stem of OD. As Likert states it, "I met Lewin at the APA annual meeting at State College, Pennsylvania, I believe in 1940. When he came to Washington during the war, I saw him several times and got to know him and his family quite well."[44] In 1944 Likert arranged a dinner at which Douglas McGregor and Kurt Lewin explored the feasibility of a group dynamics center at MIT.[45]

Likert further refers to McGregor: "I met McGregor during the war and came to know him very well after Lewin had set up the RCGD at MIT. After the war, Doug became very interested in the research on leadership and organizations that we were doing in the Institute for Social Research. He visited us frequently and I saw him often at Antioch and at MIT after he returned." Likert goes on to refer to the first NTL lab for managers that was held at Arden House in 1956: "Douglas McGregor and I helped Lee Bradford launch it. . . . Staff members in the 1956 lab were: Beckhard, Benne, Bradford, Gordon Lippitt, Malott, Shepard and I. Argyris, Blake and McGregor joined the staff for the 1957 Arden House lab."[46]

Links between group dynamics and survey feedback people were extensive, of course, after the RCGD moved to Michigan with the encouragement of Rensis Likert and members of the SRC. Among the top people in the RCGD who moved to Michigan were Leon Festinger, Dorwin Cartwright, Ronald Lippitt, and John R. P. French, Jr. Cartwright, who was selected by the group to be the director of the RCGD, was particularly knowledgeable about survey research, since he had been on the staff of the Division of Program Surveys with Rensis Likert and others during World War II.[47]

The Action Research Stem

Earlier we briefly described action research as a collaborative, client-consultant inquiry consisting of preliminary diagnosis, data gathering from the client group, data feedback to the client group, data exploration and action planning by the client group, and action. As we will describe later, there are at least four versions of action research, one of which, participant action research, is used with the most frequency in OD. The laboratory training stem in the history of OD has a heavy component of action research; the survey feedback stem is the history of a specialized form of action research; and Tavistock projects have had a strong action research thrust, as we will discuss shortly.

Because we will treat the history of action research in some detail later, we will mention only a few aspects here. For example, William F. Whyte and Edith L. Hamilton were using action research in their work with Chicago's Tremont Hotel in 1945 and 1946; John Collier, commissioner of Indian Affairs, was describing action research in a publication in 1945; Kurt Lewin and his students conducted numerous action research projects in the mid-1940s and early 1950s. The work of these and other scholars and practitioners in the invention and utilization of action research was basic in the evolution of OD.

Sociotechnical and Socioclinical Parallels

Somewhat parallel to the work of the RCGD, the SRC, and NTL was the work of the Tavistock Clinic in England. The clinic had been founded in 1920 as an outpatient facility to provide psychotherapy based on psychoanalytic theory and insights from the treatment of battle neurosis in World War I. A group focus emerged early in the work of Tavistock in the context of family therapy in which the child and the parent received treatment simultaneously.[48] The action research mode also emerged at Tavistock in attempts to give practical help to families, organizations, and communities.

W. R. Bion, John Rickman, and Others. The staff of the Tavistock Clinic was extensively influenced by such innovations as World War II applications of social psychology to psychiatry, the work of W. R. Bion and John Rickman and others in group therapy, Lewin's notions about the "social field" in which a problem was occurring, and Lewin's theory and experience with action research. Bion, Rickman, and others had been involved with the six-week "Northfield Experiment" at a military hospital near Birmingham during World War II. In this experiment each soldier was required to join a group that both performed some task, such as handicraft or map reading, and discussed feelings, interpersonal relations, and administrative and managerial problems as well. Insights from this experiment were to carry over into Bion's theory of group behavior.[49]

Eric Trist. It is of significance that Tavistock's sociotechnical approach to restructuring work grew out of Eric Trist's visit to a coal mine and his insights as to the relevance of Lewin's work on group dynamics and Bion's work on leaderless groups to mining problems.[50] Trist was also influenced by the systems concepts of Von Bertalanffy and Andras Angyal.[51] Trist's subsequent experiments in work redesign and the use of semiautonomous work teams in coal mining were the forerunners of other work redesign experiments in various industries in Europe, India, and the United States. Thus there is a clear historical link between the group dynamics field and sociotechnical approaches to assisting organizations.

Tavistock–U.S. Links. Tavistock leaders, including Trist and Bion, had frequent contact with Kurt Lewin, Rensis Likert, and others in the United States. One product of this collaboration was the decision to publish *Human Relations* as a joint publication between Tavistock and MIT's Research Center for Group Dynamics.[52] Some Americans prominent in the emergence and evolution of the OD field, for example, Robert Blake, as we noted earlier, and Warren Bennis,[53] studied at Tavistock.

Although the sociotechnical approach focused on the nonexecutive ranks of organizations and was therefore not a complete systemwide approach, many aspects were congruent with OD as we have characterized it. . . . The focus on teams and the use of action research and participation were certainly consistent with contemporary OD approaches. (As we will discuss . . . some contemporary quality of work life [QWL] programs are an amalgamation of OD, sociotechnical, and other approaches. Further, some OD efforts have been criticized as not involving rank-and-file employees; sociotechnical approaches are additions to the repertoire of improvement strategies that clearly focus on this level.)

Extent of Application

Applications emerging from one or more of the stems just described are evident in the organization development efforts now occurring in many countries, including England, Japan, Norway, Canada, Sweden, Finland, Australia, New Zealand, the Philippines, and Holland, as well as in the United States. The growing number of organizations in America that have embarked on organization development efforts include Union Carbide and Exxon (the first two companies), Connecticut General Insurance Company, Graphic Controls, Equitable Life Assurance Company, Digital Equipment Corporation, Procter & Gamble, Mountain Bell Telephone, Searle Laboratories, General Motors, Bankers Trust, Ford Motor Company, Heinz Foods, IBM, Polaroid, Sun Oil, and TRW, Inc. A random sample of half of the Fortune 500 companies, yielding 71 respondents, found 46 percent (33) of the responding firms to be using organization development techniques.[54]

Applications at the TRW Systems Group, a large research and development organization in the aerospace field, commenced in the early 1960s, have been as extensive and innovative as those found anywhere in the world, and are of major significance in the emergence and history of OD. (Three organizations have now been created out of TRW Systems Group: Electronic Systems Group, Defense Systems Group, and Space and Technology Group.) Among the key figures in the emergence of the OD effort at TRW Systems were Jim Dunlap, director of industrial relations; Shel Davis, who was later promoted to that position; Ruben Mettler, president of TRW Systems; and Herb Shepard. T-group labs conducted by internal trainers, NTL, and UCLA staff members were also important in providing impetus to the effort in its early phases. Efforts at TRW Systems and in the total organization, TRW, have included team building, intergroup team building, interface laboratories between departments and between company and customers, laboratory training, career assessment workshops, sensing, and organization redesign and restructuring for improved productivity and quality of working life. OD activities at the previous TRW Systems Group and the newly formed Three Groups to a large extent are part of the management process, with personnel department managers extensively used as facilitators.[55]

In England, Europe, Japan, and the Philippines, illustrative of the growing interest in organization development is the involvement of such companies as Imperial Chemical Industries (United Kingdom and elsewhere), J. Lyons & Company (England), the Royal Dutch Shell Group, Business Consultants, Inc. (Tokyo), and the San Miguel Corporation headquartered in Manila. Projects at Imperial Chemical Industries, a large company headquartered in London, have included job enrichment, survey research, team building, and open systems planning.

Industrial organizations, however, are by no means the only kinds of institutions involved. There are applications, for example, in public school systems; colleges; medical schools; social welfare agencies; police departments; professional associations; governmental units at the local, county, state, and national levels; various health care delivery systems; churches; and American Indian tribes.

Applications have also occurred in the U.S. military. In 1980, it was reported that the Navy was using approximately 700 officers and noncommissioned officers full time in its Human Resource Management Program. Consultants are trained in a 12-week program and are then assigned to one of five HRM centers having detachments throughout the world. The thrust of the Navy effort seems to be based on a survey feedback process, but the depth to which the process and data are used appears to vary widely depending upon commanding officer (CO) interest. In some instances, questionnaire data go only to the CO; in other instances, the consulting team works with overlapping, intact teams and uses a variety of OD interventions.[56]

Much of the thrust of the Air Force behavioral science type of consulting activities appears to have been of a technostructural nature, such as job enrichment. However, a wide variety of OD efforts has also emerged. For example, team building, intergroup development, and third-party peacemaking have been used in Air Force research laboratories, and team building and survey feedback have been used in logistics centers. Some of the OD efforts appear to involve all members of the hierarchy in a unit; others seem to have had little top-management involvement. In 1981, the Air Force's Management Consulting Program was manned by 44 consultants from lieutenant colonel to senior noncommissioned officer ranks who were part of a Leadership and Management Development Center at Maxwell Air Force Base, Alabama.[57]

The U.S. Army opened an Organizational Effectiveness Center and School at Fort Ord, California, in the mid-1970s, and between 1975 and late 1981 it had trained about 1,200 OD (OE) consultants. In 1981, there were 388 authorized OE positions at the officer rank and 100 newly created OE positions at the noncommissioned officer level. The OE Center and School also trains consultants for the National Guard and the Reserves; in 1981 there were 24 authorized OE positions in the guard. OE consultants are assigned in the Army on the basis of two per division or installation or one per brigade. Officers are assigned to a consultancy role for 18 months to a maximum of three years, at which time they return to their other military specialties. Some may be reassigned to the OE effort later on.[58] The 82nd Airborne Division, one of the first Army organizations to be involved, had an extensive OE effort, including team building at the top ranks, by 1977.[59]

Some "community development" strategies have a number of elements in common with organization development, such as the use of action research, the use of a change agent, and an emphasis on facilitating decision-making and problem-solving processes.[60] Undoubtedly, some of the commonality stems from OD practitioners working in the community development field. For example, in 1961 Herbert Shepard conducted community development laboratories at China Lake, California, sponsored by the Naval Ordnance Test Station. These one-week labs involved military persons and civilians and people of all ages and socioeconomic levels. Outcomes included the resolution of some community and intercommunity issues.[61]

In addition to emphasizing the diversity of types of systems using OD consultants, we want to emphasize that intraorganization development efforts have not focused on just top-management teams, although the importance of top-management involvement will be discussed in later chapters. The wide range of occupational roles that have been involved in OD is almost limitless and has included production workers,[62] managers, soldiers, military officers, miners, scientists and engineers, ministers, psychologists, geologists, lawyers, accountants, nurses, physicians, teachers, computer specialists, foresters, technicians, secretaries, clerical employees, and board members.

Symptomatic of the widespread application of organization development concepts is the emergence and growth of the OD Network, which began in 1964 and in late 1981 had a membership of about 2,100. Most members either have major roles in the OD efforts of organizations or are scholar-practitioners in the OD field. The network began with discussions at the Case Institute of Technology between Herbert Shepard, Sheldon Davis of TRW Systems, and Floyd Mann of the University of Michigan,[63] and through the initiative of Leland Bradford and Jerry Harvey of NTL and a number of industrial people who had attended labs at Bethel. Among the industrial founders of the organization, originally called the Industrial Trainers Network, were Sheldon Davis of TRW Systems, George Murray of Union Carbide, John Vail of Dow Chemical, and Carl Albers of the Hotel Corporation of America. Other early members were from Procter & Gamble, Weyerhaeuser, Bankers Trust, West Virginia Pulp and Paper Company, the U.S. State Department, the U.S. National Security Agency, Pillsbury, Eli Lilly, Polaroid, Esso, Parker Pen, American Airlines, Goodrich-Gulf Chemicals, RCA, Sandia, National Association of Manufacturers, General Foods, Armour & Company, Heublein, and Dupont. Jerry Harvey was the first secretary/coordinator of the emerging organization, and Warner Burke assumed that role in 1967 shortly after joining NTL on a full-time basis. There were fewer than 50 members at that time; when Warner Burke stepped aside as executive director in 1975, there were approximately 1,400 members.[64] That same year the OD Network became independent of NTL.

An OD Division of the American Society for Training and Development was established in

1968 and had more than 4,000 members by the summer of 1981. It is also significant that the Academy of Management, whose members are mostly professors in management and related areas, established a Division of Organization Development within its structure in 1971, and this unit had approximately 1,100 members in late 1983. The Division of Industrial and Organizational Psychology of the American Psychological Association has held workshops on organization development at the annual APA conventions; several annual conventions going back at least to 1965 have included papers or symposia on organization development or related topics.[65] In 1974 the *Annual Review of Psychology* for the first time devoted a chapter entirely to a review of research on organization development.[66] Other chapters on OD appeared in 1977[67] and 1982. The 1982 chapter was entitled "Organizational Development and Change" and was written by authors from the Netherlands and France.[68]

The first doctoral program devoted to training OD specialists was founded by Herbert Shepard in 1960 at the Case Institute of Technology. Originally called The Organizational Behavior Group, this program is now part of the Department of Organizational Behavior, School of Management, Case Western Reserve University. Masters degree programs in organization development or masters programs with concentrations in OD have been offered in recent years by several universities, including New York University, Brigham Young, Pepperdine, Loyola, Bowling Green, New Hampshire, Columbia, and Case Western Reserve and Sheffield Polytechnic in England. The American University and NTL Institute jointly offer a masters degree program in Human Resource Development. Many other major universities, if not most, now have graduate courses directly bearing on organization development, including UCLA, Stanford, Harvard, University of Southern California, Hawaii, Oklahoma, Colorado, Indiana, and Purdue; and in England, such courses are found at the University of Manchester Institute of Science and Technology and the University of Bath.[69]

This rapid growth in OD interest and attention has been given impetus by NTL's Program for Specialists in Organization Development (originally called PSOTD), discussed earlier in this chapter. PSOD started as an intensive four-week session held in the summer at Bethel and was partly an outgrowth of an Organization Intern Program that had included some OD training. PSOD subsequently became a two-week program for experienced practitioners with required prerequisites of T-group attendance and consultation skills training. Other professional programs in OD have been or are now being offered in the United States, Canada, the United Kingdom, Australia, New Zealand, and elsewhere under the sponsorship of universities, foundations, professional associations, and other institutions.

Summary

Organization development has emerged largely from applied behavioral sciences and has three major stems: the invention of the T-group and innovations in the application of laboratory training insights to complex organizations, the invention of survey feedback technology, and the emergence of action research. Parallel and linked to these stems was the emergence of the Tavistock sociotechnical and socioclinical approaches.

Key figures in this early history interacted with each other and across these stems and were influenced by concepts and experiences from a wide variety of disciplines and settings. These disciplines and settings included clinical and social psychology, family group therapy, military psychology and psychiatry, the theater, general semantics, systems theory, mathematics and physics, philosophy, psychodrama, nondirective counseling, survey methodology, experimental and action research, personnel and industrial relations, and general management theory.

The history of OD is emergent in that a rapidly increasing number of behavioral scientists and practitioners in organizations are building on the research and insights of the past as well as discovering the utility of some of the earlier insights. These efforts are now expanding and include a wide range of organizations, types of institutions, occupational categories, and geographical locations around the world.

In the chapters that follow, the assumptions, theory, and techniques of organization development will be examined in substantial depth along with some speculation as to its future viability.

Notes

1. The phrase "group dynamics" was coined by Kurt Lewin in 1939. See Warren Bennis, address to the Academy of Management, San Diego, California, August 3, 1981.
2. This and the next paragraph are based on Kenneth D. Benne, Leland P. Bradford, Jack R. Gibb, and Ronald O. Lippitt, eds., *The Laboratory Method of Changing and Learning: Theory and Application* (Palo Alto, Calif.: Science and Behavior Books, 1975), pp. 1–6; and Alfred J. Marrow, *The Practical Theorist: The Life and Work of Kurt Lewin* (New York: Basic Books, 1969), pp. 210–14. For additional history, see Leland P. Bradford, "Biography of an Institution," *Journal of Applied Behavioral Science* 3 (April–June 1967), pp. 127–43; and Alvin Zander, "The Study of Group Behavior During Four Decades," *The Journal of Applied Behavioral Science* 15 (July–September 1979), pp. 272–82. We are indebted to Ronald Lippitt for his correspondence, which helped to clarify this and the following paragraph.
3. Peter B. Smith, ed., *Small Groups and Personal Change* (London: Methuen & Co., 1980), pp. 8–9.
4. Robert Chin and Kenneth D. Benne, "General Strategies for Effecting Changes in Human Systems," in Warren G. Bennis, Kenneth D. Benne, and Robert Chin, eds., *The Planning of Change,* 2nd ed. (New York: Holt, Rinehardt & Winston, 1969), pp. 100–102.
5. Ibid., p. 102.
6. Correspondence with Ronald Lippitt.
7. Conversation with Lee Bradford, conference on current theory and practice in organization development, San Francisco, March 16, 1978.
8. Based largely on correspondence with Ronald Lippitt. According to Lippitt, as early as 1945 Bradford and Lippitt were conducting "three-level training" at Freedman's Hospital in Washington, D.C., in an effort "to induce interdependent changes in all parts of the same system." Lippitt also reports that Leland Bradford very early was acting on a basic concept of "multiple entry," that is, simultaneously training and working with several groups in the organization.
9. Correspondence with Robert Tannenbaum.
10. Tannenbaum correspondence; memorandum of May 12, 1952, U.S. Naval Ordnance Test Station from E. R. Toporeck to "Office, Division and Branch Heads, Test Department," and "Minutes, Test Department Management Seminar, 5 March 1953."
11. Robert Tannenbaum, Verne Kallejian, and Irving R. Weschler, "Training Managers for Leadership," *Personnel* 30 (January 1954), p. 3.
12. Verne J. Kallejian, Irving R. Weschler, and Robert Tannenbaum, "Managers in Transition," *Harvard Business Review* 33 (July–August 1955), pp. 55–64.
13. Tannenbaum correspondence.
14. Ibid.
15. See Richard Beckhard, W. Warner Burke, and Fred I. Steele, "The Program for Specialists in Organization Training and Development," p. ii, mimeographed paper (NTL Institute for Applied Behavioral Science, December 1967); and John Paul Jones, "What's Wrong with Work?" in *What's Wrong with Work?* (New York: National Association of Manufacturers, 1967), p. 8. According to correspondence with Rensis Likert, the link between McGregor and John Paul Jones occurred in the summer of 1957. Discussions took place between the two when Jones attended one of the annual

two-week seminars at Aspen, Colorado, organized by Hollis Peter of the Foundation for Research on Human Behavior and conducted by Douglas McGregor, Mason Haire, and Rensis Likert.

16. Gilbert Burck, "Union Carbide's Patient Schemers," *Fortune* 72 (December 1965), pp. 147–49. For McGregor's account, see "Team Building at Union Carbide," in Douglas McGregor, *The Professional Manager* (New York: McGraw-Hill, 1967), pp. 106–10.

17. This paragraph is based on interviews with Herbert Shepard, August 3, 1981. For a brief discussion of the career of Clarence Hicks, see Wendell French, *The Personnel Management Process,* 5th ed. (Boston: Houghton Mifflin, 1982), chap. 2.

18. Much of the historical account in this paragraph and the following three paragraphs is based on correspondence and interviews with Herbert Shepard, with some information added from correspondence with Robert Blake.

19. Correspondence with Robert Blake and Herbert Shepard. For further reference to Murray Horwitz and Paul Buchanan, as well as to comments about the innovative contributions of Michael Blansfield, see Herbert A. Shepard, "Explorations in Observant Participation," in Bradford, Gibb, and Benne, eds., *T-Group Theory,* pp. 382–83. See also Marshall Sashkin, "Interview with Robert R. Blake and Jane Srygley Mouton," *Group and Organization Studies* 3 (December 1978), pp. 401–07.

20. See Robert Blake and Jane Srygley Mouton, "The Instrumented Training Laboratory," in Irving R. Weschler and Edgar M. Schein, eds., *Selected Readings Series Five: Issues in Training* (Washington, D.C., National Training Laboratories, 1962), pp. 61–85. In this chapter, Blake and Mouton credit Muzafer and Carolyn Sherif with important contributions to early intergroup experiments. Reference is also made to the contributions of Frank Cassens of Humble Oil and Refinery in the early phases of the Esso program. For a brief description of the development of the two-dimensional Managerial Grid, see Robert Blake and Jane Srygley Mouton, *Diary of an OD Man* (Houston: Gulf 1976), pp. 332–36.

21. Based on correspondence with Robert Blake. See also Robert R. Blake and Jane Srygley Mouton, "Why the OD Movement Is 'Stuck' and How to Break It Loose," *Training and Development Journal* 33 (September 1979), pp. 12–20.

22. Blake correspondence.

23. Mouton correspondence.

24. Blake correspondence.

25. Ibid.

26. Ibid.

27. Correspondence with Richard Beckhard.

28. Ibid.

29. Based on Beckhard correspondence and other sources.

30. Interpretations of Blake correspondence, Shepard interview, Beckhard correspondence, and Larry Porter, "OD: Some Questions, Some Answers—An Interview with Beckhard and Shepard," *OD Practitioner* 6 (Autumn 1974), p. 1.

31. Blake correspondence.

32. Jane Srygley Mouton and Robert R. Blake, "University Training in Human Relations Skills," *Selected Readings Series Three: Forces in Learning* (Washington, D.C.: National Training Laboratories, 1961), pp. 88–96, reprinted from *Group Psychotherapy* 10 (1957), pp. 342–45.

33. Shepard and Blake correspondence.

34. Interview with Herbert Shepard, San Diego, California, August 3, 1981.

35. Beckhard correspondence.

36. Burck, "Union Carbide's Patient Schemers," p. 149.

37. Harry D. Kolb, "Introduction" to *An Action Research Program for Organization Improvement* (Ann Arbor, Mich.: Foundation for Research on Human Behavior, 1960), p. i. The phrase *organization development* is used several times in this monograph based on a 1959 meeting about the Esso programs and written by Kolb, Shepard, Blake, and others.

38. Based on Beckhard correspondence.

39. This history is based largely on correspondence with Rensis Likert and partially on "The Career of Rensis Likert," *ISR Newsletter,* Winter 1971; and *A Quarter Century of Social Research,* Institute for Social Research, 1971.

40. "Rensis Likert," *ISR Newsletter,* p. 6.

41. Likert correspondence. Floyd Mann later

became the first director of the Center for Research on the Utilization of Scientific Knowledge (CRUSK) when the center was established by ISR in 1964. See also Floyd C. Mann, "Studying and Creating Change," in Bennis, Benne, and Chin, eds., *Planning of Change,* pp. 605–13.

42. Mann, "Studying and Creating Change," p. 609.

43. Howard Baumgartel. "Using Employee Questionnaire Results for Improving Organizations: The Survey (Feedback) Experiment," *Kansas Business Review* 12 (December 1959), pp. 2–6.

44. Likert correspondence.

45. Marrow, *The Practical Theorist,* p. 164. This book, about the life and work of Kurt Lewin, is rich with events that are important to the history of OD.

46. Likert correspondence.

47. Ibid.

48. H. V. Dicks, *Fifty Years of the Tavistock Clinic* (London: Routledge & Kegan Paul, 1970), pp. 1, 32.

49. Based on Ibid., pp. 5, 7, 133, 140; and Robert DeBoard, *The Psychoanalysis of Organizations* (London: Tavistock 1978), pp. 35–43.

50. Eric Trist and Marshall Sashkin, "Interview," *Group & Organization Studies* 5 (June 1980), pp. 150–51.

51. Ibid., p. 155.

52. The previous three paragraphs are based largely on ibid., pp. 144–51. The brief statement about action research is also partly based on Alfred J. Marrow, "Risks and Uncertainties in Action Research," *Journal of Social Issues* 20, no. 3 (1964), p. 17.

53. Bennis address, Academy of Management, August 3, 1981.

54. Stephen R. Michael, "Organizational Change Techniques: Their Present, Their Future," *Organizational Dynamics* 11 (Summer 1982), p. 77.

55. Interview with Sam Shirley, February 4, 1982; correspondence with Sheldon A. Davis; Sheldon A. Davis, "An Organic Problem-Solving Method of Organizational Change," *Journal of Applied Behavioral Science* 3 (November 1, 1967), pp. 3–21; and the case study of the TRW Systems Group in Gene Dalton, Paul Lawrence, and Larry Greiner, *Organizational Change and Development* (Homewood, IL: Irwin-Dorsey, 1970), pp. 4–153.

56. Denis M. Umstot, "Organization Development Technology and the Military: A Surprising Merger?" *Academy of Management Review,* April 1980, pp. 193–94.

57. Ibid., pp. 196–97; and Steve Ferrier, "The U.S. Air Force Management Consulting Program: Implications for Army OE," *OE Communique* 5, no. 3 (1981), pp. 29–35.

58. Interview with Lt. Col. Ronald Sheffield, U.S. Army Organizational Effectiveness Center and School, July 1981. See also the Army's publication, *OE Communique.*

59. Presentation by Lt. Col. Robert L. Phillips, Academy of Management Annual Meeting, Orlando, Florida, August 16, 1977.

60. See Eva Schindler-Rainman, "Community Development through Laboratory Methods," in Benne, Bradford, Gibb, eds.; and Lippitt, *Laboratory Method of Changing and Learning,* pp. 445–63.

61. Shepard correspondence. Starting in 1967, Herbert Shepard was involved in the applications of OD to community problems in Middletown, Connecticut.

62. See Scott Myers, "Overcoming Union Opposition to Job Enrichment," *Harvard Business Review* 49 (May–June 1971), pp. 37–49; and Robert Blake, Herbert Shepard, and Jane Mouton, *Managing Intergroup Conflict in Industry* (Houston: Gulf, 1964), pp. 122–38.

63. Shepard correspondence.

64. Correspondence with W. Warner Burke and memoranda and attendance lists pertaining to 1967–69 network meetings furnished by Burke.

65. For example, the following topics were included in the program of the 1965 convention: "Strategies for Organization Improvement: Research and Consultation," "Managerial Grid Organization Development," and "The Impact of Laboratory Training in Research and Development Environment," *American Psychologist* 20 (July 1965), pp. 549, 562, 565.

66. Frank Friedlander and L. Dave Brown, "Organization Development," *Annual Review of Psychology* 25 (1974), pp. 313–41.

67. Clay Alderfer, "Organization Development," *Annual Review of Psychology* 28 (1977), pp. 197–223.

68. Claude Faucheux, Gilles Amanda, and André Laurent, "Organizational Development and Change," *Annual Review of Psychology* 33 (1982), pp. 343–70.

69. D. D. Warrick, ed., *OD Newsletter,* OD Division, Academy of Management, Spring 1979, p. 7.

READING 3
ORGANIZATION DEVELOPMENT IN THE 1980s

Marshall Sashkin and W. Warner Burke

The term *organization development* (OD) was not used prior to about 1960. One early attempt to review the new field was made by Clark and Krone (1972) in their paper, "Toward an Overall View of Organizational Development in the Early Seventies." They defined an "open systems" framework emphasizing adaptive change by managers in response to environmental changes and pressures. Managers would need new skills in attending to the environment and anticipating impact on the organization through "open systems planning" (Jayaram, 1978). The insights they developed would then be used to modify organizational structures and processes through "open systems redesign" (Krone, 1974). This framework, often in an expanded variation, remains at the heart of most concepts of organization development, up to and including the present review.

Since Clark and Krone, OD has developed into a widely known field of applied research and practice. OD aims involve improving both organizational performance *and* the "quality of work life" experienced by organization members. These aims are attained by applying knowledge about people in organizations, derived from the social and behavioral sciences (Burke, 1982, 1987). Although there exists a body of OD research and practice reports, it would be difficult to argue that OD is a coherent discipline. There is no single theory that encompasses most of the research and practice, for example; nor is there a code of ethics among practitioners to which most or all would subscribe, although some of us

Source: Marshall Sashkin and W. Warner Burke, "Organization Development in the 1980s," *Journal of Management,* 1987, vol. 13, no. 2 pp. 393–417. Reprinted with permission.

have attempted to address issues of ethics (e.g., Burke, 1982; Frankel, 1986; Golembiewski, 1979; Walton & Warwick, 1973; and White & Wooten, 1986). Indeed, even a definition must remain relatively general if it is to receive widespread acceptance among scholars and practitioners. Yet, as a field, OD is researched, criticized, summarized, and reviewed.

In the first section of our review we identify two critical, parallel issues that underlie OD theory and practice. The first is the focus on changes in organizational *structures* (including task structure and technology) versus changes in the ways people *behave* with and toward one another. Parallel to this first critical issue is a focus on "bottom-line" or performance and profit indicators versus a concern with "humanistic" outcomes, centering on the needs, desires, and general satisfaction of organization members. We shall see how these two parallel sets of contrapuntal themes, summarized in Table 1, are the overt and hidden aspects of a framework for integrating OD theory and practice in the 1980s.

To begin exploring this matter we turn, in the next section, to a more detailed examination of OD in the decade of the 1980s. Our review of the OD literature leads us to discuss four key research issues. On the basis of this research-focused literature review, we derive a set of ongoing trends of the 1980s. These trends are summarized in three key conclusions offered about OD in the 1980s. In conclusion, we speculate about OD from the 1980s into the 21st century, offering three scenarios and some suggestions for choosing among them.

In sum, we will in this review show how OD has developed to the present state of the art, de-

TABLE 1

Competing OD approaches and values

OD Approaches	OD Values
Change the design and structure of work	Improve performance and profit, "bottom-line" measures
OR	*OR*
Change behavioral processes in organizations (i.e., the way people work together)	Improve quality of work life of organization members, especially those at mid and lower levels

fine (to a degree) just what that state is, and suggest—at least tentatively—where the field might be heading.

Past Annual Reviews

The first *Annual Review* article on OD was prepared by Friedlander and Brown (1974), who argued that attempts to develop OD theory had generally failed, due to an all but total focus on tying research to theory. This early theory was divorced from practice and thus therefore relatively useless for informing and guiding practice. Friedlander and Brown called for a "theory of practice, which emerges from practice data and is of the practice situation, not merely about it" (p. 336).

Friedlander and Brown identified two basic OD approaches. The first, which they called the "Human-Processual" approach, centered on people and the organizational processes based in people's behavior and focused on fulfillment of human needs and values. The second, which they labeled the "Technostructural" approach, centered on technology and the manner in which technology affects organizational structures and focused on task accomplishment aims (improved performance). Finally, Friedlander and Brown observed that "the human-processual and technostructural change approaches converge at the interface of the organization process and structure" (p. 315). They illustrated this as shown in Figure 1.

The framework developed by Friedlander and Brown helps one to understand what OD is all about and why OD may or may not be successful. That is, they defined the human-processual aspect of OD as including survey feedback, several forms of group development (team building) interventions, and intergroup development activities, and concluded that, though such OD activities typically affect people's attitudes, there is rarely any substantial effect on either stable behavioral processes or on performance outcomes. In contrast, the technostructural approach, consisting of sociotechnical systems (STS) interventions, job design, and job enrichment, was seen as having substantial effects on performance. The overlap between the two OD approaches, as shown in Figure 1, suggests conflict rather than complimentarity. It has been the work of the past decade to turn this conflict into an integrative model by linking these approaches and value outcomes, as shown in Figure 2.

In their review of comparative OD studies and comprehensive case reports, Friedlander and Brown characterized successful OD as:

1. Instigated by both external and internal pressures.
2. Actively supported by top management.
3. Involving many people at many organizational levels.
4. Requiring much shared decision making throughout the organization.
5. Long-term (several years) in perspective.

FIGURE 1

Approaches to organization development.

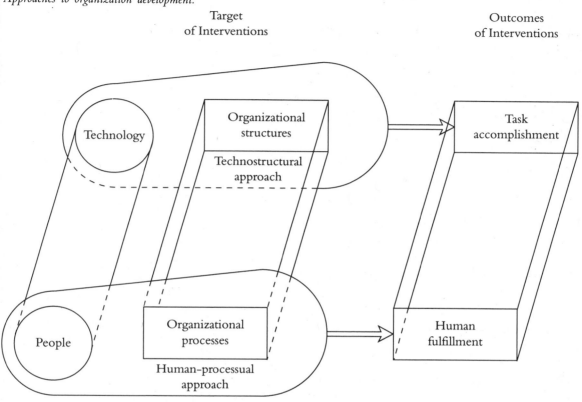

Reproduced, with permission, from the *Annual Review of Psychology* vol. 25. © 1974 by Annual Reviews, Inc.

6. Hard to evaluate in terms of clear quantitative outcomes.

The second *Annual Review* article, by Alderfer (1977), provided a detailed descriptive picture of OD research and practice in the late 1970s. He observed that, by the end of the 1970s, OD was being applied to a wide range of organizational settings in addition to the business/industry situations so typical of early OD efforts. Schools, hospitals, and even communities and countries were engaging in OD activities. At the same time, the standard OD interventions—team building, survey feedback, and structural change—were being refined. OD practitioners involved in team-building activities, for example, no longer typically assumed that everyone on the team shared the same goals prior to the intervention. Indeed, developing a common goals framework became an early focus and an integral part of team building. And research was getting much better, through new instruments, new methods, new foci, and new concepts. Such research, however, continued to be driven by academic theory, rather than being focused on practice concerns, as called for by Friedlander and Brown.

The third published *Annual Review* article

FIGURE 2

Linking organization development approaches

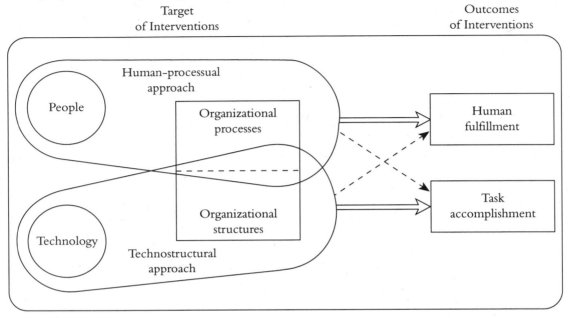

Target
of Interventions   Outcomes
of Interventions

(Faucheux, Amado, & Laurent, 1982), gives us a widely divergent and fascinating (though hard to integrate) European view of OD. The authors think of Europe as "north" ("Anglo-Saxon") versus "south" ("Latin"), rather than, as typical in the United States, "east" versus "west." Structural and especially sociotechnical themes are said to characterize Northern European/Anglo-Saxon OD (including Scandinavia, the Low Countries, and perhaps Germany, but excluding Great Britain!). In "Latin" Europe (France and Italy are the only countries mentioned) dominant OD approaches are identified as Marxist-oriented social-movement-based OD and neo-Freudian psychoanalytical frameworks. Brazil is given as an example of a "Latin bureaucracy" in which North American and Anglo-Saxon OD does not work, period. It is not clear where Great Britain fits, as the source of both sociotechnical *and* neo-Freudian OD concepts and approaches!

Faucheux et al. are most interesting when they give insights on OD in North America, insights that illuminate the blind areas that American OD has: for example, our heavy task orientation as opposed to trying "to deal with the social intricacies of human collectivities" (p. 353) more characteristic of the Latin countries of Europe. Their insights about OD in North America are summarized as follows:

> The field of planned change, which has been commensurate with OD in the U.S. for nearly 20 years, is now undergoing a very significant transformation. It may not be an exaggeration to see in the sociotechnical system approach a new paradigm (p. 365).

The most recent annual review, by Beer and Walton (1987) is in part an effort to incorporate OD into the realm of general and human resource management, rather than an exploration of OD as a unique field of organizational inquiry and practice. The present approach is similar to that of Beer and Walton in its attempt to provide a broad overview of the field and where it is headed, including—but not limited to—research findings. The present approach differs, however, in that we view OD as remaining a distinct field of study and action, rather than as becoming incorporated as an aspect of general management.

Implicit in the difference between the present review and the approach taken by Beer and Walton is the issue of values. Earlier we noted that OD has two aims, one being directed toward improved organizational performance and the other centering on improvements in the "human condition" within organizations (Table 1). This is an explicit factor in the Friedlander and Brown (1974) review, is reflected in the Alderfer (1977) review, and is a major overt and covert theme in the review by Faucheux et al. (1982). "Traditional" OD values center on the importance of people and of their roles in organizations. An OD approach to organizational improvement must include both a "people" as well as a "performance" focus (Tannenbaum & Davis, 1969). Beer and Walton (1987), however, caution OD practitioners that the latter value—performance—must become predominant, with the former—concern for people—kept in the background as a long-run strategic vision but not as an operational part of OD. Thus one might see Beer and Walton's position as an attempt to integrate the conflicting aspects of OD by eliminating some of them, by coopting OD into the broader management domain, and by relinquishing an overt concern for improving the "quality of work life" of organization members. We prefer to reemphasize the importance of both OD aims, improving organization members' quality of work life *and* improving bottom-line performance outcomes. Making this issue explicit leads us to consider the question of whether OD is distinct from what has been called "Quality of Work Life."

Quality of Work Life

The concept of quality of work life (QWL) has become increasingly popular as defining an area for study by social scientists as well as an arena for social action and organizational change. However, QWL remains a somewhat vague, fuzzy construct. What exactly *is* QWL? Is it OD? Various definitions have been offered since the term was first used in the late 1960s. Even though most people would see QWL as a part of, if not the same as OD, Carlson (1980) defined QWL so broadly that it subsumed OD, rather than vice versa.

The only empirical effort to define QWL, through a factor analytic study (Taylor, 1978), yielded a single predominant factor that could not be clearly interpreted. Perhaps the most clear and comprehensive analysis is offered by Nadler and Lawler (1983), who identify four different major definitions of QWL over the time period 1969–1980. The earliest definition used QWL as a variable, specifically as workers' reactions to the work, expressed in terms of satisfaction. Soon, however, QWL came to be seen as a particular organizational improvement approach involving labor-management cooperation. In many applications during this period, from about 1969 to 1975, performance and productivity improvements were explicitly excluded as QWL aims, in part to reassure workers and unions that this was not simply another management ploy to get more productivity out of labor at no cost. The third definition, common through the mid-70s, identified QWL with the specific changes and methods that were often involved: teams, autonomous groups, job enrichment, and sociotechnical change. Finally, beginning in the mid-to late-70s, QWL came to be seen by many as a social movement, and it is, indeed, in this context and incarnation that it was identified by Faucheux et al. (1982) as perhaps being the successor to OD. Of course, in this final definition QWL focuses on just one of the two pairs of OD aims and values (as defined in Table 1) and is therefore clearly *not* the same as OD, in our view. But the issue can, perhaps, best be expressed as one of viewpoint.

Seashore (1973) suggested that QWL can best be thought of as a set of three umbrella constructs. In each of these three constructs specific variables can be defined, but they change across the three situations. The three umbrellas are really viewpoints: the viewpoint of workers, of managers (or the organization as a whole), and of society. Table 2 presents an illustrative set of variables, listed within each viewpoint category.

Thus, a "quality" work life may mean different things to different people in different roles, or to the same person in different roles; that is, as an employee of a university—a professor—one may be concerned with how one's role as a teacher fits with one's role as a member of a profession—a researcher or scholar—and with one's other professional role as a private consultant. The dean of the college, however, is concerned with the quality of students that faculty can attract and with the number of students in a class. But consider that the professor is also a private citizen. As such, one may be concerned about how the university professor is contributing to solving the problems of socializing young adults to the traditional norms and values of society and work.

Even more troublesome, different people in the same role may have discrepant views of QWL, not merely on the basis of different personal values but as a result of different abilities and aptitudes. The same assembly job may be very low in quality from the viewpoint of a bright, intellectually gifted college graduate, moderate in quality to an "average" worker with a high school education, but high in quality to a mildly retarded individual. For one person, growth and satisfaction may mean very different things than for another.

Faucheux et al. (1982) agree most with Nadler and Lawler's (1983) fourth definition of QWL as a social movement and seem to consider QWL identical to OD. But this is actually just the reverse side of the position taken by Beer and Walton (1987), who drop the workers' and societal viewpoints and accept only the organizational perspective. In contrast, Faucheux et al. see OD as QWL for workers and society, but not for managers of the organization. The definition of OD used here makes it clear that OD is both more and less than QWL. OD, in the present view, does not include the social movement/societal viewpoint identified by Nadler and Lawler and by Seashore, but does incorporate both workers' QWL as well as QWL from an organizational viewpoint.

The confusion introduced by the varying and sometimes conflicting definitions and views of QWL is not, in our view, random noise. Rather, this confusion represents the playing out of the conflict between bottom-line and humanistic values in OD. Seashore's analysis suggests to us that both of these value positions are legitimate and that neither can be labelled true or false. It therefore seems to us to be of great importance that OD incorporate both of these value prem-

TABLE 2

Quality of work life variables: Three perspectives

Worker	Organization	Society
Health	Productivity	Effect on propensity toward deviant behavior
Security	Absenteeism	Contribution toward "full" employment
Job satisfaction	Turnover	Facilitation of positive intergenerational socialization processes
Adequate income	Development of promotable employees	Impact on older citizenry (direct and indirect, current and future)

ises, not through continual conflict but in much the same way that technology and social structure are "jointly optimized" in the sociotechnical systems approach. This is what we have tried to illustrate in Figure 2.

OD Literature in the '80s

More comprehensive reviews of the OD research literature prior to 1980 are provided in the *Annual Reviews* and in an exhaustive overview by Macy (1986a), on which we will comment later. As our aim was to examine OD trends and directions, our in-depth survey of the literature was confined to publications of the 1980s. Sources included both academic and popular literature but centered on the PsychInfo database, the past several years of the *Journal of Applied Behavioral Science* and *Group & Organization Studies,* and OD Division papers and presentations at the national Academy of Management meetings.

The PsychInfo database search yielded 210 items, of which about half were actually OD articles that included some empirical data (even if case study in nature). This was a surprisingly low number of reports for a 4½-year period (1981–85), considering that the database includes quite a few nonmainstream journals (like *Leadership and Organization Development* and *Management Education and Development*). Of the 84 reports that could clearly be called OD, the largest number were published in *Training and Development Journal* but few of these, if any, included empirical data. Of the remainder, 21 appeared in *G&OS,* 17 in *JABS,* and 6 in the next most-cited source, *Human Relations.* Perhaps encouraging, from an OD researcher's perspective, is evidence that the database failed to capture a substantial number of OD reports. Examination of the contents of the 1983 and 1984 volumes of *JABS,* all of which were supposedly in the PsychoInfo database, identified 25 (of a total of 67) articles that were, on closer examination, clearly OD research. Thus crude extrapolation suggests that the true number of OD research reports may be about

2½ times that indicated by the PsychInfo database search. In real numbers, this means that over the 1981–1985 time span there were perhaps 500 published OD-related articles, with about 250 of these representing databased research reports.

In reviewing the OD literature up to 1980, Spier, Sashkin, Jones, and Goodstein (1980) identified 717 OD references for the decade of the 1970s, 207 for the 1960s, 31 for the 1950s, and just 7 for the period up to 1950. With these figures as a baseline for comparison, the very great increase in OD reports from 1950 to 1970 was not maintained through the first half of the '80s. From about 3 reports per year in the '50s, 21 per year in the '60s, and 72 per year in the '70s, the average remains about 75 per year in the '80s. Stability also appears in the number of papers and symposia submitted to the Academy's OD Division for 1984–1986, with about 40–50 papers and 15–20 symposia. Overall, evidence from several sources suggests that the dramatic rise in OD research through the '60s, and '70s has, in the '80s, stabilized.

Until now we have considered only numbers and totals. Content categorization of OD research adds considerably to our understanding of the field. Such an examination identified four major categories. Unsurprisingly, the two outstanding ones center on *research issues*—that is, problems and methods (by far the most common topic), and *theory* (with somewhat greater than half the number of citations as research methods); these results are unexceptional.

More interesting were the major research issues to appear in the literature; we shall briefly review these in the next section. As for the development of OD theory, the relative frequency of citations may be misleading. Some, for example, limit their theoretical contribution to the use of the word *theory* in the article title. In a three-page article in *Training and Development Journal,* for example, Weisbord (1985) defines *team effectiveness theory* as the use of teams and team building activities to introduce change.

Other contributions seek to reconnect with some of the writing basic to OD. An example is provided by Mendenhall and Oddou (1983) in their paper, "The Integrative Approach to OD: McGregor Revisited." Still others hark back to fundamental OD theories and approaches of the '60s and the '70s. Sashkin, Burke, Lawrence, and Pasmore (1985), for example, sought to highlight three "neglected" OD approaches (Walton's, 1969, third-party consultation; Lawrence & Lorsch's, 1969, contingency theory; and the sociotechnical systems approach of Pasmore & Sherwood, 1978). We find no real coherence among the various theoretical contributions of the 1980s that would lead us to think that the field of OD is approaching a theoretical synthesis.

Turning to topics with lesser numbers of citations, we find two more that have enough items to be worth noting. The first is team building. This is hardly surprising; by the 1980s team building has become a standard item in the tool kit of just about every OD practitioner; the paper by Weisbord (1985), cited earlier, is one demonstration of this fact. Indeed, Friedlander and Schott (1981), along with Weisbord (1985) consider teams to be a primary vehicle for organizational change. Murrell and Valsan (1985), for example, report on the use of team building in Egypt, and Eden (1985) provides a "true field experiment" on the effects of team building, followed up by a more strongly supportive "quasi-experiment" (Eden, 1986b). And Fiedler, Bell, Chemers, and Patrick (1984) describe an OD program to increase mine productivity and safety that, though based on team building, does not even use the term in the report's title, an indication of just how deeply imbedded team building has become as a foundation stone of OD practice.

The second of these two remaining categories is unexpected. It contains reports and studies dealing with organizational cultures and change. This is a topic that we do not find in the reviews of the 1970s. Organizational culture also appeared as the single most common theme of papers and symposia at the 1985 Academy of Management OD Division meetings (followed by research methods, sociotechnical systems, and team building). However, with rare exception (e.g., see Wilkins & Ouchi, 1983), such reports lack empirical referents, let alone research data. That is, we find much in the way of concept and discussion, focused on the pragmatic (Ernest, 1985) as well as the more academic (Kilmann, Saxton, & Serpa, 1985), but little indeed that could be termed empirical research. Most of the references in this category are symposium presentations, papers in nonacademic (or nonresearch) magazines and journals (like *Personnel Administrator*), nonrefereed publications (such as chapters in annual "research" volumes; e.g., Trice & Beyer, 1986) or books. In fact, two of the most widely recognized OD practitioners in the United States, Warren Bennis and Edgar Schein, have both produced recent books dealing with organizational culture (Bennis & Nanus, 1985; Schein, 1985). We will return to this new focus on culture.

In the PsychoInfo citations there were three additional topics that received some mention. These were survey feedback, OD in schools, and ethics. The first two can be seen as continuations (with reduced emphases) of earlier OD trends (e.g., see Gavin [1984, 1985] and Fullan, Miles, & Taylor [1981]). The third topic, OD values and ethics (e.g., Frankel, 1986), may represent an attempt to deal directly with the value conflict issues we identified earlier (see Table 1 and Figure 1), issues that have long been central to OD. Another possibility is that the values/ethics issue has come to the fore in OD as a result of its emphasis in general, across Academy of Management divisions. Still another explanation might be that an ethical code is seen as an important aspect of the professionalization of OD, as an area of application and practice, just as in the fields of medicine or law (White & Wooten, 1986).

Having characterized the nature of the OD

literature, we must look a bit more closely at what it tells us with regard to our current knowledge of OD. This will highlight the means by which the themes identified in Table 1, task versus process OD aims and people-centered versus performance-centered OD values, have approached the integrated state illustrated in Figure 2.

OD Research: Issues and Answers

Topical trends in the OD literature provide leads as to where the field is going, and we shall shortly engage in some detailed speculation in that regard. However, before looking at what we might expect during the remainder of this decade and on into the next century, we should take a close and critical look at the status of OD research knowledge: What do we really know? What are the key research problems—and their solutions, if any? We identified four themes in the OD research literature, and we shall review each one in some detail.

Issue 1: How good is the research? Beginning in the late 1970s, various scholars began to examine the net findings of OD research, concentrating on whether consistent improvements as a consequence of OD activities could in fact be demonstrated (e.g., Franklin, 1976; Morrison, 1978; Porras & Berg, 1978b; White & Mitchell, 1976). They quickly, however, began to be concerned with the quality of OD research (Porras & Berg, 1978a), with some reviewers (Terpstra, 1981, 1982) concluding that much OD research shows unrealistic positive outcomes, due to weak, nonrigorous research designs that make it easy for researchers to find what they are—consciously or unconsciously—looking for. This debate over the quality of OD research raged on until quite recently, when an exceptionally careful review by Woodman and Wayne (1985) reported finding *no* relationship between research rigor and positive research findings. Indeed, tracking OD research in the early 1980s, Nicholas (1982) and Nicholas and Katz (1985)

find evidence that the quality of OD research has been consistently improving over time. Although some argue that the final word is not yet in, most scholars seem willing to conclude that general positive biases on the part of OD researchers using weak research designs have not been the primary source—and are probably not a significant cause—of positive OD research findings. Developments with respect to the second research issue, however, may make superfluous much of the concern and argument around OD research quality.

Issue 2: What are the true effects of OD interventions? Perhaps the most exciting new methodological innovation in the social sciences in this decade has been a set of methods called "meta-analysis" (Glass, McGaw, & Smith, 1982; Hunter, Schmidt, & Jackson, 1982). This approach makes use of certain quantitative data that can be gleaned from some research reports. These data are used to determine the true effects of experimental treatments, across research studies. It is important to realize that meta-analysis goes far beyond traditional integrative research reviews, whether qualitative or quantitative, allowing the strongest and clearest conclusions possible about the actual effects of specific actions.

The first meta-analysis of direct relevance to OD effects was performed by Guzzo, Jette, and Katzell (1985). Examining outcomes across more than 70 research studies, these researchers were able to assess the relative effect of several types of OD intervention. Their results were quite encouraging, showing that job design, participative management, sociotechnical systems interventions, and other OD actions all had quite positive effects on performance (output, turnover, absenteeism, and disruptions), ranging from an average improvement of one-quarter to one-half a standard deviation. This provides further, strong evidence that OD effects do not depend primarily on poorly designed or controlled research.

A more narrowly focused review of the effects

of autonomy and participative decision making (Spector, 1986), which included a number of OD efforts as well as some noninterventional studies, corroborates some of the results reported by Guzzo et al. Spector found that high levels of autonomy and participation designed into the job were associated with high satisfaction, commitment, involvement, performance, and motivation, and with low levels of physical symptoms of ill health, emotional distress, role stress, absenteeism, turnover intent, and actual turnover.

A recent, massive review of some 800 work improvement and productivity efforts by Macy (1986a) draws generally positive conclusions with respect to both performance and worker satisfaction. However, a meta-analysis by Macy, Izumi, Hurts, and Norton (1986) of the 56 studies that included the required statistical information confirmed only the productivity effects; effects of workers' self-perceived quality of work life were almost uniformly *negative*. Macy (1986b) suggests that these odd results may be due to the performance pressures placed on workers by certain effective OD "action levers" (such as the use of work teams or new work structures). With respect to performance criteria, however, the results of this meta-analysis are quite consistent with earlier reviews of OD, both traditional and meta-analytic. There is little doubt that, when applied properly, OD has substantial positive effects in terms of performance measures.

Issue 3: What is really changing? A longstanding problem has centered on the question of what really changes as a result of OD interventions. It is probable that every OD practitioner has completed a project that to all appearances was quite successful—even taking into account the sort of bias one would expect when the consultant rates his or her own work. Yet, the clients report that the situation is *worse,* not better! Golembiewski, Billingsley, and Yeager (1976) sought to explain this unsettling paradox. They defined three types of change. *Alpha* change is "true" change, a change in mea-

sured attitudes and behavior that can be shown to result from an OD intervention. *Beta* change occurs when measurement scales themselves change, in the minds of organization members. For example, what had before the OD intervention seemed to be a pretty good climate might afterward be viewed as rather poor in comparison with a newly recognized ideal. And this might be the case even though the OD intervention really *improved* the situation! Thus the outcome might appear to be little or no change, or even to be negative, although the "true" result is a positive change. This true result is, however, detectable only if the shift in organization members' internal measurement scales can be identified and taken into account. The third type of change, *gamma* change, makes quantitative OD effects almost impossible to demonstrate because the basic dimensions, the very ways in which organization members see the organization, have been changed as a result of OD activities.

There has been a modest amount of research over the decade since Golembiewski et al. (1976) published their paper on types of change, most of it dealing with how to detect the different types (e.g., Armenakis & Zmud, 1979; Lindell & Drexler, 1980; Van de Vliert, Huismans, & Stock, 1985; Zmud & Armenakis, 1978). Oddly enough, despite general acceptance of the concepts defined by Golembiewski et al., and recognition of their import (their original paper won the 1976 McGregor Award), almost no OD research appears that takes type of change into account unless the researchers are explicitly studying how to measure one or more of the three types of change. This may be due to the difficulty in applying the concepts, in actually trying to identify and take into account the type of change. The primary effect of this work may be to raise the awareness of OD practitioners and to help them explain why they may feel rotten even though objective indicators say that things are getting better.

Issue 4: Is what you want what you get? More than a decade ago King (1971, 1974) showed that the "pygmalion" or self-fulfilling prophecy (Merton, 1948) effect identified by Rosenthal (1966, 1976) applied to OD as well as to the classroom. Rosenthal's most striking illustration of the effects produced by researchers' expectations was obtained in elementary school classrooms. Twenty percent of children in each of 18 schools were *randomly* labeled as students "who would show unusual academic development during the coming school year." At the end of the school year, those who were "academic bloomers" were found to have substantially greater IQ gains compared with others in their class. Similarly, King (1971) found that when supervisors expected hard-core unemployed trainees to learn and perform well, the trainees did so; when the supervisors' expectations were for poor learning and performance, then that, too, was the result. Later, King (1974) found that an OD intervention proved effective, in terms of "hard" performance criteria, when those involved were led (by the experimenter) to expect it to, whereas the same intervention failed when organization members were led not to expect strong positive results. None of these findings implies that expectations alone can improve performance; teachers worked differently with the academic bloomers than with those not so labeled, and organization members took a different approach to the OD intervention they expected to work than to the same intervention when they were led not to expect it to work. Thus expectations are not magic and cannot in and of themselves produce the desired effects. Expectations may, however, be a *necessary* (but not sufficient) condition for OD effectiveness. This is the argument developed by Eden (1984, 1986a) and his associates (Eden & Ravid, 1982; Eden & Shani, 1982).

This issue, which, at first glance, may seem to benefit OD practice, also presents some serious problems. Expectation or experimenter effects are considered highly undesirable threats to the validity of research. Thus, as a scientist the OD practitioner is confronted with a double bind: using expectation effects may be necessary if the OD effort is to have the desired positive impact, but doing so may invalidate the worth of the OD activity as research!

Summary. OD research has, by the mid-1980s, shed quite a bit of light on the effects and effectiveness of OD. We are also in the position of understanding far more clearly than ever the key research problems in OD. Solutions are another matter. Although few today are willing to argue that OD has no real effects, there remains considerable uncertainty over how properly to measure these effects. And it may well be that effective OD is actually inconsistent with rigorous research, as some have argued (see Argyris, Putnam, & Smith, 1985). Further OD research is needed to determine whether effective OD interventions can be combined with rigorous research. Rosenthal's (1979) work suggests this is possible *if* the researcher-practitioner's expectations are taken into account as part of the research design.

We suggest that the clear research demonstration of positive OD impacts owes much to the integration of task structure and behavioral process-based OD approaches and of people-centered with profit-centered OD values. The work on types of change shows an increasingly sophisticated appreciation of the true interdependence of structure and process in OD. The newest theme, concerning the effects of expectations, may be another way of showing that the two value sets in Table 1 can be integrated if that is what we choose to expect. Future research should examine new ways of integrating or combining structural OD interventions with OD activities centered in behavioral processes (Sashkin, in press). Multivariate research is needed on the combined and interactive aspects of these two factors, which have all too often been treated only independently.

Trends in Organization Development

Some years ago, Friedlander (1976) likened OD to an adolescent going through the maturing process in the context of a strange and complex family situation, a *menage à trois*. It is now more than a decade since he used that metaphor, and in that time OD has passed through adolescence about as successfully as most adolescents do. That is to say, the field is alive and kicking, has learned a trade, has attained modest success at it, and hopes for grand successes in the future. New relationships have taken the place of the nuclear family. One might even say that arising out of a sort of *menage à trois,* OD has formed a new one, with culture and with sociotechnical systems (STS), as a means of dealing with deep and abiding value conflicts. Moreover, OD may be courting the strategy domain as well. Before going too far with this tempting metaphor, we should consider for a moment the trends and prospects for OD today in the late 1980s.

Trend 1: Systematic structure-process integration. Throughout our review we have observed increasing evidence of a marriage between task focus and process skills, not just at the level of a specific "micro-intervention" like a team building meeting or a problem solving session centered on survey feedback data, but at the larger, system level. We believe that this structure-process integration (shown in Figure 2), which was hinted at in the early review by Friedlander and Brown (1976), has developed over the past decade and has come to characterize OD practice in the 1980s. Effective OD practitioners in the 1980s use (and teach) process skills not to make people feel better about their work, one another, or the organization, but to help people learn to solve problems and get their work done more effectively. Furthermore, OD practitioners take a larger, more systematic perspective, focusing on organizational issues, such as strategic planning, reward systems, management structures, and information systems; no longer is the OD focus solely on teams, interpersonal issues, and training. The broadened perspective of OD, we should note, incorporates, rather than excludes, these "micro-issues."

Perhaps a key to the sort of task-process inte-

gration we refer to can be seen in the STS approach, which has come into much greater use in the early 1980s (see Walton, 1985). STS provides strong support for task-process integration, since it explicitly aims to "jointly optimize" the technical and social structures of the organization. And there is convincing evidence (Guzzo et al., 1985; Macy et al., 1986) that the STS approach has strong positive effects on productivity and performance. We expect the implementation of "new work structures," as Walton (1985) terms this sort of change, to proceed at an increasingly rapid rate over the remainder of this century. Effective attention to an integration of the task and process aspects of OD provides resolution to one of the two critical themes in OD that we identified at the beginning of this review.

Trend 2: Culture by design: Integrating value perspectives. Consistent with the sort of larger scale, system approach just described is the recent salience of organizational culture. Indeed, OD practitioners often find that their clients use the term *culture* before they do, even quoting Deal and Kennedy (1982) to them! The concept of culture has become more clear and has attained general acceptance due to its importance for understanding how to manage, lead, and change large and complex systems. Senior managers in many corporations are aware, as was not true a decade ago, that significant changes in organizational mission and strategy will produce great frustration, if not outright failure, unless concomitant consideration is given to modifying the organization's culture such that norms and values support the change (see Schein, 1985). Thoughtful strategy development is becoming a common aspect of OD (Eadie & Steinbacher, 1985). Such strategic designs are carried out by designing the organization's culture, a process often simply called "managing change," which has become a catchword for OD as applied to designing organizational cultures. Lest all this begin to sound rather abstract, recognize that the aim is to build a culture that values productivity, performance, and bottom-line outcome measures, a culture of "excellence" (Peters & Waterman, 1982).

Such cultures can only be developed through leadership, and for this reason leadership has come to the forefront as a critical issue at the organizational level. We refer not to the sort of academic models of leadership that actually deal with the practice of lower and mid-level supervisory management (Blake & Mouton, 1978; Fiedler, 1967; Hersey & Blanchard, 1982; Stogdill & Coons, 1957; see Yukl, 1981, for a comprehensive overview). Rather, we refer to top-level, organizational leadership (Sashkin & Fulmer, in press) of the sort that transforms organizations (Burns, 1978; Tichy & Devanna, 1986) by empowering organization members (Burke, 1986). The importance of top management for successful OD is not, of course, a new concept; nor are we really speaking of a new sort of role for the CEO. This sort of executive leadership is precisely what top-level management has always been about (e.g., see Mintzberg, 1973). The change is in conscious direction of the leadership process to attain concrete changes in organizational culture (see Schein, 1985).

We have asserted that these culture-building efforts by top-level leaders aim to incorporate organizational values of excellent performance into the culture. This takes care of the bottom-line value position of organizational management; but how is this integrated with the people-centered value position of OD, focused as it is on the quality of work life from the point of view of lower-level organization members? We have hinted at how, when we mentioned empowering employees (Burke, 1986). Such empowerment is a critical part of a broad strategy of management, that is commonly referred to as participation.

Participation in management, employee involvement, and related sorts of activities—hallmarks of OD practice and values—are more in evidence today than ever before (Hoerr, Pollack, & Whiteside, 1986; Walton, 1985).

The efficacy of participative management and its positive bottom-line effects have received empirical research support (e.g., see Miller & Monge, 1986) and the participative approach has been increasingly advocated (Sashkin, 1982, 1984, 1986).

Others, however, have pointed out that though evidence abounds that participative ways of managing pay off, at the bottom line as well as in terms of other performance indicators, the process is often resisted, especially at higher levels of management (Saporito, 1986). Saparito quotes one executive as stating that the delegating of decisions took the fun out of managing. Others appear resistant due to contradictory values (e.g., Locke, Schweiger, & Latham, 1986), even to the point of denying the positive effects of participation.

Without a greater understanding of executives' needs for power, of the dynamics of power and politics in organizations, and of the values underlying different managerial approaches, the OD emphasis on creating participative organizational cultures through top-level leadership might prove to be more of a fad than an enduring approach for building people-centered values—particularly a lower-level employee quality of work life viewpoint—into organizational cultures.

Participation encourages human development needs centered on autonomy and control of one's own actions (Argyris, 1957). It provides for satisfaction of the need for achievement and closure (McClelland & Burnham, 1976; Sashkin, 1982, 1984). And when applied in a group context (e.g., Likert, 1967) and in conjunction with a sociotechnical systems approach, participation provides for satisfaction of the need for work-relevant interpersonal contacts (Mayo, 1933; McClelland, 1955). Thus we come full circle, finding that effective integration of the conflicting value perspectives of management and workers is best accomplished in the context of effective integration of task and process foci, as was illustrated at the beginning of this review (see Figures 1 and 2). The sociotechnical approach (Pasmore & Sherwood, 1978), when combined with the development of a culture-by-design, can together serve to integrate the long-standing overt and covert conflicts in OD.

In sum, these first two critical trends suggest that OD practice may be resolving the structure versus process issue while dealing with the performance versus people concern. These ends are achieved by combining an STS design approach with a focus on changing organizational culture through executive leadership.

Trend 3: Managing conflict.   Conflict resolution and effectiveness in lateral relations have long been acknowledged as important for organizational effectiveness, and conflict management has been a basic element of OD since the 1960s (Walton, 1969, 1987). It appears to us that managing conflict is becoming even more of a focus in OD practice. There are at least three factors behind this. First, there is the tendency toward more decentralized authority structures and flatter hierarchies. In such circumstances getting the work done effectively depends more on influence skills and less on the exercise of power as a function of position or status (Kanter, 1984). Second, we see a continuing emphasis on collaborative approaches to labor-management relations and a continuing move away from the classic adversarial model (Shirom, 1983). OD is an important factor in this move. Finally, the incredible increase in organizational mergers and acquisitions in the 1980s has created many more settings in which serious conflicts are bound to occur and in which achieving some degree of smooth working relationship—if not total integration—is critical. In sum, managing conflict is a major OD trend that is likely to increase in scope in the future.

Trend 4: Better research.   As we saw from our review of OD research, there is much greater sophistication today about research in general and its relation to OD in particular. Critical issues and problems are far better and more clearly de-fined than was true a decade ago and, more important, OD practitioners are aware of those issues to a much greater degree than was true in the past. It may, however, be that awareness and understanding is as far as we can go, with respect to resolving some of the research problems (in particular, in reference to the fourth issue identified earlier), in order to have greater, more positive, and more lasting OD effects, not just to control or correct for these problems while doing "good research." Thus we may see OD practitioners making active use of expectation effects and beta change, rather than correcting research designs for these "artifacts." Indeed, some might say that practitioners will merely have new labels for (and perhaps a better understanding of) what they would do anyway.

In sum, OD research is more sophisticated, more methodologically sound, than ever. We are approaching some real syntheses of research findings, and this trend will continue as more and better meta-analyses are carried out. And OD practitioners are learning how to use experimenter effects and other research artifacts to the benefit of OD efforts in organizations.

Trend 5: Improved theory?   We are much less certain of this trend than we are of the others; perhaps it reflects our hopes more than it does reality. Our hope is that the increased interest in meta-analysis may indicate an increase in efforts at integrating not just various sets of research studies but in doing so in a way that results in good OD theory. Indeed, we hope to be seen as an example of this; it would be foolish to assert that the integration arguments just reviewed are proven fact, that they are anything other than hypotheses based on a careful review of OD research and practice.

It is our belief that OD professionals today recognize clearly—and more than they did a decade ago—that no strong integrative theory of OD exists. We have broad macro-theories of change, such as that developed by Lippitt and his associates almost 30 years ago (Lippitt, Watson,

& Westley, 1958). And we have narrow, small-scale "mid-range" theories (see chapter 2 in Burke, 1982). Still, we lack a widely accepted theory of organizational change through OD, and none seems to be on the horizon. We can only suggest and hope that the integrations and advances discussed here may eventually address this lack, too, moving us toward completion of the OD theory statement developed by Friedlander and Brown (1974).

Summary: Organization Development in the 1980s

We see three major conclusions about OD in the 1980s. First, the casual observer as well as the practitioner finds much less strangeness in the field and a much greater sense of respectability for organization development. Many OD interventions are so standard, such as off-site meetings or team building sessions, as to be familiar to any experienced manager. Rarely does one see the use of T-groups or encounter groups. And though OD research is not welcomed in the traditional research publications, there are respectable outlets and even an occasional article in the *Academy of Management Journal* or in the *Journal of Applied Psychology.*

Second, there has been an effective integration, resolving the long-standing conflict between structural OD concerns and behavioral process issues as the focus of OD activities. At the micro level this is seen most clearly with respect to team building (DeMeuse & Liebowitz, 1981). In the 1980s, team building rarely (if ever) consists of open-ended examination of interpersonal relations. Team building interventions today typically have a clear task focus; process is a way of improving how the team accomplishes its tasks, not an end in itself. On the macro level, the sociotechnical systems approach seems to be serving as a vehicle for integrating these same task structure and behavioral process concerns. Moreover, the emphases on reward

systems, management information systems, structures and strategies indicate that OD professionals have broadened their perspectives. In these ways, the "human processual" and "technostructural" cores of OD identified by Friedlander and Brown (1974) are being effectively connected.

Third, there is a greater focus on organizational culture, not from a pure process viewpoint but from the sort of structural perspective commonly used by organizational sociologists, such as Talcott Parsons (1960). Such an approach makes clear how values affect critical organizational functions. When combined with the sort of perspectives on leadership common to sociologists, such as Selznick (1957) or Perrow (1979), but unfamiliar to most of those in the field of "organizational behavior," this cultural perspective suggests some interesting new directions for OD practice. More importantly, it suggests that leaders act to create cultures that integrate the two value perspectives—organizational bottom-line and humanistic quality of employee work life—that have long been the source of covert conflict in OD theory and practice. Future OD research should focus on empirical and experimental measurement of cultural OD interventions and their effects, including especially effects on values that concern both performance and people.

Implications for Practitioners

In the 1960s and well into the 1970s, OD practitioners had to fight constantly such stereotypes as "group grope," "flakey, soft" orientations toward human behavior, and beliefs like "If people feel better, performance will be better." This strangeness about OD, as we have noted, is all but gone. In fact, the problem today may be not being different enough. The system may have co-opted us. In other words, what we face today are serious questions of values and ethics. In the face of (*a*) companies being bought and sold more rapidly than ever before, and (*b*) activities such as downsizing, undoubtedly a significant change is underway in the nature of the psychological contract between employee and employer. Loyalty to one's employer may be a thing of the past. What constitutes commitment in the workplace may be considerably different in the 1990s. What is fair treatment of employees today? Do we practitioners support the organization from whence our salary comes or the individual being considered for outplacement? Who is our client? Although we in OD have always been confronted with the conflict of the individual versus the organization, what is unprecedented is how deep this issue has become. Never before have we had to face so squarely our own beliefs, values, and ethical standards. It is far more than merely espousing Theory Y. Understanding ourselves more thoroughly and determining what stances we wish to take and under what circumstances are more important than ever.

Organizational culture is here to stay; the notion is not a passing fad. OD practitioners must immerse themselves in understanding the concept, in ways of assessing organizational culture, and in ways of changing it. There are at least two major practice areas for OD consultants. One concerns the alignment of strategy and culture. When top management decides to change to the organization's strategy without a commensurate plan to modify the culture accordingly, the new strategic thrust is likely never to materialize. The second OD practice area is the alignment of two cultures as a consequence of acquisitions/mergers or a significant reorganization. "But that's not the way we do things" is the often heard retort. OD practitioners must help the two cultures find a third, new one that is acceptable to and effective for both.

There are no doubt additional implications. In any case, for the 1980s and at least into the early 1990s, the two mentioned above seem to us to be at the top of the list.

Organization Development in the Future

Popular yet astute observers of current and future shifts in organizational effectiveness have their differences but also reflect common ground. Consider Naisbett and Aburdene's *Re-Inventing the Corporation* (1985), Rosabeth Kanter's *The Change Masters* (1984), and the latest thinking of Tom Peters (in press). They all agree that effective organizations in the future:

1. Will be flatter structurally, and organizational members will "network" more to get work done and to communicate.
2. Will involve organizational members more in decisions they are expected to implement.
3. Will be more people oriented.

If these observers are no more than half correct, OD practitioners will have plenty of work and articles like this one will continue to be written.

OD, however, is still a field in transition, as one of us wrote more than a decade ago (Burke, 1976). Even though certain principles have been delineated (e.g., change involves unfreezing, intervention, and refreezing), and most agree that OD practice follows an action research model, OD nevertheless is comparatively young. OD is no longer an adolescent, but neither is it a mature adult. So, the future is still a prediction, not a foregone conclusion. Thus, we shall provide three possible scenarios for the future, giving you, the reader, choice and involvement—in the OD fashion.

First Scenario: OD is stagnating, retrenching, and collapsing inward upon itself. Having ultimately failed to demonstrate clear and convincing bottom line effects, and with evidence that even positive attitudinal effects are ephemeral, OD as it was known from the '70s to the '80s is well on the way to being no more. The few real contributions, in terms of specific, focused "intervention" activities will become—indeed, *have* become—part of the normal functioning of a good personnel department ("human resources" department, for anyone new to the game), as well as standard elements of the management consultant's tool kit. Of course, organizations do change, and help with the problems of change is certain to be a continuing need. Such help is likely, in the future, to be more structural and technical than process-or attitude-focused. Although it is unlikely, it may be that some aspect of OD as we know it will ultimately emerge, like a phoenix, from the ashes of its own demise.

Second Scenario: To all appearances, OD is healthy and stable, entering a period of slow but steady and productive growth in which the primary task is refinement and consolidation. OD practitioners realize that they cannot work miracles, but have also come to better understand that their effort can make a difference. Some of the most generally useful bits and pieces of OD practice have become widely integrated into organizational life. The very notion of the work group or team, and of team building, has become accepted and commonplace, and it is worth noting that this was not the case 20 years ago, nor is the case in much of the industrialized world outside the United States (including Japan, as both authors were surprised to discover personally). There is now strong evidence that OD can and does make a difference and that effects are not dependent on poor research designs or chance. Although without a common theory of OD, practitioners have shown that they know what they are doing. Finally, there has been major progress in integrating structural and process-centered change interventions that may eventually lead to even stronger OD effects. In sum, OD is no longer as exciting as when it was a new and radical approach to creating change in organizations, but it has demonstrated strength, substance, and persistance.

Third Scenario: OD is moving in new, exciting directions—structure, culture, and leadership. It is about to become in fact what it has always hoped to be, a true and viable strategy for improving whole organizations, in terms of both human needs of organization members and bottom-line results. At the same time, OD is seen to be based in approaches and techniques that have been proven so effective for solving organizational problems that they stay solved and for making significant improvements in "organizational life." OD remains, as it has been for some time, the leading edge of applied behavioral science. Furthermore, and more to the point, organization culture will be the OD focus of the late '80s and of the 1990s. This will be true on a large scale, in terms of the sort of cross-cultural value differences explored in depth by Hofstede (1980), as well as on the scale of the organization, in terms of specific OD interventions, as detailed in articles such as Jaeger's (1984, 1986). But the real key to changing culture, as implied already, is not the sort of micro-OD intervention approach, like team building, that we are familiar with. As has now been recognized more appropriately, the key is in leadership, specifically the leadership of the chief executive officer. This is the focus advocated and explored for many years by Argyris (1973), who even takes the position that it is the values expressed through the actions of the CEO that ultimately drive OD.

Some of the most current culture-changing OD work (e.g., see Frohman & Sashkin, 1985) has involved a CEO and top executive team in analyzing the organization's value base, acting to make changes through a general corporate philosophy, and then carrying out that philosophy in terms of policies, programs, and personal actions. Thus, in the late 1980s and through the 1990s, the structural focus that has since the late 1970s become a stronger and more important element of OD will continue to drive major OD activities. We will continue to learn to use task-process integration and sociotechnical systems approaches to design and change organizational cultures in order to integrate the organizational value of performance and productivity with organization members' value of a high quality work life.

A Choice

Which of the above scenarios is it likely to be? We have already rejected the first, at least as a likely option, yet it cannot be completely ruled out. Without a coherent theory of OD practice and of change, the field is vulnerable, and there remains the possibility that OD will eventually become so fragmented as to have no coherence as a discipline. Thus, though not the most likely outcome, the first scenario is feasible. Still, it seems far more likely that even under the worst of circumstances OD will continue to exist as an identifiable field of research and practice. And those scholars and practitioners with some vision will be studying sociotechnical systems and culture, along with organizational leadership.

But what about a choice between the second and third scenarios? One of us predicts the second, but hopes for the third. The other hopes for no worse than the second while predicting the third. Perhaps the first is a realist and the second an idealist, if not a cockeyed optimist. In any case, we indeed agree that OD is alive and well in 1987, and all indications are that it will continue to thrive well past the millenium.

References

Alderfer, C.P. (1977). "Organization Development." In M.R. Rosenzweig & L.W. Porter (eds.), *Annual Review of Psychology* (pp. 197–223). Palo Alto, Calif.: Annual Reviews, Inc.

Argyris, C. (1957). *Personality and Organization.* New York: Harper & Row.

Argyris, C. (1973). "The CEO's Behavior: Key to Organizational Development." *Harvard Business Review* 51 (2), 55–64.

Argyris, C.; Putnam, R.; & Smith, D.M. (1985). *Action Science.* San Francisco: Jossey-Bass.

Armenakis, A.A., & Zmud, R. (1979). "Interpreting the Measurement of Change in Organizational Research." *Personnel Psychology* 32, 709–23.

Bass, B.M. (1985). *Leadership and Performance beyond Expectations.* New York: Free Press.

Beer, M., & Walton, A.E. (1987). Organization Development. In M.R. Rosenzweig & L.W. Porter (eds.), *Annual Review of Psychology* (pp. 339–67). Palo Alto, Calif.: Annual Reviews, Inc.

Bennis, W.G., & Nanus, B. (1985). *Leaders.* New York: Harper & Row.

Blake, R.R., & Mouton, J.S. (1978). *The New Managerial Grid.* Houston: Gulf.

Burke, W.W. (1976). "Organization Development in Transition." *Journal of Applied Behavioral Science* 12 (1), 22–43.

Burke, W.W. (1982). *Organization Development: Principles and Practices.* Boston, Mass.: Little, Brown.

Burke, W.W. (1986). "Leadership as Empowering Others." In S. Srivastva & Associates (eds.), *Executive Power* (pp. 51–77). San Francisco, Calif.: Jossey-Bass.

Burke, W.W. (1987). *Organization Development: A Normative View.* Reading, Mass.: Addison-Wesley.

Burke, W.W., Clark, L.P., & Koopman, C. (1984). "Improve Your OD Project's Chances for Success." *Training and Development Journal* 38 (8), 62–68.

Burns, J. McG. (1978). *Leadership.* New York: Harper & Row.

Carlson, H.C. (1980). "A Model of Quality of Work Life as a Developmental Process." In W.W. Burke & L.D. Goodstein (eds.), *Trends and Issues in OD: Current Theory and Practice* (pp. 83–123). San Diego, Calif.: University Associates.

Clark, J.V., & Krone, C.G. (1972). "Toward an Overall View of Organizational Development in the Early Seventies." In J.M. Thomas & W.G. Bennis (eds.). *The Management of Change and Conflict* (pp. 284–303). Middlesex, England: Penguin Books.

Deal, T.E., & Kennedy, A.A. (1982). *Corporate Cultures: The Rites and Rituals of Corporate Life.* Reading, Mass.: Addison-Wesley.

DeMeuse, K.P., & Liebowitz, S.J. (1981). "An Empirical Analysis of Team-Building Research." *Group & Organization Studies* 6, 357–378.

Eadie, D.C., & Steinbacher, R. (1985). "Strategic Agenda Management: A Marriage of Organizational Development and Strategic Planning." *Public Administration Review* 45, 424–30.

Eden, D. (1984). "Self-Fulfilling Prophecy as a Management Tool: Harnessing Pygmalion." *Academy of Management Review* 9, 64–73.

Eden, D. (1985). "Team Development: A True Field Experiment at Three Levels of Rigor." *Journal of Applied Psychology* 70, 94–100.

Eden, D. (1986a). "OD and Self-Fulfilling Prophecy: Boosting Productivity by Raising Expectations." *Journal of Applied Behavioral Science* 22, 1–13.

Eden, D. (1986b). "Team Development: Quasi-Experimental Confirmation among Combat Companies." *Group & Organization Studies* 11, 133–146.

Eden, D., & Ravid, G. (1982). "Pygmalion vs. Self-Expectancy: Effects of Instructor and Self-Expectancy on Trainee Performance." *Organizational Behavior and Human Performance* 30, 351–64.

Eden, D., & Shani, A.B. (1982). "Pygmalion Goes to Boot Camp: Expectancy, Leadership, and Trainee Performance." *Journal of Applied Psychology* 67, 194–199.

Ernest, R.C. (1985). "Corporate Cultures and Effective Planning." *Personnel Administrator* 30 (3), 49–60.

Faucheux, C., Amado, G., & Laurent, A. (1982). "Organizational Development and Change." In M.R. Rosenzweig & L.W. Porter (eds.), *Annual Review of Psychology* (pp. 343–370). Palo Alto, Calif.: Annual Reviews, Inc.

Fiedler, F.E. (1967). *A Theory of Leadership Effectiveness.* New York: McGraw-Hill.

Fiedler, F.E.; Bell, C.H., Jr.; Chemers, M.M.; & Patrick, D. (1984). "Increasing Mine Productivity and Safety through Management Training and Organization Development: A Comparative Study." *Basic and Applied Social Psychology* 5, 1–18.

Frankel, M.S. (1986). "Values and Ethics in Organization Development: The Case of Confidentiality." *Organization Development Journal* 4 (2), 14–20.

Franklin, J.L. (1976). "Characteristics of Successful and Unsuccessful Organization Development." *Journal of Applied Behavioral Science* 12, 471–92.

Friedlander, F. (1976). "OD Reaches Adolescence: An Exploration of Its Underlying Values." *Journal of Applied Behavioral Science* 12, 7–21.

Friedlander, F., & Brown, L.D. (1974). "Organization Development." In M.R. Rosenzweig & L.W. Porter (eds.), *Annual Review of Psychology* (pp. 313–41). Palo Alto, Calif.: Annual Reviews, Inc.

Friedlander, F., & Schott, B. (1981). "The Use of Task Groups and Task Forces in Organizational Change." In R. Payne & C. Cooper (eds.), *Groups at Work* (pp. 191–218). London: Wiley.

Frohman, M.A., & Sashkin, M. (1985, August). "Achieving Organizational Excellence: Development and Implementation of a Top Management Mind Set." Paper presented at the annual meeting of the Academy of Management, Organization Development Division, San Diego.

Fullan, M., Miles, M.B., & Taylor, G. (1981). *Organization Development in Schools: The State of the Art.* Washington, DC: U.S. Government Printing Office.

Gavin, J.F. (1984). "Survey Feedback: The Perspectives of Science and Practice." *Group & Organization Studies* 9, 29–70.

Gavin, J.F. (1985). "Observations from a Long-Term Survey-Guided Consultation with a Mining Company." *Journal of Applied Behavioral Science* 21, 201–20.

Glass, G.V., McGaw, B., & Smith, M.L. (1982). *Meta-Analysis in Social Research.* Beverly Hills, Calif.: Sage.

Golembiewski, R.T. (1979). *Approaches to Planned Change.* New York: Marcel Dekker.

Golembiewski, R.T.; Billingsley, K.; & Yeager, S. (1976). "Measuring Change and Persistance in Human Affairs." *Journal of Applied Behavioral Science* 12, 133–57.

Guzzo, R.A.; Jette, R.D.; & Katzell, R.A. (1985). "The Effects of Psychologically Based Intervention Programs on Worker Productivity: A Meta-Analysis." *Personnel Psychology* 38, 275–91.

Hersey, P., & Blanchard, K.H. (1982). *Management of Organizational Behavior* (4th ed.). Englewood Cliffs, NJ: Prentice Hall.

Hoerr, J.; Pollock, M.A.; & Whiteside, D.E. (1986, September 29). "Management Discovers the Human Side of Automation." *Business Week,* pp. 70–75.

Hofstede, G. (1980). "Motivation, Leadership, and

Organization." *Organizational Dynamics* 9 (1), 42–62.

Hunter, J.F.; Schmidt, F.L.; & Jackson, G.B. (1982). *Meta-Analysis: Cumulating Research Findings across Studies.* Beverly Hills, Calif.: Sage.

Jaeger, A.M. (1984). "The Appropriateness of Organization Development outside North America. *International Studies of Management and Organization* 14 (1), 23–35.

Jaeger, A.M. (1986). "Organization Development and National Culture." *Academy of Management Review* 11, 178–90.

Jayaram, G.K. (1978). "Open Systems Planning." In W.A. Pasmore & J.J. Sherwood (eds.), *Sociotechnical Systems: A Sourcebook* (pp. 28–38). San Diego, Calif.: University Associates.

Kanter, R.M. (1984). *The Change Masters: Innovation for Productivity in the American Corporation.* New York: Simon & Schuster.

Kilmann, R.H.; Saxton, M.J.; & Serpa, R. (1985). *Gaining Control of the Corporate Culture.* San Francisco: Jossey-Bass.

King, A.S. (1971). "Self-Fulfilling Prophecies in Training the Hard-Core: Supervisors' Expectations and the Underprivileged Workers' Performance." *Social Science Quarterly* 52,, 369–78.

King, A.S. (1974). "Expectation Effects in Organizational Change." *Administrative Science Quarterly* 19, 221–30.

Krone, G.G. (1974). "Open Systems Redesign." In J. Adams (ed.), *New Technologies in Organization Development: 2* (pp. 364–391). San Diego, Calif.: University Associates.

Lawrence, P.R., & Lorsch, J.W. (1969). *Organization and Environment.* Homewood, IL: Irwin.

Likert, R. (1967). *The Human Organization.* New York: McGraw-Hill.

Lindell, M.K., & Drexler, J.A., Jr. (1980). "Equivocality of Factor Incongruence as an Indicator of Type of Change in OD Interventions." *Academy of Management Review* 10, 269–74.

Lippitt, R.O., Watson, J., & Westley, B. (1958). *The Dynamics of Planned Change.* New York: Harcourt, Brace, & World.

Locke, E.A.; Schweiger, D.M.; & Latham, G.P. (1986). "Participation in Decision Making: When Should It Be Used?" *Organizational Dynamics* 14 (3), 65–79.

McClelland, D.C. (ed.). (1955). *Studies in Motivation.* New York: Appleton-Century-Crofts.

McClelland, D.C., & Burnham, D. (1976). "Power Is the Great Motivator." *Harvard Business Review* 54 (2), 100–10.

Macy, B.A. (1986a, August). "An Assessment of United States Work Improvement and Productivity Efforts: 1970–1985." Paper presented at the National Academy of Management meetings, Chicago.

Macy, B.A. (1986b). Personal Communication.

Macy, B.A.; Izumi, H.; Hurts, C.C.M.; & Norton, L.W. (1986, August). "Meta-Analysis of United States Empirical Organizational Change and Work Innovation Field Experiments." Paper presented at the National Academy of Management meetings. Chicago.

Mayo, E. (1933). *The Human Problems of an Industrial Civilization.* New York: Macmillan.

Mendenhall, M., & Oddou, G. (1983). "The Integrative Approach to OD: McGregor Revisited." *Group & Organization Studies* 8, 291–301.

Merton, R.K. (1948). "The Self-Fulfilling Prophecy." *Antioch Review* 8, 193–210.

Miller, K.I., & Monge, P.R. (1986). "Participation, Satisfaction, and Productivity: A Meta-Analytic Review." *Academy of Management Journal* 29, 727–753.

Mintzberg, H. (1973). *The Nature of Managerial Work.* Englewood Cliffs, NJ: Prentice Hall.

Morrison, P. (1978). "Evaluation in OD: A Review and Assessment." *Group & Organization Studies* 3, 42–70.

Murrell, K.L., & Valsan, E.H. (1985). "A Team Building Workshop as an OD Intervention in Egypt." *Leadership & Organization Development* 6 (2), 11–16.

Nadler, D.A., & Lawler, E.E. III (1983). "Quality of Work Life: Perceptions and Directions." *Organizational Dynamics* 11 (3). 20–30.

Naisbett, J., & Aburdene, P. (1985). *Re-Inventing the Corporation.* New York: Warner Books.

Nicholas, J.M. (1982). "The Comparative Impact of Organization Development Interventions on Hard Criteria Measures." *Academy of Management Review* 9, 531–43.

Nicholas, J.M., & Katz, M. (1985). "Research Methods and Reporting Practices in Organization Development: A Review and Some Guidelines. *Academy of Management Review* 10, 737–49.

Parsons, T. (1960). *Structure and Process in Modern Societies.* New York: Free Press.

Pasmore, W.A., & Sherwood, J.J. (eds.). (1978). *Sociotechnical Systems: A Sourcebook.* San Diego, Calif.: University Associates.

Perrow, C. (1979). *Complex Organizations* (2nd ed.). Glenview, IL: Scott, Foresman.

Peters, T.J. (in press). "A World Turned Upside Down." *Academy of Management Executive.*

Peters, T.J., & Waterman, R.H. Jr. (1982). *In Search of Excellence: Lessons from America's Best-Run Companies.* New York: Harper & Row.

Porras, J.I., & Berg, P.O. (1978a). "Evaluation Methodology in Organization Development: An Analytical Critique." *Journal of Applied Behavioral Science* 14, 151–73.

Porras, J.I., & Berg, P.O. (1978b). "The Impact of Organization Development." *Academy of Management Review* 3, 249–266.

Rosenthal, R. (1966). *Experimenter Effects in Behavioral Research.* New York: Appleton-Century-Crofts.

Rosenthal, R. (1976). *Experimenter Effects in Behavioral Research* (enlarged ed.). New York: Irvington.

Saparito, B. (1986). "The Revolt against " 'Working Smarter.' " *Fortune* 114 (2), 58–65.

Sashkin, M. (1982). *A Manager's Guide to Participative Management.* New York: American Management Association.

Sashkin, M. (1984). "Participative Management Is an Ethical Imperative." *Organizational Dynamics* 12 (4), 4–22.

Sashkin, M. (1986). "Participative Management Remains an Ethical Imperative." *Organizational Dynamics* 14 (4), 62–75.

Sashkin, M. (in press). "Content and Process in OD Intervention: The Message from Research." *Organization Development Journal.*

Sashkin, M.; Burke, R.J.; Lawrence, P.R.; & Pasmore, W.A. (1985). "OD Approaches: Analysis and Application." *Training and Development Journal* 39 (2), 44–50.

Sashkin, M., & Fulmer, R.M. (in press). "Toward an Organizational Leadership Theory." In J.G. Hunt et al. (eds.), *Emerging Leadership Vistas.* Boston, Mass.: Lexington Books.

Schein, E.H. (1985). *Organizational Culture and Leadership.* San Francisco: Jossey-Bass.

Seashore, S.E. (1973). Personal Communication.

Selznick, P. (1957). *Leadership in Administration.* Evanston, Ill.: Row, Peterson.

Shirom, A. (1983). "Toward a Theory of Organization Development Interventions in Unionized Work Settings." *Human Relations* 36, 743–64.

Spector, P.E. (1986). "Perceived Control by Employees: A Meta-Analysis of Studies Concerning Autonomy and Participation at Work." *Human Relations* 11, 1005–1016.

Spier, M.S.; Sashkin, M.; Jones, J.E.; & Goodstein, L.D. (1980). "Predictions and Projections for the Decade: Trends and Issues in Organization Development." In W.W. Burke & L.D. Goodstein (eds.), *Trends and Issues in OD* (pp. 12–37). San Diego, Calif.: University Associates.

Stodgill, R.M., & Coons, A.E. (eds.). (1957). *Leader Behavior: Its Description and Measurement.* Columbus, Oh.: Bureau of Business Research, Ohio State University.

Tannenbaum, R., & Davis, S.A. (1969). "Values, Man, and Organizations." *Industrial Management Review* 10 (2), 67–86.

Taylor, J.C. (1978). "An Empirical Examination of the Dimensions of Quality of Working Life." *Omega* 6 (1), 1–8.

Terpstra, D.E. (1981). "Relationship between Methodological Rigor and Reported Outcomes in Organizational Development Evaluation Research." *Journal of Applied Psychology* 66, 541–43.

Terpstra, D.E. (1982). "Evaluating Selected Organization Development Interventions: The State of the Art." *Group & Organization Studies* 7, 402–17.

Tichy, N.M., & Devanna, M.A. (1986). *The Transformational Leader.* New York: John Wiley & Sons.

Trice, H.M., & Beyer, J.M. (1986). "Charisma and Its Routinization in Two Social Movement Organizations." In B.M. Staw & L.L. Cummings (eds.), *Research in Organizational Behavior* (vol. 8, pp. 113–64). Greenwich, CT: JAI Press.

Van de Vliert, E.; Huismans, S.E.; & Stok, J.J. (1985). "The Criterion Approach to Unraveling Beta and Alpha Change." *Academy of Management Review* 10, 269–74.

Walton, R.E. (1969). *Interpersonal Peacemaking: Confrontations and Third-Party Consultation.* Reading, Mass.: Addison-Wesley.

Walton, R.E. (1985). "From Control to Commitment

in the Workplace." *Harvard Business Review* 63 (2), 76–84.

Walton, R.E. (1987). *Managing Conflict.* Reading, Mass.: Addison-Wesley.

Walton, R.E., & Warwick, D.P. (1973). "The Ethics of Organization Development." *Journal of Applied Behavioral Science* 9, 681–98.

Weisbord, M. (1985). "Team Effectiveness Theory." *Training and Development Journal* 39 (1), 27–29.

White, L.P., & Wooten, K.C. (1986). *Professional Ethics and Practices in Organizational Development.* New York: Praeger.

Wilkins, A.L., & Ouchi, W.G. (1983). "Efficient Cultures: Exploring the Relationship between Culture and Organizational Performance." *Administrative Science Quarterly* 28, 468–81.

Woodman, R.W., & Wayne, S.J. (1985). "An Investigation of Positive-Findings Bias in Evaluation of Organization Development Interventions." *Academy of Management Journal* 28, 889–913.

Yukl, G.A. (1981). *Leadership in Organizations.* Englewood Cliffs, NJ: Prentice Hall.

Zmud, R., & Armenakis, A.A. (1978). "Understanding the Measurement of Change." *Academy of Management Review* 3, 661–69.

READING 4

AN END-OF-THE-EIGHTIES RETROSPECTIVE: A COMMENTARY APPENDED TO ORGANIZATION DEVELOPMENT IN THE 1980S

Marshall Sashkin and W. Warner Burke

It was in 1985 that we began work on this overview of OD in the 1980s. Thus it is worth a brief, short-term, retrospective analysis as the decade draws to a close. We see no major differences in our original conclusions, but then it would be unlikely to find any at this time; after all, it is not that long ago that we wrote the original paper. We do, however, see some changes in emphasis that are worth mentioning.

Our first two trends, structure-process integration and culture by design, might be better expressed as the micro (task design) and macro (organization design) aspects of the same basic issue: redesigning organizations. A key issue we failed to raise in this regard is that of choice versus chance; that is, the nature of work is changing, at least in postindustrial societies, from an individual to a team focus (as we noted earlier) as well as from simpler to more complex technologies. This is true even at the lowest levels; package delivery services must, for example, now screen delivery personnel, ensuring that they can operate the miniaturized computer link devices that permit the organization to track packages in the system.

Organizations can deal with these changes the same way that changes have, for the most part, been dealt with in the past: with indifference and by making minor modifications or, as Lindblom (1959) put it, "muddling through." Of course, such an "incremental" change strat-

Source: Marshall Sashkin and W. Warner Burke, "An End-of-the-Eighties Retrospective: A Commentary Appended to Organization Development in the 1980s," *Advances in Organization Development* 1 (1990), pp. 347–49. Reprinted with permission.

egy is how the United States became involved in Vietnam and how the Soviet Union got mired down in Afghanistan. If we simply leave things to work themselves out, they will indeed do so. The outcome may, however, not be much to our liking.

Alternatively, executives can choose to take an active role in redesigning organizations and work processes within them. Such choices may be rare, but are not nonexistent. In 1988, for example, as a way to build traditional quality back into the process of manufacturing cars, Volvo began to advertise how teams are used to assemble whole subassemblies of automobiles. However, back when Volvo first experimented with this major organizational and work redesign program, the first plant was designed so that it could easily be changed back to the traditional assembly-line approach, just in case the program failed. We must learn how to approach such changes in ways that build in an escape but do not, by so doing, inculcate expectations of failure (King, 1974).

This brings us back to the issue of leadership; that is, the decision to take control over and try to design organizational cultures—and change—can only be made by top-level leaders. We can, as noted above, leave these processes to chance; the "population ecology" approach shows that some organizations will survive and others won't, depending on how well they adapt to and fit their new environments. But if we elect to try to control and design organizational change, we will need leaders who are capable of being what Bennis and Nanus (1985) call "social architects";

that is, such leaders must understand organizational culture and how to design and change it (Schein, 1985).

Having observed that the single critical role of organizational leaders may be in creating culture, Schein (1985) goes on to suggest that such a task may be impossible for most top executives. Unfortunately, both the required understanding and the necessary skills seem to be uncommon. Thus simple logic suggests that a critical prerequisite for organization development may be executive development, not in terms of traditional management training and development but as a means of producing competent social architects. In some ways this is not unlike the approach advocated for some time by Argyris (1970, 1971, 1976; Argyris & Schon, 1974). Argyris has been criticized by some (e.g., Sashkin, 1977) for an unproductive overemphasis on the chief executive as a necessary first step in organization development. He may, however, have been correct—but a generation ahead of the field!

Thus we come to the limits of our vision. The 1990s may be the period during which organization development and (a new sort of) management development are reconnected. Such a prospect raises mixed feelings in one who spent serious effort in "decoupling" the two (Burke, 1971)! Such sensations aside, both authors have been engaged in developing new approaches to identifying and training leaders who can design organizational cultures (Burke, 1988; Sashkin, 1986). It is much too soon to speculate on the ultimate success or failure of such efforts, but it is encouraging that others in our field seem to be working on the same issues (e.g., Kouzes & Posner, 1987). If we succeed in learning how to develop effective organizational leaders, and in improving organizational effectiveness through their OD efforts, then the coming century may very well be the first in which humans successfully shape their social environments in consciously chosen ways that are designed to enhance human and organizational effectiveness.

References

Argyris, C. (1970). *Intervention Theory and Method.* Reading, Mass.: Addison-Wesley.

Argyris, C. (1971). *Management and Organization Development.* New York: McGraw-Hill.

Argyris, C. (1976). *Increasing Leadership Effectiveness.* San Francisco: Jossey-Bass.

Argyris, C., & Schon, D. A. (1974). *Theory in Practice.* San Francisco: Jossey-Bass.

Bennis, W. G., & Nanus, B. (1985). *Leaders.* New York: Harper & Row.

Burke, W. W. (1971). "A Comparison of Management Development and Organization Development." *Journal of Applied Behavioral Science* 7, 569–79.

Burke, W. W. (1988). *Leadership Report* (2nd ed.). Pelham, NY: Burke Associates.

King, A. S. (1974). Expectation Effects in Organizational Change. *Administrative Science Quarterly* 19, 221–30.

Kouzes, J., & Posner, B. Z. (1987). *The Leadership Challenge.* San Francisco: Jossey-Bass.

Lindblom, C. E. (1959). The Science of "Muddling Through." *Public Administration Review* 19 (Spring), 79–88.

Sashkin, M. (1977). "Review of Argyris' 'Increasing Leadership Effectiveness.'" *Personnel Psychology* 30, 273–80.

Sashkin, M. (1988). The Visionary Leader: A New Theory of Organizational Leadership. In J. A. Conger & R. N. Kanungo (eds.), *Charismatic Leadership in Management.* San Francisco: Jossey-Bass.

Schein, E. H. (1985). *Organizational Culture and Leadership.* San Francisco: Jossey-Bass.

TOWARD THIRD-WAVE MANAGING AND CONSULTING

Marvin R. Weisbord

> The results of this generalized speedup of the corporate metabolism are multiple: shorter product life cycles, more leasing and renting, more frequent buying and selling, more ephemeral consumption patterns, more fads, more training time for workers (who must continually adjust to new procedures), more frequent changes in contracts, more negotiations and legal work, more pricing changes, more job turnover, more dependence on data, more ad hoc organization.... Under these escalating pressures, it is easy to see why so many businessmen, bankers, and corporate executives wonder what exactly they are doing and why. Brought up with Second-Wave certainties, they see the world they knew tearing apart under the impact of an accelerating wave of change.
>
> Alvin Toffler
> *The Third Wave*, 1980

We live in the midst of a historic global revolution—from physical to knowledge work, mechanical to process technologies, manufacturing to service economies, cultural sameness to greater diversity. Future-thinker Alvin Toffler calls this sea change "the third wave" to differentiate it from the agricultural and industrial revolutions of centuries past. Above all, it is a social revolution. Quality of working life (QWL)—meaning quality of products, services, and work itself—has become a worldwide aspiration. QWL is also an umbrella for every sort of "change" program—from quality circles, organization development, statistical quality control, sociotechnical systems design, and cultural transformation.

In this article I want to suggest another "bottom line" for the widespread interest in QWL. I see a hunger everywhere for community among people alienated from work and each other by new technologies and global economics. *Community*, as I use it here, means a workplace where people produce goods or services for a living. A productive community is one where people find dignity, meaning, and security in contributing to the whole.

My purpose is as old as the industrial revolution. More than 40 years ago, Elton Mayo, founder of industrial human relations, noted how "science and industry put an end to the individual's feeling of identification with his group, of satisfaction in his work." We still seek constructive responses to Mayo's diagnosis. Consider the historic 1986 agreement between the United Steelworkers of America and National Steel Corporation. Management, despite economic hard times, promised employment security. The union offered greater job flexibility to increase output. That deal marked a radical break with adversarial traditions. Both parties will be a long time, however, learning to make it work. Yet it exactly embodies the spirit of productive community.

A Practice Theory for Managers and Consultants

Here I offer some spadework toward a "third-wave" practice theory of managing and consulting grounded in these values. My ideas apply to what I know best—reorganizations and work redesign to improve output, quality, and customer focus. They synthesize my work as manager and consultant for more than 25 years with my observations of the uneasy relationship between engineering and psychology in this century. I seek a coherent way of reorganizing under what management professor Peter Vaill calls conditions of "permanent white water."

I want to shift my gaze away from "problems" like cost control *or* interpersonal conflict, that are symptomatic of needs, toward productive community—based on purposes, missions, strategies, and structures worthy of our aspirations, cooperation, and sweat. What can we do today—right now—to make work more secure and improve quality? If you had only a few hours or a few weeks, how would you use your time?

The need to build workplace communities, I'm convinced, is closely tied to preserving democratic values as global economic pressures mount and new hardware, software, and robots pump into the workplace at a furious rate. These developments encompass at once the best and the scariest aspects of American individualism. We revere entrepreneurial behavior and self-actualization. We always have been ambivalent about commitments to each other across levels, functions, lines of status, ethnicity, and class.

"We insist, perhaps more than ever before, on finding our true selves independent of any cultural or social influence," Robert Bellah and partners write in *Habits of the Heart.* "Yet we spend much of our time navigating through immense bureaucratic structures—multiversities, corporations, government agencies—manipulating and being manipulated by others."

We want things every which way. We demand freedom, equal opportunity, and the right to run our own lives, making good Jefferson's Declaration of Independence for "life, liberty, and the pursuit of happiness." We also covet personal security, dignity, support—as promised in the Constitution and Bill of Rights. In the workplace this sometimes plays out as a demand that management "give" people these qualities, when, in fact, all management has the power to do is join in searching for ways to preserve them.

We are driven together again out of necessity. Work methods change so fast now they cannot be controlled by traditional management systems. Social scientists Fred Emery and Eric Trist observed in the 1960s that firms were in increasingly "turbulent fields"—making prediction and control impossible. In *Beyond the Stable State* (1971), Donald Schon saw technology disrupting all "anchors for personal identity." Now the top is spinning faster. Companies, agencies, institutions that used to reorganize every five years now rearrange themselves annually. Many change work sites, job content, titles, and product and service concepts in a perpetual redirection of technologies and markets. How shall we manage these chaotic transactions among economics, technology, and people in the workplace? I suggest that the only steady beacons in such stormy seas are aspirations for dignity and meaning—the wellsprings of motivation—in work.

Invoking Science

For more than 100 years the image of science has been invoked as the key to human motivation. This holy grail was pursued by Frederick Taylor, "the father of scientific management," long before management became a profession. It was pursued with equal intensity by social psychologist Kurt Lewin, "the practical theorist" who invented "force field analysis," discovered participative management, and laid the intellectual groundwork for organization development (OD) in the 1940s.

Taylor, a self-taught engineer, realized that managers awash in "the second wave" could not motivate factory workers. In 1893 he invented a new profession, "consulting engineer," linking cost accounting, time study, wage incentives, and planning into a system that today influences nearly every workplace in the industrial world. Taylor sought to squeeze human discretion from work. He raised wages dramatically if people would do things "the one best way" specified by his engineers.

Taylor today is reviled for his rigid methods. His values, lost in the mists, were quite contemporary. A pacifist as a child, he hated conflict. He wanted to increase labor-management cooperation, cut out authoritarian supervision, reduce job stress, give people more equitable pay for jobs challenging their highest abilities. Taylor made industrial engineers third-party arbiters between labor and management. They devised the "correct" methods for cooperation and conflict resolution. Both organization development and sociotechnical systems design (STS), guided by Kurt Lewin's action research theories, adopted similar purposes. OD managers became the industrial engineers of group development, prescribing self-awareness and interpersonal skills and/or self-managing work teams instead of time and motion study for taking the arbitrariness out of work.

Taylor fell from grace when his descendants divorced his values and married his techniques. Similarly, many OD practitioners, seduced by social technologies, lost sight of Lewin's values—the spirit of inquiry, cooperation, and democratic principles. They were mesmerized by an innovative bag of tricks for diagnosis and intervention—survey feedback, team building, intergroup problem solving, experiential training. Like time study, these could be shoehorned into organizations without dignity, meaning, or worker commitment. In the ultimate absurdity, people were sent wholesale to learn free choice and commitment—whether they wanted to or not.

A Trip through the Forests of Change Theory

To appreciate why I want to redefine the playing field, I would like you to join me on a trip through the thickets of organizational change theory. OD case studies for 25 years have reflected two *different* theories of improvement, coexisting uneasily. One was a theory of "process" diagnosis based on the expert's data-collecting abilities, what I call "snapshooting." Another was Lewin's brilliant theory of participative change-oriented action—"movie-making" in my lingo, but very different from Hollywood's. Most practitioners know that the two theories are really one—that how we take the snapshot determines the quality of the movie. Yet all of us have one foot in what Eric Trist, the originator of sociotechnical thinking, calls the "old paradigm"—Taylor's cause-effect reasoning.

Diagnosis and Action

All consultants advocate expert diagnosis and action-taking. Engineers and behavioral scientists alike have diagnoses of organizational conflict and prescriptions for resolving it. *Diagnosis* is medical jargon for the gap between sickness and health. As biology exploded in the late 19th century, the human body, like the workplace, was divided into manageable components, too. Doctors became the industrial engineers of the human physique. Their claim to expertise was based on their ability to factor in every relevant "variable" and thus heal the sick.

It is no surprise that early psychologists thought the same way about mental processes. Indeed, until the biologist Ludwig von Bertalanffy proposed a general systems theory, people educated in Western industrial nations could hardly think any other way. Diagnosis, conceived as identifying and closing gaps between how things are and how they should be, used all the tools of science and technology. It was the ultimate expression of the industrial revolution.

Musings on Getting "Whole Systems" in a Room

1. I don't like one-shot events. School boards and town councils meet repeatedly. A one-shot conference is not adequate to the tasks of productive community in a workplace, either.

2. In planning workshops, I seek to *reduce* dynamic tensions. A decision to work with groups of 12 is a decision to train group leaders or facilitators—a step away from self-management. Subteams of three or four work well for many tasks, in which mode 100 people can easily work in one room on their own. I suggest that people make time for small groups to review each other's work and for whole system reviews—so all task forces or departments find out what the others are up to.

3. I contract to manage time boundaries and task structures. In self-managed conferences, I suggest that people monitor their own processes and be responsible for output.

4. I do better organizing the search than "the data." I don't withhold my observations, perspectives, or knowledge. But I don't want to make them the center of the action, either. I like to see "task structures"—worksheets, lists, hints, glossaries, exercises, bibliographies, handouts, overheads—devised with client help. I wish to keep them simple and use them sparingly. I aspire to give people information when they can use it, or call for it, not all at once. This does not square with what some people want from consultants. I am unable to help people who are convinced there's a lot more.

5. I aspire to keep the task front and center, directed toward output, and to shift focus to "process" only to get the task back on track. I am not against struggle, anxiety, or bewilderment. We have to go through Confusion to get to Renewal. I tend to become more involved if asked and/or when I see people running away from the task or fighting with each other. I do not always know what to do. Fortunately, someone else usually does.

6. I want to help set norms for productive learning. I reduce my involvement as people get past initial anxiety and take over the work. I have found Merrelyn Emery's advice to avoid attaching to a particular subgroup and becoming its (informal) leader a useful discipline for managing large group events.

7. I like rooms with windows and plenty of light. Hotel "dungeon rooms" depress groups and make productive community very difficult.

8. None of these practices are "the" answer to anything—except how one consultant and ex-manager seeks meaning in work.

Lewin added a new dimension to the medical model. He highlighted processes unseen through 19th-century eyes because nobody had a conceptual lens powerful enough. Lewin's force fields allowed the taking of "process" snapshots—the feelings, motives, intentions, and other intangibles accompanying "results." Lewin portrayed diagnostic gaps in dynamic terms, as an interaction of social forces—personal, group, companywide, societal. Who are the gatekeepers, asked Lewin, whose behavior must change to assure constructive action? What forces prevent or accelerate their involvement? Answers could be found through "action research"—a collaboration between activist scholars and social institutions to bring about constructive personal change.

Two Core Concepts

From Lewin I inherited two core concepts that made my consulting practice possible. Human systems, Lewin believed, were almost, but not quite, static and resistant to change. The consulting goal was to help organizations "unfreeze," "move," and "refreeze." Like all OD consultants, I learned to take diagnostic pictures that would make people want to act—to melt the ice of indifference, ignorance, or uncertainty and unfreeze the system. Once melted, it would follow more natural channels until cooled enough to refreeze in more functional patterns. All OD case studies fit that framework. At the heart of this diagnostic act was a confrontation: The client must "own" the incongruity between what is said and what is done—the demon to be exorcised before healing could begin. It was not necessary to assume sickness to use Lewin's model. However, it was not easy to avoid it either for those of us socialized to view life as one long medical model.

A second concept goes by the name of the "task/process" relationship—the subtle chicken/egg interplay between ends and means, methods and goals. A task is something concrete, observable, and thing-oriented. It can be converted into criteria, measurements, targets, and deadlines—just the way Taylor did. A task—group dynamics people were fond of saying—refers to *what* is to be done.

Process refers to *how.* It reflects perceptions, attitudes, reasoning. Process diagnosticians ask, "Why aren't we making progress?" Or, "Who feels committed to this?" They don't ask when, where, and how many but why, how, and whether. Task/process thinking can be likened to the famous visual paradox of the Old Woman/Young Woman, reproduced below. Do

you see a young beauty with her head turned or a wizened crone in profile?

You can't see both at once. By some mental gyration, you can learn to shift between them. Does one picture "cause" the other? Cause-effect thinking that gave rise both to Taylorism and the medical model led to a relentless propensity to see one form of task only as *the* "task." Western industrial managers developed an exquisite "left-brain"—linear, rational, A causes B, three steps, nine phases, finish by Tuesday, get to the bottom line. Diagnosis, even of "processes," requires structure and precision. Whether your categories are "hard" or "soft," listing and prioritizing puts the left brain into high gear.

Action, on the other hand, reflects pure process. We guide it largely on automatic pilot, fueled by little explosions of energy in the right brain—of creativity, insight, synthesis—that can't be quantified or specified as "targets." Lewin ingeniously expanded left-brain thinking. He shifted the diagnostician's viewpoint to the other picture—*processes* always present and not previously visible because nobody was looking for them. From his work came my simple practice theory: "Process" issues *always* block work on "tasks."

Through trained observation, you can diagnose ingenious linkages between task and process. When work stalls, for example, determine what is *not* being talked about—the gap between word and deed, the all-too-human shortfall between aspiration and action. You must shift attention the way a pilot scans instruments—from compass to altimeter to air speed indicator—to keep task and process synchronized. That requires skills few of us learn in school.

Unfortunately, left-brain diagnostic thinking—perfected by scientists for more than 100 years—leads people to pay attention to the compass and to consider the altimeter a frill. The diagnoser is assumed to stand outside, impartial, "objective," and aloof from what is observed. If you add to this our propensity to defer to authority—parents, bosses, experts—you have a setup for disappointment. For the authority/dependency relationship *itself* becomes a "process" issue, especially when the person invested with magical abilities lacks satisfactory "answers." Group dynamics' great contribution to management was its relentless gaze at the process picture as inseparable from the task, the diagnoser inseparable from the diagnosis, a leader's effectiveness inseparable from follower contributions.

Unfreezing, Etc.

Now, let us visit the connection between the task/process interplay and "unfreezing, moving, and refreezing." This linkage made the OD profession possible. Unresolved "process" issues accumulate in organizations like junk in an attic. People "freeze" in dysfunctional patterns—nobody listens, appreciates, communicates. Output and quality suffer. Reacting to crises drives out planning. Lewin sought to "unfreeze" this self-perpetuating ice storm over corporate headquarters with action research.

If the stored-up stuff could be got out in the open, if "undiscussable" topics could be talked about, energy would be released. People would become aware of their own contributions to their problems. New behavior would emerge, accelerated by explicit skill training. Unfrozen people could evolve strategy, policy, procedure, systems, relationships, and norms more to their liking. Implementing new action plans would refreeze the system into more functional patterns. Shifting your gaze between task and process could be-

come a "way of life." Results could be feedback loops. When you had new dilemmas, you would realize how your own assumptions contributed. You would be more inclined, for example, to involve others previously left out. This is called "learning how to learn"—studying a situation in which you assume responsibility by taking account of "data" previously ignored.

Consulting Skills and Cultural Change

In the 1950s, people began working out a new form of third-party behavior, "consulting skills," to encourage this form of learning. Technical experts diagnosed and prescribed without involving others in their analyses. Behavioral science consultants made a different deal. They proposed a "scientific" method of data collection, arrangement, and discussion derived from Lewin's insights that people are more likely to act on solutions they have helped develop. It included a minor fiction—that questions, methods of inquiry, data presentation, analysis, and action steps would be jointly planned. I say "fiction" because the methods inevitably belonged to the consultants, and so did the theories of task/process, unfreezing, etc. The "feedback meeting" became a pivotal point of social change—the payoff for action research. There the data was "owned," the system melted, and movement initiated. Those were the OD change assumptions so far as the "movie" was concerned.

As for the "snapshot," the OD consultant may have been an open-systems dreamer, but the practice did not reflect the aspiration. It was too attached to feelings, perceptions, and communications, too separated from technology, economics, and structural relations. "Social researchers," wrote William H. Whyte in *Learning from the Field,* "tended to concentrate almost exclusively on human relations. We gave lip service to the importance of technology but tended to treat it as a constant instead of as a variable, which could be changed along with changes in human relations."

However, many "sociotechnical systems"

practitioners who saw technology and people as one system lost sight of the participatory process. They prescribed complex methods of analysis and change that only trained consultants could apply. They evolved analytical tools that belied the movie's basic simplicity. Yet STS was not an "expert" invention. In 1949 Eric Trist found a British coal mine where union workers and a mine manager, driven by a change in roof-control technology, had worked out a system of self-managing teams.

Trist and Emery worked out some simple procedures embodying what they had learned—about redundant skills, managing boundaries, and full participation. In no time their successors had added checklists, analytical tools, exercises, procedures, steps, principles, team building, and other "have tos" enough to deter even the most dedicated clients. Thus we have the central paradox of the changeover from industrial to postindustrial societies—how to encourage people to solve their own problems when every simple new idea can be elaborated endlessly by specialists. What becomes of dignity, community, and meaning in work if you can't reorganize yourself without three years of full-time study? Traditional science has no answers for that paradox.

Yet second-wave ODers thought they had found one. They added up the three stages—unfreezing by third parties, movement by principals and third parties together, refreezing by the principals—that made up a "cultural change strategy." Science could be mobilized to beat back authoritarianism and bureaucracy. What made this different from Taylorism were the psychological content and participative techniques—learning to do things with others, not to them or for them.

The Snapshot Sets Up the Movie

For decades OD diagnoses were based on what might be called Lewin's law. The "snapshot" focused attention on discrepancies and pinpointed ways to close gaps. In *Productive Communities,* I recount four OD projects from 1969 to 1980 based on Lewinian action research methods. Two involved surveys and feedback of structured data and two interviews, group diagnosis, and problem-solving task forces. One project led to a reduction in employee turnover in food service cafeterias, another to a more focused research and development effort in a chemical firm, the third to production improvements in a pill factory, the fourth to strategic redirection in a solar energy company.

In all four, the consultants—with client acceptance—supplied the methods, collected and summarized data, prepared reports, created situation "maps," facilitated discussions. Eventually client groups took over, planned, and implemented changes with consulting help. Reviewing these now, I detect a subtle shift in my practice—from classical action research, based on consultant-centered problem diagnosis, toward much greater client involvement in looking at the whole system regardless of the problem. Why diagnostic technologies for systems change? The reason is not far to seek. We have assumed since Lewin that only accurate "data" and thorough analyses will "unfreeze" structures, procedures, relationships, and norms. Anything less would be unprofessional and unscientific. That is precisely what Taylor assumed about lathes and drillpresses.

Rethinking Lewin

I find my old-practice theory unsatisfying from two perspectives now. First, global markets, technologies, and worker expectations change so fast that a frozen workplace is a temporary phenomenon. Today, change goes more like a bullet train than a melting iceberg. The rate of change has accelerated since Kurt Lewin died in 1947. It occurs too fast for experts to pin down, even the "process" kind. Conventional diagnoses may serve many useful functions, but "unfreezing" systems is not one of them.

Second, we change our behavior when we are ready to do it, not because of a force field (or any) analysis. The first law of techniques is:

Everything works; nothing works. Nobody is skilled enough to push the river. That is supported by consulting experiences clear back to Frederick Taylor. The best a consultant can do is create opportunities for people to discover and do what they want to do anyway. When we apply the "bag of tricks" in a linear way, without informed cooperation and self-control, *only* the content differs from Taylor's. The process comes out uncomfortably the same.

If you accept that proposition, you will see why I worry more about responding to needs for dignity and meaning in work—which means *solving your own problems*—than about supplying "right" answers. There is considerable anxiety and confusion everywhere. I think it is wrong to assume our mutual dilemmas mean "sickness," as if only the diagnostician is whole and in control. Nothing holds still long enough to be diagnosed and "changed" anyway. So consultant-centered diagnostic activities intended to unfreeze systems, even when welcomed by clients willing to defer to authority, may inadvertently distract people from taking charge of their own lives.

Building on Lewin

To honor Lewin now, we must go beyond him. But how? We need new processes for managing and consulting that I do not fully understand. I'm conscious of profound paradoxes. I have at my fingertips diagnostic techniques for every "issue" in the cosmos. On my bookshelf I find more models for fixing things than there are stars in the galaxy. Yet I am strangely undernourished by this intellectual cornucopia. My objective, I keep reminding myself, is not to diagnose and heal "sickness," but to help people manage their work lives better—to enact productive community.

The consultants' dilemma is that we always arrive in the middle of somebody else's movie and leave before the end. It usually has many subplots and informal directors. The consultant negotiates a role—sometimes major, sometimes minor—but always limited by the willingness of others to play along. My view of the consultant's role has turned upside down from what I once thought it was. I imagine it now as helping people discover a more whole view of what they are doing than any one "discipline" or perspective can provide, *including mine.*

I find that proposition fraught with uncertainty. Is it "doable"? To the extent that I can help people integrate worthy values and tasks, I make an important contribution. Yet that means being at some level an "expert" and accepting people's projections of authority, even when I don't act the authoritarian. None of us knows, exactly, how to be both an expert and just one of the gang—when we are dedicated more to collaboration and mutual learning than to being "right." There is no substitute for learning. That any of us can teach others to "learn how to learn" is, in my opinion, a theory full of iffiness.

Toward Assessing Possibilities

We come at last to the heart of it: It is not always practical or desirable to negotiate a consulting role that, at its simplest, is helping people do what they are going to do anyway. The consultant's task in the movie is to see confusion and anxiety through to energy for constructive action and to learn along with everybody else. That has an odd ring to somebody, like me, who grew up in the "second wave." I find myself thinking that assessing conditions under which such an unusual client/consultant partnership is feasible should be the first task of consultation. I wouldn't be deciding how to help, but whether to even make the offer. That means a different kind of snapshot from the "unfreezing" variety.

Diagnosis, the gap between sickness and health, is not the right word for what I mean. The third wave of change is not a sickness, although some consequences can be. Anxiety is not a sickness. It is a sign of learning and potential energy. We need another term. Maybe *assessment* will do. Third-wave managers need simple ways for assessing the potential for action, unifying themes to focus attention, methods to help people learn together about the whole contraption. That is quite different from having a consultant build a "problem list" and prioritize it. I am not against expertise—only the assumption that the specialist (or boss, or consultant) knows *everything* required to resolve the situation defined by his or her expertise or authority without having to do anything new or risky. This is especially true in the complex activity called "reorganizing." That's a developmental task—a great deal of it governed by the right brain and not amenable, except in small details, to ordinary problem solving.

Moreover, we should not mistake "human resources management" for third-wave practices. A major limitation on action is the belief that a human resources department on the 8th floor, just like the strategic planning department on the 14th, somehow makes us immune from reductionistic, linear, rigid solutions. Staff-centered activity is not necessarily conducive to productive community, whether named "participative management," or "dynamic synergistic wholistic transformation." It doesn't matter what you call it. If people don't join in the process of planning their own work, it's old Fred Taylor all over again, only with sociopsychological window dressing instead of his time-and-motion study.

Whose Movie Is It?

It is terribly important to grasp this point if you wish to enact a productive community. An effective snapshot, seen as a dual image—task/process—portrays the whole system in relation to a worthy purpose. It can only do that accurately when the whole system, to the extent possible, takes it, appears in it, and looks it over together. When the whole system is in perpetual motion, every relationship changing, it's impossible for one person to take a coherent picture. As soon as people start making a collective self-portrait, it is no longer a snapshot. *Voilà,* it's part of the ongoing movie, a form of *cinéma vérité,* as messy as life itself.

Only those most involved can make such a movie. The best role a consultant can hope for is stage manager. Kurt Lewin showed that during World War II when he discovered participative management by having Iowa housewives decide whether to change their food habits. Nobody has improved on the principle—that the wisest decisions, given as much information as we can get, are the ones we make for ourselves. People benefit most, I'm convinced, from talking with each other and deciding what to do. I'm for any consulting methods that enhance the dialog.

Thoughts on Stage Managing Third-Wave Movies

To be part of a good movie—to influence committed action—we need a practice theory that (1) respects the past, (2) enhances productive community, and (3) is responsive to the sea change of the third wave. Such a theory requires imagining under what conditions people will work together, which is the manager's dilemma, and under what conditions a consultant can help. "Ninety percent of living," comedian Woody Allen once said, "is just showing up." Just making it possible for the right people to show up may also be 90 percent of consultation. The other 10 percent is helping people focus on worthy purposes they identify for themselves.

My task as consultant is to do the minimum needed to accomplish those objectives. I want to use my data-collecting skills to identify *essential starting conditions* rather than to codify problems. I want to move away from discrepancies between words and deeds—an act of verbal abstraction which, in my view, has very little motivating power—and focus on people's willingness to be responsible for doing important tasks together. In short, I'm more interested in figuring out whether I can make a contribution to this movie than I am in being seen as a brilliant snapshooter. I am not saying that this is the best consultation, only that I find it compatible with my faith in the metaphor of productive community.

Four Useful Practices

In reviewing my projects over 25 years, I find recurring patterns—related to leadership, energizing situations, and energizing people—under which I do better work. The leaders I have learned most from seem to me to have certain knacks. They *focus attention* on worthy aspirations; they *mobilize energy* by involving others; they seem *willing to face the unknown* without "answers."

My leadership observation underlies the first of four "useful practices" I have been experimenting with in evolving a third-wave practice theory. The other three depend on the outcome of the first. I consider these practices plausible (though far from trouble free) alternatives to more traditional consultation for reorganizing large companies and restructuring work. The four practices are to (1) assess the potential for action, (2) get the whole system into the room, (3) focus on the future, and (4) structure tasks that people can do for themselves. They focus on enacting productive community as the backdrop for finding appropriate solutions in "permanent white water." They seem to be well-known among current practitioners, though not well-articulated.

Many of us—we can hardly avoid it—continue to mix them indiscriminately with "second-wave" procedures. I believe that as we use these and similar practices more confidently we will enable "third-wave" reorganizations and work redesigns in the spirit of productive community. Yet moving away from traditional uses of expertise and authority takes us down paths riddled with potholes and pitfalls, for which there are no easy "how tos." Perhaps an explanation of each of the four third-wave practices along with examples will make things easier.

Useful Practice 1: Assess the Potential for Action.   Instead of diagnosing "gaps," I find myself asking under what conditions I could make a contribution. That leads me away from problem lists toward an assessment of leadership, business opportunities, and sources of energy.

Condition 1: committed leadership. Does the person authorized to hire me have itches he or she wants to scratch badly enough to put his or her own rear end on the line? Consultants make better contributions when a person in authority says, "I think this is so important that I'm willing to take a risk, too." I'm wary of requests to fix somebody else or to supply unilateral "expert" answers.

Condition 2: good business opportunities. Good business opportunities come in packages labeled economics and technology—the glue of productive community. So I listen sympathetically to the "people problem" list, but I don't focus on it. Rather, I focus on the opportunities for cooperative action—chances to innovate products/services and/or ways of making/delivering them. These occur most dependably in mergers, acquisitions, reorganizations, declining markets, overhead crises, structures that don't function, new technologies, the need to save jobs.

The Medical Products Division of Atomic Energy of Canada, Ltd., for example, in 1985 rescued itself from economic disaster and mass layoffs by assuring jobs for a year and employing much of its workforce in market studies, work redesign, and new employment opportunities. The payoff was a viable, $30-million-a-year business, managed participatively by employees.

These two conditions—a leader and a promising dilemma—can't be "behavioral-scienced" in, nor "engineered." Frederick Taylor understood their importance in 1900. He did not know as much as we do, though, about commitment and support. Taylor assumed that only the expert's diagnosis and prescription counted. Thanks to action research, we know a great deal more about commitment and support than our grandparents did. We have many choices about how we focus attention and mobilize energy. We know that every task needs a viable process, that every process exists only in relation to a worthy task. We also know that task and process cannot be integrated *for* people. Thus underlying theory—pure Lewin—is that involving those most affected leads to better solutions and quicker actions. Yet participative techniques, or economic ones for that matter, are useless in the absence of leadership and purposeful goals.

Condition 3: energized people. The third dimension is a little trickier. We all drag our feet some days and burst with energy on others. What can a consultant do about this? Claes Janssen, a Swedish social psychologist, has devised a simple tool for visualizing potential energy. Each person, group, department, company, says Janssen, lives in a "four-room apartment."

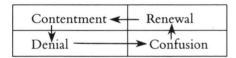

We move from room to room, depending on perceptions, feelings, and aspirations triggered by external events. The rooms represent cyclical phases, not unlike the process of death and dying. Indeed, change represents a "little death," a letting go of the past to actualize a desired future. We change rooms as we grow. However, it's not an ever upward spiral where things only get better. It's a circle game. Our feelings and behavior go up and down as outside pressures impinge on our own "life space." How much energy we have for support and commitment depends upon which room we're in.

In Contentment, we like the status quo. When that changes—through merger, reorganization, new leader, new system, market crisis, job threat—we move into Denial. We stay there until we own up to fear or anxiety. That moves us through the door into Confusion. Mucking

about in Confusion, sorting out bits and pieces, opens the door to Renewal. The passage to Renewal leads from Denial through Confusion. You can't get there from Contentment by any other route.

Anxiety, in Gestalt terminology "blocked excitement," is the emotional decor of the Confusion room. Far from a state to be avoided, it signifies readiness to learn. Anxiety is the place we store energy while deciding whether to invest it. Every new project, course correction, major change requires optimal anxiety. If there's too much, we are paralyzed; too little, unmotivated.

In every Confusion room there are people already taking constructive action. It is they who will carry the movie forward—if they can be brought together to learn how their initiatives integrate with the whole. So I seek to assess which room people live in right now, and how they are acting there. That helps me decide how I can act constructively in the situation. (See Figure 1.)

People in Contentment or Denial are not "frozen." Events will move them soon enough. Little can be done to hasten the day, though rational problem solving can certainly delay it. We can make our presence felt and accepted by acting appropriately with people in those rooms—supporting their right to stay there as long as they wish. To mobilize energy, we need to be with people in Confusion or Renewal. I believe if someone were to revisit OD cases from this perspective, they would see that "failure" correlates closely with action-research methods foisted onto people living in Contentment or Denial. The seeds of success are sown in Confusion and sprout in Renewal. Those are the rooms where people welcome flip charts, models, and OD techniques.

Even that is too simple. Any task—at some point—may shake people into Denial when the going gets rough. When that happens I don't know what to do except keep talking and wait it out. They won't be ready to work toward any

FIGURE 1

Action-taking in the four-room apartment

Contentment Room	Renewal Room
What clients say: "I like it just the way it is."	*What clients say:* "We've got more possibilities that we can ever use. I don't know what to do first."
What a consultant should do: Leave people alone, unless you think the building's on fire.	*What a consultant should do:* Offer assistance through simple, mutually arranged tasks.
Denial Room	Confusion Room
What clients say: "What, me worry?! Everything's fine—I think . . ."	*What clients say:* "This is the damnedest mess I ever saw. Helllppp!"
What a consultant should do: Ask questions. Give support. Heighten awareness. Do *not* offer advice.	*What a consultant should do:* Structure tasks. Focus on the future. Get people together. Ask for/offer help.

changes until they have moved from the Denial room to Confusion or Renewal.

The urge to hold on—to old habits, familiar patterns, relationships, and structures (whether they satisfy or not)—is as old as human history. Robert Tannenbaum and Robert Hanna have pointed out the powerful losses change represents for each of us—of identity, of certainty, of meaning itself. Under these conditions no "unfreezing" techniques are likely to help. According to Tannenbaum and Hanna, "Realistic patience and a sense of an appropriate time scale must underlie and guide the change process itself." We can help by giving people a chance to come together, to experience their mutual dilemmas more fully, to make their own choices about when and how to move.

Hooking together many activities requires only a little linear planning. If we provide the right container, people will fill it with the right elixir. This happens spontaneously as the other practices—getting the system in the room, focusing on the future, constructing doable tasks—are applied. I think it is more likely to happen when we work on important tasks, mutually de-fined, that improve our chances for survival and self-control.

"Should We/Shouldn't We" Discussions.   The activities I like best—because they involve whole systems—are joint planning of business strategy (external focus), work redesign (internal focus), and reorganizations that embody both strategy and structure. In each mode the people most affected help devise and test various structural models, using consulting help. I don't mean to make this sound easy as pie. I usually find myself in long "should we/shouldn't we" dialogs—hours or days of hashing out the pros and cons of opening the action to many others, whether there's time to do it all, whether short-term results will suffer, what good alternatives exist. Above all, each of us uses the dialogs to decide whether to become personally involved.

So I look for a leader, a business opportunity, and a "should we/shouldn't we" discussion. If we decide to team up, I help people plan how to raise a crowd, structure a task, and provide some (left brain) methods for getting started. As right brains are activated, they take care of what can't be planned in advance.

Useful Practice 2: Get the "Whole System" in the Room.   There are many ways to get a "whole system" together. A system can be there, for example, in your head—a conceptual rather than logistical feat that most people can master. Try the "All-Purpose Viewing Lens" in Figure 2, and see how fast you can become a "systems" thinker.

However, knowing what's going on is not the same as enacting productive community. People need shared perceptions to make their contributions. That means getting together to *live* the open system. How many functions, levels, managers, operators, staff, line can be mustered to work on their own organization all at once? Could customers and suppliers be involved? My inclination is to push for "more" and let others say what's "realistic." I confess I don't know how to involve a cast of thousands all at once. Yet keeping that as a benchmark helps me remember what I set out to do. Systems get better when the members cooperate on joint tasks. When people from top and bottom meet across lines of status, function, sex, race, and hierarchy, and when "problems" can be seen as systemic

rather than discrete, wonderful new (and unpredictable) things happen. These can't be "planned" except in the sense of making them more probable. Such happenings lead to more creative and committed actions, more secure and engaging work. Let's look at some examples.

In the merger that created Sovran Bank, the largest financial services institution in Virginia, the operations departments used an interlocking chain of team-development conferences, starting with three top executives from each bank, cascading to the next two levels, culminating in a mass meeting of several hundred people. People planned their own roles and divided up work—an exercise many believed was impossible.

Bethlehem Steel's Sparrows Point plate mill reorganized during a two-week training marathon attended by 80 people—managers, supervisors, and staff—who specified, in advance, which problems they wished to manage better. Together they studied every aspect of the mill—its internal dynamics, the marketplace, corporate connections, and relationships across levels and functions. They visited "suppliers" in steelmaking and customers in distant cities. As workshop "inputs" linked to their own experience, they quickly changed mill practices to serve customers better. They could do this because of an

FIGURE 2

An all-purpose viewing lens

	Inside Picture	*Outside Picture*
Economics	Are costs up or down?	Is revenue up or down?
Technology	Do systems work as intended?	How are products/services being improved?
People	How do people feel about their work?	How do customers feel about the company?

NOTE: Each question can be followed by a "why," and each person who answers these questions will provide a new slant.

unusual business opportunity—the annual maintenance shutdown. The key new management behavior: paying people to come in and learn instead of taking a two-week vacation.

A fast-growing software development company, McCormack & Dodge, lacked the structure to implement a new strategic plan. Top management convened four conferences for 50 people representing all levels and functions. Design teams organized by product line analyzed the system and created new organization designs. They included in the "design specs" a 1990 strategy, their own values about employees and customers, and their analysis of how to close information gaps, improve career paths, and develop more accountability and self-control. Then came the unpredictable part: Twenty-four hours into the first meeting they began making changes to existing practices as information gaps were discovered. Long before a design was "finalized" people were already acting in ways neither planned for nor diagnosed in advance. As a design emerged, the 50 talked over implementation issues with 1,000 other employees.

There is a further benefit to having a whole system present. New patterns of action that are achieved in the room are often carried outside of it *because* all the relevant parties enacted them together. There is less "sell" needed when three or four levels are able to come to the same conclusion at the same time.

Useful Practice 3: Focus on the Future.
This practice derives from work by the late Ronald Lippitt, the coiner, with Kurt Lewin, of the term *group dynamics* 40 years ago. In 1949 Lippitt began tape-recording planning meetings. The tapes revealed that people's voices grew softer, more stressed, depressed, as problems were listed and prioritized. You could hear the energy drain away as the lists grew longer.

In the 1950s Lippitt started using "images of potential," rather than gripes, as springboards for change. In the 1970s he created new workshops merging group dynamics with future thinking.

He has people visualize *preferred futures* in rich detail—as they wish things to be two, three, and even five years into the future. This simple concept has enormous power. While untangling present problems leads to depression, imagining scenarios energizes common values. Taking a stand for a desired future provides purposeful guidance for goal setting, planning, and skill building. Successful entrepreneurs, notes Charles Garfield in *Peak Performers,* are uniquely skilled at projecting alternative futures. They get "feedforward" from their imagination, which is a qualitatively different experience from feedback on past behavior.

This concept—"visioning" is one name for it—is so attractive that most people want to go out and run a group through a visioning training session. This technique *will not work* in the absence of committed leadership, a business opportunity, and some energized people. But don't take my word for it. Try it anyway.

Useful Practice 4: Structure Tasks That People Can Do for Themselves.
What structures make it possible for people to learn, focus on the future, and action plan for themselves (when leadership, opportunity, and energy exist)? A conference series designed by clients and consultants together is one way to bring the productive community alive. These are task-focused, working conferences to reorganize work or refocus effort; they shouldn't serve as add-ons or data dumps.

For consultants to manage such events, they need, first of all, sanction from credible parties. If that can be got, then any plausible "bag of tricks" will do. It is here—at the very last—we get to OD (or any) techniques. If the other signals say "go," then we need few of what Richard Hackman in *Work Design* calls "task performance strategies." One example (out of hundreds) is "responsibility charting," which is a simple way of symbolizing whether people are expected to be active or passive vis-à-vis a decision. Other examples include simple worksheets—which are derived from sociotechnical analysis—to help people with the process of analyzing and redesigning their own work.

Merrelyn Emery, a leading advocate of this perspective, points out that the purpose of consulting technique is to create a learning climate, not solutions. This is a subtle and important distinction. It is essential that we do nothing that would reinforce the idea—both undemocratic and unscientific—"that people cannot make sense of their own experience." Creating a learning climate, points out Emery, results in "an almost immediate increase in energy, common sense, and goodwill."

Summary Observations

Working in these ways, I find myself doing things which don't "come naturally." I have had to shift my focus—a real mental wrench—away from "content" diagnoses and problem lists, even of "process issues." I need to *understand* what a company is up against in the marketplace, what it takes to create committed customers. But I help more and faster when I can assess the potential for action rather than dictate the solution required. So I look for a leader, a business opportunity, some energized employees—conditions no consultant should leave home without. When they exist, I have faith that I can make a contribution to the most complicated reorganizations, despite my concerns that I always do too little or too much.

I have stopped fantasizing that one or two "experts"—even the process kind—are smart enough to figure out on their own the right learning structures. That's 1950s thinking. Anybody who offers to sell you an exemption from the clarifying experience of muddling through to renewal is a charlatan. The more we experts know about our own speciality, the less likely we are to see our favorite solution's impact on a system. When the "whole system" gets into one room, when people have valued tasks to accomplish, I believe the right diagnoses and action

steps occur in "real time." Designing somebody else's work is not in any way, shape, or form an expert task.

Nor do I imagine that I can take away, by any known magical mystery trick, technique, system, jargon, book, speaker, or dog-and-pony show, the travail, confusion, chaos, and anxiety that are as natural to our species as breathing. These conditions fertilize growth, excitement, creativity, joy, energy, and commitment. As a consultant I am often invested with the power to grant people exemptions from states of denial and confusion. Alas, like the Wizard of Oz (who knew he was a fraud pretending that his technologies "worked"), I can't do it.

Instead, I seek to reduce anxiety (my own and others') through simple procedures that allow people to sort through and use their own experience. I help those who wish to design their own futures. I hate to hear anxious people labeled "change resisters," as if the natural cycle of human experience is an evil legion to be defeated by superior methodological firepower on the force fields of organizational strife. Resistance is as natural as eating. I am learning to accept my own resistance, too, especially to client expectations I cannot meet.

In sum, I believe that elaborate, consultant-centered diagnoses are unnecessary to reorganize workplaces flooded by tides of change. As the author of a widely used "six-box" diagnostic model, I expect some fans will be startled by my statement. That model served its function for me long ago—translating process language into managerial tasks. I'm delighted that so many still modify and use it, for it shows that they own it—and this is a development consistent with my theory.

With or without a model, I have learned to expect frustration and anxiety, not smooth sailing, in every white-water voyage. I greet them as familiar traveling companions. I try to rejoin them each time with good humor and to forgive myself when I can't. I recall Rudyard Kipling's poem about keeping your head "when others all about you are losing theirs and blaming it on you." The productive community for me is an anchor point for dignity and meaning in democratic societies. We need to preserve, enhance, and extend it for reasons at once pragmatic, moral, humanistic, ethical, economic, technical, and social.

QWL—far from "cultural change"—can be seen as a serious effort to conserve our culture's deepest values against erosion by narrow economic and technocratic thinking. That for me is the song and dance of restructuring workplaces. I am interested in preserving economic stability beyond quarterly dividends because I believe that democratic societies depend on creating employment. Moreover, I would like to find new ways to help people manage economic and technical innovation so that all of us, myself included, find dignity and meaning in work.

In 1900, Taylor had experts solve problems for people—"scientific management." In 1950, Lewin's descendants started "everybody" solving their own problems—participative management. About 1960, experts discovered "systems" thinking—and began improving whole systems *for* other people. Now, we are learning how to get "everybody" improving whole systems. The most successful third-wave managers and consultants will be those who learn to do that soonest.

Selected Bibliography

The "generalized speedup of the corporate metabolism" has been documented with increasing frequency since World War II. Donald Schon celebrated it in *Beyond the Stable State* (Basic Books, 1971). Alvin Toffler describes it as a historic global shift in human consciousness in *The Third Wave* (Bantam Books, 1980), detailing the impact of new technologies on families, work, lifestyles, and human societies. Toffler's conclusion—more direct democracy is an imperative for survival in a high-tech age—will come as no surprise to this journal's readers.

The negative impact of technology on human aspirations for dignity, meaning, and community has been observed repeatedly from the dawn of history as an antidote to paeans of progress. Elton Mayo's *The Social Problems of an Industrial Civilization* (Harvard University Division of Research, 1945) remains a vivid statement of our own primacy over machines—although why we need to keep asserting this when people devised the contraptions to begin with troubles me. My quote is from Chapter 1, "The Seamy Side of Progress." Donald A. Schon makes the same point in *Beyond the Stable State* (Random House, 1971), adding that organizations and people have to become "learning systems" if they wish to prosper.

The tension between individualism and community in American life predates industrialization. Alexis de Tocqueville, the awed French critic of U.S. democracy, fingered this issue more than 150 years ago. For a contemporary update on his observation see *Habits of the Heart: Individualism and Commitment in American Life* (University of California, 1985) by Robert N. Bellah, Richard Madsen, William M. Sullivan, Anne Swidler, and Steven M. Tipton. This is "must reading" for anybody who cares about the future of interdependence on a shrinking planet, an old-fashioned sociology of real people above statistics in a scholarly genre I haven't seen for 20 years.

Frederick W. Taylor's values have resurfaced in a powerful way in the 1980s, even while we bury his methods for good. *The Principles of Scientific Management,* first published in 1911, is still available in paperback (W. W. Norton, 1967). It's as readable as your newspaper and just as contemporary—perhaps the earliest treatise on collaborative techniques of human resources management. If you ever believed it was anything else, you should read it for yourself—as a reminder that "participation," "commitment," and "excellence" are just as liable to "taylorization" as time-and-motion study.

For evidence of that, look what happened to Kurt Lewin's change concepts. Lewin started with a startling observation—that you can't understand a person's behavior without knowing more about the present situation he or she is in, and vice versa, embodied in "field theory." He talked "psychological ecology" before such a term was fashionable. He believed (not unlike Taylor) that an exact science could be made of human behavior. His original writings are full of obscure mathematical formulae (he used topological geometry to map social-psychological problems). It was only a short jump for appliers of his thinking to imagine (old paradigm) that "unfreezing" techniques could be divined to accelerate human development. I recommend Alfred Marrow's *The Practical Theorist* (Basic Books, 1969), an admiring, intimate, readable account of Lewin's life. In *Productive Communities,* I show Lewin's vast influence on management and the similarity of his interests to Taylor's. I think his most readable work is in *Resolving Social Conflicts: Selected Papers on Group Dynamics* (Harper & Row, 1948) edited by Gertrud Weiss Lewin.

The clearest-eyed antidote I know to megalomania about change techniques is the work of Robert Tannenbaum and Robert Hanna, accessible in "Holding On, Letting Go, and Moving On: Understanding a Neglected Perspective on Change," Chapter 6 in *Human Systems Development,* by Robert Tannenbaum, Newton Margulies, Fred Massarik and Associates (Jossey-Bass, 1985). They make the point that we can't purport to change organizations if we don't appreciate the importance of the human need to hold onto certainty, even the unpleasant kind. Their practice theory supports my belief that Douglas McGregor's Theories X and Y are not so much opposing assumptions about human nature as they are an internal dialog in each of us between our need for control and our wish to be free—a major theme of *Productive Communities.*

For consulting skills—in all areas of experience—I know of no better guide than Peter Block's *Flawless Consulting* (Learning Concepts, 1981). Block's readable follow-up, *The Empowered Manager* (Jossey-Bass, 1986) describes the choices available to those who would take initiative and risk to make their organizations great—a beacon for those who would "let go" of old assumptions and create their own futures.

There is no way to overstate the contributions of Fred Emery, Eric Trist, and colleagues to the revamping of the work world—a history I take up in my book. The best overview I know is Trist's *The Evolution of Socio-Technical Systems: A Conceptual Framework and an Action Research Program* (Ontario Quality of Working Life Centre, June 1981). These concepts will one day be seen as the most revolutionary in human history. That they are not better known now is partly a function of their dense vocabulary (e.g., "causal texture," "turbulent social field") and partly our slowness to recognize how the "new paradigm"—of necessity—is replacing the old in the same way that autos replaced buggies. To extend the analogy, our 1986 understanding of sociotechnical design in the workplace corresponds now to 1917 in the development of the car. Many people have heard of it, far fewer have seen it in action, relatively few have one, not everybody is sure they want one, and those who own one find it cranky, unpredictable, and needing constant maintenance. Eventually everybody will take new paradigm practices for granted.

The "future-oriented" book that has most influenced my practice of workplace improvement is *Building the Collaborative Community: Mobilizing Citizens for Action* (University of California Extension, 1980), by Eva Schindler-Rainman and the late Ronald Lippitt. It describes the methods used to get whole systems in the room to focus on the future and do the job for themselves in 88 community conferences for cities and states all over North America—involving thousands from all walks of life. This book is so diffident its title does not appear on the spine, making it hard to pick off a bookshelf. It deals with voluntary community action, not business firms. It shows more concretely than any work I know that what people can imagine, people can do.

ORGANIZATION DEVELOPMENT AND TRANSFORMATION

Jerry I. Porras and Robert C. Silvers

Introduction

Rapidly changing environments demand that organizations generate equally fast responses in order to survive and prosper. Planned change that makes organizations more responsive to environmental shifts should be guided by generally accepted and unified theories of organizations and organizational change—neither of which currently exists. Yet despite this absence of clear conceptual underpinnings, the field continues to evolve and grow.

In this chapter, we review recent research that improves our understanding of planned change theory and practice. We begin by proposing a new model of the change process rooted in a conception of organizations presented by Porras (1987) and Porras et al. (1990). This change model organizes our understanding of the field and guides the discussion of research presented in the second half of the chapter.[1]

A Model of Planned Change

Organizational change is typically triggered by a relevant environmental shift that, once sensed by the organization, leads to an intentionally generated response. This intentional response is "planned organizational change" and consists of four identifiable, interrelated components: (a) a change intervention that alters (b) key organizational target variables that then impact (c) individual organizational members and their on-the-job behaviors resulting in changes in (d) organizational outcomes. These broad components of planned change are shown at the top of Figure 1. The lower part of the figure adds more detail to each component and graphically summarizes our Planned Process Model;[2] we discuss each component below.

Change Interventions. Planned change interventions can be divided into two general types. The first comprises the more traditional approach, Organization Development (OD), which until recently was synonymous with the term *planned change*. The second, Organization Transformation (OT), is the cutting edge of planned change and may be called "second-generation OD." At present, OD is relatively well defined and circumscribed in terms of its technologies, theory, and research. OT, on the

---

[1] The six previous major reviews of the field (Friedlander & Brown, 1974; Beer, 1976; Alderfer, 1977; Faucheux et al., 1982; Beer & Walton, 1987; Porras et al., 1990) each used different frameworks to organize their discussions—frameworks based on change targets, strategies, functions, or theories. None, however, was based on a model of the change process itself. We hope our attempt to model the change process will interest others in doing the same. The field sorely needs a clear model of change to guide research and action.

Source: Jerry Porras and Robert Silvers, "Organization Development and Transformation," *Annual Review of Psychology* 42 (1991), pp. 51–78. Reprinted with permission.

[2] This perspective is rooted in the Stream Organization Model, a model of organizations proposed by Porras (1987) and Porras et al. (1990) as a conceptual base for planned change work. Its key assumptions include these: that individual behavior is central to producing organizational outcomes; that individual work behavior is mostly driven by the context (work setting) of individual employees; that organizational vision provides the basic rationale for the design of the work setting; and that two major outcomes, organizational performance and individual development, derive from collective behaviors.

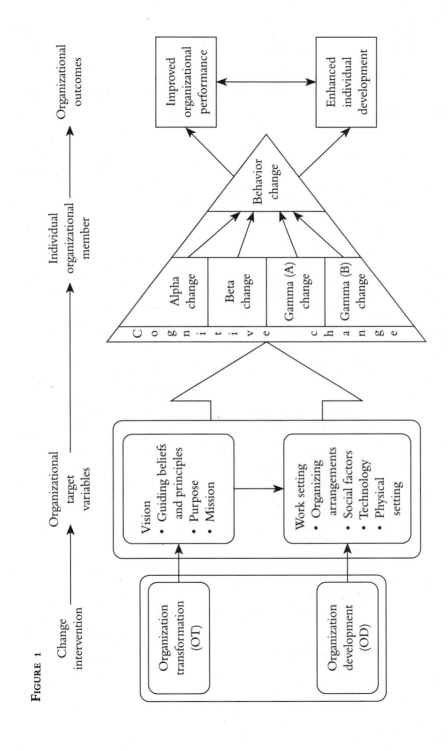

FIGURE 1

other hand, is emerging, ill-defined, highly experimental, and itself rapidly changing.[3]

Organization Development. Organization development is defined as:

1. A set of behavioral science theories, values, strategies, and techniques
2. aimed at the planned change of organizational work settings
3. with the intention of generating alpha, beta, and/or gamma (A) cognition change in individual organizational members, leading to behavioral change and thus
4. creating a better fit between the organization's capabilities and its current environmental demands, or
5. promoting changes that help the organization to better fit predicted future environments.

OD often occurs in response to modest mismatches with the environment and produces relatively moderate adjustments in those segments of the organization not congruent with the environment. This form of OD results in individuals' experiencing only alpha and beta cognition change, with a correspondingly limited change in behaviors.

Additionally, OD is triggered not only by current environmental mismatches but also by an organization's desire to fit into future desirable environmental niches. This results in the creation of new modes of functioning and impacts substantial segments of the organization. This second type of OD leads to alpha, beta,

and gamma(A) cognition change in organizational members, and behavioral changes are broader.[4]

In summary, then, OD concentrates on work-setting changes that either help an organization better adapt to its current environment or improve its fit into expected future environments. This approach to planned change produces appreciable, not radical, change in individual employees' cognitions as well as behaviors.

Organization Transformation. Organization transformation is:

1. A set of behavioral science theories, values, strategies, and techniques
2. aimed at the planned change of organizational vision and work settings.
3. with the intention of generating alpha, beta, gamma (A) and/or gamma (B) cognition change in individual organizational members, leading to behavioral change and thus
4. promoting paradigmatic change that helps the organization better fit or create desirable future environments.

OT is also planned and primarily directed at creating a new vision for the organization. Vision change occurs most effectively when an organization develops the capability for continuous self-diagnosis and change; a "learning organization" evolves—one that is constantly changing to more appropriately fit the present organizational state and better anticipate desired futures. This set of interventions leads to alpha, beta, gamma(A), and gamma(B) cognition change in organizational members, and concomitant radical change in their behaviors.

---

[3] Each of these two intervention approaches will be defined in terms of subsequent sections of the Change Process Model. As such, these definitions may not be completely clear to the reader at this point. We ask the reader to bear with us until all components are discussed.

---

[4] While this type of change is primarily caused by OD, some OT interventions focus on the work setting and also produce this pattern of change.

Organizational Target Variables. Planned change interventions impact two major types of organizational variables: organizational vision and the work setting. Taken together, these create the internal organizational environment in which individual employees function.

Vision consists of three main factors: (*a*) the guiding beliefs and principles of the organization; (*b*) the enduring organizational purpose that grows out of these beliefs; and (*c*) a catalyzing mission that is consistent with organizational purpose and, at the same time, moves the organization toward the achievement of that purpose (Collins & Porras, 1989).

The work setting consists of many dimensions and, as such, requires a parsimonious framework to organize our understanding of it. From our perspective, the organizational work setting can be subdivided into four major streams of variables: (*a*) organizing arrangements, (*b*) social factors, (*c*) technology, and (*d*) physical setting (Porras, 1987). Table 1 lists the subvariables that constitute each of these streams. These four streams of variables are themselves shaped by the organization's vision, which gives them coherence and direction.

Individual Organizational Members. Individual organizational members must change

TABLE 1

Organizational components in the stream organizational model

Organizing Arrangements (OA)	Social Factors (SF)	Technology (T)	Physical Setting (PS)
A. goals	A. culture	A. tools, equipment, & machinery	A. space configuration
B. strategies	1. basic assumptions	B. technical expertise	1. size
C. formal structure	2. values	C. job design	2. shape
D. administrative policies & procedures	3. norms	D. work flow design	3. relative locations
E. administrative systems	4. language & design	E. technical policies & procedures	B. physical ambiance
F. formal reward systems	5. rituals	F. technical systems	1. light
1. evaluation system	6. history		2. heat
2. pay systems	7. stories		3. noise
3. benefits packages	8. myths		4. air quality
G. ownership	9. symbols		5. cleanliness
	B. interaction processes		C. interior design
	1. interpersonal		1. decorations
	2. group		2. furniture
	3. intergroup		3. window coverings
	C. social patterns & networks		4. floor coverings
	1. communication		5. colors
	2. problem solving/ decision making		a. floors
	3. influence		b. walls
	4. status		c. ceilings
	D. individual attributes		D. architectural design
	1. attitudes & beliefs		
	2. behavioral skills		
	3. feelings		
	E. management style		

SOURCE: Adapted from Porras, J. I. 1987. *Stream Analysis*. Reading, Mass.: Addison-Wesley: p. 52, Table 3–1.

their on-the-job behaviors in order for the organization to change over a longer term. The complex environment surrounding individuals at work is the primary catalyst for behaviors on the job (moderated, as discussed below, by cognitive change). Organizational behaviors are generated by individuals behaving in response to the signals received directly from their work setting and indirectly from organizational vision. Therefore, successful planned change efforts must alter these two components of the internal organizational environment such that new signals influence individuals to produce new behaviors. Employees consciously process work setting cues and modify their behavior as a result.

Individual Cognition and Planned Change. The types of individual cognitive change that occur as a result of planned change activities have been discussed in the management and organization literature for over four decades (e.g. Lindblom, 1959; Vickers, 1965; Greiner, 1972; Sheldon, 1980). For our purposes, the most useful conceptualization appeared in the OD literature 15 years ago when Golembiewski and his colleagues proposed alpha, beta, and gamma change as the three possible measurable outcomes of OD interventions (Golembiewski et al., 1976):

1. "Alpha change involves a variation in the level of some existential state, given a constantly calibrated measuring instrument related to a constant conceptual domain" (p. 134).

2. "Beta change involves a variation in the level of some existential state complicated by the fact that some intervals of the measurement continuum associated with a constant conceptual domain have been recalibrated" (p. 135).

3. "Gamma change involves a redefinition or reconceptualization of some domain, a major change in the perspective or frame of reference within which phenomena

are perceived and classified, in what is taken to be some relevant slice of reality" (p. 135).

This perspective is primarily oriented toward framing change in the context of measurement issues, but it highlights some important principles. Alpha change is a perceived change in objective circumstances, while beta change is that type of change coupled with changing standards of individual interpretation. Gamma change is a radical shift in an individual's assumptions about causal relationships, the values attached to various dimensions of reality, and the interpretive frameworks that describe reality. In other words, gamma change describes a "paradigm shift" in organizational members' mental constructs (Kuhn, 1970).

The notion of paradigm is useful for conceptualizing the change process. An organizational paradigm may be defined as:

> a prevailing worldview or collective belief system. The fundamental set of beliefs or organizing principles which are unquestioned and unexamined assumptions about the nature of reality (Adams, 1984, p. 278).[5]

Integrating the construct of organizational paradigm with the notions of alpha, beta, and gamma change is a useful way to develop a new typology that conceptualizes individual cognitive change processes. The focus here is not on measurement but on broad categories of individual cognitive change. This leads to the following four types:

---

[5] Kuhn (1970) defined a knowledge paradigm as "the collection of ideas within the confines of which scientific inquiry takes place, the assumed definition of what are legitimate problems and methods, the accepted practice and point of view with which the student prepares for membership in the scientific community, the criteria for choosing problems to attack, the rules and standards of scientific practice" (p. 11). This definition of paradigm, which is widely cited in both the natural and social sciences, is consistent with Adam's definition, which focuses specifically on organizations.

1. Alpha change: change in the perceived levels of variables within a paradigm without altering their configuration (e.g. a perceived improvement in skills).

2. Beta change: change in people's view about the meaning of the value of any variable within an existing paradigm without altering their configuration (e.g. change in standards).

3. Gamma(A) change: change in the configuration of an existing paradigm without the addition of new variables (e.g. changing the central value of a "production-driven" paradigm from "cost containment" to "total quality focus"; this results in the reconfiguration of all variables within this paradigm).

4. Gamma(B) change: the replacement of one paradigm with another that contains some or all new variables (e.g. replacing a "production-driven" paradigm with a "customer-responsive" paradigm).

Each of these cognitive changes leads to corresponding changes in behavior. As an illustration, a change in standards (the example given above for beta change) causes behavior to change in order to meet these new standards. As another example, a paradigm shift from "production-driven" to "customer-responsive" alters existing behaviors, creates new behaviors, and gives individual employees a totally new way of viewing their work. The level and depth of behavior change will therefore correspond to the shift in individual cognitions.

Organizational Outcomes. Two kinds of organizational outcomes are central to our model. The first is organizational performance, captured in such factors as productivity, profitability, efficiency, effectiveness, quality, and so on. The second is individual development, an actualization of the self that occurs as individuals alter their world views, expand their repertoire of behaviors, and/or improve their skills and abilities.

Summary. The Change Process Model identifies the key components of a change process and organizes them in a way that improves one's understanding of the field as a whole. We use this model to categorize our review of recent research by analyzing articles according to the intervention approach used, the variables targeted for change, the type of individual cognitive change that occurs, and the organizational outcomes derived from the intervention activity. Unfortunately, much of the research does not give enough detail to fully analyze work by the last two above-mentioned categories, so we categorize articles primarily by intervention approach and target variables.

Research Findings

This review examines articles concerning OD and OT that were published between 1985 and 1989 in journals with an organizational behavior and/or organization development focus (e.g., the *Journal of Applied Behavioral Science, Human Relations, Group and Organizational Studies, Journal of Applied Psychology, Academy of Management Journal, Academy of Management Review, Organizational Dynamics,* and more). Because little literature on OT was found in these sources, we reviewed books and other journals that do contain work on OT (e.g., Levy & Merry, 1986; Adams, 1984).

Organization Development. We first focus our discussion on OD research and structure our comments using the change targets (i.e., organizing arrangements, social factors, technology, physical space) as subcategories in our review. Articles that do not fit these categories are reviewed at the end of this section.

Organizing Arrangements. Research on a variety of interventions focuses on this stream of target variables. Quality circles (QCs), gain-sharing interventions, and other forms of employee involvement are the topics most prevalent in the period reviewed. Some research also focused on other OA dimensions, such as alternative work schedules, new design tools, and new design options. We review the key articles that further our understanding of these various interventions and/or discuss innovative practices and ideas.[6]

Quality circles. Generally, the literature on QCs lacks empirical and statistical rigor. One important cause of this appears to be the absence of a clear theoretical foundation to guide research. Initial attempts at theory have been made that primarily classified QCs as focusing on work technology, with productivity as its end target (Steel & Shane, 1986). Later attempts to strengthen QC theory provided a more detailed model of the QC process, focusing on both structural and processual variables. However, the empirical evidence supporting these models has been mixed (Steel & Lloyd, 1988).

Other additions to QC theory emphasize the conditions leading to failure in QC implementation. One approach views disappointments with QCs as due to flawed assumptions (e.g., that groups always outperform individuals) and a lack of understanding regarding the cultural differences between the United States and Japan (Ferris & Wagner, 1985). Another proposes that a myriad of organizational factors hamper QC success, such as supervisory resistance, lack of volunteers, departmental transfer of employees (leading to less QC continuity), unskilled meeting facilitation, et cetera (Meyer & Stott, 1985). A third suggests that QCs are an employee-involvement strategy leading to minimal changes in organizational power and should be used primarily when conditions are not favorable for more extensive employee involvement (Lawler & Mohrman, 1987; Lawler, 1988). These perspectives all imply that changes in both structure and process are necessary to improve QC success rates.

Additional empirical research investigating QC efficacy has focused on assessing the impact of QC interventions on a variety of attitudinal and perceptual variables. QC membership significantly affects attitudes specific to QC functioning, such as communication, participation (Marks et al., 1986), and influence (Rafaeli, 1985); changes in more general attitudes, such as satisfaction and commitment, have also been found (Griffin, 1988).[7]

Findings on the effects of QCs on task perceptions have been contradictory. Rafaeli (1985) showed significant effects from QC membership on task perceptions while, in a similar study, Head et al. (1986) did not. Overall, the evidence regarding QCs is most positive for attitudinal and behavioral impacts directly related to QC functioning; the evidence is contradictory about QC impact on task perceptions.

Gainsharing. Theory and research on gainsharing has emphasized its motivational effects on performance. Although the theory base for this approach is relatively weak, there have been recent attempts at strengthening it. For example, Florkowski (1987) proposed a theoretical model explaining the connection between profit sharing and behavioral and attitudinal outcomes. Drawing on expectancy theory and labor relations theory, he hypothesizes that profit sharing is a motivator for individual employees to the extent that it is a salient and important part of earnings and/or based on subunit performance.

Empirical investigations of this motivation dimension have not yielded highly positive findings. For example, Pearce et al. (1985) found that merit pay for federal agency managers had no effect on improved performance in the manager's units. Jordan (1986) examined the effects of performance-contingent rewards and found that this type of pay for social service workers

---

[6] This same criteria will be applied to each of the following sections.

[7] It should be noted, however, that these findings were reported for the second and third years of a longitudinal study. By the fourth year, the measures of these indicators did not differ from the first year.

decreased intrinsic motivation and did not affect satisfaction with pay. However, positive effects were reported in a study of a manufacturing firm that had employed the Scanlon Plan for approximately a decade. Miller & Schuster (1987) found that the plan had statistically significant effects on employment stability along with positive effects on productivity and labor-management cooperation.

The negative empirical findings regarding gainsharing theory appear to be derived from change projects of more limited scope and duration. On the other hand, much more positive findings seem to obtain when gainsharing is part of a long-term, broad-based program (i.e., the Scanlon Plan study). It appears that gainsharing has the greatest effect when it is part of a larger-scale and more extensive change process.

Employee ownership. Research on employee ownership is expanding and developing a stronger theory base. Some of the most substantial work in this arena was done by Klein (1987), who tested three competing models relating employee stock ownership to employee attitudes. She found that the financial benefits and influence opportunities of ownership most strongly impacted attitudes. This evidence supported extrinsic and instrumental models of ownership, but not an intrinsic model where ownership is satisfying in and of itself.

Regarding the influence effects of employee ownership, some research contradicts the "expected" link between employee ownership and desire for influence in organizational policies. For example, French (1987) characterized employees as investors who only seek influence when it is in their best financial interests to do so. As a consequence, he concludes that ownership may not be a solution for increasing power equalization within the firm.

In summary, research on employee ownership has grown and illustrates a promising and innovative approach to organizing in this country. However, it still lacks a strong theory base, one that is much needed to guide both practice and research.

Alternative work schedules. Researchers here have primarily investigated the impact of alternative work schedules on attitudes and productivity. Attitude changes about the schedule and free time have been found to be a primary effect of work schedule changes, with smaller impacts on general attitudes and effectiveness (Dunham et al., 1987). The process used to implement alternative work schedules is also important. As would be expected, the greater the participation in the implementation process, the more favorable the attitudes toward the change (Latack & Foster, 1985).[8] Regarding only the relationship between alternative work schedules and productivity, positive effects of flextime on productivity occur when resources are scarce and productivity is measured at the group level (Ralston et al., 1985).

In summary, although this approach to organizational improvement has existed for over a decade, there has been little research on it. Alternative schedules appear to improve attitudes and performance, but more research is needed to determine the conditions under which these effects extend beyond variables specific to the intervention.

Organizational structure. Changes in organizational structure have been discussed in the literature from a variety of perspectives. One approach has foused on the development of new structural options. Ackoff (1989) proposed the "circular organization," where each manager reports to a "board of directors" consisting of his or her immediate superiors, subordinates, and important peers or outsiders. These boards are responsible for planning and coordination with other units, and, in some cases, for evaluating managerial performance. This approach to organization structure highlights one way that de-

---

[8] Latack & Foster (1985) also propose an interesting unanticipated consequence of altering work schedules—that if they are compressed schedules they will tend to lead to job enrichment, since workers on duty at any one time will have to perform more tasks.

mocracy and responsiveness need not conflict in modern organizations.

A second perspective focuses on new tools for design, rather than the final design itself. Two such tools have been proposed by McDaniel et al. (1987) and Nelson (1988). The former examined the usefulness of decision analysis for interventions involving organizational design. They found this tool helped participants to identify problems and resolve them productively. The latter discussed the uses of "blockmodeling" (a form of network analysis found primarily in sociology) for structural diagnosis, coalition identification, and intergroup relations analysis. Network analysis uncovers groupings and patterns not easily identified by traditional OD diagnostic methods. These two approaches to the problem of organization design are creative and should set the stage for additional (and much needed) development in this area.[9]

Summary. While it is encouraging to see more theory related to organization-level issues and structural interventions, most of the above research consists of "little studies." Although these further knowledge of a specific intervention and its particular effects, no attempt is made to explore multifaceted interventions and systemic outcomes. Intervention research in this and other areas would be more profitable if it explored broader and more complex system change and its outcomes (e.g., the effects of gainsharing on social factors variables, such as culture). In addition, research needs to expand its focus from direct effects to more pervasive and indirect impacts in order to assess the overall effectiveness of organizing arrangement interventions.

Social Factors. The social factors (SF) variables have historically been the most frequent targets of OD in organizations, but research in this area has decreased somewhat in recent years. In addition, the particular dimensions of interest have shifted; team interventions and group variables (which used to be the primary focus of this area) do not dominate the more current literature.

We begin our discussion with interventions oriented toward the alteration of individual attributes, next review research on group change, and then treat work focusing on culture change.

Personality theory. An exciting development in the SF area is the increased integration of personality theory with OD. Personality theory research reported in the period reviewed has been applied to all levels of analysis: to the individual employee, the manager, the small group, and the overall organization.

At the individual level, personality theory has been applied to identifying traits that might moderate the acceptance and effects of planned change. One that has been identified is the employee's "focus of attention" (Gardner et al., 1987). Employees may either focus on the job, the work unit, or off-the job; each focus leads to different effects from various interventions. It was hypothesized that job design interventions would positively affect individuals focused on their jobs, with similar types of predictions made for the other foci. Empirical evidence indicated that job focus and job change impacted hard measures, whereas work unit focus and job change impacted soft measures. Off-the-job focus impacted both types of measures negatively.

An important application of personality theory to the understanding of manager behavior has been made by Fisher et al. (1987), who drew on developmental psychology to create a four-stage model of the managerial life cycle. Their

---

[9] It is useful to note that, irrespective of the technique used to design organizational structures, their implementation is strongly enhanced through the use of employee involvement and process consultation work. Stebbins & Shani (1989) reviewed four major approaches to organizational design (Galbraith's Information Processing Model; MacKenzie's ABCE model and OA&A process; Kilmann's MAPS technology; and Sociotechnical Systems consulting) and found that while all four methods varied in their foci and key variables, they all incorporated process consultation and employee involvement principles in their implementation process.

research showed that few managers have reached the final two stages (which emphasize a tolerance for ambiguity and "transformational" leadership); therefore, problems in the organization may indicate a mismatch between organizational needs and managers' development. This framework could be useful as a diagnostic tool to identify dysfunctional matches.

Krantz (1985) used a Tavistock Institute approach to explore how unconscious group processes, such as defenses against anxiety, serve to create a specific organizational structure and culture. Examples of organizational decline were used to elucidate this process. This analysis provides an innovative method for understanding resistance to change and implementing more effective organizational designs.

These three articles further our understanding of the impact of individual differences on intervention efficacy. They also highlight the link between organizational form and individual personality. However, this area (like many others) needs substantially more attention than it has been given. Other personality factors should be explored, and a more comprehensive model of personality related to OD should be developed.

Team building. We found relatively few studies of team building. Those we identified were clustered into three broad groups: one that investigated the effects of team building on group process variables, a second that explored the impact of team building on the productivity or performance of the group, and a third that presented new perspectives on team building dynamics and appropriate research methods.

The impact of team building interventions on process measures was explored in two studies by Eden (1985, 1986a). Working with Israel Defense Forces (IDF) officers, Eden found that team building significantly affected self-perceptions of the efficacy of the intervention but did not effect actual changes (as rated by subordinates). A follow-up study (Eden, 1986a) showed significant effects on teamwork, conflict handling, and information about plans but not on other variables less directly related to the intervention itself (such as challenge, officer support, and so on). These studies provide only mixed evidence for the efficacy of the team building intervention.

The impact of team building on performance measures was examined in three different investigations. Bottger & Yetton (1987) studied the impact of individual training in problem solving on group performance and found significantly positive effects. Mitchell (1986) showed that revealing one's "internal frame of reference" leads to improved task accomplishment. However, these results were not significantly better than a traditional team building intervention. Research by Buller & Bell (1986) examined a team building/goal setting intervention with miners and found only marginally significant effects on outcomes such as productivity. It appears that narrowly focused team building interventions have a positive effect on performance. This suggests that the creative combination of some of these more narrowly focused intervention techniques could produce a substantially greater impact.

Contributions to the theory base of team building were made by Buller (1986), who utilized concepts from force-field analysis and participative decision making to develop a more precise definition of team building. He proposed that the effect of "team building–problem solving" on task performance occurs due to a variety of individual, group, task, and organizational factors. Finally, Buller suggests that team building research can be substantially improved through the development of clear operational definitions of variables, clear conceptualization of causal mechanisms, increased use of experimental designs, and the development of objective performance measures. We agree with these recommendations, except for the use of experimental designs. The reality of field research often precludes the use of true experiments; in addition, there are strong arguments against the use of these types of designs in OD (Bullock & Svyantek, 1987).

Multilevel issues. Social factor interventions that attempt to affect more complex organizational problems or arenas were reported in two studies. The first (Evans, 1989) dealt with multinational corporate development, where there has been a shift from structural to processual approaches. This is because the major challenge faced today by multinational corporations is to couple global integration with local responsiveness. For OD to be relevant in this arena, it must focus more on macro/substantive issues and become more culturally sensitive.

In contrast to the multinational setting, Golembiewski et al. (1987) discussed an intervention within a large company where the human resources staff was experiencing high levels of burnout. Both the sources and solutions to the situation were multilevel and required that a complex set of actions be undertaken. Active intervention into the culture, processes, and structure of the unit not only reduced the incidence of burnout but also improved working conditions.

New tools. An interesting new tool in OD demonstrates the time-honored principle that the sounder the theory base, the more potent any tool derived from it will be. Bernstein & Burke (1989) began with a theory of meaning systems in organizations; an implication of this theory is that belief systems must change in order to produce behavioral change in organizations. The authors used survey data and multivariate methods to uncover basic belief structures held by individuals and groups within organizations, and stated that making beliefs explicit allows for their conscious change. We encourage the use of new tools in OD, especially when these tools are derived from a sound theoretical base.

Technology.   Research focusing on interventions in the technology area has utilized primarily sociotechnical systems (STS) and quality of work life (QWL) approaches. These approaches have, over time, been more broadly applied to change of entire organizations or major subsystems. A more recent variant of these two approaches uses parallel organizations (POs) as a key mechanism to implement change. We begin our discussion by focusing on studies where POs were used.

Parallel organizations. Research on POs focuses on the contingencies and outcomes associated with their success or failure. Scholars such as Herrick (1985) view POs as a "metapractice" of STS theory. If successful, POs serve as models leading to the implementation of STS concepts across the whole organization. Bushe (1987) studied a QWL intervention involving POs and found that they were more effective when a permanent middle-management problem-solving group was also created; these groups led to greater feelings of empowerment and security for the managers, who were then less threatened by changes in employees' power. Shani & Eberhardt (1987) examined the implementation of the PO in a hospital, and employees who were a part of the PO became highly involved with organizational issues and suggestions for change. Ironically, this very interest proved threatening to top management, and this aspect of POs must be carefully managed in order to ensure their effective use. Bushe (1988), in a later study, examined the implementation of five QWL projects within a large organization and showed that QWL projects utilizing POs outperformed projects involving QCs.[10]

Quality of work life.   Bocialetti (1987) examined a QWL intervention in a unionized metals processing plant and found younger workers more satisfied with the intervention because it allowed them to circumvent both the seniority system and the adversarial relations between management and older workers. Ondrack & Evans (1987) examined the effects of QWL in both greenfield and redesigned plants in the pet-

---

[10] Bushe also found the evidence mixed regarding the usefulness of traditional QWL theory and proposed intergroup theory as a better way to understand QWL.

rochemical industry in Canada. No differences were found in either job enrichment or satisfaction between traditional and QWL plants. Sorenson et al. (1985) examined the effects of QWL on a small organization and found positive changes in attitudes and performance over a four-year period. These results suggest that QWL interventions frequently have positive effects on attitudes but that performance effects are somewhat more mixed.

Sociotechnical systems. Two studies explored theoretical issues about STS interventions. Kolody & Stjernberg (1986) drew upon case studies to develop a model of the STS process that highlights specific organizational subsystems as important to design efforts in plant settings. Susman & Chase (1986) explored the technical and social challenges that computer-integrated manufacturing poses for traditional STS plant design. The authors suggest changes in the STS process that will result in more successful implementation. Unfortunately, no subsequent research appears to be guided by either approach.

Other research explored STS interventions in a variety of settings. Pasmore et al. (1986) found that negative results from an STS intervention in a health care setting were due to the consultants' lack of sensitivity to the unique dynamics of this setting. Wall et al. (1986) instituted an autonomous workgroup design in a greenfield plant site and found positive effects only for intrinsic job satisfaction. Other individual-level measures showed no positive and/or lasting effects. Conversely, Taylor (1986) created an STS intervention in a computer operations department that did not involve semiautonomous work groups (a mainstay of typical STS interventions). Positive effects on turnover and production were demonstrated.

Reviewing the technology interventions as a whole, we are heartened that, by and large, they increasingly focus on whole-system issues and change. At the same time, the mixed success of these interventions means that their theoretical base still needs more refinement. Questions regarding the appropriateness of STS to different settings as well as the efficacy of QWL arrangements in creating both satisfaction and productivity are prime targets for further examination.

Physical Setting. Although planned change interventions focusing on physical settings have been part of the OD literature for over 15 years (e.g., Steele, 1973), we located only two more recent studies that focused on this intervention strategy. Oldham, one of the more active researchers in this area, investigated the effects of changing from a normal open office plan to either a more spacious open office plan or partitioned cubicles (Oldham, 1988). Both approaches resulted in positive effects on variables specific to the change (such as privacy satisfaction); individual differences in privacy needs and stimulus screening were significant moderators of these relations. In a somewhat similar study, Zalesny & Farace (1987) examined the effects of moving from closed offices to an open office plan for governmental employees. Symbolic theory (i.e., that work environments communicate information symbolically) best explained the results because those with higher positions were less satisfied (i.e., managers felt losing their offices indicated a loss of position).

Other Areas of Interest. A substantial amount of theory and research in OD focuses on general processes and issues.

New settings for OD. Gray & Hay (1986) extended political analysis to interorganizational domains to explicate the necessary conditions and actions for successful interventions in this arena. For interventions to be successful, powerful and legitimate stakeholders must participate in domain definition and action. Key environmental forces must also be successfully managed. Some have focused on how well OD might fit with other cultures. Boss & Mariono (1987) examined the history and practice of OD in Italy and showed that it has primarily occurred in large organizations that train their own professionals. Italian work culture appears to be oriented more toward role-oriented and structural interventions than does the United States. Jaeger (1986) drew upon Hofstede's work (1980) on national values to determine the fit of OD with various cultures. He concluded that some areas, such as Scandinavia, have values very consonant with OD; while others, such as Latin America, do not.[11] The author suggests that the success of OD in other nations will be determined by its adaptation to the dominant local values.

The applicability of OD to settings other than traditional corporate ones has also been examined. Leitko & Szczerbacki (1987) found that applying traditional OD strategies in professional bureaucracies (such as found in human service organizations) often fails. Traditional OD typically uses interpersonal interventions that loosen the constraints imposed by the "machine" bureaucracies found in industry. However, as the authors note, professional bureaucracies are often loosely integrated, and interventions that create more bounded systems are more appropriate here. Shamir & Salomon (1985) investigated telecommuting (i.e., work at home employing computer technology) and concluded that home work is not a panacea for the problems of modern organization. Thus research needs to consider carefully both the problems and benefits of home work before it is suggested as a desirable alternative. These studies explore the role of OD in situations that require the development of new concepts and new techniques for intervention.

Research methods.   Methodology issues in OD have also been researched. One controversy in this area concerns the appropriateness of different measurement approaches. Bullock & Svyantek (1987) argued persuasively that evaluating OD interventions using random strategies fundamentally contradicts the need for collabo-

ration and participation found in effective OD. Therefore the authors suggest the use of more appropriate research methods such as case meta-analysis (discussed below). Eden (1986b) suggested that rigorous research designed to eliminate "expectation effects" associated with interventions is misguided. He argues that these effects are an important part of OD's success and should be studied and clarified, rather than removed from research. Woodman (1989) takes the position that research should be useful to both practitioners and academics, and therefore should require both "thick" description and generalizable propositions. He proposes a "combined paradigm" approach (using both qualitative and quantitative methods), with stream analysis (Porras, 1987) and appreciative inquiry (Cooperrider & Srivasta, 1987) as possible examples for this.

Appreciative inquiry is an exciting new method of inquiry that deserves mention. Cooperrider & Srivasta view action research as impotent in generating alternative forms for organizing that can lead to social betterment. They propose appreciative inquiry as a revitalization of action research that both improves practice and generates theory. It does this by highlighting areas where an organization "works" and, using collaborative inquiry processes, determines directions for growth and renewal. This approach is distinct from the organizational pathology model implicit in most OD.

Stream analysis is also an important new intervention method. Porras (1987) has developed a graphical tool that maps organizational problems into the four streams (OA, SF, T, and PS), and then diagrams the links between them. By doing this, core problems are identified and targeted for change. A stream diagram is then developed mapping out the intervention's time-line and targets. This approach is a simple yet powerful way to diagnose and intervene in organizational issues.

Research in this period has also focused on better measurement of the Golembiewski et al.

---

[11] Faucheux et al. (1982), in their review of OD, also emphasized the substantial differences in change approaches between Latin and Anglo-Saxon countries.

(1976) typology. Millsap & Hartog (1988) propose a methodology based on factorial structures within a structural equation framework to determine whether either gamma or beta change has occurred. Van de Vliert et al. (1985) propose a method to distinguish between alpha and beta change in which, once gamma change is ruled out (by examining the construct validity of pre- and post-test measures), dynamic correlations are used to separate alpha and beta change.

An exciting innovation in OD research is the use of both quantitative and case meta-analysis to combine results across many different studies. Case meta-analysis (Bullock & Tubbs, 1987) integrates OD case studies (still the most prevalent form of OD research) by coding study variables and then performing correlational analysis on them. Quantitative meta-analysis uses the statistics provided in more quantitative research and determines "effect sizes" due to interventions on outcome variables.

Guzzo et al. (1985) performed a meta-analysis that examined the effects of psychologically based interventions on "hard" measures. Interventions such as team building showed strong effects on productivity (in contrast to the team building research cited above) but not on withdrawal or disruption (e.g., absenteeism, grievances, et cetera). Beekun (1989) conducted a meta-analysis of STS interventions and demonstrated generally positive effects on productivity and withdrawal behaviors. Several moderator variables were also important to STS success but, interestingly enough, workgroup autonomy was not one of them. This again indicates the need for some rethinking of STS theory. Finally, Neuman et al. (1989) conducted a meta-analysis of OD interventions on attitudinal outcomes. The authors find the primary effects on attitudes to be due to human processual, not techno-structural interventions.

Some authors have investigated measures to improve OD research. Porras & Hoffer (1986) conducted a survey of leading OD professionals and found substantial agreement among them on a set of nine behaviors that correlate with successful interventions. Hoffer (1986) operationalized the behaviors into a questionnaire that she then used to explore the relationship between them and hard measures of organizational performance. Her results showed a highly significant relationship between an index representing the entire set of behaviors and various hard measures of organizational performance, such as sales levels, market share, costs, profits, et cetera. This indicates that these behaviors hold promise for providing a common base upon which to aggregate findings from disparate change studies.

Nicholas & Katz (1985) also focused on the same "aggregation" issue. They reviewed OD research from 1948 to 1982 and suggested a set of reporting standards to make cross-study comparison much more effective. It is clear that one of the challenges facing OD research is to find ways to aggregate the research findings of the field. In turn, this aggregation process will help to improve the quality of theory found in OD.

The generation of theory and new methodology in OD should be encouraged. At the same time, much of this research is fragmented and does not build on work done by other authors laboring in a similar arena. More effort should be directed at the development of a paradigm for OD, and thus researchers must build more consciously on each other's work.

Organization Transformation

OT has emerged over the last decade as a distinct form of planned change. It is an advancement over OD owing to its focus on precipitating more profound change in organizations. This occurs because the variables targeted by OT approaches (organizational beliefs, purpose, and mission, the components of organizational vision) affect a "deeper" level in the organization than those traditionally targeted for change by OD (i.e., work setting variables).

First we examine interventions focused on organizational vision. We then discuss the practice of industrial democracy in Norway. This type of intervention has not usually been considered part of OT, but recent developments indicate that the types of change pursued here are transformational. Finally, we survey other areas of interest in the OT field. The literature on OT was quite limited, reflecting the newness of this area.

Organizational Vision.   Organizational-level views of vision examine the processes through which organizations are able to change and learn. Individual-level perspectives assume that organizational transformation is dependent upon individual workers radically shifting their typical ways of thinking and doing.

Levy & Merry (1986) identify two distinct approaches to individual consciousness change: reframing (which draws from theory in family therapy—e.g., Watzlawick et al., 1974) and consciousness raising (which has many roots—e.g., Harrison, 1984). Reframing consists of organizational interventions that change an organization member's perceptions of reality. Reframing does not change current organizational reality; instead, it alters the way individuals view the world. This new worldview leads to corresponding changes in attitudes and behaviors, and organizational transformation follows.

Consciousness raising, on the other hand, makes the processes of transformation visible to organization members. Thought is viewed as the source of both existing circumstances and potential change; therefore, individuals with more awareness of transformative processes are better able to guide them. Theory here has been primarily adapted from transpersonal psychology (e.g., Walsh & Vaughan, 1980). Techniques such as meditation and creativity exercises are suggested as practice interventions in this approach.

Other work on organizational transformation focuses on creating organizations that understand how (and when) to initiate radical change and have strategies and structures in place to produce this change. Beer (1987) examined three cases of organizational transformation where successful change included the concurrent development of a vision of the future and a heightened dissatisfaction with the status quo throughout the whole organization. These factors, coupled with a well-managed change process, led to successful transformation. Nadler & Tushman (1989) developed a model of the transformation process similar to Beer's; however, these authors also stressed diagnosis and provided more detail regarding implementation steps. For example, they stress the need for a "magic leader," who serves as a focus for the change effort, followed by a diffusion of energy for change throughout the organization.

Bartunek & Moch (1987) and Levy & Merry (1986) examined transformation caused by changing the organizational "paradigm." Transformation is accomplished here by increasing the system's ability to analyze and change current paradigms, as well as to envision desirable future paradigms. Lundberg (1989) discussed organizational learning in OD and proposed a cyclical process of learning occurring at three successively deeper levels: organizational change, development, and transformation. His model provides a useful set of analytical tools for implementing transformative processes.

The differences between the micro and macro approaches to organizational vision reflect a "top-down" versus "bottom-up" orientation. Organizational-level approaches typically view top management as the catalyst for changes in organizational vision; these changes then spread throughout the whole organization. Individual-level approaches view vision change as decentralized; when enough organizational members change their consciousness, organizational change occurs. We believe that whether an intervention focuses on the macro or micro level matters less than how effective it is at producing change; it is also likely that interventions combining both strategies will have the greatest impact.

Industrial Democracy.   The theory and practice of industrial democracy developed outside the United States and has not been generally considered part of either OD or OT. However, the change processes initiated by this approach result in paradigm shifts. The techniques that constitute the industrial democracy change strategy all relate to the shifting of power in the organization toward the end goal of democratizing the work setting. The intervention techniques used in this approach have their roots in STS and QWL concepts and technology but have evolved to the point where they focus primarily on gamma(A) and gamma(B) change.

Perhaps the most interesting and innovative work in this area has occurred in Norway and increasingly centers on "local theory" (Gustavsen & Engelstad, 1986). Local theory evolved when change projects based on general OD, STS, and QWL theory were not successful. This led to the realization that theories of democracy not generated by employees themselves are, in some sense, not democratic. Thus generative capacity (i.e., the ability of people to develop solutions to their own organizational problems) is most important, and interventions should be designed to increase this capacity. Gustavsen & Engelstad view "the conference" (an off-site meeting involving managers and employees from several companies) as an ideal setting for the practice of industrial democracy. Successes at such conferences can then be translated into practices appropriate for individuals' home organizations.

Elden (1986), in a very insightful piece, discussed how these ideas have become a part of public policy in Norway. Empowering participation is the key phrase in the Norwegian efforts; workers shape the actual conditions of their work through participatory STS activity. Participation is seen as second-order [gamma (A) and gamma (B)] change in this new framework. In this way, the change thrust has moved from empowerment through structure (e.g., instituting autonomous work groups) to empowerment through process (workers making local-level decisions about appropriate work practices). Some necessary conditions for empowering participa-

tion include institutional and political support at higher levels, participatory research, researchers as co-learners, empowering the less powerful, and rejecting conventional OD and STS.

Other Areas of Interest.   An interesting area of OT research examines disequilibrium models, where transformation is the rule, rather than the exception. Gemmill & Smith (1985) developed a dissipative structure model of transformation, where turbulent conditions prevent organizations from damping change and reaching equilibrium. When this happens, old forms of organizing break down and experimentation with many new forms occurs. Eventually, the most successful experiment reorganizes the system at a higher functional level. Leifer (1989) also proposed a dissipative structure model but stressed that a vision of the future is needed to mobilize the energy for experimentation. The premise of these articles is that organizations move from transformation to transformation, with only brief periods of stability (characterized by efficiency concerns) in between.

Several other authors have proposed intervention methods appropriate for OT work. Argyris et al. (1985) described "action science," an approach that attempts to catalyze double-loop learning [roughly equivalent to gamma(B) change] in individuals and organizations. The theoretical underpinning of this work parallels work discussed above on individual consciousness change and paradigm shifts. Pava (1986) proposed the concept of "normative incrementalism," an intervention method appropriate when both high complexity and high conflict exist in organizations (a condition ripe for transformation). These conditions only allow for interventions that are incremental and not threatening to current interests. This intervention therefore introduces some general theme (such as "quality of working life") without specifying how this translates into day-to-day organizational practice. However, this theme triggers employees to engage in activities that begin to clarify it retrospectively. This is a dialectic process that leads to the reformulation of values and ultimately to major organizational change.

After reviewing the breadth of ideas in OT, it is apparent how much vitality exists in this emerging approach to planned change. Although the broad outlines of the field may be sketched (e.g., a focus on vision, consciousness change, et cetera), there is still considerable diversity in this area and consequently many different directions for future development. It is therefore difficult to predict where the field will be in 10 years, but we are certain that it will still be generating excitement and interest for both scholars and practitioners.

Summary

There was much research on OD in the period reviewed, while relatively little published literature exists in the area of OT. OD is still vigorous, as judged by the number of publications in this area, but the field has moved (since the late 1960s) from an energetic adolescence to a somewhat sedate maturity. In categorizing OD intervention approaches and target variables, we noticed two interesting patterns (noted only regarding the OA and SF streams). First of all, SF interventions dominated OD in the 1960s and early 1970s. However, in the period reviewed there had been a definite shift in emphasis from interventions emphasizing individual and group processes to interventions focusing on structural arrangements and reward systems (i.e., a shift from SF to OA research). OD research has, over time, increasingly emphasized organizational-level factors, and this is reflected by the increased volume of work on OA interventions.

The second pattern we noted concerned the target variables of research. OA research, although examining newer types of interventions in OD, typically focuses on "traditional" variables. These include participation (e.g., Marks et al., 1986), motivation (e.g., Jordan, 1986), task perceptions (e.g., Rafaeli, 1985), etc. In addition, OA

research typically investigates the connection between these variables and outcomes such as productivity (e.g. Ralston et al 1985). In contrast, SF research has focused on a more innovative set of variables. These include internal frames of reference (Mitchell, 1986), managerial life cycles (Fisher et al., 1987), organizational embodiments of ego defenses (Krantz, 1985), et cetera. OA research seems to "lag" SF research in its choice of variables, and we suggest more integration of organizational-level intervention research with newer variables. At the same time, SF research can be criticized for not more explicitly theorizing and researching the link between innovative target variables and organizational outcomes (Buller's 1986 study was an exception).

Although there are some innovative areas of OD research in the period reviewed, no fundamental new paradigms have been developed and embraced by the field, and major new insights are rare. OT, on the other hand, is exciting precisely because it involves dramatically new premises for planned change. OT draws on more recent developments in psychology, transpersonal psychology, and systems theory, and often challenges traditional concepts in OD regarding models and methods. However, since this area is so underdeveloped, it is our hope that an increasing amount of rigorous theory development and research will appear in the near future.

Future Directions in Planned Change

Our analysis of the last five years of organizational change research has led us to a series of conclusions about where the field should head.

An important arena for future research concerns organizational paradigms. Paradigms are a key concept in OT work, but no clear conceptualization or research strategy for them has been developed. Specifying the mechanisms and boundaries of paradigm change is also important.

Organizational vision is another crucial area where research could improve OT theory and practice. Collins & Porras (1989) discuss vision and its component parts (guiding beliefs, purpose, mission) in detail, but more work needs to be done. The role of vision in maintaining organizational coherence should be explored, as should the dynamics of vision change in organizational change.

Concepts from Asian philosophy underlie some types of OT practice (e.g., the use of meditation as a tool for consciousness change). However, these concepts are not rigorously integrated into OT theory, and more theory development exploring Eastern conceptions of individual and group change should be done.

Planned change theory in general also needs much more development. The Change Process Model is one attempt to improve this area, but we encourage other attempts at developing theoretical models of change. In addition to general models of change, research should focus on how interventions impact important organizational variables and how change in these variables cascades throughout the organizational system.

The dynamics and effects of new organizational forms need much more research. Exploring Ackoff's (1989) circular organization, parallel organizations, and other innovations will increase the knowledge bases of both OD and OT. Another important area of research concerns changes in ownership, rather than in governance. More employee ownership research on ESOPs and their outcomes is needed, as well as research on organizations that are fully employee owned.

Finally, as mentioned above, more research is needed on the direct effects of physical-setting change. Beyond that, exploring the interrelationship of physical setting and other organizational factors (such as structure and culture) has important implications for change theory and practice. Research should investigate the contingencies that make different types of physical setting optimal under different conditions.

There are also some important directions in which research methods and measures should head. Of course theory building that results in

testable models is a key to improving research. Such models are the best guides for research, and can lead to more productive exploration of OD and OT issues.

In addition to better theory, developing a common set of variables upon which to aggregate findings is important. Meta-analysis provides the analytical tools for cross-study comparison, but meaningful comparisons can only be made when common measures are employed. We believe that the behaviors of individual organizational members are a useful and easily measured set of variables that could serve this function. The set of behaviors proposed by Porras & Hoffer (1986) are an example of this.

The Golembiewski et al. (1976) typology of alpha, beta, and gamma change would be another way to develop a common set of measures. Given the amount of interest generated by this typology in the last 15 years, it was shocking to find no studies in our review that used these measures. One reason may be that methodologists are still exploring the optimal way to measure these types of change (e.g. Millsap & Hartog 1988); however, several such measures already exist, and this typology provides another common metric for more integration of research. Better reporting standards (Nicholas & Katz 1985) also would aid in promoting cross-study comparison. All in all, better theory coupled with more integration of findings would immeasurably improve the effectiveness of planned change interventions.

Literature Cited

Ackoff, R. L. 1989. "The Circular Organization: An Update." *Acad. Manage. Exec.* 3:11–16.

Adams, J. D., ed. 1984. *Transforming Work: A Collection of Organizational Transformation Readings.* Alexandria, VA: Miles River Press.

Alderfer, C. P. 1977. "Organization Development." *Annu. Rev. Psychol.* 28:197–223

Argyris, C.; Putnam, R.; Smith, D. M. 1985. *Action Science*. San Francisco: Jossey-Bass.

Bartunek, J. M.; Moch, M. K. 1987. "First-Order, Second-Order, and Third-Order Change and Organization Development Interventions: A Cognitive Approach." *J. Appl. Behav. Sci.* 23:483–500.

Beekun, R. I. 1989. "Assessing the Effectiveness of Sociotechnical Intervention: Antidote or Fad?" *Hum. Relat.* 42:877–97.

Beer, M. 1976. "The Technology of Organization Development." In *Handbook of Industrial and Organizational Psychology,* ed. M. Dunnette. Chicago: Rand McNally College Publishing.

Beer, M. 1987. "Revitalizing Organizations: Change Process and Emergent Model." *Acad. Manage. Exec.* 1:51–55.

Beer, M., Walton, A. E. 1987. "Organization Change and Development." *Annu. Rev. Psychol.* 38: 339–67.

Bernstein, W. M.; Burke, W. W. 1989. "Modeling Organizational Meaning Systems." See Woodman & Pasmore, 1989, pp. 117–59.

Bocialetti, G. 1987. "Quality of Work Life: Some Unintended Effects on the Seniority Tradition of an Industrial Union." *Group Organ. Stud.* 12: 386–410.

Boss, R. W., Mariono, M. V. 1987. "Organization Development in Italy." *Group Organ. Stud.* 12: 245–56.

Bottger, P. C., Yetton, P. W. 1987. "Improving Group Performance by Training in Individual Problem Solving." *J. Appl. Psychol.* 72:651–57.

Buller, P. F. 1986. "The Team Building-Task Performance Relation: Some Conceptual and Methodological Refinements." *Group Organ. Stud.* 11: 147–68.

Buller, P. F., Bell, C. H., Jr. 1986. "Effects of Team Building and Goal Setting on Productivity: A Field Experiment." *Acad. Manage. J.* 29:305–28.

Bullock, R. J., Svyantek, D. J. 1987. "The Impossibility of Using Random Strategies to Study the Organization Development Process." *J. Appl. Behav. Sci.* 23:255–62.

Bullock, R. J., Tubbs, M. E. 1987. "The Case Meta-Analysis Method for OD." See Woodman & Pasmore, 1987, pp. 171–228.

Bushe, G. R. 1987. "Temporary or Permanent Middle-Management Groups? Correlates with Attitudes in QWL Change Projects." *Group Organ. Stud.* 12:23–37.

Bushe, G. R. 1988. "Developing Cooperative Labor-Management Relations in Unionized Factories: A Multiple Case Study of Quality Circles and Parallel Organizations within Joint Quality of Work Life Projects." *J. Appl. Behav. Sci.* 24:129–50.

Collins, J. C., Porras, J. I. 1989. "Making Impossible Dreams Come True." *Stanford Bus. Sch. Mag.* 57:12–19.

Cooperrider, D. L., Srivasta, S. 1987. "Appreciative Inquiry in Organizational Life." See Woodman & Pasmore, 1987, pp. 129–69.

Dunham, R. B.; Pierce, J. L.; Castaneda, M. B. 1987. "Alternative Work Schedules: Two Field Experiments." *Personnel Psychol.* 40:215–41.

Eden, D. 1985. "Team Development: A True Field Experiment at Three Levels of Rigor." *J. Appl. Psychol.* 70:94–100.

Eden, D. 1986a. "Team Development: Quasi-Experimental Confirmation among Combat Companies." *Group Organ. Stud.* 11:133–46.

Eden, D. 1986b. "OD and Self-Fulfilling Prophecy: Boosting Productivity by Raising Expectations." *J. Appl. Behav. Sci.* 22:1–13.

Elden, M. 1986. "Sociotechnical Systems Ideas as Public Policy in Norway: Empowering Participation through Worker-Managed Change." *J. Appl. Behav. Sci.* 22:239–55.

Evans, P. A. L. 1989. "Organizational Development in the Transnational Enterprise." See Woodman & Pasmore, 1989, pp. 1–39.

Faucheux, C., Amado, G., Laurent, A. 1982. "Organizational Development and Change." *Annu. Rev. Psychol.* 33:343–70.

Ferris, G. R., Wagner, J. A. III. 1985. "Quality Circles in the United States: A Conceptual Reevaluation." *J. Appl. Behav. Sci.* 21:155–67.

Fisher, D.; Merron, K.; Torbert, W. R. 1987. "Human Development and Managerial Effectiveness." *Group Organ. Stud.* 12:257–73.

Florkowski, G. W. 1987. "The Organizational Impact of Profit Sharing." *Acad. Manage. Rev.* 12:622–36.

French, J. L. 1987. "Employee Perspectives on Stock Ownership: Financial Investment or Mechanism of Control?" *Acad. Manage. Rev.* 12:427–35.

Friedlander, F., Brown, L. D. 1974. "Organization Development." *Annu. Rev. Psychol.* 25:313–41.

Gardner, D. G.; Dunham, R. B.; Cummings, L. L.; Pierce, J. L. 1987. "Employee Focus of Attention and Reactions to Organizational Change." *J. Appl. Behav. Sci.* 23:351–70.

Gemmill, G., Smith, C. 1985. "A Dissipative Structure Model of Organizational Transformation." *Hum. Relat.* 38:751–66.

Golembiewski, R. T.; Billingsley, K.; Yeager, S. 1976. "Measuring Change and Persistence in Human Affairs: Types of Change Generated by OD Designs." *J. Appl. Behav. Sci.* 12:133–57.

Golembiewski, R. T.; Hilles, R.; Daly, R. 1987. "Some Effects of Multiple OD Interventions on Burnout and Work Site Features." *J. Appl. Behav. Sci.* 23:295–313.

Gray, B., Hay, T. M. 1986. "Political Limits to Interorganizational Consensus and Change." *J. Appl. Behav. Sci.* 22:95–112.

Greiner, L. 1972. "Evolution and Revolution as Organizations Grow." *Harv. Bus. Rev.* 50:39–46.

Griffin, R. W. 1988. "Consequences of Quality Circles in an Industrial Setting: A Longitudinal Assessment." *Acad. Manage. J.* 31:388–58.

Gustavsen, B., Engelstad, P. H. 1986. "The Design of Conferences and the Evolving Role of Democratic Dialogue in Changing Work Life." *Hum. Relat.* 39:101–16.

Guzzo, R. A.; Jette, R. D.; Katzell, R. A. 1985. "The Effects of Psychologically Based Intervention Programs on Worker Productivity: A Meta-Analysis." *Personnel Psychol.* 38:275–91.

Harrison, R. 1984. "Leadership and Strategy for a New Age." In *Transforming Work,* ed. J. Adams. Alexandria, VA: Miles River Press.

Head, T. C.; Molleston, J. L.; Sorenson, P. F., Jr.; Gargano, J. 1986. "The Impact of Implementing a Quality Circle Intervention on Employee Task Perceptions." *Group Organ. Stud.* 11:360–73.

Herrick, N. Q. 1985. "Parallel Organizations in Unionized Settings: Implications for Organizational Research." *Hum. Relat.* 38:963–81.

Hoffer, S. J. 1986. *"Behavior and Organizational Performance: An Empirical Study."* PhD thesis. Stanford Univ. Grad. Sch. Educ.

Hofstede, G. 1980. *Culture's Consequences: International Differences in Work Related Values.* Beverly Hills, CA: Sage.

Jaeger, A. M. 1986. "Organization Development and National Culture: Where's the Fit?" *Acad. Manage. Rev.* 11:178–90.

Jordan, P. C. 1986. "Effects of an Extrinsic Reward on Intrinsic Motivation: A Field Experiment." *Acad. Manage. J.* 29:405–12.

Klein, K. J. 1987. "Employee Stock Ownership and Employee Attitudes: A Test of Three Models." *J. Appl. Psychol.* 72:319–32.

Kolodny, H.; Stjernberg, T. 1986. "The Change Process of Innovative Work Designs: New Design and Redesign in Sweden, Canada, and the U.S." *J. Appl. Behav. Sci.* 22:287–301.

Krantz, J. 1985. "Group Processes under Conditions of Organizational Decline." *J. Appl. Behav. Sci.* 21:1–17.

Kuhn, T. 1970. *The Structure of Scientific Revolution.* Chicago: Univ. Chicago Press. 2nd ed.

Latack, J. C.; Foster, L. W. 1985. "Implementation of Compressed Work Schedules: Participation and Job Redesign as Critical Factors for Employee Acceptance." *Personnel Psychol.* 38:75–92.

Lawler, E. E. III. 1988. "Choosing an Involvement Strategy." *Acad. Manage. Exec.* 2:197–204.

Lawler, E.E. III; Mohrman, S. A. 1987. "Quality Circles: After the Honeymoon." *Organ. Dyn.* 15:42–54.

Leifer, R. 1989. "Understanding Organizational Transformation Using a Dissipative Structure Model." *Hum. Relat.* 42:899–916.

Leitko, T. A.; Szczerbacki, D. 1987. "Why Traditional OD Strategies Fail in Professional Bureaucracies." *Organ. Dyn.* 15:52–65.

Levy, A.; Merry, U. 1986. *Organizational Transformation.* New York: Praeger.

Lindblom, C. 1959. "The Science of Muddling Through." *Public Admin. Rev.* 21:78–88.

Lundberg, C. C. 1989. "On Organizational Learning: Implications and Opportunities for Expanding Organizational Development." See Woodman & Pasmore, 1989, pp. 61–82.

Marks, M. L.; Mirvis, P. H.; Hackett, E. J.; Grady, J. F. Jr. 1986. "Employee Participation in a Quality Circle Program: Impact on Quality of Work Life, Productivity, and Absenteeism." *J. Appl. Psychol.* 71:61–69.

McDaniel, R. R. Jr.; Thomas, J. B.; Ashmos, D. P.; Smith, J. P. 1987. "The Use of Decision Analysis for Organizational Design: Reorganizing a

Community Hospital." *J. Appl. Behav. Sci.* 23: 337–50.

Meyer, G. W., Stott, R. G. 1985. "Quality Circles: Panacea or Pandora's Box?" *Organ. Dyn.* 13: 34–50.

Miller, C. S., Schuster, M. 1987. "A Decade's Experience with the Scanlon Plan: A Case Study." *J. Occup. Behav.* 8:167–74.

Millsap, R. E.; Hartog, S. B. 1988. "Alpha, Beta, and Gamma Change in Evaluation Research: A Structural Equation Approach." *J. Appl. Psychol.* 73: 574–84.

Mitchell, R. 1986. "Team Building by Disclosure of Internal Frame of Reference." *J. Appl. Behav. Sci.* 22:15–28.

Nadler, D. A.; Tushman, M. L. 1989. "Organizational Frame Bending: Principles for Managing Reorientation." *Acad. Manage. Exec.* 3:194–204.

Nelson, R. E. 1988. "Social Network Analysis as an Intervention Tool: Examples from the Field." *Group Organ. Stud.* 13:39–58.

Neuman, G. A.; Edwards, J. E.; Raju, N. S. 1989. "Organization Development Interventions: A Meta-Analysis of Their Effects on Satisfaction and Other Attitudes." *Personnel Psychol.* 42: 461–89.

Nicholas, J. M.; Katz, M. 1985. "Research Methods and Reporting Practices in Organization Development: A Review and Some Guidelines." *Acad. Manage. Rev.* 10:737–49.

Oldham, G. R. 1988. "Effects of Changes in Workspace Partitions and Spatial Density on Employee Reactions: A Quasi-Experiment." *J. Appl. Psychol.* 73:253–58.

Ondrack, D. A.; Evans, M. G. 1987. "Job Enrichment and Job Satisfaction in Greenfield and Redesign QWL Sites." *Group Organ. Stud.* 12:5–22.

Pasmore, W.; Petee, J.; Bastian, R. 1986. "Sociotechnical Systems in Health Care: A Field Experiment." *J. Appl. Behav. Sci.* 22:329–39.

Pava, C. 1986. "New Strategies of Systems Change: Reclaiming Nonsynoptic Methods." *Hum. Relat.* 39:615–33.

Pearce, J. L.; Stevenson, W. B.; Perry, J. L. 1985. "Managerial Compensation Based on Organizational Performance: A Time Series Analysis of the Effects of Merit Pay." *Acad. Manage. J.* 28:261–78.

Porras, J. I., 1987. *Stream Analysis: A Powerful New Way to Diagnose and Manage Change.* Reading, MA: Addison-Wesley.

Porras, J. I.; Hoffer, S. J. 1986. "Common Behavior Changes in Successful Organization Development Efforts." *J. Appl. Behav. Sci.* 22:477–94.

Porras, J. I.; Robertson, P.; Goldman, L. 1990. "Organization Development." In *Handbook of Industrial and Organizational Psychology,* ed. M. Dunnette. Palo Alto, CA: Psychological Press.

Rafaeli, A. 1985. "Quality Circles and Employee Attitudes." *Personnel Psychol.* 38:603–15.

Ralston, D. A.; Anthony, W. P.; Gustafson, D. J. 1985. "Employees May Love Flextime, But What Does It Do to the Organization's Productivity?" *J. Appl. Psychol.* 70:272–79.

Shamir, B.; Salomon, I. 1985. "Work-at-Home and the Quality of Working Life." *Acad. Manage. Rev.* 10:455–64.

Shani, A. B.; Eberhardt, B. J. 1987. "Parallel Organization in a Health Care Institution." *Group Organ. Stud.* 12:147–73.

Sheldon, A. 1980. "Organizational Paradigms: A Theory of Organizational Change." *Organ. Dyn.* 8:61–80.

Sorenson, P. F. Jr.; Head, T. C.; Stotz, D. 1985. "Quality of Work Life and the Small Organization: A Four-Year Case Study." *Group Organ. Stud.* 10:320–39.

Stebbins, M. W.; Shani, A. B. 1989. "Organization Design: Beyond the Mafia Model." *Organ. Dyn.* 17:18–30.

Steel, R. P.; Lloyd, R. F. 1988. "Cognitive, Affective, and Behavioral Outcomes of Participation in Quality Circles: Conceptual and Empirical Findings." *J. Appl. Behav. Sci.* 24:1–17.

Steel, R. P.; Shane, G. S. 1986. "Evaluation Research on Quality Circles: Technical and Analytical Implications." *Hum. Relat.* 39:449–68.

Steele, F. I. 1973. *Physical Settings and Organization Development.* Reading, MA: Addison-Wesley.

Susman, G. I.; Chase, R. B. 1986. "A Sociotechnical Analysis of the Integrated Factory." *J. Appl. Behav. Sci.* 22:257–70.

Taylor, J. C. 1986. "Long-Term Sociotechnical Systems Change in a Computer Operations Department." *J. Appl. Behav. Sci.* 22:303–13.

Van de Vliert, E.; Huismans, S. E.; Stok, J. J. L. 1985. "The Criterion Approach to Unraveling Beta and Alpha Change." *Acad. Manage. Rev.* 10:269–74.

Vickers, G. 1965. *The Art of Judgment.* New York: Basic Books.

Wall, T. D.; Kemp, N. J.; Jackson, P. R.; Clegg, C. W. 1986. "Outcomes of Autonomous Workgroups: A Long-Term Field Experiment." *Acad. Manage. J.* 29:280–304.

Walsh, R. N.; Vaughan, F. 1980. *Beyond Ego: Transpersonal Dimensions in Psycology.* Los Angeles: J. P. Tarcher.

Watzlawick, P.; Weakland, J.; Fisch, R. 1974. *Change.* New York: W. W. Norton.

Woodman, R. W. 1989. "Evaluation Research on Organizational Change: Arguments for a 'Combined Paradigm' Approach." See Woodman & Pasmore, 1989, pp. 161–80.

Woodman, R. W.; Pasmore, W. A., eds. 1987. *Research in Organizational Change and Development,* vol. 1. Greenwich, CT: JAI Press.

Woodman, R. W.; Pasmore, W. A., eds. 1989. *Research in Organizational Change and Development,* vol. 3. Greenwich, CT: JAI Press.

Zalesny, M. D.; Farace, R. V. 1987. "Traditional versus Open Offices: A Comparison of Sociotechnical, Social Relations, and Symbolic Meaning Perspectives." *Acad. Manage. J.* 30:240–59.

P   A   R   T

II THE FOUNDATIONS OF OD: THEORY AND PRACTICE ON CHANGE IN ORGANIZATIONS

The field of organization development came into being as advances were made in understanding the nature of change and the nature of organizational dynamics. We examine those topics in Part II.

Organization development is an applied behavioral science discipline that attempts to translate knowledge from the basic and applied behavioral sciences into action programs intended to solve problems, correct deficiencies, and seize opportunities in ongoing organizations. In the broadest and most general sense, the objective of organization development programs is to increase short-term and long-term organizational effectiveness. Operationally this means the client system (organization) must be able to "sense" the current state of affairs, must be able to solve the current problems it faces—usually consisting of two major types, deficiencies to be corrected and opportunities to be exploited—and must build the capacity to be able to do this over time as conditions, demands, and exigencies change. To cope successfully with current events requires effective problem-solving and action-taking skills; to adjust successfully to future events requires the ability to sense environmental demands, the ability to respond to those demands, and the ability to maintain this adaptive flexibility over time. This latter skill is called "organizational self-renewal." The role of the OD practitioner is to help the organization members solve current problems and develop the competence for self-renewal.

At least four kinds of knowledge are required of OD practitioners or managers who desire to create problem-solving, self-renewing organizations: knowledge of how organizations work; knowledge of how change occurs; knowledge of how to intervene in an organization to produce desired change; and knowledge of how to diagnose and solve problems.

The knowledge of how organizations work comes mainly from basic behavioral science research and theory. It entails an understanding of the dynamics of individuals, groups, and goal-oriented social systems. Knowledge of how change occurs involves understanding the processes of change and changing. Such knowledge is required in all applied disciplines. In the case of organization development, gaining this knowledge was made more difficult because the phenomena are so complex and are themselves changing as they are being studied. But it was progress in the theory and practice of change that helped launch the field of OD. Knowledge of how to intervene in an ongoing organization relates to change but goes beyond it to investigate the consultation or helping process. How does one intervene effectively? What are the ingredients of effective client-consultant relationships? When is help helpful? Other applied disciplines, such as education, psychotherapy, and social work, provided numerous insights about intervening in organizations. Knowledge of diagnosis and problem solving comes from many sources, but culminates in the ability to answer the questions: What is wrong? What made it wrong? What must be done to correct the situation? Competent problem solving and action taking require being able to do two things: classify problem situations accurately, and select appropriate remedies. This competence in turns rests on the prior existence of two bodies of knowledge: valid diagnostic categories (having a good classification scheme for different kinds of problems), and an efficacious set of remedial treatments (having an array of different solutions or actions that will solve different problems). In relatively advanced applied sciences, such as medicine, great progress has been made in refining diagnostic categories and in discovering appropriate treatments. Less progress has been made in OD, but advances have been substantial.

It is not possible to explore all the foundations of organization development in this section. Instead, we concentrate on the nature of change and the nature of organizational dynamics.

The Nature of Planned Change

The action arena of OD is organizations. The name of the game is planned change. Organization improvement requires an understanding of change processes and a knowledge of the nature of organizations.

Kurt Lewin was the great practical theorist whose action and research programs provided much of the early foundation for understanding change processes in social situations.[1] Lewin (1890–1947) was a personality theorist, a social psychologist, and a man who wanted to improve the lot of humankind through behavioral science knowledge and application. To improve things means to change them; to change them requires knowledge of the structure and dynamics of change. Lewin's work had a significant impact on group dynamics, intergroup relations, and applied social psychology. Lewin once said, "If you want to understand a phenomenon, try to change it." And he devoted a considerable part of his career trying to understand processes of change.

Two concepts proposed by Kurt Lewin are especially useful in thinking

---

[1] Alfred J. Marrow, *The Practical Theorist: The Life and Work of Kurt Lewin* (New York: Basic Books, 1969).

about change. The first idea suggests that what is occurring at any point in time is the result of a field of opposing forces. Thus, for example, the production level of a manufacturing plant or the level of morale in a work group should be thought of as *equilibrium points* in a field of forces, some forces pushing toward higher and some pushing toward lower levels of production or morale. In order to understand a problematic situation the investigator must know what major forces are operating in that particular instance. A technique called the Force Field Analysis diagrams the field of forces and shows how to develop actions plans for moving the equilibrium point in one direction or another. This is a useful model for understanding what is going on in complex situations.

The second idea proposed by Lewin analyzes what must occur for permanent change to take place. He conceptualized change as a three-stage process: *unfreezing* the old behavior, *moving* to a new level of behavior, and *freezing* the behavior at the new level. This is a useful model for knowing how to move an equilibrium point to a new, desired level and *keep it there*. These two simple ideas undergird the theories of change of most OD practitioners.

Ronald Lippitt, Jeanne Watson, and Bruce Westley later refined Lewin's three phases into a seven-phase model of the change process as follows:

Phase 1. The development of a need for change. This phase corresponds to Lewin's *unfreezing* phase.

Phase 2. The establishment of a change relationship. This is a crucial phase in which a client system in need of help and a "change agent" from outside the system establish a working relationship with each other.

Phase 3. The clarification or diagnosis of the client system's problem.

Phase 4. The examination of alternative routes and goals; establishing goals and intentions of action.

Phase 5. The transformation of intentions into actual change efforts. Phase 3, 4, and 5 correspond to Lewin's *moving* phase.

Phase 6. The generalization and stabilization of change. This corresponds to Lewin's *freezing* phase.

Phase 7. Achieving a terminal relationship.[2]

The models of change developed by Lewin and by Lippitt, Watson, and Westley have advanced both theory and practice in organization development. They are foundations of the discipline. Causing change in organizations presents additional challenges, however. In an article entitled "Change Does Not Need to be Haphazard," Kenneth Benne and Max Birnbaum suggest some principles that form a strategy for effecting organizational change. Their principles are as follows:

---

[2] Ronald Lippitt, Jeanne Watson, and Bruce Westley, *The Dynamics of Planned Change* (New York: Harcourt Brace Jovanovich, 1958). See chapter 6 for a discussion of the phases of planned change.

1. To change a subsystem or any part of a subsystem, relevant aspects of the environment must also be changed.

2. To change behavior on any one level of a hierarchical organization, it is necessary to achieve complementary and reinforcing changes in organization levels above and below that level.

3. The place to begin change is at those points in the system where some stress and strain exist. Stress may give rise to dissatisfaction with the status quo and thus become a motivating factor for change in the system.

4. If thoroughgoing changes in a hierarchical structure are desirable or necessary, change should ordinarily start with the policy making body.

5. Both the formal and the informal organization of an institution must be considered in planning any process of change.

6. The effectiveness of a planned change is often directly related to the degree to which members at all levels of an institutional hierarchy take part in the factfinding and the diagnosing of needed changes and in the formulating and reality testing of goals and programs of change.[3]

The Nature of Organizational Dynamics

Organization development efforts are directed toward deliberately established social systems called organizations. Organizations exist to accomplish specific purposes or goals—a mission, task, products, or services. In most organizations the decision to belong is a voluntary choice made by the individual. There is division of labor and responsibility in organizations, with the consequence that a social structure of roles, duties, and offices is created. Individuals perform "role behaviors"; they are expected to do some things and not others by virtue of the positions they hold. One cannot know how organizations function simply by knowing how individuals function and then "summing across" individuals, because organizations have unique characteristics of their own.

One characteristic of organizations is that much of the work gets done by teams consisting of bosses and subordinates. Work teams are the basic building blocks of organizations. If teams function well, it is more likely that the organization as a whole will function well. Advances in understanding the dynamics of groups served as a foundation for the development of OD. Insights, theories, and techniques concerning group processes formed a large part of the basic toolkit of early OD practitioners.

Relations between groups in organizations are often problematic and dysfunctional. Another characteristic of organizations is that these relations are very

---

[3] Kenneth D. Benne and Max Birnbaum, "Change Does Not Need to be Haphazard," *Notebook for Summer Participants*, NTL Institute for Applied Behavioral Science.

important for organizational performance. As knowledge about intergroup dynamics was developed, it was incorporated into organization development.

A fundamental tenet of OD is that organizations are open systems. Russell Ackoff defines a system as "a set of interrelated elements. Thus a system is an entity which is composed of at least two elements and a relation that holds between each of its elements and at least one other element in the set. Each of a system's elements is connected to every other element, directly or indirectly."[4] Systems (and organizations) must be treated from a holistic point of view, because certain properties derive from the *relationships* between the parts of the system and cannot be discovered from an analysis of the components themselves. In addition, organizations are open systems—they are in interaction with and in exchange with their environments. Organizations are impacted by and have an impact on their environments. As Katz and Kahn state: "Organizations as a special class of open systems have properties of their own, but they share other properties in common with all open systems. These include the importation of energy from the environment, the throughput or transformation of the imported energy into some product form that is characteristic of the system, the exporting of that product into the environment, and the reenergizing of the system from sources in the environment."[5]

The organization development practitioner must understand the nature of the client systems in which he or she works. That is a basic prerequisite. The selections in this section provide a start in that direction.

Readings in Part II

The readings in this section are classic statements that improve with age and with each reading.

The first article, written by Robert Chin and Kenneth D. Benne, describes three broad general strategies for effecting changes in human systems—the empirical-rational strategy, the normative-reeducative strategy, and the power-coercive strategy. This elegant and erudite essay was written for the book, *The Planning of Change*, edited by Warren Bennis, Kenneth Benne, and Robert Chin. The historical development of the three strategies of change is traced in detail and examples of each strategy in operation are given. It is our opinion that the organization development approach to planned change rests primarily on a normative-reeducative strategy and secondarily on an empirical-rational strategy. For this reason, understanding the three general strategies for change is important for the OD practitioner as well as for managers who may be interested in OD efforts in their organizations.

---

[4] Russell L. Ackoff, "Toward a System of Systems Concepts," *Management Science,* July 1971, p. 662.

[5] Daniel Katz and Robert L. Kahn, *The Social Psychology of Organizations,* 2nd ed. (New York: John Wiley & Sons, 1978), p. 33.

The next selection is an exerpt from Kurt Lewin's highly influential book, *Field Theory in Social Science.* Lewin's field theory approach postulates that any phenomenon is the resultant in a field of opposing forces—a model that has proved very useful for organizational change. A technique called the Force Field Analysis allows one to map the field of forces and build action plans to change the field of forces.

Chris Argyris has made significant contributions to the field of organization development and transformation. This reading is from a very influential book published in 1970. OD practitioners intervene in ongoing organizations to help produce positive results. But the intervention process itself was mainly based on rules of thumb and principles derived from experience until Argyris formulated a systematic statement of intervention theory and method. Argyris sees three primary tasks of the interventionist: to help the client system generate valid information; to help ensure that client system members act on the basis of free and informed choice; and to help ensure internal commitment to the choices made. What is the practitioner trying to do? What theory is available to guide behavior and give overall direction? The reading by Argyris addresses these issues.

The brief piece by Carl Rogers looks at the dynamics of two-person conflict. He describes four elements that will almost always be found in such situations. Becoming aware of these elements is the first step in resolving interpersonal disputes.

Intergroup relations are especially important phenomena in organizations. Just as individuals may be interdependently related on a work team for task accomplishment, entire teams are interdependently related to other teams for task accomplishment. The ways groups work together can either help or hinder organizational performance. The selection by Edgar Schein summarizes much of the literature on cooperation and competition between groups. Schein has packaged a wealth of empirical research, much of it conducted by Muzafer Sherif and Robert Blake and Jane Syrgley Mouton, in such a way that the OD practitioner and the manager alike can gain insights into this important area.

The article on organizational culture is also by Edgar Schein, who has written extensively on the subject. OD practitioners have recognized the importance of culture since the early days of the field, but it was not until the 1980s that serious and systematic attention was given to this important determinant of behavior. The reading by Schein defines organizational culture, shows how to analyze culture, and describes how to think about culture change.

The final reading in Part II "puts it all together." Ralph Kilman proposes a comprehensive, holistic approach to organization development and transformation in which he identifies the critical stages, the five "tracks" of activities that must take place, and several key success factors. He writes: "Today, managers are realizing 'future shock' is upon them. They can no longer ignore the need for fundamental systemwide changes. Their entire organizations must be transformed into market-driven, innovative, and adaptive systems if they are to survive and prosper in the highly competitive, global environment of the next decades." He then tells how to accomplish such systemwide planned change.

READING 7
GENERAL STRATEGIES FOR EFFECTING CHANGES IN HUMAN SYSTEMS

Robert Chin and Kenneth D. Benne

Discussing general strategies and procedures for effecting change requires that we set limits to the discussion. For, under a liberal interpretation of the title, we would need to deal with much of the literature of contemporary social and behavioral science, basic and applied.

Therefore we shall limit our discussion to those changes which are planned changes—in which attempts to bring about change are conscious, deliberate, and intended, at least on the part of one or more agents related to the change attempt. We shall also attempt to categorize strategies and procedures which have a few important elements in common but which, in fact, differ widely in other respects. And we shall neglect many of these differences. In addition, we shall look beyond the description of procedures in commonsense terms and seek some genotypic characteristics of change strategies. We shall seek the roots of the main strategies discussed, including their variants, in ideas and idea systems prominent in contemporary and recent social and psychological thought.

One element in all approaches to planned change is the conscious utilization and application of knowledge as an instrument or tool for modifying patterns and institutions of practice. The knowledge or related technology to be applied may be knowledge of the nonhuman environment in which practice goes on or of some knowledge-based "thing technology" for controlling one or another feature of the practice environment. In educational practice, for exam-

ple, technologies of communication and calculation, based upon new knowledge of electronics—audiovisual devices, television, computers, teaching machines—loom large among the knowledges and technologies that promise greater efficiency and economy in handling various practices in formal education. As attempts are made to introduce these new thing technologies into school situations, the change problem shifts to the human problems of dealing with the resistances, anxieties, threats to morale, conflicts, disrupted interpersonal communications, and so on, which prospective changes in patterns of practice evoke in the people affected by the change. So the change agent, even though focally and initially concerned with modifications in the thing technology of education, finds himself in need of more adequate knowledge of human behavior, individual and social, and in need of developed "people technologies," based on behavioral knowledge, for dealing effectively with the human aspects of deliberate change.

The knowledge which suggests improvements in educational practice may, on the other hand, be behavioral knowledge in the first instance—knowledge about participative learning, about attitude change, about family disruption in inner-city communities, about the cognitive and skill requirements of new careers, and so forth. Such knowledge may suggest changes in school grouping, in the relations between teachers and students, in the relations of teachers and principals to parents, and in counseling practices. Here change agents, initially focused on application of behavioral knowledge and the improvement of people technologies in school settings, must face the problems of using people technologies in planning, installing, and evaluating such changes

Source: "General Strategies for Effecting Changes in Human Systems" from *The Planning of Change,* 3rd ed., by Warren G. Bennis, Kenneth D. Benne, Robert Chin, and Kenneth E. Corey, copyright © 1976 by Holt, Rinehart, and Winston, Inc. Reprinted by permission of the publisher.

in educational practice. The new people technologies must be experienced, understood, and accepted by teachers and administrators before they can be used effectively with students.

This line of reasoning suggests that, whether the focus of planned change is in the introduction of more effective thing technologies or people technologies into institutionalized practice, processes of introducing such changes must be based on behavioral knowledge of change and must utilize people technologies based on such knowledge.

Types of Strategies for Changing

Our further analysis is based on three types or groups of strategies. The first of these, and probably the most frequently employed by men of knowledge in America and Western Europe, are those we call empirical-rational strategies. One fundamental assumption underlying these strategies is that men are rational. Another assumption is that men will follow their rational self-interest once this is revealed to them. A change is proposed by some person or group which knows of a situation that is desirable, effective, and in line with the self-interest of the person, group, organization, or community which will be affected by the change. Because the person (or group) is assumed to be rational and moved by self-interest, it is assumed that he (or they) will adopt the proposed change if it can be rationally justified and if it can be shown by the proposer(s) that he (or they) will gain by the change.

A second group of strategies we call normative-reeducative. These strategies build upon assumptions about human motivation different from those underlying the first. The rationality and intelligence of men are not denied. Patterns of action and practice are supported by sociocultural norms and by commitments on the part of individuals to these norms. Sociocultural norms are supported by the attitude and value systems of individuals—normative outlooks which undergird their commitments. Change in a pattern of practice or action, according to this

view, will occur only as the persons involved are brought to change their normative orientations to old patterns and develop commitments to new ones. And changes in normative orientations involve changes in attitudes, values, skills, and significant relationships, not just changes in knowledge, information, or intellectual rationales for action and practice.

The third group of strategies is based on the application of power in some form, political or otherwise. The influence process involved is basically that of compliance of those with less power to the plans, directions, and leadership of those with greater power. Often the power to be applied is legitimate power or authority. Thus the strategy may involve getting the authority of law or administrative policy behind the change to be effected. Some power strategies may appeal less to the use of authoritative power to effect change than to the massing of coercive power, legitimate or not, in support of the change sought.[1]

Empirical-Rational Strategies   A variety of specific strategies are included in what we are calling the empirical-rational approach to effecting change. As we have already pointed out, the rationale underlying most of these is an assumption that men are guided by reason and that they

---

[1] Throughout our discussion of strategies and procedures, we will not differentiate these according to the size of the target of change. We assume that there are similarities in processes of changing, whether the change affects an individual, a small group, an organization, a community, or a culture. In addition, we are not attending to differences among the aspects of a system, let us say an educational system, which is being changed—curriculum, audiovisual methods, team teaching, pupil grouping, and so on. Furthermore, because many changes in communities or organizations start with an individual or some small membership group, our general focus will be upon those strategies which lead to and involve individual changes.

We will sidestep the issue of defining change in this paper. As further conceptual work progresses in the study of planned change, we shall eventually have to examine how different definitions of change relate to strategies and procedures for effecting change. But we are not dealing with these issues here.

will utilize some rational calculus of self-interest in determining needed changes in behavior.

It is difficult to point to any one person whose ideas express or articulate the orientation underlying commitment to empirical-rational strategies of changing. In Western Europe and America, this orientation might be better identified with the general social orientation of the enlightenment and of classical liberalism than with the ideas of any one man. On this view, the chief foes to human rationality and to change or progress based on rationality were ignorance and superstition. Scientific investigation and research represented the chief ways of extending knowledge and reducing the limitations of ignorance. A corollary of this optimistic view of man and his future was an advocacy of education as a way of disseminating scientific knowledge and of freeing men and women from the shackles of superstition. Although elitist notions played a part in the thinking of many classic liberals, the increasing trend during the 19th century was toward the universalization of educational opportunity. The common and universal school, open to all men and women, was the principal instrument by which knowledge would replace ignorance and superstition in the minds of people and become a principal agent in the spread of reason, knowledge, and knowledge-based action and practice (progress) in human society. In American experience, Jefferson may be taken as a principal, early advocate of research and of education as agencies of human progress. And Horace Mann may be taken as the prophet of progress through the institutionalization of universal education opportunity through the common school.[2]

---

[2] We have indicated the main roots of ideas and idea systems underlying the principal strategies of changing and their subvariants on a chart which appears as Figure 1 at the end of this essay. It may be useful in seeing both the distinctions and the relationships between various strategies of changing in time perspective. We have emphasized developments of the past 25 years more than earlier developments. This makes for historical foreshortening. We hope this is a pardonable distortion, considering our present limited purpose.

Basic Research and Dissemination of Knowledge through General Education. The strategy of encouraging basic knowledge building and of depending on general education to diffuse the results of research into the minds and thinking of men and women is still by far the most appealing strategy of change to most academic men of knowledge and to large segments of the American population as well. Basic researchers are quite likely to appeal for time for further research when confronted by some unmet need. And many people find this appeal convincing. Both of these facts are well illustrated by difficulties with diseases for which no adequate control measure or cures are available—poliomyelitis, for example. Medical researchers asked for more time and funds for research and people responded with funds for research, both through voluntary channels and through legislative appropriations. And the control measures were forthcoming. The educational problem then shifted to inducing people to comply with immunization procedures based on research findings.

This appeal to a combination of research and education of the public has worked in many areas of new knowledge-based thing technologies where almost universal readiness for accepting the new technology was already present in the population. Where such readiness is not available, as in the case of fluoridation technologies in the management of dental cavities, general strategy of basic research plus educational (informational) campaigns to spread knowledge of the findings do not work well. The cases of its inadequacy as a single strategy of change have multiplied, especially where "engineering" problems, which involve a divided and conflicting public or deep resistances due to the threat by the new technology to traditional attitudes and values, have thwarted its effectiveness. But these cases, while they demand attention to other strategies of changing, do not disprove the importance of basic research and of general educational opportunity as elements in a progressive and self-renewing society.

We have noted that the strategy under discussion has worked best in grounding and diffusing generally acceptable thing technologies in society. Some have argued that the main reason the strategy has not worked in the area of people technologies is a relative lack of basic research on people and their behavior, relationships, and institutions and a corresponding lack of emphasis upon social and psychological knowledges in school and college curricula. It would follow in this view that increased basic research on human affairs and relationships and increased efforts to diffuse the results of such research through public education are the ways of making the general strategy work better. Auguste Comte, with his emphasis on positivistic sociology in the reorganization of society, and Lester F. Ward in America may be taken as late 19th-century representatives of this view. And the spirit of Comte and Ward is by no means dead in American academia or in influential segments of the American public.

Personnel Selection and Replacement. Difficulties in getting knowledge effectively into practice may be seen as lying primarily in the lack of fitness of persons occupying positions with job responsibilities for improving practice. The argument goes that we need the right person in the right position, if knowledge is to be optimally applied and if rationally based changes are to become the expectation in organizational and societal affairs. This fits with the liberal reformers' frequently voiced and enacted plea to drive the unfit from office and to replace them with those more fit as a condition of social progress.

That reformers' programs have so often failed has sobered but by no means destroyed the zeal of those who regard personnel selection, assessment, and replacement as a major key to program improvement in education or in other enterprises as well. This strategy was given a scientific boost by the development of scientific testing of potentialities and aptitudes. We will use Binet as a prototype of psychological testing and Moreno as a prototype in sociometric testing, while recognizing the extensive differentiation and elaboration which have occurred in psychometrics and sociometrics since their original work. We recognize, too, the elaborated modes of practice in personnel work which have been built around psychometric and sociometric tools and techniques. We do not discount their limited value as actual and potential tools for change, while making two observations on the way they have often been used. First, they have been used more often in the interest of system maintenance rather than of system change, since the job descriptions personnel workers seek to fill are defined in terms of system requirements as established. Second, by focusing on the role occupant as the principal barrier to improvement, personnel selection and replacement strategies have tended not to reveal the social and cultural system difficulties which may be in need of change if improvement is to take place.

Systems Analysts as Staff and Consultants. Personnel workers in government, industry, and education have typically worked in staff relations to line management, reflecting the bureaucratic, line-staff form of organization which has flourished in the large-scale organization of effort and enterprise in the 20th century. And other expert workers—systems analysts—more attuned to system difficulties than to the adequacies or inadequacies of persons as role occupants within the system, have found their way into the staff resources of line management in contemporary organizations.

There is no reason why the expert resources of personnel workers and systems analysts might not be used in nonbureaucratic organizations or in processes of moving bureaucratic organizations toward nonbureaucratic forms. But the fact remains that their use has been shaped, for the most part, in the image of the scientific management of bureaucratically organized enterprises. So we have placed the systems analysts in our chart under Frederick Taylor, the father of scientific management in America.

The line management of an enterprise seeks

to organize human and technical effort toward the most efficient service of organizational goals. And these goals are defined in terms of the production of some mandated product, whether a tangible product or a less tangible good or service. In pursuing this quest for efficiency, line management employs experts in the analysis of sociotechnical systems and in the laying out of more efficient systems. The experts employed may work as external consultants or as an internal staff unit. Behavioral scientists have recently found their way, along with mathematicians and engineers, into systems analysis work.

It is interesting to note that the role of these experts is becoming embroiled in discussions of whether or not behavioral science research should be used to sensitize administrators to new organizational possibilities, to new goals, or primarily to implement efficient operation within perspectives and goals as currently defined. Jean Hills has raised the question of whether behavioral science when applied to organizational problems tends to perpetuate established ideology and system relations because of blinders imposed by their being "problem centered" and by their limited definition of what is "a problem."[3]

We see an emerging strategy, in the use of behavioral scientists as systems analysts and engineers, toward viewing the problem of organizational change and changing as a wide-angled problem, one in which all the input and output features and components of a large-scale system are considered. It is foreseeable that with the use of high-speed and high-capacity computers, and with the growth of substantial theories and hypotheses about how parts of an educational system operate, we shall find more and more applications for systems analysis and operations research in programs of educational change. In fact, it is precisely the quasi-mathematical character of these modes of research that will make possible the rational analysis of qualitatively different aspects of educational work and will bring them into the range of rational planning—masses of students, massive problems of poverty and educational and cultural deprivation, and so on. We see no necessary incompatibility between an ideology which emphasizes the individuality of the student and the use of systems analysis and computers in strategizing the problems of the total system. The actual incompatibilities may lie in the limited uses to which existing organizers and administrators of educational efforts put these technical resources.

Applied Research and Linkage Systems for Diffusion of Research Results. The American development of applied research of a planned system for linking applied researchers with professional practitioners and both of these with centers for basic research and with organized consumers of applied research has been strongly influenced by two distinctive American inventions—the land-grant university and the agricultural extension system. We, therefore, have put the name of Justin Morrill, author of the land-grant college act and of the act which established the cooperative agricultural extension system, on our chart. The land-grant colleges or universities were dedicated to doing applied research in the service of agriculture and the mechanic arts. These colleges and universities developed research programs in basic sciences as well and experimental stations for the development and refinement of knowledge-based technologies for use in engineering and agriculture. As the extension services developed, county agents—practitioners—were attached to the state land-grant college or university that received financial support from both state and federal governments. The county agent and his staff developed local organizations of adult farm men and women and of farm youth to provide both a channel toward informing consumers concerning new and better agricultural practices and toward getting awareness of unmet consumer needs and unsolved problems back to centers of knowledge and research. Garth Jones has made one of the more compre-

---

[3] Jean Hills, "Social Science, Ideology and the Purposes of Educational Administration," *Education Administration Quarterly,* Autumn 1965, pp. 23–40.

hensive studies of the strategies of changing involved in large-scale demonstration.[4]

All applied research has not occurred within a planned system for knowledge discovery, development, and utilization like the one briefly described above. The system has worked better in developing and diffusing thing technologies than in developing and diffusing people technologies, though the development of rural sociology and of agricultural economics shows that extension workers were by no means unaware of the behavioral dimensions of change problems. But the large-scale demonstration, through the land-grant university cooperative extension service, of the stupendous changes which can result from a planned approach to knowledge discovery, development, diffusion, and utilization is a part of the consciousness of all Americans concerned with planned change.[5]

Applied research and development is an honored part of the tradition of engineering approaches to problem identification and solution. The pioneering work of E. L. Thorndike in applied research in education should be noted on our chart. The processes and slow tempo of diffusion and utilization of research findings and inventions in public education is well illustrated in studies by Paul Mort and his students.[6] More recently, applied research, in its product development aspect, has been utilized in a massive way

to contribute curriculum materials and designs for science instruction (as well as in other subjects). When we assess this situation to find reasons why such researches have not been more effective in producing changes in instruction, the answers seem to lie both in the plans of the studies which produced the materials and designs and in the potential users of the findings. Adequate linkage between consumers and researchers was frequently not established. Planned and evaluated demonstrations and experimentations connected with the use of materials were frequently slighted. And training of consumer teachers to use the new materials adaptively and creatively was frequently missing.

Such observations have led to a fresh spurt of interest in evaluation research addressed to educational programs. The fear persists that this, too, may lead to disappointment if it is not focused for two-way communication between researchers and teachers and if it does not involve collaboratively the ultimate consumers of the results of such research—the students. Evaluation researches conducted in the spirit of justifying a program developed by expert applied researchers will not help to guide teachers and students in their quest for improved practices of teaching and learning, if the concerns of the latter have not been taken centrally into account in the evaluation process.[7]

Recently, attempts have been made to link applied research activities in education with basic researchers on the one hand and with persons in action and practice settings on the other through some system of interlocking roles similar to those suggested in the description of the land-grant extension systems in agriculture or in other fields where applied and development researches have flourished.

The linking of research-development efforts

[4] Garth Jones, "Planned Organizational Change, a Set of Working Documents," Center for Research in Public Organization, School of Public Administration (Los Angeles: University of Southern California, 1964).

[5] For a review, see Ronald G. Havelock and Kenneth D. Benne, "An Exploratory Study of Knowledge Utilization," in *The Planning of Change,* 2nd ed. Warren G. Bennis, Kenneth D. Benne, and Robert Chin (New York: Holt, Rinehart & Winston, 1969), chap. 3, p. 124.

[6] Paul R. Mort and Donald R. Ross, *Principles of School Administration* (New York: McGraw-Hill, 1957). Paul R. Mort and Francis G. Cornell, *American Schools in Transition: How Our Schools Adapt Their Practices to Changing Needs* (New York: Bureau of Publications, Teachers College, Columbia University Press, 1941).

[7] Robert Chin, "Research Approaches to the Problem of Civic Training," in *The Adolescent Citizen,* ed. F. Patterson (New York: Free Press, 1980).

with diffusion-innovation efforts has been gaining headway in the field of education with the emergence of federally supported research and development centers based in universities, regional laboratories connected with state departments of education, colleges and universities in a geographic area, and with various consortia and institutes confronting problems of educational change and changing. The strategy of change here usually includes a well-researched innovation which seems feasible to install in practice settings. Attention is directed to the question of whether or not the innovation will bring about a desired result, and with what it can accomplish, if given a trial in one or more practice settings. The questions of *how* to get a fair trial and *how* to install an innovation in an already going and crowded school system are ordinarily not built centrally into the strategy. The rationalistic assumption usually precludes research attention to these questions. For, if the invention can be rationally shown to have achieved desirable results in some situations, it is assumed that people in other situations will adopt it once they know these results and the rationale behind them. The neglect of the above questions has led to a wastage of much applied research effort in the past.

Attention has been given recently to the roles, communication mechanisms, and processes necessary for innovation and diffusion of improved education practices.[8] Clark and Guba have formulated very specific processes related to and necessary for change in educational practice following upon research. For them, the necessary processes are: *development,* including invention and design; *diffusion,* including dissemination and demonstration; *adoption,* including trial, installation, and institutionalization. Clark's earnest conviction is summed up in this statement: "In a sense, the educational research community will be the educational community, and the route to educational progress will self-evidently be research and development."[9]

The approach of Havelock and Benne is concerned with the intersystem relationships between basic researchers, applied researchers, practitioners, and consumers in an evolved and evolving organization for knowledge utilization. They are concerned especially with the communication difficulties and role conflicts that occur at points of intersystem exchange. These conflicts are important because they illuminate the normative issues at stake between basic researchers and applied researchers, between applied researchers and practitioners (teachers and administrators), between practitioners and consumers (students). The lines of strategy suggested by their analysis for solving role conflicts and communication difficulties call for transactional and collaborative exchanges across the lines of varied organized interests and orientations within the process of utilization. This brings their analysis into the range of normative-reeducative strategies to be discussed later.

The concepts from the behavioral sciences upon which these strategies of diffusion rest come mainly from two traditions. The first is from studies of the diffusion of traits of culture from one cultural system to another, initiated by the American anthropologist, Franz Boas. This

[8] Matthew B. Miles, *Some Propositions in Research Utilization in Education* (March 1965), in press. Kenneth Wiles, paper for seminar on Strategies for Curriculum Change (Columbus: Ohio State University, 1965). Charles Jung and Ronald Lippitt, "Utilization of Scientific Knowledge for Change in Education," in *Concepts for Social Change* (Washington, D.C.: National Educational Association, National Training Laboratories, 1967). Havelock and Benne, "Exploratory Study of Knowledge Utilization," in Bennis et al., *Planning of Change*, chap. 3, p. 124. David Clark and Egon Guba, "An Examination of Potential Change Roles in Education," seminar on Innovation in Planning School Curricula (Columbus: Ohio State University, 1965).

[9] David Clark, "Educational Research and Development: The Next Decade," in *Implications for Education of Prospective Changes in Society,* a publication of "Designing Education for the Future—an Eight State Project" (Denver, Colo., 1967).

type of study has been carried on by Rogers in his work on innovation and diffusion of innovations in contemporary culture and is reflected in a number of recent writers, such as Katz and Carlson.[10] The second scientific tradition is in studies of influence in mass communication associated with Carl Hovland and his students.[11] Both traditions have assumed a *relatively passive recipient of input* in diffusion situations. And actions within the process of diffusion are interpreted from the standpoint of an observer of the process. Bauer has pointed out that scientific studies have exaggerated the effectiveness of mass persuasion since they have compared the total number in the audience to the communications with the much smaller proportion of the audience persuaded by the communication.[12] A clearer view of processes of diffusion must include the actions of the receiver as well as those of the transmitter in the transactional events which are the units of diffusion process. And strategies for making diffusion processes more effective must be transactional and collaborative by design.

Utopian Thinking as a Strategy of Changing. It may seem strange to include the projection of utopias as a rational-empirical strategy of chang-

ing. Yet inventing and designing the shape of the future by extrapolating what we know of in the present is to envision a direction for planning and action in the present. If the image of a potential future is convincing and rationally persuasive to men in the present, the image may become part of the dynamics and motivation of present action. The liberal tradition is not devoid of its utopias. When we think of utopias quickened by an effort to extrapolate from the sciences of man to a future vision of society, the utopia of B. F. Skinner comes to mind.[13] The title of the Eight State Project, "Designing Education for the Future," for which this paper was prepared, reveals a utopian intent and aspiration and illustrates an attempt to employ utopian thinking for practical purposes.[14]

Yet it may be somewhat disheartening to others as it is to us to note the absence of rousing and beckoning normative statements of what both can and ought to be in man's future in most current liberal-democratic utopias, whether these be based on psychological, sociological, political, or philosophical findings and assumptions. The absence of utopias in current society, in this sense, and in the sense that Mannheim studied them in his now classical study,[15] tends to make the forecasting of future directions a problem of technical prediction, rather than equally a process of projecting value orientations and preferences into the shaping of a better future.

Perceptual and Conceptual Reorganization through the Clarification of Language. In classical liberalism, one perceived foe of rational change and progress was superstition. And superstitions are carried from man to man and from generation to

[10] Elihu Katz, "The Social Itinerary of Technical Change: Two Studies on the Diffusion of Innovation," in Bennis et al., *Planning of Change,* chap. 5, p. 230. Richard Carlson, "Some Needed Research on the Diffusion of Innovations" (paper at the Washington Conference on Educational Change, Columbus, Ohio, Ohio State University). Everett Rogers, "What Are Innovators Like?" in *Change Processes in the Public Schools,* Center for the Advanced Study of Educational Administration (Eugene: University of Oregon, 1965). Everett Rogers, *Diffusion of Innovations* (New York: Free Press, 1962).

[11] Carl Hovland, Irving Janis, and Harold Kelley, *Communication and Persuasion* (New Haven, Conn.: Yale University Press, 1953).

[12] Raymond Bauer, "The Obstinate Audience: The Influence Process from the Point of View of Social Communication," in Bennis et al., *Planning of Change,* chap. 9, p. 507.

[13] B. F. Skinner, *Walden Two* (New York: Crowell-Collier and Macmillan, 1948).

[14] "Designing Education for the Future—an Eight State Project" (Denver, Colo., 1967).

[15] Karl Mannheim, *Ideology and Utopia* (New York: Harcourt Brace Jovanovich, 1946).

generation through the agency of unclear and mythical language. British utilitarianism was one important strand of classical liberalism, and one of utilitarianism's important figures, Jeremy Bentham, sought to purify language of its dangerous mystique through his study of fictions.

More recently, Alfred Korzybski and S. I. Hayakawa, in the general semantics movement, have sought a way of clarifying and rectifying the names of things and processes.[16] While their main applied concern was with personal therapy, both, and especially Hayakawa, were also concerned with bringing about changes in social systems as well. People disciplined in general semantics, it was hoped, would see more correctly, communicate more adequately, and reason more effectively and thus lay a realistic common basis for action and changing. The strategies of changing associated with general semantics overlap with our next family of strategies, the normative-reeducative, because of their emphasis upon the importance of interpersonal relationships and social contexts within the communication process.

Normative-Reeducative Strategies of Changing. We have already suggested that this family of strategies rests on assumptions and hypotheses about man and his motivation which contrast significantly at points with the assumptions and hypotheses of those committed to what we have called rational-empirical strategies. Men are seen as inherently active, in quest of impulsive and need satisfaction. The relation between man and his environment is essentially transactional, as Dewey[17] made clear in his famous article on "The Reflex-Arc Concept."

[16] Alfred Korzybski, *Science and Sanity,* 3rd ed. (International Non-Aristotelian Library Publishing Company, 1948). S. I. Hayakawa, *Language in Thought and Action* (New York: Harcourt Brace Jovanovich, 1941).

[17] John Dewey, *Philosophy, Psychology and Social Practice,* ed. Joseph Ratner (New York: Capricorn Books, 1967).

Man, the organism, does not passively await given stimuli from his environment in order to respond. He takes stimuli as furthering or thwarting the goals of his ongoing action. Intelligence arises in the process of shaping organism-environmental relations toward more adequate fitting and joining of organismic demands and environmental resources.

Intelligence is social, rather than narrowly individual. Men are guided in their actions by socially funded and communicated meanings, norms, and institutions, in brief by a normative culture. At the personal level, men are guided by internalized meanings, habits, and values. Changes in patterns of action or practice are, therefore, changes, not alone in the rational informational equipment of men, but at the personal level, in habits and values as well and, at the sociocultural level, changes are alterations in normative structures and in institutionalized roles and relationships, as well as in cognitive and perceptual orientations.

For Dewey, the prototype of intelligence in action is the scientific method. And he saw a broadened and humanized scientific method as man's best hope for progress, if men could learn to utilize such a method in facing all of the problematic situations of their lives. *Intelligence,* so conceived, rather than *reason* as defined in classical liberalism, was the key to Dewey's hope for the invention, development, and testing of adequate strategies of changing in human affairs.

Lewin's contribution to normative-reeducative strategies of changing stemmed from his vision of required interrelations between research, training, and action (and, for him, this meant collaborative relationships, often now lacking, between researchers, educators, and activists) in the solution of human problems, in the identification of needs for change, and in the working out of improved knowledge, technology, and patterns of action in meeting these needs. Man must participate in his own reeducation if he is to be reeducated at all. And reeducation is a normative change as well as a cognitive and perceptual change. These convictions led Lewin[18] to emphasize action research as a strategy of changing, and participation in groups as a medium of reeducation.

Freud's main contributions to normative-reeducative strategies of changing are two. First, he sought to demonstrate the unconscious and preconscious bases of man's actions. Only as a man finds ways of becoming aware of these nonconscious wellsprings of his attitudes and actions will he be able to bring them into conscious self-control. And Freud devoted much of his magnificent genius to developing ways of helping men to become conscious of the main springs of their actions and so capable of freedom. Second, in developing therapeutic methods, he discovered and developed ways of utilizing the relationships between change agent (therapist) and client (patient) as a major tool in reeducating the client toward expanded self-awareness, self-understanding, and self-control. Emphasis upon the collaborative relationship in therapeutic change was a major contribution by Freud and his students and colleagues to normative-reeducative strategies of changing in human affairs.[19]

Normative-reeducative approaches to effecting change bring direct interventions by change agents, interventions based on a consciously worked out theory of change and of changing, into the life of a client system, be that system a person, a small group, an organization, or a community. The theory of changing is still crude, but it is probably as explicitly stated as possible, granted our present state of knowledge about planned change.[20]

Some of the common elements among variants within this family of change strategies are the following. First, all emphasize the client system and his (or its) involvement in working out programs of change and improvement for himself (or itself). The way the client sees himself and his problem must be brought into dialogic relationship with the way in which he and his problem are seen by the change agent, whether the latter is functioning as researcher, consultant, trainer, therapist, or friend in relation to the client. Second, the problem confronting the client is not assumed a priori to be one which can be met by more adequate technical information, though this possibility is not ruled out. The problem may lie rather in the attitudes, values, norms, and the external and internal relationships of the client system and may require alteration or reeducation of these as a condition of its solution. Third, the change agent must learn to intervene mutually and collaboratively along with the client into efforts to define and solve the client's problem(s). The here and now experience of the two provide an important basis for diagnosing the problem and for locating needs for reeducation in the interest of solving it. Fourth, nonconscious elements which impede problem solution must be brought into consciousness and publicly examined and reconstructed. Fifth, the methods and concepts of the behavioral sciences are resources which change agent and client learn to use selectively, relevantly, and appropriately in learning to deal with the confronting problem and with problems of a similar kind in the future.

These approaches center in the notion that people technology is just as necessary as thing technology in working out desirable changes in human affairs. Put in this bold fashion, it is obvious that for the normative-reeducative change agent, clarification and reconstruction of values is of pivotal importance in changing. By getting the values of various parts of the client system, along with his own, openly into the arena of change, and by working through value conflicts responsibly, the change agent seeks to avoid ma-

[18] Kurt Lewin, *Resolving Social Conflicts* (New York: Harper & Row, 1948). Kurt Lewin, *Field Theory in Social Science* (New York: Harper & Row, 1951).

[19] For Freud, an interesting summary is contained in Otto Fenichel, *Problems of Psychoanalytic Technique* (Albany: NT Psychoanalytic Quarterly, 1941).

[20] W. Bennis, K. Benne, and R. Chin, *The Planning of Change*, 1st ed. (New York: Holt, Rinehart & Winston, 1961). R. Lippitt, J. Watson, and B. Westley, *The Dynamics of Planned Change* (New York: Harcourt Brace Jovanovich, 1958). W. Bennis, *Changing Organizations* (New York: McGraw-Hill, 1966).

nipulation and indoctrination of the client, in the morally reprehensible meanings of these terms.

We may use the organization of the National Training Laboratories (NTL) in 1947 as a milestone in the development of normative-reeducative approaches to changing in America. The first summer laboratory program grew out of earlier collaborations among Kurt Lewin, Ronald Lippitt, Leland Bradford, and Kenneth Benne. The idea behind the laboratory was that participants, staff, and students would learn about themselves and their back-home problems by collaboratively building a laboratory in which participants would become both experimenters and subjects in the study of their own developing interpersonal and group behavior within the laboratory setting. It seems evident that the five conditions of a normative-reeducative approach to changing were met in the conception of the training laboratory. Kurt Lewin died before the 1947 session of the training laboratory opened. Ronald Lippitt was a student of Lewin's and carried many of Lewin's orientations with him into the laboratory staff. Leland Bradford and Kenneth Benne were both students of John Dewey's philosophy of education. Bradford had invented several technologies for participative learning and self-study in his work in WPA adult education programs and as training officer in several agencies of the federal government. Benne came out of a background in educational philosophy and had collaborated with colleagues prior to 1943 in developing a methodology for policy and decision making and for the reconstruction of normative orientations, a methodology which sought to fuse democratic and scientific values and to translate these into principles for resolving conflicting and problematic situations at personal and community levels of human organization.[21] Benne and his colleagues

had been much influenced by the work of Mary Follett,[22] her studies of integrative solutions to conflicts in settings of public and business administration, and by the work of Karl Mannheim[23] on the ideology and methodology of planning changes in human affairs, as well as by the work of John Dewey and his colleagues.

The work of the National Training Laboratories has encompassed development and testing of various approaches to changing in institutional settings, in America and abroad, since its beginning. One parallel development in England which grew out of Freud's thinking should be noted. This work developed in efforts at Tavistock Clinic to apply therapeutic approaches to problems of change in industrial organizations and in communities. This work is reported in statements by Elliot Jaques[24] and in this volume by Eric Trist. Another parallel development is represented by the efforts of Roethlisberger and Dickson to use personal counseling in industry as a strategy of organizational change.[25] Roethlisberger and Dickson had been strongly influenced by the pioneer work of Elton Mayo in industrial sociology[26] as well as by the counseling theories and methodologies of Carl Rogers.

Various refinements of methodologies for changing have been developed and tested since the establishment of the National Training Laboratories in 1947, both under its auspices and under other auspices as well. For us, the modal developments are worthy of further discussion here. One set of approaches is oriented focally to

---

[21] Raup, Benne, Smith, and Axtelle, *The Discipline of Practical Judgment in a Democratic Society,* Yearbook No. 28 of the National Society of College Teachers of Education (Chicago: University of Chicago Press, 1943).

[22] Mary Follett, *Creative Experience and Dynamic Administration* (New York: David McKay, 1924).

[23] Karl Mannheim, *Man and Society in an Age of Reconstruction* (New York: Harcourt Brace Jovanovich, 1940).

[24] Elliot Jaques, *The Changing Culture of a Factory* (New York: Holt, Rinehart & Winston, 1952).

[25] William J. Dickson and F. J. Roethlisberger, *Personal Counseling in an Organization: A Sequel to the Hawthorne Researchers* (Boston: Harvard Business School, 1966).

[26] Elton Mayo, *The Social Problems of an Industrial Civilization* (Cambridge, Mass.: Harvard University Press, 1945).

the improvement of the problem-solving processes utilized by a client system. The other set focuses on helping members of client systems to become aware of their attitude and value orientations and relationship difficulties through a probing of feelings, manifest and latent, involved in the functioning and operation of the client system.[27] Both approaches use the development of "temporary systems" as a medium of reeducation of persons and of role occupants in various ongoing social systems.[28]

Improving the Problem-Solving Capabilities of a System. This family of approaches to changing rests on several assumptions about change in human systems. Changes in a system, when they are reality oriented, take the form of problem solving. A system to achieve optimum reality orientation in its adaptations to its changing internal and external environments must develop and institutionalize its own problem-solving structures and processes. These structures and processes must be tuned both to human problems of relationship and morale and to technical problems of meeting the system's task requirements, set by its goals of production, distribution, and so on.[29] System problems are typically not social *or* technical but actually sociotechnical.[30] The problem-solving structures and processes of a human system must be developed to deal with a range of sociotechnical difficulties, converting them into problems and organizing the relevant

processes of the data collection, planning, invention, and tryout of solutions, evaluation and feedback of results, replanning, and so forth, which are required for the solution of the problems.

The human parts of the system must learn to function collaboratively in these processes of problem identification and solution and the system must develop institutionalized support and mechanisms for maintaining and improving these processes. Actually, the model of changing in these approaches is a cooperative, action-research model. This model was suggested by Lewin and developed most elaborately for use in educational settings by Stephen M. Corey.[31]

The range of interventions by outside change agents in implementing this approach to changing is rather wide. It has been most fully elaborated in relation to organizational development programs. Within such programs, intervention methods have been most comprehensively tested in industrial settings. Some of these more or less tested intervention methods are listed below. A design for any organizational development program, of course, normally uses a number of these in succession or combination.

1. Collection of data about organizational functioning and feedback of data into processes of data interpretation and of planning ways of correcting revealed dysfunctions by system managers and data collectors in collaboration.[32]

2. Training of managers and working

---

[27] Leland Bradford, Jack R. Gibb, and Kenneth D. Benne, *T-Group Theory and Laboratory Methods* (New York: John Wiley & Sons, 1964).

[28] Matthew B. Miles, "On Temporary Systems," in *Innovation in Education,* ed. M. B. Miles (New York: Bureau of Publications, Teachers College, Columbia University Press, 1964), pp. 437–92.

[29] Robert R. Blake and Jane S. Mouton, *The Managerial Grid* (Houston: Gulf Publishing, 1961).

[30] Jay W. Lorsch and Paul Lawrence, "The Diagnosis of Organizational Problems," in Bennis et al., *Planning of Change,* chap. 8, p. 468.

[31] Stephen M. Corey, *Action Research to Improve School Practices* (New York: Bureau of Publications, Teachers College, Columbia University Press, 1953).

[32] See contributions by Miles et al., "Data Feedback and Organizational Change in a School System," in Bennis et al., *Planning of Change,* chap. 8, p. 457; and Lorsch and Lawrence, "Diagnosis of Organizational Problems," in Bennis et al. *Planning of Change,* chap. 8, p. 468.

organizational units in methods of problem solving through self-examination of present ways of dealing with difficulties and through development and tryout of better ways with consultation by outside and/or inside change agents. Usually, the working unit leaves its working place for parts of its training. These laboratory sessions are ordinarily interspersed with on-the-job consultations.

3. Developing acceptance of feedback (research and development) roles and functions within the organization, training persons to fill these roles, and relating such roles strategically to the ongoing management of the organization.

4. Training internal change agents to function within the organization in carrying on needed applied research, consultation, and training.[33]

Whatever specific strategies of intervention may be employed in developing the system's capabilities for problem solving, change efforts are designed to help the system in developing ways of scanning its operations to detect problems, of diagnosing these problems to determine relevant changeable factors in them, and of moving toward collaboratively determined solutions to the problems.

Releasing and Fostering Growth in the Persons Who Make Up the System to Be Changed.   Those committed to this family of approaches to changing tend to see the person as the basic unit of social organization. Persons, it is believed, are capable of creative, life-affirming, self-and other-regarding and respecting responses, choices, and

actions, if conditions which thwart these kinds of responses are removed and other supporting conditions developed. Rogers has formulated these latter conditions in his analysis of the therapist-client relationship—trustworthiness, empathy, caring, and others.[34] Maslow has worked out a similar idea in his analysis of the hierarchy of needs in persons.[35] If lower needs are met, higher need-meeting actions will take place. McGregor[36] has formulated the ways in which existing organizations operate to fixate persons in lower levels of motivation and has sought to envision an organization designed to release and support the growth of persons in fulfilling their higher motivations as they function within the organizations.

Various intervention methods have been designed to help people discover themselves as persons and commit themselves to continuing personal growth in the various relationships of their lives.

1. One early effort to install personal counseling widely and strategically in an organization has been reported by Roethlisberger and Dickson.[37]

2. Training groups designed to facilitate personal confrontation and growth of members in an open, trusting, and accepting atmosphere have been conducted for individuals from various back-home situations and for persons from the same back-home setting. The

---

[33] C. Argyris, "Explorations in Consulting-Client Relationships," in Bennis et al., *Planning of Change,* chap. 8, p. 434. See also Richard Beckhard, "The Confrontation Meeting," in Bennis et al., *Planning of Change,* chap. 8, p. 478.

[34] Carl Rogers, "The Characteristics of a Helping Relationship," in Bennis et al., *Planning of Change,* chap. 4, p. 153.

[35] Abraham Maslow, *Motivation and Personality* (New York: Harper & Row, 1954).

[36] Douglas M. McGregor, "The Human Side of Enterprise," in W. Bennis et al., *The Planning of Change,* 1st ed. (New York: Holt, Rinehart & Winston, 1961), pp. 422–31.

[37] Dickson and Roethlisberger, *Personal Counseling in an Organization.*

processes of these groups have sometimes been described as "therapy for normals."[38]

3. Groups and laboratories designed to stimulate and support personal growth have been designed to utilize the resources of nonverbal exchange and communication among members along with verbal dialogue in inducing personal confrontation, discovery, and commitment to continuing growth.

4. Many psychotherapists, building on the work of Freud and Adler, have come to use groups, as well as two-person situations, as media of personal reeducation and growth. Such efforts are prominent in mental health approaches to changing and have been conducted in educational, religious, community, industrial, and hospital settings. While these efforts focus primarily upon helping individuals to change themselves toward greater self-clarity and fuller self-actualization, they are frequently designed and conducted in the hope that personal changes will lead to changes in organizations, institutions, and communities as well.

We have presented the two variants of normative-reeducative approaches to changing in a way to emphasize their differences. Actually, there are many similarities between them as well, which justify placing both under the same general heading. We have already mentioned one of these similarities. Both frequently use temporary systems—a residential laboratory or workshop, a temporary group with special re-

sources built in, an ongoing system which incorporates a change agent (trainer, consultant, counselor, or therapist) temporarily—as an aid to growth in the system and/or in its members.

More fundamentally, both approaches emphasize experience-based learning as an ingredient of all enduring changes in human systems. Yet both accept the principle that people must learn to learn from their experiences if self-directed change is to be maintained and continued. Frequently, people have learned to defend against the potential lessons of experience when these threaten existing equilibria, whether in the person or in the social system. How can these defenses be lowered to let the data of experience get into processes of perceiving the situation, of constructing new and better ways to define it, of inventing new and more appropriate ways of responding to the situation as redefined, of becoming more fully aware of the consequences of actions, of rearticulating value orientations which sanction more responsible ways of managing the consequences of actions, and so forth? Learning to learn from ongoing experience is a major objective in both approaches to changing. Neither denies the relevance or importance of the noncognitive determinants of behavior— feelings, attitudes, norms, and relationships— along with cognitive-perceptual determinants, in effecting behavioral change. The problem-solving approaches emphasize the cognitive determinants more than personal growth approaches do. But exponents of the former do not accept the rationalistic biases of the rational-empirical family of change strategies, already discussed. Since exponents of both problem-solving and personal growth approaches are committed to reeducation of persons as integral to effective change in human systems, both emphasize norms of openness of communication, trust between persons, lowering of status barriers between parts of the system, and mutuality between parts as necessary conditions of the reeducative process.

Great emphasis has been placed recently upon

[38] James V. Clark "A Healthy Organization," in Bennis et al., *Planning of Change*, chap. 6, p. 282. Irving Weschler, Fred Massarik, and Robert Tannenbaum, "The Self in Process: A Sensitivity Training Emphasis," in *Issues in Training*, ed. I. R. Weschler and E. Schein. Selected Reading Series No. 5 (Washington, D.C.: National Training Laboratories).

the releasing of creativity in persons, groups, and organizations as requisite to coping adaptively with accelerated changes in the conditions of modern living. We have already stressed the emphasis which personal growth approaches put upon the release of creative responses in persons being reeducated. Problem-solving approaches also value creativity, though they focus more upon the group and organizational conditions which increase the probability of creative responses by persons functioning within those conditions than upon persons directly. The approaches do differ in their strategies for releasing creative responses within human systems. But both believe that creative adaptations to changing conditions may arise *within* human systems and do not have to be imported from *outside* them as in innovation-diffusion approaches already discussed and the power-compliance models still to be dealt with.

One developing variant of normative-reeducative approaches to changing, not already noted, focuses on effective conflict management. It is, of course, common knowledge that differences within a society which demand interaccommodation often manifest themselves as conflicts. In the process of managing such conflicts, changes in the norms, policies, and relationships of the society occur. Can conflict management be brought into the ambit of planned change as defined in this volume? Stemming from the work of the Sherifs in creating intergroup conflict and seeking to resolve it in a field-laboratory situation,[39] training in intergroup conflict and conflict resolution found its way into training laboratories through the efforts of Blake and others. Since that time, laboratories for conflict management have been developed under NTL and other auspices and methodologies for conflict resolution and management, in keeping with the values of planned change, have been devised. Blake's and Walton's work represents

some of the findings from these pioneering efforts.[40]

Thus, without denying their differences in assumption and strategy, we believe that the differing approaches discussed in this section can be seen together within the framework of normative-reeducative approaches to changing. Two efforts to conceptualize planned change in a way to reveal the similarities in assumptions about changing and in value orientations toward change underlying these variant approaches are those by Lippitt, Watson, and Westley and by Bennis, Benne, and Chin.[41]

Another aspect of changing in human organizations is represented by efforts to conceive human organization in forms that go beyond the bureaucratic form which captured the imagination and fixed the contours of thinking and practice of organizational theorists and practitioners from the latter part of the 19th through the early part of the 20th century. The bureaucratic form of organization was conceptualized by Max Weber and carried into American thinking by such students of administration as Urwick.[42] On this view, effective organization of human effort followed the lines of effective division of labor and effective establishment of lines of reporting, control, and supervision from the mass base of the organization up through various levels of control to the top of the pyramidal organization from which legitimate authority and responsibility stemmed.

The work of industrial sociologists like Mayo threw doubt upon the adequacy of such a model of formal organization to deal with the realities of organizational life by revealing the informal

---

[39] Muzafer and Carolyn Sherif, *Groups in Harmony and Tension* (New York: Harper & Row, 1953).

[40] Robert Blake et al., "The Union Management Inter-Group Laboratory," in Bennis et al., *Planning of Change*, chap. 4, p. 176. Richard Walton, "Two Strategies of Social Change and Their Dilemmas," in Bennis et al., *Planning of Change*, chap. 4, p. 167.

[41] Lippitt et al., *Dynamics of Planned Change*. Bennis et al., *Planning of Change*, 1st ed.

[42] Lyndall Urwick, *The Pattern of Management* (Minneapolis: University of Minnesota Press, 1956).

organization which grows up within the formal structure to satisfy personal and interpersonal needs not encompassed by or integrated into the goals of the formal organization. Chester Barnard may be seen as a transitional figure who, in discussing the functions of the organizational executive, gave equal emphasis to his responsibilities for task effectiveness and organizational efficiency (optimally meeting the human needs of persons in the organization).[43] Much of the development of subsequent organizational theory and practice has centered on problems of integrating the actualities, criteria, and concepts of organizational effectiveness and of organizational efficiency.

A growing group of thinkers and researchers have sought to move beyond the bureaucratic model toward some new model of organization which might set directions and limits for change efforts in organizational life. Out of many thinkers, we choose four who have theorized out of an orientation consistent with what we have called a normative-reeducative approach to changing.

Rensis Likert has presented an intergroup model of organization. Each working unit strives to develop and function as a group. The group's efforts are linked to other units of the organization by the overlapping membership of supervisors or managers in vertically or horizontally adjacent groups. This view of organization throws problems of delegation, supervision, and internal communication into a new light and emphasizes the importance of linking persons as targets of change and reeducation in processes of organizational development.[44]

We have already stressed McGregor's efforts to conceive a form of organization more in keeping with new and more valid views of human nature and motivation (Theory Y) than the limited and

false views of human nature and motivation (Theory X) upon which traditional bureaucratic organization has rested. In his work he sought to move thinking and practice relevant to organization and organizational change beyond the limits of traditional forms. "The essential task of management is to arrange organizational conditions and methods of operation so that people can achieve their own goals best by directing their own efforts toward organizational objectives."[45]

Bennis has consciously sought to move beyond bureaucracy in tracing the contours of the organizations of the future.[46] And Shephard has described an organizational form consistent with support for continual changing and self-renewal, rather than with a primary mission of maintenance and control.[47]

Power-Coercive Approaches to Effective Change.   It is not the use of power, in the sense of influence by one person upon another or by one group upon another, which distinguishes this family of strategies from those already discussed. Power is an ingredient of all human action. The differences lie rather in the ingredients of power on which the strategies of changing depend and the ways in which power is generated and applied in processes of effecting change. Thus what we have called rational-empirical approaches depend on knowledge as a major ingredient of power. In this view, men of knowledge are legitimate sources of power and the desirable flow of influence or power is from men who know to men who don't know through processes of education and of dissemination of valid information.

Normative-reeducative strategies of changing do not deny the importance of knowledge as a

---

[43] Chester I. Barnard, *The Functions of the Executive* (Cambridge, Mass.: Harvard University Press, 1938).

[44] Rensis Likert, *New Patterns of Management* (New York: McGraw-Hill, 1961).

[45] McGregor, "Human Side of Enterprise," pp. 422–31.

[46] W. G. Bennis, "Changing Organizations," in Bennis et al., *Planning of Change,* chap. 10, p. 568.

[47] H. A. Shephard, "Innovation-Resisting and Innovation-Producing Organizations," in Bennis et al., *Planning of Change,* chap. 9, p. 519.

source of power, especially in the form of knowledge-based technology. Exponents of this approach to changing are committed to redressing the imbalance between the limited use of behavioral knowledge and people technologies and the widespread use of physical-biological knowledge and related thing technologies in effecting changes in human affairs. In addition, exponents of normative-reeducative approaches recognize the importance of noncognitive determinants of behavior as resistances or supports to changing—values, attitudes, and feelings at the personal level and norms and relationships at the social level. Influence must extend to these noncognitive determinants of behavior if voluntary commitments and reliance on social intelligence are to be maintained and extended in our changing society. Influence of noncognitive determinants of behavior must be exercised in mutual processes of persuasion within collaborative relationships. These strategies are oriented against coercive and nonreciprocal influence, both on moral and on pragmatic grounds.

What ingredients of power do power-coercive strategies emphasize? In general, emphasis is upon political and economic sanctions in the exercise of power. But other coercive strategies emphasize the utilization of moral power, playing upon sentiments of guilt and shame. Political power carries with it legitimacy and the sanctions which accrue to those who break the law. Thus getting a law passed against racial imbalance in the schools brings legitimate coercive power behind efforts to desegregate the schools, threatening those who resist with sanctions under the law and reducing the resistance of others who are morally oriented against breaking the law. Economic power exerts coercive influence over the decisions of those to whom it is applied. Thus federal appropriations granting funds to local schools for increased emphasis upon science instruction tend to exercise coercive influence over the decisions of local school officials concerning the emphasis of the school curriculum. In general, power-coercive strategies

of changing seek to mass political and economic power behind the change goals which the strategists of change have decided are desirable. Those who oppose these goals, if they adopt the same strategy, seek to mass political and economic power in opposition. The strategy thus tends to divide the society when there is anything like a division of opinion and of power in that society.

When a person or group is entrenched in power in a social system, in command of political legitimacy and of political and economic sanctions, that person or group can use power-coercive strategies in effecting changes which they consider desirable, without much awareness on the part of those out of power in the system that such strategies are being employed. A power-coercive way of making decisions is accepted as in the nature of things. The use of such strategies by those in legitimate control of various social systems in our society is much more widespread than most of us might at first be willing or able to admit. This is true in educational systems as well as in other social systems.

When any part of a social system becomes aware that its interests are not being served by those in control of the system, the coercive power of those in control can be challenged. If the minority is committed to power-coercive strategies, or is aware of no alternatives to such strategies, how can they make headway against existing power relations within the system? They may organize discontent against the present controls of the system and achieve power outside the legitimate channels of authority in the system. Thus teachers' unions may develop power against coercive controls by the central administrative group and the school board in a school system. They may threaten concerted resistance to or disregard of administrative rulings and board policies or they may threaten work stoppage or a strike. Those in control may get legislation against teachers' strikes. If the political power of organized teachers grows, they may get legislation requiring collective bargaining between organized teachers and the school board on some range of educational issues. The power struggle then shifts to the negotiation table, and compromise between competing interests may become the expected goal of the intergroup exchange. Whether the augmented power of new, relevant knowledge or the generation of common power through joint collaboration and deliberation are lost in the process will depend on the degree of commitment by all parties to the conflict and to a continuation and maintenance of power-coercive strategies for effecting change.

What general varieties of power-coercive strategies, to be exercised either by those in control as they seek to maintain their power or to be used by those now outside a position of control and seeking to enlarge their power, can be identified?

Strategies of Nonviolence.   Mahatma Gandhi may be seen as the most prominent recent theorist and practitioner of nonviolent strategies for effecting change, although the strategies did not originate with him in the history of mankind, either in idea or in practice. Gandhi spoke of Thoreau's *Essay on Civil Disobedience* as one important influence in his own approach to nonviolent coercive action. Martin Luther King was perhaps America's most distinguished exponent of nonviolent coercion in effecting social change. A minority (or majority) confronted with what they see as an unfair, unjust, or cruel system of coercive social control may dramatize their rejection of the system by publicly and nonviolently witnessing and demonstrating against it. Part of the ingredients of the power of the civilly disobedient is in the guilt which their demonstration of injustice, unfairness, or cruelty of the existing system of control arouses in those exercising control or in others previously committed to the present system of control. The opposition to the disobedient group may be demoralized and may waver in their exercise of control, if they profess the moral values to which the dissidents are appealing.

Weakening or dividing the opposition through moral coercion may be combined with economic sanctions—like Gandhi's refusal to buy salt and other British manufactured commodities in India or like the desegregationists' economic boycott of the products of racially discriminating factories and businesses.

The use of nonviolent strategies for opening up conflicts in values and demonstrating against injustices or inequities in existing patterns of social control has become familiar to educational leaders in the demonstrations and sit-ins of college students in various universities and in the demonstrations of desegregationists against de facto segregation of schools. And the widened use of such strategies may be confidently predicted. Whether such strategies will be used to extend collaborative ways of developing policies and normative-reeducative strategies of changing, or whether they will be used to augment power struggles as the only practical way of settling conflicts, will depend in some large part upon the strategy commitments of those now in positions of power in education systems.

Use of Political Institutions to Achieve Change. Political power has traditionally played an important part in achieving changes in our institutional life. And political power will continue to play an important part in shaping and reshaping our institutions of education as well as other institutions. Changes enforced by political coercion need not be oppressive if the quality of our democratic processes can be maintained and improved.

Changes in policies with respect to education have come from various departments of government. By far the most of these have come through legislation on the state level. Under legislation, school administrators have various degrees of discretionary powers, and policy and program changes are frequently put into effect by administrative rulings. Judicial decisions have played an important part in shaping educational policies, none more dramatically than the Supreme Court decision declaring laws and policies supporting school segregation illegal. And the federal courts have played a central part in seeking to implement and enforce this decision.

Some of the difficulty with the use of political institutions to effect changes arises from an overestimation by change agents of the capability of political action to effect changes in practice. When the law is passed, the administrative ruling announced, or the judicial decision handed down legitimizing some new policy or program or illegitimizing some traditional practice, change agents who have worked hard for the law, ruling, or decision frequently assume that the desired change has been made.

Actually, all that has been done is to bring the force of legitimacy behind some envisioned change. The processes of reeducation of persons who are to conduct themselves in new ways still have to be carried out. And the new conduct often requires new knowledge, new skills, new attitudes, and new value orientations. And, on the social level, new conduct may require changes in the norms, the roles, and the relationship structures of the institutions involved. This is not to discount the importance of political actions in legitimizing changed policies and practices in educational institutions and in other institutions as well. It is rather to emphasize that normative-reeducative strategies must be combined with political coercion, both before and after the political action, if the public is to be adequately informed and desirable and commonly acceptable changes in practice are to be achieved.

Changing through the Recomposition and Manipulation of Power Elites.   The idea or practice of a ruling class or of a power elite in social control was by no means original with Karl Marx. What was original with him was his way of relating these concepts to a process and strategy of fundamental social change. The composition of the ruling class was, of course, for Marx those who owned and controlled the means and processes of production of goods and services in a society.

Since, for Marx, the ideology of the ruling class set limits to the thinking of most intellectuals and of those in charge of educational processes and of communicating, rationales for the existing state of affairs, including its concentration of political and economic power, is provided and disseminated by intellectuals and educators and communicators within the system.

Since Marx was morally committed to a classless society in which political coercion would disappear because there would be no vested primate interests to rationalize and defend, he looked for a counterforce in society to challenge and eventually to overcome the power of the ruling class. And this he found in the economically dispossessed and aliented workers of hand and brain. As this new class gained consciousness of its historic mission and its power increased, the class struggle could be effectively joined. The outcome of this struggle was victory for those best able to organize and maximize the productive power of the instruments of production—for Marx this victory belonged to the now dispossessed workers.

Many of Marx's values would have put him behind what we have called normative-reeducative strategies of changing. And he recognized that such strategies would have to be used after the accession of the workers to state power in order to usher in the classless society. He doubted if the ruling class could be reeducated, since reeducation would mean loss of their privileges and coercive power in society. He recognized that the power elite could, within limits, accommodate new interests as these gained articulation and power. But these accommodations must fall short of a radical transfer of power to a class more capable of wielding it. Meanwhile, he remained committed to a power-coercive strategy of changing until the revolutionary transfer of power had been effected.

Marxian concepts have affected the thinking of contemporary men about social change both inside and outside nations in which Marxism has become the official orientation. His concepts

FIGURE 1

Strategies of deliberate changing

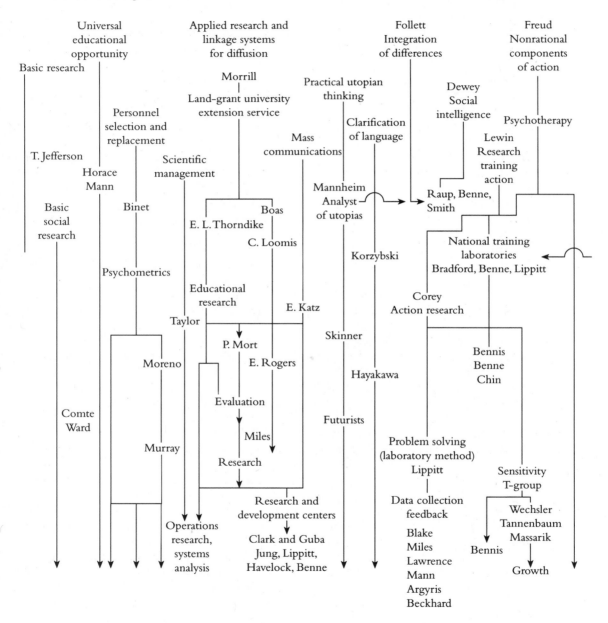

A. Rational-Empirical
Views of the enlightenment and classical liberalism

B. Normative
Views of therapists

FIGURE 1
(concluded)

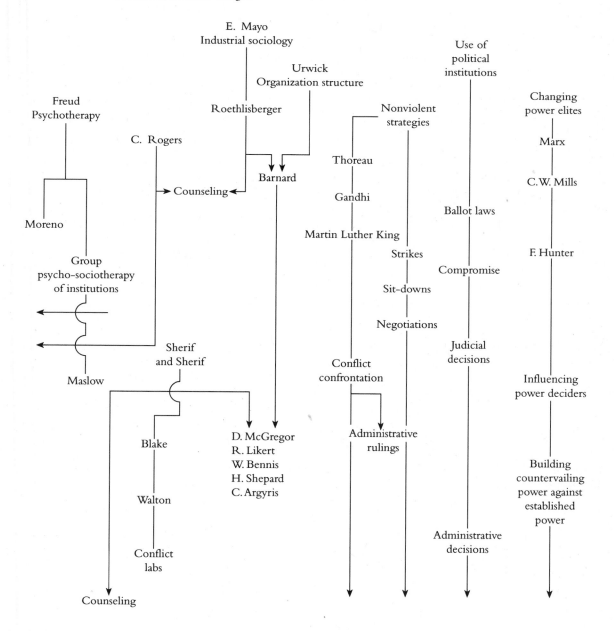

have tended to bolster assumptions of the necessity of power-coercive strategies in achieving fundamental redistributions of socio-economic power or in recomposing or manipulating power elites in a society. Democratic, reeducative methods of changing have a place only after such changes in power allocation have been achieved by power-coercive methods. Non-Marxians as well as Marxians are often committed to this Marxian dictum.

In contemporary America, C. Wright Mills has identified a power elite, essentially composed of industrial, military, and governmental leaders, who direct and limit processes of social change and accommodation in our society. And President Eisenhower warned of the dangerous concentration of power in substantially the same groups in his farewell message to the American people. Educators committed to democratic values should not be blinded to the limitations to advancement of those values, which are set by the less than democratic ideology of our power elites. And normative-reeducative strategists of changing must include power elites among their targets of changing as they seek to diffuse their ways of progress within contemporary society. And they must take seriously Marx's questions about the reeducability of members of the power elites, as they deal with problems and projects of social change.

The operation of a power elite in social units smaller than a nation was revealed in Floyd Hunter's study of decision making in an American city. Hunter's small group of deciders, with their satellite groups of intellectuals, front men,

and implementers, is in a real sense a power elite. The most common reaction of educational leaders to Hunter's "discovery" has been to seek ways in which to persuade and manipulate the deciders toward support of educational ends which educational leaders consider desirable— whether bond issues, building programs, or anything else. This is non-Marxian in its acceptance of power relations in a city or community as fixed. It would be Marxian if it sought to build counter power to offset and reduce the power of the presently deciding group where this power interfered with the achievement of desirable educational goals. This latter strategy, though not usually Marxian inspired in the propaganda sense of that term, has been more characteristic of organized teacher effort in pressing for collective bargaining or of some student demonstrations and sit-ins. In the poverty program, the federal government in its insistence on participation of the poor in making policies for the program has at least played with a strategy of building countervailing power to offset the existing concentration of power in people not identified with the interests of the poor in reducing their poverty.

Those committed to the advancement of normative-reeducative strategies of changing must take account of present actual concentrations of power wherever they work. This does *not* mean that they must develop a commitment to power-coercive strategies to change the distribution of power except when these may be necessary to effect the spread of their own democratically and scientifically oriented methods of changing within society.

Reading 8
The Field Approach: Culture and Group Life as Quasi-Stationary Processes

Kurt Lewin

This question of planned change or of any "social engineering" is identical with the question: What "conditions" have to be changed to bring about a given result and how can one change these conditions with the means at hand?

One should view the present situation—the status quo—as being maintained by certain conditions or forces. A culture—for instance, the food habits of a certain group at a given time—is not a static affair but a live process like a river which moves but still keeps a recognizable form. In other words, we have to deal, in group life as in individual life, with what is known in physics as "quasi-stationary" processes.[1]

Food habits do not occur in empty space. They are part and parcel of the daily rhythm of being awake and asleep; of being alone and in a group; of earning a living and playing; of being a member of a town, a family, a social class, a religious group, a nation; of living in a hot or a cool climate, in a rural area or a city, in a district with good groceries and restaurants, or in an area of poor and irregular food supply. Somehow all of these factors affect food habits at any given time. They determine the food habits of a group every day anew just as the amount of water supply and the nature of the river bed determine from day to day the flow of the river, its constancy, or its change.[2]

Food habits of a group, as well as such phenomena as the speed of production in a factory, are the result of a multitude of forces. Some forces support each other, some oppose each other. Some are driving forces, others restraining forces. Like the velocity of a river, the actual conduct of a group depends upon the level (for instance, the speed of production) at which these conflicting forces reach a state of equilibrium. To speak of a certain culture pattern—for instance, the food habits of a group—implies that the constellation of these forces remains the same for a period or at least that they find their state of equilibrium at a constant level during that period.

Neither group "habits" nor individual "habits" can be understood sufficiently by a theory which limits its consideration to the processes themselves and conceives of the "habit" as a kind of frozen linkage, an "association' between these processes. Instead, habits will have to be conceived of as a result of forces in the organism *and* its life space, in the group *and* its setting. The structure of the organism, of the group, of the setting, or whatever name the field might have in the given case, has to be represented and the forces in the various parts of the field have to be analyzed if the processes (which might be either

---

[1] For the general characteristics of quasi-stationary processes see Wolfgang Koehler, *Dynamics in Psychology* (New York: Liveright Publishing, 1940).

Source: Kurt Lewin, *Field Theory in Social Science* (New York: Harper & Row, 1951), pp. 172–74.

---

[2] The type of forces, of course, is different; there is nothing equivalent to "cognitive structure" or "psychological past" or "psychological future" in the field determining the river.

constant "habits" or changes) are to be understood scientifically. The process is but the epiphenomenon, the real object of study is the constellation of forces.

Therefore, to predict which changes in conditions will have what result we have to conceive of the life of the group as the result of specific constellations of forces within a larger setting. In other words, scientific predictions or advice for methods of change should be based on an analysis of the "field as a whole," including both its psychological and nonpsychological aspects.

Chris Argyris

A Definition of Intervention

To intervene is to enter into an ongoing system of relationship, to come between or among persons, groups, or objects for the purpose of helping them. There is an important implicit assumption in the definition that should be made explicit: the system exists independently of the intervenor. There are many reasons one might wish to intervene. These reasons may range from helping the clients make their own decisions about the kind of help they need to coercing the clients to do what the intervenor wishes them to do.

Our view acknowledges interdependencies between the intervenor and the client system but focuses on how to maintain, or increase, the client system's autonomy; how to differentiate even more clearly the boundaries between the client system and the intervenor; and how to conceptualize and define the client system's health independently of the intervenor's. This view values the client system as an ongoing, self-responsible unity that has the obligation to be in control over its own destiny. An intervenor, in this view, assists a system to become more effective in problem solving, decision making, and decision implementation in such a way that the system can continue to be increasingly effective in these activities and have a decreasing need for the intervenor.

Basic Requirements for Intervention Activity

Are there any basic or necessary processes that must be fulfilled regardless of the substantive is-

Source: Chris Argyris, *Intervention Theory and Methods: A Behavioral Science View* (Reading, Mass.: Addison-Wesley Publishing, 1970), pp. 15–20. © 1970, Addison-Wesley. Reprinted with permission.

sues involved, if intervention activity is to be helpful with any level of client (individual, group, or organizational)? One condition that seems so basic as to be defined axiomatic is the generation of *valid information*. Without valid information, it would be difficult for the client to learn and for the interventionist to help.

A second condition almost as basic flows from our assumption that intervention activity, no matter what its substantive interests and objectives, should be so designed and executed that the client system maintains its discreteness and autonomy. Thus *free, informed choice* is also a necessary process in effective intervention activity.

Finally, if the client system is assumed to be ongoing (that is, existing over time), the clients require strengthening to maintain their autonomy not only vis-à-vis the interventionist but also vis-à-vis other systems. This means that their commitment to learning and change has to be more than temporary. It has to be so strong that it can be transferred to relationships other than those with the interventionist and can do so (eventually) without the help of the interventionist. The third basic process for any intervention activity is therefore the client's *internal commitment* to the choices made.

In summary, valid information, free choice, and internal commitment are considered integral parts of any intervention activity, no matter what the substantive objectives are (for example, developing a management performance evaluation scheme, reducing intergroup rivalries, increasing the degree of trust among individuals, redesigning budgetary systems, or redesigning work). These three processes are called the primary intervention tasks.

135

Primary Tasks of an Interventionist

Why is it necessary to hypothesize that, in order for an interventionist to behave effectively and in order that the integrity of the client system be maintained, the interventionist has to focus on three primary tasks, regardless of the substantive problems that the client system may be experiencing?

Valid and Useful Information.   First, it has been accepted as axiomatic that valid and useful information is the foundation for effective intervention. Valid information is that which describes the factors, plus their interrelationships, that create the problem for the client system. There are several tests for checking the validity of the information. In increasing degrees of power they are public verifiability, valid prediction, and control over the phenomena. The first is having several independent diagnoses suggest the same picture. Second is generating predictions from the diagnosis that are subsequently confirmed (they occurred under the conditions that were specified). Third is altering the factors systematically and predicting the effects upon the system as a whole. All these tests, if they are to be valid, must be carried out in such a way that the participants cannot, at will, make them come true. This would be a self-fulfilling prophecy and not a confirmation of a prediction. The difficulty with a self-fulfilling prophecy is its indication of more about the degree of power an individual (or subset of individuals) can muster to alter the system than about the nature of the system when the participants are behaving without knowledge of the diagnosis. For example, if an executive learns that the interventionist predicts his subordinates will behave (*a*) if he behaves (*b*), he might alter (*b*) in order not lead to (*a*). Such an alteration indicates the executive's power but does not test the validity of the diagnosis that if (*a*), then (*b*).

The tests for valid information have important implications for effective intervention activity. First, the interventionist's diagnoses must strive to represent the total client system and not the point of view of any subgroup or individual. Otherwise, the interventionist could not be seen only as being under the control of a particular individual or subgroup, but also his predictions would be based upon inaccurate information and thus might not be confirmed.

This does not mean that an interventionist may not begin with, or may not limit his relationship to, a subpart of the total system. It is totally possible, for example, for the interventionist to help management, blacks, trade union leaders, etc. With whatever subgroup he works he simply should not agree to limit his diagnosis to its wishes.

It is conceivable that a client system may be helped even though valid information is not generated. Sometimes changes occur in a positive direction without the interventionist having played any important role. These changes, although helpful in that specific instance, lack the attribute of helping the organization to learn to gain control over its problem-solving capability.

The importance of information that the clients can use to control their destiny points up the requirement that the information must not only be valid, it must be useful. Valid information that cannot be used by the clients to alter their system is equivalent to valid information about cancer that cannot be used to cure cancer eventually. An interventionist's diagnosis should include variables that are manipulable by the clients and are complete enough so that if they are manipulated effective change will follow.

Free Choice.   In order to have free choice, the client has to have a cognitive map of what he wishes to do. The objectives of his action are known at the moment of decision. Free choice implies voluntary as opposed to automatic; proactive rather than reactive. The act of selection is rarely accomplished by maximizing or optimizing. Free and informed choice entails what Simon has called "satisficing"; that is, selecting the alternative with the highest probability of succeeding, given some specified cost constraints. Free choice places the locus of decision making in the client system. Free choice makes it possible for the clients to remain responsible for their destiny. Through free choice the clients can maintain the autonomy of their system.

It may be possible that clients prefer to give up their responsibility and their autonomy, especially if they are feeling a sense of failure. They may prefer, as we shall see in several examples, to turn over their free choice to the interventionist. They may insist that he make recommendations and tell them what to do. The interventionist resists these pressures because, if he does not, the clients will lose their free choice and he will lose his own free choice, also. He will be controlled by the anxieties of the clients.

The requirement of free choice is especially important for those helping activities where the processes of help are as important as the actual help. For example, a medical doctor does not require that a patient with a bullet wound participate in the process by defining the kind of help he needs. However, the same doctor may have to pay much more attention to the processes he uses to help patients when he is attempting to diagnose blood pressure or cure a high cholesterol. If the doctor behaves in ways that upset the patient, the latter's blood pressure may well be distorted. Or, the patient can develop a dependent relationship if the doctor cuts down his cholesterol—increasing habits only under constant pressure from the doctor—and the moment the relationship is broken off, the count goes up.

Effective intervention in the human and social sphere requires that the processes of help be congruent with the outcome desired. Free choice is important because there are so many unknowns, and the interventionist wants the client to have as much willingness and motivation as possible to work on the problem. With high client motivation and commitment, several different methods for change can succeed.

A choice is free to the extent the members can make their selection for a course of action with minimal internal defensiveness; can define the path (or paths) by which the intended consequence is to be achieved; can relate the choice to their central needs; and can build into their choices a realistic and challenging level of aspiration. Free choice therefore implies that the members are able to explore as many alternatives as they consider significant and select those that are central to their needs.

Why must the choice be related to the central needs and why must the level of aspiration be realistic and challenging? May people not choose freely unrealistic or unchallenging objectives? Yes, they may do so in the short run, but not for long if they still want to have free and informed choice. A freely chosen course of action means that the action must be based on an accurate analysis of the situation and not on the biases or defenses of the decision makers. We know, from the level of aspiration studies, that choices which are too high or too low, which are too difficult or not difficult enough will tend to lead to psychological failure. Psychological failure will lead to increased defensiveness, increased failure, and decreased self-acceptance on the part of the members experiencing the failure. These conditions, in turn, will tend to lead to distorted perceptions by the members making the choices. Moreover, the defensive members may unintentionally create a climate where the members of surrounding and interrelated systems will tend to provide carefully censored information. Choices made under these conditions are neither informed nor free.

Turning to the question of centrality of needs, a similar logic applies. The degree of commitment to the processes of generating valid information, scanning, and choosing may significantly vary according to the centrality of the choice to the needs of the clients. The more central the choice, the more the system will strive to do its best in developing valid information and making free and informed choices. If the research from perceptual psychology is valid, the very perception of the clients is altered by the needs involved. Individuals tend to scan more, ask for more information, and be more careful in their choices when they are making decisions that are central to them. High involvement may produce perceptual distortions, as does low involvement. The interventionist, however, may have a greater probability of helping the clients explore possible distortion when the choice they are making is a critical one.

Internal Commitment. Internal commitment means that course of action or choice that has been internalized by each member so that he experiences a high degree of ownership and has a feeling of responsibility about the choice and its implications. Internal commitment means that the individual has reached the point where

he is acting on the choice because it fulfills his own needs and sense of responsibility, as well as those of the system.

The individual who is internally committed is acting primarily under the influence of his own forces and not induced forces. The individual (or any unity) feels a minimal degree of dependence upon others for the action. It implies that he has obtained and processed valid information and that he has made an informed and free choice. Under these conditions, there is a high probability that the individual's commitment will remain strong over time (even with reduction of external rewards) or under stress, or when the course of action is challenged by others. It also implies that the individual is continually open to reexamination of his position because he believes in taking action based upon valid information.

READING 10
TWO-PERSON DISPUTES

Carl Rogers

When persons are in serious discord, whether we are speaking of a discordant marital relationship, friction between an employer and an employee, a formal and icy dispute between two diplomats, or tension growing out of some other base, we tend to find certain very common elements:

1. In such a dispute there is no doubt at all but that I am right and you are wrong. I am on the side of the angels, and you belong with the forces of darkness.

2. There is a breakdown of communication. You do not hear what I say, in any understanding way; and I am unwilling and unable to hear what you are really saying.

3. There are distortions in perception. The evidence which is taken in by my senses—your words, your actions, your responses to my words and actions—is trimmed and shaped by my needs to fit the views of you which I already hold. Evidence which is clearly and openly contradictory to my rigidly held views is conveniently ignored or made acceptable by being grossly distorted. Thus, a real gesture toward reconciliation on your part can be perceived by me as only another deceitful trick.

4. Implicit in all this is the element of distrust. While whatever *I* do is obviously done with honorable intent, whatever *you* do is equally obviously done with an underlying evil intent, no matter how sweetly reasonable it may appear on the surface. Hence, from the perspective of each opponent, the whole relationship is shot through with suspicion and mistrust.

I believe I am correct in saying that in any serious two-person dispute, these four elements are invariably present and often make the situation appear hopeless. Yet there are knowledge and skill available which can be applied to such a situation. If there is to be progress in reducing this kind of tension, we have learned that the first necessity is a facilitative listener—a person who will listen empathically and will understand the attitudes of each disputant.

Source: Reprinted with permission from NTL Institute, "Dealing with Psychological Tensions," by Carl Rogers, pp. 12–13, *Journal of Applied Behavioral Science* 1, no. 1, copyright 1965.

INTERGROUP PROBLEMS IN ORGANIZATIONS

Edgar H. Schein

The first major problem of groups in organizations is how to make them effective in fulfilling both organizational goals and the needs of their members. The second major problem is how to establish conditions between groups which will enhance the productivity of each without destroying intergroup relations and coordination. This problem exists because as groups become more committed to their own goals and norms, they are likely to become competitive with one another and seek to undermine their rivals' activities, thereby becoming a liability to the organization as a whole. The overall problem, then, is how to establish collaborative intergroup relations *in those situations where task interdependence or the need for unity makes collaboration a necessary prerequisite for organizational effectiveness.*

Some Consequences of Intergroup Competition

The consequences of intergroup competition were first studied systematically by Sherif in an ingeniously designed setting (Sherif, Harvey, White, Hood, & Sherif, 1961). He organized a boys' camp in such a way that two groups would form and would gradually become competitive. Sherif then studied the effects of the competition and tried various devices for reestablishing collaborative relationships between the groups. Since his original experiments, there have been many replications with adult groups; the phenomena are so constant that it has been possible to make a demonstration exercise out of the experiment (Blake & Mouton, 1961). The effects can be described in terms of the following categories:

Source: Edgar H. Schein, *Organizational Psychology,* 3rd ed., 1980, pp. 172–80. Reprinted by permission of Prentice Hall, Inc., Englewood Cliffs, NJ.

A. What happens *within* each competing group?

1. Each group becomes more closely knit and elicits greater loyalty from its members; members close ranks and bury some of their internal differences.

2. The group climate changes from informal, casual, playful to work and task oriented; concern for members' psychological needs declines while concern for task accomplishment increases.

3. Leadership patterns tend to change from more democratic toward more autocratic; the group becomes more willing to tolerate autocratic leadership.

4. Each group becomes more highly structured and organized.

5. Each group demands more loyalty and conformity from its members in order to be able to present a "solid front."

B. What happens *between* competing groups?

1. Each group begins to see the other group as the enemy, rather than merely a neutral object.

2. Each group begins to experience distortions of perception—it tends to perceive only the best parts of itself, denying its weaknesses, and tends to perceive only the worst parts of the other group, denying its strengths; each group is likely to develop a negative stereotype of the other ("they don't play fair like we do").

3. Hostility toward the other group increases while interaction and communication with the other group

decreases; thus it becomes easier to maintain the negative stereotype and more difficult to correct perceptual distortions.

4. If the groups are forced into interaction—for example, if they are forced to listen to representatives plead their own and the others' cause in reference to some task—each group is likely to listen more closely to their own representative and not to listen to the representative of the other group, except to find fault with his or her presentation; in other words, group members tend to listen only for that which supports their own position and stereotype.

Thus far, we have listed some consequences of the competition itself, without reference to the consequences if one group actually wins out over the other. Before listing those effects, I would like to draw attention to the generality of the above reactions. Whether one is talking about sports teams, interfraternity competition, labor-management disputes, or interdepartmental competition as between sales and production in an industrial organization—or about international relations and the competition between the Soviet Union and the United States—the same phenomena tend to occur. These responses can be very useful to the group, by making it more highly motivated in task accomplishment, but they also open the door to group think. Furthermore, the same factors which improve intragroup effectiveness may have negative consequences for intergroup effectiveness. For example, as we have often seen in labor-management disputes or international conflicts, if the groups perceive themselves as competitors, they find it more difficult to resolve their differences, and eventually both become losers in a long-term strike or even a war.

Let us next look at the consequences of winning and losing, as in a situation where several groups are bidding to have their proposal ac-

cepted for a contract or as a solution to some problem. Many intraorganizational situations become win-or-lose affairs, hence it is of particular importance to examine their consequences.

C. What happens to the *winner*?

1. Winner retains its cohesion and may become even more cohesive.
2. Winner tends to release tension, lose its fighting spirit, become complacent, casual, and playful (the condition of being "fat and happy").
3. Winner tends toward high intragroup cooperation and concern for members' needs, and low concern for work and task accomplishment.
4. Winner tends to be complacent and to feel that the positive outcome has confirmed its favorable stereotype of itself and the negative stereotype of the "enemy" group; there is little motivation for reevaluating perceptions or reexamining group operations in order to learn how to improve them, hence the winner does not learn much about itself.

D. What happens to the *loser*?

1. If the outcome is not entirely clear-cut and permits a degree of interpretation (say, if judges have rendered it or if the game was close), there is a strong tendency for the loser to *deny or distort the reality of losing*; instead, the loser will find psychological escapes like "the judges were biased," "the judges didn't really understand our solution," "the rules of the game were not clearly explained to us," "if luck had not been against us at the one key point, we would have won," and so on. In effect, the loser's first response is to say "we didn't really lose!"
2. If the loss is psychologically accepted, the losing group tends to seek someone or something to blame; strong forces

toward scape-goating are set up; if no outsider can be blamed, the group turns on itself, splinters, surfaces previously unresolved conflicts, fights within itself, all in the effort to find a cause for the loss.

3. Loser is more tense, ready to work harder, and desperate (the condition of being "lean and hungry").

4. Loser tends toward low intragroup cooperation, low concern for members' needs, and high concern for recouping by working harder in order to win the next round of the competition.

5. Loser tends to learn a lot about itself as a group because its positive stereotype of itself and its negative stereotype of the other group are disconfirmed by the loss, forcing a reevaluation of perceptions; as a consequence, the loser is likely to reorganize and become more cohesive and effective once the loss has been accepted realistically.

The net effect of the win-lose situation is often that the losers refuse psychologically to accept their loss, and that intergroup tension is higher than before the competition began.

Intergroup problems of the sort we have just described arise not only out of direct competition between clearly defined groups but are, to a degree, intrinsic in any complex society because of the many bases on which a society is stratified. Thus we can have potential intergroup problems between men and women, between older and younger generations, between higher and lower ranking people, between blacks and whites, between people in power and people not in power, and so on (Alderfer, 1977). Any occupational or social group will develop "ingroup" feelings and define itself in terms of members of an "outgroup," toward whom intergroup feelings are likely to arise. Differences between nationalities or ethnic groups are especially strong, particularly if there has been any conflict between the groups in the past.

For intergroup feelings to arise we need not belong to a psychological group. It is enough to feel oneself a member of what has been called a "reference group"; that is, a group with which one identifies and compares oneself or to which one aspires. Thus, aspirants to a higher socioeconomic level take that level as their reference group and attempt to behave according to the values they perceive in that group. Similarly, members of an occupational group uphold the values and standards they perceive that occupation to embody. It is only by positing the existence of reference groups that one can explain how some individuals can continue to behave in a deviant fashion in a group situation. If such individuals strongly identify with a group that has different norms they will behave in a way that attempts to uphold those norms. For example, in Communist prison camps some soldiers from elite military units resisted their captors much longer than draftees who had weak identification with their military units. In order for the Communists to elicit compliant behavior from these strongly identified prisoners, they had to first weaken the attachment to the elite unit— that is, destroy the reference group—by attacking the group's image or convincing the prisoner that it was not a group worth belonging to (Schein, 1961). Intergroup problems arise wherever there are any status differences and are, therefore, intrinsic to all organizations and to society itself.

Reducing the Negative Consequences of Intergroup Competition

The gains of intergroup competition may, under some conditions, outweigh the negative consequences. It may be desirable to have work groups pitted against one another or to have departments become cohesive loyal units, even if interdepartmental coordination suffers. Often, however, the negative consequences outweigh the gains, and management seeks ways of reducing intergroup tension. Many of the techniques proposed to accomplish this come from the basic researches of Sherif, Blake, Alderfer, and others; they have been tested and found to be successful.

The chief stumbling block remains not so much being unable to think of ways for reducing intergroup conflict as being *unable to implement some of the most effective ways.*

Destructive intergroup competition results basically from a conflict of goals and the breakdown of interaction and communication between the groups. This breakdown in turn permits and stimulates perceptual distortion and mutual negative stereotyping. The basic strategy of reducing conflict, therefore, is to locate goals which the competing groups can agree on and to reestablish valid communication between the groups. Each of the tactical devices that follows can be used singly or in combination.

Locating a Common Enemy. For example, the competing teams in a league can compose an all-star team to play another league, or conflicts between sales and production can be reduced if both can harness their efforts to helping their company successfully compete against another company. The conflict here is merely shifted to a higher level.

Bringing Leaders or Subgroups of the Competing Groups into Interaction. An isolated group representative cannot abandon his or her group position, but a powerful leader or a subgroup that has been delegated power not only can permit itself to be influenced by its counterpart negotiation team, but also will have the strength to influence the remainder of its home group if negotiation produces common agreements. This is the basis for "summit meetings" in international relations.

Locating a Superordinate Goal. Such a goal can be a brand-new task which requires the cooperative effort of the previously competing groups, or it can be a task like analyzing and reducing the intergroup conflict itself. For example, the previously competing sales and production departments can be given the task of developing a new product line that will be both cheap to produce and in great customer demand; or, with the help of an outside consultant, the

competing groups can be invited to examine their own behavior and reevaluate the gains and losses from competition (Walton, 1969).

Experiential Intergroup Training. The procedure of having the conflicting parties examine their own behavior has been tried by a number of psychologists, notably Blake and Mouton (1962), with considerable success. Assuming the organization recognizes that it has a problem, and assuming it is ready to expose this problem to an outside consultant, the experiential workshop approach to reducing conflict might proceed with the following steps:

1. The competing groups are both brought into a training setting and the common goals are stated to be an exploration of mutual perceptions and mutual relations.

2. The two groups are then separated and each group is invited to discuss and make a list of its perceptions of itself and the other group.

3. In the presence of both groups, representatives publicly share the perceptions of self and other which the groups have generated, while the groups are obligated to remain silent (the objective is simply to report to the other group as accurately as possible the images that each group has developed in private).

4. Before any exchange has taken place, the groups return to private sessions to digest and analyze what they have heard; there is a great likelihood that the representatives' reports have revealed discrepancies to each group between its self-image and the image that the other group holds of it; the private session is partly devoted to an analysis of the reasons for these discrepancies, which forces each group to review its actual behavior toward the other group and the possible consequences of that behavior, regardless of its intentions.

5. In public session, again working through

representatives, each group shares with the other what discrepancies it has uncovered and the possible reasons for them, focusing on actual, observable behavior.

6. Following this mutual exposure, a more open exploration is then permitted between the two groups on the *now-shared goal* of identifying further reasons for perceptual distortions.

7. A joint exploration is then conducted of how to manage future relations in such a way as to minimize a recurrence of the conflict.

Interspersed with these steps are short lectures and reading assignments on the psychology of intergroup conflict, the bases for perceptual distortion, psychological defense mechanisms, and so on. The goal is to bring the psychological dynamics of the solution into conscious awareness and to refocus the groups on the common goal of exploring jointly the problem they share. In order to do this, they must have valid data about each other, which is provided through the artifice of the representative reports.

Blake's model deals with the entire group. Various other approaches begin by breaking down group prejudices on an individual basis. For example, groups A and B, each proposing an alternative product (idea), can be divided into pairs composed of an A and a B member. Each pair can be given the assignment of developing a joint product that combines the best ideas from the A product and the B product. Or, in each pair, members may be asked to argue for the product of the opposing group. It has been shown in a number of experiments that one way of changing attitudes is to ask a person to play the role of an advocate of the new attitude to be learned (Janis & King, 1954). The very act of arguing for another product, even if it is purely an exercise, makes the person aware of some of its virtues which he or she can now no longer deny. A practical application of these points might be to have some members of the sales department spend time in the production department and be asked to represent the production point of view to some third party, or to have some production people join sales teams to learn the sales point of view.

Most of the approaches cited depend on a *recognition* of some problem by the organization and a *willingness* on the part of the competing groups to participate in some program to reduce negative consequences. The reality, however, is that most organizations neither recognize the problem nor are willing to invest time and energy in resolving it. Some of the unwillingness also arises from each competing group's recognition that in becoming more cooperative it may lose some of its own identity and integrity as a group. Rather than risk this loss, the group may prefer to continue the competition. This may well be the reason why, in international relations, nations refuse to engage in what may seem like perfectly simple ways of resolving their differences. They resist partly in order to protect their integrity—that is, save face. For all these reasons, the *implementation* of strategies and tactics for reducing the negative consequences of intergroup competition is often a greater problem than the initial development of such strategies and tactics.

Preventing Intergroup Conflict

Because of the great difficulties of reducing intergroup conflict once it has developed, it may be desirable to prevent its occurrence in the first place. How can this be done? Paradoxically, a strategy of prevention challenges the fundamental premise upon which organization through division of labor rests. Once it has been decided by a superordinate authority to divide up functions among different departments or groups, a bias has already been introduced toward intergroup competition; for in doing its own job well, each group must, to some degree, compete for scarce resources and rewards from the superordinate authority. The very concept of division of labor implies a reduction of communication and interaction between groups, thus making it possible for perceptual distortions to occur.

The organization planner who wishes to avoid intergroup competition need not abandon the concept of division of labor, but should follow some of the steps listed below in creating and handling the different functional groups.

1. Relatively greater *emphasis should be given to total organizational effectiveness* and the role of departments in contributing to it; departments should be measured and rewarded on the basis of their contribution to the total effort, rather than their individual effectiveness.

2. *High interaction and frequent communication* should be stimulated between groups to work on problems of intergroup coordination and help; organization rewards should be given partly on the basis of help rendered to other groups.

3. *Frequent rotation of members* among groups or departments should be encouraged to stimulate a high degree of mutual understanding and empathy for one another's problems.

4. *Win-lose situations should be avoided* and groups should never be put into the position of competing for some scarce organizational reward; emphasis should always be placed on pooling resources to maximize organizational effectiveness; rewards should be shared equally with all the groups or departments.

Most managers find the fourth point particularly difficult to accept because of the strong belief that performance can be improved by pitting people or groups against one another in a competitive situation. This may indeed be true in the short run, and may even on occasion work in the long run, but the negative consequences described above are undeniably the product of the win-lose situation. Thus, if managers wish to prevent such consequences, they must face the possibility that they may have to abandon com-

petitive relationships altogether and seek to substitute intergroup collaboration toward organizational goals. The more *interdependent* the various units are, the more important it is to stimulate collaborative problem solving.

Implementing a preventing strategy is often more difficult, partly because most people are inexperienced in stimulating and managing collaborative relationships. Yet observations of organizations using the Scanlon Plan not only reveal that it is possible to establish collaborative relationships, even between labor and management, but also that when this has been done, organizational and group effectiveness have been as high as or higher than under competitive conditions. Training in how to set up collaborative relations may be a prerequisite for any such program to succeed, especially for those managers who have themselves grown up in a highly competitive environment.

References

Alderfer, C. P. (1977). Group and Intergroup Relations. In J. R. Hackman, & J. L. Suttle (eds.). *Improving Life at Work.* Santa Monica, CA: Goodyear.

Blake, R. R., & Mouton, J. S. (1961). "Reactions to Intergroup Competition under Win-Lose Conditions." *Management Science* 7, 420–35.

Blake, R. R., & Mouton, J. S. (1962). "Headquarters-Field Team Training for Organizational Improvements. *Journal of the American Society of Training Directors* 16.

Janis, I. L., & King, B. T. (1954). The Influence of Role Playing on Opinion Change. *Journal of Abnormal and Social Psychology* 69, 211–18.

Schein, E. H. (1961). Management Development as a Process of Influence. *Industrial Management Review* 2, 59–77.

Sherif, M., Harvey, O. J., White, B. J., Hood, W. R., and Sherif, C. (1961). *Intergroup Conflict and Cooperation: The Robbers' Cave Experiment.* Norman, OK: University Book Exchange.

Walton, R. E. (1969). *Interpersonal Peacemaking: Confrontations and Third Party Consultation.* Reading, MA: Addison-Wesley.

READING 12
ORGANIZATIONAL CULTURE

Edgar H. Schein

To write a review article about the concept of organizational culture poses a dilemma because there is presently little agreement on what the concept does and should mean, how it should be observed and measured, how it relates to more traditional industrial and organizational psychology theories, and how it should be used in our efforts to help organizations. The popular use of the concept has further muddied the waters by hanging the label of "culture" on everything from common behavioral patterns to espoused new corporate values that senior management wishes to inculcate (e.g., Deal & Kennedy, 1982; Peters & Waterman, 1982).

Serious students of organizational culture point out that each culture researcher develops explicit or implicit paradigms that bias not only the definitions of key concepts but the whole approach to the study of the phenomenon (Barley, Meyer, & Gash, 1988; Martin & Meyerson, 1988; Ott, 1989; Smircich & Calas, 1987; Van Maanen, 1988). One probable reason for this diversity of approaches is that culture, like role, lies at the intersection of several social sciences and reflects some of the biases of each— specifically, those of anthropology, sociology, social psychology, and organizational behavior.

A complete review of the various paradigms and their implications is far beyond the scope of this article. Instead, I will provide a brief historical overview leading to the major approaches currently in use and then describe in greater de-

tail one paradigm, firmly anchored in social psychology and anthropology, that is somewhat integrative in that it allows one to position other paradigms in a common conceptual space.

This line of thinking will push us conceptually into territory left insufficiently explored by such concepts as "climate," "norm," and "attitude." Many of the research methods of industrial/ organizational psychology have weaknesses when applied to the concept of culture. If we are to take culture seriously, we must first adopt a more clinical and ethnographic approach to identify clearly the kinds of dimensions and variables that can usefully lend themselves to more precise empirical measurement and hypothesis testing. Though there have been many efforts to be empirically precise about cultural phenomena, there is still insufficient linkage of theory with observed data. We are still operating in the context of discovery and are seeking hypotheses, rather than testing specific theoretical formulations.

A Historical Note

Organizational culture as a concept has a fairly recent origin. Although the concepts of "group norms" and "climate" have been used by psychologists for a long time (e.g., Lewin, Lippitt, & White, 1939), the concept of "culture" has been explicitly used only in the last few decades. Katz and Kahn (1978), in their second edition of *The Social Psychology of Organizations,* referred to roles, norms, and values but presented neither climate nor culture as explicit concepts.

Organizational "climate," by virtue of being a more salient cultural phenomenon, lent itself to direct observation and measurement and thus has had a longer research tradition (Hellriegel &

Source: Edgar H. Schein, "Organizational Culture," *American Psychologist* 45, no. 2 (February 1990), pp. 109–19. Copyright 1990 by the American Psychological Association. Reprinted by permission. Table 1 and Table 2 originally appeared in E. H. Schein's *Organizational Culture and Leadership: A Dynamic View,* pp. 52, 86. Copyright © 1985 by Jossey-Bass, Inc., Publishers. Reprinted by permission.

Slocum, 1974; A. P. Jones & James, 1979; Litwin & Stringer, 1968; Schneider, 1975; Schneider & Reichers, 1983; Tagiuri & Litwin, 1968). But climate is only a surface manifestation of culture, and thus research on climate has not enabled us to delve into the deeper causal aspects of how organizations function. We need explanations for variations in climate and norms, and it is this need that ultimately drives us to "deeper" concepts such as culture.

In the late 1940s social psychologists interested in Lewinian "action research" and leadership training freely used the concept of "cultural island" to indicate that the training setting was in some fundamental way different from the trainees' "back home" setting. We knew from the leadership training studies of the 1940s and 1950s that foremen who changed significantly during training would revert to their former attitudes once they were back at work in a different setting (Bradford, Gibb, & Benne, 1964; Fleishman, 1953, 1973; Lewin, 1952; Schein & Bennis, 1965). But the concept of "group norms," heavily documented in the Hawthorne studies of the 1920s, seemed sufficient to explain this phenomenon (Homans, 1950; Roethlisberger & Dickson, 1939).

In the 1950s and 1960s, the field of organizational psychology began to differentiate itself from industrial psychology by focusing on units larger than individuals (Bass, 1965; Schein, 1965). With a growing emphasis on work groups and whole organizations came a greater need for concepts such as "system" that could describe what could be thought of as a *pattern* of norms and attitudes that cut across a whole social unit. The researchers and clinicians at the Tavistock Institute developed the concept of "socio-technical systems" (Jaques, 1951; Rice, 1963; Trist, Higgin, Murray, & Pollock, 1963), and Likert (1961, 1967) developed his "Systems 1 through 4" to describe integrated sets of organizational norms and attitudes. Katz and Kahn (1966) built their entire analysis of organizations around systems theory and systems dynamics,

thus laying the most important theoretical foundation for later culture studies.

The field of organizational psychology grew with the growth of business and management schools. As concerns with understanding organizations and interorganizational relationships grew, concepts from sociology and anthropology began to influence the field. Cross-cultural psychology had, of course, existed for a long time (Werner, 1940), but the application of the concept of culture to organizations *within* a given society came only recently as more investigators interested in organizational phenomena found themselves needing the concept to explain (*a*) variations in patterns of organizational behavior, and (*b*) levels of stability in group and organizational behavior that had not previously been highlighted (e.g., Ouchi, 1981).

What has really thrust the concept into the forefront is the recent emphasis on trying to explain why U.S. companies do not perform as well as some of their counterpart companies in other societies, notably Japan. In observing the differences, it has been noted that national culture is not a sufficient explanation (Ouchi, 1981; Pascale & Athos, 1981). One needs concepts that permit one to differentiate between organizations within a society, especially in relation to different levels of effectiveness, and the concept of organizational culture has served this purpose well (e.g., O'Toole, 1979; Pettigrew, 1979; Wilkins & Ouchi, 1983).

As more investigators and theoreticians have begun to examine organizational culture, the normative thrust has been balanced by more descriptive and clinical research (Barley, 1983; Frost, Moore, Louis, Lundberg, & Martin, 1985; Louis, 1981, 1983; Martin, 1982; Martin, Feldman, Hatch, & Sitkin, 1983; Martin & Powers, 1983; Martin & Siehl, 1983; Schein, 1985a; Van Maanen & Barley, 1984). We need to find out what is actually going on in organizations before we rush in to tell managers what to do about their culture.

I will summarize this quick historical overview by identifying several different research streams that today influence how we perceive the concept of organizational culture.

Survey Research.   From this perspective, culture has been viewed as a property of groups that can be measured by questionnaires leading to Likert-type profiles (Hofstede, 1980; Hofstede & Bond, 1988; Kilmann, 1984; Likert, 1967). The problem with this approach is that it assumes knowledge of the relevant dimensions to be studied. Even if these are statistically derived from large samples of items, it is not clear whether the initial item set is broad enough or relevant enough to capture what may for any given organization be its critical cultural themes. Furthermore, it is not clear whether something as abstract as culture can be measured with survey instruments at all.

Analytical Descriptive.   In this type of research, culture is viewed as a concept for which empirical measures must be developed, even if that means breaking down the concept into smaller units so that it can be analyzed and measured (e.g., Harris & Sutton, 1986; Martin & Siehl, 1983; Schall, 1983; Trice & Beyer, 1984; Wilkins, 1983). Thus organizational stories, rituals and rites, symbolic manifestations, and other cultural elements come to be taken as valid surrogates for the cultural whole. The problem with this approach is that it fractionates a concept whose primary theoretical utility is in drawing attention to the holistic aspect of group and organizational phenomena.

Ethnographic.   In this approach, concepts and methods developed in sociology and anthropology are applied to the study of organizations in order to illuminate descriptively, and thus provide a richer understanding of certain organizational phenomena that had previously not been documented fully enough (Barley, 1983; Van Maanen, 1988; Van Maanen & Barley, 1984). This approach helps to build better theory but is

time consuming and expensive. A great many more cases are needed before generalizations can be made across various types of organizations.

Historical.   Though historians have rarely applied the concept of culture in their work, it is clearly viewed as a legitimate aspect of an organization to be analyzed along with other factors (Chandler, 1977; Dyer, 1986; Pettigrew, 1979; Westney, 1987). The weaknesses of the historical method are similar to those pointed out for the ethnographic approach, but these are often offset by the insights that historical and longitudinal analyses can provide.

Clinical Descriptive.   With the growth of organizational consulting has come the opportunity to observe in areas from which researchers have traditionally been barred, such as the higher levels of management where policies originate and where reward and control systems are formulated. When consultants observe organizational phenomena as a byproduct of their services for clients, we can think of this as "clinical" research even though the client is defining the domain of observation (Schein, 1987a). Such work is increasingly being done by consultants with groups and organizations, and it allows consultants to observe some of the systemic effects of interventions over time. This approach has been of how members of the organization react. We can see and feel that one company is much more formal and bureaucratic than another, but that does not tell us anything about why this is so or what meaning it has to the members.

For example, one of the flaws of studying organizational symbols, stories, myths, and other such artifacts is that we may make incorrect inferences from them if we do not know how they connect to underlying assumptions (Pondy, Boland, & Thomas, 1988; Pondy, Frost, Morgan, & Dandridge, 1983; Wilkins, 1983). Organizational stories are especially problematic in this regard because the "lesson" of the story is not clear if one does not understand the underlying assumptions behind it.

Through interviews, questionnaires, or survey instruments one can study a culture's espoused and documented *values,* norms, ideologies, charters, and philosophies. This is comparable to the ethnographer's asking special "informants" why certain observed phenomena happen the way they do. Open-ended interviews can be very useful in getting at this level of how people feel and think; but questionnaires and survey instruments are generally less useful, because they prejudge the dimensions to be studied. There is no way of knowing whether the dimensions one is asking about are relevant or salient in that culture until one has examined the deeper levels of the culture.

Through more intensive observation, through more focused questions, and through involving motivated members of the group in intensive self-analysis, one can seek out and decipher the taken-for-granted, underlying, and usually unconscious *assumptions* that determine perceptions, thought processes, feelings, and behavior. Once one understands some of these assumptions, it becomes much easier to decipher the meanings implicit in the various behavioral and artifactual phenomena one observes. Furthermore, once one understands the underlying taken-for-granted assumptions, one can better understand how cultures can seem to be ambiguous or even self-contradictory (Martin & Meyerson, 1988).

As two case examples I present later will show, it is quite possible for a group to hold conflicting values that manifest themselves in inconsistent behavior while having complete consensus on underlying assumptions. It is equally possible for a group to reach consensus on the level of values and behavior and yet develop serious conflict later because there was no consensus on critical underlying assumptions.

This latter phenomenon is frequently observed in mergers or acquisitions where initial synergy is gradually replaced by conflict, leading ultimately to divestitures. When one analyzes these examples historically one often finds that there was insufficient agreement on certain basic assumptions, or, in our terms, that the cultures were basically in conflict with each other.

Deeply held assumptions often start out historically as values but, as they stand the test of time, gradually come to be taken for granted and then take on the character of assumptions. They are no longer questioned and they become less and less open to discussion. Such avoidance behavior occurs particularly if the learning was based on traumatic experiences in the organization's history, which leads to the group counterpart of what would be repression in the individual. If one understands culture in this way, it becomes obvious why it is so difficult to change culture.

Deciphering the "Content" of Culture

Culture is ubiquitous. It covers all areas of group life. A simplifying typology is always dangerous because one may not have the right variables in it; but if one distills from small group theory the dimensions that recur in group studies, one can identify a set of major external and internal tasks that all groups face and with which they must learn to cope (Ancona, 1988; Bales, 1950; Bales & Cohen, 1979; Benne & Sheats, 1948; Bennis & Shepard, 1956; Bion, 1959; Schein, 1988). The group's culture can then be seen as the learned response to each of these tasks (see Table 1).

Another approach to understanding the "content" of a culture is to draw on anthropological typologies of universal issues faced by all societies. Again there is a danger of overgeneralizing these dimensions (see Table 2), but the comparative studies of Kluckhohn and Strodtbeck (1961) are a reasonable start in this direction.

If one wants to decipher what is really going on in a particular organization, one has to start more inductively to find out which of these dimensions is the most pertinent on the basis of that organization's history. If one has access to the organization, one will note its *artifacts* readily

TABLE 1

The external and internal tasks facing all groups

External Adaption Tasks	Internal Integration Tasks
Developing concensus on:	Developing concensus on:
1. The core mission, functions, and primary tasks of the organization vis-à-vis its environments.	1. The common language and conceptual system to be used, including basis concepts of time and space.
2. The specific goals to be pursued by the organization.	2. The group boundaries and criteria for inclusion.
3. The basic means to be used in accomplishing the goals.	3. The criteria for the allocation of status, power, and authority.
4. The criteria to be used for measuring results.	4. The criteria for intimacy, friendship, and love in different work and family settings.
5. The remedial or repair strategies if goals are not achieved.	5. The criteria for the allocation of rewards and punishments.
	6. Concepts for managing the unmanageable— ideology and religion.

NOTE: Adapted from *Organizational Culture and Leadership* (pp. 52, 56) by E. H. Schein, 1985, San Francisco: Jossey-Bass. Copyright 1985 by Jossey-Bass. Adapted by permission.

but will not really know what they mean. Of most value in this process will be noting *anomalies* and things that seem different, upsetting, or difficult to understand.

If one has access to members of the organization, one can interview them about the issues in Table 1 and thereby get a good roadmap of what is going on. Such an interview will begin to reveal *espoused values,* and, as these surface, the investigator will begin to notice inconsistencies between what is claimed and what has been observed. These inconsistencies and the anomalies observed or felt now form the basis for the next layer of investigation.

Pushing past the layer of espoused values into underlying *assumptions* can be done by the ethnographer once trust has been established or by the clinician if the organizational client wishes to be helped. Working with motivated insiders is essential, because only they can bring to the surface their own underlying assumptions and articulate how they basically perceive the world around them.

To summarize, if we combine insider knowledge with outsider questions, assumptions can be brought to the surface; but the process of inquiry has to be interactive, with the outsider continuing to probe until assumptions have really been teased out and have led to a feeling of greater understanding on the part of both the outsider and the insiders.

Two Case Examples

It is not possible to provide complete cultural descriptions in a short article, but some extracts from cases can be summarized to illustrate particularly the distinctions between artifacts, values, and assumptions. The "Action Company" is a rapidly growing high-technology manufacturing concern still managed by its founder roughly 30 years after its founding. Because of its low turnover and intense history, one would expect to find an overall organizational culture as well as functional and geographic subcultures.

A visitor to the company would note the open office landscape architecture; a high degree of informality; frenetic activity all around; a high degree of confrontation, conflict, and fighting in meetings; an obvious lack of status symbols, such as parking spaces or executive dining rooms; and a sense of high energy and emo-

TABLE 2

Some underlying dimensions of organizational culture

Dimension	Questions to be answered
1. The organization's relationship to its environment	Does the organization perceive itself to be dominant, submissive, harmonizing, searching out a niche?
2. The nature of human activity	Is the "correct" way for humans to behave to be dominant/pro-active, harmonizing, or passive/fatalistic?
3. The nature of reality and truth	How do we define what is true and what is not true; and how is truth ultimately determined both in the physical and social world? By pragmatic test, reliance on wisdom, or social concensus?
4. The nature of time	What is our basic orientation in terms of past, present, and future, and what kinds of time units are most relevant for the conduct of daily affairs?
5. The nature of human nature	Are humans basically good, neutral, or evil, and is human nature perfectible or fixed?
6. The nature of human relationships	What is the "correct" way for people to relate to each other, to distribute power and affection? Is life competitive or cooperative? Is the best way to organize society on the basis of individualism or groupism? Is the best authority system autocratic/paternalistic or collegial/participative?
7. Homogeneity vs. diversity	Is the group best off if it is highly diverse or if it is highly homogeneous, and should individuals in a group be encouraged to innovate or conform?

NOTE: Adapted from *Organizational Culture and Leadership* (p. 86) by E. H. Schein, 1985, San Francisco: Jossey-Bass. Copyright 1985 by Jossey-Bass. Adapted by permission.

tional involvement, of people staying late and expressing excitement about the importance of their work.

If one asks about these various behaviors, one is told that the company is in a rapidly growing high-technology field where hard work, innovation, and rapid solutions to things are important and where it is essential for everyone to contribute at their maximum capacity. New employees are carefully screened; and when an employee fails, he or she is simply assigned to another task, not fired or punished in any personal way.

If one discusses this further and pushes to the level of assumptions, one elicits a pattern or paradigm such as that shown in Figure 1. Because of the kind of technology the company manufactures, and because of the strongly held beliefs and values of its founder, the company operates on several critical and coordinated assumptions: (*a*) Individuals are assumed to be the source of all innovation and productivity. (*b*) It is assumed that truth can only be determined by pitting fully involved individuals against each other to debate ideas until only one idea survives; and it is further assumed that ideas will not be implemented unless everyone involved in implementation has been convinced through the debate of the validity of the idea. (*c*) Paradoxically, it is also assumed that every individual must think

FIGURE 1

The Action Company paradigm

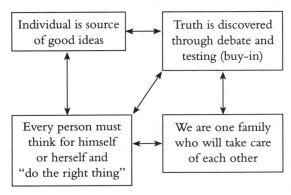

for himself or herself and "do the right thing" even if that means disobeying one's boss or violating a policy. (*d*) What makes it possible for people to live in this high-conflict environment is the assumption that the company members are one big family who will take care of each other and protect each other even if some members make mistakes or have bad ideas.

Once one understands this paradigm, one can understand all of the different observed artifacts, such as the ability of the organization to tolerate extremely high degrees of conflict without seeming to destroy or even demotivate its employees. The value of the cultural analysis is that it provides insight, understanding, and a roadmap for future action. For example, as this company grows, the decision process may prove to be too slow, the individual autonomy that members are expected to exercise may become destructive and have to be replaced by more disciplined behavior, and the notion of a family may break down because too many people no longer know each other personally. The cultural analysis thus permits one to focus on those areas in which the organization will experience stresses and strains as it continues to grow and in which cultural evolution and change will occur.

By way of contrast, in the "Multi Company," a 100-year-old multidivisional, multinational chemical firm, one finds at the artifact level a high degree of formality; an architecture that puts great emphasis on privacy; a proliferation of status symbols and deference rituals, such as addressing people by their titles; a high degree of politeness in group meetings; an emphasis on carefully thinking things out and then implementing them firmly through the hierarchy; a formal code of dress; and an emphasis on working hours, punctuality, and so on. One also finds a total absence of cross-divisional or cross-functional meetings and an almost total lack of lateral communication. Memos left in one department by an outside consultant with instructions to be given to others are almost never delivered.

The paradigm that surfaces, if one works with insiders to try to decipher what is going on, can best be depicted by the assumptions shown in Figure 2. The company is science based and has always derived its success from its research and development activities. Whereas "truth" in the Action Company is derived through debate and conflict and employees down the line are expected to think for themselves, in the Multi Company truth is derived from senior, wiser heads and employees are expected to go along like good soldiers once a decision is reached.

The Multi Company also sees itself as a fam-

FIGURE 2

The Multi Company paradigm

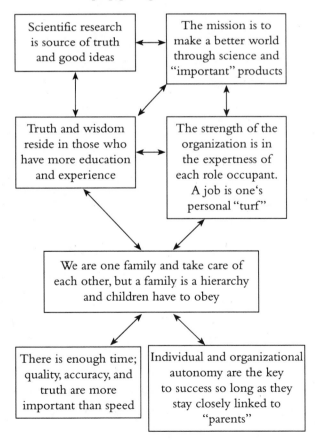

ily, but its concept of a family is completely different. Whereas in the Action Company, the family is a kind of safety net and an assurance of membership, in the Multi Company it is an authoritarian/paternalistic system of eliciting loyalty and compliance in exchange for economic security. The paradoxical absence of lateral communication is explained by the deeply held assumption that a job is a person's private turf and that the unsolicited providing of information to that person is an invasion of privacy and a potential threat to his or her self-esteem. Multi Company managers are very much on top of their jobs and pride themselves on that fact. If they ask for information they get it, but it is rarely volunteered by peers.

This cultural analysis highlights what is for the Multi Company a potential problem. Its future success may depend much more on its ability to become effective in marketing and manufacturing, yet it still treats research and development as a sacred cow and assumes that new products will be the key to its future success. Increasingly, the company finds itself in a world that requires rapid decision making, yet its systems and procedures are slow and cumbersome. To be more innovative in marketing it needs to share ideas more, yet it undermines lateral communication.

Both companies reflect the larger cultures within which they exist, in that the Action Company is an American firm whereas the Multi Company is European; but each also is different from its competitors within the same country, thus highlighting the importance of understanding *organizational* culture.

Cultural Dynamics: How Is Culture Created?

Culture is learned; hence learning models should help us to understand culture creation. Unfortunately, there are not many good models of how groups learn—how norms, beliefs, and assumptions are created initially. Once these exist, we can see clearly how leaders and powerful members embed them in group activity, but the process of learning something that becomes shared is still only partially understood.

Norm Formation Around Critical Incidents.   One line of analysis comes from the study of training groups (Bennis & Shepard, 1956; Bion, 1959; Schein, 1985a). One can see in such groups how norms and beliefs arise around the way members respond to critical incidents. Something emotionally charged or anxiety producing may happen, such as an attack by a member on the leader. Because everyone witnesses it and because tension is high when the attack occurs, the immediate next set of behaviors tends to create a norm.

Suppose, for example, that the leader counterattacks, that the group members "concur" with silence or approval, and that the offending member indicates with an apology that he or she accepts his or her "mistake." In those few moments a bit of culture has begun to be created—the norm that "we do not attack the leader in this group; authority is sacred." The norm may eventually become a belief and then an assumption if the same pattern recurs. If the leader and the group consistently respond differently to attacks, a different norm will arise. By reconstructing the history of critical incidents in the group and how members dealt with them, one can get a good indication of the important cultural elements in that group.

Identification with Leaders.   A second mechanism of culture creation is the modeling by leader figures that permits group members to identify with them and internalize their values and assumptions. When groups or organizations first form, there are usually dominant figures or "founders" whose own beliefs, values, and assumptions provide a visible and articulated model for how the group should be structured and how it should function (Schein, 1983). As these beliefs are put into practice, some work out and some do not. The group then learns from its own experience what parts of the "founder's" belief system work for the group as a whole. The joint learning then gradually creates shared assumptions.

Founders and subsequent leaders continue to attempt to embed their own assumptions; but increasingly they find that other parts of the organization have their own experiences to draw on and, thus, cannot be changed. Increasingly the learning process is shared, and the resulting cultural assumptions reflect the total group's experience, not only the leader's initial assumptions. But leaders continue to try to embed their own views of how things should be, and, if they are powerful enough, they will continue to have a dominant effect on the emerging culture.

Primary embedding mechanisms are (a) what leaders pay attention to, measure, and control; (b) how leaders react to critical incidents and organizational crises; (c) deliberate role modeling and coaching; (d) operational criteria for the allocation of rewards and status; and (e) operational criteria for recruitment, selection, promotion, retirement, and excommunication. *Secondary articulation and reinforcement mechanisms* are (a) the organization's design and structure; (b) organizational systems and procedures; (c) the design of physical space, facades, and buildings; (d) stories, legends, myths, and symbols; and (e) formal statements of organizational philosophy, creeds, and charters.

One can hypothesize that, as cultures evolve and grow, two processes will occur simultaneously: a process of differentiation into various kinds of subcultures that will create diversity, and a process of integration, or a tendency for the various deeper elements of the culture to become congruent with each other because of the human need for consistency.

Cultural Dynamics: Preservation Through Socialization

Culture perpetuates and reproduces itself through the socialization of new members entering the group. The socialization process really begins with recruitment and selection in that the organization is likely to look for new members who already have the "right" set of assumptions, beliefs, and values. If the organization can find such presocialized members, it needs to do less formal socialization. More typically, however, new members do not "know the ropes" well enough to be able to take and enact their organizational roles, and thus they need to be trained and "acculturated" (Feldman, 1988; Ritti & Funkhouser, 1987; Schein, 1968, 1978; Van Maanen, 1976, 1977).

The socialization process has been analyzed from a variety of perspectives and can best be conceptualized in terms of a set of dimensions that highlight variations in how different organizations approach the process (Van Maanen, 1978; Van Maanen & Schein, 1979). Van Maanen identified seven dimensions along which socialization processes can vary:

1. *Group versus individual:* the degree to which the organization processes recruits in batches, as in boot camp, or individually, as in professional offices.

2. *Formal versus informal:* the degree to which the process is formalized, as in set training programs, or is handled informally through apprenticeships, individual coaching by the immediate superior, or the like.

3. *Self-destructive and reconstructing versus self-enhancing:* the degree to which the process destroys aspects of the self and replaces them, as in boot camp, or enhances aspects of the self, as in professional development programs.

4. *Serial versus random:* the degree to which role models are provided, as in apprenticeship or mentoring programs, or are deliberately withheld, as in sink-or-swim kinds of initiations in which the recruit is expected to figure out his or her own solutions.

5. *Sequential versus disjunctive:* the degree to which the process consists of guiding the recruit through a series of discrete steps and roles versus being open-ended and never letting the recruit predict what organizational role will come next.

6. *Fixed versus variable:* the degree to which stages of the training process have fixed timetables for each stage, as in military academies, boot camps, or rotational training programs, or are open-ended, as in typical promotional systems where one is not advanced to the next stage until one is "ready."

7. *Tournament versus contest:* the degree to which each stage is an "elimination tournament" where one is out of the organization if one fails or a "contest" in which one builds up a track record and batting average.

Socialization Consequences.   Though the goal of socialization is to perpetuate the culture, it is clear that the process does not have uniform effects. Individuals respond differently to the same treatment, and, even more important, different combinations of socialization tactics can be hypothesized to produce somewhat different outcomes for the organization (Van Maanen & Schein, 1979).

For example, from the point of view of the organization, one can specify three kinds of outcomes: (*a*) a *custodial orientation,* or total conformity to all norms and complete learning of all assumptions; (*b*) *creative individualism,* which implies that the trainee learns all of the central and pivotal assumptions of the culture but rejects all peripheral ones, thus permitting the individual to be creative both with respect to the organization's tasks and in how the organization performs them (role innovation); and (*c*) *rebellion,* or the total rejection of all assumptions. If the rebellious individual is constrained by external circumstances from leaving the organization, he or she will subvert, sabotage, and ultimately foment revolution.

We can hypothesize that the combination of socialization techniques most likely to produce a custodial orientation is (1) formal, (2) self-reconstructing, (3) serial, (4) sequential, (5) variable, and (6) tournament-like. Hence if one wants new members to be more creative in the use of their talents, one should use socialization techniques that are informal, self-enhancing, random, disjunctive, fixed in terms of timetables, and contest-like.

The individual versus group dimension can go in either direction in that group socialization methods can produce loyal custodially oriented cohorts or can produce disloyal rebels if countercultural norms are formed during the socialization process. Similarly, in the individual apprenticeship the direction of socialization will depend on the orientation of the mentor or coach.

Efforts to measure these socialization dimensions have been made, and some preliminary support for the above hypotheses has been forthcoming (Feldman, 1976, 1988; G. R. Jones, 1986). Insofar as cultural evolution is a function of innovative and creative efforts on the part of new members, this line of investigation is especially important.

Cultural Dynamics: Natural Evolution

Every group and organization is an open system that exists in multiple environments. Changes in the environment will produce stresses and strains inside the group, forcing new learning and adaptation. At the same time, new members coming into the group will bring new beliefs and assumptions that will influence currently held assumptions. To some degree, then, there is constant pressure on any given culture to evolve and grow. But just as individuals do not easily give up the elements of their identity or their defense mechanisms, so groups do not easily give up some of their basic underlying assumptions merely because external events or new members disconfirm them.

An illustration of "forced" evolution can be seen in the case of the aerospace company that prided itself on its high level of trust in its employees, which was reflected in flexible working hours, systems of self-monitoring and self-control, and the absence of time clocks. When a number of other companies in the industry were discovered to have overcharged their government clients, the government legislated a system of controls for *all* of its contractors, forcing this company to install time clocks and other control mechanisms that undermined the climate of trust that had been built up over 30 years. It remains to be seen whether the company's basic assumption that people can be trusted will gradually change or whether the company will find a way to discount the effects of an artifact that is in fundamental conflict with one of its basic assumptions.

Differentiation. As organizations grow and evolve they divide the labor and form functional, geographical, and other kinds of units, each of which exists in its own specific environment. Thus organizations begin to build their own subcultures. A natural evolutionary mechanism, therefore, is the differentiation that inevitably occurs with age and size. Once a group has many subcultures, its total culture increasingly becomes a negotiated outcome of the interaction of its subgroups. Organizations then evolve either by special efforts to impose their overall culture or by allowing dominant subcultures that may be better adapted to changing environmental circumstances to become more influential.

Cultural Dynamics: Guided Evolution and Managed Change

One of the major roles of the field of organization development has been to help organizations guide the direction of their evolution; that is, to enhance cultural elements that are viewed as critical to maintaining identity and to promote the "unlearning" of cultural elements that are

viewed as increasingly dysfunctional (Argyris, Putnam, & Smith, 1985; Argyris & Schon, 1978; Beckhard & Harris, 1987; Hanna, 1988; Lippitt, 1982; Walton, 1987). This process in organizations is analogous to the process of therapy in individuals, although the actual tactics are more complicated when multiple clients are involved and when some of the clients are groups and subsystems.

Leaders of organizations sometimes are able to overcome their own cultural biases and to perceive that elements of an organization's culture are dysfunctional for survival and growth in a changing environment. They may feel either that they do not have the time to let evolution occur naturally or that evolution is heading the organization in the wrong direction. In such a situation one can observe leaders doing a number of different things, usually in combination, to produce the desired cultural changes:

1. Leaders may unfreeze the present system by highlighting the threats to the organization if no change occurs, and, at the same time, encourage the organization to believe that change is possible and desirable.

2. They may articulate a new direction and a new set of assumptions, thus providing a clear and new role model.

3. Key positions in the organization may be filled with new incumbents who hold the new assumptions because they are either hybrids, mutants, or brought in from the outside.

4. Leaders systematically may reward the adoption of new directions and punish adherence to the old direction.

5. Organization members may be seduced or coerced into adopting new behaviors that are more consistent with new assumptions.

6. Visible scandals may be created to discredit sacred cows, to explode myths

that preserve dysfunctional traditions, and to destroy symbolically the artifacts associated with them.

7. Leaders may create new emotionally charged rituals and develop new symbols and artifacts around the new assumptions to be embraced, using the embedding mechanisms described earlier.

Such cultural change efforts are generally more characteristic of "midlife" organizations that have become complacent and ill adapted to rapidly changing environmental conditions (Schein, 1985a). The fact that such organizations have strong subcultures aids the change process, in that one can draw the new leaders from those subcultures that most represent the direction in which the organization needs to go.

In cases where organizations become extremely maladapted, one sees more severe change efforts. These may take the form of destroying the group that is the primary cultural carrier and reconstructing it around new people, thereby allowing a new learning process to occur and a new culture to form. When organizations go bankrupt or are turned over to "turnaround managers," one often sees such extreme measures. What is important to note about such cases is that they invariably involve the replacement of large numbers of people, because the members who have grown up in the organization find it difficult to change their basic assumptions.

Mergers and Acquisitions.   One of the most obvious forces toward culture change is the bringing together of two or more cultures. Unfortunately, in many mergers and acquisitions, the culture compatibility issue is not raised until after the deal has been consummated, which leads, in many cases, to cultural "indigestion" and the eventual divestiture of units that cannot become culturally integrated.

To avoid such problems, organizations must either engage in more premerger diagnosis to de-termine cultural compatibility or conduct training and integration workshops to help the meshing process. Such workshops have to take into account the deeper assumption layers of culture to avoid the trap of reaching consensus at the level of artifacts and values while remaining in conflict at the level of underlying assumptions.

The Role of the Organizational Psychologist

Culture will become an increasingly important concept for organizational psychology. Without such a concept we cannot really understand change or resistance to change. The more we get involved with helping organizations to design their fundamental strategies, particularly in the human resources area, the more important it will be to be able to help organizations decipher their own cultures.

All of the activities that revolve around recruitment, selection, training, socialization, the design of reward systems, the design and description of jobs, and broader issues of organization design require an understanding of how organizational culture influences present functioning. Many organizational change programs that failed probably did so because they ignored cultural forces in the organizations in which they were to be installed.

Inasmuch as culture is a dynamic process within organizations, it is probably studied best by action research methods, that is, methods that get "insiders" involved in the research and that work through attempts to "intervene" (Argyris et al., 1985; French & Bell, 1984; Lewin, 1952; Schein, 1987b). Until we have a better understanding of how culture works, it is probably best to work with qualitative research approaches that combine field work methods from ethnography with interview and observation methods from clinical and consulting work (Schein, 1987a).

I do not see a unique role for the traditional industrial/organizational psychologist, but I see great potential for the psychologist to work as a team member with colleagues who are more ethnographically oriented. The particular skill that will be needed on the part of the psychologist will be knowledge of organizations and of how to work with them, especially in a consulting relationship. Organizational culture is a complex phenomenon, and we should not rush to measure things until we understand better what we are measuring.

References

Ancona, D. G. (1988). "Groups in Organizations: Extending Laboratory Models." In C. Hendrick (ed.), *Annual Review of Personality and Social Psychology: Group and Intergroup Processes*. Beverly Hills, CA: Sage.

Argyris, C., Putnam, R., & Smith, D. M. (1985). *Action Science*. San Francisco: Jossey-Bass.

Argyris, C., & Schon, D. A. (1978). *Organizational Learning: A Theory of Action Perspective*. Reading, MA: Addison-Wesley.

Bales, R. F. (1950). *Interaction Process Analysis*. Chicago: University of Chicago Press.

Bales, R. F., & Cohen, S. P. (1979). SYMLOG: *A System for the Multiple Level Observation of Groups*. New York: Free Press.

Barley, S. R. (1983). "Semiotics and the Study of Occupational and Organizational Cultures." *Administrative Science Quarterly, 28,* 393–413.

Barley, S. R.; Meyer, C. W.; & Gash, D. C. (1988). "Culture of Cultures: Academics, Practitioners and the Pragmatics of Normative Control." *Administrative Science Quarterly* 33, 24–60.

Bass, B. M. (1965). *Organizational Psychology*. Boston: Allyn & Bacon.

Beckhard, R. (1969). *Organization Development: Strategies and Models*. Reading, MA: Addison-Wesley.

Beckhard, R., & Harris, R. T. (1977). *Organizational Transitions: Managing Complex Change*. Reading, MA: Addison-Wesley.

Beckhard, R., & Harris, R. T. (1987). *Organizational Transitions: Managing Complex Change* (2nd. ed.). Reading, MA: Addison-Wesley.

Benne, K., & Sheats, P. (1948). "Functional Roles of Group Members." *Journal of Social Issues* 2, 42–47.

Bennis, W. G. (1966). *Changing Organizations*. New York: McGraw-Hill.

Bennis, W. G. (1969). *Organization Development: Its Nature, Origins, and Prospects*. Reading, MA: Addison-Wesley.

Bennis, W. G., & Shepard, H. A. (1956). "A Theory of Group Development." *Human Relations* 9, 415–37.

Bion, W. R. (1959). *Experiences in Groups*. London: Tavistock.

Bradford, L. P.; Gibb, J. R.; & Benne, K. D. (eds.). (1964). *T-Group Theory and Laboratory Method*. New York: John Wiley & Sons.

Chandler, A. P. (1977). *The Visible Hand*. Cambridge, MA: Harvard University Press.

Deal, T. W., & Kennedy, A. A. (1982). *Corporate Cultures*. Reading, MA: Addison-Wesley.

Durkin, J. E. (ed.). (1981). *Living Groups: Group Psychotherapy and General Systems Theory*. New York: Brunner/Mazel.

Dyer, W. G., Jr. (1986). *Cultural Change in Family Firms*. San Francisco: Jossey-Bass.

Feldman, D. C. (1976). "A Contingency Theory of Socialization." *Administrative Science Quarterly* 21, 433–52.

Feldman, D. C. (1988). *Managing Careers in Organizations*. Glenview, IL: Scott, Foresman.

Festinger, L. (1957). *A Theory of Cognitive Dissonance*. New York: Harper & Row.

Fleishman, E. A. (1953). "Leadership Climate, Human Relations Training, and Supervisory Behavior." *Personnel Psychology* 6, 205–22.

Fleishman, E. A. (1973). "Twenty Years of Consideration and Structure." In E. A. Fleishman & J. G. Hunt (eds.). *Current Developments in the Study of Leadership* (pp. 1–39). Carbondale: Southern Illinois University Press.

French, W. L., & Bell, C. H. (1984). *Organization Development*. 3rd ed. Englewood Cliffs, NJ: Prentice Hall.

Frost, P. J.; Moore, L. F.; Louis, M. R.; Lundberg, C. C.; & Martin, J. (eds.). (1985). *Organizational Culture*. Beverly Hills, CA: Sage.

Hanna, D. P. (1988). *Designing Organizations for High Performance*. Reading, MA: Addison-Wesley.

Harris, S. G., & Sutton, R. I. (1986). "Functions of

Parting Ceremonies in Dying Organizations." *Academy of Management Journal* 29, 5–30.

Hebb, D. (1954). "The Social Significance of Animal Studies." In G. Lindzey (ed.), *Handbook of Social Psychology,* vol. 2, pp. 532–61. Reading, MA: Addison-Wesley.

Heider, F. (1958). *The Psychology of Interpersonal Relations.* New York: John Wiley & Sons.

Hellriegel, D., & Slocum, J. W., Jr. (1974). "Organizational Climate: Measures, Research, and Contingencies." *Academy of Management Journal,* 17, 255–80.

Hirschhorn, L. (1987). *The Workplace Within.* Cambridge, MA: MIT Press.

Hofstede, G. (1980). *Culture's Consequences.* Beverly Hills, CA: Sage.

Hofstede, G., & Bond, M. H. (1988). "The Confucius Connection: From Cultural Roots to Economic Growth." *Organizational Dynamics* 16(4), 4–21.

Homans, G. (1950). *The Human Group.* New York: Harcourt Brace Jovanovich.

Jaques, E. (1951). *The Changing Culture of a Factory.* London: Tavistock.

Jones, A. P., & James, E. R. (1979). "Psychological Climate: Dimensions and Relationships of Individual and Aggregated Work Environment Perceptions." *Organizational Behavior and Human Performance* 23, 201–50.

Jones, G. R. (1986). "Socialization Tactics, Self-Efficacy, and New-Comers' Adjustments to Organizations." *Academy of Management Journal* 29, 262–79.

Katz, D., & Kahn, R. L. (1966). *The Social Psychology of Organizations.* New York: John Wiley & Sons.

Katz, D., & Kahn, R. L. (1978). *The Social Psychology of Organizations* (2nd ed.). New York: John Wiley & Sons.

Kets de Vries, M. F. R., & Miller, D. (1984). *The Neurotic Organization.* San Francisco: Jossey-Bass.

Kets de Vries, M. F. R., & Miller, D. (1986). "Personality, Culture, and Organization." *Academy of Management Review* 11, 266–79.

Kilmann, R. H. (1984). *Beyond the Quick Fix.* San Francisco: Jossey-Bass.

Kluckhohn, F. R., & Strodtbeck, F. L. (1961). *Variations in Value Orientations.* New York: Harper & Row.

Lewin, K. (1952). "Group Decision and Social Change." In G. E. Swanson, T. N. Newcomb, & E. L. Hartley (eds.), *Readings in Social Psychology* (rev. ed., pp. 459–73). New York: Holt, Rinehart & Winston.

Lewin, K.; Lippitt, R.; & White, R. K. (1939). "Patterns of Aggressive Behavior in Experimentally Created 'Social Climates.'" *Journal of Social Psychology* 10, 271–99.

Likert, R. (1961). *New Patterns of Management.* New York: McGraw-Hill.

Likert, R. (1967). *The Human Organization.* New York: McGraw-Hill.

Lippitt, G. (1982). *Organizational Renewal* (2nd ed.). Englewood Cliffs, NJ: Prentice Hall.

Litwin, G. H., & Stringer, R. A. (1968). *Motivation and Organizational Climate.* Boston: Harvard Business School, Division of Research.

Louis, M. R. (1981). "A Cultural Perspective on Organizations." *Human Systems Management* 2, 246–58.

Louis, M. R. (1983). "Organizations as Culture Bearing Milieux." In L. R. Pondy, P. J. Frost, G. Morgan, & T. C. Dandridge (eds.), *Organizational Symbolism* (pp. 39–54). Greenwich, CT: JAI Press.

Martin, J. (1982). "Stories and Scripts in Organizational Settings." In A. Hastorf & A. Isen (eds.), *Cognitive Social Psychology.* New York: Elsevier.

Martin, J.; Feldman, M. S.; Hatch, M. J.; & Sitkin, S. (1983). "The Uniqueness Paradox in Organizational Stories." *Administrative Science Quarterly* 28, 438–54.

Martin, J., & Meyerson, D. (1988). "Organizational Cultures and the Denial, Channeling, and Acknowledgement of Ambiguity." In L. R. Pondy, R. J. Boland, & H. Thomas (eds.). *Managing Ambiguity and Change.* New York: John Wiley & Sons.

Martin, J., & Powers, M. E. (1983). "Truth or Corporate Propaganda: The Value of a Good War Story." In L. R. Pondy, P. J. Frost, G. Morgan, & T. C. Dandridge (eds.), *Organizational Symbolism* (pp. 93–108). Greenwich, CT: JAI Press.

Martin, J., & Siehl, C. (1983). "Organizational Culture and Counter-Culture: An Uneasy Symbiosis." *Organizational Dynamics* 12, 52–64.

Menzies, I. E. P. (1960). "A Case Study in the Functioning of Social Systems as a Defense against Anxiety." *Human Relations,* 13, 95–121.

O'Toole, J. J. (1979). "Corporate and Managerial Cultures." In C. L. Cooper (ed.), *Behavioral Problems in Organizations*. Englewood Cliffs, NJ: Prentice Hall.

Ott, J. S. (1989). *The Organizational Culture Perspective*. Chicago: Dorsey Press.

Ouchi, W. G. (1981). *Theory Z*. Reading, MA: Addison-Wesley.

Pascale, R. T., & Athos, A. G. (1981). *The Art of Japanese Management*. New York: Simon & Schuster.

Peters, T. J., & Waterman, R. H., Jr. (1982). *In Search of Excellence*. New York: Harper & Row.

Pettigrew, A. M. (1979). "On Studying Organizational Cultures." *Administrative Science Quarterly*, 24, 570–81.

Pondy, L. R.; Boland, R. J.; & Thomas, H. (1988). *Managing Ambiguity and Change*. New York: John Wiley & Sons.

Pondy, L. R.; Frost, P. J.; Morgan, G.; & Dandridge, T. C. (eds.). (1983). *Organizational Symbolism*. Greenwich, CT: JAI Press.

Rice, A. K. (1963). *The Enterprise and Its Environment*. London: Tavistock.

Ritti, R. R., & Funkhouser, G. R. (1987). *The Ropes to Skip and the Ropes to Know*. 3rd. ed. New York: John Wiley & Sons.

Roethlisberger, F. J., & Dickson, W. J. (1939). *Management and the Worker*. Cambridge, MA: Harvard University Press.

Schall, M. S. (1983). "A Communication-Rules Approach to Organizational Culture." *Administrative Science Quarterly*, 28, 557–81.

Schein, E. H. (1965). *Organizational Psychology*. Englewood Cliffs, NJ: Prentice Hall.

Schein, E. H. (1968). "Organizational Socialization and the Profession of Management." *Industrial Management Review (MIT)* 9, 1–15.

Schein, E. H. (1969). *Process Consultation*. Reading, MA: Addison-Wesley.

Schein, E. H. (1978). *Career Dynamics*. Reading, MA: Addison-Wesley.

Schein, E. H. (1983). "The Role of the Founder in Creating Organizational Culture." *Organizational Dynamics* 12, 13–28.

Schein, E. H. (1985a). *Organizational Culture and Leadership*. San Francisco: Jossey-Bass.

Schein, E. H. (1985b). "Organizational Culture: Skill, Defense Mechanism or Addiction?" In F. R. Brush & J. B. Overmier (eds.), *Affect, Condition-*

ing, and Cognition (pp. 315–23). Hillsdale, NJ: Erlbaum.

Schein, E. H. (1987a). *The Clinical Perspective in Fieldwork*. Beverly Hills, CA: Sage.

Schein, E. H. (1987b). *Process Consultation* (vol. 2). Reading, MA: Addison-Wesley.

Schein, E. H. (1988). *Process Consultation* (rev. ed.). Reading, MA: Addison-Wesley.

Schein, E. H., & Bennis, W. G. (1965). *Personal and Organizational Change through Group Methods*. New York: John Wiley & Sons.

Schneider, B. (1975). "Organizational Climate: An Essay." *Personnel Psychology* 28, 447–79.

Schneider, B., & Reichers, A. E. (1983). "On the Etiology of Climates." *Personnel Psychology* 36, 19–40.

Smircich, L., & Calas, M. B. (1987). "Organizational Culture: A Critical Assessment." In F. M. Jablin, L. L. Putnam, K. H. Roberts, & L. W. Porter (eds.), *Handbook of Organizational Communication* (pp. 228–63). Beverly Hills, CA: Sage.

Tagiuri, R., & Litwin, G. H. (eds.). (1968). *Organizational Climate: Exploration of a Concept*. Boston: Harvard Business School, Division of Research.

Trice, H., & Beyer, J. (1984). "Studying Organizational Cultures through Rites and Ceremonials." *Academy of Management Review* 9, 653–69.

Trist, E. L., Higgin, G. W., Murray, H., & Pollock, A. B. (1963). *Organizational Choice*. London: Tavistock.

Van Maanen, J. (1976). "Breaking in: Socialization to Work." In R. Dubin (ed.), *Handbook of Work, Organization and Society* (pp. 67–130). Chicago: Rand McNally.

Van Maanen, J. (1977). "Experiencing Organizations." In J. Van Maanen (ed.). *Organizational Careers: Some New Perspectives* (pp. 15–45). New York: John Wiley & Sons.

Van Maanen, J. (1978). "People Processing: Strategies of Organizational Socialization." *Organizational Dynamics*, 7, 18–36.

Van Maanen, J. (1988). *Tales of the Field*. Chicago: University of Chicago Press.

Van Maanen, J., & Barley, S. R. (1984). "Occupational Communities: Culture and Control in Organizations." In B. M. Staw & L. L. Cummings (eds.), *Research in Organizational Behavior* (vol. 6). Greenwich, Conn.: JAI Press.

Van Maanen, J., & Schein, E. H. (1979). "Toward a

Theory of Organizational Socialization." In B. M. Staw & L. L. Cummings (eds.), *Research in Organizational Behavior* (vol. 1, pp. 204–64). Greenwich, Conn.: JAI Press.

Walton, R. (1987). *Innovating to Compete.* San Francisco: Jossey-Bass.

Werner, H. (1940). *Comparative Psychology of Mental Development.* New York: Follett.

Westney, D. E. (1987). *Imitation and Innovation.* Cambridge, MA: Harvard University Press.

Wilkins, A. L. (1983). "Organizational Stories as Symbols Which Control the Organization." In L. R. Pondy, P. J. Frost, G. Morgan, & T. C. Dandridge (eds.), *Organizational Symbolism* (pp. 81–91). Greenwich, Conn.: JAI Press.

Wilkins, A. L., & Ouchi, W. G. (1983). "Efficient Cultures: Exploring the Relationship between Culture and Organizational Performance." *Administrative Science Quarterly* 28, 468–81.

READING 13
A COMPLETELY INTEGRATED PROGRAM FOR CREATING AND MAINTAINING ORGANIZATIONAL SUCCESS

Ralph H. Kilmann

Consultants and managers alike had high hopes for the field of organization development as it first emerged in the 1950s. Its methods for systemwide change were hailed as the organizational cure-all that would significantly improve the functioning of entire companies. For the most part, however, this majestic vision soon faded and eventually disappeared.

What happened? During the 1960s and 1970s, efforts at improving organizations became increasingly specialized, leading to fragmentation. This happened primarily because the methods of improvement focused on the narrow use of single approaches, such as team building, survey feedback, and performance appraisal. Academics, following traditional guidelines for rigorous research, tended to develop improvement methods suited to tightly controlled, isolated parts of the organization—thereby ignoring systemwide perspectives. Executives found this approach consistent with their own inclinations, of course, since it did not require them to examine either the corporate culture or the power structure of their organizations.

Today, managers are realizing "future shock" is upon them: They can no longer ignore the need for fundamental systemwide changes. Their entire organizations must be transformed into market-driven, innovative, and adaptive systems if they are to survive and prosper in the highly competitive, global environment of the next decades. As organizations gear up to greet the

1990s, many are beginning to face this urgent need to rejuvenate the vision and practice of organization development: to supply systemwide programs of planned change.

To Begin a Program of Planned Change

The first step in developing a completely integrated program for improving organizations entails identifying at least three sets of elements: (1) all the controlable variables—pinpointed via a systems perspective—that determine organizational success, (2) all the multiple approaches—techniques, instruments, and procedures—that can alter these controllable variables, and (3) all the ongoing activities that drive organization-wide change.

The first set of elements—the controlable variables—can be pinpointed by taking a systematic, *holistic* view of the barriers (problems) and channels (opportunities) management must address for the organization to be successful. It is these variables that managers and consultants can subsequently use as leverage for improving organizations.

Second, a completely integrated program must include multiple approaches for directly influencing the full range of leverage points that can *change* individual, group, and organizational behavior. A variety of techniques, instruments, and procedures for achieving organizational success can be organized into a sequence of five tracks: (1) the culture track, (2) the management skills track, (3) the team-building track, (4) the strategy-structure track, and (5) the reward system track. As a whole, these five tracks can alter all the controlable variables from the environ-

Source: Ralph H. Kilmann, "A Completely Integrated Program for Creating and Maintaining Organizational Success." Reprinted, by permission of publisher, from *Organizational Dynamics,* Summer 1989, pp. 5–19. Copyright © 1989 by American Management Association, New York. All rights reserved.

ment outside the organization to the psyche inside the individual.

The third element essential to a completely integrated program specifies *how* systemwide change can be managed in an organization—given the complexities and dynamics of a living system. While the process of change can be managed by an arbitrary number of stages, phases, or steps (from the very beginning of the program to the end), I have found it useful to organize the "how" of planned change into five critical stages: (1) initiating the program, (2) diagnosing the problems, (3) scheduling the tracks, (4) implementing the tracks, and (5) evaluating the results. Only by viewing the organization holistically (the first ingredient) and surrounding the five tracks (the second ingredient) with the ongoing stages of planned change (the third ingredient) will continuous adaptability become ingrained in an organization—thereby creating and maintaining organizational success.

Exhibit 1 shows these five stages of planned change as a recurring cycle of activity. To be successful, all programs for improving organiza-

tions must devote sufficient time and effort to complete each stage. Movement from one stage to the next, shown by the single arrows, should not take place until all the criteria for the earlier stages have been satisfied. Otherwise, any stages that are glossed over will result in more difficulties later. Since most organizations have lagged far behind the dramatic changes that have taken place in their environment, major transformational changes occur during the first cycle of the program. In subsequent cycles, organizations undertake mostly incremental—evolutionary—change, since they are then able to keep pace with a rapidly shifting environment.

Stage 1: Initiation

The critical issue during "initiation" is ascertaining whether the organization is ready for a successful improvement effort. Several key conditions must exist before the second "diagnosis" stage gets underway. Through informal one-on-one dialogues, small group meetings, and formal sessions with top executives of the whole organization and senior executives of business units, consultants can determine whether the following conditions exist indicating that management is ready to commit to a program of planned change.

Senior executives must understand the holistic approach, the five tracks, the critical stages of planned change, and the effort involved in implementing such a large-scale effort. It would be unrealistic to expect executives to make a well-informed decision about whether to implement a completely integrated program of planned change if they do not have the concepts and the language to debate the key issues. It is crucial to the ultimate success of any program of planned change that top executives know beforehand exactly what the program entails.

Senior executives must fully commit to implementing the whole program of planned change. Once the executives know what to expect, the program's success requires their full commitment: Execu-

EXHIBIT 1

The Five Stages of Planned Change

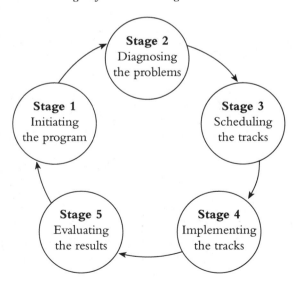

tives who will merely pay lip service to the change effort are not truly ready to transform the organization. Another shortcoming senior managers may exhibit is that, despite a commitment to follow through on the complete program, they may see the program as more relevant to their employees than to themselves. True commitment is demonstrated when the senior executives openly acknowledge that they are also part of "the problem" and need to change as well. Such an admission sets the best example for the rest of the employees and encourages everyone in the organization to participate in a learning mode.

Senior executives must be willing to have consultants diagnose the organization's full range of barriers to success. While managers may believe they can conduct the diagnosis of problems themselves, this is the one area in which it is imperative to get an objective, independent reading of the organization's health. All the remaining stages of planned change rely on the diagnosis as the basis for choosing among various techniques, instruments, and procedures—to bring about change and improvement. If the diagnosis is biased, inaccurate, or simplistic, the remaining stages of planned change will be jeopardized.

The implementation of the improvement program must be led by senior executives who will take full responsibility for its success. While most improvement efforts seem to be led by various staff groups—human resources, personnel, industrial relations, or employee relations—a completely integrated program for long-term organizational success should be led by line management, preferably by top management. With top management behind the change, the resources needed to conduct the whole program are more likely to be forthcoming. Moreover, with top management leading the charge, top priority will be assigned to the improvement effort in spite of all the pressures to concentrate on the here-and-now business problems and operational issues.

For example, if the organization is undergoing hard times because of a recent crisis or financial setback, involvement in the program might take a back seat to other priorities. The program is most likely to be successful if it is presented by top management as the number-one priority and is viewed as such by the rest of the membership.

Stage 2: Diagnosing Problems

When the key executives and consultants believe that all the conditions for success are present— that the program has been initiated properly— the diagnostic stage of planned change can proceed. The objective at this stage is to develop a deep understanding of the full range of problems (barriers) facing the organization as well as its opportunities (channels) for success.

Many organizations make use of various employee opinion surveys to learn what members think about their jobs, their respective division, and the organization as a whole. While the information gathered from such questionnaires is certainly systematic, surveys alone do not uncover the true experiences employees face in a complex organization. One-on-one, face-to-face discussions are a more effective method of capturing the full range of issues that impact on organizational members. Although it may seem more efficient to interview groups of members instead of individuals, this method is also lacking since employees are less apt to voice their true feelings in front of other co-workers unless the organization already has an open and trusting culture.

Consultants, with the aid of managers, must develop a plan to gather diagnostic information from members throughout the organization. The objective is to sample each level in the hierarchy—and each division and department—to obtain a representative view of the organization. Everyone in the top management group should be interviewed, simply because their views, and especially their commitment to change, are so critical to the program. If there are as many as 5,000 members in an organization, interviewing about 250 members should provide enough information to diagnose the organization's problems and opportunities adequately. For smaller organizations or divisions, 50 to 150 interviews should be sufficient.

Interviewers must be carefully instructed in the proper techniques of asking questions and recording responses. If the interviewers see organizations only as a collection of interpersonal relationships, they will only ask questions and record responses with regard to interpersonal issues. The same holds true if the interviewer should view the organization as merely a document-producing system (strategies, organization charts, or job descriptions), a cultural system, or a collection of management styles. *Any* perceptual filter that hampers the search for a full understanding of the organization's problems will limit the variety of controllable variables—leverage points—that are identified and used subsequently in the change process utilized.

Locating Barriers.   Exhibit 2 shows organizational life through a three-dimensional lens. This model is used for discovering the full range

Exhibit 2

Barriers to Success

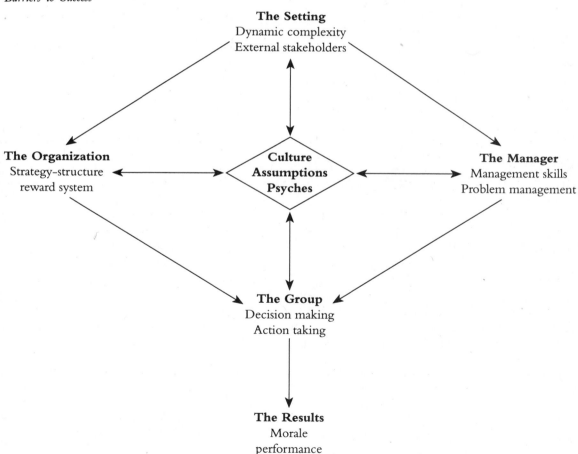

The Setting
Dynamic complexity
External stakeholders

The Organization
Strategy-structure
reward system

**Culture
Assumptions
Psyches**

The Manager
Management skills
Problem management

The Group
Decision making
Action taking

The Results
Morale
performance

of barriers to success that can be transformed into channels for success. The model consists of five broad categories representing the at-the-surface aspects of an organization along with three aspects that operate below the surface of experience. The five broad categories are the setting, the organization, the manager, the group, and the results. The three aspects at work below the surface are culture, assumptions, and psyches.

The setting. The broadest category of the Barriers to Success model is the setting. It includes every outside event and force that can affect the success of the organization. Any diagnosis that does not put the internal dynamics of the organization in the context of its external setting is treating the organization as if it were a simple machine—not a living, breathing entity that is in a symbiotic relationship with its environment. Moreover, the history of the organization—when and how it was founded and the various environmental obstacles it has had to overcome since then—helps in determining how the organization is likely to respond to the world today.

Two aspects of the setting deserve further discussion. *Dynamic complexity*—rapid change and interdependence in a global marketplace—is having an increasingly powerful impact on all organizations. Playing into this added complexity are *external stakeholders*—any individual, group, organization, or community that has some stake in what the focal organization does. Stakeholders vary according to the organization being studied. And new stakeholders can enter into the organization's setting at any time. For example, competitors with improved products, government agencies with new regulations, research groups developing new production methods, or new customers with different tastes may suddenly appear in an organization's arena. A critical diagnostic issue in assessing an organization's barriers to success is determining whether it anticipates the actions of its external stakeholders or merely reacts to their initiatives.

The organization. The formal organization's barriers to success can be diagnosed by examining its strategy-structure and reward system. *Strategy* refers to all the documents that indicate direction: statements of vision, mission, purpose, goals, and objectives. *Structure* refers to the way resources are organized into action: organization charts, policy statements, job descriptions, formal rules and regulations, and work procedures. The *reward system* includes all documented methods to attract and retain employees and, in particular, to motivate them to high levels of performance. The essential diagnostic issue is whether all these documented systems are barriers (or channels) to success: Does too much bureaucratic red tape strangle creative, innovative, and discretionary behavior? Are members asking for more clarity about their objectives and for more guidelines on how to perform their tasks?

The manager. As shown on the righthand side of the Barriers to Success model, managers can be diagnosed according to how well their styles and skills fit with the types of people and problems in the organization. Until recently, managers have been thought of primarily as decision makers—persons who must choose from a set of alternatives to arrive at an optimal or satisfactory solution. This works well if the alternatives are already determined and the rules for choosing among them are clear-cut. In a setting of dynamic complexity, however, the essential problem may not be clear, let alone the choices for solving it. Today's managers need to be problem managers, who must sense and define problems *before* they select and implement solutions. The critical diagnostic issue here is whether managers throughout the organization are applying the right skills for addressing complex problems.

Culture, assumptions, psyche. At the center of the Barriers to Success model, are aspects of the organization at work below the surface. Each of these aspects functions at a different level of depth.

Just below the surface, and thus easiest of the three to diagnose and manage, is culture. As the invisible force behind the tangibles and observables in an organization, culture is the social energy that moves the membership into action. Culture is defined as *shared* values, beliefs, expectations, and norms. Norms are easiest to define. They are the unwritten rules of the game: Don't disagree with your boss; don't rock the boat; don't share information with other groups. Often, work groups pressure their members to follow such dysfunctional norms out of habit. One consequence of this pressure is that culture—as manifested in norms of behavior—greatly affects how formal statements are interpreted and provides what written documents leave out. The fundamental diagnostic question, therefore, is this: Does the organization's culture support the behavior that is needed for organizational success today (or does it pressure members to live according to what worked yesterday)?

Assumptions—found at the next level of depth—are beliefs that are taken for granted to be true but that may turn out to be false under closer analysis. Underlying every decision and every action is a vast set of generally unstated and untested assumptions. Managers may well assume the following unstated beliefs are unquestionably true: No new competitors will enter the industry; the economy will steadily improve; the consumer will buy whatever the firm produces; employees will continue to accept the same working conditions. The key diagnostic question to be asked is whether the critical assumptions that affect all major business decisions are up to date, explicit, understood, and used by members throughout the organization.

Psyche, the third aspect at the center of the Barriers to Success model, operates at the deepest level of the organization. While the innermost qualities of the human mind and spirit cannot be changed in a short period of time, if at all, an accurate understanding of human nature is essential to manage organizations and solve problems. In essence, the assumptions that members make concerning the psyche—what people want, fear, resist, support, and defend—underlie the eventual success or failure of every decision and action. A useful diagnostic test is to find out whether managers are frequently surprised when their proposed solutions are not accepted by their employees—suggesting inaccurate assumptions about some aspect of their psyche.

The group. The lower part of the Barrier to Success model illustrates the central role that groups must play in organizational decision making and action taking. It also indicates the close link between the group and the results. While individuals do act on their own volition, today's organization requires multiple contributions from members of one or more groups to manage complex problems. The synergistic team approach will result in high-quality decisions *and* employee commitment to implement these decisions for organizational success.

As Exhibit 2 illustrates, the team approach will fail in most organizations where all the other barriers to success are still in place. If a manager does not use the proper styles and skills to manage complex problems, group decisions will be made by majority rule or by the dictates of the manager. If the culture pressures employees to withhold information in the interest of protecting their own turf, the quality of decisions will again be adversely affected. If the organization's strategy is rooted in false assumptions about the consumer and the firm's competitors, every group decision will be moving the organization in the wrong direction. If the organization's structure makes it difficult for members in different departments to meet and discuss important issues, the group will simply lack the expertise and information needed to make high-quality decisions. Furthermore, if the reward system encourages individual versus team efforts, members will not be motivated to commit themselves to the group decision-making process in the first place. Indeed, only if an organization is composed of well-functioning teams, with negligible barriers to success in every category, can it become a truly breakaway company in a competitive world.

These interrelated dynamics, as captured by the Barriers to Success model, show the variety of issues that arise again and again while diagnosing organizations. Naturally, the problems vary from one organization to the next. Nevertheless, an uncanny pattern has emerged in all the work I have done in organizations: Rarely do I find that teaching managers new skills about complex problems will by itself solve the organization's performance and morale problems. I have never encountered a case anywhere in the world in which only the culture lagged behind and there was an effective formal organization already in place with managers applying up-to-date skills. The culture problem has *always* been associated with problems in the organization, the group, and the manager as well. Organizations are interrelated sets of above-and below-the-surface problems and opportunities that must be considered and dealt with as whole systems.

Once all the interviews have been conducted, the consultants organize the variety of problems they have discovered by sorting them into the categories of the Barriers to Success model. This is in preparation for proposing how a specially tailored, five-track program can remove these barriers by building on the channels to success (the positive aspects of the organization that should be retained). The consultants prepare a report and present it first to the top managers. When the top managers have accepted the general diagnosis, it is time to discuss these findings with the entire membership. Top managers' convictions and willingness to present the diagnosis to the employees is critical, for it demonstrates managers' commitment to the plan.

Stage 3: Scheduling the Tracks

The next stage of planned change is scheduling the five tracks (culture, management skills, team-building, strategy-structure, and reward system). Scheduling involves (1) selecting the first unit to participate in the program and planning the spread of change to the remaining units and (2) selecting the methods (techniques, instruments, and procedures for bringing about

change) that will make up each of the five tracks into a timed sequence of activity to promote effective learning and change in each organizational unit. Once a plan for action has been formalized, managers, employees, and consultants will work together to apply it in the next stage: implementing the tracks.

The best approach for scheduling business units for planned change is to apply the changes to a *primary* business unit first. This will add credibility to the change program. Often managers will instead select a business unit isolated from the core business of the organization. Perhaps this represents a safe strategy: If the program fails, the whole organization is hardly affected. If the program *is* successful, however, the other business units will not regard the pilot project as a relevant example of what they should be doing. If the intent is to spread change throughout the organization, units should be chosen that are critical to the success of the whole enterprise—even though this necessarily involves greater risk. This risk, however, should be reason enough for top executives to do whatever it takes to make the program a success.

A plan is then developed that specifies the ways in which change can be spread throughout the organization. This plan should outline not only the order in which the remaining units will be scheduled but also the supporting techniques and procedures that will be used once the pilot project is underway (and as other units begin the process)—for example, the rest of the organization can be kept informed of what is taking place and why. Some managers or members from the pilot project might be temporarily transferred to the next unit to help facilitate the changes. Moreover, various rewards and perquisites might be offered to units participating in the program to convey its importance.

The five tracks, in all cases, are scheduled in the prescribed order. The first three tracks (culture, management skills, and team building) adjust the behavioral infrastructure of the organization—the blood and guts of how people behave toward one another on the job. The last two tracks (strategy structure and reward system) adjust the organization's tangible features—the documents, technologies, systems, and resources that guide people's behavior toward an agreed-on mission. Without first developing an adaptive *inner* organization, any adjustments to the outer organization would be cosmetic and, therefore, short-lived.

What does each track do for the organization? The culture track enhances trust, communication, information sharing, and willingness to change among members—the conditions that must exist before any other improvement effort can succeed. The management-skills track provides all management personnel with new ways of coping with complex problems and hidden assumptions. The team-building track infuses the new culture and updated management skills into each work unit—thereby instilling cooperation organizationwide so that complex problems can be addressed with all the expertise and information available. The strategy-structure track develops either a completely new or a revised strategic plan for the firm and then aligns divisions, departments, work groups, jobs, and all resources with the new strategic direction. The reward-system track establishes a performance-based reward system that sustains all improvements by officially sanctioning the new culture, the use of updated management skills, and cooperative team efforts within and among all work groups.

While the reward-system track is often viewed as the "bottom line" for employees, conducting this last track is futile if all the other tracks have not accomplished their intended outcomes—thereby illustrating just how critical it is to schedule (and implement) the five tracks in sequence *and* in total. Without an adaptive culture, members will not believe that rewards are tied to performance. Instead, they will believe that it is useless to work hard and do well. Similarly, if managers do not have the skills required to conduct performance appraisal, any well-intentioned reward system will be thwarted. If the work groups in the organization do not tolerate individual differences, it will be most difficult to distinguish high and low performers—which is what every pay-for-performance system must do. Furthermore, if the strategy and structure of the organization are not developed and aligned properly, the reward system cannot measure performance objectively as close to the individual level as possible. The latter condition is essential to make the pay-for-performance link a reality in everyone's eyes.

While all five tracks are *always* relevant to planned change in today's competitive world, what makes each application of the program different are the various methods used in each of the five tracks. Just as the diagnosis varies for each organizational unit, so does the choice of method to address each problem. In some cases the management-skills track will include material or leadership styles, conflict-handling modes, and ways of minimizing defensive communication. If the managers have already acquired these skills, management training moves directly to teaching methods for managing complex problems. Clearly, managers and consultants should be aware of the diversity of methods that exist so they can choose the ones that best fit the problems in each organizational unit.

Exhibit 3 provides a sample timeframe for scheduling the five tracks. The horizontal line for each track signifies an ongoing series of off-site meetings (in a workshop environment) and on-site meetings (organized at the workplace) set up to pursue the topic in question (for example, cultural change). As the exhibit shows, a track does not have to be completed before the next track is initiated. The guiding principle is that the earlier track should have established the conditions necessary for the next track to succeed.

Scheduling the five tracks also requires numerous choices regarding personnel. Who will be involved in each track? Typically, the culture track includes every work group in the organization (or business unit). As might be expected,

Exhibit 3

Scheduling the five tracks

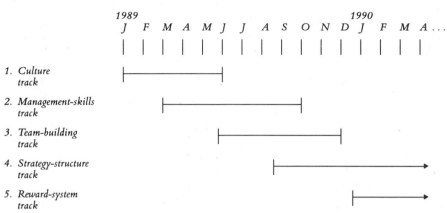

ensuring every member's involvement in workshop sessions is the only way to change something as ingrained as corporate culture. Since, in most cases, an open and trusting culture will not be evident in the organization for several months to come (at least not until the team-building track is initiated), every work group is subdivided into peer groups for each workshop in the culture track. Generally, these peer groups are formed by separating superiors from their subordinates, since these subgroups provide the best opportunity for candid discussions.

Scheduling the management-skills track usually involves all the managers in the organization (or designated business units)—from first-line supervisors through the chief executive officer. Sometimes, key professional personnel and potential managers are included in the interest of career development. Just as in the culture track, however, all group discussions take place in peer groups—to foster open communication before the culture has changed.

Scheduling the team-building track brings managers back together with their subordinates in their formal organizational units. This is the only way to ensure that the new knowledge gained from the workshop sessions can be transferred directly to the job. If, however, the managers and employees are brought together too early, before the new culture and skills have been internalized, almost everyone will fall back into old routines. It does take some time—in a relatively safe environment—for people to learn new behavior and skills before they can approach emotionally charged situations in new ways.

Scheduling the last two tracks, strategy-structure and reward-system, generally involves the formation of two separate task forces of about 25 persons each. One task force addresses strategy-structure problems that were revealed during the diagnostic stage, while the other task force addresses reward-system problems. The people chosen for these special missions not only represent all levels and areas in the company, but they also have demonstrated leadership during the prior tracks of the program. Following their deliberations, these two task forces present their recommendations to top management for improving the organization's strategy structure and reward system. Subsequently, these groups play a key role in helping to implement the recommended changes.

Stage 4: Implementing the Tracks

It is one thing to schedule the five tracks but quite another to adjust the schedule as the tracks are being implemented. The plan *never* takes place exactly as intended—there are always surprises. Human nature and human systems do not lend themselves to an entirely predictable path. Besides, if people feel they are being programmed in any way, they may purposely do something illogical or unexpected just to show how independent they really are.

The key issue throughout implementation, therefore, is flexibility. As the schedule is implemented, the managers and consultants must look for cues, take suggestions and, in short, adapt. For example, special requests will be made for counseling sessions, feedback sessions for staff meetings, additional culture sessions, more management-skills training, and so forth. In each case, managers and consultants must consider the request and respond according to their principles and their sense of what will work.

The detailed methods—techniques, instruments, and procedures—for implementing each of the five tracks in a flexible, adaptive manner are provided in my book: *Managing Beyond the Quick Fix.* The following discussion, therefore, only presents some general approaches for managing the implementation process.

A "shadow" track (running parallel to all the five tracks) is recommended to ensure the successful implementation of the program; this track places primary responsibility for the program on the shoulders of the "shadow" group. This group of approximately 10 to 15 employees, mostly senior executives but also members of other levels and areas in the organization, meets regularly to monitor the program and discover ways of improving the whole process of implementation. The shadow group is encouraged to be as proactive and imaginative as possible in making sure that the program succeeds.

A fundamental issue that always arises during implementation is whether employees will take personal responsibility for change. Even after having participated in several workshops on culture and management skills, employees often keep waiting for something to happen: "My boss still doesn't keep me informed of what goes on." "The other groups still don't cooperate with us." "My staff still doesn't complete work on time." "When will this organization change?"

Julian Rotter's distinction between internal and external control is exceedingly useful in challenging employees to look at themselves, rather than point the finger at others. *External control* is when people believe that what happens to them is determined by outside forces (luck, politics, other people's behavior). *Internal control* is when people believe that what happens to them is determined by what they do (their own decisions, attitudes, behavior). Naturally, internal control helps people take responsibility for change; external control shifts all the attention to someone else.

Who *is* the source of organizational change? Discussions of this question, usually during the first two tracks of the program, translate into action when they are supplemented by this exercise: First, each person lists the things he or she has done differently since the improvement program began. Then each employee shares this list with the rest of the work group members. Next each member asks co-workers if they have witnessed what he claims. If they have not observed these changes, the member must be prepared to act on his good intentions—to demonstrate internal control and personal responsibility for change. Gradually, employees begin to talk about their experiences in a very different way from before: "I've convinced my boss that I can do a better job if I know more about her priorities." "I've spent more time getting to know the people in other departments." "I now tell my staff the reasons why I need something done on a given date." "This organization is really changing!"

After a number of months go by, it will become increasingly apparent that the employees have internalized the desired behavior. Now the new ways are enacted quite automatically as the new behavior becomes easier to put into everyday practice. At a certain point—typically sometime during the team-building track when the new culture and skills become internalized—the hump is crossed and the old gives way to the new. So long as these behavioral changes are subsequently guided and rewarded by the formal organization (the last two tracks), continuous adaptability will have become ingrained in the organization—for both present and future members.

How long will the process of implementation take? One can expect the first cycle of implementing all five tracks to take anywhere from one to five years. A period of less than one year might work for a small division in which the barriers to success are minimal. A program taking more than five years might be necessary for a large, older organization that must break with its past in practically every way. If the program were to take more than 10 years, I would assume there was insufficient commitment over this time period—and hence no momentum for change to prevail.

Stage 5: Evaluating the Results

One reason for evaluating the results of the program is to improve the implementation process for the remaining units. The shadow group should keep a close watch on the pilot project so new insights and methods can be adopted as one unit after another embarks on the path of planned change.

Planned change is never complete. Thus a second reason for evaluation is to discover barriers that still need attention. An evaluation might reveal, for example, the need to improve the culture in a few of the more troublesome work groups. Or, if new managers enter an organizational unit after most of the program has been implemented, additional skill-training sessions can be conducted to bring the new managers up to speed with the rest of the membership. Typically, cycling through the stages of planned

change a second or third time, as guided by the evaluation stage, is a process of fine tuning (incremental change), rather than corporate transformation (revolutionary change).

Both the first and second types of evaluation can be accomplished by engaging in another round of face-to-face interviews. If diagnostic interviews were the most effective way to learn about the organization's barriers (and channels) at the beginning of the program, the same approach can be applied again to assess what could have been done differently and to discover what still needs to be done to remove any remaining barriers to success. I find it useful to have internal consultants conduct these evaluation interviews, rather than the external consultants who conducted the diagnostic interviews.

The third purpose for evaluation is to determine whether the program has achieved the intended results: improved organizational success. From the viewpoint of stakeholders—consumers, stockholders, suppliers, federal agencies, the community—one usually can suggest some "hard" outcome measures: returns on investments, earnings per share, profit, sales, number of clients served, market share, budget increases, number of patents and new products, new contracts and orders, productivity gains, and so on. Making a before-and-after comparison on any of these measures should provide a solid basis for assessing the program's impact. If the whole endeavor was successful, the differences in these measures should be evident—or so the argument goes.

While these bottom-line measures certainly can be convincing, one has to recognize their limitations. One should not overlook the time lag between decisions and actions on the one hand and performance on the other. Some of the bottom-line measures will not be affected until months or years after a key decision has been made. Improved decision making that results in new approaches to product development is an example of a result that will take years to be felt. If the before-and-after comparisons are made right after the improvement program has concluded, one cannot expect external stakeholders to notice any observable differences. Ironically, if such before-and-after comparisons were to suggest significant improvements (or declines), they probably would be spurious. Only if these measurements are made over a long enough period of time—a period in which *true* effects can be expected—can one take the results of such an "objective" evaluation seriously.

The New Bottom Line

While the five stages of planned change are certainly complex, so are the problems that this program is designed to resolve. A completely integrated program must be able to affect every controllable variable in the organization, not just one or two. At the same time, if the whole program is not initiated properly with top management's support and if the organization's problems are not diagnosed correctly, the program cannot produce its potential benefits. Moreover, the program's implementation must be *integrated* and *flexible*. Attempting to shortcut a program for planned change would do the field of organizational development—and the organization in question—a great disservice.

Selected Bibliography

This article is adapted from *Managing Beyond the Quick Fix* by Ralph H. Kilmann (Jossey-Bass, 1989). Other books by Kilmann that contain various approaches to large-scale organizational change include *Gaining Control of the Corporate Culture* (Jossey-Bass, 1985) and *Corporate Transformation* (Jossey-Bass, 1988).

Related discussions on the general topic of systemwide change can be found in *Organization Change and Development: A Systems View* by Michael Beer (Goodyear, 1980); *The Planning of Change* by Warren G. Bennis, Kenneth D. Benne, and Robert Chin (Holt, Rinehart & Winston, 1976); *Organization Development: Behavioral Science Interventions for Organi-* zation Improvement by Wendell L. French and Charles H. Bell (Prentice Hall, 1978); *Managing Strategic Change: Technical, Political, and Cultural Dynamics* by Noel M. Tichy (John Wiley & Sons, 1983). Perhaps one of the most significant contributions on the topic of large-scale change is Richard Beckhard and Rubin Harris's *Organizational Transitions: Managing Complex Change* (Addison-Wesley, 1977).

Regarding the five stages of planned change, the following sources are recommended for further reading. The first stage, initiating the program, is typically spearheaded by a "transformational leader" or a small group of key advocates of organizational improvement as described in "The Leadership Challenge—A Call for the Transformational Leader," by Noel M. Tichy and David Ulrich (*Sloan Management Review*, Fall 1984). The second stage, diagnosing the problems, is examined very systematically in *Organizational Diagnosis* by Harry Levinson (Harvard University Press, 1972). The third stage, scheduling interventions (with the intention of spreading change), is addressed most explicitly by Richard Walton's "The Diffusion of New Work Structures: Explaining Why Success Didn't Take" (*Organizational Dynamics*, Winter 1975). The fourth stage, implementing the interventions, is documented most thoroughly in *Organization Development and Change* by Edgar Huse (West, 1980), as supported by the crucial ingredient of assuming personal responsibility for change: "External Control and Internal Control," by Julian B. Rotter (*Psychology Today*, June 1971). The fifth stage, evaluating the results, is explored in classic form by C. Weiss in *Evaluation Research* (Prentice Hall, 1972).

Regarding each of the five tracks (the core of the completely integrated program), the following sources are recommended for further reading. For the culture track, see Robert F. Allen and Charlotte Kraft's *The Organizational Unconscious: How to Create the Corporate Culture You Want and Need* (Prentice Hall, 1982). For the management skills track, see Richard O. Mason and Ian I. Mitroff's *Challenging Strategic Planning Assumptions: Theory, Cases, and Techniques* (John Wiley & Sons, 1981). For the team-building track, see William G. Dyer's *Team Building Issues and Alternatives* (Addison-Wesley, 1977). For the strategy-structure track, see Jay Galbraith's *Designing Complex Organizations* (Addison-Wesley, 1973). For the reward system track, see Edward E. Lawler's *Pay and Organizational Development* (Addison-Wesley, 1981).

III   Basic OD Interventions

Part III is central to this volume because it includes fairly detailed descriptions of the OD interventions that tend to be widely used in contemporary OD practice. Team building, intergroup activities, survey feedback, and other interventions are described. Although diagnostic activities underlie all of these interventions, diagnosis is so fundamental that additional attention is paid to it.

The introduction to Part III first defines intervention, then looks at different ways of classifying interventions, and then looks at diagnosis as a special, but pervasive, kind of intervention in OD. A discussion of the essays in the Part III sections then follows.

A Definition of "Intervention"

Argyris defines "intervention" as follows: "To intervene is to enter into an ongoing system of relationships, to come between or among persons, groups, or objects for the purpose of helping them."[1] More specifically related to OD, the term *OD interventions* refers to the range of planned, programmatic activities clients and consultants participate in during the course of an organization development program. Largely these are diagnostic and problem-solving activities that ordinarily occur with the assistance of a consultant who is not a regular member of the particular system or subsystem culture. However, many of the activities become absorbed by the client system as the process unfolds.

---

[1] Chris Argyris, *Intervention Theory and Method: A Behavioral Science View* (Reading, MA: Addison-Wesley Publishing, 1970), p. 15.

Classifications of OD Interventions

There are a number of ways of classifying OD interventions, depending on the dimensions one wishes to emphasize.[2] One classification method is based on the *type of causal mechanism* hypothesized to underlie the particular technique used. For example, feedback, which refers to receiving new data about oneself, others, or group dynamics, is assumed to have potential for constructive change if it is not too threatening. Techniques for providing more *awareness of changing organizational norms* are assumed to result in modification of behavior, attitudes, and values. *Increased interaction* and communication may effect changes in attitudes and behavior. Homans, for example, suggests that increased interaction leads to positive sentiments,[3] and Murphy refers to "tunnel vision" or "autism," which develops in individuals and groups in isolation.[4] *Confrontation,* a surfacing and addressing of differences in perceptions, values, attitudes, feelings, or norms, is assumed to help remove obstacles to effective interaction if handled in constructive ways. *Education* is designed to upgrade (1) knowledge and concepts, (2) outmoded beliefs and attitudes, and/or (3) skills, and has long been accepted as a change mechanism.

Depth of intervention is another useful dimension for classifying interventions. In an essay by Roger Harrison that appears in Part V, interventions can be distinguished in terms of the accessibility of the data and the degree of individuality or self-exposure involved. For example, we see a family T-group involving a work group and formal leader ("family" group) as a deeper intervention than a task-oriented team-building (problem-solving) workshop with such a group. The use of a collage may be a deeper intervention than an interview that includes general questions about how things are going in a unit.

A different approach to classifying OD interventions is provided by Robert Blake and Jane Mouton when they list the major interventions in terms of their *underlying themes.*[5] They describe the following kinds of interventions: (1) a *discrepancy intervention,* which calls attention to a contradiction in action or attitudes that then leads to exploration; (2) a *theory intervention,* in which behavioral science knowledge and theory are used to explain present behavior and assumptions underlying the behavior; (3) a *procedural intervention,* which represents a critiquing of how something is being done to determine whether the best methods are being used; (4) a *relationship intervention,* which focuses attention on interpersonal relationships (particularly ones where there are strong negative feelings) and surfaces the issues for exploration and possible resolution; (5) an *experimentation in-*

---

[2] For a more detailed discussion of several of these dimensions, see Wendell French and Cecil Bell, *Organization Development: Behavioral Science Interventions for Organization Improvement,* 4th ed. (Englewood Cliffs, NJ: Prentice Hall, 1990), chap. 9.

[3] George C. Homans, *The Human Group* (New York: Harcourt Brace Jovanovich, 1950).

[4] G. Murphy, "The Freeing of Intelligence," *Psychological Bulletin* 42 (1945), pp. 1–19.

[5] Robert R. Blake and Jane Srygley Mouton, *The Managerial Grid* (Houston: Gulf Publishing, 1964), pp. 282–83.

tervention, in which two different action plans are tested for their consequences before a final decision on one is made; (6) a *dilemma intervention,* in which an imposed or emergent dilemma is used to force close examination of the possible choices involved and the assumptions underlying them; (7) a *perspective intervention,* which draws attention away from immediate actions and demands and allows a look at historical background, context, and future objectives in order to assess whether or not the actions are still on target; (8) an *organization structure intervention,* which calls for examination and evaluation of structural causes for organizational ineffectiveness; and (9) a *cultural intervention,* which examines traditions, precedents, and practices—the fabric of the organization's culture—in a direct, focused approach. These are largely process consultation interventions and they tend to occur within the context of a broader intervention, such as team building or in intergroup activities.

The *time and comprehensiveness* involved in the intervention can be another way of distinguishing between interventions. Some interventions, such as the use of a simple questionnaire, may take only minutes; others, such as the Role Analysis Technique may take two hours relative to one job incumbent. Team building of different varieties may be an intervention taking place over one to three or more days and will include within it a variety of brief interventions. It should be added that successful interventions will probably always have a broader context; even the simplest of interventions needs to occur in the setting of some prework, which serves to make the intervention acceptable to the client, and needs follow-up to maximize the odds of success.

Another way of classifying OD interventions, although somewhat spurious, might be in terms of the emphasis on *task* versus *process.* Some team-building activities, for example, may have a high focus on interpersonal and group processes, such as the quality of communications or the dynamics of informal leadership and influence processes occurring in the group. Other activities might have a more task-related orientation, such as goal setting or the reallocating of responsibilities. This dichotomy of task and process can be somewhat misleading, however, because they are highly interrelated.

Finally, another way of classifying OD interventions, and a way we will use, is in terms of the *size and complexity of the client group.* For example, the client group may consist of *(a) individuals, (b) dyads or triads, (c) a self-managed team, (d) an intact work team,* including the formal leader, *(e) intergroup configurations* (two or more interfacing units), or *(f) the total organization.* As we move from interventions with individuals, to dyads, to group, to intergroups and then to the total organization, the interdependencies and the number of dimensions to be concerned about obviously increases. For example, an intervention which is successful in dealing with two groups that are in conflict must also successfully deal with the intragroup communications problems and conflict that become manifest. That is one reason why assistance to teams in helping them with internal problems and in increasing their interpersonal and group skills is usually a wise step before intergroup activities are undertaken.

A simple classification scheme based on the size and complexity of the client group is shown in Figure 1. Some interventions appear in more than one category because they have utility with more than one type of client group. What the table does not show are the many "mini" interventions used by the OD consultant within the context of broader interventions like team building, or even within techniques used in team building (e.g., the Role Analysis Technique)—that is, there are interventions within interventions. For example, this table says nothing about the consultant's ability to point out a discrepancy, or to provide support, or to clarify, or to use subgroups, or to have data made visible on newsprint, or, for that matter, to know when to use their interventions. (A number of these professional skills are discussed in Part V.)

This classification scheme generally underlies the organization of Part III. The first essay is on T-groups, which are vehicles for training individuals (usually in a stranger-group setting), and then the next several essays are on team interventions. Part III then moves to intergroup interventions and then to more comprehensive interventions, such as survey feedback and the use of the collateral

FIGURE 1

Typology of interventions based on the size and complexity of the client group

Client Group	Types of Interventions
Interventions designed to improve the effectiveness of *individuals* (although most are conducted in group settings).	Life and career-planning activities. Role analysis technique. Coaching and counseling. T-group (sensitivity training). Training to increase technical skills, relationship skills, group process skills, or decision-making, problem-solving, planning, goal-setting skills. Grid OD phase 1.* Transactional analysis. Behavior modeling.
Interventions designed to improve the effectiveness of *dyads/triads*.	Process consultation. Third-party peacemaking. Third-party peacemaking. Transactional analysis.
Interventions designed to improve the effectiveness of *teams and groups*.	Interviews or questionnaires. Team building. Responsibility charting. Survey feedback. Process consultation. Role negotiation. Role analysis technique. Collages. "Start-up" team-building activities. Training in decision making, problem solving, planning, goal setting in group settings. Grid OD phase 2. Appreciative inquiry.

organization. At the end of Part III the readings take us back again to teams—in this case self-managed teams—or, as Thomas Cummings calls them, "self-regulating work groups." Essays in Part IV will deal with Total Quality Management (TQM) and how this broad, continuous improvement process can be linked to such matters as self-managed teams, gainsharing, quality circles, and team building.

Notes on Diagnosis

As will be evident in the essays that follow, diagnostic activities are pervasive aspects of the collaborative action research model that underlies most organization development interventions. Basically, to diagnose is to identify the underlying forces or conditions giving rise to the present state of affairs. Diagnosis may pertain broadly to the present state of a system, including the many positive forces giving rise to desirable outcomes, or it may be narrower in the sense of focusing on the dysfunctional forces that are producing undesirable outcomes, or it may focus on changes in the state of the system over time.

FIGURE 1

(continued)

Client Group	*Types of Interventions*
Interventions designed to improve the effectiveness of *intergroup relations.*	Interviews or questionnaires. Intergroup activities. Organizational mirroring (three or more groups). Process consultation. Third-party peacemaking at group level. Grid OD phase 3. Survey feedback.
Interventions designed to improve the effectiveness of the *total organization.*	Interviews or questionnaires. Sensing. "Confrontation" meetings (Beckhard). Team building at all levels. Appreciative inquiry. Strategic planning activities. Grid OD phases 4, 5, 6. Survey feedback. OD strategy planning. Quality of Work Life programs. Total Quality Management programs.

* For a discussion of the Managerial Grid® approach to OD, see Robert R. Blake and Jane Srygley Mouton, *Consultation* (Reading, Mass.: Addison-Wesley Publishing, 1976), chap. 27.

SOURCE: Modified from Wendell L. French and Cecil H. Bell, Jr., *Organization Development: Behavioral Science Interventions for Organization Improvement,* 4th ed. (Englewood Cliffs, NJ: Prentice Hall, 1990, p. 122).

Three Types of Theories

As Ronald Lippitt has stated, "Every consultant has a cluster of ideas, or a set of concepts, which guide his perception of 'what exists' and 'what is going on' when he comes in contact with a particular group or organization"; this *descriptive-analytic theory,* to whatever degree of refinement, assists the consultant in understanding and interpreting the complexities of group or organization functioning. Lippitt goes on to say that every consultant has, in addition, some form of *diagnostic theory* that assists in identifying symptoms of disturbances in the system and what some of the probable causes might be. A diagnostic theory, to Lippitt then, is a set of notions that relate more to the dysfunctional or anomalous aspects of organizational life than does descriptive analytic theory.[6] We might add that OD consultants also need some form of *change theory* that assists in understanding the consequences of the interaction of various forces over time. This would be congruent with Lippitt's ideas. Thus organizational diagnosis stems from some theoretical base, however partially or completely formulated.

An illustration of a descriptive analytic theory (perhaps combined with a diagnostic theory) is the theory underlying the "Survey of Organizations" questionnaire developed by the Institute for Social Research at the University of Michigan. The survey is based, as Taylor and Bowers describe, on a "metatheory of organizational system functioning" as presented by Rensis Likert and others in various writings. Part of the theory is represented by a model, which includes the notions of causal variables, intervening variables, and end-result variables. Questionnaire categories and items are related to these broader concepts and to the underlying theory.[7]

Dimensions to Consider in Diagnosis

In addition to the importance of the consultant having descriptive, analytic, and diagnostic theories, a number of other dimensions of diagnosis are important for the consultant to consider. A description of seven such dimensions follows.

Timing of the diagnostic activities is a significant dimension. For example, it is one thing to collect and analyze organizational climate data and then to develop a strategy for how to use it, but quite another to gather data about the perceived usefulness and timeliness of doing a climate survey in the first place. Much time (and therefore resources) can be wasted if organizational participants are not prepared to work with the data.

Extent of participation is a key aspect of diagnosis. Who, in a preliminary way, decided that diagnosis should take place? Who decided how it should be done? Which people were systematically involved in supplying data, and further, in an-

---

[6] Ronald Lippitt, "Dimensions of the Consultant's Job," in *The Planning of Change,* 1st ed., ed. Warren G. Bennis, Kenneth D. Benne, and Robert Chin (New York: Holt, Rinehart & Winston, 1961), p. 157.

[7] James C. Taylor and David G. Bowers, *Survey of Organizations* (Ann Arbor: Institute for Social Research, University of Michigan, 1972), pp. 1–6.

alyzing and describing the dynamics revealed by the data? One person? Two people? The top team? The top team plus others? One or more people in conjunction with a consultant? All of the members of the system or subsystem? Customers of the system? One of the underlying assumptions in OD is the efficacy of participative problem identification and diagnosis in contrast to unilateral problem identification and diagnosis.

The dimension of *confidentiality,* or individual-anonymous versus group surfacing of data, has important facets. In the early stages of an OD effort, when trust between group members may be low and their feedback skills inadequate, the situation may call for individual interviews, with responses kept anonymous and only reported to the group in terms of themes. As trust is earned and grows, people can become more open in terms of surfacing attitudes, feelings, and perceptions about organizational dynamics in group settings.

The degree to which there was *preselection of variables versus an emergent selection of variables* to be considered is another important dimension. The University of Michigan version of survey feedback utilizes the questionnaire, "Survey of Organizations," which taps some 19 dimensions subsumed under three broad categories: leadership, organizational climate, and satisfaction. Another approach, Grid OD, depends heavily in early phases on an analysis of leadership style using a questionnaire called the "Managerial Grid." This analysis focuses on two dimensions: concern for people and concern for production. On the other hand, data gathering can be more emergent with less structuring of questions. Some OD consultants will use interviews that are structured only to the extent that two or three general questions are asked at the outset, such as: What things are going well in the organization? What problems do you see? Follow-up probes are then used to pursue important issues uncovered.

The extent to which data gathering and analysis are isolated events in contrast to being part of a long-range strategy is also important. One usual assumption in OD efforts is that diagnostic activities should be part of an overall plan. Diagnostic activities lead to action programs that in turn call for diagnostic activities—this is the action research model. Diagnostic activities that are not part of any such plan or that are prompted by someone's whim to know "what they are thinking" may produce resentment and resistance and can seriously hinder attempts to get valid data from system members.

The nature of the target population in both preliminary and later systematic data gathering and analysis is also a key dimension. The size and nature of the target group can affect the acceptability of the diagnostic process, what kinds of interdependencies can be examined, and what kinds of issues can be worked successfully. The data-providing group can be different from the data-analyzing group, of course, but in OD, suppliers of the information usually work with their own data in intact work teams.

And finally, *the type of technique used* obviously has a number of important ramifications. By type we mean questionnaire-versus-interview techniques, individual-versus-group surfacing of data, or other categories of techniques that can be differentiated in major ways. We have already discussed how the type of instrument, such as the Survey of Organizations, can structure the responses. As another example of the importance of technique selection, an interview can be used for trust building as well as collecting data; a face-to-face conversation is a better vehicle for building a relationship than sending someone a questionnaire. Concerns can be expressed and responded to, questions can be answered, assurances can be provided as to how the data will be used, and so on. As another example of the importance of the type of technique selected, giving diagnostic assignments to subgroups in a workshop setting can be a powerful diagnostic technique. But the way these groups are constituted—for example, heterogeneous versus homogeneous in terms of rank, position, or aggressiveness-reticence—can be crucial to the amount and candor of the data generated.

Elliot Aronson

Broadly speaking, the term *T-group* refers to the more conservative, more traditional group, in which the primary emphasis is on verbal behavior and the group discussions are almost exclusively confined to the here and now. It is associated with East Coast centers, principally the National Training Laboratories in Bethel, Maine. The term *encounter group* is most often associated with the more radical wing of the human potential movement; the activities of such groups often include such nonverbal procedures as touching, body movement, dance, and massage. Although they tend to be associated with such West Coast centers as Esalen Institute, encounter groups may be found throughout the United States. In recent years, many of the more traditional T-groups have incorporated some of these nonverbal procedures, but they still remain relatively conservative. I will use the term *T-group* throughout this chapter; the groups that I will be describing are more toward the traditional end of the spectrum, although they may use some of the more recent innovations usually associated with the encounter group.

The first T-group was an accident. But, like most productive accidents, it occurred in the presence of a brilliant and creative person who was quick to appreciate the importance and potential utility of what he had stumbled upon. In 1946, Kurt Lewin, perhaps the greatest innovator and theorist in the brief history of social psychology, was asked to conduct a workshop to explore the use of small group discussions as a way of addressing some of the social problems of the day. The participants were educators, public officials, and social scientists. They met during

Source: From Elliot Aronson, *The Social Animal,* 3rd ed., W. H. Freeman and Company, Copyright © 1976, 1980.

the day in small groups. The small groups were observed by several of Lewin's graduate students, who met in the evenings to discuss their interpretation of the dynamics of the group discussions they had observed during the day.

One evening, a few of the participants asked if they could sit in and listen while the graduate students discussed their observations. Lewin was a little embarrassed by the request, but, much to the surprise of his graduate students, he allowed the visitors to sit in. As it happened, one of the educators joined the group just as the observers were discussing her behavior and interpreting an episode that she had participated in the preceding morning. She became very agitated and said that the observer's interpretation was all wrong. She then proceeded to give her version of the episode. The discussion proved very exciting. The next night, all 50 of the participants showed up and gleefully joined the discussion, frequently disagreeing with the observations and interpretations of the trained observers. The session was both lively and illuminating.

Lewin and his students were quick to grasp the significance of that event: A group engaged in a problem-solving discussion can benefit enormously by taking time out to discuss its own dynamics or "group process" without special training as observers. Indeed, the participants themselves are much better observers of their own process because each is privy to his or her own intentions—something that is not easily available to outside observers, no matter how astute and well trained they are. After a time, what evolved was the agendaless group: The group could meet with maximum benefit if it had no formal agenda and no problems to discuss other than its own dynamics.

Interest in T-groups has grown rapidly since 1946. They are conducted in all sections of the country, and their members include individuals from all walks of life. There have been specialized groups consisting solely of college students, high-school teachers, corporation presidents, police officers, members of the State Department, and delinquents; there have been groups for married couples, unmarried couples, and families; there have been confrontation groups of street people and police, blacks and whites, and managers and their employees. But most groups have been heterogeneous—the same group might contain a lawyer, a laborer, a nun, a housewife, a bank teller, a college student, and a smattering of male and female business executives, teachers, and drop-outs. T-groups have become a phenomenon of the 1960s and 1970s—they have received wide (and often sensational) publicity; they have been treated with an uncritical, cultish, almost religious zeal by some of their proponents; and they have been castigated by the right-wing as an instrument of the devil, as a subversive form of brainwashing that is eating away at the fabric and soul of the nation. In my judgment, sensitivity-training groups are neither the panacea nor the menace that they frequently are made out to be. When properly used, they can be enormously useful as a means of learning communication skills, increasing self-awareness, and enriching human relations. With this in mind, the distinguished psychotherapist Carl Rogers characterized the T-group as "the most significant social invention of the century," and the social historian William Thompson considered the T-group "a rehearsal for the complete transformation of human nature and civilization." When abused, they can be a waste of time—or, in extreme cases, they might even provide people with some very painful experiences, whose effects can persist long beyond the termination of the group.

The primary focus in this chapter will be on the sensitivity-training group as an instrument of communication. Although there are all kinds of groups, I will discuss only the traditional T-groups. I will attempt to describe them from within and from without and discuss what happens in a group, what gets learned, and what the inherent problems and dangers are.

The Content and Process of a T-group

A T-group experience is educational, but educational in a different way from what most of us have grown accustomed to. It is different both in the *content* of the material that is learned and in the *process* by which the learning takes place.

The Content: What Gets Learned.   Generally, individuals in a T-group learn things about themselves and their relations with other people. It can be said that, in a college psychology course, I learn how people behave; in a T-group, I learn how *I* behave. But I learn much more than that: I also learn how others see me, how my behavior affects them, and how I am affected by other people.

The primary purpose of T-groups is to learn how to communicate effectively, to listen carefully, and to understand one's own feelings and those of other people. In addition, many people are motivated to participate in a T-group not only to learn to communicate but because they believe that there may be something missing in their lives. A person may feel alienated from other people; he may feel that life is going by too quickly; he may feel that he wants something more out of life than waking up in the morning, eating breakfast, going to work, coming home, watching television, and going to sleep. In short, many people are searching for greater self-awareness and greater enrichment of their lives through these groups. This does not mean that a person has to be in the middle of an existential crisis in order to join a group; many people join because they have specific confusions and are searching for specific answers: "Why do I have trouble getting along with my children (or my employees, or the opposite sex)?" "Why do other people make friends easily, while I tend to be alone?" "Why do I have difficulty opening up to people?" "What is there about people that makes them so untrustworthy?" "How can I handle my anger?" "What do I do that turns people off?" "Why is it that, when I meet a guy, all he wants to do is take me to bed?"

Interacting with other people in a competently led T-group *can,* and frequently *does,* provide individuals with answers to specific questions like these. But, more generally, the T-group provides the first step toward the achievement of a number of goals and forms the basis for the clarification of a wide range of confusions. Among the major goals of a T-group are:

1. To develop ways of communicating that are clear, straight, and nonattributional.

2. To develop a spirit of inquiry and a willingness to examine one's own behavior and to experiment with one's role in the world.

3. To develop an awareness of more things about more people.

4. To develop greater authenticity in interpersonal relations; to feel freer to be oneself and not feel compelled to play a role.

5. To develop the ability to act in a collaborative and mutually dependent manner with peers, superiors, and subordinates, rather than in an authoritarian or submissive manner.

6. To develop the ability to resolve conflicts and disputes through problem solving, rather than through coercion or manipulation.

The Process: How Things Are Learned. The single most important distinguishing characteristic of a T-group is the method by which people learn. Again, a T-group is not a seminar or a lecture course. Although a great deal of learning *does* occur, it's not the kind of learning

that can be easily transmitted verbally in a traditional teacher-student relationship. It is learning through doing, learning through experience. In a T-group, people learn by trying things out, by getting in touch with their feelings, and by expressing those feelings to other people, either verbally or nonverbally. "Trying things out" not only helps individuals understand their own feelings, it also allows them the opportunity of benefitting from learning about how their behavior affects other people. If I want to know whether or not people find me to be a cold, aloof, unemotional person, I simply *behave*—and then others in the group will tell me how my behavior makes them feel.

An implicit assumption underlying these groups is that very little can be gained if someone tells us how we are *supposed* to feel, how we are *supposed* to behave, or what we are *supposed* to do with our lives. A parallel assumption is that a great deal can be gained if we understand *what* we're feeling, if we understand the kinds of interpersonal events that trigger various kinds of feelings, if we understand how our behavior is read and understood by other people, and if we understand the wide variety of options available to us. The role of the T-group leader is not to present us with answers but simply to help establish an atmosphere of trust and intensive inquiry in which we are willing to look closely at our own behavior and the behavior of others.

It is in this sense that a T-group is not a therapy group. The leader does not attempt to interpret our motives or probe into our experiences outside the group; in addition, he tends to discourage other group members from doing this. Instead, he simply encourages us to behave and to react to the behavior of others.

The Cultural Island.   As we race through life, we are frequently distracted. Thoughts about the work we must do compete for our attention with the person we are supposedly listening to now; thoughts about the person we must see during the *next* hour distract us from the work we are trying to do now; as we stand at the cocktail party, balancing a drink in one hand and holding a cigarette in the other, "listening" to the pompous fellow in the flashy suit, we glance over his shoulder to see who else is at the party, and we begin to wonder why we didn't go to that other party instead. This kind of distraction is minimized in a T-group, because there is literally no alternative to paying attention. Here, we are in a room—on a "cultural island"—with several other people for two weeks (or 10 days, or a weekend) with nothing to do and no agenda and no one directing us toward any specific action. We are meeting for 12 to 16 hours a day—there's nothing else happening. Initially, this can be somewhat frightening, as we realize how difficult it is to interact with people in the absence of conversational crutches (the weather, have you seen any good films lately, and so on). Then, as we learn to pay attention to others, to listen, to look, we begin to pick up nuances of speech and behavior that we didn't think we were capable of noticing. We also begin to listen to ourselves more—to pay attention to those rumblings in our gut and to try to make sense out of them in the context of what is going on in the room, *outside* our gut.

OK, but what happens? How do people get started? What is there to talk about? Typically, the group begins with the leader (trainer) outlining the "housekeeping" schedule—when meals will be served, how long each session will last before it breaks, and so on. She may or may not proceed to outline her philosophy of groups and the limits of her own participation. She may or may not discuss the "contract"—what the participants do *not* have to do. In any case, she soon falls into silence. Minutes pass. They seem like hours. The group members may look at each other or out the window. We are not accustomed to being left to our own devices by people in leader-teacher roles. Typically, the participants will look to the trainer for guidance or direction. None is forthcoming. After several minutes, someone might express his discomfort. This may

or may not be responded to. Eventually, in a typical group, someone will express some annoyance at the leader: "I'm getting sick of this. This is a waste of time. How come you're not doing your job? What the hell are we paying you for? Why don't you tell us what we're supposed to do?" There may be a ripple of applause in the background. But someone else might jump in and ask the first person why he's so bothered by a lack of direction—does he need someone to tell him what to do? And the T-group is off and running.

Learning from Each Other

How does learning occur? How can we learn from people who are not experts? We learn through communicating. There are many ways for communications to become distorted. Occasionally, in our everyday lives, when we think we are communicating something to a person, that person is hearing something entirely different. Suppose, for example, that Fred has warm feelings for Jack, but, out of shyness or out of a fear of being rejected, he finds it difficult to express these feelings directly. He may choose to communicate those warm feelings by engaging in a teasing, sarcastic kind of banter. Jack may not understand this as warmth, however; indeed, the sarcasm might hurt him. As I indicated earlier, in our culture, it is difficult to communicate hurt feelings because it indicates weakness and vulnerability. So Jack keeps quiet. Thus Fred, oblivious to the fact that his behavior is disturbing to Jack, continues to express his warmth via sarcastic jocularity—continuing to hurt the person he likes—until he succeeds in driving Jack away. Not only does Fred lose out on what could have been a warm friendship but he may also fail to learn from this experience and may continue to alienate the very people toward whom he feels most warmly.

It may be useful to view the interaction between two people as a chain of events, as illustrated in Figure 1. The Person (P) has some

FIGURE 1

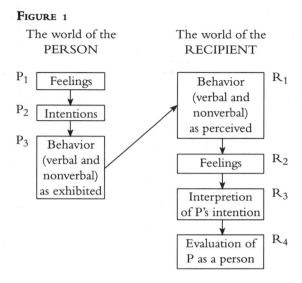

The world of the
PERSON

The world of the
RECIPIENT

P_1 Feelings

P_2 Intentions

P_3 Behavior (verbal and nonverbal) as exhibited

Behavior (verbal and nonverbal) as perceived R_1

Feelings R_2

Interpretion of P's intention R_3

Evaluation of P as a person R_4

feelings about the Recipient (R). He intends to communicate a particular feeling. This manifests itself in some kind of behavior—some words, a gesture, a smile, a look, or whatever. The Recipient perceives this behavior in his own way, based upon his own needs, feelings, past history, opinions about P, and so on. This perception of P's behavior evokes a feeling in R (warmth, anger, annoyance, love, fear, or whatever). This feeling is quickly translated into an interpretation of what P's intentions were, which in turn flows into an evaluation of what kind of a person P is.

There are possibilities for error or distortion along any point in the links of this chain. Thus, to return to our example, Fred (P) has some warm, loving feelings (P_1) toward Jack. He intends to communicate these (P_2), but he does it in an oblique, noncommittal, self-protective way: He teases Jack, makes fun of his clothes, is jocular and sarcastic (P_3). Jack perceives this sarcasm and teasing (R_1); it causes him pain (R_2); and he decides that Fred was trying to put him down (R_3). He concludes, therefore, that Fred is a cruel, aggressive, unfriendly person (R_4).

Error can occur in a different part of the chain. Imagine a totally new situation in which Fred is completely direct and honest, but Jack is suspicious. Suppose that Fred expresses his warmth directly—by putting his arm around Jack's shoulder, by telling Jack how much he likes him, and so on. But, in this case, such behavior may be too fast for Jack. Accordingly, Jack may feel uncomfortable, and, instead of simply admitting his discomfort, he may interpret Fred's behavior as manipulative in its intent. He may evaluate Fred as an insincere, political, manipulative person.

The process described above may be familiar to readers of this book. If we see a person behaving in a particular way, we have a strong tendency to attribute some motive or personality disposition to him on the basis of his behavior. If this process can be explored and examined, there is a great deal of potential learning in the encounter for both Fred and Jack. Is Fred too scared to display his warm feelings openly? Is Jack too suspicious to accept genuine warmth without vilifying Fred? These are important questions whose answers can produce a lot of insight, *but the opportunity for gaining this insight rarely occurs in the real world.* This learning can occur only if Fred and Jack share their feelings with each other. The T-group provides an atmosphere in which these feelings can be expressed and worked through. The group accomplishes this by encouraging the participants to stay with their feelings and to avoid "short-circuiting" the process by skipping from Fred's behavior (P_3) all the way to Jack's attribution (R_3) and ultimately to Jack's evaluation of Fred (R_4) without exploring the preceding and intervening events.

Openness and the Need for Privacy

Basically, then, a T-group is a setting in which people are provided with the opportunity to talk straight to each other—and to listen straight. The emphasis is on the *here and now,* rather than on past history. Thus a participant is *not* encouraged, for example, to explain to everyone the kind of person she is, nor is she encouraged to reveal her childhood experiences, her job anxieties, or the intricacies of her sex life. She *may* talk about these things if she chooses; but she usually learns more if she simply allows events to happen, reacts to the events openly as she experiences them, and allows others to respond to her as she *is,* rather than as she describes herself to be. "Openness" is the key aspect of behavior in a T-group. Many critics of T-groups have reacted against the emphasis on openness, because they believe that it violates the dignity of the individual and his need for privacy. But, in this context, openness does not mean detailed self-revelation; it simply means straight talk between two or more people. In a competently conducted T-group, a norm is established that provides each member with the right to as much physical and emotional privacy as that person desires. Participants are encouraged to resist any pressure to make them reveal things that they would rather hold private. But a member who wishes to express something in a group is helped to learn how to express it directly, rather than obliquely. For example, if Bill is angry at Ralph, it is his right to keep that anger to himself, if he so chooses. But if he chooses to express his anger, it is much more useful (for Bill, for Ralph, and for everyone else concerned) if he expresses it directly by telling Ralph about his feelings than it is if he expresses it by any one of a number of indirect means—such as making snide remarks or sarcastic statements, grunting whenever Ralph talks, making

fun of Ralph covertly, or lifting his eyes toward the ceiling, so that everyone can be made aware of his contempt for Ralph. If Bill makes a snide remark, someone in the group will almost invariably ask him if he has any feelings about Ralph that he wants to share with the group. He is not forced to share his feelings—but he's discouraged from talking in riddles and encouraged to translate the muddy language of sarcasm into straight talk.

This is not to deny that, in some groups, a great deal of coercion is used to make people reveal things that they might prefer not to reveal. Sigmund Koch, a vocal and erudite critic of group encounter, provides a graphic description of some of the more lurid and extreme examples of coercive groups. But he goes beyond that and asserts that *all* T-groups constitute a threat to human dignity and "a challenge to any conception of the person that would make life worth living." Koch has sounded a warning siren that is well worth heeding. Personally, I would choose not to participate in a group that invaded my privacy and pressured me to make self-revealing statements against my better judgment; but I believe that Koch's condemnation of all T-groups on these grounds is based on a misunderstanding of the term *openness* and an overgeneralization of his limited exposure to the goings on in "far-out" groups. At the same time, I would agree with Koch to the extent of advising people to steer clear of encounter groups unless they are competently conducted and unless they practice the value that no one has to do anything that he doesn't want to do.

Jack K. Fordyce and Raymond Weil

This section contains seven basic methods for collecting information. They include:

- Questionnaires and Instruments.
- Interviewing.
- Sensing.
- Polling.
- Collages.
- Drawings.
- Physical Representation of Organizations.

The methods are ranked in order of degree of confrontation. Thus Questionnaires are generally relatively impersonal because the source of the information is not publicly revealed, while Physical Representations (in which, for example, participants literally position themselves according to degree of influence) are highly confronting.

As a rule of thumb, the more confronting the method, the richer the response and the stronger the impulse to change. But groups vary considerably in their readiness to work with intimate methods.

Another important method for collecting information is Subgrouping. However, Subgrouping has more general uses and consequently it is described in the section on Methods for Better Meetings.

1. Questionnaires and Instruments

Questionnaires are an old standby for detecting opinion and sentiment. We send out questionnaires to customers, production workers, the professional staff, constituents, television and

Source: Jack K. Fordyce and Raymond Weil, *Managing with People,* 2nd ed. (Reading, MA: Addison-Wesley Publishing, 1979), pp. 143–58. Reprinted with permission.

movie viewers, lower levels of management, people who sojourn at motels and ride in planes, and others.

Unfortunately, traditional questionnaires have often been disappointing as a means of bringing about significant change within organizations. They do not create the kind of personal involvement and discussion that is so valuable in changing hearts and minds. The information garnered by questionnaires tends to be canned, anonymous, ambiguous, and detached—cool data rather than hot. The replies may be interesting but they lack punch. It is too easy to hold them at arm's length, put them off until another day, or take token action. And the questionnaire asks the person only what *we* want to know, not what he or she thinks we should know. You might say a filled-out questionnaire amounts to half a conversation. The employee opinion questionnaire is regarded by many as a device that some managements use to avoid coming to grips with strong opinions and sentiments.

Nevertheless, to our mind the questionnaire can be useful when it is developed jointly by the manager and representatives of the population to be canvassed.

The *instrument* as used in organization development is similar to the questionnaire, with the important addition that it is constructed around a theory of management in such manner as to help the respondent understand the theory and rate himself or herself or the organization in terms of that theory. Thus in "Grid Organization Development," the manager answers questions which help to place himself or herself in the grid model of management styles. Others in the group rate the manager, too. In this manner, instruments are a means by which a group can collect information from itself about itself. This information then provides the starting point for feedback and confrontation within the group.

Uses.

As a primary vehicle for learning in one complete system of organization development (Grid Organization Development).

To collect information as part of a specific, planned strategy of change, preferably jointly managed.

Instruments may be used by a group to collect information quickly about itself, as part of a diagnostic or team-building meeting. In this use, the instrument is the same as Polling except that the instrument is predesigned and may incorporate criteria for evaluation.

Benefits.

Questionnaires and instruments are economical means for gathering information from a large population.

They lend themselves readily to legitimate statistical use.

Instruments are valuable for self-confrontation, for learning, and as stepping stones to interpersonal confrontations.

You can more readily afford to spend time and money on the quality of the questionnaires or instruments because the unit cost is low.

There is wide acceptance of these methods.

They reduce reliance on expert third parties.

Anonymity may bring to light previously undisclosed strong sentiment.

Limitations.

Questionnaires and instruments produce findings which seem canned, a quality which is mitigated if they are used, as in Grid Organization Development, as a steppingstone to confrontation. The hazard is that the parties involved may merely imitate the motions of engaging with one another—shadowbox, so to speak.

One becomes too readily dependent on the questionnaire, pressing upon it (and thrusting away from oneself) a load it can't carry: direct human communication.

Operating Hints.   Unless the objective is purely personal learning, be sure the questionnaire or instrument leads to real engagement among people. Make sure that those involved are really hearing one another well enough—both heart-to-heart and head-to-head—so that their communication may have consequences in constructive action.

2.   Interviewing

Before a team-building or similar meeting, it is common practice to interview the participants. The interviewer is generally a third party. The purpose of the interview is to explore ways in which the group can be more effective. The interviews uncover both positive and negative opinions and sentiments about a wide range of subjects—for example, clarify of individual and group goals, impact of the manager's style, and personal concerns that have never been aired.

The question should help the interviewee to express whatever is on his or her mind about life in the organization. Examples of general opening questions:

"How are things going around here?"

"What changes would you like to see?"

"How do you think this organization could be more effective? What do you feel it does best? Does poorly?"

The interviewer may also ask about management:

"How would you describe the management style of X? How do you think he or she could be more effective?"

Questions may also be asked about relationships within the organization:

"Whom do you like to work with most? Least?"

"Who is most influential in your organization?"

"Are you kept informed of what goes on?"

And about relationships with other organizations:

"When there are problems with other organizations, what can you do about them?"

"Can you give examples of unresolved issues with other organizations?"

"Do you think you could give them advice that would help them do a better job?"

Information from the interviews is fed back to the total group, usually at the beginning of the meeting.

Uses.   Interviewing is a way to get private views and feelings on the table. The information collected often furnishes the principal basis for the meeting agenda.

Benefits.   The interview is an excellent way to probe for the problems and opportunities of the organization. Interviewing has the virtue of facilitating private expression. A sensitive interviewer can also invite ideas and emotions that the subject has not previously formulated in any conscious way. Interviewing also furnishes an occasion to develop trust between the third party and members of the organization; such trust is valuable in later work.

Limitations.

A good interview often takes one to two hours. For a large organization,

interviewing can therefore consume a lot of time.

Skillful interviewing runs the risk of turning up more information of a personal and perhaps threatening nature than the group is ready to deal with. When confronted with the interview findings, the group may close up, reject the information, and attack the interviewers.

If the interviewer is clumsy or is not trusted as impartial, interviewing may worsen matters. Under these circumstances, it is best to gather information by open group process. (See methods 3–7 in this section.)

Operating Hints.

There should be an understanding between the interviewer, the manager, and members of the team as to how the information will be used, especially with respect to protecting the privacy of sources. Normally, interviewees are promised that the information will be presented anonymously. The interviewer must keep that promise.

The information can be presented verbatim or thematically. The former has greater impact but does not protect privacy as well, and some data may be too hot for the group to handle. Thematically presented material has the opposite virtues: it's cooler, protects privacy better, has a softer impact. It is usually easily summarized, and hence easier to grasp.

One variation in reporting is to present themes and to back them up with supporting verbatim quotes.

If the findings are highly critical of the manager or another member of the group, it is advisable for the interviewer to disclose enough of the information to the manager in advance of the group meeting so that he or she will not feel ambushed.

Interviews may be carried out on an individual or subgroup basis, the latter having the obvious advantage of saving time. Interviewing of subgroups does not confer the same advantages of privacy and sensitivity, but the information disclosed tends to be of a character that the group is ready and willing to deal with. Moreover, the person who volunteers data in a subgroup interview normally feels committed to confirm it in a larger meeting.

A way to disseminate the interview findings is to type and distribute copies to all members of the group. Summary statements and corroborative information can then be posted on chart pads.

3.   Sensing

Sensing is an organized method by which a manager can learn about the issues, concerns, needs, and resources of persons in any suborganization with which he or she has limited personal contact. It takes the form of an unstructured group interview and is usually tape-recorded. The recording may be then used to educate others.

Example.   The general manager of an organization which employs 2000 wants to make an annual report to employees highly pertinent to their interests. To discover what subjects most concern them, the personnel manager schedules a series of meetings with a sampling of employees.

The personnel manager schedules four meetings, each two hours in length and each with a different group of 12 employees. To aid the general manager get a "feel" for people in all parts of the organization, the personnel manager selects the attendees as follows:

Group I—Nonsupervisory, shop and service, and technical and office employees.
Group II—Professional employees and staff specialists.

Group III—Supervisors.
Group IV—A diagonal cross section (i.e., one person from each organizational level; no one of the persons selected reports to any other).

Before scheduling the meetings, the personnel manager contacts the supervisor of each prospective participant. He or she explains the purpose of the meeting and the intention that no direct actions will ensue which might affect the supervisor or people who report to the supervisor.

Each meeting begins with a statement from the personnel manager who says that the general manager will arrive in half an hour. The personnel manager explains the general manager's purpose for the meeting and the hope that the conversation will be open and informal. The personnel manager suggests: "Suppose you board an airplane to Europe and you happen to find yourself sitting next to the general manager. What would you say?" The personnel manager also tells the group that, unless they object, to ease the burden of notetaking, the meeting will be tape-recorded. The general manager may also later use the tape as an aid to memory or to present illustrative excerpts to the division's top staff. If any member of the group prefers, the recorder will be promptly turned off now or at any time during the conversation.

During the meeting, the general manager spends most of the time listening, sometimes asking clarifying questions. The general manager also expresses his or her own thoughts and intentions regarding the various topics introduced.

Another Example.   A manager has been hearing from outsiders that recently hired engineers in the organization are dissatisfied. To better understand the nature of their complaints, the manager asks the personnel manager to rearrange sensing sessions with several groups of engineers and a group of engineering supervisors.

Another Example.   A third party uses the sensing procedure to make a quick assessment of the health of a company. He or she meets with four representative small groups from different parts of the organization, asking each group to discuss what is going well in the company and what needs to be changed. To avoid inhibiting the discussion, the third party does not record it but periodically stops the conversation and, in front of the group, dictates into the tape recorder a digest of what they have said. Then, with the recorder still running, he or she asks if they have been heard correctly and records their response. In a day's time, a 15-minute tape can summarize the four discussions. This tape is given to the top-management group of the company.

If the consultant were collecting information for a team-building meeting, he or she might use a different question, such as: "The general manager and the division directors are going to hold an off-site meeting to work on improving their performance as a management team. What issues do you think they should take up?"

Uses.

To collect information as part of a general diagnosis of the organization.

To learn the desires and agonies of a group that seems to be dissatisfied.

To learn how organization objectives are understood by diverse people within an organization.

To test a proposed course of action for its effect on various groups of people.

To collect information for a team-building meeting.

Benefits.

The interaction of the group often produces rich information and ideas.

More economical than individual interviews.

May provide a quick glimpse of what's going on.

Allows for communication of impressions and feelings as well as opinions and ideas.

Provides a check on conventional and more formal communication channels.

Admits the rumble of humanity into the ivory tower.

Tapes from sensing sessions communicate more vividly to later listeners than second-hand transmission, written reports, or questionnaires.

Limitations.

Won't work well unless the relations at various levels in the organization are basically trusting.

Is not as statistically rigorous or as economical as a questionnaire.

May be suspected as "snooping."

Success of the meeting is highly dependent on the manager's ability to listen effectively and on a willingness to engage with the members of the group in a personal way.

The meeting may fail to get at the attendees' real concerns because for one reason or another they are not willing to reveal them.

Operating Hints.

Make sure that all intermediate supervisors understand the objectives and possible outcomes of the meeting so that they will not feel "spied on." Be clear and explicit about the objectives of the meeting and what is to become of the information.

Notetaking may interfere with easy, informal discussion while the tape recorder is less likely to. But tape-record the session only if the group is willing. Be explicit about how the tape will be used and make a commitment to control its use.

Don't try to use sensing as a substitute for maintaining effective communication channels throughout the organization, or to "get the boss's message across," or to reprimand or judge.

Allow about two hours (enough time for a comfortable discussion).

Provide some warm-up time with a third party, especially for people who have never seen the big boss.

Convene the session in a comfortable setting and one that is not strange or intimidating to the group. (Don't meet in the boss's office.)

Establish a single and limited objective for a given sensing session. Don't try to cover too much at once. Start the meeting in an open-ended way. This will permit individuals to express their viewpoints (e.g., "How does it feel to work around here?" or "I'm interested in how things are going," rather than, "Do you like the company benefits plan?").

If the manager doing the sensing is a poor listener, include a third party who, by prearrangement, can intervene if the manager seems to be blocking the group's efforts to express itself.

Don't do a lot of sensing unless the groups sensed can see positive results coming from it. Overuse of sensing can be as bad as overuse of questionnaires. Sensing may be conducted by persons other than a key manager; for example, by a third party or someone from the personnel department.

4. Polling

Sometimes a group becomes uneasy with itself. The members may feel anxious, bored, or in some way out of tune with one another. Such conduct is a common symptom of a buried issue. The way out is to move the discussion to the unspoken agenda item. Polling is a way to reveal it. Or, in a more positive way, a group may wish to evaluate its current state as a prelude to action.

One approach is to poll the group on a question that calls attention to its present condition. The third party might float a tentative question

and, with the help of the group, modify the question so that it becomes one that the group wants to deal with. The participants must also decide upon the procedure for conducting the poll.

Example.   The group has been planning goals for improvement. At this time, the discussion is agreeable but lethargic. The third party suggests polling the group members on their optimism about whether they can agree upon and later achieve a goal involving significant change. The group consents. He or she suggests a procedure and draws on the chalkboard a scale of optimism:

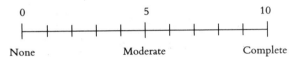

Each member is asked to assign a number to his or her degree of optimism. The third party will mark each response on the scale.

The responses cluster around 2½. Now the group members begin to comment on their pessimism, on their history of past failures at meeting their goals. They begin to analyze weaknesses in their methods of planning and execution of change. More than one member acknowledges a feeling of guilt at not having been able to subscribe to the manager's wishes, having done instead what seemed fitting and necessary.

The truth begins to sink in. As a group, they have a way to travel before they can plan realistic goals to which they will feel strongly committed.

Another Example.   One person remarks that participation in the meeting has been uneven. Some have said little or nothing. Others have made important comments to which there was no response; perhaps they have not been heard. One or two have dominated the conversation.

The group determines to poll itself on this concern. The members will score one another (from 1 to 5) on two questions:

- Amount of participation?
- Quality of participation?

Each member writes a self-rating and a rating of the others with respect to the two questions. The results are presented to the group on grids, one grid for each question (See Figure 1). Following the poll, the group members agree on the need to police themselves better. They also decide to rotate responsibility for calling attention to weaknesses in future meetings.

FIGURE 1

Raters

	John	Betty	Ted	Sam	Francis	Fred
John	②	1	1	1	2	1
Betty	5	⑤	5	5	5	5
Ted	4	5	③	4	4	5
Sam	2	1	2	①	2	2
Frances	1	2	1	1	③	1
Fred	1	1	1	1	1	②

Subjects

Circled numbers are self-ratings

Another Example. One member wonders aloud about how effective the group is as a team. The third party suggests that the members first decide upon the attributes of an effective team (in their situation) and then rate themselves on each attribute. The group now *develops its own* questionnaire, which is posted. Each member now marks his or her ratings (see Figure 2). Now the group members reflect on why the ratings came out as they did. They become specific about what they do well and what they do poorly as a team.

Another Example. The third party asks on what questions would the members like to know the position of the others. The group arrives at a set of questions:

- Should we do something about our relationship with organization X?
- Am I able to influence what goes on in this organization?
- Do I plan to leave this organization in the next two years?

Each member jots down a yes or no reply to each question, and then predicts the number of yes and no answers for the total group. The results are tabulated and posted on the wall (see

FIGURE 2

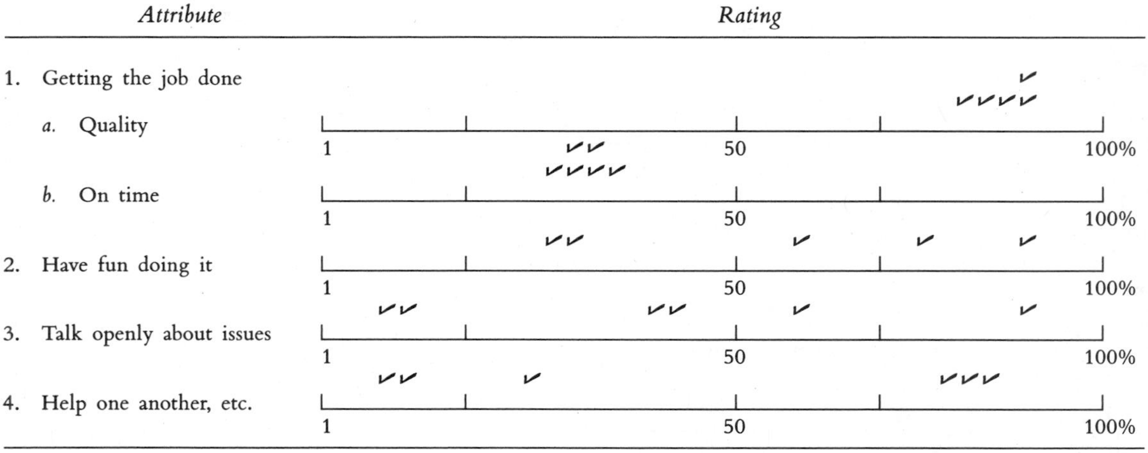

Attribute	Rating
1. Getting the job done	
a. Quality	
b. On time	
2. Have fun doing it	
3. Talk openly about issues	
4. Help one another, etc.	

Figure 3). The range of the *predictions* is an indicator of common understanding. The *actual count* starts the group working on some real problems.

Another Example.   After an effort lasting some period of time, the group has reached a fairly high level of trust and mutual helpfulness. However, one member is troubled by certain relationships among members, and feels the group has been avoiding the subject.

The third party invites each group member to pursue two questions:

- Which two persons in the group do I *like* working with the *most*?
- Which two persons in the group do I *like* working with the *least*?

The responses are collected on signed slips of paper and tabulated on a grid (see Figure 4). In the ensuing discussion, the group deals with the intensity of the choices, the reasons for them, and perhaps what sort of conduct can improve the relationships.

Uses.   Polling is a quick way of bringing buried issues to light. Such issues may be of two types:

- Those which are interfering with the progress of a meeting.
- Chronic problems in the organization.

Benefits.

Polling is fast, interesting, and simple. Anyone can devise his or her own questions and polling procedure.

The whole group takes part in the process and feels greater commitment to the results. It is an easy way to get issues out into the open, and a good way to move from general, inconclusive discussions to specifics that can be dealt with. It is a highly flexible method that can be improvised to suit the needs of the moment.

Limitations.   The questions aren't as carefully thought out as those on professionally developed questionnaires, and they don't lend themselves to large groups. They are most useful in groups of 5 to 30.

Operating Hints.

Don't rush into polling at your next meeting to suit *your* interests. The questions and the procedure must make sense to the group. If not, the responses won't be very useful, and other members will start wondering about *you*.

Group involvement is important for another reason. As the examples show, polls can touch people where they are quite sensitive. The group's OK to go ahead is the only evidence that they feel up to it.

FIGURE 3

	Actual Count		Predicted Count (range)	
Question	Yes	No	Yes	No
1. Organization X	5	5	3–8	2–7
2. Influence	3	7	1–4	6–9
3. Leaving, etc.	4	6	2–5	5–8

FIGURE 4

		Choosers					
		Jane	Frank	Nan	Mary	Ken	Mark
Chosen	Jane		✔		X	X	X
	Frank	✔		✔			✔
	Nan	✔	✔		✔	✔	✔
	Mary	X		✔		✔	
	Ken		X	X	✔		X
	Mark	X	X	X	X	X	

✔ = Most   X = Least

If sensitive relationships are to be taken up, it's wise to have a competent third party present.

Be cautious about secretive methods of collecting information. An occasional secret ballot may be all right, but beware of raising issues which the group is unwilling to confront openly.

Once the questions have been answered, move the discussion to specifics as soon as possible. General discussions leave a lot of fog in the atmosphere.

5. Collages

Individuals, subgroups, or groups may be asked to prepare collages around a theme (e.g., "How do you feel about this team?", "How do you feel about yourself in this organization, and this organization in the company?", "What is happening to this organization and the team?"). Materials for the collage include large sheets of paper, magazines from which pictures and words may be clipped, crayons, felt pens, glue, scissors, and so on. Each finished collage is then described for the total group by the individual or subgroup preparing it. If a single, large collage is prepared by the total group, it becomes the focal point for a total group discussion.

Uses.

As an instrument for tracing the cultural and emotional topography of a group. The collage allows the members to express themselves to one another on a fairly deep, personal level. Common themes from collages tend to find their way onto group agendas.

Benefits.

Collages can be quite effective in breaking the ice. Afterward, the group may be more willing to deal with personal and interpersonal issues. Besides, they are fun to do.

When the group produces a large single collage, the members are apt to be proud of their accomplishment. The experience is unifying.

Limitations.

Groups that are formal in behavior may resist what first appears to be a children's game.

As noted, collages are highly expressive. On the other hand, they may reveal little that is hard and specific.

Operating Hints.

Lead boldly into the assignment to help the group overcome its resistance to this "child's play."

If they want, let the participants suggest the theme for the collage. Provide plenty of magazines and ample space, and be prepared to wind up with a cluttered room.

Suggest to the participants that they cut out any pictures or words which "ring a bell' without giving much thought to why they do so.

The time for preparing the collages should be approximately one-half hour to an hour and a half. Judge the time by whether the participants seem productively employed, but apply deadline pressure to discourage excessive deliberation.

Don't let the responses to the presentation turn into a game of interpretation. The object is to understand the presenter without putting words into his or her mouth and without awakening defensiveness.

The boss's collage should be presented last so as not to set the tone for others.

6. Drawings

One member of the group (or some, or all members) is asked to make a drawing about an aspect of the individual's life, or something about the nature of the organization. The drawings are made on large sheets of paper posted on the walls. The authors are then asked to discuss their drawings in the presence of the group. Members of the group may ask questions to clarify the author's intent. Common themes and problems, or significant differences of opinion, are then culled from the drawings and posted on chart pads. Here is an example of an instruction given to all members of a group:

> Draw a circle for each person in the group, including your boss and your boss's boss. Make the circle proportionately larger for those individuals who seem to have greater influence over the way the group does its work.
>
> Place the circles near or far apart, depending on how closely you feel those individuals must work together to get their job done. Label the circles with the names of the people.
>
> With a blue line, connect those people who are personally close to one another. Connect with a red line those people who are far apart (i.e., individuals who communicate very little with one another or between whom you feel there is friction).

Other Examples.

> Draw a picture of how it feels to be in your organization.
>
> Draw a picture of your organization today and another picture of what you would like it to be in five years.
>
> The drawings may vary in style from conventional organization charts to imaginative symbolic representations.

Uses.

> Drawings of the sort suggested can be a powerful way of unearthing for the group issues that have been buried alive—for

example, the presence of cliques, inappropriate competition, or personal influence contrary to organizational goals. While they may be used to describe a current situation, drawings can also display what people want and hope for in place of what they have now.
>
> Drawings can be used for building an agenda for team-building or similar meetings.

Benefits.

Pictures are often rich compressions of meaning. Moreover, they are inherently stimulating to work with. Drawings may also afford an easy entry into discussion of tender subjects.

Limitations.
Drawings are an expressive medium. But they are difficult for some to enter into unless the directions are quite literal and easy to follow.

Operating Hints.

> Don't attempt to cover too many subjects in a single drawing or it will become difficult to understand.
>
> Spend enough time on the instructions so that the members understand the *objectives* of the activity. Don't discourage people from departing from your rules; they may do better in their own fashion.
>
> When a person presents a drawing to the group, encourage clarifying questions. *Discourage* general discussion, debate, or clever interpretation of the drawing by other members of the group.
>
> Keep in readiness large sheets of paper, colored markers, and tape.
>
> Some groups need more guidance than others. A group that is esthetically inclined is apt to respond swiftly to the assignment. Others may want more specific instruction.

7. Physical Representation of Organization

Members of a group are asked to arrange themselves physically in the room according to some group characteristic they are troubled about. For example, if the participants are apparently concerned about cliques, they may be asked to position themselves in the room so that each stands nearest to those he or she feels warmest about and farthest from those he or she feels coolest about. Or, if inappropriate influence is an issue, they may be asked to arrange themselves closer or farther from the boss according to the amount of influence they feel they have. Usually, the manager takes a position in the middle of the room as a starting point. Members are asked to call attention to any aspect of the deployment which they believe to be inaccurate. Usually no further instructions are given. Discussion normally occurs spontaneously.

Uses.   For bringing into the open relationship issues which are bothering the group. These may include cliques, feelings about being "in" or "out" of the group, influence, competitiveness, communication channels, and the like.

Benefits.

A good, rapid, and dramatic diagnostic tool for disclosing interpersonal issues that are hindering a group.

Creates strong motivation to improve the situation.

Limitations.   Many groups find this sort of thing too "far out," so the method isn't useful to them and may do more harm than good.

Operating Hints.   You will need a qualified third party.

READING 16
OPERATION KPE: DEVELOPING A NEW ORGANIZATION

Ishwar Dayal and John M. Thomas

It was ... decided that analysis of each role in the organization might be facilitated if, as a group, we could strive for an atmosphere in these sessions where individuals could express disagreement with the manner in which a particular role was being defined or currently being performed by the focal role incumbent, particularly in terms of how this performance either failed to meet expectations from others or convey obligations to others. Analysis of the role system could best be accomplished alongside some critical analysis of current role performance, with a view toward helping individuals understand how they might alter their characteristic styles of working with others. Our hope here was to be able to assist the group in developing a climate where it could begin to undertake analysis of the interpersonal sphere in conjunction with analysis of its task interdependencies: in other words, how the group might begin to share and work together on these concerns about interpersonal needs discussed with us in individual counseling sessions. In addition to ideas of one's own role, it would be valuable for each other member of the group to think about the role under discussion in terms of its specific linkages with his role.

As a model for role analysis in the group we attempted to integrate the Glacier formulations of *prescribed* and *discretionary* components of roles (Brown, 1960) with that of Kahn, et al. (1964). This included discussion of the following:

Source: Reproduced by special permission from *The Journal of Applied Behavioral Science,* "Operation KPE: Developing a New Organization," by Ishwar Dayal and John M. Thomas. Volume 4, number 4 (1968), pp. 473–505. Copyright by NTL Institute for Applied Behavioral Science.

1. Analysis of why a particular role is needed and what purpose in the organization it would serve. This point has relevance to the expressed individual problem of identity.
2. The expectations and obligations of related roles in relation to a focal role (Kahn, et al., 1964).

Thus each role analysis consisted of three parts: discussion of purpose of the role, its prescribed and discretionary components, and its linkages with other roles.

Beginning with the GM as the first focal role, the phase aimed at developing what we have termed interdependence was launched. To date, each member of the management group has taken sessions in which he has been a focal role under discussion. The live format evolved for these discussions came to include the following steps:

The focal role individual initiates discussion and the group begins an analysis of the purpose of the role in the organization, how it fits into the overall objectives of the company, and its rationale.

The focal role individual lists on the blackboard the activities which he feels constitute his role; other members discuss this and ask for clarification; additions and subtractions are often made to this list. The group agrees upon the prescribed elements of the role and helps the role incumbent analyze its discretionary elements. Often this enables the individual to clarify the responsibility he must take on himself for decisions, the choices open to him for alternative courses of action, and new competencies he must develop in his assigned role. For example, during discussion of the role of the sales manager, he thought that the GM should initiate contact with major customers because he was more likely to influence them by virtue of his social contacts with top management in those companies. In contrast, the consultants suggested that the sales manager might, for various reasons, be taking "flight" from this responsibility and wondered whether he had any feelings about this matter that he could explore with the group. This led to an intensive, useful clarification of the relationship of the general manager with customers and with the sales manager. Similar issues came to center stage while discussing the roles of the purchasing and personnel officers. These discussions often led the group to examine the social customs prevailing in business firms which seem to require members of the group to establish social contacts with key people. These discussions also helped the GM and the members of the management team visualize what kind of support they would have to give to one another in this activity. For example, the sales and purchasing role incumbents discussed the development of a formal system for effective exchange of information about customers and suppliers.

The focal role individual then lists his expectations from each of those other roles in the group which he feels most directly affect his own role performance. Often a lively dialogue ensues at this point between the focal role incumbent and the role sender under discussion. They may disagree over expectations and obligations. Other group members enter in to help clarify by adding their own perceptions of that role relationship. In the end a workable formula is evolved describing mutual expectations and obligations.

Each role sender then presents his list of expectations from the focal role. This consists of their views of his obligations to them in role performance, and much the same process as in the previous step is repeated.

Upon concluding an individual role analysis, the focal role incumbent is held responsible for writing up

the major points evolved during the group discussion. This consists of *(a)* a set of activities classified as to the prescribed and discretionary elements of the role, *(b)* the obligations of the role to each role in its set, and *(c)* the expectations of this role from others in its set. Viewed in toto, this provides a comprehensive understanding of each individual's "role space." In addition, note is made of procedures and suggestions which may have been brought out as to how the role incumbent might more effectively implement his role activities. This write-up is done with the aid of the consultants and is circulated to all group members.

Briefly, at the next meeting, before another focal role is taken up, the previous role write-up is discussed and points are clarified. This statement is then accepted as a picture of the responsibilities and activities of that position in the organization. Unlike the traditional job description, however, this statement has been evolved live and entirely in the context of the *interaction* of that role with others. It expresses the group's views of how that role fits into the internal structure of the organization.

References

Argyris, C. *Interpersonal Competence and Organizational Effectiveness.* Homewood, IL: Irwin-Dorsey, 1962.

Bamforth, K. "Some Experiences of the Use of T-Groups and Structured Groups within a Company." *Working paper no. 3.* University of Leeds, U.K.: Industrial Management Division, 1963.

Benne, K. "Deliberate Changing as the Facilitation of Growth." In Bennis, W. G., Benne, K., & Chin, R., eds. *The Planning of Change.* New York: Holt, Rinehart & Winston, 1961.

Bennis, W. G. *Changing Organizations.* New York: McGraw-Hill, 1966.

Brown, W. *Explorations in Management.* London: Heinemann, 1960.

Burns, T., & Stalker, G. *The Management of Innovation.* London: Tavistock, 1961.

Dayal, I. "Organization of Work." In Baumgartel, H., Bennis, W., & De, N., eds. *Readings in Group Development for Managers and Trainers.* Bombay: Asia Publishing House, 1967.

Deutsch, M. "Cooperation and Trust: Some Theoretical Notes." In Bennis, W., Schein, E., Berlew, D., & Steele, F., eds. *Interpersonal Dynamics.* Homewood, IL: Dorsey Press, 1964.

Jaques, E., & Brown, W. *The Glacier Project Papers.* London: Heinemann, 1965.

Kahn, R., & Rosenthal, R. *Organizational Stress,* New York: John Wiley & Sons, 1964.

Lorsch, J., & Lawrence, P. "Organizing for Product Innovation." *Harvard Business Review* 43, no. 1 (1965) pp. 109–22.

Rogers, C., & Roethlisberger, F. J. "Barriers and Gateways to Communication." *Harvard Business Review* 30, no. 4 (1952), pp. 46–52.

Schultz, W. *FIRO—B.* New York: Holt, Rinehart & Winston, 1958.

Selznick, P. *Leadership in Administration.* New York: Harper & Row, 1957.

Shepard, H., & Blake, R. "Changing Behavior through Cognitive Change." *Human Organization* 21, no. 2 (1962), pp. 88–96.

Walker, C. *Modern Civilization and Technology.* New York: McGraw-Hill, 1958.

Richard Beckhard and Reuben T. Harris

From new structures, multiple roles, and new reporting relationships emerge problems of job definitions, reporting lines, accountability, and performance review. In managing a change effort in a large system, the point of pressure for change will probably occur at some organizational interface. Significant changes occur when: (1) the task relationships between, say, market research and market development are reorganized; (2) it is necessary to superimpose programs on top of functional organizations; or (3) there are mergers of different organizations with different backgrounds or cultures. Such reorganizations tend to have some characteristics of a matrix organization—increased ambiguity, role confusion, problems with decision making, and communications problems.

The typical ways of resolving these dilemmas are to:

1. Try to get clearer job descriptions of each job or position involved.
2. Use a mediating mode (e.g., upper management defines the responsibilities of the various roles).
3. Utilize intergroup development activities designed to clarify responsibilities, authority, and rewards.

Most of these efforts do not succeed too well, however, because they are focused on improving the decision making *or* the communications *or* the power. They are not focused directly on *optimizing work,* although they may appear to.

Source: Richard Beckhard and Reuben T. Harris, *Organizational Transitions: Managing Complex Change,* (Reading, Mass.: Addison-Wesley Publishing, 1977), pp. 76–82. © 1977, Addison-Wesley. Reprinted with permission.

Responsibility Charting

In recent years a new technique has emerged which does focus on allocating work responsibilities; this technique is called *responsibility charting.* The first step is to construct a grid; the types of decisions and classes of actions that need to be taken in the total area of work under discussion are listed along the left-hand side of the grid, and the actors who might play some part in decision making on those issues are identified across the top of the grid (see Figure 1).

The process, then, is one of assigning a behavior to each of the actors opposite each of the issues. There are four classes of behavior:

1. *Responsibility (R)*—the responsibility to initiate action to ensure that the decision is carried out. For example, it would be a department head's responsibility (R) to initiate the departmental budget.
2. *Approval required, or the right to veto (A–V)*—the particular item must be reviewed by the particular role occupant, and this person has the option of either vetoing or approving it.
3. *Support (S)*—providing logistical support and resources for the particular item.
4. *Inform (I)*—*must be* informed and, by inference, cannot influence.

Each item is considered and responsibility (R) assigned. A very important aspect of the technique is that there can be only *one* R on any one horizontal line. Therefore, a consensus must be reached or an authoritarian decision made on who has the responsibility. If the group is unable to agree about where the R should go, there are three options:

FIGURE 1

Responsibility chart

CODE:	R–	Responsibility (initiates)
	A–V	Approval (right to veto)
	S–	Support (put resources against)
	I–	Inform (to be informed)

Actors → Decisions ↓																		

1. Break the problem out—always the most desirable alternative. For example, the R for a large capital expenditure might be different from the R for a small capital expenditure.

2. Move the R up one level in the organization hierarchy. For example, if the marketing manager and production manager cannot agree which one of them should have the R for defining monthly production targets, move the R up to their boss, the division general manager.

3. Move the *decision about assigning the* R up one level. In the previous example, the division general manager would assign the R for setting production targets rather than define the targets themselves.

Once the R has been assigned, the next step is to take a new item and assign a behavior for the various actors. In addition to R-A-S-I alternatives, it is possible that an actor has no assigned behavior opposite a particular type of activity, and this situation should be indicated by a dash (—).

Completion of the horizontal line gives one a de facto modus operandi for handling that particular class of task and its associated roles. Completion of a responsibility chart for all of the tasks relevant to the interfaces between departments or organizations and reading down a column vertically reveals the consensus role description of a particular actor on all those matters in which he or she is interdependent with other roles.

Some Further Guidelines in the Process

1. If an item has several As—for example, one R, six As, one S, and one I—undoubtedly it will be very difficult to accomplish that task. For example, one organization decided to increase its benefits plan for management. The plan was agreed to by all levels of the organization; the board approved it, and the compensation people were told to install the plan. Nine months later, the plan was still not in. A responsibility-charting exercise indicated that each of the major profit centers had defined itself as having an A because it was an independent profit center with a budget commitment to the center. Because this new program required investment of funds not budgeted, each profit center's manager felt it was his or her choice to decide whether or not to institute the program this year or next year. It did not take long for the managing director to indicate, and for the profit center managers to see, that S rather than A was the appropriate symbol to describe the profit center's role. Then the program got instituted very quickly.

2. Depending on who is filling out the chart, one might find a skewing of A's under the senior executive. Subordinate managers tend to give their bosses more As than in fact the bosses want. It is desirable to try to minimize the number of As for any task if one wishes to facilitate the accomplishment of the task.

3. The decision about who can allocate a letter to a role can be tricky. In one situation, for example, the management group decided that first-line supervisors in the production organization should be held accountable for weekly scrap losses and various other things and should have timely information about their progress toward their objectives and organization standards. However, the controller's department, which was part of the general headquarters, refused to develop and introduce a new cost-accounting system. The department's requirements for accounting systems were focused primarily on the needs of the top of the organization, the tax people, and the like, and another system would have to be added in order to provide this new type of information. The department felt that as the top financial resource, it should have responsibility for deciding whether or not such a system, with the attendant costs, would be introduced.

At a responsibility-charting session, it became clear that the department had defined itself as having an A, whereas others lower in the organization felt strongly that the department should have an S—that it should be required to produce the system. At the meeting, the general manager supported those who were arguing for the S on the basis that the task required it. This changed the basis for making decisions from hierarchy position to task accomplishment.

Some Applications

Illustration One: A Change in Structure. A large consumer company identified with a particular product orientation decided to "go to market" in a different way. Previously the company had sold its product, which was used in interior decorating, through specialty stores. Instead of being known as a single-product company, the company now wanted to be known as a decorating company. This meant changing the products in the stores, changing the relationship of the franchised stores to the corporation, differentiating the various types of buyers—housewives, contractors, and so on—and providing outlets for customers' different needs.

The prechange organization was a marketing-sales-functional organization. All selling was done in the geographic regions under the direction of division and, ultimately, regional sales-managers. Plants made products on demand from the different regions. The technical-service organization made the special blends of products required by the sales organization.

The company's top management felt that, given the new marketing plan and corporate image, a new organizational structure was needed. Accordingly, the sales organization was maintained, but purely as a selling organization. Product managers were created within the marketing organization and were given worldwide responsibility for sales in their particular product or market area. Also created were product-technical managers, who came from the technical organization but also had a product or business orientation. People in the new technical-service role would now receive all of their instructions from the product-technical director, rather than from the sales organization.

Everyone in the organization, with the exception of the production and finance organizations, now had a new role, a new set of task responsibilities, and new relationships. Much confusion could be expected.

The strategy for dealing with the confusion was to conduct a series of *responsibility-charting conferences*. The first two-day conference focused on the new roles—the product managers from marketing, the technical-product managers, and the top of the organization (i.e., the directors of marketing, manufacturing, technical and finance, and the group vice president). After opening re-marks by the group vice president, the participants proceeded to do a responsibility-charting exercise. They identified areas of decision and activities that needed to be done, made a list of the actors, and then assigned behaviors to these actors. Because the top of the organization was also present, the assigned behavior could be "reality-tested" right then. The output of the two days was a "map" of the general modus operandi as seen by the top management and the occupants of the new roles.

Next, the two sets of roles in marketing—sales and product management—and the two sets of technical roles—product management and technical service—met to work through responsibilities and to assign behaviors for their roles in the new setup. Difficulties arising with the earlier models and maps were resolved by the top-management group that had attended the first workshops. The results were then distributed to everybody and became the basis for work.

The change, a massive one involving several thousand managers, was in effect. People were operating in their new roles within six weeks of the announcement of the change. The process of having all of the key people sit down together and develop the new modus operandi was credited by most as having a significant effect on the efficiency of the change.

APPRECIATIVE INQUIRY: AN ALTERNATIVE TO PROBLEM SOLVING

David L. Cooperrider and Suresh Srivasta

Many of us have come to look upon traditional, stepwise problem-solving methodologies as, at best, reactive, deficient, and certainly incapable of fully harnessing our creative energies to resolve major organizational challenges. Long immersed in the "felt need" paradigm, we too often regard pain as a requisite stimulus for action. We do this even though we know that (1) most organizations would benefit by addressing potential challenges well before the organization reaches its ill-defined and often fluctuating minimum pain threshold and (2) most people appreciate the sense of awe, exhilaration, and joy that comes from handling challenges in more optimistic, creative and holistic ways.

One alternative to the "felt need" model is David L. Cooperrider and Suresh Srivastva's model of Appreciative Inquiry, which begins with what we do well, rather than what we need to repair:

> Appreciative inquiry seeks out the very best of "what is" to help ignite the imagination of "what might be." The aim is to generate new knowledge which expands "the realm of the possible" and helps the partners of an organization envision a collectively desired future and then to carry forth that vision in ways which successfully translate intention into reality and belief into practice.

This model replaces our focus on problems with an appreciation for the best of *what is* and *what might be,* followed by agreement on *what*

Source: David L. Cooperrider and Suresh Srivastva, "Appreciative Inquiry in Organizational Life," *Research in Organizational Change and Development,* vol. 1, R. W. Woodman and W. A. Pasmore (eds) (Greenwich, CT: JAI Press, 1987), pp. 129–69. Reprinted with permission.

should be and *what will be.* At the organization level, Appreciative Inquiry is an action research model that uses affirmative data as a basis of dialogue from which new knowledge and theory is generated. These are then used to bring about positive organizational change. The following very briefly and simply describes the process.

The starting point is to ground our inquiry in actual experience, the best of what is. We identify our peak experiences and then delineate those life-giving forces that give value to these experiences. Next, we allow the best of what is to inspire a vision of what might be. Grounded appreciation helps us envision an ideal future which clearly goes beyond our current peak experiences.

Then we dialogue about our discoveries and possibilities. Here we may discover new knowledge as we slowly move toward shared understandings—from individual insight to group insight, from individual appreciation to collective appreciation, from individual vision to organization vision. The bonds of collective will are forged and embraced as we determine what should be.

Finally, we create the vision. We confidently make things happen, allowing our common vision of what should be to empower our creativity, commitment and energy toward what will be.

Appreciative Inquiry may be, for many of us, the paradigm shift we need to truly focus on the best in our lives and to empower ourselves to do even better. The visioning phase will challenge our somewhat atrophied imaginations. The dialogue phase will challenge our inhibitions around talking in organizations about what re-

Problem Solving	**Appreciative Inquiry**
1. Find a felt need. Identify the problem.	1. Appreciate the best of "What Is."
2. Analyze causes.	2. Envision: "What Might Be."
3. Analyze solutions.	3. Dialogue for new knowledge and theory "What Should Be."
4. Develop an action plan.	4. Create the vision "What Will Be."

ally matters, our values. And the action phase will challenge us to recall the vision and the process of receiving the vision as we do our work. We are adept at reacting to demands, but can we as readily perceive ourselves surrounded by exciting opportunities for creative sense making and then act according to the positive selves we have chosen to be?

READING 19
WHEN POWER CONFLICTS TRIGGER TEAM SPIRIT

Roger Harrison

Getting people to work together in harmony is no easy task. Modern management techniques abound with new approaches to improving the working relationship between employees. In the United States, sensitivity training has had quite a vogue, and various techniques such as the T-group or the managerial grid have been brought forth to encourage managers to abandon their competitiveness and to create mutual trust and egalitarian approaches to decision making.

Or managers have been urged to change their motivations from reliance upon monetary reward or punishment to more internal motivation based on intrinsic interest in the job and personal commitment to meeting work objectives: for example, in Management by Objectives and programs of job enrichment. Still other practitioners have developed purely rational approaches to group problem solving: for example, Kepner Tregoe in the United States, and Coverdale in Britain.

Running through these approaches is the tendency to ignore or explain away competition, conflict and the struggle for power and influence. They assume people will be cooperative and productive if they are taught how, or if the barriers to their so being are removed. These approaches may be called *tender minded,* in that they see power struggles as a symptom of a managerial *mistake,* rather than a basic and ubiquitous process in organizations.

The problem of organizational change is seen as one of *releasing* human potential for collaboration and productivity, rather than as one of controlling or checking competition for advantage and position.

Source: Roger Harrison, *European Business*, Spring 1972, pp. 57–65.

However, consider the case of the production and engineering managers of a plant who had frequent disagreements over the work that was done by the latter for the former. The production manager complained that the engineering manager set maintenance priorities to meet his own convenience and reduce his own costs, rather than to make sure production targets were met. The engineering manager maintained that the production manager gave insufficient notice of jobs which could be anticipated, and the production operators caused unnecessary breakdowns by failure to carry out preventive maintenance procedures faithfully. The two men aired their dissatisfaction with one another's performance from time to time; but, according to both parties, no significant change has occurred.

Or take the case of the scientist in a development department, who complains of overly close supervision by his section manager. According to the scientist, the manager intervenes to change the priorities he assigns to work, or to interfere with his development of promising lines of enquiry, and to check up with insulting frequency to see whether the scientist is carrying out the manager's instructions.

The scientist is actively trying to get a transfer to another section, because he feels he cannot do a proper job with so much hampering interference from above.

On the other hand, the section manager says the scientist does competent work but is secretive and unwilling to heed advice. He fails to let the manager know what he is doing and deviates without discussion from agreements the manager thought they had reached about how the work should be carried out. The manager feels he has to spend far too much time checking up on the scientist and is beginning to wonder whether his otherwise good work is worth the trouble required to manage him.

In both of these examples, the men are concerned with either gaining increased control over the actions of the other, reducing control by the other or both. And they know it. A consultant talking to them about communication problems or target setting would no doubt be listened to politely, but in their hearts, these men would still feel it was a question of who was going to have the final say, who was going to be boss.

And, in a way, they are more intuitively right than any outside consultant could be. They know where the power and influence lie, whether people are on their side or against them. They are aware of those with whom they can be open and honest and those who will use information against them. And these concerns are much more accurate and real than an outsider's suggestions for openness and collaboration.

Knowing Where the Power and Coercion Lie

Does this mean that most behavioral science approaches to business are too optimistic? What is certain is that they fail to take into account the forces of power, competitiveness, and coercion. In this article, I shall propose a method that does work directly with these issues, a method that gets tough with the team spirit.

This program is based on role negotiation. This technique describes the process that involves changing through *negotiation* with other interested parties the *role* that an individual or group performs in the organization. By an individual's or a group's *role,* I mean what activities he is supposed to perform, what decisions he can make, to whom he reports and about what and how often, who can legitimately tell him what to do and under what circumstances, and so on. Some people would say that a man's *job* is the same as what I have called his *role,* and I would

partially agree with this. But what I mean by *role* includes not only the formal job description but also all the informal understandings, agreements, expectations, and arrangements with others which determine the way one person's or group's work affects or fits in with another's.

Role negotiation intervenes directly in the relationships of power, authority, and influence within the group. The change effort is directed at the work relationships among members. It avoids probing into the likes and dislikes of members for one another and their personal feelings about one another. In this it is more consonant with the task-oriented norms of business than are most other behavioral approaches.

The Fear of Touchy Emotional Confrontations

When I first developed the technique, I tried it out on a client group which was proving particularly hard to work with. They were suspicious and mistrustful of me and of each other, and said quite openly that talking about their relationships was both "irrelevant to our work problems" and "dangerous—it could split the group apart." When I introduced them to role negotiation, they saw ways they could deal with issues that were bothering them without getting into touchy emotional confrontations they could not handle. They dropped their resistance dramatically and turned to work with a will that surprised and delighted me.

I have used role negotiation successfully with top management groups, project teams, even between husbands and wives. The technique can be used with very small or quite large groups—although groups of over 8 or 10 should be broken down.

The technique makes one basic assumption: *most people prefer a fair negotiated settlement to a state of unresolved conflict,* and they are willing to invest some time and make some concessions in order to achieve a solution. To operate the program a modest but significant risk is called for from the participants: they must be open about the changes in behavior, authority, responsibility, and so on they wish to obtain from others in the situation.

If the participants are willing to specify concretely the changes they desire from others, then significant changes in work effectiveness can usually be obtained.

How does this program work in reality? First of all, the consultant must have the participants' sufficient confidence in his motives and competence so that they are willing at his behest to try something new and a bit strange. It also stands to reason that the consultant should know enough about the people, their work system, and their relationship problems to satisfy himself that the members of the group are ready to make a real effort towards improvement. No technique will work if the clients don't trust the consultant enough to give it a fair try or if the members of the group (particularly the high-influence members) devote most of their effort to maintaining the status quo. In the description that follows I am assuming that this confidence and readiness to work have been established. Although this is a rather large assumption, these problems are universal in consulting and not peculiar to role negotiation. If anything, I have found that role negotiation requires somewhat less preparation than other team development techniques I have used.

Let us say we are working with a group of five to seven people, including a manager and his subordinates, two levels in the formal organization. Once basic assumptions of trust are established, I try to get at least a day with the group away from the job location to start the role negotiation process going. A two-day session with a commitment to follow up in three to four weeks is best. If the group is not felt to be quite prepared to undertake serious work, the session may be made longer with some trust building and diagnostic activities in the beginning, work-ing into the role negotiation when and if the group is ready for it.

No Probing into People's Feelings

The first step in the actual role negotiation is *contract setting*. Its purpose is to make it clear between the group and the consultant what each may expect from the other. This is a critical step in the change process. It controls and channels everything that happens afterwards.

My contract is usually based on the following provisions, which should be written down, if only as a first practice step in the formal way of working which I try to establish.

It is not legitimate for the consultant to press or probe anyone's *feelings*. We are concerned about work: who does what, how, and with whom. How people *feel* about their work or about others in the group is their own business, to be introduced or not according to their own judgment and desire. The expression or nonexpression of feelings is not part of the contract.

Openness and honesty about behavior are expected and essential for achieving results. The consultant will insist that people be specific and concrete in expressing their expectations and demands for the behavior of others. Each team member is expected to be open and specific about what he wants others to do *more* or *do better* or *do less* or *maintain unchanged*.

No expectation or demand is adequately communicated until it has been *written down* and is clearly understood by both sender and receiver, nor will any change process be engaged in until this has been done.

The full sharing of expectations and demands does not constitute a completed change process. It is only the precondition for change to be agreed through negotiation. It is unreasonable for anyone in the group, manager or subordinate, to expect that any change will take place merely as a result of communicating a demand or expectation. Unless a team member is willing to change his own behavior in order to get what he wants from the other(s), he is likely to waste his and the group's time talking about the issue. When a member makes a request or demand for changed behavior on the part of another, the consultant will always ask what quid pro quo (something for something) he is willing to give in order to get what he wants. This goes for the manager as well as for the subordinates. If the former can get what he wants simply by issuing orders or clarifying expectations from his position of authority, he probably does not need a consultant or a change process.

The change process is essentially one of bargaining and negotiation in which two or more members each agree to change behavior in exchange for some desired change on the part of the other. This process is not complete until the agreement can be *written down* in terms which include the agreed changes in behavior and make clear what each party is expected to give in return.

Threats and pressures are neither illegitimate nor excluded from the negotiation process. However, group members should realize that overreliance on threats and punishment usually results in defensiveness, concealment, decreased communication and retaliation, and may lead to breakdown of the negotiation. The consultant will do his best to help members accomplish their aims with positive incentives wherever possible.

The Secret Game of Influence Bargaining

Each member has power and influence in the group, both positively to reward and collaborate with others, and negatively to resist, block or punish. Each uses his power and influence to create a desirable and satisfying work situation for himself. Most of the time this process is gone about secretly. People use a lot of time and energy trying to figure out how to influence another person's behavior covertly; but since they rarely are aware of others' wants and needs, their attempts fail.

Although in stable organizations, employees can learn what works on others just through trial and error over long periods of time, nowadays the fast personnel turnover makes this primitive process obsolete.

Role negotiation tries to replace this old process with a more efficient one. If one person knows because it has been made public what another's wants or intentions are, he is bound to be more effective in trying to influence that person. In addition, when someone tries to influence him, the quid pro quo put forward is more likely to be one he really wants or needs. I try to show my clients that, by sharing the information about desires and attempts, *role negotiation increases the total amount of influence group members have on one another.*

The next stage is *issue diagnosis.* Each member spends some time thinking about the way business is conducted between himself and the others in the group. What would he change if he could? What would he like to keep as is? Who and what would have to change in order to improve things? I ask the participants to focus especially on the things which might be changed to improve their *own effectiveness,* since these are the items to be discussed and negotiated.

After he has spent 20 minutes or so thinking about these matters and perhaps making a few notes, each member fills out one Issue Diagnosis Form (like the one in Figure 1) for each other member, listing those things he would like to see the other person:

1. Do more or do better.
2. Do less or stop doing.
3. Keep on doing, maintain unchanged.

All of these messages are based on the sender's increasing his own effectiveness in his job.

These lists are exchanged so that each person has all the lists pertaining to his work behavior.

FIGURE 1

Issue Diagnosis Form

Messages from ___Jim Farrell___

to ___David Sills___

1. If you were to do the following things <u>more</u> or <u>better</u>, it would help me to increase my own effectiveness:

   - Being more receptive to improvement suggestions from the process engineers.
   - Give help on cost control (see 2).
   - Fight harder with the G.M. to get our plans improved.

2. If you were to do the following things <u>less</u>, or were to <u>stop</u> doing them, it would help me to increase my own effectiveness:

   - Acting as judge and jury on cost control.
   - Checking up frequently on small details of the work.
   - Asking for so many detailed progress reports.

3. The following things which you have been doing help to increase my own effectiveness, and I hope you will continue to do them:

   - Passing on full information in our weekly meetings.
   - Being available when I need to talk to you.

Each member makes a master list for himself on a large piece of paper itemizing the behavior which each other person desires him to do *more* or *better, less,* or *continue unchanged* (Figure 2).

These are posted so that the entire group can peruse and refer to each list. Each member is allowed to question the others who have sent messages about his behavior, querying the what, why, and how of their requests; *but no one is allowed a rebuttal, defense or even a yes or no reply to the messages he has received.* The consultant must assure that only clarification is taking place; argument, discussion, and decision making about issues must be engaged in at a later stage.

Defensiveness Just to Save Face

The purpose of the consultant's rather rigid and formal control on communication is to prevent the group from having a negative problem-solving experience, and members from becoming polarized on issues or taking up extreme positions which they will feel impelled to defend just to save face. Communication is controlled to prevent escalation of actual or potential conflicts. Channeling the energy released by the sharing of demands and expectations into successful problem solving and mutual influence is behind this strategy of control.

The consultant intervenes to inhibit hostile and destructive expression at this point and later to facilitate constructive bargaining and negotiation of mutually beneficial agreements.

This initial sharing of desires and change goals among group members leads to a point at which the team development process is most vulnerable. If sufficient anger and defensiveness are generated by the problem sharing, the consultant will not be able to hold the negative processes in check long enough for the development of the positive problem-solving spiral on which the process depends for its effectiveness. It is true that such an uncontrollable breakthrough of hostility has not yet occurred in my experience with the method. Nevertheless, concern over the negative possibilities is in part responsible for my slow, deliberate, and rather formal development of the confrontation of issues within the group.

FIGURE 2

Summary of messages to James Farrell from other group members

MORE OR BETTER:	LESS OR STOP:	CONTINUE AS NOW:
Give information on project progress (completion date slippage) Bill, Tony, David.	Let people go to other good job opportunities — stop hanging on to your good engineers — Tony, Bill.	Training operators on preventive maintenance—Henry.
Send progress reports or Sortair project — Bill.	Missing weekly planning meetings frequently — Jack, Henry, David.	Good suggestions in meetings — Tony, Henry.
Make engineers more readily available when help needed — Jack, Henry.	Ignoring memos and reports re cost control — David.	Asking the difficult and awkward questions — Tony, Jack.
Keep better informed re plans and activities — David.	Setting aside my priorities on engineering work — Henry, Jack.	Willingness to help on design problems — Bill, Jack.
Enforce safety rules on engineers when in production area — Henry.	Charging time on Sortair to other accounts — David.	Good quality project work—Bill, Henry, David, Jack.
Push harder on the Sensiter project — David, Henry, Tony, Jack.	Overrunning agreed project budget without discussing beforehand — David.	

The Influence Trade

After each member had had an opportunity to clarify the messages he has received, the group selects the issues for negotiation. The consultant begins this phase by reemphasizing that, unless a quid pro quo can be offered in return for a desired behavior change, there is little point in having a discussion about it: *unless behavior changes on both sides the most likely prediction is that the status quo will continue.*

If behavior changes merely as the result of an exchange of views between men of good will, all the better. However, one cannot count on it.

Each participant is asked to choose one or more issues on which he particularly wants to get some changes on the part of another. He is also asked to select one or more issues on which he feels it may be possible for him to move in the direction desired by others. He does this by marking his own flip chart and those of the other members. In effect, *each person indicates the issues upon which he most wants to exert influence and those on which he is most willing to accept influence.* With the help of the consultant, the group then goes through the list to select the most negotiable issues, those where there is a combination of a high desire for change on the part of an initiator and a willingness to negotiate on the part of the person whose behavior is the target of the change attempt. The consultant asks for a group of two or more persons who are involved in one such issue to volunteer for a negotiation demonstration before the rest of the group.

The negotiation process consists of the parties making contingent offers to one another such as "If you do X, I will do Y." The negotiation ends when all parties are satisfied that they will receive a reasonable return for whatever they are agreeing to give. The consultant asks that the agreement be formalized by writing down specifically and concretely what each party is going to give and receive in the bargain (Figure 3). He also asks the participants to discuss openly what sanctions can be applied in the case of nonfulfillment of the bargain by one or another party. Often this involves no more than reversion of the status quo, but it may involve the application of pressures and penalties as well.

After the negotiation demonstration, the members are asked to select other issues they wish to work on. A number of negotiations may go on simultaneously, the consultant being involved at the request of any party to any negotiation. All agreements are published to the entire group, however, and questioned by the consultant and the other members to test the good faith and reality orientation of the parties in making them. Where agreement proves impossible, the consultant and other group members try to help the parties find further incentives (positive or, less desirably, coercive) which they may bring to bear to encourage agreement.

This process is, of course, not as simple as it sounds. All kinds of difficulties can occur, from bargaining in bad faith, to refusal to bargain at all, to escalation of conflict. In my experience, however, group members tend to be rather wise about the issues they can and cannot deal with, and I refrain from pushing them to negotiate issues they feel are unresolvable. My aim is to light the sparks of team development with a successful experience which group members can look on as a fruitful way of improving their effectiveness and satisfaction.

The Consultant Withers Away

The cycle ends here. Each group must then try living with their agreements. There is always, of course, the occasion to meet later with the consultant to work out new agreements or renegotiate old ones.

Ideally, the group should learn this process so thoroughly that the consultant's role withers away. To do this, though, they must be so fully aware of the dangers and pitfalls involved in the negotiation process that a third party's arbitration is no longer needed.

So far this has not occurred in my experience. The positive results are expressed mostly in terms of less backsliding between visits than has occurred in groups where I have applied more interpersonal behavior-change methods. Role negotiation agreements have more teeth in them.

What are the advantages of role negotiation? First of all, participants seem more at home with problems of power and influence than other interpersonal issues. They feel more competent and less dependent on the consultant in dealing

FIGURE 3

Final agreement between James Farrell and David Sills

Jim agrees to let David know as soon as agreed completion dates and cost projections look as though they won't be met, and also to discuss each project's progress fully with David on a bi-weekly basis.

In return, David agrees not to raise questions about cost details and completion dates, pending a trial of this agreement to see if it provides sufficient information soon enough to deal with questions from above.

with the problems and so they are ready to work sooner and harder.

Furthermore, the consultant's or referee's amount of skill and professional training which is required to conduct role negotiation is less than for more sensitive approaches.

That does not mean that role negotiation poses no threat to organization members. The consultant asks participants to be open about matters that are often kept secret in everyday life. This requires more than the normal amount of trust and confidence. If not, these matters would have been talked about before the group ever got to the role negotiation.

There also seems to be some additional discomfort involved in *writing down* the changes one would like to see another make in his work behavior. Several times participants have questioned the necessity of doing this, because one feels so *exposed* when his concerns are written out for all to see, and there is the fear that others will think them silly, childish or odd (though this never seems to happen). If the matter comes up, I point out that one need not write down *all* the concerns he has, but only those he would like to work on with others at this time.

Of course, role negotiation, like any other process that changes relationships, does pose a threat to the participants. The members are never sure they will personally be better off after the change than before. In the case of role negotiation, most of these fears arise around losing power and influence, or losing freedom and becoming more controlled by others. Particular resistance to talking openly about issues occurs when someone is trying to manipulate another person to his own advantage, or when he feels that he might want to do this in the future. I think this is the main reason participants in role negotiation so often try to avoid the step of writing down their agreements. If things aren't down in black and white, they feel, it will be easier to ignore the agreement later on if it becomes inconvenient. Also, writing down agreements seems to dispel the aura of trust and good

fellowship which some groups like to create on the surface and below which they engage in quite a lot of cutthroat competition.

Role negotiation is of course no panacea for power problems in groups and between people. People may bargain in bad faith; agreements once reached may be broken; circumstances and personnel may change so that the work done becomes irrelevant. Of course, these problems can exist in any group or organization. What role negotiation *does* is try to deal with the problems directly and to identify and use constructively those areas of *mutual* advantage where both sides can benefit from discussion and agreement. These areas are almost always larger than people think they are, and when they find that they can achieve something *for* themselves by open negotiation which they could not achieve by covert competition, then the more constructive process can begin to grow.

Avoiding the Consultant's High Fees

One other likely advantage of role negotiation is the ease and economy with which it can be introduced into the firm.

One disadvantage of most behavioral approaches to team development is that the consultant's level of skill and experience must be very high indeed. Managers themselves are not confident in dealing with these issues, and because they feel uneasy in this area they reasonably want to have as much safety and skill as money can buy. This demand for skilled consultants on interpersonal and group processes has created a shortage and a meteoric rise in consulting fees. It seems unlikely that the supply will soon catch up with the demand.

The shortage of highly skilled workers in team development argues for deskilling the requirements for effective consultant performance. I see role negotiation as a way of reducing the skill requirements for team development consultation. Preliminary results by internal consultants using the approach have been promising.

For example, one management development manager teamed up with a colleague to conduct a successful role negotiation with his own top management. He reported that his main problem was getting up enough confidence to take on the job. The team development session itself went smoothly. Although I cannot say whether this experience was typical (I suspect it was not), it does lead me to hope that role negotiation will prove to be practical for use by internal consultants without professional training in the behavioral sciences.

What then are the main points about role negotiation? First, role negotiation focuses on work relationships: what people do, and how they facilitate and inhibit one another in the performance of their jobs. It encourages participants to work with problems using words and concepts they are used to using in business. It avoids probing to the deeper levels of their feelings about one another unless this comes out naturally in the process.

Second, it deals directly with problems of power and influence which may be neglected by other behavioral approaches. It does not attempt to dethrone the authority in the group, but other members are helped to explore realistically the sources of power and influence available to them.

Also, unlike some other behavioral approaches to team development, role negotiation is highly action-oriented. Its aim is not just the exposing and understanding of issues as such, but achieving changed ways of working through mutually negotiated agreements. Changes brought about

through role negotiation thus tend to be more stable and lasting than where such negotiated commitments are lacking.

In addition, all the procedures of role negotiation are clear and simple if a bit mechanical, and can be described to participants in advance so they know what they are getting into. There is nothing mysterious about the technique, and this reduces participants' feelings of dependency upon the special skill of the consultant.

Furthermore, role negotiation actually requires less skill from the consultant than some other behavioral approaches. Internal consultants can suitably use the technique without lengthy special training in the behavioral sciences. It can therefore be a moderate cost approach to organization change.

It's important to understand that role negotiation does not necessarily replace other "soft" behavioral approaches to organization change. Work groups can be effective and achievement-oriented and at the same time allow open and deeply satisfying interpersonal relationships.

However, resolving conflict successfully at the interpersonal level can only be done by first attacking the ever-present issues of power and influence among members. Role negotiation does this and provides a sound and effective base on which to build more satisfying relationships.

If role negotiation is an effective first or "basic" approach to team development, it goes without saying that employee growth means moving beyond this stage into a deeper exploration of intergrating work and relationships.

READING 20
INTERVENTIONS TO CHIP SUCCESSFULLY OUT OF TEAM-BUILDING "SAND-TRAPS"

Marilyn E. Harris
Ross N. Nicholson

The challenge of assisting organisations to address team building is no easy task, as it might appear on the surface. Consultants and people in organisations often fall into traps which can impede the effectiveness of their efforts. This article outlines key traps of which consultants must be aware and identifies ways in which to respond to them.

An organisation in a highly competitive environment needs to develop anticipatory and participatory behaviour. Greater participation in decision making generates commitment and motivation to excel during the implementation of those decisions, and pride in high accomplishment. To increase anticipatory behaviour a team must stop dwelling on past accomplishments or failures (e.g., reports) and set its sights on future developments, not only to anticipate the future but also, having anticipated the future, to make decisions that will have a successful impact on that future.

The process of team building is probably the best-known feature of organisational development, and possibly the one that shows the most promise for increasing the effectiveness of many contemporary organisations. Effective intragroup collaboration and problem solving are becoming increasingly important as organisations became more complex and more information-intensive; teamwork steadily becomes a more valuable asset.

In order to understand how team building

Source: Marilyn E. Harris and Ross N. Nicholson, "Interventions to Chip Successfully Out of Team-Building 'Sand-Traps,'" *Journal of Organizational Change Management* 3, no. 3 (1990), pp. 14–24. Reprinted with permission.

works, it is first necessary to have a clear idea of what team effectiveness really is. We can say a group of people have worked effectively as a team, in some circumstances, if they have met two important conditions. First, they have accomplished something of value; they reached the worthwhile goal they set for themselves or had presented to them. Second, they have maintained or increased their sense of cohesion or group integrity, and willingness to work together.

Whether the members of a certain group of people work together routinely as part of an intact work unit, or they have just come together to work as an ad hoc problem-solving group or task force, they can learn some basic techniques for good teamwork. The process of team building usually employs an outside person in the role of a coach, working with the team members for one or more concentrated sessions to help them build both their problem-solving capability and their cohesion.

The key to team building is helping people to learn to monitor their own interaction processes, rather than having them preoccupy themselves solely with the "content" of those processes (i.e., with the specific subject-matter or problems with which they are dealing). This "content-process" distinction is rather subtle and difficult to grasp for some people at first, and this is why an external consultant can prove to be a resource to them. The consultant can observe and participate as they go about their task and can help them develop process-type techniques and ground rules, such as to clarify objectives, agree on roles and interactions, disagree without fighting, solve problems collectively and collaboratively, focus their energies on outcomes, and commit themselves to concrete plans.

We can specify the basic conditions for a team to function effectively in terms of three primary factors: goals, roles, and attitude. Briefly, they are:

1. *Goals:* The group must have a clear-cut purpose or outcome which its members have set out to achieve. If they do not have a definite and firmly stated goal, then their first objective must be to establish their group's goal and then develop a plan to achieve that goal. The plan must spell out the timetable of their actions, with various tasks clearly related to the goal they want to achieve.

2. *Roles:* Sooner or later, they must extract what has to be done and divide up the work amongst themselves. They need to establish a clearly defined role or task assignment for each member, including that of the team leader. The group members need a clearly identified leader who has the skills to coordinate their activities while maintaining positive interpersonal relations. They need an agreed basis for dealing with one another when they meet as a group, as well as when they work on their own.

3. *Attitude:* An effective team has a distinctive, high-energy atmosphere in their meeting environment. Each member contributes to this ambience through his or her participation, and particularly "how" they participate (e.g., if one member is abrupt in talking to another, it may indicate a past conflict that still exists between them, but signals to others in the team to stay away from that type of interaction or the specific content, which will lower the energy in the environment). Using "group affect level" as a thermometer regularly to

check a team's health is important. Members and leaders can both monitor the quality of the interaction in this way, by drawing attention to the situation and checking to see if that is a ground rule by which the group wishes to abide in the future.

We use the metaphor of the sand-trap (or bunker, in English golfing parlance) in understanding the common blocks and problems in team building. This frames our understanding of the blocks in a distinctive way, demonstrating that there are ways to avoid the trap or to chip out easily, thereby resolving the problem. Further, it highlights the reality that getting into the sand-trap need not be an everlasting problem or one that occurs regularly: that, in fact, it is the type of potential problem which one should not expect to experience almost every time one begins team building in an organisation. We believe that it has relevance for understanding the complex and paradoxical phenomena of organisational life, and of the management of organisations. Finally, the metaphor brings a lightness to the serious business of working in the organisation and attempting to build teams.

This brief introduction is intended to provide a common ground on which to base consultation in team building in organisations. We have tried to outline a few of the critical interventions that consultants and eventually organisation members may make, either to avoid the sand-trap or successfully to chip out of it in the shortest time and with the least problem. The interventions noted are in no way intended to be inclusive, and we invite you to add your successful experiences to the list.

Sand-Trap 1: Stalled Starting Owing to Lack of a Key Person's Approval

Sometimes an organisation hesitates to initiate a team-building process until one last key person has given his or her approval. The result is institutional inertia. The consultant is faced with the dilemma of needing that key person's involvement, whilst at the same time understanding the importance of moving forward with the team-building process.

In one instance of a large bank with many branches throughout the state, where team building had been planned as a second phase in management development to cascade through the several levels of management emanating from the success of the executive team-building experience, it was repeatedly stalled. The chairman had not had a good experience in the off-site team building and therefore continually offered other priorities for the change team to address, putting off the team-building experience for the executive team members. The chairman was able to avoid the issue for some time, and everybody was afraid to go ahead without his blessing. Finally, the chief consultant pointed out to the chairman the number of second-tier teams that wanted to go ahead and indeed had made a formal request to do so. After repeated questioning by the chairman relative to the potential of other teams' success, considering that the top team had not been successful using this approach, he was assured it was worth the risk and that his team might like to try team-building there on-site as well. He then suggested that five teams go ahead and have one three-day team-building session, from which he would get reports.

When a stalling action occurs, consultants must enlist their supporters within the organisation in the effort to get that key person involved, while at the same time urging that work begins or continues. It may be sufficient to have that key person's verbal or financial support for team building, rather than waiting for his or her active participation.

In chipping out, consultants must learn to make maximum use of minimal or token gestures from key people. Sometimes, getting key people to experiment, to try out without great

risk, and to get some data for making future decisions is necessary.

Sand-Trap 2: Short-Team Training or a "Quick Fix" to Build Teams

Team building is a long-term ongoing process, and it is a tall order in almost all cases where teams are just beginning to be used. It is particularly difficult in organisations that have not been using group meetings effectively and that tend to work mainly through individuals (as noted later, in Sand-trap 10: The Big Sand-trap in the Sky, Rewarding Individuals). Conceptualising the task of building effective teams with the client is usually an important first step, particularly where the sense of "quick fix" is quite prevalent in the organisational thinking. However, in some cases, implementation of teams can be counterproductive. In reality the organisation may not be aware that it rewards only individual behaviour, not team or group efforts, and does not effectively use groups or teams in any place in the organisation; thus conceptualising the long-term developmental process in team building may simply be for naught. And although they may use the words quite effectively and articulate team approaches to solving problems, their behaviour belies them.

In still other situations, where the need is very high and time appears to be of the essence, consultants may be coerced into trying out a short-term training programme on a pilot basis without any commitment as to taking next steps and following through on developing an ongoing process. The seduction may then be based on the reality that there is too little time that they are willing to make available to do the real team building, or an unwillingness to pay a consultant for the time required to undertake team building. They may be operating out of the experience that they have been able to coerce other consultants into doing things in a shorter time, and do not see the necessity or the value of using more time.

The high risk here is that a trial balloon or a shortened "quick fix" may meet with such resistance that the team-building effort is dismantled before it can be broadened and achieve any measurable results. The consultant involved, or others following, are going to have a much more difficult job convincing the client that team building is an ongoing process and that it simply takes time. Essentially, learning process skills takes much more time than gaining substantive knowledge. A process commercial that is helpful in this situation is: "You have to go slow to go fast."

Obviously it is best to avoid this sand-trap by religiously practising Argyris's three intervention tasks with the client (i.e., to provide valid data, to allow for a free and informed decision, and to develop commitment to that decision before taking action). In most situations this will work if the consultant is willing not to contract with clients who for whatever reason are not willing to go through these tasks systematically, and to take the time that is necessary for teams to practise the team-building process. Providing the valid data for making an honest decision about team building can be a difficult and arduous educational task. It may be difficult to convince some clients, regardless of what the data are and how they are presented. Often this is the best clue that this is not a worthwhile contract for the consultant or the client in which to engage at this time.

Once recognising that you are in this sand-trap is another situation, and it requires adroit manoeuvring as close as possible to the point of recognition of your position. Ideally the consultant should lightly chip out by calling "time" or "stop action," and ask for a joint diagnosis of "where are we?", attempting to point out that what is happening is not going to get them where they want to go in the time allotted for it. Otherwise, renegotiating a new contract with

the team to build it successfully in an appropriate amount of time is important. If this does not work then a deeper wedge is required, intending to get out of the sand-trap in the shortest possible time. The extreme may be to postpone team building until a better time or to terminate the contract, in order to prevent a failure for the organisation in team building. This is a judgement call the consultant must make, given his or her understanding of what is best for the organisation at that point.

In essence, an organisation must learn to replace the norm which values only short-term training or quick fix interventions with the realisation that effective team building is a developmental process that can be achieved only through people learning and taking the responsibility to monitor their own team interaction process, rather than being solely preoccupied with the "content" of those processes, the problems or the specific subject-matter. To facilitate an organisation moving in this direction, a consultant should develop a long-range plan and choose a small cluster of process-type issues to work thoroughly, such as clarifying objectives, agreeing on roles and interactions, disagreeing without fighting, and solving problems collectively. Visible movements on those issues will encourage the organisation to be receptive to team building.

Sand-Trap 3: Good Intentions without Action

One organisation with which we worked announced that from then on "the contributions of each and every worker will be listened to and respected. We have been top-down too long and we need to work from the bottom up. We need to act like a team, pulling together for common goals." Six months later the top team (CEO and senior vice presidents) came out with mission statements, goals, and objectives for the whole organisation, including those for divisions and departments, without any consultation at the lower levels of the organisation.

The attitude expressed by top management indicated their good intentions. However, their actions indicated that nothing had changed. They were clearly not "walking what they talked."

The external consultant is the appropriate party to confront the discrepancy between articulation and action. The norms for this kind of intervention must be set at the beginning. At the start of a team-building programme we are clear with the leader that, if his team does not give him adequate feedback on his behaviour, it is our roles as a consultants to do so. It is our consulting practice intentionally to set up interim meetings with the leader to provide feedback. So it becomes a natural part of the process to confront discrepancies between his or her good intentions and action or lack of action, specifically any lack of change in behaviour.

Sand-Trap 4: The Untouchables

The sand-trap involving the untouchables is a delicate one with which to deal for consultants and people in the organisation at almost any time. Untouchables are critical people entrenched in the old order, which does not include team building, who are blocks to the team-building process and change. They are standard-bearers for the old ways of interacting with people, for the most part on an individual and secretive basis. They may be key producers, or merely ensconced in positions of influence within the organisation.

Untouchables may be individuals who are known to be against the team-building process. Because they occupy powerful positions, others fear confronting their unacceptable behaviour. When an organisation fails to respond to such individuals, it sends a clear message: being a top producer or having power carries a great deal more weight than does team building.

To chip out of the sand-trap, untouchables must be touched. Consultants who discover untouchables must be willing to challenge the norms that keep those individuals protected and prevent the organisation from moving forward. Consultants who are unwilling to risk a confrontation collude in maintaining the status quo. If removal of the untouchable is impossible, his or her influence must be minimised and team building must go on.

Sand-Trap 5: Team Building Always Ends Up Happy

Team members often fall into the trap of believing that, once they have created a "team" and learned to monitor their interactions, balancing content and process to reach their objective, problems will disappear and struggles will cease. They fail to realise, however, that team building is dynamic. Consultants must teach team members that the happy ending is a myth. A well-managed team-building effort will produce fortuitous results, and new dilemmas, issues, and challenges will emerge. The team-building process entails living in a vibrant ever-changing organisation.

Closely related to the myth that team building always ends up happy is the common sand-trap of "we like each other and therefore we are a team." Teamwork for organisational effectiveness is sometimes taken lightly. Statements often heard are "If we get to know each other, then we will trust each other and then we will be a team" or "We get along so well together we make a good team" implying little or no conflict.

The trap is that acceptance of the mediocre understanding of a team will keep an organisation from developing high-performing highly skilled teams. The consultant must constantly confront such narrow understandings and push for skill development, work integration, openness, and candour. High-performing creative teams conflict openly and completely change the decision-making process. Work life cannot continue as it has in the past. The intervention for change pushes the organisation out of the sand-trap and back into the game.

Sand-Trap 6: Control Mechanism versus Empowerment

In one of the automobile companies, we were introducing Performance Team Building on the line. The foremen were impressed with the possibility of higher production and better quality. As the line teams were developing autonomy and sensing empowerment, the foreman would move in and set production and quality standards to "encourage them to do better." The team would pull back and lose momentum. The foreman, in trying to be helpful, was stifling the process.

The excitement of team development comes through internal commitment to the work and to the team, rather than external pressure from the foreman. The foreman needs extensive skill development in working with people via encouragement, influence, challenge, and motivation, rather than control through directives. The foreman's role must be redefined so that he or she is the "facilitator of internal commitment," rather than the enforcer through external control.

The intervention for the consultant to deal with this sand-trap is to begin with a clear positive redefinition of the leader's role in the team relationship, and with *appropriate skill development* in coaching. This sand-trap needs constant surveillance and intervention by the consultant. Leaders often fall back into the old patterns of wanting to control, rather than to facilitate and empower.

Sand-Trap 7: Team-Work Is Done only in Meetings

Often when teams find that they like working together early in their development, they fall into the trap of not wanting to do any work until they are all together in order to understand and agree on what should be done on the task. They become concerned about "permission" to do something on their own, not wanting to detract from the value of the synergic output of the team.

The ebb and flow of the team together and the team apart must be orchestrated by the leader. The "team together" is a time to make decisions about the work, but it is with the "team apart" that much of the "real work" is accomplished. Whether it is one person working independently, or two or three members working separately from other members of the team, it is the "team at work", and not only when they are physically gathered together.

Even when this has been addressed in the team preparation and plan, teams still fall into this trap. If it has not been avoided, the best "chipping" club to use is to add an interim process review session to the beginning of the meeting and a reporting summary of interim task assignments to the end of the meeting. These may be supplemented with meeting notes that outline interim tasks and the people responsible for each one. An important warning is not to make *only one person responsible—many* may be accountable for getting each task done, which does not preclude inviting others to help to do the work of the task in the interim between meetings.

Sand-Trap 8: From Directive to Permissive

The strong authoritarian leader is often the most frustrated when developing a team. The reaction is "if they want it (participation in decision making), they can have it," and he or she dumps responsibility on the team or abdicates authority without communicating support or setting the limitations and parameters related to the decision in hand.

The intervention here is two-dimensional. First, it is to recognise that there are choices for team decision making other than directive and permissive. The leader needs skills in the use of other methods of decision making—delegating styles, such as consultative (e.g., "I need your input, but I will make the decision"), collaborative (e.g., "We will make this decisions together as a team"), and facilitative (e.g., "You [the team or sub-team] can decide without me; I will support by clarifying requirements, options and strategies"). Usually, these other choices require skill development to be used effectively and can be developed within the team-building programme.

The second dimension for intervention here is one of appropriateness. Which style of decision making is appropriate for each situation? The manager will continue to be directive and make independent decisions for most of the ongoing day-to-day situations. So when is it appropriate to use team decision making, and which style will give the best results in each situation? The intervention is to broaden the base of well-honed decision-making skills for the team and chip out of the trap of unlimited choice between directive and permissive styles.

Sand-Trap 9: Team-Building Fatigue

The effort involved in continuing to do the regular job plus a major team-building programme can sometimes be overwhelming to participants, leading to team-building fatigue.

A data processing group of managers and directors were dragging their feet with the learning model. Pre-work not done, limited and hesitant participation, and irritable responses all decreased the value of the team-building effort. When we stopped and asked the group to assess what was wrong, they said "We learn all this great stuff and then go back into that whirlwind of work where nobody seems to care even when it works well."

One intervention to get out of this sand-trap is to develop a pattern of celebration even for small victories. The tradition of visiting the 19th hole for some camaraderie allows players to relive the highlights of the game, to enjoy one another's success, and especially to enjoy the sand-traps out of which they have learned to chip. Appropriate appreciation and celebration help to instil a sense of satisfaction for a job well done. This becomes a stronger motivator than a pay rise and will develop commitment to the next change effort with enthusiasm.

Another intervention is to establish the norm of networking relationships. Persons who are struggling with the same team-building issues can use each other as sounding-boards. The network experience can be stimulating and energy-regenerating, counteracting team-building fatigue.

Sand-Trap 10: The Big Sand-Trap in the Sky—Rewarding Individuals

The culture of most organisations is still highly individualised and is for that matter structurally dissonant from building teams. The larger American cultural environment surrounding organisations still supports individual aggressiveness and competitiveness. This is a very subtle sand-trap, not immediately obvious to many team-building consultants. We have tried to picture this in the diagram of our short course showing the first nine sand-traps (see Figure 1). The 10th sand-trap is shown as the shaded background in which the other 9 sand-traps are embedded. It is one thing to be aware of this sand-trap from the beginning, and to share its existence with the people who are involved in team building in the organisation as well as with those who are responsible for the decision to use and develop teams; but it is a very different issue to consider chipping out of this subtle, but overarching, sand-trap in the sky which exists in most organisations.

Chipping out is difficult, for it actually involves eventual restructuring of the golf-course and/or organisation. Until very recently this has been a rare choice for most organisations, despite the many built-in "advantages" for the team approach. In considering teams and small groups over individuals as basic design units around which to build organisations, one must realise that:

FIGURE 1

Team-building sand-traps: avoid or chip out

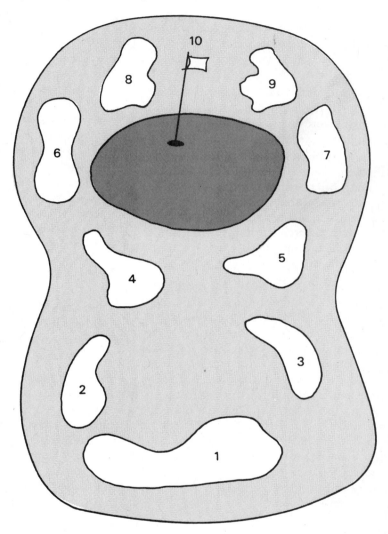

1. Teams seem to be good for people. They can satisfy important membership needs. They can provide a moderately wide range of activities for individual members. They can provide support in times of stress and crisis. They are settings in which people can learn, not only cognitively but also empirically, to be reasonably trusting and helpful to one another.

2. Teams seem to be good problem-solving tools. They seem to be useful in promoting innovation and creativity.

3. In a wide variety of decision situations they make better decisions than do individuals.

4. They are great tools for implementation. They gain commitment from their members, so that group decisions are likely to be carried out willingly.

5. They can control and discipline members in ways that are often extremely difficult through more impersonal quasi-legal disciplinary systems.

6. As organisations grow, small groups appear to be useful mechanisms for fending off many of the negative effects of size. They help prevent communication lines from growing too long, the hierarchy from growing too steep, and the individual from getting lost in the crowd.

Chipping out of sand-trap 10 will require several educational "chips" carefully planned, with restructuring alternatives and successful experiences close at hand. Many organisations are willing to consider restructuring, based on teams after considerable success with teams has been experienced, and will restructure a division or department accordingly. This sand-trap is discussed not only to alert consultants to the existence and the subtlety of this overarching sand-trap but also to help them understand the built-in resistance that they may experience from team and organisation members. It is far better to be forewarned and prepared than to be surprised and overwhelmed.

Checklist of Consultant Interventions

The consultant works her or his way out of the sand-traps using intervention skills. The following types of interventions are basic approaches to the client and consultant working together, chipping out of the sand-traps with aplomb:

- *Collaborative:* The consultant involves the client in joint exploration of the blocking forces that prevent the organisation development process from moving forward. Having identified those obstacles, they then strategise together to turn them around.

- *Facilitative:* The consultant helps the client to develop a basic sense of personal security so that he or she can express him or herself freely in an atmosphere without fear of rejection.

- *Theoretical:* By building with the client a theoretical base pertinent to the client's situation, the consultant aids the client in internalising systematic and empirically tested ways of understanding and acting that will impact on the long-range goals of the organisation development process.

- *Confrontational:* The consultant challenges the client to examine the foundations of his or her thinking, especially the value-laden assumptions which may be distorting his or her view of the situation. Alternative approaches can then be generated for more effective long-term solutions to organisational problems.

In conclusion, as in a game of golf, avoid the sand-traps and, when you do get into one, chip cleanly out. Anticipation and planning for the avoidance of these team-building sand-traps will give teams the best chance of success. If you get into one of them, chip your way out with an intentional intervention and get back into the game.

Bibliography

Albrecht, K. (1983). *Organization Development: A Total Systems Approach to Positive Change in any Business Organization.* Englewood Cliffs, NJ: Prentice Hall.

Buchholz, S. and Roth, T. (1987). *Creating the High Performance Team.* New York: John Wiley & Sons.

Dyer, W.G. (1977). *Team Building: Issues and Alternatives,* Reading, MA: Addison-Wesley.

Leavitt, H.G., (1975). "Suppose We Took Work Groups Seriously?" In E.G. Cass, and F.G. Zimmer (eds.), *Man and Work in Society.* New York: Van Nostrand, pp. 67–77.

Likert, R. (1961), *New Patterns of Management.* New York: McGraw-Hill.

Patten, T.H. Jr. (1981). *Organizational Development through Team-building,* New York: John Wiley & Sons.

Phillips, S.L., and R.L. Elledge. (1989). *The Team-Building Source Book.* San Diego: University Associates.

Scholtes, P.R. (1988). *The Team Handbook.* Madison, WI: Joiner Associates.

READING 21
STRATEGIES FOR IMPROVING HEADQUARTERS-FIELD RELATIONS

Robert Blake, Herbert A. Shepard, and Jane S. Mouton

Organizations whose operations extend over great distances encounter complex problems in maintaining effective integration between the headquarters facility and field installations.[1] Geographical distance makes communications difficult. Differences in regional experience are hard for the person at a distance to comprehend. Psychological distance develops to enhance the mechanical difficulties created by geography.

In all other parts of an organization, superordinate groups are joined to subordinate groups by a common member (i.e., the leader of a subordinate group is himself a subordinate in the group consisting of himself, his peers, and his boss).[2] The linkpin between groups of unequal power, while more responsive to those above than below, nonetheless has a powerful mediating effect. He is placed in personal conflict and stress if the two groups in which he has membership are in conflict. The stresses on the foreman are so great that in many organizations he loses membership in both groups; that is, he has little influence up or down. Clearly, there is no linkpin between union and management, and, through unionization and legislative supports, union and management are approximately equal in power.

Most headquarter-field relationships lack this cement, and it is not uncommon for negative attitudes to develop between the parties. In formal theory, field units are subordinate to headquarters, but field units can acquire great informal power. This is particularly true if one field organization is very much larger than other field divisions and accounts for a majority, or at least a large portion, of the company's business. In such cases, the head of the field division may be given formal membership in the top corporate group, thus providing the missing cement. But if, as is more often the case, there are several large or many small field units, headquarters maintains its power by placing them in competition with one another. Building good relations and a good record with headquarters can lead to promotion for key executives in a field unit and to a favored position when headquarters contemplates new investment.

Field groups can develop resentment toward headquarters for many reasons. For example, each field unit is, in most companies, treated as a profit center. However, the profitability of the whole corporation may sometimes require that a given field unit do something which reduces its own profitability. Similarly, new investment by headquarters in one field unit can arouse feelings of injustice in others.

Such problems were causing severe deterioration of relationships between headquarters and a large division in the Tennex Corporation. The following pages describe the problem-solving procedures employed to bring about adequate working relationships. The design was, of course, adapted to the particular set of problems being experienced by Tennex. A different design would be used, for example, if the object were to build better team relations among several field units, and between them and headquarters.

[1] R. R. Blake and J. S. Mouton, "Headquarters-Field Team Training for Organizational Improvement." *ASTD J.* 16, no. 3 (1962), pp. 3–11.

[2] R. R. Blake and J. S. Mouton, *The Managerial Grid* (Houston: Gulf Publishing, 1964); and R. Likert, *New Patterns of Management* (New York: McGraw-Hill, 1961).

Source: Robert Blake, Herbert A. Shepard, and Jane S. Mouton, *Managing Intergroup Conflict in Industry* (Houston: Gulf Publishing, 1964), pp. 114–21.

The Scofield Case

The following example illustrates an approach to the improvement of working relationships between headquarters and field. The Scofield Division is one of several subsidiaries of the Tennex Corporation. The Tennex Corporation is a highly diversified organization, moderately decentralized.

Since World War II, Tennex has grown quite rapidly, partly by acquisition. Corporate efforts to develop strategies in marketing and production which took advantage of its diverse resources brought many changes which affected Scofield, one of the divisions. Over a period of years, a number of points of friction had developed between the division's management and the top corporate management.

Headquarters personnel felt the division managers were "secretive" and "unresponsive." The division was looked upon as unwilling to provide information that headquarters felt it needed. In turn, Scofield Division management saw the headquarters management as "prying" and "arbitrary." For example, headquarters was critical of the labor relations practices of the division. The division management resented the criticism, regarding it as prejudiced and ill-informed. Again, headquarters felt that Scofield managers had been "dragging their feet" in implementing corporate marketing policies. Scofield felt that headquarters' demands in the area were unrealistic and that the corporate marketing group was behaving "unilaterally," and so on.

The behavioral science consultants called in to help first acquainted themselves with key management in both locations and were exposed to the patterns of action and reaction, frustration, and negative stereotypes, which characterize a deteriorating intergroup working relationship. Some of the headquarters executives were considering replacing certain Scofield managers. The latter, in their turn, were attempting to influence other top corporate officers in Scofield's behalf.

Gaining Perspective on Intergroup and Intragroup Dynamics. In separate three-day conferences with each group, the consultants provided intragroup (or "team") and intergroup training experiences and theory. The intergroup training had two effects. First, managers were able to see the headquarters-field problem in sufficient perspective to analyze the destructive consequences of the win-lose trap which had been dictating their actions. Second, an intergroup experiment and its analysis created a degree of openness within each group of managers that enabled them to review their own intragroup relationships and to develop greater mutual understanding and acceptance. This teamwork training is an important prelude to intergroup confrontation, because friction, "politics," or inability to level within each team clouds and confuses intergroup communication when the two groups are brought together.

The Headquarters-Field Laboratory. As a next step after the separate three-day conferences, the two teams met together, again for a three-day period. It will be convenient to describe their work as a sequence of phases.

Phase I: Listing Issues Requiring Joint Problem Solving. The laboratory opened with a joint session in which members discussed those issues they felt the group should debate. These were then listed in order of priority to provide an overview of the work to be accomplished over the three-day period.

Phase II: Preparation of Group Self-Images and Images of the Other Group. Each group met separately to prepare a description of itself as viewed by its members. The issues listed in Phase I provided a basis for elaborating and giving substance to the self-image descriptions.

Next, each group constructed a verbal image *of the other group.* Scofield's "secretiveness" as experienced by headquarters and headquarters' "prying" as experienced by Scofield could thus be bought into open communication.

Finally, each group built a description of the relationship between Tennex headquarters and the Scofield Division.

These images were developed to provide a background statement of existing attitudes, feelings, and difficulties which needed to be examined, understood, and overcome.

Phase III: Exchange of Images. During this phase, each group in turn exposed its own image of itself, and in turn listened to the image as perceived by the other group. The process of bringing these images into the open created a background of understanding and brought a new atmosphere of mutual acceptance into the discussion.

Finally, a review was undertaken of relationship problems with respect to the issues that had been listed at the beginning of the conference. Since most of these were related to specific functions and activities, they provided the basis for moving to the subgroup meetings of Phase IV.

Phase IV: Subgroup Meetings Based on Similarity of Function in Field and Headquarters. During Phase IV, members from the headquarters staff with functional responsibilities at the corporate level met with Scofield managers who had responsibility for the corresponding function in the plant.

The purpose of these discussions was akin to the "team development" of the earlier three-day conferences: to explore relationship problems between individuals whose responsibilities make them interdependent. Once interpersonal relationship issues had been explored and sources of difficulty had been cleared out of the way, it was possible to discuss functional problems in a climate conducive to understanding and collaboration.

The latter part of Phase III and beginning of Phase IV brought out dramatically how confused and inadequate communication between Scofield

and headquarters had been in many areas. The headquarters group seized on the relationship-image exchange as an excellent opportunity to "explain" to Scofield things that they believed Scofield did not understand. As the discussion proceeded, however, the tables were turned. When the field group presented its view of the relationship it began to "get through" to headquarters. By the end of Phase IV, headquarters staff members were *really* able to understand operational difficulties from a field point of view. They were also able to see more clearly how they might serve as consultants in the field, rather than as persons who attempt to "control" field operations.

Phase V: Review and Planning. In this phase the two groups met to prepare an overall summary of problems that had been identified and defined. This led to a joint discussion of the kinds of changes required to bring about improvements. Some of the problems implied changes in the behavior of only one of the groups, but most required joint implementation by functional subgroups.

The most significant product of this phase was that it provided a new concept of the way to bring about change and innovation. For instance, prior to the headquarters-field conference, it was accepted that "headquarters formulates policy; the field implements it." The inappropriateness of this concept for policies which had long been in force was evident to both parties. Reports from the field told headquarters whether the policy was being implemented adequately and enabled the headquarters to take special action where departures from policy were detected.

Conference discussions clearly disclosed that this control was woefully inadequate during a period of policy changing, policy making, or during implementation of new or changed policies. Communication distortions and breakdowns, areas of mutual frustration with the accompanying charges of "foot-dragging" and "arbitrariness," were seen to be the result of those methods which had been used in developing and implementing new policies.

Both sides came to see clearly that making and implementing new or changed policy is a complex process requiring continuous feedback among those involved. Efforts to implement a change are experiments, the results of which need to be quickly available to the organization. They are reality tests which may lead to policy modification, and they are explorations to find sufficient methods of implementation. The policy-making-and-implementing process was thus seen as an innovation phase requiring open communication and collaboration among members of the leadership groups.

Phase VI: Followup. By the end of Phase V, much had been accomplished in the areas of mutual trust, respect, and understanding. Moreover, the groups had made a number of commitments to new ways of working and had reached a number of agreements in defining certain problems and the courses of action to be taken in solving them.

Realizing that planning is insufficient to bring about desired results, the groups established some means for operational followup. The groups also agreed to reconvene for review and evaluation after a period of implementation. The purpose of this meeting would be to insure that they could find ways to handle possible difficulties in carrying out the plans of Phase V, and in "checking on the health" of the relationship. Thus, if new sources of friction were to arise for which no problem-solving procedure was available, they could be dealt with appropriately.

Summary

The normal day-by-day working arrangements between the headquarters facilities and field units often generate many problem areas. Some of the problems tend to become chronic. As a rule, formal communication and decision-making arrangements are insufficient for correcting these chronic difficulties.

Headquarters-field training situations as described in this article are useful devices for exploring and improving organizational interrelationships, including: headquarters interrelations and operations, field interrelations and operations, problems at the general level between headquarters and the field, and functional and concrete operational difficulties within those segments of the organization which are responsible for smooth working arrangements between headquarters and field.

Appendix: Postscript for "Strategies for Improving Headquarters-Field Relations"

This article represented one of the series of spinoff applications of the basic intergroup confrontation and resolution design that we pioneered in the mid-50s. We see no revisions, based on our experience with it over 25 years, that constitute fundamental improvements. However, consultants using this design implement it in short-cut ways that may fail to solve problems underlying headquarters-field tensions. Limitations such as this in using the design are most likely to derive from the consultant's failure to sense the depth of intergroup tensions, and therefore to prompt premature informality in a way that is not present in the design itself. This is likely to lead to mutual accusations and defensive retaliations, rather than to constructive efforts to resolve the underlying problems.[3]

---

[3] Robert Blake and Jane Mouton, personal correspondence.

READING 22
THE CONFRONTATION MEETING

Richard Beckhard

One of the continuing problems facing the top-management team of any organization in times of stress or major change is how to assess accurately the state of the organization's health. How are people reacting to the change? How committed are subordinate managers to the new conditions? Where are the most pressing organization problems?

In the period following a major change—such as that brought about by a change in leadership or organization structure, a merger, or the introduction of a new technology—there tends to be much confusion and an expenditure of dysfunctional energy that negatively affects both productivity and morale.

At such times, the top-management group usually spends many hours together working on the business problems and finding ways of coping with the new conditions. Frequently, the process of working together under this pressure also has the effect of making the top team more cohesive.

Concurrently, these same managers tend to spend less and less time with their subordinates and with the rest of the organization. Communications decrease between the top and middle levels of management. People at the lower levels often complain that they are less in touch with what is going on than they were before the change. They feel left out. They report having less influence than before, being more unsure of their own decision-making authority, and feeling less sense of ownership in the organization. As a result of this, they tend to make fewer decisions,

take fewer risks, and wait until the "smoke clears."

When this unrest comes to the attention of top management, the response is usually to take some action such as:

Having each member of the top team hold team meetings with his subordinates to communicate the state of affairs, and following this procedure down through the organization.

Holding some general communication improvement meetings.

Conducting an attitude survey to determine priority problems.

Any of these actions will probably be helpful, but each requires a considerable investment of time, which is competitive with the time needed to work on the change problem itself.

Action Plans

Recently I have experimented with an activity that allows a total management group, drawn from all levels of the organization, to take a quick reading on its own health, and—*within a matter of hours*—to set action plans for improving it. I call this a "confrontation meeting."

The activity is based on my previous experience with an action-oriented method of planned change in which information on problems and attitudes is collected and fed back to those who produced it, and steps are taken to start action plans for improvement of the condition.

Sometimes, following situations of organizational stress, the elapsed time in moving from identification of the problem to collaborative action planning must be extremely brief. The confrontation meeting can be carried out in 4½ to 5 hours' working time, and it is designed to include the entire management of a large system in a joint action planning program.

I have found this approach to be particularly practical in organization situations where there are large numbers in the management group and/or where it is difficult to take the entire group off the job for any length of time. The activity has been conducted several times with a one evening and one morning session—taking only 2½ hours out of a regular working day.

The confrontation meeting discussed in this article has been used in a number of different organization situations. Experience shows that it is appropriate where:

There is a need for the total management group to examine its own workings.

Very limited time is available for the activity.

Top management wishes to improve the conditions quickly.

There is enough cohesion in the top team to ensure follow-up.

There is real commitment to resolving the issues on the part of top management.

The organization is experiencing, or has recently experienced, some major change.

In order to show how this technique can speed the process of getting the information and acting on it, let us first look at three actual company situations where this approach has been successfully applied. Then we will examine both the positive results and the possible problems that could occur through the use and misuse of this technique. Finally, after a brief summary there are appendixes for the reader interested in a more elaborate description of the phasing and scheduling of such a meeting.

Case Example A.   The initial application of the confrontation meeting technique occurred in

1965 in a large food products company. Into this long-time family-owned and closely controlled company, there was introduced for the first time a nonfamily professional general manager. He had been promoted from the ranks of the group that had previously reported to the family-member general manager.

This change in the "management culture," which had been carefully and thoroughly prepared by the family executives, was carried out with a minimum number of problems. The new general manager and his operating heads spent many hours together and developed a quite open problem-solving climate and an effective, cohesive team. Day-to-day operations were left pretty much in the hands of their immediate subordinates, while the top group focused on planning.

A few months after the change, however, the general manager began getting some information that indicated all was not well further down in the organization. On investigation, he discovered that many middle-level managers were feeling isolated from what was going on. Many were unclear about the authority and functions of the "management committee" (his top team); some were finding it very difficult to see and consult with their bosses (his operating heads); others were not being informed of decisions made at his management committee meetings; still others were apprehensive that a new power elite was developing which in many ways was much worse than the former family managers.

In discussing this feedback information with his operating heads, the general manager found one or two who felt these issues required immediate management committee attention. But most of the members of the top team tended to minimize the information as "the usual gripping," or "people needing too many decisions made for them," or "everybody always wanting to be in on everything."

The general manager then began searching for some way to:

Bring the whole matter into the open.

Determine the magnitude and potency of the total problem.

Give his management committee and himself a true picture of the state of the organization's attitudes and concerns.

Collect information on employee needs, problems, and frustrations in some organized way so that corrective actions could be taken in priority order.

Get his management committee members in better tune with their subordinates' feelings and attitudes, and put some pressure on the team members for continued two-way communication within their own special areas.

Make clear to the total organization that he—the top manager—was personally concerned.

Set up mechanisms by which all members of the total management group could feel that their individual needs were noticed.

Provide additional mechanisms for supervisors to influence the whole organization.

The confrontation meeting was created to satisfy these objectives and to minimize the time in which a large number of people would have to be away from the job.

Some 70 managers, representing the total management group, were brought together for a confrontation meeting starting at 9:00 in the morning and ending at 4:30 in the afternoon. The specific "design" for the day, which is broken down into a more detailed description in Appendix A, had the following components:

1. Climate setting—establishing willingness to participate.
2. Information collecting—getting the attitudes and feelings out in the open.
3. Information sharing—making total information available to all.
4. Priority setting and group action planning—holding work-unit sessions to set priority actions and to make timetable commitments.
5. Organization action planning—getting commitment by top management to the working of these priorities.
6. Immediate follow-up by the top management committee—planning first actions and commitments.

During the daylong affair, the group identified some 80 problems that were of concern to people throughout the organization; they selected priorities from among them; they began working on these priority issues in functional work units, and each unit produced action recommendations with timetables and targets; and they got a commitment from top management of actions on priorities that would be attended to. The top-management team met immediately after the confrontation meeting to pin down the action steps and commitments.

(In subsequent applications of this confrontation meeting approach, a seventh component—a progress review—has been added, since experience has shown that it is important to reconvene the total group four to six weeks later for a progress review both from the functional units and from the top-management team.)

Case Example B. A small company which makes products for the military had been operating at a stable sales volume of $3 million to $4 million. The invention of a new process and the advent of the war in Vietnam suddenly produced an explosion of business. Volume rose to the level of $6 million within six months and promised to redouble within another year.

Top management was desperately trying to (a) keep raw materials flowing through the line, (b) get material processed, (c) find people to hire, (d) discover quicker ways of job training, and (e) maintain quality under the enormously increased pressure.

There was constant interaction among the

five members of the top-management team. They were aware of the tension and fatigue that existed on the production line, but they were only vaguely aware of the unrest, fatigue, concern, and loneliness of the middle manager and foreman groups. However, enough signals *had* filtered up to the top team to cause concern and a decision that something needed to be done right away. But, because of the pressures of work, finding the time to tackle the problems was as difficult as the issues themselves.

The entire management group agreed to give up one night and one morning; the confrontation meeting was conducted according to the six component phases described earlier, with phases 1, 2, and 3 being held in the evening and phases 4, 5, and 6 taking place the following morning.

Case Example C.   A management organization took over the operation of a hotel which was in a sorry state of affairs. Under previous absentee ownership, the property had been allowed to run down; individual departments were independent empires; many people in management positions were nonprofessional hotel people (i.e., friends of the owners); and there was very low competence in the top management team.

The general manager saw as his priority missions the need to:

Stop the downhill trend.

Overcome a poor public image.

Clean up the property.

Weed out the low-potential (old friends) management.

Bring in professional managers in key spots.

Build a management team.

Build effective operating teams, with the members of the top-management team as links.

He followed his plan with considerable success. In a period of one year he had significantly cleaned up the property, improved the service, built a new dining room, produced an enviable food quality, and begun to build confidence in key buyers, such as convention managers. He had acquired and developed a very fine, professional, young management team that was both competent and highly motivated. This group had been working as a cohesive team on all the hotel's improvement goals; differences between them and their areas seemed to have been largely worked through.

At the level below the top group, the department and section heads, many of whom were also new, had been working under tremendous pressure for over a year to bring about improvements in the property and in the hotel's services. They felt very unappreciated by the top managers, who were described as "always being in meetings and unavailable," or "never rewarding us for good work," or "requiring approval on all decisions but we can't get to see them," or "developing a fine top-management club but keeping the pressure on us and we're doing the work."

The problem finally was brought to the attention of the top managers by some of the department heads. Immediate action was indicated, and a confrontation meeting was decided on. It took place in two periods, an afternoon and the following morning. There was an immediate follow-up by the top-management team in which many of the issues between departments and functions were identified as stemming back to the modus operandi of the top team. These issues were openly discussed and were worked through. Also in this application, a follow-up report and review session was scheduled for five weeks after the confrontation meeting.

Positive Results

The experience of the foregoing case examples, as well as that of other organizations in which the confrontation meeting technique has been applied, demonstrates that positive results— particularly, improved operational procedures and improved organization health—frequently occur.

Operational Advantages. One of the outstanding plus factors is that procedures which have been confused are clarified. In addition, practices which have been nonexistent are initiated. Typical of these kinds of operational improvement, for example, are the reporting of financial information of operating units, the handling of the reservation system at a hotel, and the inspection procedures and responsibilities in a changing manufacturing process.

Another advantage is that task forces, and/or temporary systems, are set up as needed. These may be in the form of special teams to study the overlap in responsibilities between two departments and to write new statements and descriptions, or to work out a new system for handling order processing from sales to production planning, or to examine the kinds of information that should flow regularly from the management committee to middle management.

Still another improvement is in providing guidance to top management as to specific areas needing priority attention. For example, "the overtime policy set under other conditions is really impeding the achievement of organization requirements," or "the food in the employee's cafeteria is really creating morale problems," or "the lack of understanding of where the organization is going and what top management's goals are is producing apathy," or "what goes on in top management meetings does not get communicated to the middle managers."

Organization Health. In reviewing the experiences of companies where the confrontation meeting approach has been instituted, I have perceived a number of positive results in the area of organization health:

A high degree of open communication between various departments and organization levels is achieved very quickly. Because people are assigned to functional units and produce data together, it is possible to express the real feeling of one level or group toward another, particularly if the middle echelon believes the top wants to hear it.

The information collected is current, correct, and "checkable."

A real dialogue can exist between the top management team and the rest of the management organization, which personalizes the top manager to the total group.

Larger numbers of people get "ownership" of the problem, since everyone has some influence through his unit's guidance to the top-management team; thus people feel they have made a real contribution. Even more, the requirement that each functional unit take personal responsibility for resolving some of the issues broadens the base of ownership.

Collaborative goal setting at several levels is demonstrated and practiced. The mechanism provides requirements for joint goal setting within each functional unit and between top and middle managers. People report that this helps them to understand "management by objectives" more clearly than before.

The top team can take corrective actions based on valid information. By making real commitments and establishing check or review points, there is a quick building of trust in management's intentions on the part of lower level managers.

There tends to be an increase in trust and confidence both toward the top-management team and toward colleagues. A frequently appearing agenda item is the "need for better understanding of the job problems of other departments," and the output of these meetings is often the commitment to some "mechanism for systematic interdepartmental communication." People also report a change in their stereotypes of people in other areas.

This activity tends to be a "success experience" and thus increases total morale. The process itself, which requires interaction, contribution, and joint work on the problems and which rewards constructive criticism, tends to produce a high degree of enthusiasm and commitment. Because of this, the follow-up activities are crucial in ensuring continuation of this enthusiasm.

Potential Problems

The confrontation meeting technique produces, in a very short time, a great deal of commitment and desire for results on the part of a lot of people. Feelings tend to be more intense than in some other settings because of the concentration of time and manpower. As a result, problems can develop through misuse of the techniques.

If the top-management team does not really use the information from its subordinates, or if there are great promises and little follow-up action, more harm can be caused to the organization's health than if the events were never held.

If the confrontation meeting is used as a manipulative device to give people the "feeling of participation," the act can boomerang. They will soon figure out management's intentions, and the reaction can be severe.

Another possible difficulty is that the functional units, full of enthusiasm at the meeting, set unrealistic or impractical goals and commitments. The behavior of the keyman in each unit—usually a department manager or division head—is crucial in keeping suggestions in balance.

One more possible problem may appear when the functional units select a few priority issues to report out. While these issues may be the most *urgent,* they are not necessarily the most *important.* Mechanisms for working *all* of the information need to be developed within each functional unit. In one of the case examples cited earlier, the groups worked the few problems they identified very thoroughly and never touched the others. This necessitated a "replay" six months later.

In Summary

In periods of stress following major organization changes, there tends to be much confusion and energy expended that negatively affects productivity and organization health.

The top-management team needs quick, efficient ways of sensing the state of the organization's attitudes and feelings in order to plan appropriate actions and to devote its energy to the most important problems.

The usual methods of attitude surveys, extended staff meetings, and so forth demand extensive time and require a delay between getting the information and acting on it.

A short micromechanism called a "confrontation meeting" can provide the total management group with:

An accurate reading on the organization's health.

The opportunity for work units to set priorities for improvement.

The opportunity for top management to make appropriate action decisions based on appropriate information from the organization.

An increased involvement in the organization's goals.

A real commitment to action on the part of subgroups.

A basis for determining other mechanisms for communication between levels and groups, appropriate location of decisions, problem solving within subunits, as well as the machinery for upward influence.

Appendix A: Confrontation Meeting

Here is a detailed description of the seven components which make up the specific "design" for the day-long confrontation meeting.

Phase 1. Climate Setting (45 minutes to one hour).   At the outset, the top manager needs to communicate to the total management group his goals for the meeting, and his concern for and interest in free discussion and issue facing. He also has to assure his people that there is no punishment for open confrontation.

It is also helpful to have some form of information session or lecture by the top manager or a consultant. Appropriate subjects might deal with the problems of communication, the need for understanding, the assumptions and the goals of the total organization, the concept of shared responsibility for the future of the organization, and the opportunity for and responsibility of influencing the organization.

Phase 2. Information Collecting (one hour).

The total group is divided into small heterogeneous units of seven or eight people. If there is a top-management team that has been holding sessions regularly, it meets as a separate unit. The rest of the participants are assigned to units with a "diagonal slice" of the organization used as a basis for composition—that is, no boss and subordinate are together, and each unit contains members from every functional area.

The assignment given to each of these units is along these lines:

> Think of yourself as an individual with needs and goals. Also think as a person concerned about the total organization. What are the obstacles, "demotivators," poor procedures or policies, unclear goals, or poor attitudes that exist today? What different conditions, if any, would make the organization more effective and make life in the organization better?

Each unit is instructed to select a reporter to present its results at a general information-collecting session to be held one hour later.

Phase 3. Information Sharing (one hour).

Each reporter writes his unit's complete findings on newsprint, which is tacked up around the room.

The meeting leader suggests some categories under which all the data from all the sheets can be located. In other words, if there are 75 items, the likelihood is that these can be grouped into six or seven major categories—say, by type of problem, such as "communications difficulties"; or by type of relationship, such as "problems with top management"; or by type of area involved, such as "problems in the mechanical department."

Then the meeting breaks, either for lunch or, if it happens to be an evening session, until the next morning.

During the break all the data sheets are duplicated for general distribution.

Phase 4. Priority Setting and Group Action Planning (one hour and 15 minutes).

The total group reconvenes for a 15-minute general session. With the meeting leader, they go through the raw data on the duplicated sheets and put category numbers by each piece of data.

People are now assigned to their functional, natural work units for a one-hour session. Manufacturing people at all levels go to one unit, everybody in sales to another, and so forth. These units are headed by a department manager or division head of that function. This means that some units may have as few as 3 people and some as many as 25. Each unit is charged to perform three specific tasks:

1. Discuss the problems and issues which affect its area. Decide on the priorities and early actions to which the group is prepared to commit itself. (They should be prepared to share this commitment with their colleagues at the general session.)
2. Identify the issues and/or problems to which the top-management team should give its priority attention.
3. Decide how to communicate the results of the session to their subordinates.

Phase 5. Organization Action Planning (one to two hours).

The total management group reconvenes in a general session, where:

1. Each functional unit reports its commitment and plans to the total group.
2. Each unit reports and lists the items that its members believe the management team should deal with first.
3. The top manager reacts to this list and makes commitments (through setting targets or assigning task forces or timetables, and so on) for action where required.
4. Each unit shares briefly its plans for communicating the results of the confrontation meeting to all subordinates.

Phase 6. Immediate Follow-Up by Top Team (one to three hours). The top-management team meets immediately after the confrontation meeting ends to plan first follow-up actions, which should then be reported back to the total management group within a few days.

Phase 7. Progress Review (two hours). Follow-up with total management group four to six weeks later.

Appendix B: Sample Schedule

9:00 A.M. Opening Remarks, by general manager.
 Background, goals, outcomes.
 Norms of openness and "leveling."
 Personal commitment to follow-up.
9:10 General Session.
 Communications Problems in Organizations, by general manager (or consultant).
 The communications process.
 Communications breakdowns in organizations and individuals.
 Dilemmas to be resolved.
 Conditions for more openness.

10:00 Coffee.
10:15 Data Production Unit Session.
 Sharing feelings and attitudes.
 Identifying problems and concerns.
 Collecting data.
11:15 General Session.
 Sharing findings from each unit (on newsprint).
 Developing categories on problem issues.
12:15 P.M. Lunch.
 2:00 General Session.
 Reviewing list of items in categories.
 Instructing functional units.
 2:15 Functional Unit Session.
 Listing priority actions to be taken.
 Preparing recommendations for top team.
 Planning for presentation of results at general meeting.
 3:15 General Session.
 Sharing recommendations of functional units.
 Listing priorities for top team action.
 Planning for communicating results of meeting to others.
 4:15 Closing Remarks, by general manager.
 4:30 Adjournment.

READING 23
COLLATERAL ORGANIZATION: A NEW CHANGE STRATEGY

Dale E. Zand

Part One: Concepts

Many organization development specialists who emphasize behavioral rather than structural or technical change contend that free-form organizations, participative leadership, and humanistic values should—indeed, will—displace hierarchical organizations, directive leadership, and mechanistic values (Argyris, 1970; Bennis, 1965, 1966; Golembiewski, 1972; Likert, 1961, 1967; McGregor, 1960; Marguilies & Raia, 1972; Slater & Bennis, 1964; Tannenbaum & Davis, 1969). It is their view that knowledge rather than level of authority should (or will) determine decisions, and that environmental complexity and turbulence should (or will) cause one-man decision making to give way to group decision making.

These assertions have merit and are especially attractive to social scientists, but they are controversial to managers. Indeed, the idea of totally displacing existing systems may well have diverted managers into choosing sides, and thereby seriously interfered with their learning to improve their organization's adaptability and effectiveness. There is increasing evidence of a need for flexibility in structure and leadership style across different tasks and individuals; the superiority of any one approach above all others cannot be defended (Fiedler, 1967; Lawrence & Lorsch, 1967). The key issue is: How can OD specialists help managers design creative, problem-solving organizations and use them flexibly?

This article seeks to clarify and extend our concepts of organizational form and behavior by introducing the strategy of *collateral organization*[1] as a means of increasing flexibility. I shall present supporting theory and research; describe two field cases which illustrate methods of introducing collateral modes of organization; contrast collateral organizations with task forces, temporary systems, and matrix organizations; and finally, discuss their impact on the use of groups for solving problems and on the role of middle managers.

Collateral Mode Defined. Research into the relation between the structure of a problem and the effectiveness of different organizations suggests that a work group benefits from using more than one mode of organization. To state it simply: authority/production-centered organizations work best with "well-structured" problems; knowledge/problem-centered organizations work best with "ill-structured" problems. These organizational modes and problem structures will be described in greater detail later; the important point is that, since problems vary in structure, managers can and should operate in more than one organizational mode.

The concept of a secondary mode of working will be called a collateral organization. Hence a collateral organization is a supplemental organization coexisting with the usual, formal organization.[2] Of course a manager may develop more

Source: Reprinted with permission from NTL Institute, "Collateral Organization: A New Change Strategy?" by Dale E. Zand, pp. 63–69, *Journal of Applied Behavioral Science* 10, no. 1, copyright 1974.

[1] I shall use the word *organization* to mean the communication channels, relationships, and the inner workings of a group composed of a superior and his subordinates, and the working relationships between such groups—rather than the distinct major divisions of a company.

[2] *Collateral*, when used as a noun, denotes assets pledged as security for a loan. It is used here as an adjective, meaning to exist at the same time and level as, hence in association with, another organization.

than one collateral organization, but to keep matters simple we will talk of only one collateral mode in the remainder of this article.

Typically, a group has a chain of command and a division or responsibilities designed primarily for coping with well-defined, repetitive problems. Continued changes in consumers' desires, competitors' tactics, and product technology introduce unforeseen, ill-defined problems and opportunities. The hierarchical organizational structure is not designed to discover and solve these "ill-structured" problems. Managers, regardless of organizational level, therefore need collateral modes.

But managers hesitate to depart from the formal hierarchy to use a collateral mode because they are rarely given concepts explaining and legitimizing such departures. Traditional organization theory, for example, offers only the vague concept of "informal organization" (Pfiffner & Sherwood, 1960). Moreover, managers are advised to avoid and suppress informal organization because it is unsanctioned, unplanned, and unpredictable (Delbecq, 1968).

The manager's confusion is sometimes compounded by laboratory-method organizational development programs. Sensitivity training, grid laboratories, and variations of group methods focus on improving the manager's skill in individual and group behavior, but rarely introduce relevant organization theory. When a manager applies his new knowledge to his formal organization, he usually encourages open questioning of goals and methods, which blurs formal boundaries between jobs. Other managers interpret his actions as undermining authority and disrupting the formal organization, so they resist and discard his changes. The manager is in a theoretical limbo; without concepts, he cannot explain to other managers what he is doing in terms they can understand.

The concept of collateral organization is offered to aid managerial understanding and use of organizational development efforts. To explain and illustrate it, I shall first discuss the relationship between organizational problems and organizational structures, and the characteristics of a collateral organization.

Matching Problems and Modes. A problem is a dilemma and an organization is an instrument. It is useful to think of a problem and an organization as a set which is poorly or well matched. If the manager is to choose the right instrument for the job, it is important to understand when a problem and an organization are matched.

A problem can be classified as either well structured or ill structured. Some problems of course will have characteristics found in both categories, but analysis of the pure types will contribute most to understanding the matching process.

A well-structured problem—for example, preparing a customer's bill from a list of items and prices or putting values into a computer program which calculates the present worth of a capital investment—has the characteristics of physical or routine mental work.

In contrast, an ill-structured problem—for example, determining what new products should be added to a line over the next three years, preparing a schedule of prices for products that do not exist in any market, or projecting the long-range organizational, financial, and employment effects of a new marketing strategy—has the characteristics of complex, nonroutinized mental work. The elements of well-and ill-structured problems are outlined in Figure 1.

Usually a manager assumes that he has only one organization, which he must use for all problems. That is like a carpenter who uses a hammer for all jobs. A more effective manager first classifies a problem and then chooses an instrument best suited for it.

An organization (work group) can be classified as *(a)* authority/production centered or *(b)* knowledge/problem centered. Of course, some organizations will cross both categories, but again we learn the most from studying the two

FIGURE 1

Characteristics of well-structured and ill-structured problems

Element	Well-Structured Problems	Ill-Structured Problems
Variation of output with hours of work	Known. Proportional.	Unknown. Nonproportional.
Variation of output with number of people	Known. Proportional.	Unknown. Nonproportional.
Characteristics of input and output	Countable. Quality accurately measurable. Errors detected quickly, precisely.	Not countable. Quality difficult to measure. Errors difficult to detect.
Information available	Relevant. Accurate. Complete.	Uncertain. Inaccurate. Incomplete.
Solutions	Few are feasible. All are known. Best one determined easily.	Many are feasible. Few are known. Best one difficult to determine.
Experts	Past solution of similar problems is a reliable indication of expertise.	Many claim to be expert, but past experience is an unreliable guide to expertise.
Methods of control	External standards such as output targets, hours allowed, cost goals can effectively control performance.	External standards are inapplicable and misleading.
Feedback about results	Occurs shortly after action. Can be attributed to the action.	Occurs long after the action. Cannot be attributed only to the action.

pure types. The authority/production form is concerned with mobilizing people and equipment to maximize output of a finished product. The knowledge/problem form is concerned with processing or inventing knowledge to solve problems. Elements of the two organizational forms are compared in Figure 2.

Research Findings. Experimental research with small groups suggests that some combinations of organizations and problems are more productive than others. Communication network studies are especially relevant because they simulate many of the properties of the two types of organizations described in Figure 2, and the problems used fit well into one or the other of the two classes of problems described above. Transfer of results from experimental settings to operating organizations requires caution; so the findings summarized here can be viewed only as suggestive. They are presented in condensed

form for purposes of theory development, with some of the complex differences in morale and other factors set aside.

For well-structured problems, it appears that groups in the authority/production mode produce more output, more rapidly, than groups in the knowledge/problem mode (Bavelas, 1950; Christie, Luce, & May, Jr., 1952; Leavitt, 1951). And when groups organized in the knowledge/problem mode are given a series of well-structured problems and are allowed to reorganize, they shift toward the authority/production mode. They install a hierarchy, divide labor, and cut unused communication links (Guetzkow & Dill, 1957; Guetzkow & Simon, 1955).

For ill-structured problems, however, groups in the knowledge/problem mode devise solutions of better quality, more rapidly, than do groups in the authority/production mode (Shaw, Rothchild, & Strickland, 1957). The hierarchy, the division of labor, and the rules that make the

FIGURE 2

Types of organizations

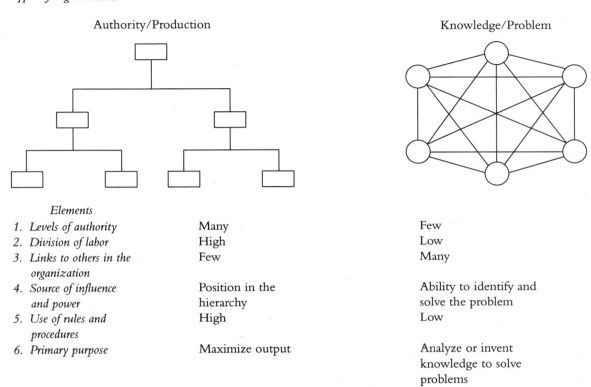

Authority/Production   Knowledge/Problem

Elements		
1. *Levels of authority*	Many	Few
2. *Division of labor*	High	Low
3. *Links to others in the organization*	Few	Many
4. *Source of influence and power*	Position in the hierarchy	Ability to identify and solve the problem
5. *Use of rules and procedures*	High	Low
6. *Primary purpose*	Maximize output	Analyze or invent knowledge to solve problems

authority/production mode effective for well-structured problems seem to interfere with the group's ability to devise quality solutions to ill-structured problems.

Another characteristic of the authority/production mode makes it unsuitable for ill-structured problems: it tends to reject unsolicited innovation. In this mode managers view an uninvited proposal for improvement as a distraction that will reduce output. In contrast, the knowledge/problem group tends to accept and use unsolicited innovations to improve productivity (Bavelas, 1950).

There are no experimental data on whether authority/production groups, given ill-structured problems, shift to a knowledge/problem mode. Observation of authority/production organizations suggests that when they are confronted with an ill-structured problem, such as entering a volatile market undergoing rapid technical change, managers do not shift to another mode but try to redefine the problem, forcing it to fit the existing hierarchy and division of labor. Burns and Stalker (1961) found that companies unable to shift to a knowledge/problem mode were unsuccessful in the new environment.

The most effective combinations (see Figure 3) are well-structured problems with authority/production organization (Quadrant I), and ill-structured problems with knowledge/problem

FIGURE 3

Relationship between type of problem and type of organization

Type of Problem	Type of Organization	
	Authority/Production	*Knowledge/Problem*
Well-Structured	**I** High output. Rapid processing. Small number of errors in output. Members low in authority report low satisfaction. Tends to reject unsolicited innovations.	**II** Lower output. Slower processing. More errors in output. More satisfying. Accepts unsolicited innovations.
Ill-Structured	**IV** Lower output. Slower processing. Low-quality solutions. Low in creativity. Orderly, but not functional.	**III** High output. Rapid processing. High-quality solutions. High creativity. Appears disorderly but is functional.

organization (Quadrant III). The other combinations (II and IV) are not so well matched.

Displacement Trap. Contrary to the "displacement belief," there is little likelihood that the authority/production mode, which is characteristic of most business organizations, will vanish. It works for well-structured problems and minimally disrupts the organization. There is, however, a limit to how far it can be stretched; and when a problem keeps recurring, that limit has by definition been exceeded. The challenge is: Can a manager and his group shift to a secondary mode before their primary mode becomes ineffective?

Many managers who make the shift to a new mode of organization are led to believe by poorly conceptualized OD efforts that they and their subordinates never again need directive behavior, specialized assignments, and limited communication. Such expectations prove unrealistic. Upon "regressing" to the authority/production mode, managers feel guilty and disappointed. Subordinates are frustrated and dissatisfied at relinquishing their newly found influence. Managers and subordinates frequently conclude that organizational development is a sham.

There may be a similar lack of realism about shifting even when the primary mode is knowledge/problem centered. For example, research units and educational institutions resist using the authority/production mode when it is needed, fearing that the primary, participative mode would not only be displaced but would be unrecoverable.

An understanding of collateral organization can help managers integrate needed changes while maintaining the primary organization.

Relation of Collateral Organization to Formal Organization.   In the remainder of this paper, for discussion purposes, I shall assume that the formal organization is in the authority/production mode. The collateral organization will be the knowledge/problem mode. (This state of affairs may of course be reversed in some organizations; e.g., research units and educational organizations.)[3]

In Tandem.   A collateral organization is distinguishable from and linked to the formal organization as follows:

1. The purpose of the collateral organization is to identify and solve problems not solved by the formal (primary) organization.
2. A collateral organization creatively complements the formal organization. It allows new combinations of people, new channels of communication, and new ways of seeing old ideas.
3. A collateral organization operates in parallel or in tandem with the formal organization. Both the collateral and the formal organizations are available; a manager chooses one or the other, depending on the problem. A collateral organization does not displace the formal organization.
4. A collateral organization consists of the same people who work in the formal organization. There are no new people.

5. The outputs of the collateral organization are inputs to the formal organization. The ultimate value of a collateral organization depends on successfully linking it to the formal organization, so its outputs are used.
6. A collateral organization operates with norms (that is, expectations of how people will behave) that are different from the norms in the formal organization. The different norms facilitate new ideas and new approaches to obstacles.

Characteristics.   A collateral organization has the following characteristics:

1. All channels are open and connected. Managers and specialists are free to communicate without being restricted to formal channels in the hierarchy.
2. There is a rapid and complete exchange of relevant information.
3. Norms encourage careful questioning and analysis of goals, assumptions, methods, alternatives, and criteria for evaluation.
4. A manager can approach and enlist others in the organization to help solve a problem, without being restricted to his formal subordinates.

Part Two: Applications

The two cases that follow illustrate different social technologies for introducing collateral organization. They are brief descriptions of change efforts in the field. They do not have the benefit of control groups or the statistical data characteristic of rigorous experimental research, though information is presented about end results—ill-structured problems identified and solved, and productivity. The cases do not dwell on the interpersonal dynamics of group-based change efforts, which are described in other studies (e.g., Argyris, 1970; Golembiewski, 1972).

---

[3] When the knowledge/problem mode is primary, the organization requires and attracts individuals who value individual contribution, creativity, self-motivation, and low interdependence. Going from a knowledge/problem mode to an authority/production mode introduces complex problems of coordination, reduction of individual freedom, group operation, and conflicts with personal values. It is not simply the reverse of going from the authority/production mode to the knowledge/problem mode.

Silver City Bank.   In August of 1968, Ralph Brady, vice president of Silver City Bank,[4] was concerned about future strategy for the international banking department. He wanted to improve the department's ability to compete with well-established competitors in a changing, worldwide market. At this stage in his thinking he felt the issues, problems, and opportunities were ill structured. He discussed his concern, in general terms, with his superiors, who encouraged him to recommend changes in strategy.

His work group functioned primarily in an authority/production mode. He and his subordinates were amiable and cooperative and deeply involved in getting work out. Although there was the glamour of international travel and negotiating loans of large dollar value, most of the situations were well structured.

Mr. Brady discussed strategy with several key subordinates but felt he and they were not able to dig into issues in any depth. Each could focus only on short-term obstacles close to his own group's productivity. The ill-structured problems of analyzing long-term strategy seemed to elude the problem-solving capability of his group. Finally, Mr. Brady consulted an OD specialist (the author) who had been working with another department in the bank.

Preparation for Introduction of Collateral Mode.
The specialist interviewed Mr. Brady and his division managers. He observed that their daily work required many immediate decisions and was extremely demanding. They could not be away from a telephone. He concluded they would have great difficulty establishing the relationships needed to identify and solve the ill-structured issues of strategy. Although the managers were competent problem solvers with extensive knowledge of international banking, they could not direct their skills

---

[4] Names in this case and the one that follows are fictitious.

toward analyzing strategy. Somehow, they would have to depart from the norms of their intensive authority/production-centered work.

The OD specialist explained the need for a collateral organization to Mr. Brady and his group. He proposed an initial three-day meeting, at which strategy and operating issues would be discussed, analyzed, and if possible, resolved. (The men were so busy they insisted it be from Friday afternoon to Sunday evening.) Aware that collateral organizations frequently fail because managers may have unrealistic expectations and cannot foresee the difficulties of a mode, the specialist stressed setting limited, attainable goals. He suggested that the group try to identify key issues but discuss only two or three priority issues in detail. Since there would be many unanswered questions after the meeting, they would also have to approve some structure which could be used to work on finding answers after they returned to work. Finally they should discuss how they could organize to solve ill-structured problems more effectively in the future.

Ten days before the meeting, the OD specialist interviewed each manager, gathering information for the meeting and answering questions about format. Each manager described the issues he most wanted discussed, the outcomes that would make him feel the meeting was worthwhile, and the difficulties that might interfere with managers' being reasonably open about important issues. The interview process itself stimulated managers to think about norms that departed from those of the primary mode.

Learning the Collateral Mode.
At the start of the meeting, the specialist made the following statements to clarify the norms of the collateral mode and to assure its proper connection to the primary mode.

The power differences in the formal organization would still exist when the managers returned to work.

Mr. Brady, the vice president, was the group's superior, and this was his meeting, not the consultant's.

The group or its members could make recommendations, but Mr. Brady would have to approve any proposal before it could be implemented.

Regardless of formal position, managers usually have valuable insights and proposals that cut across many different areas. It would be the responsibility of the higher managers to facilitate expression and use of these views.

The OD specialist would suggest procedures and ask questions to help the group's problem solving.

The OD specialist then reported a summary of the issues managers wanted to discuss. At first, the group operated in an authority/production mode. Managers frequently proposed solutions before a problem had been clearly defined. The specialist made process observations to alter these norms. Discussion was brought back to managers whose views had not been heard adequately. There was regular testing to ensure that any problem was understood by all before solutions were discussed in depth. Regardless of status, managers began contributing important information and insights. This helped the senior managers see how the open channels of the collateral mode improved problem solving.

On the second day, the managers agreed to experiment with a collateral mode after they returned to work. They would set aside "unstructured" time (multichannels, free questioning, and so on) to study several ill-structured problems. Based on their new experience, they also adopted a special norm for their collateral mode: incomplete ideas, although not thoroughly reasoned and defendable, were welcomed. This was a deliberate and significant departure from behavior in their primary organization. It was intended to stimulate search and creativity. They

reiterated, however, that in the hierarchical (primary) organization, a recommendation would still have to be supported by thorough reasoning and documentation. They had grasped the distinction between primary and collateral modes without falling into the trap of insisting that one had to displace the other.

Connecting to the Hierarchical Organization. After returning to work at the bank, Mr. Brady and his group used their collateral mode to analyze ill-structured problems one morning each week for the first six weeks. This helped stabilize the collateral mode and increase cohesion. They worked out a long-term agenda, which they used to enlarge their collateral organization with several task forces for specific problems. The daytime meetings were conflicting with work, so they reviewed their needs and shifted to one evening a month. They also convened three-day, off-site, collateral meetings at five-month intervals to review progress and react to task force reports. The task forces made proposals to Mr. Brady and the full group during the year; gradually a comprehensive international banking strategy was formulated.

There were differences of opinion within the task forces, and sometimes there were conflicting responses to reports from the task forces. The process had its difficulties, and in two instances Mr. Brady encouraged and arranged for the transfer of two individuals who were personally dissatisfied by and unable to contribute to the collateral mode. In general, the managers at this level were bright and aggressive and enjoyed the opportunity to do a better job of planning their department's future. At their daily work, the nature of their activities, however, impelled them toward an authority/production mode. (Incidentally, this did not mean that they were not caring, friendly, and thoughtful of one another and their subordinates.)

In any case, the primary and the collateral mode remained quite distinct. Managers were well aware of the distinct properties of the two modes and when one or the other was in use. The department was relatively autonomous and top management stayed out of its internal activities, so the use of the collateral mode caused no problems and raised no outside concerns.

Results. The original stimulus for the collateral organization was the need to develop a strategy for international banking. No before-after measures were taken of attitudes, perceptions, share in influence, or other intervening variables. At the time of the intervention, gathering data about casual variables was secondary to the change effort. Nevertheless, in terms of the criterion measure—quality of the strategy—the decisions made in 1969 are impressive, in view of the political and economic developments in Latin America, the Far East, and Europe in the early 1970s. The group decided to expand in Latin America and the Orient, where competition was thin, demand was growing, and the bank could effectively use its existing relationships to tap an expected increase in U.S. trade with countries in those areas. In Europe, where competition was heavy for the existing large market, a strategy of affiliating with strong foreign banks, and selectively establishing a few home office branches was instituted. To support the new strategy, relations between international banking officers and domestic banking officers who served U.S. companies with large overseas affiliates or subsidiaries were reviewed and significantly improved. Procedures in the bank's main European office were also substantially changed, facilitating more accurate and rapid responses to customers. The department's formal structure was changed to fit the new strategies. Several divisions were eliminated, others were combined. Finally, a manpower development plan which systematically rotated upcoming managers to selected world areas and headquarters assignments was instituted. Since 1968, top management has rated the international banking

department's performance as outstanding each year. Mr. Brady was promoted to senior vice president and a subordinate moved into his job.

Of course, without control groups we cannot assert that an equally good strategy would not have developed without a collateral mode. Using Mr. Brady's group as its own control, however, we recall that it had repeatedly tried to formulate strategy while working in its primary mode but had been dissatisfied with the results.

Another interesting result is that the collateral organization concept spread during the three years following its initial use by Mr. Brady. Each of his five division managers developed collateral organizations with their own subordinates.

Ajax Corporation. Now we turn to the introduction of a complex multistage collateral organization. Again our purpose is to illustrate the usefulness of the collateral organization concept and to outline some social technology for introducing one. We do not intend to delve deeply into the interpersonal or social dynamics of the development process.

Fred Anderson, manager of the Maintenance and Laboratory Service Division of Ajax Corporation, a large research and development company, was concerned about the cost effectiveness of his unit. His division had been performing more work with the same budget, and although objective standards were difficult to establish, he felt improvement was possible. Since the Service Division employed 300 of the 3,000 people in Ajax, it was a major expense.

The Service Division had been formed two years earlier by consolidating into one unit activities that had previously been performed by small groups in each of the major research and engineering divisions of Ajax. After consolidation, the foreman's job changed from supervising only craftsmen in one specialty (such as machinists or electricians) to supervising a team which could completely build and repair complex laboratory facilities. Thus, at the level of the foremen and below, the organization took on some properties of a *matrix*. Specialized craftsmen were assigned to different projects as needed, and they usually worked on several projects with groups of varying size and membership. In addition, for the first time, foremen and craftsmen were rotated between the company's two locations, 20 miles apart.

Middle managers advised Mr. Anderson that the foremen were at the crux of the division's difficulties and would be the key to any improvement effort. They described the foremen as unwilling to stress high output, reluctant to discipline workers, resistant to cost reduction and work changes, and tending to promise work dates that frequently were not met.

Mr. Anderson consulted organization development specialists, who observed that foremen were affected by the behavior and attitudes of their managers and that the problems Mr. Anderson was trying to solve were complex, ill defined, and substantially different from the well-structured routines of daily manager-foreman relations.[5] The consultants proposed, and management accepted, a sequence of collateral organizations involving both managers and foremen (Figure 4).

Collateral Phase 1. All 16 managers in the division met for three days away from the plant in order to (1) identify and solve work problems of concern to managers and foremen and (2) learn a collateral mode of problem solving.

To help introduce the collateral mode, the OD specialists constrained the managers to work on one element of problem solving at a time, in a method called "staged problem solving." They

also facilitated information flow, wider use of resources, and norms that encouraged questioning and creativity by placing managers in different groups with varying membership.

First, the managers developed an inventory of problems while working in three "diagonal slice" groups (no manager and immediate subordinate in the same group). Then, in a plenary meeting of all 16 managers, the groups discussed their problem inventories and consolidated them. At first the small groups were "stiff" and concerns were stated indirectly. However, with the aid of process observations by the OD specialists, role-playing, small-group exercises, and the discipline of discussing each group's product in plenary session, this stiffness disappeared.

Next each group diagnosed causes of a subset of problems. A written summary of each diagnosis was immediately duplicated and distributed to all the managers. The managers met again in plenary session and each group explained and discussed its diagnosis. By this time the managers were deeply involved in the effort. Highly relevant problems had been identified, and causes were being discussed without disguising names or incidents. The managers were stimulated by the open exchange of views and the increasing probability that several important problems might be solved.

On the second day of the meeting, the OD team arranged for the managers to meet in three peer groups. The groups were given the following tasks: (1) assign priorities to problems, (2) nominate managers to task forces that would recommend solutions to Mr. Anderson at the meeting, and (3) nominate managers to a steering committee that would take control of the remainder of the meeting and also guide the collateral organization after returning to the plant and the hierarchical (primary) organization.

Linking to the Formal Organization. To assure that the collateral organization would tie into the formal one, the managers were asked to use the following criteria for nominating candidates

---

[5] I acknowledge my gratitude to Matthew B. Miles and William O. Lytle, Jr., who were the OD team with me. This case is based upon Enlarging Organization Choice through Use of a Temporary Problem-Solving System, by D. E. Zand, M. B. Miles, and W. O. Lytle, Jr. (mimeo, available from author).

FIGURE 4

Multiphase collateral organization

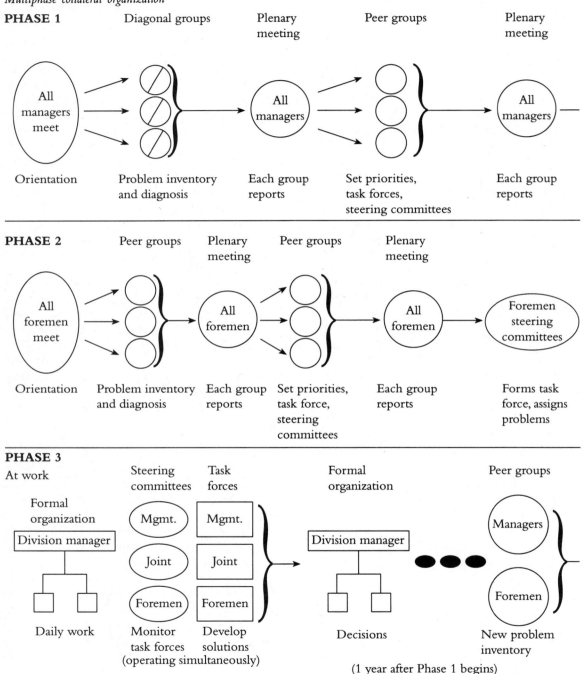

FIGURE 4
(concluded)

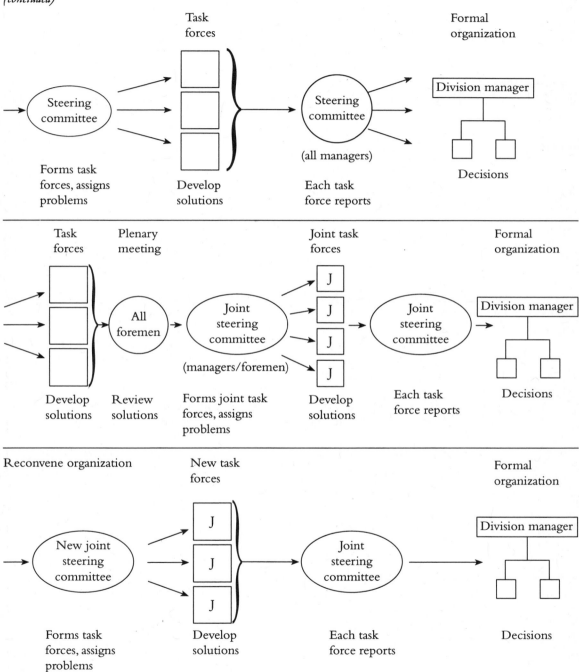

to a task force: *(a)* at least one manager should have formal authority to act on the problem; *(b)* several should be technical and procedural experts on the problem; *(c)* at least one should know and represent the views of people who would be affected by a solution.

The managers elected a five-man steering committee and asked the division manager to serve as chairman. Thus they connected the collateral organization's steering committee to the highest authority in their formal organization.

The steering committee formed task forces for the high-priority problems and assigned every manager (including themselves) to a task force. The task forces rediagnosed their assigned problems and developed solutions.

Then, in plenary session, each task force presented and discussed its progress. All managers freely questioned, commented, and provided additional inputs. The task forces absorbed the new inputs and met again to refine their proposals. By this stage, involvement was intense. Groups worked late into the night to prepare their recommendations for the next day. The norms in these groups very closely followed the knowledge/problem-centered mode: A manager's position was secondary to his contribution.

During the last half day, each task force presented its recommendations in plenary session. To clarify that the organization was shifting back to its primary mode, the OD team explicitly stated that the division manager, Mr. Anderson, could respond in any of the following ways: (1) He could accept the task force recommendation, designate a manager to implement it, specify a completion date, and state how a report of progress would be given to all the managers. (2) He could suggest modifications, discuss them, and approve a modified recommendation. (3) He could withhold a decision, pending additional information or alternatives, and authorize the task force to continue its work back at the plant. (4) He could withhold a decision if in his judgment the proposal was not appropriate now but might be at a later date. (5) He could reject the recommendation and not give any reasons.

There was a good deal of excitement and joking as Mr. Anderson stood at the front of the room waiting to hear each group's statement of the problem, review of causes, and recommended solutions. During the presentations, managers freely called from the floor for clarification or elaborated a point when they felt it was misunderstood. The cohesiveness of the managers was noticeably higher than before the three-day meeting.

By this time much information that had been known only in isolated pockets of the formal hierarchy had been exchanged across the organization. Managers had demonstrated their trust in one another through the openness of their discussions during the preceding two and one-half days. With this background, solutions that were not feasible or not integrative were readily discarded in the task forces. As a result, the final recommendations were appropriate and well thought out. Mr. Anderson neither rejected nor withheld a decision on any of the recommendations.

Results: Collateral Phase 1. A new information system for managers was instituted. A new strategy for recruiting engineering and scientific specialists was approved. Middle managers were delegated additional decision powers. A task force was established to redesign the division's organizational structure.

The managers also made plans to follow up in the hierarchical organization problems they had identified but did not have time to solve during the three-day meeting. Finally, they agreed they would join the foremen in a collateral organization if the foremen invited them. They discussed how they might work with the foremen in a collateral mode.

Collateral Phase 2.   One week after the managers' collateral organization experience, all 18 foremen met for three days at the off-site location. The OD specialists had decided to separate managers from foremen to prevent tension and distorted communication between levels from interfering with learning to work in a collateral mode. The managers' collateral organization was developed first so they could decide from personal experience whether to approve a collateral organization for foremen.

The procedure and activities in the foremen's meeting were similar to the managers' meeting. Some minilectures and demonstration exercises were eliminated to save time, but in all other ways the foremen's collateral organization used the same "staged problem solving," small-group discussions, and plenary sessions.

The foremen, like the managers, developed their own inventory of problems, diagnosed causes, set priorities, and elected their own steering committee to take control of their meeting. The steering committee established foremen task forces, which began work at the meeting. At first, like the managers, the foremen were resistant and indirect. Again with the aid of process observations from the OD specialists, exercises, and the regimen of having to present their group's deliberations to all other foremen, the norms of the groups changed toward those in a knowledge/problem mode.

Linking Two Collateral Organizations. Anticipating the need to link the managers' collateral organization to the foremen's collateral organization for work on common problems, management had agreed to the OD specialists' recommendation that foremen be permitted to invite managers to join them the last day and a half. The foremen (contrary to management's stereotype of foremen as insensitive) did not wish to offend any manager by not inviting him and negotiated with management to have all managers join them, except for five who were left to run the division.

A joint steering committee of foremen and managers assigned both foremen and managers to joint task forces. Comprehensive, ill-structured issues had been identified for work. Sample items which both managers and foremen agreed were adversely affecting the performance of foremen included: confusion about foremen's authority to work crews overtime, purchase inexpensive materials which were delaying completion of a job, or grant workers time off;

misunderstandings about the scope of the foreman's job; need for a better system for screening and assigning priorities to incoming jobs; inadequate engineering services on complex, technical jobs; inadequate pay differentials between foremen and craftsmen; conflict about the merit pay system; need for a better manpower assignment system; conflict about training of foremen and craftsmen. There was tension within the joint task forces as managers and foremen who knew each other by name but had never worked closely together before prepared to discuss problems that had been suppressed, distorted, or circumvented in the formal organization. Some foremen became guarded when a manager tried to dominate, but the issues and the withheld information that had been constraining the organization were nevertheless introduced via the "impersonal" written task force reports.

During the last half day, the joint task forces presented their recommendations to Mr. Anderson (format as before), who immediately made several important decisions. Procedures for working on unsolved problems after returning to the plant were also established.

Results: Collateral Phase 2. The recommendations approved by Mr. Anderson included the following: Foremen were given wider latitude in authorizing overtime to complete a job without their supervisor's approval; they could authorize workers' time off without pay; they could purchase parts that were delaying job completion up to $200 per job without going through time-consuming formal purchasing procedures. These measures cut costs and sped completion of jobs.

Mr. Anderson also decided that task forces concerned with the responsibilities of foremen, the training of foremen, the merit and performance review system, providing proper engineering support, and reviewing pay differentials between foremen and workers were to continue their investigation after they returned to the plant and the hierarchical organization.

Much misinformation about foremen attitudes and behavior had been dispelled, and managers had tested some of their stereotyped reactions to foremen and found them inappropriate. The outcome was a concerted effort on the part of both groups to provide the conditions that would enable foremen to be effective, rather than to blame them for inadequacies not under their control.

Thirty important problems had been identified, nine had been assigned to task forces, three had been resolved. Completion and review dates had been established for the others, and procedures had been developed for following through on the remaining problems. An attitude survey showed that managers and foremen felt they had learned much about one another and about problem solving. They were enthusiastic about the collateral organization.

Collateral Phase 3. After returning to the plant and the hierarchical organization, task forces of managers, foremen, and joint membership continued their work. Progress was slower than expected because of daily work pressures.

There also was testing of the authority/production mode. Some foremen task forces, impressed with their new influence potential, attempted to circumvent middle managers and moved directly to the joint steering committee or the division manager with short-term work issues. Senior foremen quickly sensed the resentment this was arousing among middle managers and redirected the foremen task forces to the issues they had been assigned. Managers of other divisions in the laboratory were skeptical about allowing foremen on task forces. They were also concerned that foremen might usurp higher management's authority. Mr. Anderson was able to reassure the other divisions that this dual mode of operation need not spread to other divisions unless they wanted it. He was also able to convince them on the basis of preliminary results that the performance of the Maintenance Division would improve over the long run.

Based on the measure of identifying and solving ill-structured problems, the collateral mode contributed to the organization's effectiveness.

After nine months, six of the nine original high-priority and five secondary problems were solved. All but three task forces had completed their assignments and were dissolved. Work was to begin on 12 less-critical problems.

The collateral organization was self-operating; no OD specialists were used. One year after the first meetings, a new division manager (promoted from within the division) continued the collateral organization with the aid of the joint steering committee. Using small groups, a new inventory of problems was developed, three new task forces were formed, and progress was reviewed with the steering committee until the new problems were solved.

To obtain information about attitudes toward the collateral mode, interviews were conducted 18 months after the start of the project. Five managers and five foremen representing all levels of management, every task force, and both steering committees were interviewed. Each respondent felt strongly that the collateral mode was extremely useful and strongly supported its continuation.

Additional Issues. These two cases, one relatively simple, the other more complexly structured, illustrate strategies for using collateral organization. Using the case material as reference, some additional issues deserve discussion: the distinction between collateral organization and related concepts such as "matrix organization" and "temporary systems," and some problems which may arise in the use of collateral organization.

Relation to Matrix Organization. Managers may sometime confuse a matrix organization with a collateral mode. A matrix organization is intended to provide a project manager with easier access to functional specialists. Nevertheless it may operate primarily in an authority/production mode, as in the Ajax case. Internal competition for resources and conflicts among functional managers and project managers are heightened in a matrix organization (Galbraith, 1971). These conditions stimulate managers to overstate needs, to hoard resources, to withhold information, and to block others from access to needed manpower, in short, to behave in an authority/production mode with high conflict. Thus a matrix organization may itself need a collateral problem-solving mode. Much of the organizational development activity at TRW Systems can be interpreted as an effort to build collateral modes to complement its matrix (primary) organization (Davis, 1967).

Relation to Task Forces.   In both Silver City and Ajax, each collateral organization created task forces as part of its structure. This can be confusing, because a manager may assume he can install a collateral organization simply by forming a task force. The important question is: Does the task force operate with norms different from those in the hierarchical (primary) organization? Many task forces, spun off by conventional hierarchies, operate in the same authority/ production mode as the primary organization. Individuals project their provincial interests and minimally question values, assumptions, methods, and criteria of evaluation. Such a task force contributes to restricted flow of information, legitimizes restricted use of resources, and adds little creativity to the hierarchical organization. The task forces in both Silver City Bank and Ajax worked in a collateral mode. They had learned the foundation for this mode in their initial off-site meeting. If they had not, it is doubtful that they would have contributed so creatively to the development of strategy. Indeed, a task force which operates under the authority/ production norms prevailing in its primary organization will need a collateral mode for itself.

Relation to Temporary Systems.   The relationship between collateral organization and a temporary system (Miles, 1964) also merits clarification. A temporary system is brought into existence with the understanding it will have limited duration. Its dissolution may be linked to (1) time (a two-day conference), (2) the occurrence of an event (the completion of a report), or (3) the attainment of a condition or level of functioning (a marketing unit solves its sales training problems without further aid from headquarters staff). A collateral organization is likely to terminate for one of two reasons. First, the ill-structured problems it is intended to solve are solved and there are no more. Second, the permanent, primary organization has internalized the norms and the competence of the collateral organization. In the second instance, the primary organization has attained a new level of functioning, thereby making the collateral mode redundant.

A collateral organization will be useful so long as it performs two functions: *(a)* it compensates for a deficiency in the primary system; *(b)* it is a vehicle for introducing needed changes in the primary system. In Silver City Bank, for example, the collateral mode was used intensively for strategy problems for about a year and a half. Then it was used to examine problems of implementation for about a year, but much less intensively. After that, it was used at semiannual intervals to take stock of unresolved, ill-structured problems, with the understanding that its shift to more intensive use would be made if the problems warranted it.

Operating Problems.   Collateral organization tends to increase the use of groups, at least initially, puts more stress on middle managers, and surfaces problems of individual tolerance and flexibility.

Need for Groups. A manager may be concerned that introducing a collateral organization will increase the number of problems going to groups for solution. This may happen initially for two reasons. First, there appears to be a temporary increase in the number of problems, because a collateral organization identifies problems that were previously diffused or unshared. Second, collateral organizations concentrate on high-priority, organizationwide problems, which are usually solved better by a group than by one person working alone. After an initial surge, the need for groups rapidly decreases, because the collateral mode diligently separates problems that should go to one manager (or a pair of managers) from those that should go to a larger group.

Stress on Middle Managers.   When a collateral organization permits lower and higher managers to interact directly, the stress on middle managers increases. Higher managers may discover that middle managers have been distorting and editing the upward flow of information. Lower managers may discover they can influence higher management decisions more easily than they thought possible. Both higher and lower managers discover they need less time to identify and solve complex problems. Management may be prompted to redesign the hierarchical organization and redefine the role of middle managers.

In the Silver City Bank, after working in a collateral mode, managers discovered they could expand operations more rapidly than planned because an anticipated shortage of managers could be met by freeing several middle managers for other assignments. In the Ajax case, managers in the collateral mode concluded that several middle-management positions were redundant but should be kept for back-up purposes and for training.

Individual Flexibility.   Some subordinates have a strong need for structure and a relationship with their superior that does not change. They are comfortable only when working in one mode all the time—either authority/production or knowledge/problem solving. The important element for them is stability and consistency (Adorno, Frenkel-Brunswick, Levinson, & Sanford, 1950; Vroom, 1959). Even though problems may change and require organizational versatility, they find shifting from one mode to another confusing. Most subordinates, however, can be productive in more than one organizational mode provided they understand the pur-

poses of a collateral mode, know which mode they are in, and know when it will end.

Sometimes a superior may not have the flexibility to work in more than one mode. If this is the case, attempts to use a collateral organization will meet strong resistance. The majority of managers, however, seem to have enough flexibility to use collateral organizations. The achievements in the two cases described above were heavily dependent on the flexibility of Mr. Brady and Mr. Anderson.

Too often, a manager's skepticism toward attempts to displace one organizational mode with another have been misconstrued as a sign of deep-seated personal rigidity. This "rigidity" usually fades when the manager understands the concept of collateral organization. When he sees how it can productively complement the hierarchical organization without displacing or destroying it, he can be remarkably flexible. As a matter of fact, after a manager experiences his first successful collateral organization, the problem is usually not one of rigidity but of overoptimism. He feels he and his group have broken through to a new form of relationship and productivity, and he easily develops overly optimistic expectations of future accomplishment. The demands of daily work, however, quickly intrude, as they must, making continued use of the collateral mode an infrequent, disjointed activity. Some ill-structured problems are solved, but, because of interruptions, solutions take longer to implement than he planned. New ill-structured problems that are identified take much greater effort to solve than he expected. He discovers that time for the collateral mode must be fought for and taken from the primary mode.

After using a collateral mode, the manager and his subordinates learn that the hierarchical organization can continue. Disorder does not take over. Directive behavior can still be used, but there is better understanding of how to integrate participation and group effort with the formal organization through use of a collateral mode. Perhaps most important, organization members learn concepts and methods which enable them to freely invent and use new modes for solving ill-structured problems.

References

Adorno, T. W.; Frenkel-Brunswick, E.; Levinson, D. J.; and Sanford, R. N. *The Authoritarian Personality*. New York: Harper & Row, 1950.

Argyris, C. *Intervention Theory and Method*. Reading, MA: Addison-Wesley Publishing, 1970.

Bavelas, A. "Communication Patterns in Task-Oriented Groups." *Journal of Acoustical Society of America* 22, (1950), pp. 725–30.

Bennis, W. G. "Beyond Bureaucracy." *Trans-Action,* July–August 1965.

Bennis, W. G. *Changing Organizations*. New York: McGraw-Hill, 1966.

Burns, T., & Stalker, G. M. *Management of Innovation*. London: Tavistock, 1961.

Christie, L. S.; Luce, R. D.; & May, J., Jr. "Communications and Learning in Task-Oriented Groups. Cambridge, MA: Research Laboratory Electronics, 1952.

Davis, S. A. "An Organic Problem-Solving Method of Organizational Change." *Journal of Applied Behavioral Science* 3 (1967), pp. 3–21.

Delbecq, A. L. "How 'Informal' Organization Evolves: Interpersonal Choice and Subgroup Formation." *Business Perspectives,* 1968, *IV* (3), 17–21.

Fiedler, F. E. *A Theory of Leadership Effectiveness*. New York: McGraw-Hill, 1967.

Galbraith, J. R. "Matrix Organization Designs." *Business Horizons,* February 1971, pp. 24–40.

Golembiewski, R. T. *Renewing Organizations: The Laboratory Approach to Planned Change*. Itasca, IL: Peacock, 1972.

Guetzkow, H., & Dill, W. R. "Factors in the Organizational Development of Task-Oriented Groups." *Sociometry* 20 (1957), pp. 175–204.

Guetzkow, H., & Simon, H. A. "The Impact of Certain Communication Nets upon Organization and Performance in Task-Oriented Groups." *Management Science* 1 (1955), pp. 233–50.

Lawrence, P. R., & Lorsch, J. W. "New Management Job: The Integrator." *Harvard Business Review,* November–December 1967, p. 142.

Leavitt, H. J. "Some Effects of Certain Communication Patterns on Group Performance." *Journal of Abnormal and Social Psychology,* 46 (1951), pp. 38–50.

Likert, R. *New Patterns of Management*. New York: McGraw-Hill, 1961.

Likert, R. *The Human Organization*. New York: McGraw-Hill, 1967.

McGregor, D., *The Human Side of Enterprise*. New York: McGraw-Hill, 1960.

Margulies, N., & Raia, A. P. *Organizational Development*. New York: McGraw-Hill, 1972.

Miles, M. B. "On Temporary Systems." In M. B. Miles, ed., *Innovation in Education*. New York: Columbia University Press, 1964, pp. 437–92.

Pfiffner, J. M., & Sherwood, F. P. *Administrative Organization*. Englewood Cliffs, NJ: Prentice Hall, 1960, pp. 16–32.

Shaw, M. E.; Rothchild, G. H.; & Strickland, J. F. "Decision Process in Communication Nets." *Journal of Abnormal and Social Psychology* 54 (1957) pp. 323–30.

Slater, P. E., & Bennis, W. G. "Democracy Is Inevitable." *Harvard Business Review,* March–April 1964, p. 51.

Tannenbaum, R., & Davis, S. A. "Values, Men, and Organizations." *Industrial Management Review,* Winter 1969, pp. 67–83.

Vroom, V. H. "Some Personality Determinants of the Effects of Participation." *Journal of Abnormal and Social Psychology* 59 (1959), pp. 322–27.

SURVEY-GUIDED DEVELOPMENT: USING HUMAN RESOURCES MEASUREMENT IN ORGANIZATIONAL CHANGE

David G. Bowers and Jerome L. Franklin

As it exists today, organizational development (OD) in various forms and practices includes many common values and goals. However, there is also a considerable degree of difference in the various concepts, procedures, and assumptions that are identified within this field. The common elements reflect to some extent the fact that those engaged in the field share some aspects of their backgrounds. The differences reflect different evolutionary streams from which the practice of OD has emerged. Much of what is currently considered within the realm of OD can be traced to the fields of adult education, personnel training, industrial consultation, and clinical psychology. Organizational development now represents a crystallization of the experiences of practitioners from these fields. Examples of the techniques and procedures that have evolved in this way include sensitivity training, human relations training, team development training, process consultation, and role-playing.

Some portion of what presently may be considered organizational development came into existence through a different route, which is perhaps best described as a concern for the utilization of scientific knowledge. This data-based type of development and, specifically, the survey feedback technique, originated not from the search by practitioners for more effective helping tools, but from the concern of organizational management researchers for better ways of moving new scientific findings from the producers (researchers) to the consumers (organizational managers.)

This view is clearly spelled out in the prospectus which launched the organizational behavior research program at the Institute for Social Research over 25 years ago:

> The general objective of this research program will be to discover the underlying principles applicable to the problems of organizing and managing human activity. *A second important objective of the project will be to discover how to train persons to understand and skillfully use these principles* [9, p. 2].

> The major emphasis during the last four years of the project will be on the experimental verification of the results and *especially on learning how to make effective use of them in everyday situations. . . .* Each experiment will be analyzed in terms of measures made before and after the experiment, and often a series of measures will be made during the experiment [9, p. 10].

> The entire progress of our society depends upon our skill in organizing our activity. Insofar as we can achieve efficiently through systematic research new understandings and skills instead of relying on trial and error behavior, we can speed the development of a society capable of using constructively the resources of an atomic age. Unless we achieve this understanding rapidly and intelligently, we may destroy ourselves in trial and error bungling. Understanding individual behavior is not enough, nor is an understanding of the principles governing the behavior of men in small groups. We need generalizations and principles which will point the way to organizing human activity on the scale now required [9, p. 12].

This same prospectus also stated that the basic measurement tool to be used in the proposed

Source: David G. Bowers and Jerome L. Franklin, "Survey-Guided Development: Using Human Resources Measurement in Organizational Change," *Journal of Contemporary Business* 1, no. 3 (Summer 1972), pp. 43–55. School of Business Administration, University of Washington, DJ-10, Seattle. Reprinted with permission.

studies would be the sample survey, employing procedures that the proposers had developed during their years with the Program Surveys Division of the Department of Agriculture. It was also stated that the study design would be generally like that employed by Rensis Likert in the Agency Management Study [7].

Thus the stage was set for an organizational development emphasis that first engaged in scientific search for principles of organizational management, and then, once such principles were established, set forth to identify effective implementation strategies for them. This plan was provided impetus by real-life circumstances. Researchers rapidly discovered that the generation of sound findings regarding organizational management was one thing and their implementation quite another. Two factors seriously diminished the effective use of early findings. First, although survey items referred to work-world events, there was often no readily accepted "map" tying what was measured to operating realities in ways that were readily understood. Second, because there was a lack of implementation procedures geared to the data, presentation of findings normally involved a narrative report. As a result of both these factors, there was a great propensity either to file the report away, to pass it along to lower levels accompanied by vague directives to "use it," or simply to seize selectively upon bits which reinforced managers' existing biases [3].

The Nature of Survey Feedback

In an effort to solve this problem, Floyd Mann and his colleagues at the Institute for Social Research developed the *survey feedback* procedure as an implementation tool. No authoritative volume has as yet been written about this development tool. Partially as a result of this absence of detailed description, many persons mistakenly believe that survey feedback consists of a rather superficial handing back of tabulated numbers and percentages, but little else. On the contrary, where the survey feedback is employed with skill and experience, it becomes a sophisticated tool for using the data as a springboard to development. Data are typically tabulated for each and every work group in an organization, as well as for each combination of groups that represents an area of responsibility, including the total organization.

Each supervisor and manager receives a tabulation of this sort, containing data based on the responses of *his own* immediate subordinates, together with documents describing their interpretation and use. A resource person, sometimes from an outside (consulting) agency and at other times from the client system's own staff, usually counsels privately with the supervisor-recipient about the contents of the package and then arranges a suitable time when the supervisor can meet with his subordinates to discuss the findings and their implications. The resource person attends that meeting to provide help to the participants, both in the technical aspects of the tabulations and in the process aspects of the discussion.

Procedures by which the feedback process progresses through an organization may vary from site to site. In certain instances a "waterfall" pattern is adhered to, in which the process substantially is completed at high-level groups before moving down to subordinate groups. In other instances, feedback is more or less simultaneous to all groups and echelons.

By whichever route it takes, an effective survey feedback operation depicts the organization's groups as moving, by a discussion process, from the tabulated perceptions, through a cataloging of their implications, to commitment for solutions to the problems that the discussion has identified and defined.

The Necessity of Differential Diagnosis

From these general and specific concerns there has emerged a viewpoint, largely identified with persons associated with the Institute for Social

Research, that constructive change is measurement-centered, beginning with a quantitative reading of the state of the organization and direction of movement. Even more than this, change is, throughout, a rational process that makes use of information, pilot demonstrations, and the persuasive power of evidence and hard fact.

A successful change effort begins with rigorous measurement of the way in which the organization presently is functioning. These measurements provide the material for a diagnosis, and the diagnosis forms the basis for the design of a program of change activities. Likert has stated this quite pointedly in an early publication:

> One approach that can be used to apply the findings of human relations research to your own operation can be described briefly. Your medical departments did not order all of your supervisors nor all of your employees to take penicillin when it became available, even though it is a very effective antibiotic. They have, however, administered it to many of your employees. But note the process of deciding when it should be administered. The individual was given certain tests and measurements obtained—temperature, blood analysis, etc. The results of these measurements were compared with known facts about diseases, infections, etc., and the penicillin was prescribed when the condition was one that was known or believed to be one that would respond to this antibiotic.
>
> We believe the same approach should be used in dealing with the human problems of any organization. This suggests that human relations supervisory training programs should not automatically be prescribed for all supervisory and management personnel. Nor should other good remedies or methods for improvement be applied on a blanket basis to an entire organization hoping it will yield improved results [5, p. 35].

One of the reasons for the importance of the diagnostic step early in the life of a change program is stated explicitly in the preceding quotation: it will increase the probability of focusing upon the right, not the wrong, problems, and it will add to the likelihood of the right, not the wrong, course of treatments being prescribed. A clear statement of the problems, courses of action, and change objectives, based on sound measurements allied to the best possible conceptualization from research and theory, will maximize the likelihood that true causal conditions, rather than mere symptoms, will be dealt with [2].

The Rationale for Survey-Guided Development

The preceding sections have pointed to the existence of two somewhat different approaches to organization development. One, growing out of applied practice, is identified more obviously with the laboratory approach to education. It uses the *immediate* behavior (verbal and nonverbal) of the participants as the source material around which development forms. It focuses much more on the "here-and-now" than on the "there-and-then" and emphasizes experience-based learnings. It focuses more sharply on issues related to interpersonal processes than those less observable issues of role and structure.

The other approach, which we propose to elaborate on in greater detail, is related more obviously to an information-systems approach to adaptation. This approach uses participants' summarized perceptions of behavior and situation as the source material around which development is focused. It focuses on the there-and-then at least as much as on the here-and-now, attaches considerably more importance to cognitive understanding than does the other approach, and is concerned with such issues as role and structure, at least as much as with those of interpersonal process.

These brief identifications are more descriptive than explanatory. A true understanding of the survey-guided approach requires that we look more closely at the assumptions which it appears to make and the operating propositions which it derives from those assumptions.

Like most organization development techniques, survey feedback is only one aspect of a measurement-guided approach to change. As a tool or procedure, it emerged as a response to a practical need to see research findings implemented. It did not emerge as the logical conclusion of a formal body of scientific thought, and it remains for us presently to search, after the fact, for a rationale about how and why it works.

In this vein, two bodies of scientific thought seem relevant. One comes from the research done in the area of perception and involves the fundamental concept that a difference between perceptions is motivating—an idea originally and most clearly stated by Peak [8]. This is perhaps illustrated by the following example: if I perceive, on the one hand, that I cannot complete a particular piece of work by the end of the normal workday and perceive, on the other hand, that that work must be complete by the start of office hours in the morning, I am motivated to work late or to take home a work-loaded briefcase.

According to this view, the perceptions must be associated (i.e., they must be seen as belonging to the same "domain"). I may perceive that I do not play the piano as well as Arthur Rubenstein, but this discrepancy is hardly motivating, because I do not consider myself to be a professional concert pianist. Although associated, the perceptions must be different, yet not so different as to destroy their association. The perceptions may be related to emotion-laden or "feelings" issues, or they may consist of different perceptions of conditions in the external world. Peak illustrates the process by drawing an analogy:

> Think of a thermostat. Here there are two events. One is the temperature setting (an expected state if you will). The other event or term in the system is the height of the mercury in the tube, representing the present state of affairs (room temperature). These are analogous then to the two events in our motive construct, and disparity exists between them when there is a difference in the setting and in the temperature reading. Now, the second fea-

ture of our motive construct, which is called contact or association, is provided by the structure of the thermostat and is not modifiable in this system as it is in the motive system. In other words, the two terms (or events) remain in association. Only disparity can vary, and when there is disparity there is "motivation" and action; i.e., the furnace starts to run. The results of this action are fed back to produce change in one of the terms of the disparity relation (the mercury level). When the disparity disappears through rise in temperature or resetting of the thermostat, action ceases. . . . But since the thermostat lacks the capacity to stop action through isolation, and in the simple design we have described, cannot select different actions, the model must be regarded merely as illustrative . . . [8, pp. 172–73].

Another closely related set of ideas comes from engineering psychology and begins with the observation that human behavior is goal-seeking or goal-oriented. As such, behavior is characterized by a search for processes by which the human being controls his environment (i.e., means by which he reshapes it toward more constructive or productive ends).

Oversimplifying the control process greatly, at least four elements are involved: (1) a model, (2) a goal, (3) an activity, and (4) feedback. The *model* is a mental picture of the surrounding world, including not only structural properties, but cause-and-effect relations. It is built by the person(s) from past accumulations of information, stored in memory. From the workings of the model and from the modeling process which he employs, alternative possible future states are generated, of which one is selected as a *goal*. At this point what is called the "goal selection system" ends and that is known as the "control system" per se begins. *Activities* are initiated to attain the goal, and *feedback*, which comes by some route from the person's environment, is used to compare, confirm, adjust, and correct responses by signaling departures from what was expected.

The process as just described is beguilingly simple. However, in actual life it is often extremely complex. The thermostat example, although embodied in a marvelous and valuable piece of equipment, is basically a simple instance of an adaptive system. Others are much more complicated, such as that contained in the role of a Mississippi river boat pilot. The shifting character of currents and channels make this adaptive task quite complex. Therefore the difficulty in this as in other complex systems stems from not having learned how to predict system performance under various conditions. As one of the foremost human factors writers has described it, "The ability to predict system performance is in major respects the same as the ability to control the system" [4, p. 42]

The human organization reflects the same type of a complex, difficult control system, in part for these same reasons. Activity is only as good as the model which leads to it, yet human organizations are often managed according to grossly imperfect models (models which ignore much of what is known from research about organizational structure and functioning). Predictability is enhanced, in human systems as elsewhere, by quantification, yet many of the relationships are often not quantified, if, indeed, they are recognized at all.

In the absence of a sound model, what is expected varies with immediate experience. It is for this reason that objective feedback on organizational functioning is absolutely essential in organizational development. In its absence, true deviations are unknown because expectations constantly adjust to incurred performance.

From this very condensed discussion, it is apparent that, when organizational change is viewed as a problem in optimal control or adaptation (which it inherently is) several things are required:

1. An adequate model—one which is a valid representation of that external reality known as "the organization," including both structural properties, knowledge of cause-effect relations, and predictive capability.

2. A goal—a preferred potential future state, generated by the model.

3. An activity—selected as instrumental to attaining that goal.

4. Objective feedback—about deviations from what the model would lead us to expect.

These two sets of concepts—the one drawn from basic work in the area of perception, the other taken from the human factors work of engineering psychology—provide jointly a plausible rationale for survey-guided development. As in the human factors area, feedback of information about the actual state of functioning provides key input to selecting development goals and making mid-course corrections. It tells the developing system what needs to be done. The power source, which in human factors descriptions is shown as an external input, is in survey-guided development provided by the sort of discrepancy described by Peak. Survey feedback, by pointing to the existence of differences between what is actually going on and what the model indicates one wants and needs, provides the energy (motivation) to undertake change activities.

In detail, as in general, organizational development (as the survey-guided approach envisions) may be seen as an analog of adaptation as described by human factors theorists. What they have termed the "goal selection system" is, in survey-based development, the *diagnostic* process. What they have referred to as the "control system" is the *therapeutic* process.

To serve its function within the diagnostic process, the work group draws inputs from the same sorts of areas drawn upon by all adaptive systems:

From higher-level systems: from the larger organization, its top management, and from society in general in the form of performance trends, top-management evaluations, labor relations trends, changes in laws or regulations, and so on.

From its own information about the model which they have thus far accepted, as well as information concerning past experiences and results.

From a reading of how things actually are: from the survey; through what we have described as survey feedback, which deals largely with intragroup behavior, attitudes, and relationships; and from a more formal *diagnosis* (an analytic report prepared by persons skilled in the survey data area), which deals with intergroup and systemic properties.

From the environment: in many forms, but particularly from the "change agent," the organizational development scientist-consultant who helps to catalyze the overall change process.

Each of these input sources has potential impact by virtue of its presence or comparative absence, its kind, and its quality. For example, the higher-level system inputs ordinarily create some degree of felt urgency. Often, discrepancy generated by this input motivates the initial search and culminates in serious consideration of organizational development as a possible course of action. The extent to which these inputs encourage the development efforts of the client entity is also critical. Many of the development failures occur in instances in which higher-level system inputs are either lacking, which indicates acquiescence, or instead, are signaling outright disapproval of organizational development. A general example of such an instance might involve a supervisor who verbally acquiesces to an organizational development effort for his subordinates but behaves and rewards his subordinates for behaving in ways which are incongruent with the values, assumptions, and goals that are emphasized in organizational development. Efforts that proceed in the face of such higher-level system inputs run a great risk of death by neglect.

From the group's own information storage comes the model of organizational functioning already held by group members. This includes information regarding past organizational practices (behaviors, interaction patterns, managerial styles) as well as outcomes at various levels of finality (absenteeism, turnover, profit, production efficiency, growth, et cetera).

The survey provides a means by which multiple perceptions of behaviors and organizational conditions related to effectiveness can be gathered, compiled, and compared. As has been indicated above, one must consider not one, but two, separate input streams from the survey. One of these input streams consists of the survey feedback process itself, in which tabulations of the group's *own data,* especially concerning its internal functioning, is used as a springboard to the identification, understanding, and solving of problems. The other consists of a more formal diagnosis, prepared by persons skilled in multivariate analysis, and focuses on those problem streams which occur in the system as a whole and which can be seen only by careful comparison of the tabulated data of many groups.

The Change Agent's Role

The change agent, as an adjunct person, seems to have no exact counterpart in *manual* control problems. The reason for his presence in organizational development is that a model of organizational functioning and human behavior is not as simple or programmable as that involved in manual control. Reading and digesting survey data are not the same as reading a gauge. Accomplishing an organizational "correction" is much more complicated than pushing a button or turning a wheel a certain number of degrees. In most instances the controller in organizational change—the client group—must be shown what the "gauge" says and how to read it, and must be guided through the operations of making the desired changes. The survey discrepancy, properly digested with the aid of the change agent, both builds the *motivation* to make the change and indicates *what* changes in functioning must occur.

However, the change agent helps the client group learn *how* to make the necessary changes.

The primary role of the change agent in survey-guided development is that of a transducer (i.e., an energy link between scientific knowledge regarding principles of organizational functioning and the particular organization or group with which he is working). As such, the change agent enters into both the diagnostic and therapeutic phases of the development effort. During the diagnostic phase, the model that the change agent presents must be reasonably complete, predictive, and adequate to provide the client with useful information. If the model lacks any of these characteristics, the change agent will be supplying the system with little more than noise.

In addition to having these characteristics, the model must be presented to the members of the group or organization accurately and adequately. The issue of acceptance is critical: the best model loses its value unless it is understood in useful ways by members of the system. The model and evidence in its support must be presented in such a manner that acceptance is based upon rational evaluations of the evidence as well as the experiences and insights of those involved in the organization. During this activity, the change agent must have the model clearly in mind, must be able to present the model and its evidence clearly, and must also be able to call upon his group process and related skills to facilitate understanding and acceptance.

As in any other situation in which the talents and knowledge of one man are to be made available to assist another, the manner in which that occurs is, of course, important. In the area of human organizational development, of all places, it is important that the knowledge be made available in a supportive, not a demeaning, fashion; it is not to be "laid on," ordered into place, or delivered as some form of speech from a pretentious throne. Skill in patient explanation, in aiding understanding, and in helping the client entities themselves to come to grips with

reality—in short, the whole array of interpersonal skills—are extremely important. But the change agent must have the knowledge of what must be explained, the grasp of what must be understood, and the comprehension of what that reality is.

In this vein, the change agent facilitates the understanding and digesting of diagnostically useful information. In the survey-guided approach, this role involves helping members of the system to understand better the survey feedback information. It also may involve a range of activities, from a detailed explanation of the meaning and relevance of certain content areas to helping group members understand information from the survey in terms of the here-and-now of the feedback meeting process. In addition, he aids the client group members in setting goals and formulating action plans for the development effort. In this activity, as in the others, the change agent may serve both as a source of information (e.g., suggesting potential actions to be undertaken or considered) and as a facilitator who focuses upon the group's processes.

The change agent also serves as a transducer in the therapeutic phase of survey-guided organizational development. Once a diagnosis has pointed to problem areas in organizational functioning, the change agent provides a link between scientific knowledge regarding effective methods of correcting specific problems and the problems exhibited in the immediate situation. A variety of activities may be undertaken during this phase. Each has, as its ultimate goal, movement toward the model of organizational functioning held (after its initial establishment) by both change agent and clients.

In part, the specific type of activity undertaken depends on the stage in the therapeutic phase. In the early stages, the change agent is likely to be involved largely with supplying informational inputs regarding specific possible activities, helping organizational members cope with attitudinal shifts, and handling defensive reactions. The motivation to change created by a discrepancy between the ideal model and the actual state of the organization is alone not sufficient to produce change. Methods of actually accomplishing the change must also be evident to organizational members. In this respect, the change agent in part fulfills his transducer role by informing members of the client system of the available alternatives.

In later stages the change agent is often involved with skill acquisition and perfection by group members. The range and variety of potentially necessary skills is large. Problem solving, giving and receiving personal feedback, listening, general leadership, goal-setting, resolving conflict, and diagnosing group processes are but a few of those which might be cited. The change agent must not only know which skills are needed but also must be competent in guiding their acquisition. It is as a result of this acquisition and perfection of skill that organizational members come to rely less on the change agent and more on themselves in movement toward the goal.

In addition to the emphasis on skills, the change agent provides and facilitates informal intermediate-phase feedback during the therapeutic phase. For example, he may provide the group with feedback in the form of process comments inserted during or after key intragroup interactions. He may also facilitate attempts by the members themselves to gather and understand information regarding their progress toward accepted goals.

A Recapitulation

As the preceding pages have indicated, the survey-guided approach suggests several general propositions regarding: (1) certain basic assumptions of organizational development; (2) change processes; and (3) the change agent's role.

Basic Assumptions of OD.   There are systemic properties (i.e., characteristics of the organization as a total system) not definable by the simple sum of individual and/or group behaviors.

A *model* of organizational functioning, which includes these systemic properties, reflecting available evidence and testable by quantifiable and scientific means, should be used as a basis for development efforts.

Systemic properties in particular can improve only as a result of *carefully sequenced planned interventions.*

Valid information about the state of group and organizational functioning (objectives and useful reflections of reality) is best obtained from summarized, quantified longtudinal perceptions. (There-and-then data are at least as useful as here-and-now data.)

A *diagnosis* based upon a quantitative comparison with the model and prepared by competent professionals should be used to evaluate the organization on both intragroup and systemic levels.

Prescription of intervention activities should be *diagnostically based.*

Change Processes.   *Motivation* is created by the realization that the actual state differs from the accepted model (i.e., a discrepancy exists between that which is desired and that which exists).

The discrepancies exist in terms of both *intragroup* and *systemic* processes and properties.

Change involves a *sequence of events,* including: informational inputs; formation of a model; selection of a goal; assessment of the situation; formation of a diagnosis, feedback; adjustment; and reevaluation.

Change Agent's Role and Activities.   The change agent acts as *transducer* between scientific knowledge regarding organizational functioning and change processes, on the one hand, and the particular situation, on the other.

He has a *model* of organizational functioning and *works toward* its realization.

Except in those rare instances which require a

nondirective stance, the change agent is an *active advocate of goal-oriented behavior.* He evaluates and helps the client group to *evaluate progress toward the goals,* but he is not punitive.

He must have a *wide range of knowledge and skills* and not be bound to one or two particular techniques.

These general propositions of survey-guided development are illustrated as a flow of events in Figure 1.

Perspective and Prologue

We conclude by offering an apology to the reader who anticipated a less-labored description. What has been written has been, in many ways, a rather technical document. It reflects our strong belief that organizational development rightfully is becoming more a science than an art. This view was expressed several years ago by one of the authors:

> By science I mean discernible in replicatable terms—objective, understandable (rather than "mystique"), verifiable, and predictive. Should these conditions for organizational develpment fail to be met, it will go the way of the Great Auk and the "Group Talking Technique." In short, organizational development will die, having been remembered as one more fad.
>
> Organizational development cannot survive on the goodwill of top management persons who are already sold on its potential and effectiveness. It can survive only if it proves its method and its contribution beyond reasonable doubt to the hard-headed skeptics. Organizational development must prove with hard, rigorous evidence that it can beneficially affect: *(a)* the volume of work done by the organization, *(b)* the cost per unit of doing the organization's work, and *(c)* the quality of work done [1, p. 62].

The same article described barriers which, up to that time, had impeded the progress of organizational development as a science:

> The lack of a "critical mass" of knowledge in the field.

> The tendency for organizational development to take the form of a single general practitioner, operating on an isolated island.

> The absence of an adequate measuring instrument, geared to an adequate model of organizational functioning, for use in organizational development efforts.

Within the last decade, considerable progress has been made on each of these fronts. Books and articles, describing and integrating findings in this field, have appeared in increasing numbers and richness. This present journal issue is a case in point.

To the extent that our own experience is typical, opportunities for researchers and change agents to collaborate in multifaceted, large system development efforts have emerged.

Efforts have similarly been undertaken by a number of persons to develop procedures and instruments for rigorous description of change agent interventions and their immediate effects.

Finally, we feel that survey-guided development has pressed, from its own necessity, the construction of reliable, valid, standardized instruments for assessing organizational functioning.

The availability of such instruments, together with the accumulating critical mass of knowledge, leads us to considerable optimism concerning the future of organizational development in general and concerning the survey-guided approach, in particular.

References

1. Bowers, D. G. "The Scientific Data-Based Approach to Organization Development," Part 2, in A. L. Hite, ed. *Organizational Development: The State of the Art.* Ann Arbor, MI: Foundation for Research on Human Behavior, 1971.
2. Bowers, D. G. *System 4: The Ideas of Rensis Likert.* New York: Basic Books, 1972.
3. Katz, Daniel, and Kahn, Robert L. *The Social*

FIGURE 1

Survey-guided development

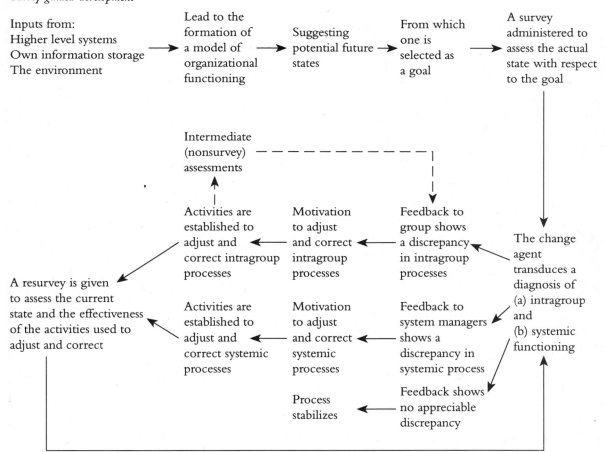

Psychology of Organizations. New York: John Wiley & Sons, 1966.

4. Kelley, C. R. *Manual and Automatic Control.* New York: John Wiley & Sons, 1968.

5. Likert, R. "Findings of Research on Management and Leadership." *Proceedings, 43,* Pacific Coast Gas Assn., 1952.

6. Likert, R. *The Human Organization.* New York: McGraw-Hill, 1967.

7. Likert, R., and Willets, J. M. *Morale and Agency Management.* Hartford, Conn.: Life Insurance Agency Management Association, 1940. 4 vols.

8. Peak, H. "Attitude and Motivation," in M. R. Jones, ed., *Nebraska Symposium on Motivation.* Lincoln, NE: University of Nebraska Press, 1955.

9. Survey Research Center. *A Program of Research on the Fundamental Problems of Organizing Human Behavior.* Ann Arbor: University of Michigan, 1947.

10. Taylor, J. C., and Bowers, D. G. *The Survey of Organizations: A Machine-Scored, Standardized Questionnaire Instrument.* Ann Arbor: Institute for Social Research, 1972.

READING 25
SELF-REGULATING WORK GROUPS: A SOCIOTECHNICAL SYNTHESIS

Thomas G. Cummings

Since its conception about 25 years ago at the Tavistock Institute of Human Relations in London, England, sociotechnical systems theory has emerged as a significant approach for designing organizations, especially at the people and technology interface [27; 28]. This body of theoretical and empirical work seeks to improve productivity and human enrichment through a design process that focuses on the interdependencies between and among people, technology, and environment. A concrete outcome of this theoretical perspective is development of self-regulating work groups. Variously referred to as "autonomous" [12; 13; 17; 26], or "composite" [28], or "self-managing" [14] work groups, these work designs generally include: a relatively whole task; members who each possess a variety of skills relevant to the group task; worker discretion over such decisions as methods of work, task schedules, and assignment of members to different tasks; and compensation and feedback about performance for the group as a whole [14]. These attributes are intended to provide the work group with the task boundary, autonomy, and feedback necessary to control variances from goal achievement within the unit, rather than external to it. This self-regulating capacity is hypothesized to lead to greater productivity and worker satisfaction.

Existing evidence suggests that self-regulating work groups are productive and satisfying [7]. Current knowledge about such applications is limited primarily to their overall effects, with relatively little practical understanding of how self-regulating groups operate or how they are

Source: Thomas G. Cummings, *Academy of Management Review* 3, no. 3 (July 1978), pp. 625–34.

implemented. This lack of comprehension frequently leads organizations to apply self-regulating designs inappropriately, resulting in confusion and other unintended consequences. Moreover, the literature in this area is somewhat fragmented, making it difficult to develop a coherent theory of self-regulating groups or to conduct research in a cumulative manner.

This article outlines the theory behind self-regulating work groups, their implementation strategy, and the kind of supervision appropriate to their management. Such knowledge is needed if self-regulating designs are to emerge from loose metaphors for worker autonomy to scientifically sound and practical operational strategies for work design.

Theory of Self-Regulating Groups

Sociotechnical Design. Self-regulating work groups are a direct outgrowth of sociotechnical systems theory and design. Briefly, this perspective views production systems as comprised of both technological and social parts. The former consists of the equipment and methods of operations used to transform raw materials into products or services; the latter includes the work structure that relates people to the technology and to each other. A traditional division-of-labor work design, for example, relates workers to limited and highly prescribed parts of the production process and to a narrow set of physically proximate employees performing similar jobs. The concept of a sociotechnical system arises from the consideration that any production system requires both a technology and a work structure [22]. Since the work structure ties people to the technology, its design has a major impact on both of these substantive dimensions of work.

Based on this simple yet often neglected premise, sociotechnical experimenters attempt to design work structures so that a "best match" is obtained between employees and technology [12]. This may involve changes in the technology (i.e., equipment and process layout), the work structure (i.e., work roles and their interrelationships), or both. The primary aim is to design a work structure that is responsive to the task requirements of the technology and the social and psychological needs of employees: a structure that is both productive and humanly satisfying. A division-of-labor work design, for instance, may well meet the task demands of a mechanized assembly line and the needs of individuals who prefer direction and social isolation; yet, it is questionable whether this work structure would satisfy the task requirements of a research team or the needs of employees who desire autonomy and social interaction.

Beyond matching the social and technical dimensions of work, sociotechnical systems must also relate effectively to their task environment—those external elements that are relevant to the setting and achievement of system goals [9]. For many work systems, such as lower-level production units, the task environment consists primarily of other organizational units internal to the total organization. Conversely, other work systems, such as higher-level staff groups, engage a task environment that is predominately external to the organization.

Given this system and environment interdependence, sociotechnical designers attempt to structure work systems so that they can meet environmental demands while remaining relatively resilient to external disruptions. This may involve changes in the system or the task environment. A work group may be given discretion to alter its production methods to account for changes in the quality of its raw materials; similarly, it may pressure the purchasing department

to tighten the quality standards for raw materials inventory. The essential design issue is to match the work system to its task environment.

Unit of Design and Locus of Control. Self-regulating work groups are an attempt to design effective relationships between the social and technical components of work systems and between the systems and their task environments. Although such designs have been employed in a variety of work settings, at least two issues underlie their use: the relevant unit of design (i.e., groups versus individual jobs) and the locus of control (i.e., internal versus external to the system).

Sociotechnical designers typically use the work group, rather than the individual job, as the basic building block of work design. The tendency is to group employees who perform interdependent tasks into a common work unit that is relatively differentiated from other units. This grouping appears necessary when the technology is such that interdependence among workers is essential [14]. Referred to as "technically required cooperation" [20], this dimension is present in production systems where workers must share, in addition to time, the same equipment or materials to achieve a productive outcome. Examples of this include oil refineries, where employees are responsible for materials flowing through the plant; coal mines, where workers are sequentially dependent on the output of previous employees; and hospitals, where a combination of techniques are applied concurrently to the same material. Under these conditions, group designs that account for necessary task interdependencies seem more appropriate than individual job designs. The obverse appears to hold in those situations where technically required cooperation is low (e.g., key punching, telephone installation, and field sales).

An underlying objective in designing any work system is to reduce variance from goal attainment [5]. This involves a choice between two fundamental forms of system control: elaborating external mechanisms of control (i.e., hierarchical supervision, scheduling, and standardization) or increasing the internal control of members of the system (i.e., giving employees the autonomy needed for self-regulation [11]. Sociotechnical designers tend to structure work so that variance is controlled within the work system, rather than external to it. This seems necessary when external control mechanisms are unable to reduce the uncertainty facing work systems. Specifically, two major sources of uncertainty affect goal achievement: those concerned with transactions across the system's boundary (e.g., scheduling input and output exchanges with the task environment) and those involved with the conversion of raw materials into finished output (e.g., operating production technology) [26]. Boundary-transaction uncertainty is likely to be high when the work system's task environment is relatively complex and changing. Since the parts of the environment are richly interconnected and fused with a change gradient, it is difficult to know what, where, and when inputs and outputs will enter or leave the work system (e.g., the number and characteristics of students enrolling in a particular university course may be difficult to predict and control). Similarly, conversion uncertainty is likely to be high when there is incomplete technical knowledge about how to produce a desired outcome (e.g., surgery, psychotherapy, education, and the like). When either boundary-transaction or conversion uncertainty is high, external controllers, such as supervisors and technical staff, find it difficult to program the flow of inputs and outputs or the conversion activities of the work system. Rather, these regulatory functions are more effectively performed by those employees who are closer to the sources of uncertainty.

Conditions for Self-Regulation. The design of self-regulating work groups depends on at least three conditions that enhance technically required cooperation and employees' capacity to

control variance from goal attainment: task differentiation, boundary control, and task control [6]. Task differentiation refers to the extent to which the group's task is itself autonomous forming a self-completing whole. The more autonomous the group's task, the more differentiated its task boundary from other organizational units. This task discontinuity facilitates technically required cooperation by bounding interdependent tasks into a common unit and aids variance control by increasing the likelihood that technical variances will be contained within the work group's boundaries, rather than exported across them [21]. For example, an assembly line may be divided into relatively differentiated task groups through expedient placement of buffer stocks and inventories; this may in turn help to restrict technical variances to discrete segments of the line. The opportunity to form whole task groups may be limited by such technological constraints as equipment size and location and length of the production cycle.

Boundary control involves the extent to which employees can influence transactions with their task environment (e.g., the types and rate of inputs and outputs). The major factors contributing to boundary control include: a well-defined work area, which individuals can identify as their own territory [22]; competent members who possess an adequate repertoire of skills, which frees them from having to rely on external resources of task performance [18]; and group responsibility for boundary control decisions (e.g., quality assurance), which reduces dependence on external boundary regulators (e.g., inspectors). The combination of these characteristics helps group members protect their work boundaries from external intrusions and perform selective environmental transactions.

Task control refers to the extent to which employees can regulate their behavior to convert raw materials into finished products. This factor is enhanced when group members are given: freedom to choose work methods and to adjust work activities to match task and environmental demands [17]; influence over production goals, allowing employees to modify their output as emergent situations are encountered, such as unpredictable breakdowns and stressful working periods [10]; and feedback of relevant measures of group performance, which provides the knowledge of results necessary for goal-directed behavior [10; 17].

The above mentioned conditions—task differentiation, boundary control, and task control—relate directly to a group's capacity for self-regulation. Since the extent to which these conditions must be met to consider a group self-regulating is currently unknown, they are probably most useful in determining the relevance of particular organizational variables for self-regulation. This is a pertinent point, for many attempts to implement self-regulating groups have involved a number of organizational changes [7]. Given this variety of potentially relevant organizational variables, it is important to know which factors are necessary for self-regulation and which are redundant or extraneous. The conditions discussed here can serve as a guide for identifying relevant changes and for understanding them conceptually.

Conceptual clarity concerning the interrelationship of self-regulating conditions is especially needed. Task differentiation and boundary control probably are related curvilinearly. Groups that score low on the task dimension may have such highly diffuse task boundaries that members are unable to differentiate themselves clearly from other organizational units, making boundary control difficult, if not impossible. Conversely, groups that score high on the task variable may have such highly differentiated task boundaries that mutual relations with external units are severely restricted [1]. This may impede environmental exchanges required for task performance (e.g., the attainment of needed raw materials). One would expect a similar relationship between task differentiation and task control. Highly diffuse task boundaries may make it so difficult to separate the group's task from the

task of related units that members are unable to control task-related variables, such as production scheduling. Highly differentiated task boundaries may lead to such high group cohesion that members reduce their openness to task-related inputs, such as performance feedback and managerial support. Such rigidity may also cause external others, such as management, to retaliate by withholding resources, information, or freedom needed for task control. The final relationship, between boundary control and task control, is likely to be positive. The more members influence transactions with their task environment, the more they regulate their behavior toward task achievement. Presumably, increased boundary control enhances members' ability to engage with external units, including management, to obtain relevant feedback and freedom to control task variables. This depends on whether such attempts at environmental influence are perceived and acted upon positively by external others. If boundary control is experienced positively by external others, it is likely to improve task control; otherwise, it may thwart it.

The above discussion suggests possible relationships among the self-regulating conditions. Further study is needed to clarify these interactions. Specific information about the shape, direction, and strength of the relationships would provide a more accurate account of how the different properties of self-regulating groups affect each other systemically. Moreover, research into this issue would likely uncover a variety of other variables that moderate these relationships, such as group size, organization climate, and type of technology. Such knowledge is a necessary step toward explaining the conditions needed for self-regulation and how these operate in organizational settings.

While the previous discussion was aimed at how self-regulating groups promote required cooperation and employees' competence to respond to technical and environmental variances, how such designs affect the social and psychological needs of employees is equally important.

Hackman and Oldham's [15] theory of job design suggests a framework for understanding how self-regulating groups affect individuals motivationally. They identify three psychological conditions that lead to both work effectiveness and personal satisfaction: *(a)* personally meaningful work; *(b)* responsibility for work conditions; and *(c)* knowledge of results. These states are present when the work content is high on the following five core dimensions: *(a)* skill variety; *(b)* task identity (i.e., ability to complete a whole piece of work); *(c)* task significance (i.e., degree to which the job has a substantial impact on the lives or work of other people); *(d)* autonomy; and *(e)* feedback.

When the conditions for self-regulation are implemented effectively, they seem to score high on all these work characteristics. They provide group members with the opportunity to use different skills, to complete a meaningful piece of work, to perform tasks that affect other team members, to make important work-related decisions, and to learn how well they are doing. Therefore, the combination of these work elements is likely to satisfy employees' needs for responsible autonomy over a meaningful task, at least for those individuals who have such needs.

The similarity of Hackman and Oldham's [15] job design characteristics and the self-regulating conditions of work groups suggest a common ground for integrating these two streams of theory and research. The former perspective views work variables primarily from a concern for individual motivation and the latter from a need for required cooperation and control of technical and environmental variances. This contrast, relatively neglected in other attempts to integrate these approaches [14; 23], suggests that each work characteristic may have two distinct yet complementary facets: one related to motivation and the other to self-regulation. For example, skill variety, task identity, and task significance each contribute to the psychological condition of personally meaningful work. They also enhance self-regulation: skill variety pro-

vides the behavioral flexibility necessary to develop group strategies for coping with changing task and environmental conditions; task identity furnishes the differentiated task boundary needed for grouping interdependent tasks and containing technical variances within a common work unit; task significance provides the social interdependence needed to relate individual task contributions to those of other workers. This distinction between motivational and self-regulating views of work characteristics raises the issue of how the work variables affect individual performance and satisfaction. Do they affect work outcomes primarily through their impact on individual psychological needs, or on workers' ability to develop a work structure for coping with technical and environmental demands, or on some combination of both? Research into this complex issue is an important starting point for integrating these so far separate perspectives.

Implementation of Self-Regulating Groups

Developmental System Design. The formation of self-regulating work groups typically follows a design strategy that facilitates group development toward responsible autonomy. Referred to as "developmental system design" [18], this process recognizes that self-regulation cannot be created in a one-step mechanical manner. Rather, the conditions for self-regulation (i.e., task differentiation, boundary control, and task control) may require considerable time and diagnosis to implement fully. This is especially relevant for the social aspects of work groups, such as group decision making, task interaction, and other internal dynamics that occur among group members. These social conditions are not created by design fiat, but through careful attention to the processes by which group members develop their own ways of working together and of adjusting their internal activities to changing task and environmental circumstances. Given the substantial evidence about the ways that groups can thwart work effectiveness and members' well-being [2; 19; 29], development of an effective social system needs to be an explicit part of the design process. Indeed, it is probably the most salient feature distinguishing the design of self-regulating groups from that of enriched jobs.

Developmental system design starts from diagnosis and specification of the structural properties needed to form self-regulating work groups. These include a clearly differentiated group task, a well-defined work area, and relevant measures of performance. These provide the physical and task boundaries for the group and the standards against which variances are monitored and controlled. Training employees to perform the requisite tasks is also a preliminary design issue. Although it seems desirable that all members initially learn all the tasks for which the group is responsible, it is probably more realistic to assume that each worker will acquire the full complement of skills on the job.

The design properties outlined above are aimed primarily at structuring the technical component of the work group and providing employees with the skills necessary to operate it. The problem of forming an effective social system is a more process-oriented task. This requires an understanding of how groups develop from a loose aggregate of individuals into a well-integrated, problem-solving unit. Although this issue has not received adequate attention in the sociotechnical literature [14], there is a substantial body of theory and research about group development. Heinen and Jacobson [16] have integrated much of this literature into a pragmatic framework that is particularly relevant to self-regulating groups, since it accounts for the different kinds of issues that such groups are likely to face at each stage of their development—that is, from an initial forming stage to a more mature phase.

Although it is beyond the scope of this article to present the strategy more fully, it is important to note that such process interventions are best used to support and maintain a self-regulating group that is initially well-designed [14] (i.e., that has a clearly differentiated task boundary, that is staffed with competent members who possess requisite skills, that has relevant feedback of performance, and so on). Given these conditions, a group consultant or leader who is trained in group process skill (e.g., a process consultant [25]) can help members work through their interpersonal and procedural problems and devise performance strategies [14] appropriate to carrying out the group's conversion and boundary-transaction tasks.

Organizational Context. This discussion has concentrated on self-regulating groups in relative absence of their organizational context. The larger organization has a major impact on whether such structures can be implemented effectively. Foremost among these external conditions is the structure of the organization. This appears to affect both the internal dynamics of the group and its relationships with other organizational units. Since self-regulating groups tend to be organic in character [4], an organization structure with similar dimensions would likely support and enhance the group's internal development [14] (i.e., a structure with flexibility among units, decentralized authority, few formal rules and procedures, and so on). Moreover, an organic form of organization where there is a network structure of control, authority, and communication would also tend to promote interdependence among parts of the organization. This would increase the likelihood that a self-regulating group's boundaries remain permeable to mutual relationships with other organizational units, such as plant maintenance, procurement, and technically related groups. A more mechanistic form of organization [4] would tend to place severe constraints on self-regulation. A hierarchic structure of authority and control, a precise definition of rights and obligations, and a functional specialization of tasks would likely thwart a group's autonomy and flexibility, reducing its capacity for self-regulation [14]. Group members would also tend to withdraw from the organization and enact rigid boundaries to protect their autonomy, thus reducing their mutual contacts with other organizational units.

The climate of the organization also affects implementation of self-regulating groups [8]. Since such work designs may involve changes in the organization's reward system, power relationships, communication flows, work flows, and status hierarchies, organizational members must be capable of dealing with these related issues if work is to be redesigned effectively. Argyris [3] suggests that an organizational climate that fosters interpersonal openness, experimentation, trust, and risk-taking behavior is conducive to such structural changes. A review of 16 selected autonomous group experiments seems to support this premise [7]. In most cases, successful implementation of self-regulating designs followed from an organizational change strategy where experimentation, trust, and collaboration among workers and managers were relatively high.

Beyond the structure and climate of the organization, a number of more pragmatic organizational practices are likely to enhance self-regulating groups. Specific organizational measures that tend to promote group (as opposed to individual) forms of work include a group-based pay scheme, performance data relevant to the group as a whole, self-selection of group members, and low turnover of group personnel [26]. Similarly, organizational practices that are likely to nurture learning and responsible autonomy are protection of the group during its early growth stages (e.g., reduced pressures to perform); wage and job security (e.g., a formal agreement among workers and management guaranteeing that no reductions in wages or employment will result from experimenting with new ways to work); and alternative work opportunities for those group members who become disenchanted with group forms of work [8].

Supervision of Self-Regulating Groups

Self-regulating work groups are designed to take on many of the functions traditionally ascribed to management (e.g., assigning members to individual tasks, determining methods of work, controlling task variances, and so on), but this does not mean that external supervision is unnecessary. The supervisory role emerging under such conditions involves two major functions: developing group members and helping the group maintain its boundaries [8; 26].

Developing group members for a self-regulating system requires a consultative style of management. The supervisor helps members organize themselves into an effective team that is capable of responsible autonomy. The essential task is to provide the group with clear boundaries for the exercise of discretion and to assist members to acquire the skills and knowledge to carry out the work assigned. Since first-level management is the critical link between the wider organization and the group, the supervisor's behavior largely determines how much autonomy workers can experience and how much support and encouragement is received from the organization.

Helping the group maintain its boundaries is necessary if members are to sustain sufficient autonomy to control variances and relate to their task environment. Referred to as "boundary management" [8; 26], this supervisory function operates in two directions: outward to the group's task environment and inward to its conversion activities. Since work groups have limited control over their task environment, supervision must help to reduce the environmental uncertainty facing the group. This may include a number of strategies for controlling the flow and acceptability of the group's inputs and outputs (e.g., maintaining alternative sources of raw material, scheduling inventories, negotiating delivery dates for finished products, and so on). It may also involve mediating relationships with other organizational units that affect the group's performance, such as higher-level management, plant maintenance, and related groups in other territories or on other work shifts. Research into the management of lateral and horizontal relationships with the task environment suggests that the former may be more difficult, more lengthy, and involve more negotiation contacts than the former [24].

Focusing on the group's conversion activities, management may assist group members to control those variances that are beyond their knowledge and skills (e.g., handling raw materials with unusual properties, deciding whether to scrap or rework an expensive product, et cetera). Supervision may also help the group to formulate a task definition appropriate to the group's technology and acceptable to the larger organization (e.g., defining textile weaving in terms of a set of looms for a group of workers [22]). Finally, management may assist group members to plan for a desired future and to *problem-solve ways* to bring this about, which may result, in turn, in redefining the group's task or redesigning the group itself.

The above discussion suggests that the supervision of self-regulating work groups may require skills and expertise that are not familiar to traditional line managers [8; 14]. Among these skills are: knowledge of group dynamics and sociotechnical principles; understanding the group's technology and task environment; an ability to intervene in the group and develop members' capacity for responsible autonomy.

Conclusion

Self-regulating work groups are a valuable contribution from sociotechnical systems theory and practice. Their growing use in organizations in a number of industrialized countries suggests that they are a unique and viable alternative to traditional forms of work design. Their popularity, however, may lead organizational members to overestimate the general applicability of self-regulating groups or to underestimate the condi-

tions necessary for their implementation and continued effectiveness. This article has attempted to provide a clearer understanding of the conditions, implementation strategy, and supervision needed for effective self-regulation.

The discussion suggests some preliminary propositions that may lead to much-needed research in this area:

1. To the extent that technically required cooperation and boundary-transaction or conversion uncertainty are high, self-regulating work groups are more task effective than individual job designs.

2. Self-regulating groups are more task effective to the extent that members have (a) a moderately differentiated task, (b) high boundary control, and (c) high task control.

3. Self-regulating groups are more personally satisfying to the extent that members have (a) the conditions in Proposition 2 and (b) needs for responsible autonomy over a meaningful task.

4. Self-regulating groups are more effectively implemented to the extent that (a) attention is given to the social processes by which members develop their own ways of working together and of adjusting their activities to task and environmental conditions; (b) their organizational context is organic; and (c) their organizational climate fosters experimentation, trust, and collaboration among workers and managers.

5. Management of self-regulating groups is more effective to the extent that supervisors (a) provide clear boundaries to the exercise of discretion, (b) assist members to acquire the skills and knowledge to carry out the work assigned, and (c) manage group boundaries both outward to the task

environment and inward to conversion
activities.

References

1. Alderfer, C. P. "Change Processes in Organizations." In M. D. Dunnette (ed.), *Handbook of Industrial and Organizational Psychology.* Chicago: Rand McNally, 1976, pp. 1591–1638.
2. Alderfer, C. P. "Group and Intergroup Relations." In J. R. Hackman and J. L. Suttle (eds.), *Improving Life at Work: Behavioral Science Approaches to Organizational Change.* Santa Monica: Goodyear, 1977, pp. 227–96.
3. Argyris, C. *The Applicability of Organizational Sociology.* London: Cambridge University Press, 1972.
4. Burns, T., and G. M. Stalker. *The Management of Innovation.* London: Tavistock Publications, 1961.
5. Cooper, R., and M. Foster, "Sociotechnical Systems." *American Psychologist,* vol. 26 (1971), pp. 467–74.
6. Cummings, T. G., and W. Griggs. "Worker Reactions to Autonomous Work Groups: Conditions for Functioning, Differential Effects, and Individual Differences." *Organization and Administration Sciences,* vol. 7 (Winter 1977), pp. 87–100.
7. Cummings, T. G., and E. S. Molloy. *Improving Productivity and the Quality of Work Life.* New York: Praeger, 1977.
8. Cummings, T. G., and S. Srivastva. *Management of Work: A Socio-Technical Systems Approach.* Kent, Ohio: The Comparative Administration Research Institute of Kent State University, 1977.
9. Dill, W. R. "Environment as an Influence on Managerial Authority." *Administrative Science Quarterly,* vol. 2 (1958), pp. 409–43.
10. Emery, F. E. "Some Hypotheses about the Way Tasks May Be More Effectively Put Together to Make Jobs." Doc. 527. Tavistock Institute of Human Relations, 1959.
11. Emery, F. E. "The Next Thirty Years: Concepts, Methods and Applications." *Human Relations,* vol. 20 (1967), pp. 199–237.
12. Emery, F. E., and E. L. Trist, "Socio-Technical Systems." In F. E. Emery (ed.), *Systems Thinking.* London: Penguin Books, 1969, pp. 281–96.
13. Gulowsen, J. "A Measure of Work Group Autonomy." In L. E. Davis and J. C. Taylor (eds.), *Design of Jobs.* Middlesex, England: Penguin Books, 1972, pp. 374–90.
14. Hackman, J. R. "The Design of Self-Managing Work Groups." *Technical Report No. 11.* New Haven, CT: School of Organization and Management, Yale University, December 1976.
15. Hackman, J. R., and G. R. Oldham, "Motivation through the Design of Work: Test of a Theory." *Organizational Behavior and Human Performance,* vol. 16 (1976), pp. 250–79.
16. Heinen, J. S., and E. Jacobson. "A Model of Task Group Development in Complex Organizations and a Strategy for Implementation." *The Academy of Management Review* 1, no. 4 (1976), pp. 98–111.
17. Herbst, P. G. *Autonomous Group Functioning.* London: Tavistock Publications, 1962.
18. Herbst, P. G. "Socio-Technical Unit Design." *Doc. 899.* Tavistock Institute of Human Relations, 1966.
19. Janis, I. L. *Victims of Groupthink: A Psychological Study of Foreign Policy Decisions and Fiascos.* New York: Houghton Miffin, 1972.
20. Meissner, M. *Technology and the Worker: Technical Demands and Social Processes in Industry.* San Francisco: Chandler, 1969.
21. Miller, E. J., and A. K. Rice. *Systems of Organization.* London: Tavistock Publications, 1967.
22. Rice, A. K. *Productivity and Social Organization: The Ahmedabad Experiments.* London: Tavistock Publications, 1958.
23. Rosseau, D. M. "Technical Differences in Job Characteristics, Employee Satisfaction, and Motivation: A Synthesis of Job Design Research and Sociotechnical Systems Theory." *Organizational Behavior and Human Performance,* vol. 19 (1977), pp. 18–42.
24. Sayles, L. *Managerial Behavior.* New York: McGraw-Hill, 1964.
25. Schein, E. H. *Process Consultation.* Reading, MA: Addison-Wesley, 1969.

26. Sussman, G. I. *Autonomy at Work.* New York: Praeger, 1976.

27. Trist, E. L. and K. W. Bamforth. "Some Social and Psychological Consequences of the Longwall Method of Coal Getting." *Human Relations,* vol. 4 (1951), pp. 3–38.

28. Trist, E. L.; G. W. Higgin; H. Murray; and A. B. Pollock. *Organizational Choice.* London: Tavistock Publications, 1963.

29. Whyte, W. F. *Money and Motivation.* New York: Harper & Row, 1955.

IV   Cutting Edge Change Strategies

In our third edition of this book we labeled this part "Structural Interventions vis-à-vis OD" because we believed, at the time, that a number of contemporary organization improvement strategies or techniques could be subsumed under that label. Those interventions were consulting activities aimed at improving organization effectiveness through changes in structure. We broadly defined structure to mean such aspects of organizations as how the overall work is divided among units, spatial arrangements of machines and people, work flow, operating procedures, who reports to whom, role definitions and expectations, and goal setting and compensation procedures. Thus we viewed structure broadly as consisting of procedures or devices that channel, direct, or constrain activities.

Further, we depicted some of the variables that tend to characterize OD in contrast to non-OD. That depiction is presented in Figure 1.

Some structural interventions visible in the literature and in practice in 1989 were quality circles, quality of work life (QWL) projects, work redesign, management by objectives (MBO), the use of task forces, and collateral organizations. While these OD interventions continue to have merit and usually have a time perspective of two to three years and beyond, we observed that there is a major shift towards a shorter time perspective, such as 18 months, for interventions, and the organization that can learn faster than its competitors will have a strategic competitive advantage. An example of a consultant trained with the longer time perspective is a director for McKinsey & Company who stated in the April 6, 1993, *Wall Street Journal* "A major change typically takes five years or more, and is marked as much by management missteps as breakthroughs." [1] Since 1989, we observed that <u>sucessful</u> interventions, such as total quality management (TQM), self-directed teams (SDTs), gainsharing, organizational learning, and reengineering [2], all contain most of the elements of second-generation OT. The one element of first-generation OD that is being questioned by practitioners is the *time perspective*. During 1950 through the 1980s, OD consultants had the luxury of time; in the 1990s, time will give the firm a competitive advantage; therefore, consultants who continue to "preach" a longer time perspective may not survive in this decade.

Figure 1

Organizational improvement strategies

	Organization Development (OD)	Non-OD (Examples)
Target of intervention	Work-related groups.	Individuals, or noninterdependent persons in a group or audience setting.
Consultant model used	Collaborative equal power (change agent model)	Expert or "purchase" model.
Task or structure versus process orientation	Focuses largely on processes such as group interaction, norms, leadership, decision making; outcomes may be task/structural changes.	Focuses largely on changing tasks or structure.
Depth of culture managed	Attempt to manage culture in depth; both formal aspects and informal (e.g., cognizance of attitudes, perceptions, feelings).	Primary focus on one selected aspect of formal system (e.g., structure, technology, tasks, or goals).
Time perspective	Two to three years and beyond.	Ad hoc, short-range orientation.
Systems perspective	High systems orientation (i.e., high cognizance of interdependencies).	Narrow attention to functional organizational subsystem or problem.

As we move from OD with its well-defined theory, technologies, and research to OT that is more experimental, developing, and self-learning, with a shorter time perspective, we included in this section eight timely articles that describe this new paradigm shift toward a major redirection for the organization of the future.

The first essay, by Lawrence Schein, provides some key linkages between successful total quality programs and successful organizational change. This essay is critical because quality programs led by such authorities as Deming, Juran, and Crosby took on a tone of the next quick fix in the 1980s, and expectations were exceptionally high because of the need for organizations to compete on quality at the international level. However, by 1992 the total quality movement, "one of the biggest fads in corporate management, is [was] floundering, a broad study suggests." [3] It is our experience that where TQM is successful it has a heavy OD and OT flavor.

The second essay, by David Chaudron, builds on how to successfully implement TQM by defining the commonalities with OD, which are teamwork, management-labor cooperation, customer satisfaction, employee empowerment, trust, and a focus on the process.

The third essay, by Robert A. Zawacki and Carol A. Norman, explores the relationship between successful self-directed teams and planned change. They begin their article with an overview on the transition from first-generation planned change (OD) to second-generation planned change (OT) and then suggest that SDTs are growing extremely fast in popularity with managers because SDTs are a strategy for second-generation planned change that are demonstrating significant increases in productivity when implemented effectively. They also discuss the law and SDTs, the guidelines for implementing successful SDTs, and end with a detailed checklist for SDTs.

The fourth essay, by Brian Dumaine, further explores the dynamics of SDTs and the experiences of such organizations as Texas Instruments and 3M. One example of success is General Mills, which reports productivity in its plants that use SDTs is as much as 40 percent higher than its traditional units. This article also discusses the shortcomings of SDTs, such as less opportunities for promotion to management by individual contributors.

The key to successful implementation of TQM and SDTs maybe in tieing compensation to behaviors that help implement these programs. The fifth essay, by Elizabeth M. Doherty, Walter R. Nord, and Jerry L. McAdams, describes two types of gainsharing programs: performance improvement programs (PIPs) and team suggestion programs (TSPs). The PIP rewards improvements in actual performance of the team, whereas the TSP rewards were directly linked to the implementation of the suggestion. Rewards from both programs were not increases in base pay but were points that could be traded for merchandise. Their research indicated that the two programs led to increased productivity, quality, and attendance. The authors conclude their essay with a discussion on the similarities between OD and gainsharing.

The sixth essay, by Chris Argyris, discusses the important concept of learning. He labels his theory as "single loop" and "double loop" learning. He maintains that some of the most successful professionals will have a difficult time adjusting to the faster pace of change, such as random change. The very behaviors that resulted in success in the past (single loop learning) will be a handicap in the future. His essay is especially important as our discipline moves from OD to OT.

The seventh article in this part, by Ray Stata, continues with the theme of organizational learning. Mr. Stata argues "that the rate at which individuals and organizations learn may become the only sustainable competitive advantage, especially in knowledge-intensive industries." [4] In this article he shares with the reader how Analog Devices applied innovative ideas to improve its performance and competitiveness.

The final essay was written by Gary E. Jusela especially for this edition. He presents an informative review of the two main contrasting views of the organization: machine bureaucracy and the systems model. Then he describes large-scale systems change at Ford Motor Company and at Boeing Aerospace using many of the elements of planned change and team building.

References

1. Daniel Machalaba. "Learning Curve." *The Wall Street Journal,* April 6, 1993, p. 1.
2. Susan Albers Mohrman and Thomas G. Cummings. *Self-Designing Organizations: Learning How to Create High Performance.* Reading, MA: Addison-Wesley Publishing, 1990. And Michael Hammer and James Champy. *Reengineering the Corporation.* New York: Harper Collins Publishers, 1993.
3. Gilbert Fuchsberg. "Quality Programs Show Shoddy Results." *The Wall Street Journal,* May 14, 1992, p. B9.
4. Ray Stata. "Organizational Learning—The Key to Management Innovation." *Sloan Management Review,* Spring 1989, pp. 63–74.

READING 26
THE ROAD TO TOTAL QUALITY: VIEWS OF INDUSTRY EXPERTS

Lawrence Schein

Highlights

Few major manufacturers in the United States, or in the world for that matter, lack experience with quality control or quality assurance in production. Traditionally, however, quality was the business of specialists—of engineers who developed product specifications; of statisticians who determined "acceptable" levels of product variability; and of inspectors on the shop floor. Quality control was one of many separate corporate functions. Total quality, by contrast, is everybody's business. It is sought for both products and services, involves every corporate function, and is the business of management. In fact, some executives view quality as a way of managing the firm (i.e., as a management system). In the transition from quality control/assurance to total quality, the focus shifts from inside the business organization to listening to, understanding, and pleasing the customer outside.

This report is based on interviews with the members of The Conference Board's U.S. Quality Council, conducted in 1988. These senior quality process executives represent 12 firms that have made serious commitments to quality improvement and whose achievements and experiences can provide valuable insights for other firms.

In particular, the report examines these executives' views on the key concepts in the total quality approach and strategies for the implementation of quality within the company.

Source: Lawrence Schein, "The Road to Total Quality: Views of Industry Experts," *The Conference Board Research Bulletin*, no. 239 (1990), pp. 3–17. Reprinted with permission.

Among the major points of agreement were:

- A conviction that total quality is the strategy of choice for assuring the economic position of the United States in the global marketplace.
- Dedication to quality as a long-term process.
- Concern over the lack of top-level involvement in quality in many companies.

Why the Change to Total Quality?

What persuaded the major firms interviewed to undertake what most concede to be an arduous corporate journey? One common motive, according to the Quality Council, is competition. As one executive remarked:

> Korean workers work 56 hours a week for an average $1.75 an hour and produce higher quality goods at lower prices. They can take away business from U.S. firms, in the United States and abroad, and eliminate U.S. jobs and companies in the process. There is nothing that clears the mind as quickly as fear.

Council executives stress, in particular, the threat of Japanese competition. "They beat the pants off us." "They really cleaned our clocks." And the Japanese have done something else. They have changed, probably forever, the U.S. view of product cycle life, traditionally measured in decades, occasionally in years, but rarely in months.

The total quality approach, mounted by Quality Council companies from the late 1970s to the mid-1980s was also motivated by back-to-back recessions; deregulation; a growing trade deficit; low productivity; downsizing, which required firms to do more with less; and the upward spiraling of consumer awareness and sophistication.

Much of the inspiration for the adoption of total quality programs occurred in the late 1970s and early 1980s. From 1978 to 1982, Ford's sales of cars and trucks in the United States plummeted by 49 percent to 2.1 million units. Ford sustained worldwide operating losses of $3.3 billion between 1980 and 1982. Xerox, which had pioneered the paper copier, saw its U.S. market share drop from 93 percent in 1971 to 40 percent in 1981. Corning's financial performance in the early 1980s was sluggish. The Japanese had made serious inroads into several of the company's key markets. For example, although Corning had developed the ceramic substrates used in automobile emission control and had become a primary supplier to Ford, within 33 months the Japanese were offering a better product.

At American Express, management feared that the company's explosive growth in the late 1970s might cause employees to become overly confident and possibly lose focus on the principle that made them so successful—making the customer their number one priority. No financial threat faced 3M, but corporate leadership saw total quality as the best way to position the firm for the future. Their vision was world-class quality. Toward this vision, 3M positioned quality as a positive business strategy. At Celanese, prior to the merger with Hoechst, inconsistent market performance, customer complaints, and a profit squeeze prompted a new look. At Management Science America (MSA), the software manufacturer, new waves of competition mandated a strengthened industry presence. Quality was perceived as a way to absorb recent acquisitions while maintaining a market image. According to MSA's vice president, Quality and Management Systems, Edward J. Kane, quality was the way to

manage, but the basic motivation was "to take advantage of the opportunity presented by industry changes to increase competitiveness and build new customer partnerships." Johnson & Johnson's management sought ways to maintain and improve quality at lower costs in the face of rising domestic and foreign competition.

Attention to quality began to address these problems. The interviewed executives credit the total quality effort with contributing to major operational improvements and to a healthier bottom line in their companies. For example:

- Ford's share of the U.S. new car market was 18.8 percent when the Taurus was launched in 1985. By the end of 1989, Ford's share is expected to reach 22.5 percent. Between 1985 and 1987, the company's total earnings were $10.4 billion.

- Corning has recovered its Detroit ceramic substrate business and is currently shipping product to Japan. At one time, audits indicated a substrate defect rate approaching 6 percent (60,000 parts per million, or PPM). Today, some substrate customers report defect levels below 100 PPM. Corning is also shipping television glass to Japan. Says David Luther, senior vice president and corporate director, Quality: "The superb competition required us to run a four-minute mile and we did."

- In its remittance banking or lockbox business, First Chicago's accuracy rate is nearly three times the industry standard.

- Florida Power & Light (FPL) has reduced customer complaints by 60 percent and improved reliability of electric services to customers by 40 percent since 1983. In 1986, FPL received the U.S. Electric Utility Industry's highest award, the Edison Award, for excellence and quality achievements. In 1987, the firm was rated by 156 utility CEOs as the best-managed utility in the nation. FPL's St. Lucie 2 nuclear power plant, licensed in 1983, came in on schedule and under budget—$600 million less costly than any other similarly sized plant in the United States and three and one-half years ahead of the industry average.

- All the major franchises of Johnson & Johnson (J&J) are market leaders.

- Westinghouse is well on its way to reducing average gross inventory from 24 percent of sales prior to 1982 to 10 percent in 1993.

- One and a half years into the total quality process, Arthur Nichols, formerly director of Quality Management at Hoechst Celanese, reports favorable results in the Hoechst Celanese operation's bottom line: improvement in conversion efficiencies in plants and reduction in wastes. Customer complaints are also sharply down.

- Xerox has started to regain its market share in copiers from the Japanese—the only U.S. company in an industry targeted by the Japanese to accomplish this without government support. Return on assets has improved, manufacturing costs are down, and incoming parts quality stands at 99.96 percent. In a recent survey of a sample of 140 Xerox managers, 97 percent said that total quality is the correct company strategy. John Kelsch, director of quality, points to what is perhaps the best result of all: "TQC [total quality control] has gone so deeply into the organization that it would be extremely difficult to change."

Quality Council members go on to discuss the basic concepts and underlying values upon which the total quality approach is built.

Key Concepts

The executives identify several key areas that influenced their companies' adoption of total quality programs and that continue to be the focal points of their quality strategies.

Customer Satisfaction. According to those interviewed, customer satisfaction begins with a clear identification of customer constituency and with the desire to understand and speak the customer's language. Who customers are and what they want are determined in a variety of ways. Companies conduct extensive market research, including surveys and focus groups; review reports of sales calls; analyze complaints about products and services; and hold meetings with customers to discuss priorities and obtain suggestions. When the customer is another company, personnel of both firms often meet during the planning phase of a new product or service. In the early days of total quality, the emphasis was on meeting customer specifications. Later, "specifications," with roots in engineering, were replaced by "requirements," attesting to the customer's power to choose among competing suppliers. More recently, "requirements," now viewed as too static, have given way to the more dynamic concept of "expectations." What the customer needs and wants can change and grow in complexity. Successful companies anticipate changing expectations and more demanding standards. According to council members, customer expectations are met by doing the right things the right way the first time and 100 percent of the time at a cost that represents value to the customer. From this standard of performance flow all of the measures, tools, techniques, and training and staffing methods in the quality arsenal. Some executives speak of going even further and "delighting" the customer by providing a useful product feature or service dimension that the customer has neither requested nor expected.

Internal Customers. The quality experts also stress the concept of the internal customer, which originated with the total quality movement. Managers and employees often cannot focus constructively on improving quality to external customers until they understand the importance of meeting each other's requirements within and across departments and functions. Often, this is a difficult concept to communicate in the organization. Xerox's director of quality likens internal customership to a fire bucket brigade. Each member of the brigade line receiving the bucket is a customer who expects the bucket to be safely delivered without spillage. But when that person turns to hand the bucket to the next person in the line, the "customer" becomes a "supplier" from whom speedy and safe handling is expected. Within the company each customer is also a supplier—and vice versa.

As firms develop norms of meeting the expectations of both internal and external customers, they also begin to look more critically at the output and performance standards of their own external suppliers or vendors. In companies such as Xerox, Ford, and FPL, this has led to certification programs under which vendors who must meet rigorous criteria. In the best of circumstances, total quality companies seek a cooperative partnership with their suppliers.

The Need for Continuous Improvement.

The senior quality executives are quick to stress that quality is a "process" not a "program." Programs end; processes are continuous, and, in the increasingly competitive marketplace, continuously improved. In the older quality control environment, a margin of error was allowable. The production line or run would be shut down only if defects exceeded set limits. Total quality strives for perfection and thus emphasizes zero defects—the total elimination of error, scrap, rework, defects. The Japanese maxim is: "No error is too small to ignore." Executives note that, as awareness has grown and as quality has improved, the margin of error in the United States has shifted from the number of defects per 10,000 or per 100,000 total units produced to the number of defects per million units. This is not to say that the drive toward continuous quality improvement has been easy. Attitudinal and behavioral changes come hard, cautions IBM's program director of Quality, Les Papay. People tend to cling to the status quo, to rest on the laurels of improvement, and to resist the pressure to change constantly. Defining and meeting customer requirements continuously reflects a culture of constant change that is also a culture of uncertainty. Continuous quality improvement generates a momentum to take calculated risks in uncharted waters and to expose one's self to the possibility of failure.

The Cost of Quality.

The cost of quality includes the cost of making mistakes in both manufacturing and service operations—duplication; missed, late, and wrong delivery; scrap and repairs. The cost of quality also includes the cost of inspection to locate errors, as well as the cost of preventing errors—creating error-free designs and training programs in problems-solving skills. The cost of quality, estimated at 20 to 30 percent of sales, is in itself a powerful inducement to quality improvement. IBM's program director of Quality notes that, in a "culture of prevention," the cost of quality declines—as defects decrease, costs decrease, as shown in Figure 1.

Some executives also include inventory as a cost of quality. Inventory occupies valuable space, requires movement, and incurs maintenance costs. Large inventories are the result of a "collection of mistakes"—poor planning, unreliable delivery from suppliers, lack of confidence to get the job done on time. Elimination of inventory by "just-in-time" methods, adapted from Japanese manufacturing, is strongly associated with driving down product costs.

FIGURE 1

Two views of the cost of quality

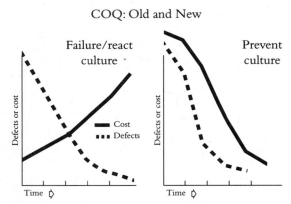

COQ: Old and New

SOURCE: **IBM Corporation.**

Quality as a Management System. Companies such as MSA and FPL have integrated quality with management. In the broadest sense, quality embraces management systems and performance indicators covering all functions and results—costs, delivery, scheduling, benefits. According to W. Kent Sterrett, FPL's former director of Quality Improvement, the principal goal of quality improvement is the improvement of the organization which, in turn, increases the reliability of service to the customer and raises customer satisfaction. The quality management system is the key to long-term survival and profitability.

Instilling a Quality Culture. The participants agree that success also hinges on instilling a quality culture—the values, beliefs, and assumptions that underlie key quality concepts. Ideally, the goals of the quality effort and the supporting practices become the daily norm and are embedded in the line organization. When quality becomes everybody's business, a participative work culture begins to emerge. Employees at all levels are enabled or "empowered" to par-

ticipate in decisions affecting their work. In the culture of involvement, the team is the organization of choice—quality circles, quality improvement teams, corrective action teams, autonomous work teams. Teams range in scope and responsibility from problem-solving groups to self-managed work teams that schedule work, assign jobs, hire members, and set the standards and volume of output.

The former director of Quality Management at Hoechst Celanese observes that one particular function of the team is the reduction of adversary relationships among disparate functions. Executives also describe the culture of quality as a culture of trust and courtesy. More open com-

Gurus

Four authorities stand out in the quality movement: W. Edwards Deming, Joseph Juran, Philip Crosby, and Armand Feigenbaum.

Deming and Juran, who contributed so heavily to the quality process in Japan after World War II, tend to concentrate on statistical process control; Feigenbaum pioneered the concept of total quality control; and Crosby has addressed the management issues in quality.

munication through publicity about quality goals and management's sharing of business information with workers contribute to the growth of trust, as does the encouragement to make use of one's abilities in the service of improved performance. Courtesy, extended to the external customer as a condition of the relationship, becomes an expectation governing conduct within the firm.

One of the most dramatic examples of culture change among total quality companies is the turn-around in labor-management relations at Ford. Ford's cooperative labor-management agreement and the development of the Employee Involvement Program is one of the key elements in the company's quality thrust. James Bakken, Ford's vice president of Corporate Quality, now retired, says that it took the auto industry 50 years to see it was not going to succeed in an adversary stance with labor. Management views the movement from an adversary relationship and confrontation with the unions to cooperation and the creation of an environment where people are involved in creating meaningful change as a "gigantic" step. A result is the continuous improvement of products and services provided to customers.

Involvement and empowerment are not limited to employees. Increasingly, customers and suppliers are sought out for their ideas. At Ford, for example, vendors and dealers are explicitly brought into the quality improvement process.

Managing Total Quality. The council companies differ more in their implementation efforts than in their overall dedication to total quality or in the key concepts to which they subscribe. Some of the differences are traceable to industry type. Quality, like productivity, has had a longer history in manufacturing, where processes tend to be more easily measurable than in services. Other differences result from the amount of resources invested in total quality. In one member firm, the corporate quality "organization" consists of a single full-time executive and a secretary. Contrast this with the staff of 120 at the Westinghouse Productivity and Quality Center, which is housed in a separate facility. The center provides expert information and analytic and applications support for operating systems and management.

The diffusion of quality—the extent to which the process spreads through the organization—

also varies by company. In diversified firms and in those expanding through acquisition, quality is likely to be more advanced in some parts of the firm than in others. Currently, 100 of Johnson & Johnson's 170 constituent companies have begun a total quality process. When Hoechst acquired Celanese, quality in the parent firm was largely concentrated in manufacturing, in contrast to the new subsidiary, which addressed quality at many levels. At the other end of the spectrum are several companies that have involved every organizational unit. Within the constraints of its culture, industry, and financial position, each of the interviewed firms has developed a strategy for implementing its quality agenda. No two strategies are identical, but most embrace common elements. For example, Corning's four total quality principles and 10 quality actions are shown in Figure 2.

Top-Management Commitment. The *sine qua non* of a successful approach, in the eyes of quality executives, is the dedication of senior management beyond public pronouncements. It is usually the management or executive committee that signals a change toward total quality. Typically, these committees go off-site to develop new missions and strategies. Xerox's 25 top executives met for a special two-day session to hammer out the new corporate policy and strategy on total quality. MSA executives held several off-site meetings, first to develop a quality vision by the management committee and then to design function-specific missions by senior functional executives.

According to quality executives, senior management must periodically and actively review the work of the organization against stated quality goals. It is also up to top management to ensure that their successors are equally committed. Long-term quality improvement is equated with support by several generations of managers.

Leadership of total quality requires highly visible and articulate champions. Such spokesper-

FIGURE 2

Corning's quality principles and actions

The Four Total Quality Principles

I. Meet the Customer's Requirements

First, **understand** and **agree** on the requirements; then meet them. People often confuse beauty, price or luxury with quality. For example, a Steuben® vase meets the requirements for a memorable gift, while a Pyrex© beaker meets the requirements for an experiment in a science lab. The vase is costly. The beaker is not. Yet each is a quality item; each meets the requirements.

II. Error-Free Work

This defines the standard for meeting the requirements: the first time, every time. It does not mean that errors will not happen. It does mean **an attitude that errors are not acceptable.** There's no more "Acceptable Quality Level" with its allowable percentage of defects. This new attitude leads to asking "why?" when an error occurs, tracking down the root cause, and taking action to keep it from happening again.

III. Manage by Prevention

Quality must be built into the work. It cannot be "inspected in," "improvised in" or "repaired in." This means anticipating problems and making permanent changes to prevent errors. The more emphasis that is placed on preventing errors, the more often the customer's requirements will be met the first time, every time.

IV. Measure by the Cost of Quality

The cost of quality is made up of three parts: error cost, detection cost, and prevention cost. Error cost includes the cost of doing work over. Detection cost is the cost of inspecting for errors. Prevention cost is the cost of building quality into the work. The goal is to cut the cost of quality by reducing error and detection costs. Measuring by the cost of quality accomplishes three things: it focuses people's attention on problems, it helps to set priorities for error correction, and it marks progress toward eliminating problems.

FIGURE 2

(concluded)

Turning Principles into Results

The Ten Total Quality Actions

Commitment: A continuing personal action in support of Total Quality.

Teams: The organization of people to manage Total Quality at each location.

Education: Programs to create awareness and teach the skills and techniques needed for Total Quality.

Measure/Display: Using charts and other displays of error rates to focus on the need for corrective action.

Cost of Quality: Use of procedures to measure error, detection and prevention costs, so problems can be prioritized and solved.

Communication: Keeping everyone informed of company and unit progress, and the ways employees can become involved.

Corrective Action: Establishment of a system in which the individual and the organization can identify and eliminate problems. An essential element of the system is that it is able to respond to individual employee suggestions.

Recognition: Recognizing individual and group participation in, and contributions to, Total Quality.

Event: A gathering of employees to celebrate and rededicate themselves to Total Quality.

Goals: Establishment of error reduction goals by everyone.

---

sons can be CEOs like David Kearns of Xerox, James Houghton of Corning, and Donald Peterson of Ford. The style of leadership appropriate to total quality is what Douglas Anderson, 3M's Corporate Quality director, calls "commitment and involvement." Quality is not strictly a top-down or bottom-up proposition. Top man-agement sets the strategy, but others are motivated to "catch the ball and run with it once it has been thrown." Leadership fashions the environment for change.

In stating their expectations of top management, senior quality executives emphasize concrete behaviors—sharing information with employees, taking the same courses in quality skills as shop workers, recognizing and rewarding superior performance, and assuming leadership on the national quality scene (see Figure 3). At Xerox, all echelons of management—including middle and supervisory levels—are expected to be fully committed. According to

FIGURE 3

Excerpts from mission statements and corporate credos of three companies

These statements are intended to convey to employees, to industry and to the public that quality is serious business. They often imply a commitment by top management and a corporate dedication to a long-term endeavor. According to Ford's Vice President, Corporate Quality, when his CEO named quality as the company's number one priority in 1979, the message pulled the organization together and provided a common language and sense of direction for the firm. Such statements from Xerox, Hoechst Celanese and Johnson & Johnson are shown in this exhibit.

XEROX

Leadership Through Quality:

A Total Quality Process For Xerox Corporation

"Xerox is a quality company. Quality is the basic business principle for Xerox. Quality means providing our external and internal customers with innovative products and services that fully satisfy their requirements. Quality improvement is the job of every Xerox employee."

Values

Performance

- Preferred supplier, dedicated to understanding and meeting customer expectations
- Commitment to safety, employee health and protection of the environment
- Responsible corporate citizen
- Earnings to support long-term growth
- Consistently superior to competition
- Commitment to continual improvement

People

- Respect for individuals and appreciation for contributions each can make
- Diversity accepted and valued
- Concern and fair treatment for individuals in managing business change
- Equal opportunity for each employee to achieve his or her potential
- Employee pride and enthusiasm
- Informed employees through open communication

Process

- Openness and trust in all relationships
- Innovation, creativity and risk taking encouraged
- Teamwork throughout the organization
- Participative goal setting, measurement and feedback
- Decision making at the lowest practical level
- Actions consistent with clearly understood mission and long-term goals
- Recognition for quality achievements
- Resources committed to ongoing training and development

Striving for "10 out of 10"

Hoechst Celanese

Hoechst

Johnson & Johnson

Our Credo

We believe our first responsibility is to the doctors, nurses and patients,
to mothers and all others who use our products and services.
In meeting their needs everything we do must be of high quality.
We must constantly strive to reduce our costs
in order to maintain reasonable prices.
Customers' orders must be serviced promptly and accurately.
Our suppliers and distributors must have an opportunity
to make a fair profit.

Xerox's director of Quality, management is the critical driving force for quality; it is imperative for top executives to "walk the way they talk."

To this end, the Xerox corporate quality team, using survey techniques, identified a set of management behaviors that are considered supportive of total quality. Managerial performance is rated by subordinates through confidential surveys. Behaviors include encouragement of teamwork, openness, and trust; respect for co-workers; and recognition of work well done.

Organizing for Quality.   There are two ways in which quality is ingrained in the structure of the firm: through the full-time quality managers and professionals at corporate and operational levels, and through the councils and committees that form the quality management organization.

Quality Staff.   The Board's council members' backgrounds reflect the interdisciplinary nature of the quality effort. Several of the executives have engineering and plant management backgrounds; three have financial training; while others come from management consulting, marketing, sales, and personnel. Staff size and scope of responsibility vary considerably. Xerox, starting with a 15-member corporate quality team, now has over 300 specialists worldwide, a number of whom are part-time. At 3M, 20 quality professionals work within the company; an additional 20 consult with other companies in a profit center arrangement. At Hoechst Celanese, the quality staff is organized as a council—the director at the corporate level has a counterpart in each operating division. The Quality Assurance Office in the American Express (Amex) Travel Related Services (TRS) Company is worldwide in scope. This company's corporate quality officer has six direct reports for policy, customer service, and quality observation on a worldwide basis. Amex quality assurance staff are present in every country in which a card operations center exists. At J&J, the director of the Quality Improvement Process is assisted by a

four director-level staff who operate out of the company's Quality Institute. J&J also has international Quality Institute staff centrally located in Europe and Latin America to provide support to its companies in these regions.

Full-time quality executives in council companies and their subordinates perform a variety of tasks. They help in formulating quality guidelines and standards, teach and develop training materials, measure process and customer satisfaction, and interpret customer feedback. Jack Fooks, Westinghouse's vice president of Corporate Productivity and Quality, notes that the Productivity and Quality Center has an artificial intelligence capability and CAD/CAM technology, providing a laboratory setting for new quality tools and techniques. In general, quality staff consider themselves internal consultants and facilitators to the corporate staff and to the line organization. But quality staff roles have also changed over time. In the 1970s, for example, the Corporate Quality Office at Ford focused on developing corporate policy and on monitoring and auditing results. The office now provides "expert consultant services in development and deployment of a total quality improvement process to the company worldwide," in the words of the vice president, Corporate Quality.

The Quality Management Organization.   The comparatively small corporate quality staffs are amplified organizationally in two ways. First, the corporate quality office is integrated with the larger management system of committees and councils that administer the quality process within the company. Second, the management system represents many organizational levels and functions. Although variations exist among companies, the divisional/departmental organization may have full-time quality managers in staff and operational jobs. The Corning chart (see Figure 4) illustrates this type of structure.

In Amex's TRS Company, the quality assurance staff in operational card centers report directly to country managers, with dotted-line

FIGURE 4

Corning quality management organization

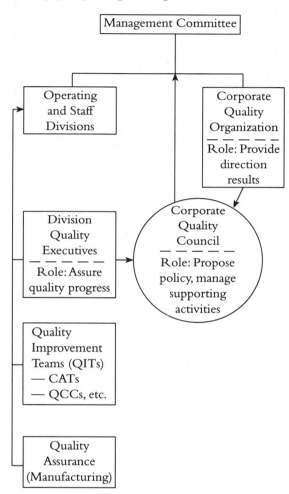

Management Committee

Operating and Staff Divisions

Corporate Quality Organization
— — — — — —
Role: Provide direction results

Division Quality Executives
— — — — — —
Role: Assure quality progress

Corporate Quality Council
— — — — — —
Role: Propose policy, manage supporting activities

Quality Improvement Teams (QITs)
— CATs
— QCCs, etc.

Quality Assurance (Manufacturing)

relationships to regional centers and to the corporate quality assurance office.

Managing the Quality Process.   Wringing waste out of processes and shortening production and delivery time satisfy two objectives: a superior product at a lower cost. One way to improve the process is to manage by prevention, rather than by inspection. Ways are constantly being sought to build in quality at the design stage. Error-free designs, for example, sharply reduce the need for costly after-the-fact inspections.

Focusing on process, rather than on products or services per se, is referred to as "process management." In manufacturing, say the quality professionals, the process should generate a reliable and durable product that performs a specific function over time without breaking down, and that holds up under heavy usage. MaryAnne Rasmussen, senior vice president of Worldwide Service Quality at American Express, and Aleta Holub, vice president and manager of Quality Assurance at The First National Bank of Chicago, identify three critical factors in the service process: accuracy, timeliness, and responsiveness. Holub notes that customer responsiveness includes clarity and conciseness of communication.

According to process quality management; which is now being practiced by IBM, MSA, and Westinghouse, among others, operational problems in all areas—accounting, finance, marketing, sales, purchasing, personnel, etc.—are traceable to a failure in internal processes. Poor process management is characterized by an absence of ownership and accountability, a lack of measurement and objectives, and by uninformed employees.

For example, a firm with a heavy customer base in the East expanded its services nationwide but had not increased the number of switchboard operators during the lunch hour in the New York headquarters. This led to delays in responses to telephone inquiries, and customers became increasingly exasperated. In short, a process in office services was "out of control." The problem was easily resolved once a "process owner" was designated—in this case, the director of office services who, assisted by computer data, established a monitoring system to assure an effective match between switchboard staff and call volume over the working day. Data analysis revealed an upsurge in calls at the end of the day, as midwestern and far-western customers rushed to call before the offices closed. Additional staff for this time period led to improvement in the process, and complaints virtually disappeared.

The continuous improvement model (another form of process quality management) in use at Ford is shown in Figure 5. In explaining the model, the vice president of Corporate Quality stresses that it is not intended to be generic, but to fit the needs of Ford's changing quality culture:

> The model is suited to Ford's culture of "graphically" displaying the concept that the continuous improvement of products/services can only be achieved by making meaningful changes to the processes and systems that generate these products and services.
>
> At Ford, every process is thought of as having five generic inputs: people, equipment, materials, methods, and the environment (physical and cultural). What is inside the model's large box is, in Ford vernacular, "the way we work" and "the blending of resources"—what some academics refer to as "the transformation process." The outputs are the products and services that meet customers'

needs and expectations. Note the important feedback loop that is utilized to bring the voice of the customer back into the planning process. Once a process is stable and in control, it will not improve unless change is made to one or more of the inputs. The model depicts an ongoing cycle of activity—planning, doing, checking, and acting—that generates continuous improvement. The model also suggests that management's job is changing from managing the status quo to leadership of people in creating meaningful changes in the way business is conducted that result in products and services that provide greater customer satisfaction.

The vice president of Quality and Management Systems at MSA views process management as part of his company's formula for competitiveness, which is effectiveness, efficiency, and adaptability. Effectiveness is relevance, efficiency is the cost of being effective, and adaptability is being effective and efficient over time.

Quality executives agree that the management of quality requires a participative environment in

FIGURE 5

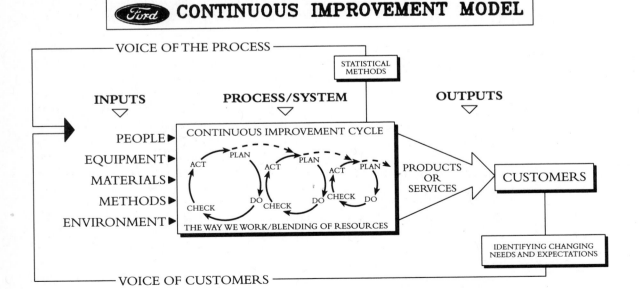

which teamwork is strongly encouraged. The work of teams and other parts of the organization toward quality goals needs continuous review and feedback. Managers must also be careful to link the quality process to business objectives and the way the company's business is conducted. And managers must also support the quality process with appropriate training, reward, and recognition.

Teams. The team structure is the most visible form of employee involvement in the quality process. According to Ford's vice president of Corporate Quality, the voluntary team approach is a way for employees to be meaningfully involved in continuously improving their processes and systems, leading to higher quality products and services and customer satisfaction. 3M's Corporate Quality director values teams for producing functional and cross-functional improvements. Xerox's director of Quality recalls that quality circles at Xerox had struggled prior to total quality because of middle-manager antipathy. With TQC and its participative emphasis, quality circles and quality improvement teams have taken off.

Teams do proliferate. At Corning there are approximately 1,500 temporary teams at any given time actively involved in corrective action. At 3M there are several thousand teams of varying types: voluntary and semivoluntary, short term and long term, ranging from quality circles to self-managed groups. There are several thousand quality improvement teams in action at Xerox at any one time. In addition to quality improvement teams of employees at Hoechst Celanese, special teams also involve customers. At FPL, the team is a major vehicle for continuous quality improvement, and teams are found at all levels including senior management. FPL's 1,800 teams involve 60 percent of the 15,000 member work force.

A recent example of a cross-functional team with a successful product is related by Ford's representative on the Quality Council:

Everyone was on Team Taurus—financial people, product planners, product engineers, purchasing staff, manufacturing engineers, quality control specialists, and our supplier and dealer partners. The team was assembled early in the product conceptualization stage. The identity was the team, not the functional unit. Team Taurus operated through the development cycle and into the product introduction stage. Employee involvement such as this is becoming a way of life at Ford: we are a team.

At MSA, cross-functional teams are organized under the auspices of functional quality councils (FQCs). The FQC on development, for instance, consists of the vice president of Development and the people who directly report to him. The vice president is the "executive owner" of the development process. On the cross-functional team is an FQC member responsible for development methodology. He is the "working owner" of the process. Other members of the team come from other functions/disciplines whose input is essential. The team is assisted by a quality coordinator. Both the working owner and the other team members may belong to teams serving FQCs in other areas. The cross-functional team proposes and implements solutions, subject to the approval of its FQC. The management committee reviews the work of all the functional councils, and thus, indirectly, the work of the teams. In the future, it is anticipated that the quality councils will be absorbed in the normal management structure. Quality objectives become simply management objectives, thereby hastening the integration of quality and strategic management.

The Review. The review is a periodic meeting at a department or unit level, attended by senior management, at which the quality process is reviewed in painstaking detail. The purpose is twofold: to implement total quality in the line and to improve it by continuous feedback.

At First Chicago, the review takes the form of a weekly performance measurement meeting in the Bank's Services Products Group, which deals with noncredit products for corporate and institutional customers. These product lines include management of payables and receivables and security and trade-related services. Each week, 500 measures of timeliness, accuracy, and customer service responsiveness are tracked. Levels of minimal acceptable performance and superior performance (goals) have been established for each indicator. Product areas present charts to senior managers showing unacceptable and above-average performance. Both problems and successes are analyzed. The minimums and standards of superior performance are constantly adjusted upward. Figure 6 shows some of the measures used by the Remittance Banking Division.

According to First Chicago's top quality officer, these meetings permit senior managers to wander about without moving, a highly desired time-saving arrangement. The meetings give nonmanagers and middle managers "a chance to shine" if their news is good and opportunity to get participatory, high-level feedback and support if the news is bad. The concentration on quality has become part of the daily culture at Services Products Group.

The senior vice president of Quality Assurance describes the business review she conducts in the Amex Travel Related Services Company on a country-by-country basis:

> If we're performing a review in the UK, we'll go to the operations site in Brighton and spend a month there. On day one, we'll sit down with the appropriate executive—the general manager or division president—and discuss strategy: where we are going, where we have been, where we are with competition, whether the business is growing as it should, how our one-and five-year plans stack up, and what our budget looks like. During the next 29 days, we do a complete analysis of the business to see how we are focusing on quality.

The review covers:

- Marketing techniques.
- Monitoring of customer phone calls.
- Monitoring of customer correspondence.

- Analysis of market research.
- A critical review of the work of the local quality assurance staff, including an examination of the quality of performance provided to individual customers for specific customer service transactions.

Some of the measures used in country/regional evaluations are shown in Figure 7. The Amex review probes continuously for indications of customer dissatisfaction and for ways of upgrading services:

> These types of business reviews really get underneath all aspects of service delivery and we walk out with a 50 point action program for implementation. Our whole philosophy about quality isn't doing one or two things right; it's doing lots of small things right.

At Westinghouse, a total quality fitness review is conducted under the leadership of the Productivity and Quality Center at operating unit levels. Each operation is rated against 12 criteria or conditions of excellence (see Figure 8).

The rating on information, for example, shows the extent to which a unit's required information is clear, complete, accurate, timely, useful, and accessible. The reviews are voluntary, the results confidential, and all levels of personnel in the unit are included in the structured interviews. Each member of the review team fills out a score sheet independently; the raters then reach a consensus on the final score. Feedback is used to improve processes and customer satisfaction. The center makes follow-up services available to help implement actions based on the fitness review.

The Business Process. Executives at FPL, IBM, MSA, Amex, and Westinghouse have taken the position that managing quality is managing the entire business with customer needs in mind. It is quality that should drive the business since quality is a process of constant improvement. At

FIGURE 6

The First National Bank of Chicago: Selected Performance Indicators, January–June, 1989

Lockbox/Remittance Banking

Comprehensive remittance processing services allow clients to quickly convert payments to available funds while capturing critical accounts receivable information. First Chicago offers a wide range of remittance services through our sophisticated technology and nationwide processing network in Charlotte, Chicago, Dallas, Newark and Pasadena.

Shown here is a representative sampling of the performance charts for our nationwide product delivery and customer service.

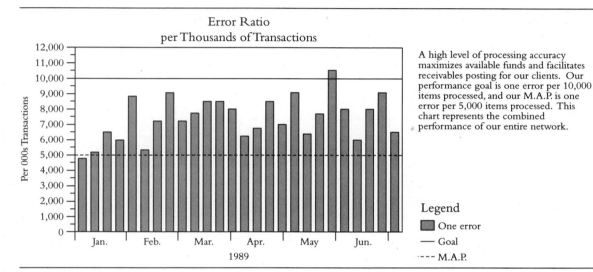

A high level of processing accuracy maximizes available funds and facilitates receivables posting for our clients. Our performance goal is one error per 10,000 items processed, and our M.A.P. is one error per 5,000 items processed. This chart represents the combined performance of our entire network.

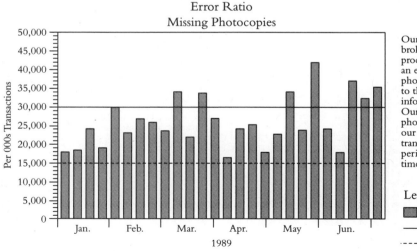

Our error ratio measurement is further broken down by error types and processing locations. This chart reflects an error ratio by type—missing photocopies. Clients apply cash receipts to their accounts receivables based upon information from their photocopies. Our goal for this measure is one missing photocopy per 30,000 transactions, and our M.A.P. is one per 15,000 transactions. During this reporting period, we made our M.A.P. 100% of the time.

FIGURE 6

(concluded)

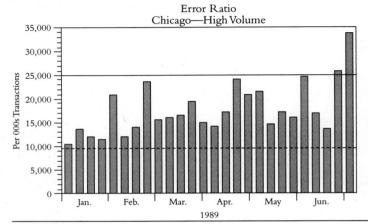

Error Ratio
Chicago—High Volume

Processing accuracy is charted in the various production units in our Chicago site, as well as in each of our wholly-owned network sites. This documentation gives us the control we need to measure all units by the same standard of excellence. The chart shown reflects the error ratio per 1,000 transactions processed for our Chicago High Volume Unit. This unit processes clients' accounts with more than 5,000 transactions per month or with complex processing instructions.

Legend

■ One error
— Goal
--- M.A.P.

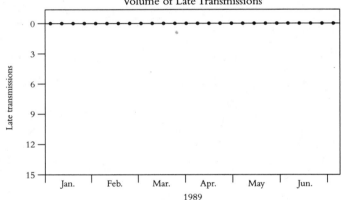

Firstcash Transmissions
Volume of Late Transmissions

Our FirstCash clients depend on timely information to make informed cash management decisions. Lockbox deposit information is transmitted to the FirstCash System in accordance with key deposit deadlines that occur throughout the day. In the first half of 1989, as shown on this chart, no deadlines were missed.

Legend

● Volume
— Goal

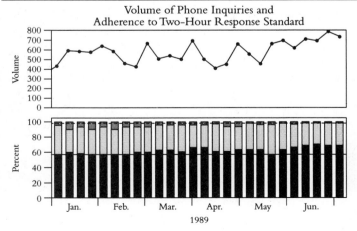

Volume of Phone Inquiries and
Adherence to Two-Hour Response Standard

So that clients receive a timely response to their inquiries, our M.A.P. for this measure is that our service consultants return all client phone calls within two hours. During this reporting period, we met our M.A.P. 100% of the time. For 24 of the 26 weeks, we met our goal of responding to 55% of the inquiries during the client's initial call.

Legend

● Calls
□ 2+ hours
▨ 2 hours
▦ 1 hour   — Goal
■ Initial call   --- M.A.P.

FIGURE 7

Key Service Performance Measures for Card Products at American Express, 1986 and 1987

KEY SERVICE PERFORMANCE MEASURES
CARD PRODUCTS

1987 ■
1986 ▨

Timeliness of Processing Basic Applications

Percentage of Standard Achieved
Average number of days from receipt of applications to mailing of plastic or decline notifications.

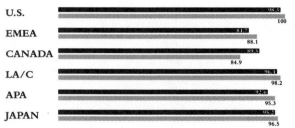

Higher than anticipated volumes were received in many Divisions due to successful marketing campaigns. Consequently, some delays occurred. Staff shortages and conversion to new accounts systems in LAROC and Hong Kong caused additional delays. Some improvement was achieved in Canada, where Operations and Data Entry management worked together to address issues affecting processing timeliness. Actions to improve results included use of overtime, temporary and borrowed staff, as well as the filling of open positions.

Timeliness of Processing Emergency Card Replacements

Percentage of Standard Achieved
Percentage of replacement Cards available on the same business day as the emergency request, or available on the day specified by the Cardmember.

Most markets continued to achieve good results. In the few situations when emergency Card replacements were not available on time, the primary reasons were delays and inaccuracies in transmitting embossing information between Centers and internal routing delays. To ensure that we continue to meet our worldwide service commitments, Canada revised procedures and staff schedules, Thailand changed internal workflows, and all Divisions reinforced procedures and emphasized the importance of accuracy and prompt receipt of embossing information.

Timeliness of Processing Replacement Cards

Percentage of Standard Achieved
Average number of days from request for normal replacements to mailing of plastic.

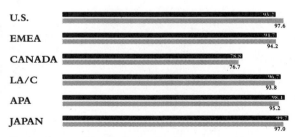

Good results were achieved in Japan, and performance was stable or improved in most other Divisions. In Canada, staff shortages and delays in sorting replacement requests have been addressed through staff recruitment and implementation of revised workflows. In the U.S., additional embossing equipment was installed and staff schedules were revised to offset the effects of equipment problems and unexpectedly high volumes associated with the introduction of the Optima Card.

Timeliness of Mailing Cardmember Statements

Percentage of Standard Achieved
Average number of days from cycle cut-off to mailing of statements.

Relatively stable performance was achieved, except in the U.S., where software implementation and acceptance testing associated with the introduction of Enhanced Country Club Billing caused delays in mailing Cardmember statements. Staff shortages affected results in New Zealand, as well as in Canada, where additional delays were caused by significant equipment downtime in March.

Note: U.K. results are included in the EMEA Division

FIGURE 8

Total quality fitness review at Westinghouse

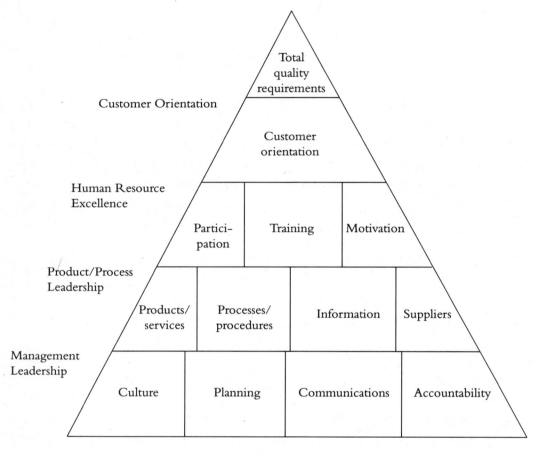

Conditions of Excellence

FPL, senior management "prioritizes" the areas that represent major opportunities for improvement, then deploys time and resources accordingly. This process is termed *policy deployment.* In 1988, FPL selected 13 areas on which to focus improvement. Figure 9 shows three of these areas (under short-term plans) within the longer-range objective of achieving customer satisfaction. The goal of deployment is to fulfill

the corporate vision for the next decade— "becoming the best-managed electric utility in the United States."

At IBM and MSA, the concept of business management takes quality a step beyond process management. The latter is appropriate in managing quality within specific functions (e.g., engineering, manufacturing, and marketing). But a different order of magnitude emerges when mul-

FIGURE 9

Policy deployment at Florida Power & Light, 1988: Achieving customer satisfaction (excerpt)

FPL Corporate Vision

During the next decade, we want to become the best managed electric utility in the United States and an excellent company overall and be recognized as such.

Mid-term plans (5–7)	Short-term plans (1 year)	Indicators	Details of implementation
	Improve the reliability of electric service.	Service unavailability. Transmission forced outages.	Reduce the frequency of customer interruptions. Reduce the duration of customer interruptions. Improve the collection and analysis of data to determine cause of interruptions. Target preventive maintenance resources to activities with high potential for improving service reliability.
I. Achieve Customer Satisfaction	Improve public perception of our nuclear programs.	Percent of customers surveyed satisfied with our safety performance.	Increase public confidence in our continued safe operations of nuclear power plants. Enhance public awareness programs.
	Improve customer satisfaction.	Number of customer inquiries to PSC (excluding current diversion).	Increase level of customer satisfaction with FPL's products and services.

tiple processes have to be managed simultaneously. Product development is a case in point. It requires integration of customer and engineering input, product design, manufacturing, marketing, distribution, and customer feedback.

This complex process really requires the "management and administration of the resources of the business and quality plays a key role in improving the process," according to the vice president of Quality and Management Systems of MSA, who was formerly with IBM. "Cross-functional processes," he adds, "are the primary means to carry out the strategic direction of the business unit." Business process, or policy deployment, allows the concentration or "optimization" of resources in companies whose traditional organizational structure causes work to be done vertically through functions and div-

isions. The cross-functional approach cuts through the slow-moving hierarchy. But, cautions the executive, this requires a "disciplined environment," like the MSA business process methodology shown in Figure 10.

Learning and Training. Continuous quality improvement requires continuous training, retraining, and skills upgrading. Learning is highly valued in total quality companies, which, on the whole, allocate substantial resources toward teaching their employees teamwork and problem-solving skills. Executives visit other quality companies to learn more about the growth process. They also retain consultants, send their managers to quality institutes, visit Japanese operations, join learning networks, and listen to suggestions from employees.

FIGURE 10

Effective process management at Management Science America

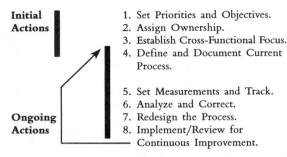

Initial Actions
1. Set Priorities and Objectives.
2. Assign Ownership.
3. Establish Cross-Functional Focus.
4. Define and Document Current Process.

Ongoing Actions
5. Set Measurements and Track.
6. Analyze and Correct.
7. Redesign the Process.
8. Implement/Review for Continuous Improvement.

Meetings between the company and its supplier staffs and with customers further advance the learning process. American Express and First Chicago use detailed, continuously applied measures to gauge customer satisfaction with service quality. Gerald Cianfrocca, Johnson & Johnson's director of Quality Improvement, in establishing a worldwide quality process in this diversified company, has drawn on Ford's experience with continuous quality improvement and IBM's leadership in process management. As a preliminary step in planning for a quality organization, FPL invited presentations from other companies that had embarked on the total quality effort. Several firms, FPL among them, regularly schedule day-long orientation programs on quality at corporate headquarters for executives from other companies, the government, and the military.

Council executives believe training programs are essential for orienting employees to quality and for teaching them fundamental skills. Training is also seen as the key to continuous quality improvement through the upgrading of skills and mastery of new methods. Typically, quality training falls into three categories:

- *Awareness:* raising consciousness of quality, cost of quality, and group dynamics.

- *Skills:* group problem solving, team building, decision making.
- *Statistical techniques:* data collection, process control, advanced statistics.

At FPL, for example, problem solving for quality improvement combines both interpersonal skills and statistics. The process proceeds from interviewing and data collection, to data analysis and presentation.

Corning, IBM, and J&J have established quality institutes or colleges. Training is Corning's principal method for changing to a culture of total quality; training programs extend throughout the organization. For example, starting with the CEO and the management committee, all of the firm's 28,000 employees worldwide have been trained in the first phase of quality awareness in two-to-three day sessions. Instructional staff are all Corning employees, trained at the Quality Institute. Instruction is given in six languages. Corning employees are also well into the process of a second round of training in communications and group dynamics, problem solving, and statistical skills. The goal—part of the corporate vision for 1991—is to have *all* employees spend 5 percent of their working time in training to meet job requirements. The current percentage is 3.4. The 5 percent level is regarded by several council members as an appropriate standard. Others, however, question whether nonexempt employees need such extensive preparation.

Training for all is mandatory at Corning. At other firms, quality seminars are mandatory for managers and for supervisors who will serve as team leaders. Also, special training is customarily provided for facilitators who work as resource personnel in the quality team structure. Several members view the training systems at Corning, IBM, and FPL as "highly disciplined."

Reward and Recognition. On the whole, the quality executives tend to favor recognition for quality improvement over financial reward. Financial remuneration is perceived as setting up a win/lose situation that can polarize the work force. Council executives have found that employees respond enthusiastically to publicity and nonmonetary awards for superior performance. In one company, about 1,000 suggestions were received per year prior to total quality. Of these, approximately 25 percent were accepted and the employees received cash payments. After total quality was instituted, cash rewards were discontinued, but the number of suggestions rose to 8,000 annually. In the experience of one executive, involvement in the quality process has brought company recognition to many workers for the first time in their lives. One very powerful form of recognition in such firms is the team or individual presentation of proposals or success stories to upper-level management. At Amex, an executive is available to coach employees in making effective presentations to senior management.

Although nonmonetary recognition is highly valued, most council companies are working to develop compensation strategies that reflect quality achievements. At the executive level, 8 of the 12 council companies have begun to tie compensation to performance on quality indicators. One approach is to designate a percentage of bonus for performance against quality targets. Another is a variable pay system, in which the bulk of salary is fixed with a variable percentage that moves up or down depending on corporate profitability. At Xerox, managers' eligibility for promotion is influenced by their acting as role models in quality.

Several of the companies have explored gain-sharing methods, whereby all employees receive a portion of cost savings as a bonus. But the trend with respect to the nonexempt labor force seems to be in the direction of profit sharing. Ford has such a plan in place, with an average bonus of $5,500 paid out in 1987 and 1988.

Assessment of Progress to Date

In commenting on the general quality movement in the United States, the members of the

Tools and Techniques for Monitoring Quality Improvement

Among the newer tools mentioned in the interviews:

Competitive Benchmarking: A technique pioneered by Xerox that compares a company's performance to that of leading competitors, and to noncompeting firms viewed as outstanding in their industry. Xerox, for example, uses L.L. Bean as its competitive benchmark in distribution systems.

Cost of Quality: Used by many companies to target (or "prioritize") opportunities for quality improvement—for example, the highest error rate or the most wasteful process.

Avoidable Input Analysis: Used by Amex to eliminate unnecessary customer inquiries, which are due to a variety of causes, such as billing disputes or unclear marketing programs. Amex analyzes 147 different types of customer phone calls to root out the causes for the input and take appropriate action to reduce the unnecessary input. Amex equates avoidable input with "rework" and "scrap" in the manufacturing sector.

Value to Price Ratio: A measure of customer satisfaction, developed by Westinghouse, expressing the perceived value to the customer (relative to competition) compared to the price the customer pays.

Structured Business Analysis: Also developed by Westinghouse and named "Cost-Time Profiling," this is a method for shrinking cost and time in both blue-collar and white-collar operations leading to higher investment turnover and higher profit margins.

board's U.S. Quality Council are most troubled by the lack of top-level commitment in many companies. Overemphasis on the short term, continued insensitivity to customers, and business school failure to teach process skills are among the failures cited.

Council executives are also concerned that too many business leaders believe that increasing productivity is the principal means to improving competitiveness. Quality experts see higher productivity as a result of improved quality. Quality, to them, addresses customer satisfaction; productivity does not. Other issues within and beyond council firms include how to:

- Overcome resistance to accepting quality as an integral part of the business—"Quality is fine, but I've got to get back to work."
- Overcome the attitude that attention to quality is over when training ends.
- Maintain and improve quality levels during an economic downturn or a corporate restructuring.
- Better link performance appraisal and reward to quality improvement.
- Enlist greater support and commitment to total quality within the human resources function.

Several issues surfaced on which there was disagreement:

- Not everyone is happy with the terminology of "zero defects," a concept first popularized in the United States in the aerospace industry. Certain employees, particularly professionals, are said to believe that the concept is applicable to manufacturing and not to intellectual activity.

- It is not clear how much or what kind of training is suitable for the nonmanagerial ranks.
- Executives dispute the correct strategy of measurement. Some executives emphasize the "vital few" approach in which quality improvement is limited to the usual handful of factors that account for 80 to 90 percent of a problem. Others maintain that no measurable factor is too inconsequential for consideration.

Although concerns remain, and differences of opinion exist, results in quality companies are impressive. Besides, as executives in council companies and other quality firms—Milliken, Disney, Motorola—will say, the quality movement is in its early days and the steep upward road to total quality still lies ahead. The immediate outlook is positive and the interviewed quality executives share the view that they have begun a journey from which there is no turning back.

It is the more distant future that harbors uncertainty about the success and consequences of the total quality approach. When the process begins, impressive gains are usually registered rather quickly. Executives caution that the going will get very hard when the defect rate or the late delivery rate is pushed down to the 5 percent level. Further movement toward zero defects will require extraordinary innovation. New strategies and techniques will be needed. Quality executives use the analogy of the football game—"the going is toughest inside the 10-yard line."

These executives also agree that as quality continuously improves, the tempo of competition will quicken. An unspoken possibility is that in trying to go "the last 10 yards," the competition may become so severe that even some of the current total quality players may not survive.

READING 27
HOW OD CAN HELP IMPLEMENT TQM: OPPORTUNITIES FOR OD PROFESSIONALS

David Chaudron

Total quality management (TQM) is a buzzword receiving increasing publicity. Many organizations indicate that TQM is a potent mechanism to increase performance and customer satisfaction. This article will describe key TQM concepts and opportunities for OD professionals.

TQM Concepts

Focus on Quality and Prevention. Many definitions of quality exist. For purposes of this article, quality is defined as consistently producing what the customer wants while minimizing errors before and after customer delivery.

TQM emphasizes detecting potential problems before they occur. Failure has several consequences:

1. The necessity to inspect other people's finished work, rather than relying on the worker's own motivation and skill. This inspection requires extra people and resources.

2. If the inspection finds errors, the errors must either be fixed, causing extra time and workload, or scrapped with all the accompanying waste.

3. If customers find the errors, this can cause dissatisfaction, loss of customer confidence, and perhaps loss of the customers themselves.

Source: David Chaudron, "How OD Can Help Implement TQM: Opportunities for OD Professionals," *Organization Development Practitioner,* March 1992, pp. 14–18 (publication of the National Organization Development Network, P.O. Box 69329, Portland, OR. 97201). Reprinted with permission.

To be successful in preventing defects, quality must be designed in before it is produced. During the design phase of product development, get input from customers, marketing, and those that assemble or produce the final product.

Cooperate with your suppliers and customers. Another element of TQM emphasizes cooperative relationships with suppliers of products and services to the organization, and a focus on customer satisfaction. In many organizations, suppliers are treated with indifference, and often with hostility. Instead of having a large number of potential suppliers, each competing to give the organization the cheapest price, TQM emphasizes a different relationship. In an organization that has implemented TQM, vendors are treated as business partners, with all parties working to deliver a quality product. Suppliers are chosen based on consistently delivering a quality product. This means that, for an organization to succeed, its suppliers must implement TQM as well.

A key philosophy in dealing with customers is that it is they who define quality. The quality control department doesn't define it; the president doesn't define it; the customer, and only the customer defines it. According to TQM, the secret of success is to consistently deliver to customers what they need (see Figure 1).

In organizations implementing TQM, the concepts of *customers* and *suppliers* include relationships inside the organizations. Manufacturing can be considered the customer of engineering; patients can be the customers of doctors. The "products" departments produce for other departments must satisfy the quality require-

FIGURE 1

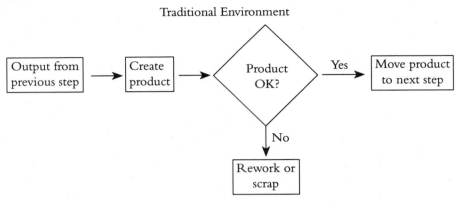

Traditional Environment

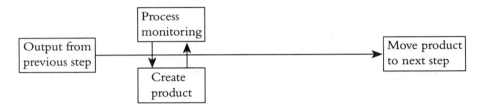

TQM Environment

ments of their customers. A report that the finance organization produces must satisfy external auditors; but those reports must also give accurate, needed information to manufacturing, product support and sales. If it doesn't, the customer is not getting what he wants.

Continuously improve. Not only is quality defined by the customer, but it is a moving target. Cars that were thought of as reliable in the past are now of average quality. What is now a rare feature offered only by you, will soon become commonplace and expected. To meet dynamic customer needs, the organization itself must be dynamic.

Eliminate nonvalue added steps. One of the chief tools of TQM is the flowchart. With it, intact and cross-functional work groups diagram the steps and decisions that make up their work life. After a flowchart is developed, group members

examine it for redundant products, steps, decisions, and processes. Elements without value are eliminated or minimized based on efficiency and customer need.

Flowcharting can be an excellent opportunity to empower line employees by changing who makes decisions. Negative consequences can exist as well. Elimination of nonvalue-added steps can mean the elimination of positions or whole classes of work.

It is a fundamental tenant of TQM that most problems are caused by poor process (OD professionals can read "systems" here) not the lack of motivation by employees.

Encourage the proper climate. In order for continuous improvement to work, people must be empowered, willing to innovate and act in an atmosphere of trust and respect. Without motivated employees in a facilatative climate, all of

FIGURE 2

The problem-solving/prevention cycle

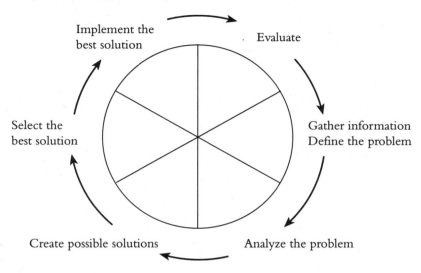

the other components can be in place, and TQM will still fail.

Use the problem-solving/problem-prevention cycle (see Figure 2). This cycle describes the general steps that TQM problem-solving/prevention groups use. Its major elements are:

1. The gathering of information and its analysis before actions are taken.
2. The use of brainstorming (creating possible solutions) before evaluating ideas.
3. Evaluation of success. (This cycle, using somewhat different terminology, is called the Deming cycle, where its components are PDCA: Plan, Do, Check, and Act).

This cycle can be used in:

1. Cross-functional teams, to clarify and refine processes that cross organizational boundaries.
2. Design teams, to create or modify organizationwide systems.
3. Intact family work groups working to

improve their day-to-day operations;
4. Newly formed and intact work groups to improve their interpersonal functioning.

Use statistics to back decisions. The key to success is to consistently deliver your customer's need. To find out whether we are successful, we ask our customers how well we are doing. In TQM, this data can be graphed in pareto charts, run charts, and control charts. With this data, trained employees can use it:

1. Spot trends before problems are caused.
2. As part of problem solving, to find out why the problem occurred and what can be done to prevent it from happening again. These graphs are the tools of Statistical Process Control (SPC).
3. In product design: The use of experiments at this stage of product development can identify key characteristics that can affect and optimize product development. This use of experimentation in product design can

dovetail into an organization's attempts at "concurrent engineering." Concurrent engineering attempts to design and develop a product with input from customers, vendors, and line operators occurring simultaneously, rather than sequentially.

When an organization uses statistics to make decisions, it can avoid making knee-jerk reactions to small, random changes in outcome. Statistics allow decision-makers to tell the difference between chance occurrences and systematic factors that significantly affect product quality.

Commonalities with OD

TQM and OD emphasize the same things:

- Teamwork.
- Management-labor cooperation.
- Customer satisfaction.
- Employee empowerment.
- Trust instead of fear.
- A focus on process, not solely on outcomes.

How OD Can Help

Avoiding the Training Hammer. The old saying goes, "If you have a hammer, you think everything is a nail." One of the most frequently overused implementation strategies in TQM is training. Though the goals of TQM have much in common with OD, techniques to implement these goals are different. Many TQM implementation programs recommend training in "top-down" fashion, with a person's manager training his or her subordinates in problem solving. As most OD professionals acknowledge, training will solve only skill and knowledge problems. Skills training won't solve problems in the reward system or of poor organization.

Assessing Organizational Climate. Another way OD professionals can help is in a thorough understanding of an organization's climate. All too often, organizational change is implemented without a good knowledge of the environment. Without this understanding, any "canned program" can end up as a square peg in a round hole. This assessment will also give the organization a clearer idea what to implement. This goes hand in hand with avoiding the training hammer.

Change Planning and Management. After an organization decides what it will implement, OD professionals can develop the change management plan. Such elements as communication, stakeholder buy-in, and possibly outplacement assistance are all critical in implementing TQM.

Using a Systems Approach. Another contribution our profession can make is helping the organization take a systems perspective. Organizational change often has unintended effects, both positive and negative. Thinking through these consequences will increase the chances of a successful implementation.

Initial pilot projects may spur the interest of top management, who wish to see the techniques of successful efforts spread elsewhere. What often is not understood, however, is that not only a quantitative increase must be made (more groups using problem-solving techniques, for example), but qualitative changes as well. In order for TQM to become an integral part of an organization's life, selection, reward and communication systems must support it. Drastic changes in organizational structure must be necessary to align the organization with its customers.

Career Development and Employee Selection. TQM requires new behaviors of employees. Some employees will have the necessary skills, style, and motivation; others will be required to develop those skills. Employees must be carefully selected for new positions. OD professionals can assist in this process by helping management make individual selection decisions and by developing systemwide selection systems.

Individual Coaching on Management Style. Valued members of management may have been promoted on the basis of their technical skills; TQM requires much more. Coaching, counseling and empowering others may be strange terms and even stranger behaviors to many. Individual coaching can improve the performance of "old-line" management.

Teambuilding.   This may be necessary in:

1. The top-management team to air and resolve interpersonal issues that inhibit implementing TQM.
2. Intact "family" work groups before and during their use of TQM tools.
3. Cross-functional groups whose task it is to optimize processes that cross departments.
4. Newly formed family groups created as a result of restructuring.

Sadly, the author knows of several TQM interventions whose "team building" consists solely of teaching stranger groups meeting management skills!

Considerations in Implementation

Top Down Implementation.   Many involved in TQM implementation insist that "top-down" implementation is the only way. Though implementation of some elements must involve the CEO or other top management, TQM efforts do not often start this way. Often initial, small-scale projects come to the attention of someone with influence who then gets top-management involvement.

Schisms between the TQM Folks and the HR Folks.   Interest in TQM can often arise spontaneously at the operator level of an organi-

zation, usually with small-scale interventions focused on one or two natural work teams. At other times, initial interest in TQM can begin with middle management of the operations department, or perhaps with the operations vice president. As a result, much activity can go on about which that top management of human resources is unaware.

As a result, many employees who have worked on these small-scale projects may be interested in TQM and feel somewhat isolated. They learn through informal communication channels that others are doing similar work. Some leaders among these employees may have had sporadic training in TQM concepts.

Human resource departments in many organizations are not aware of the day-to-day happenings on the shop floor. As a result, HR departments are often unaware of the initial stirrings of interest in TQM. Once the effort gathers more momentum, the HR department can be seen as marginal, because "We have gone so far without them, so who needs them now?"

As a result, the TQM folks and the HR folks can end up in a nasty political imbroglio both groups should deplore. When an organization finds itself in this position, both groups can ask several questions:

- How did this occur in the first place? What can be done to prevent it from happening again?
- How can we keep each other informed?
- In what ways can we cooperate with each other?
- How do we get top management involved?

If the situation between the two groups has deteriorated significantly, third-party consultation using intergroup team-building techniques may need to be used.

Expansion of TQM beyond Day-to-Day Operations.   TQM interest may start in the departments most concerned with day-to-day operations. Examples of this include assembly and fabrication for manufacturing organizations; teller transactions and customer interface in financial organizations; or paperwork reduction efforts in public organizations. In order for TQM to succeed, it must permeate the efforts of all employees, in all departments. Because operations functions receive so much scrutiny, and have often been the efforts of many cost reduction and simplification efforts in the past, little "fat" may be left to trim. Large opportunities may exist in billing, research & development, engineering, financial, human resources, and legal functions.

This attempted expansion may have several consequences:

- Initial resistance by support departments.
- Support departments, and those departments not on the original pilot projects, may feel resentful and reject TQM, because "it wasn't invented here."
- Failure of previously used techniques.

Often little diagnosis is made before TQM implementation techniques successfully used in one group are implemented by other groups.

- Ambiguity regarding the identity of the customer, the nature of the product, and the measures of customer satisfaction. Support departments often have a more difficult time than line organizations defining their products. This is the same challenge felt by service organizations as a whole.
- Failure to make qualitative changes. Initial expansion efforts tend to be "more of the same." Pilot projects tend to be technical in nature: fixing machinery and reducing production time. When efforts expand, management expects the next pilot project to be the same kind of effort. Management often fails to realize the challenge is to make systematic changes to the organization so that TQM becomes a way of life—not start other pilot projects.

READING 28
SUCCESSFUL SELF-DIRECTED TEAMS AND PLANNED CHANGE: A LOT IN COMMON

Robert A. Zawacki and Carol A. Norman

Organization development is moving from a first-generation response to change to a second-generation response to change, which is labeled "organization transformation" (OT). "At present, OD is relatively well defined and circumscribed in terms of its technologies, theory, and research. OT, on the other hand, is emerging, ill-defined, highly experimental, and itself rapidly changing." [1]

We believe there are certain human technologies, such as self-directed teams (SDTs), when implemented as a planned change strategy, that are very supportive of OT. Further, we believe that OT is emerging as the second-generational response to a new kind of change, that is extremely rapid, because of market, technology, international competition, and profit realities.

The purpose of this article is to explain how to so design and implement successful SDTs that the organization of the future can better adapt to random/faster change yet maintain some degree of order, stability, and internal equity. Then, we present a brief history of SDTs, next we will describe how to transition from traditional top-down management to SDTs, and we conclude our dissertation with the linkage between successful SDTs and planned change.

———
The authors express their sincere thank you to Professors John F. Milliman and D. D. Warrick for their helpful comments on this manuscript.

Source: Written especially for this volume.

Adaptive, Rapid, and Random Change

D. Verne Morland, in his article "Lear's Fool: Coping with Change Beyond Future Shock," [2] introduces the concept that, in the past, change flowed along a reasonably predictable course and individual contributors in the organization adjusted by working harder and smarter to stay ahead of the changes. Recently, however, organizations are facing high-speed change that is frequently changing the direction and behaviors of individual contributors. Further, Chris Argyris builds on this idea of random change and discusses how the very behavior that has been reinforced by yesterday's performance can become a liability in the organization of the future. [3]

In Figure 1, line 1 illustrates organizational change in the decades of the 1950s and 1960s. It was during the period of the birth of OD that change was incremental and people adapted to the change and were rewarded for their new behavior, and generally they perceived those rewards as reinforcing successful behavior. Then, during the decades of the 1970s and 1980s, change became more rapid (line 2) and individual contributors responded by working harder and smarter. The organization's managers helped their people stay ahead of the increasing rate of change by introducing more and better technologies, such as personal computers, networks, and some general movement toward empowering employees.

Line 3 illustrates what is happening in the 1990s. Change is becoming more rapid/random and seems to lack cause and effect for people in our society. This decade can be labeled

FIGURE 1

Impact of change over time

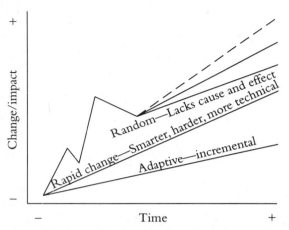

SOURCE: This is a modification of D. Verne Morland, "Lear's Fool: Coping with Change beyond Future Shock," *New Management* 2, no. 2 (1984).

"continuous/discontinuous change." Three brief examples highlight our contention about change in line 3. First, we have neighbors whose son attended a major university at some financial sacrifice on the part of the family. The son majored in aeronautical engineering, studied hard, and graduated first in his class. As an honor graduate, he only had two job interviews and received one job offer as a programmer. When he entered the university, engineers were in demand; when he graduated after the ending of the cold war, there was no demand for engineers. To him and his family this change lacked cause and effect!

A second example—an engineer joined a large electronic company after graduating from a major engineering school. For the next eight years he worked very hard, received outstanding performance reviews, and was promoted to management ahead of his peers. When another company formed an alliance with his company, he was told that the new organization no longer needed his services. To him, with a wife and two children, this alliance lacked cause and effect!

A third example is IBM. This organization was extremely successful delivering large computers to clients during the periods represented by lines 1 and 2. However, when the pace of change quickened, this computer giant was not flexible enough to perform effectively on line 3. In fact, the very behaviors that made IBM successful on the first two lines, now became a handicap on line 3.

It was during the four decades in lines 1 and 2 that OD was born, grew, and matured. We believe that the key variable, as organizations and people move from adaptive and rapid change to random change, is time. In first-generation OD, change agents and organizations had time to respond to change. Numerous planned change programs were designed over a period of three or more years. As we move to extremely rapid (random) change, business leaders do not have the luxury of three or more years. It is our thesis that out of this extreme need for more timely change was born second-generation OT with its experimental feel and self-designing emphasis. Organizational technologies—such as SDTs, total quality management, business process reengineering, organizational architecture, self-designing organizations, and employee empowerment—are strategies designed to cope with random change.

History of Self-Directed Teams (SDTs)

Self-directed teams are an outcome of the research of Kurt Lewin at the Research Center for Group Dynamics and the Tavistock Institute of Human Relations whose members conceptualized socio-technical systems theory as an approach to designing organizations. [4] Under the direction of Kurt Lewin, the Research Center for Group Dynamics was founded in 1945 at MIT. This initial group dynamics effort at RCGD evolved into the National Training Laboratory in Group Development, which introduced the idea of feedback to group members and the effect of feedback on individual and group behavior. [5]

At about the same time that the RCGD was experimenting with the effect of feedback on attitudes and performance, the Tavistock group began to look at the interdependencies between technology and the human interface. "A concrete outcome of this theoretical perspective is development of self-regulating work groups." [6] Various authors have named these groups—for example, autonomous, self-managed, self-regulating, composite, self-directed teams (SDTs), or work teams. A common pattern in all of this research is that the goal is to transfer control of work and process from the traditional control manager to the individual members in the work unit over time.

Our research indicates the key to successful SDTS is that the change program must be planned and implemented over time with managers who have the ability to make the transition into coaches. It is our experience that many managers, coaches, and OD consultants view SDTs as binary; you either don't have them or you have them. In fact, successful SDTs evolve through five stages. In Figure 2, we show the evolution from a control model to a self-directed model and the corresponding organizational structure at the bottom of the figure. Stage 1 is the typical hierarchical organization. In Stage 2, we introduce the group manager, whose role is to "transition" into team coordinator/coach. In Stage 4, the team assumes most of the duties of the previous manager, who now become a boundary interface. And finally, in Stage 5, the manager is a resource for the SDT. Thus a typical organization will have SDTs in all five stages at various times. Further, a SDT can be at Stage 4 and, when a key technical member of the SDT is transferred, the SDT may revert back to Stage 3 while the team leader assumes more control until the team can again assume more of the leadership tasks.

Thomas G. Cummings adds to the history of SDTs in his excellent article, "Self-Regulating Work Groups: A Socio-Technical Synthesis" (Reading 25 in this book). In Cummings's article he states that "the design of self-regulating work groups depends on at least three conditions that enhance technically required cooperation and employees' capacity to control variance from goal attainment: task differentiation, boundary control, and task control." [6] Task differentiation refers to the autonomous nature of the teams' work. This permits the SDT to develop an identity, and technical specialists emerge within the team to solve technical problems. Boundary control is defined as the ability of the individual contributors to control quality decisions, staffing, and performance appraisal issues, rather than relying on outside resources. Also, a well-defined work area increases the boundary control of the SDT. Task control is the degree of control that the team members have over how they change inputs into a completed product or service. It is our experience that many organizations that profess to having SDTs in fact do not. A further examination of their teams reveals that they violated one or usually all three of these conditions. Thus what some organizations claim are SDTs are really only people going to staff meetings. Many organizations are chasing the latest quick-fix and do not plan properly or even understand the dimensions of successful SDTs.

Based on our research and experience with successful SDTs, we will add a fourth condition to Cummings's list. The fourth condition is the ability of the control manager to transition into a coach. Our early experience indicates that only about 50 percent of control managers can make this transition, because of the need to unlearn old behavior and learn new helping, negotiation, and conflict resolution skills.

Combined with this lack of understanding of the dimensions of successful SDTs is the impatience of top management. Top management is generally looking for the next quick-fix, because they usually are rewarded on a quarterly basis and are unwilling to "stay the course" for a long-term planned change program, such as

FIGURE 2

From management control to self-control model

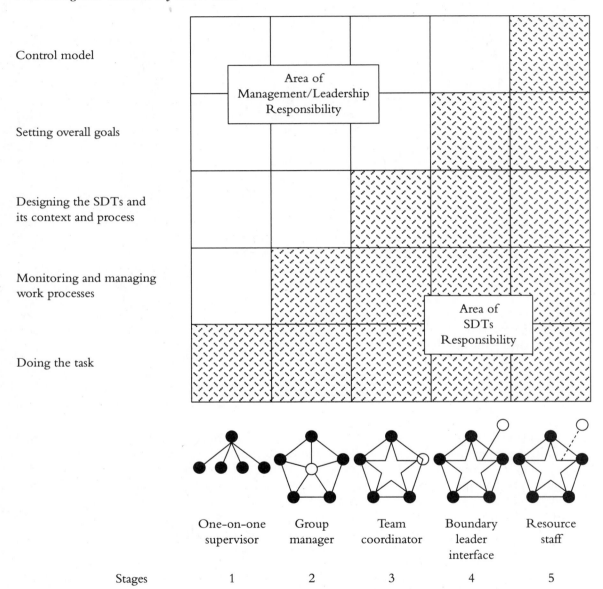

Control model

Setting overall goals

Designing the SDTs and
its context and process

Monitoring and managing
work processes

Doing the task

	One-on-one supervisor	Group manager	Team coordinator	Boundary leader interface	Resource staff
Stages	1	2	3	4	5

SDTs. Cummings recognizes the need to plan for SDTs and implement them over time. He refers to this process as "developmental system design," which came out of the early Tavistock research.

Development System Design

For the last six years we have experimented with SDTs in organizations from small manufacturing firms to large service companies. Our experience is that SDTs can succeed or fail, regardless of the core technology. The key is to have people who believe they are valued and empowered, managers who can transition into coaches over time, and a well-designed plan. Although they are rare, there are managers who have the ability to sense the timing and training required before individual contributors share in some of the leadership tasks. In other words, a group of leadership competencies must be performed within a SDT: the key to a successful SDT is to transfer those competencies with a plan over time. Figure 3 illustrates this transfer of competencies.

FIGURE 3

Checklist for self-directed work teams (SDTs)

Activity	Before Designing/ Implementation	3 mo.	6 mo.	12 mo.	18 mo.	24 mo.	30 mo.
1. Steering committee	X	X	X	X	X	X	X
2. Leadership/coach responsibilities	X						
3. Team members responsibilities	X						
4. Goals	X						
5. Assumptions:	X						
a. About SDTs							
b. About people							
6. Training:							
a. Technical and quality		X					
b. People skills:							
Problem solving		X					
Team building			X	X	X	X	X
Conducting meetings			X				
Presentation skills			X				
Conflict resolution				X			
Change skills				X			X
c. Management skills:							
Interviewing				X			
Feedback and coaching				X			
Performance appraisal					X		
Group rewards		X			X		
Budgets							X
d. Teach managers coaching skills		X					
7. Measurement:							
a. Internal		X	X	X	X		
b. Customer service				X		X	
8. Feedback:							
a. Team		X	X	X	X	X	X
b. Other STDS	X	X	X	X	X	X	X

SOURCE: Dr. Robert A. Zawacki and Carol A. Norman.

The critical activities are transferred from the leader to the individual contributors over a period of 30 months. Our experience suggests that 30 months is an optimum goal, and OD consultants should experiment with reducing this time even more if they are to be perceived in the 1990s as adding value to the organization. As we indicated earlier, it is our thesis that we are in the second generation of OD and on the third level of random change. Although OD consultants may be "pushing the envelope" of change, can we help organizations introduce and sustain planned change faster? We believe that with a good plan and checklist we can load the experiment for success!

The first activity we recommend is to establish a steering committee that consists of a few top organizational leaders, some middle managers, some technical people, and some individual contributors. Normally this steering committee is not larger than 12 people and reports directly to the president or CEO. In some organizations, this steering committee even becomes a SDT, because they want to function as a role model for the rest of the organization. If the senior officer of the company or a senior vice president is not willing to chair this committee, this is a signal to the change agent that there maybe a lack of top-level support. The primary purpose of the steering committee is to demonstrate top-level support but also to provide linkages to other parts of the organization. Therefore we recommend a steering committee meeting every three to six months, and even have the SDTs brief the steering committee on their successes.

The other activities on the checklist are all extremely important. However, we will briefly discuss the training activities that are critical to successful SDTs. Training costs normally increase by a factor of four, and the money is usually targeted for the softer area of people skills. Many leaders of technical organizations have a tendency to attempt to save money by not committing to sufficient training before and during the evolution of SDTs. One top leader, who attempted to save money, stated to us later, "If only I would have listened to you and approved of the training before we started SDTs. Now we are playing catch-up as the team grew without any planned way to deal with conflict."

After the decision to implement SDTs, the first training program must be a course on problem solving. The content of this course should become the basis for making decisions within the SDT. Next, there must be team building, followed up with courses on how to conduct team meetings and how to make presentations. As the group matures, the need will arise for training on interviewing skills, performance appraisal, and feedback. For example, we recommend that at the 12-month point the interviewing and hiring process transfer from the leader/coach to a subteam of approximately six team members. This transfer must not happen until the team members have been trained.

A second example is performance appraisal. Traditional managers tend to resist performance appraisal and usually are late doing the performance appraisals of their subordinates. Further, in the traditional hierarchical organization, individual contributors report that they do not receive sufficient feedback. After training, we recommend transferring the performance appraisal process from the leader/coach to the team members at about the 18-month point in the evolution of SDTs. Our article, "Team Appraisals— Team Approach" [7] describes the process for a peer evaluation system within SDTs. Our early findings are that, although the coach may be threatened or at best be hesitant to turn this process over to the team, once the new process is in place the coach becomes a strong advocate, because it relieves the coach of a burden— getting those performance appraisals into personnel on time.

A final but very important point: Internal and external measures of performance are critical to the success of SDTs. Those things that get measured get done! If the leaders of an organization support a pilot SDT, invariably someone will sooner or later ask for measures of effectiveness or value added. There are many good measures of customer service, and one of those measures should be administered every six months. Further, the measures should be simple and quick so the customer is not burdened with bureaucracy. Internal measures of team satisfaction usually are administered every week during the early stages of the SDT; as the SDT matures, the team should measure and feedback the results to the team every two weeks and, at about the sixth month, go to a three-or four-month cycle.

Teams and the Law

On December 16, 1992, the National Labor Relations Board (NLRB) issued a decision in Electromation, Inc., 309 NLRB No. 163 (1992). Electromation raised the issue of whether employee committees are labor organizations as defined in the 1935 National Labor Relations Act. The decision of the NLRB was that Electromation violated the 1935 act against setting up a company union by establishing and dominating five employee representation committees. Unfortunately, the NLRB's decision is a setback for organizations looking to teams to increase motivation and productivity. However, the decision will continue to be challenged in the courts or addressed by Congress because the NLRB's decision "was narrowly focused on the particular facts of the case, which was a disappointment to many who had hoped the board would provide general guidelines for lawfully creating and maintaining employee involvement committees." [9]

It appears to us that the problem is that the National Labor Relations Act of 1935 as a statute "largely written in the days of wrenches and blast furnaces, can be read as outlawing these groups." [10] OD and OT consultants should continue to help organizations design SDTs; however, they must be aware of this outdated law and use every opportunity to communicate with their representatives in Congress of the need for a change to this 1935 law.

The popular press reported that union leaders praised the decision, saying it will help labor relations by increasing the right of unions to organize and bargain collectively. During 1993, three of the members of the NLRB will probably be appointed by the Clinton Administration and, if those members are pro-union, this maybe a setback for SDTs. [11] Our advice to change agents is to watch the OD and human resource journals for further comment on this extremely serious development regarding teams. For example, recently the NLRB, in a case involving DuPont's Chambers Works plant in New Jersey and the plant's Chemical Workers Association, ordered DuPont to disband seven committees that had been formed to deal with recreation and safety issues.

Guideline for Implementing Successful SDTs

Successful OD (OT) programs and SDTs have a lot in common. For example, both have elements of the key words in the definition of OD by French and Bell [8], such as long-range effort, top-management support, improve problem solving, emphasis on teams, the assistance of a facilitator, and the use of theory to guide the change agents. Using the above key words, successful SDTs require:

1. Setting up a steering committee with top-management support and planning a long-range effort with a pilot SDT. Further, select a natural work group committed to employee empowerment and who are involved in a technology/product/service with task interdependencies.

2. Establishing base line measures of internal team satisfaction and customer service.

3. Visiting other organizations with SDTs to determine "best practices."

4. Making certain that the pilot SDT is congruent with organizational values and goals. Recognize that designing and implementing SDTs is a Theory Y philosophy and this may be a cultural shift for the organization.

5. Thinking beyond cutting costs. There usually is an actual drop in productivity during the early stages of a SDT, because the team members are learning new skills, conducting staff meetings, and so on. Be patient—as the team grows and the individual members feel they are truly empowered, the gains are greater productivity, lower costs, higher-quality products, greater customer service, and more adaptability. It may be 18 to 24 months before the organization begins to see the positive results of the change program.

6. Recognize that many managers are threatened by even the mention of SDTs. No longer the experts, now managers must become coaches and problem solvers or facilitators. It is our experience that only about one-half of existing managers can make the transition, even after training in the new competencies. Organization leaders must clearly state expectations up front: that good performers who cannot make the transition to coaches will be retained as individual contributors as long as they add value to the bottom line.

7. Review the reward system. Consider greater employee participation into reward decisions and designing gainsharing plans or profit-sharing schemes that encourage horizontal organizational structures based on process, rather than function. At about the 18-month point, consider changing the reward from individual to part group/individual. Consider a bonus for the volunteers in the first pilot SDT.

8. Establish feedback systems to inform all members of the organization on the progress of the pilot and future SDTs. Consider having SDT members brief top leaders on their progress. Feedback permits the program to adjust, grow, and remain viable over time. [12]

References

1. Jerry I. Porras and Robert C. Silvers. "Organization Development and Transformation." *Annual Review of Psychology* 42 (1991), pp. 51–78.
2. D. Verne Morland. "Lear's Fool: Coping with Change beyond Future Shock." *New Management* 2, no. 2 (1984).
3. Chris Argyris. "Teaching Smart People How to Learn." *Harvard Business Review,* May–June 1991, pp. 99–109.
4. E. L. Trist and K. W. Bamforth. "Some Social and Psychological Consequences of the Longwall Method of Coal Getting." *Human Relations* 4 (1951), pp. 3–38.
5. Wendell L. French and Cecil H. Bell, Jr. "A History of Organization Development." In *Organization Development: Behavioral Science Interventions for Organization Improvement,* 3rd. ed. Englewood Cliffs, N.J.: Prentice Hall, 1984, pp. 24–44.
6. Thomas G. Cummings. "Self-Regulating Work Group: A Socio-Technical Synthesis." *Academy of Management Review,* no. 3 (July 1978), pp. 625–34.
7. Carol A. Norman and Robert A. Zawacki. "Team Appraisals—Team Approach." *Personnel Journal,* September 1991, pp. 101–04.
8. French and Bell, "A History of Organization Development," p. 17.
9. "Electromation Appeals NLRB Ruling." *Human Resources Management,* Issue no. 293, January 20, 1993, p. 9.
10. David Frum. "Union Rules." *Forbes,* January 4, 1993, p. 88.
11. Stephenie Overman. "NLRB Ruling on Teams Fails to End Dispute." *HR News,* January 1993, p. A3. Also see "Manager's Newsfront." *Personnel Journal,* February 1993, p. 20.
12. Paul S. Goodman and James W. Dean, Jr. "Why Productivity Efforts Fail." Paper presented at the American Psychological Association, August 1981.

Brian Dumaine

Many American companies are discovering what may be *the* productivity breakthrough of the 1990s. Call the still-controversial innovation a self-managed team, a cross-functional team, a high-performance team, or, to coin a phrase, a superteam. Says Texas Instruments CEO Jerry Junkins: "No matter what your business, these teams are the wave of the future." Corning CEO Jamie Houghton, whose company has 3,000 teams, echoes the sentiment: "If you really believe in quality, when you cut through everything, it's empowering your people, and it's empowering your people that leads to teams."

We're not talking here about the teamwork that's been praised at Rotary Club luncheons since time immemorial, or the quality circles so popular in the 1980s, where workers gathered once a week to save paper clips or bitch about the fluorescent lights. What makes superteams so controversial is that they ultimately force managers to do what they had only imagined in their most Boschian nightmares: give up control. Because if superteams are working right, *mirabile dictu,* they manage themselves. No boss required. A superteam arranges schedules, sets profit targets, and—gulp—may even know everyone's salary. It has a say in hiring and firing team members as well as managers. It orders material and equipment. It strokes customers, improves quality, and, in some cases, devises strategy.

Superteams typically consist of between three and 30 workers—sometimes blue collar, sometimes white collar, sometimes both. In a few cases, they have become a permanent part of the work force. In others, management assembles

Source: Brian Dumaine, "Who Needs a Boss?" *Fortune,* May 7, 1990, pp. 52–59. Reprinted with permission.

Cheering on the Team

If Harvard awarded MBAs to factory workers for their expertise, this team at a General Mills cereal plant in Lodi, California, would graduate with honors. They do just about everything middle managers do, and do it well: Since General Mills introduced teams to the plant, productivity has risen up to 40 percent. Carmen Gomez, Ruby Liptack, and Bill Gerstner operate machinery to make cereal (that's Oatmeal Crisp). Denny Perak is a manager, but he doesn't supervise in the traditional sense. He coaches the team on management techniques and serves as their link with headquarters. Donald Owen and William Walker help maintain the machinery, which Irma Hills operates. Team members like the added responsibility, but also feel more pressure. Says Owen: "I work a lot harder than I used to. You have to worry about the numbers."

the team for a few months or years to develop a new product or solve a particular problem. Companies that use them—and they work as well in service or finance businesses as they do in manufacturing—usually see productivity rise dramatically. That's because teams composed of people with different skills, from different parts of the company, can swoop around bureaucratic obstacles and break through walls separating different functions to get a job done.

Ten years ago there were practically no super-teams. Only a handful of companies—Procter & Gamble, Digital Equipment, TRW—were experimenting with them. But a recent survey of 476 Fortune 1,000 companies, published by the American Productivity & Quality Center in Houston, shows that, while only 7 percent of the work force is organized in self-managed teams, half the companies questioned say they will be relying significantly more on them in the years ahead. Those who have already taken the plunge have seen impressive results:

- At a General Mills cereal plant in Lodi, California, teams such as the one pictured on *Fortune's* cover schedule, operate, and maintain machinery so effectively that the factory runs with no managers present during the night shift.
- At a weekly meeting, a team of Federal Express clerks spotted—and eventually solved—a billing problem that was costing the company $2.1 million a year.
- A team of Chaparral Steel millworkers traveled the world to evaluate new production machinery. The machines they selected and installed have helped make their mill one of the world's most efficient.
- 3M turned around one division by creating cross-functional teams that tripled the number of new products.
- After organizing its home office operations into superteams, Aetna Life & Casualty reduced the ratio of middle managers to workers—from 1 to 7 down to 1 to 30—all the while improving customer service.
- Teams of blue-collar workers at Johnsonville Foods of Sheboygan, Wisconsin, helped CEO Ralph Stayer make the decision to proceed with a major plant expansion. The workers told

Stayer they could produce more sausage, faster than he would have ever dared to ask. Since 1986, productivity has risen at least 50 percent.

Like latter-day Laocoöns, the companies using superteams must struggle with serpentine problems. How do you keep a team from veering off track? How should it be rewarded for inventing new products or for saving money? How much spending authority should a team have? What happens to the opportunity for team members to advance as the corporate hierarchy flattens? How should disputes among its members be resolved? Answers vary from company to company. Read on to see how some organizations are coping.

Superteams aren't for everyone. They make sense only if a job entails a high level of dependency among three or more people. Complex manufacturing processes common in the auto, chemical, paper, and high-tech industries can benefit from teams. So can complicated service jobs in insurance, banking, and telecommunications. But if the work consists of simple assembly line activity like stuffing pimentos into olives, teams probably don't make sense. Says Edward Lawler, a management professor at the University of Southern California: "You have to ask, 'How complex is the work?' The more complex, the more suited it is for teams."

Lawler is getting at the heart of what makes superteams tick: cross-functionalism, as the experts inelegantly put it. The superteam draws together people with different jobs or functions—marketing, manufacturing, finance, and so on. The theory is that by putting their heads together, people with different perspectives on the business can solve a problem quickly and effectively.

Contrast that to the Rube Goldberg approach a hierarchical organization would usually take. A person with a problem in one function might have to shoot it up two or three layers by memo to a vice president who tosses it laterally to a vice president of another function who then kicks it down to the person in his area who knows the answer. Then it's back up and down the ladder again. Whew.

Federal Express has been particularly successful using superteams in its back-office operations in Memphis. Two years ago, as part of a companywide push to convert to teams, Fedex organized its 1,000 clerical workers into superteams of 5 to 10 people, and gave them the training and authority to manage themselves. With the help of its teams, the company cut service glitches, such as incorrect bills and lost packages, by 13 percent in 1989.

At lunch with one team, this reporter sat impressed as entry-level workers, most with only high school educations, ate their chicken and dropped sophisticated management terms like *kaizen,* the Japanese art of continuous improvement, and *pareto,* a form of problem solving that requires workers to take a logical step-by-step approach. The team described how one day during a weekly meeting, a clerk from quality control pointed out a billing problem. The bigger a package, he explained, the more Fedex charges to deliver it. But the company's wildly busy delivery people sometimes forgot to check whether customers had properly marked the weight of packages on the air bill. That meant that Fedex, whose policy in such cases is to charge customers the lowest rate, was losing money.

The team switched on its turbochargers. An employee in billing services found out which field offices in Fedex's labyrinthine 30,000-person courier network were forgetting to check the packages, and then explained the problem to the delivery people. Another worker in billing set up a system to examine the invoices and make sure the solution was working. Last year alone the team's ideas saved the company $2.1 million.

In 1987, Rubbermaid began to develop a so-called auto office, a plastic, portable device that straps onto a car seat; it holds files, pens, and other articles and provides a writing surface. The company assembled a cross-functional team composed of, among others, engineers, designers, and marketers, who together went into the field to ask customers what features they wanted. Says Rubbermaid vice president Lud Huck: "A designer, an engineer, and a marketer all approach research from a different point of view."

Huck explains that, while a marketer might ask potential customers about price, he'd never think to ask important design questions. With contributions from several different functions, Rubbermaid brought the new product to market last year. Sales are running 50 percent above projections.

Companies making the move to superteams often discover middle managers who feel threatened, and refuse—even for a millisecond—to think outside their narrow functional specialties, or chimneys, as they're labeled at some companies. Understandable, since the managers probably made it to where they are by being marketing whizzes or masters of the bean-counting universe. Why help some poor slob in engineering? For superteams to work, functional chimneys must be broken down and middle managers persuaded to lend their time, people, and resources to other functions for the good of the entire corporation.

Robert Hershock, a group vice president at 3M, is an expert chimney breaker. In 1985 he introduced teams to his division, which makes respirators and industrial safety equipment, because it was desperately in need of new products. The old boss had simply told his underlings what to develop. R&D would sketch it up and deliver the concept to sales for comment, leaving manufacturing and marketing scrambling to figure out how to make or position the new offering. Says Hershock: "Every function acted as if it didn't need anyone else."

He formed an operating team made up of himself and six top managers, each from a different function. With suggestions from all interested parties, he hoped to chart new-product strategies that everyone could get behind. Under the operating team he established 10 self-managed "action teams,' each with 8 to 10 people, again from different functions. They were responsible for the day-to-day development of new products.

It wasn't all sweetness and light. Hershock says one manager on the operating team dragged his feet all the way. "He'd say he wasn't in favor of this or that," recalls Hershock. "He'd say to his people, 'Meet with the action teams because Hershock said so, but don't commit to anything. Just report back to me what was said.'" Hershock worked to convince the man of the benefits of the team approach, but to no avail. Eventually the manager went to Hershock and said, "I didn't sleep all weekend. I'm upset." The manager found a good job in another division. "You need to have a sense of who's not buying in and let the teams kick people off who aren't carrying their weight," Hershock concludes. Today his division is one of 3M's most innovative and fastest growing.

It's easier to build superteams into a new office or factory than to convert an old one to them. When an operation is just starting up, a company can screen people carefully for educational skills and the capacity to work on a team, and can train them without worrying about bad old work habits like the "it's not my problem" syndrome. Nonetheless, General Mills is organizing superteams in all its existing factories. Randy Darcy, director of manufacturing, says transforming an old plant can take several years, versus only a year to 18 months for a new plant. Says Darcy: "It costs you up front, but you have to look at it as a capital project. If you consider the productivity gains, you can justify it on ROE."

Can you ever. General Mills says productivity in its plants that use self-managed teams is as much as 40 percent higher than at its traditional factories. One reason is that the plants need fewer middle managers. At one of General Mills' cereal plants in Lodi, workers on the night shift take care of everything from scheduling to maintenance. The company has also found that superteams sometimes set higher productivity goals than management does. At its Carlisle, Pennsylvania, plant, which makes Squeezit juice, superteams changed some equipment and squeezed out a 5 percent production increase in a plant management thought was already running at full capacity.

But you will never get large productivity gains unless you give your teams real authority to act. This is a theme that Johnsonville's Stayer, who teaches a case on teams at the Harvard business school, preaches with messianic zeal. "The strategic decision," he explains, "is who makes the decision. There's a lot of talk about teamwork in this country, but we're not set up to generate it. Most quality circles don't give workers responsibility. They even make things worse. People in circles point out problems, and it's someone else's problem to fix."

In 1986 a major food company asked Johnsonville to manufacture sausage under a private label. Stayer's initial reaction was to say no, because he thought the additional volume would overload his plant and force his people to work grueling hours. But before declining, he assembled his 200 production workers, who are organized in teams of five to 20, and asked them to decide whether *they* wanted to take on the heavier workload. Stayer discussed the pros: Through economies of scale, the extra business would lower costs and thus boost profits; since everyone's bonus was based on profitability, everyone would make more money. And the cons: long hours, strained machinery, and the possibility of declining quality.

After the teams deliberated for 10 days, they came back with an answer: "We can do it. We'll have to work seven days a week at first, but then the work will level off." The teams decided how much new machinery they would need and how many new people; they also made a schedule of how much to produce per day. Since Johnsonville took on the new project, productivity has risen over 50 percent in the factory. Says Stayer:

"If I had tried to implement it from above, we would have lost the whole business."

Some large organizations still feel a need to exercise oversight of superteams' activities. What to do with a team that louses up quality or orders the wrong machinery? James Watson, a vice president of Texas Instruments' semiconductor group, may have the answer. At one of TI's chip factories in Texas, Watson helped create a hierarchy of teams that, like a shadow government, works within the existing hierarchy.

On top is a steering team consisting of the plant manager and his heads of manufacturing, finance, engineering, and human resources. They set strategy and approve large projects. Beneath the steering team, TI has three other teams: corrective-action teams, quality-improvement teams, and effectiveness teams. The first two are cross-functional and consist mainly of middle managers and professionals like engineers and accountants. Corrective-action teams form to tackle short-lived problems and then disband. They're great for those times when, as the technophantasmic novelist Thomas Pynchon writes, there's fecoventilatory collision: the s—hits the fan.

By contrast, TI's quality-improvement teams work on long-term projects, such as streamlining the manufacturing process. The corrective-action and quality-improvement teams guide and check effectiveness teams, which consist of blue-collar employees who do day-to-day production work, and professional workers.

What's to keep this arrangement from becoming just another hierarchy? "You have to keep changing and be flexible as business conditions dictate," says Watson. He contends that one of the steering team's most important responsibilities is to show a keen interest in the teams beneath it. "The worst thing you can do to a team is to leave it alone in the dark. I guarantee that if you come across someone who says teams didn't work at his company, it's because management didn't take interest in them."

Watson suggests that the steering team periodically review everyone's work, and adds, "It doesn't have to be a big dog-and-pony show. Just walk around and ask, 'How are you doing.'"

Last spring a group of executives from a Fortune 500 manufacturer traveled to Midlothian, Texas, to learn how Chaparral Steel managed its teams. Efficient superteams have helped make Chaparral one of the world's most productive steel companies. During the tour, one executive asked a Chaparral manager, "How do you schedule coffee breaks in the plant?"

"The workers decide when they want a cup of coffee," came the reply.

"Yes, but who tells them when it's okay to leave the machines?" the executive persisted.

Looking back on the exchange, the Chaparral manager reflects, "The guy left and still didn't get it."

Why do Chaparral workers know when to take a coffee break? Because they're trained to understand how the whole business operates. Earl Engelhardt, who runs the company's educational program, teaches mill hands "The Chaparral Process," a course that not only describes what happens to a piece of steel as it moves through the company but also covers the roles of finance, accounting, and sales. Once trained, a worker understands how his job relates to the welfare of the entire organization. At team meetings, many of which are held in the company's modest boardroom, talk is of backlogs and man-hours per ton. Financial statements are posted monthly in the mill, including a chart tracking operating profits before taxes—the key measure for profit sharing.

In the early 1980s the company sent a team leader and three millworkers, all of whom had been through "The Chaparral Process," to Europe, Asia, and South America to evaluate new mill stands. These large, expensive pieces of equipment flatten and shape hot steel as it passes through the mill, much as the rollers on old washing machines used to wring clothes. After team members returned from their first trip, they discussed the advantages and disadvantages of various mill stands with other workers and with top management. Then they narrowed the field and flew off again. Eventually the team agreed on the best mill stand—in this case a West German model—and top management gave its blessing.

The team then ordered the mill stands and oversaw their installation, even down to negotiating the contracts for the work involved. At other companies it can take as long as several years to buy and install such a complicated piece of equipment. The Chaparral team got the job done in a year. Perhaps even more amazing, the mill stands—notoriously finicky pieces of machinery—worked as soon as they were turned on.

There remains considerable debate among employees, managers, and consultants over the best way to compensate team members. Most companies pay a flat salary. And instead of handing out automatic annual raises, they often use a pay-for-skills system that bases any increase not on seniority but on what an employee has learned. If, say, a steelworker learns how to run a new piece of equipment, he might get a 5 percent raise.

While the young and eager tend to do well with pay-for-skills, some old-school blue-collar workers like Chaparral Steel's Neil Parker criticize aspects of the system. Says he: "New guys come in who are aggressive, take all the courses, and get promoted ahead of guys who have been here years longer and who showed up for overtime when the company really needed us. It's not fair." As Parker suggests, pay-for-skills does set up a somewhat Darwinian environment at the mill, but that's just the way Chaparral's management likes it.

When teams develop a hot new product, like Rubbermaid's auto office, or save money, like the Federal Express team that caught $2.1 million in billing errors, you would think they would clamor for rewards. Not necessarily. In many cases, surprisingly, a little recognition is reward enough. The Fedex team members seem perfectly content with a gold quality award pin and their picture in the company newsletter. Says one: "We learn more in teams, and it's more fun to work in teams. It's a good feeling to know someone is using your ideas."

In his book *Managing New Products,* Thomas Kuczmarski, a consultant to many of the Fortune 500 industrials, argues that recognition isn't enough. "In most companies multidisciplinary teams are just lip service because companies don't provide the right motivation and incentive. Most top managers think people should just find 20 percent more time to work on a new team project. It's a very naive and narrow-minded approach." His modest proposals: If a new product generates $1 million in profits, give each of the five team members $100,000 the first year. Or have each member write a check for $10,000 in return for 2 percent of the equity in the new product. If it flies they're rich; if it flops they lose their money.

Kuczmarski admits that no major corporation has adopted his provocative system, although he says a few are on the verge of doing so. One objection: Jack Okey, a Honeywell team manager, flatly states that it would be bad for morale to have, say, a junior engineer making more than a division vice president. "If you want to be an entrepreneur, there are plenty of entrepreneurial opportunities outside the company. You can have entrepreneurial spirit without entrepreneurial pay."

Perhaps. Awards dinners and plaques for jobs well done are common in the world of teams, but Texas Instruments vice president James Watson thinks more can be done. He cites the example from Japan, where there is a nationwide competition among manufacturers' teams. Sponsored by the Union of Japanese Scientists and Engineers, the competition pits teams selected by their companies against one another. Once a year the teams travel to Tokyo to make presentations before judges, who decide which performs best at everything from solving quality problems to continuously improving a manufacturing process. The winners get showered with prizes and media coverage.

Sometimes, despite everyone's best efforts, teams get hung up. Leonard Greenhalgh, a professor of management at Dartmouth's Tuck School, says the most common problem is the failure by team members to understand the feelings and needs of their co-workers. At GTE's training center in Connecticut, Greenhalgh had middle managers do role-playing to bring out how such problems can creep up. In a fictionalized case, a team of six pretended they were Porsche managers who had to set next year's production schedule. Each was given a different function and agenda. The Porsche sales manager, for instance, wanted to manufacture more of the popular Carrera convertibles, but the general counsel thought it a bad idea because of the liability problems generally associated with convertibles.

The GTE managers spent several hours arriving at a consensus. Says Greenhalgh: "Typically, a team lacks skills to build a strong consensus. One coalition tries to outvote the other or browbeat the dissenters." To make sure everyone is on board, says Greenhalgh, it's important that each team member feel comfortable airing his opinions. But that can take some training for all group members in how to respond. For instance, the GTE managers learned it's better not to blurt out an intimidating, "I disagree," but rather, "That's an interesting way to look at it; what about this?"

Companies using teams sometimes run into another problem: With fewer middle-manager positions around, there's less opportunity for advancement. The experts say they need to emphasize that because team members have more responsibility, their work is more rewarding and challenging. Harvard business school professor

Anne Donnellon, who is doing a major new study of teams, sees this approach already working at some Fortune 500 companies: "People are adjusting to career-ladder shortening. If a team is operating well, I hear less talk about no opportunity for promotion and more about the product and the competition. They're focusing on getting the work done. After all, people want rewarding work."

If you've done all you can think of, and your team is still running on only three cylinders, you might consider something as prosaic as changing the office furniture. Aetna Life recently reorganized its home office operations into self-managed teams—combining clerks, technical writers, underwriters, and financial analysts—to handle customer requests and complaints. To facilitate teamwork, Aetna is using a new line of "team" furniture designed by Steelcase.

The furniture establishes small areas that the folks at Steelcase call "neighborhoods." A central work area with a table lets teams meet when they need to, while nearby desks provide privacy. Says William Watson, an Aetna senior vice president: "I can't tell you how great it is. Everyone sits together, and the person responsible for accounting knows who prepares the bills and who puts the policy information in the computers to pay the claims. You don't need to run around the building to get something done."

The most important thing to remember about teams is that organizing them is a long, hard process, not a quick fix that can change your company in a few weeks. Says Johnsonville's Stayer: "When I started this business of teams, I was anxious to get it done and get back to my real job. Then I realized that, hey, this *is* my real job"—letting the teams loose. For those up to the challenge, there will be real results as well.

READING 30
GAINSHARING AND ORGANIZATION DEVELOPMENT:
A PRODUCTIVE SYNERGY*

Elizabeth M. Doherty, Walter R. Nord, and Jerry L. McAdams

Behavioral scientists have long urged managers to tie compensation to performance. Consistent with this advice, many organizations have planned or introduced a wide variety of reward-for-performance systems (O'Dell, 1987). Many of these systems are called "gainsharing," meaning that they measure the value to the organization of improved performance by a particular work group and distribute some percentage of these benefits to the work group members—that is, the gains are shared.

Beyond the contingency of the rewards and the "sharing of the gains," gainsharing programs vary considerably (Lawler, 1988; Miller & Schuster, 1987; O'Dell, 1987). Lawler (1988, p. 326) notes, "Perhaps the most important thing known about gainsharing plans is that they work," and he and other authorities have commented on how little is known about the factors affecting the success of these interventions (Bullock & Bullock, 1982; Bullock & Lawler, 1984;

*The authors are deeply indebted to the many persons at "Progress, Inc." (a pseudonym) who devoted much time and effort to making this study possible. They regret that protecting the identity of this firm prevents them from crediting these persons by name. The authors also thank Sharon Tucker, Nicholas Baloff, Elisabeth Case, Joe Dobson, Gideon Sjoberg, David Austin, and the anonymous *JABS* reviewers for their comments on earlier versions of this article.

Source: Reprinted with permission from NTL Institute, "Gainsharing and Organization Development: A Productive Synergy," by Elizabeth M. Doherty, Walter R. Nord, and Jerry L. McAdams, pp. 209–229, *Journal of Applied Behavioral Science* 25, no. 3, copyright © 1989.

Lawler, 1988). In particular, Lawler (1988, p. 332) states, "Little is known about the key process issues that are involved in the installation and maintenance of a gainsharing plan."

This article describes a study conducted to determine which factors affect the successful implementation of gainsharing. Because we had so little to build on, we took an inductive approach. We investigated interventions in four organizations, searching for elements affecting their success. This search produced both expected and unexpected findings. As we had expected, the interventions produced significant improvements in quantifiable measures of performance and had positive "side effects" (e.g., increased employee awareness of the firm's mission, trust, and cooperation). We had not expected, however, to find that process issues apparently affected the interventions' success to a far greater degree than previous research on gainsharing suggested they should. These results indicate the benefits of integrating knowledge and practice from two major branches of applied behavioral science that, to date, have proceeded independently of each other: gainsharing and organization development (OD). We argue that these benefits move in both directions, for knowledge about the process of planned change can improve gainsharing interventions markedly, and planned organizational change can be enhanced by the introduction of the quantitative standards and measures central to gainsharing. We conclude this article by arguing for a synthesis, although our point of departure is the study of gainsharing.

Gainsharing in Perspective

Gainsharing is now used as a generic label for various reward-for-performance systems (Hauck, 1987; Miller & Schuster, 1987). Indeed, Miller and Schuster use the terms *gainsharing* and *productivity plans* synonymously. Although most programs determine gains by comparing current performance with some historical base, O'Dell (1987, p. 35) notes that gainsharing "is often used to denote any plan for sharing gains with employees, including small group and individual incentives and other pay for performance practices." [1]

This article focuses mainly on the implementation of gainsharing, rather than on a psychological explanation of why gainsharing works. Because so many versions of gainsharing exist, however, we consider it useful to locate our study by describing our assumptions as to why gainsharing works, for these assumptions led us to study the particular program we did.

To us, a central feature of all gainsharing programs is the introduction of systems that increase the contingency of rewards upon performance. Although seldom recognized explicitly in the gainsharing literature, this emphasis on making rewards contingent upon performance suggests a close link between gainsharing and operant conditioning as advanced by B. F. Skinner and others advocating behavior modification (Luthans & Kreitner, 1975).

Although the details of gainsharing plans differ from one another, they share a common core. For example, commonly used plans (e.g., Scanlon, Rucker,® and Improshare®) feature a financial or physical (i.e., nonmonetary) formula for measuring performance (e.g., labor costs) that assesses improvements in productivity and shares the benefits with employees according to a predetermined agreement. Although the plans use different formulas (see Doyle, 1982; Jenkins & Gupta, 1982; Ross & Ross, 1984), they all calculate appropriate rewards for progress toward targeted objectives.

The form of the contingency also varies. Typically, gainsharing programs distribute rewards to employees on the basis of group performance. The group measured may vary from a small work group to an entire organization. Moreover, although many types of rewards and schedules are possible, most of the reported systems award cash payments at set intervals (e.g., monthly), which are generally considered part of a company's compensation plan. Some programs, however, use noncash incentives, which are viewed as "add-ons" to normal wages. Despite these differences, we perceive of gainsharing programs as sharing a key ingredient that contributes significantly to their success: They increase the degree to which rewards are made contingent upon performance.

A second aspect of many gainsharing plans that may account for their success is employee participation. For example, employee committees and/or work teams are often chosen to solicit ideas for improving operations, reducing costs, and the like. One must recognize that in most of these programs no direct relationship exists between the suggestions generated and the distribution of rewards. Instead, a good idea is expected to improve operations and to be reflected in the measure of performance. One must also note, however, that at least one widely used gainsharing system—Improshare—does not include such participation (Miller & Schuster, 1987). Moreover, the link between participation and improved performance is unclear (Locke & Schweiger, 1979). Thus, participation may contribute to improved performance in many gainsharing applications, but not in all cases.

In sum, the specifics of gainsharing programs vary widely. Most prominent writers addressing this topic agree, however, that these programs represent attempts to improve performance by both sharing responsibility among employees and management and making rewards contingent upon improvements (Bullock & Bullock, 1982; Doyle, 1982; Graham-Moore & Ross, 1983; Lawler, 1981).

Previous Research on Gainsharing. The literature reports little systematic research on gainsharing, but the findings available support the potential of the approach. Bullock and Lawler (1984) reviewed 500 to 1,000 plans and noted that of these, only 33 cases were reported in enough detail to permit even preliminary assessment, and methodological problems made interpreting those cases difficult. Nevertheless, a consistent pattern of positive findings suggests the potential value of these systems. In 74 percent of the 33 cases, improvement on an indicator of overall success was found, and in more than half of the cases improvements were found on five dimensions: organizational effectiveness, quality of work life, innovation, labor-management cooperation, and pay. Similarly, Preiwisch (1981) has reported that gainsharing was associated with increased productivity and product quality, improved labor-management relations, better use of materials, greater employee interest and performance, and more cost-saving suggestions. More recently, O'Dell (1987) found that in more than 200 uses of gainsharing, respondents reported highly positive outcomes on various performance dimensions for all types of plans.

Factors Affecting Success. Several studies have assessed the causes and correlates of the success or failure of gainsharing. Lawler (1981) notes that small organizations (i.e., those with fewer than 500 employees) that have existed long enough to establish a performance history tend to benefit most from gainsharing plans. Moreover, gainsharing generally fits well with organizations having simple financial measures, limited use of overtime, little new investment planned, stable products and markets, product costs controllable by employees, and a market that can absorb additional production. Furthermore, gainsharing's success is likely to be associated with moderate to high levels of work flow interdependence, high levels of trust, participa-

tive styles of management, and communication policies that support openness and the sharing of financial results. Finally, Lawler indicates that managers and employees who are interested, committed, and technically competent in their areas are generally more receptive to and capable of conducting gainsharing programs.

White (1979) found that the success of the Scanlon Plan in 23 organizations was positively related to employee participation in decision making, managerial attitudes toward participative management policies, and the number of years an organization had used the plan. White also reports that although expectations of instant changes can have a negative effect on a Scanlon Plan's success, neither technology nor company size (at least within the ranges presented for the various studies) were correlated with the success of an implementation.

Preiwisch (1981) has identified many factors that may prevent gainsharing from succeeding. These factors include situational constraints (e.g., market fluctuation, changing business conditions), design problems (e.g., the failure to develop appropriate accounting, reporting, or bonus systems), and process issues (e.g., employee and/or management resistance, poor program administration, lack of commitment). Six of 36 firms investigated had discontinued their gainsharing efforts, offering the following major reasons for doing so: financial difficulties, lack of dedication, inadequate plan design or implementation, the small number of bonus payments made, poor communication between labor and management about the program, insufficient monitoring of performance, and bonus formula difficulties.

Ross (1983) delineates the following three sets of problems with gainsharing: organization variables; social, cultural, and institutional factors; and difficulties related to finances, information, and competition. Many of the variables Ross found were associated with gainsharing's failure (e.g., low trust or confidence in management by employees, lack of accountability, low levels of participation by workers, poor internal communication and information systems, low control by employees over sales, unstable markets and employment, poor industrial relations, and little understanding of the financial systems) overlap substantially with the conclusions of Lawler, White, and Preiwisch.

Finally, Goodman and Dean (1983) found that five processes had the greatest impact on the success and implementation of gainsharing: training, commitment, reward allocation, diffusion, and feedback and correction. Their suggestions for the permanence of gainsharing mirror the concerns of the other researchers cited above.

In sum, research has begun to identify variables that influence the success of gainsharing. These variables relate primarily to situational or organizational characteristics, program design, process or implementation issues, and participant attitudes. Bullock and Lawler, however, conclude, "The amount of available research data is insignificant compared to the potential utility of organizational gainsharing plans" (1984, p. 32). To increase our understanding of the factors that affect the success of gainsharing efforts, the research reported in this article examined four interventions in detail.

Overview of the Interventions

We studied two applications of two types of gainsharing programs: performance improvement programs (PIPs) and team suggestion programs (TSPs). All four interventions were tailored to meet the specific objectives of an organization. These programs were designed and sold by "Progress, Inc." (a pseudonym used in this article to protect the firm's identity). Progress, Inc., which has a staff of program designers, analysts, trainers, and communications experts, custom designs and helps implement gainsharing systems for a wide variety of organizations.

PIPs and TSPs use different formats. A PIP rewards improvements in actual performance, whereas a TSP rewards suggestions and includes a high degree of employee participation. Despite this contrast, both incorporate the fundamental component of gainsharing: systems that reward individuals based on the performance of their work units according to a predetermined formula used to calculate gains and/or savings from employee performance.

Both types of programs differ from commonly used programs in several ways. First, instead of focusing solely on an entire company or plant, PIPs and TSPs measure and reward the performance of individual teams. Second, instead of cash payments for rewards, these programs prefer to award points that winners can use toward the purchase of merchandise (e.g., appliances, clothing, furniture). By using award points, the programs seek to underscore that participants' rewards are not part of their compensation packages, but additions to them. Third, in TSPs rewards are directly linked to the acceptance of an idea, with the amount of the reward tied directly to the estimated value of the idea. Fourth, unlike many popular plans, PIPs and TSPs provide ongoing communication and feedback to educate employees and sustain their interest while the programs are in operation. Finally, the programs are not designed to be permanent: PIPs generally run for less than two years, and TSPs for several months.

PIPs and TSPs differ from each other in several important ways. The following descriptions reveal contrasts between the general objectives, duration, award structures, monitoring and feedback processes, communications design, and training schedules of the two types of programs.

Performance Improvement Programs.

General Objectives and Duration. Typical objectives of PIPs are related to productivity, quality, costs, and attendance. Each intervention usually runs for 12 to 24 months.

Team Assignment and Award Structure. Teams are specified based on the job performed (e.g., machine operators, nursing staff on a given floor). Two types of teams may be designated. "Direct teams" do work for which a quantitative base line for prior performance (usually the previous year) can be established. "Nondirect teams" consist of personnel in support positions (e.g., secretarial staff). The latter receive a fixed proportion of the awards earned by the direct teams they support, as well as rewards based on criteria such as attendance and overall performance. For both groups, earned awards are usually distributed monthly (sometimes quarterly), with the amount varying according to the degree of improvement over the direct team's base line.

Monitoring and Feedback. The organization's management monitors and tracks results for the program's measures, and appoints a liaison to the consultants from Progress, Inc., to coordinate the activities and expedite communications. The consultants compute the earnings and provide award vouchers for management to distribute. In addition to the awards, personnel receive feedback on performance outcomes through notices from the top administrator, progress charts, promotional posters, newsletters, and feedback from department heads.

Communications. The intervention is introduced through announcements and a "kickoff" session in which the gainsharing program is explained, employee involvement is stimulated, and small awards (e.g., coffee mugs) are distributed as incentives to employees. During the program, newsletters, messages from the administration, and various spurt activities—such as intense promotion and additional reward opportunities for achieving a particular program objective during a short time period—are employed to maintain enthusiasm and provide feedback.

Training. Usually, Progress, Inc., retains a second consulting group to provide training in behavioral methods to all managers and supervisors. One month before the program begins, four four-hour classroom sessions teach participants to identify significant behavioral events, to provide feedback, reinforcement, and punishment, and to graph and assess performance. To follow up on this training, a trainer generally meets with each trainee to review that person's progress and discuss any problems.

Team Suggestion Programs.

General Objectives and Duration. TSPs seek to increase revenues or reduce costs by generating ideas toward these ends. Each intervention generally lasts 10 to 16 weeks.

Team Assignment and Award Structure. All the employees who agree to participate in the program are organized into teams of five to seven members. The organization provides these teams with one hour a week in which to meet and develop research ideas for generating revenue or reducing expenses (any other time employees devote to this endeavor must be their own). The teams are responsible for obtaining all information needed to calculate the amount their ideas will produce or save. Once they develop suggestions, the teams submit them to an evaluation committee of middle-level managers, which reviews the proposals, verifies the potential cost benefits, and accepts or rejects each idea within 10 to 20 days. If the committee accepts an idea that will save the organization at least $500, each member of the team that developed it receives award points based on the estimated net savings or revenues the idea is expected to yield in the first year after implementation. If an idea is rejected, the team can revise and resubmit it.

Program Monitoring and Feedback. Consultants provide the system for tracking the ideas generated, but the organization's management oversees the administration of the program. Employees receive feedback through newsletters and displays, as well as through award vouchers when ideas are accepted.

Communications. Approximately three months before the program begins, information campaigns explain the plan. A "kick-off" event is held one month before the program begins, which usually includes a welcome speech by the chief executive officer, an audiovisual presentation about the program, a summary of the program's rules, and an opportunity for employees to ask questions. Time is then provided to enable employees to sign up for the program and to distribute awards to those who volunteer to participate.

Training. The training includes a three-hour overview of the program for top management; a full-day session in which program coordinators (who are general managers or appointees of top management) explain the program's concept and their roles; a full-day session in which the evaluation committee members (who are top and middle-level managers) learn about the process of accepting, rejecting, or returning ideas and about communicating with team leaders and maintaining enthusiasm among the participants. After the kick-off event, the team leaders (generally nonsupervisory personnel selected by management because of their leadership potential) receive a full day of training. The training includes discussion of roles, leadership, techniques for encouraging creativity, and procedures for determining the financial savings of ideas and submitting them.

The Research

Method. Out of the 70 programs Progress, Inc. had completed in a five-year period, two

PIPs and two TSPs were selected for study. Their selection was based on several criteria. First, we wished to study how each type of program was implemented in a manufacturing organization and in a service organization. Second, the files and tracking reports for the programs had to be relatively complete. Third, at least one key person who had worked on each program had to still be associated with Progress, Inc. Using these criteria, we selected two programs from manufacturing firms (which we call PIP-1 and TSP-1) and two from service firms (which we call PIP-2 and TSP-2).

Because each program is custom-designed to fit the particular objectives and technology of each organization, we have difficulty labeling any given program "typical." Several data, however, suggest that the four selected for study were reasonably representative of the programs done by Progress, Inc. First, two of the three TSPs that had been completed were investigated. Second, the programs all followed the intervention formats described above. Third, interviews with managers at Progress, Inc., indicated that the overall results of the programs selected were comparable to those of other programs, with the possible exception being that the two PIPs might have been slightly better integrated into their organizations' operations (e.g., they made continued use of the programs' measurement systems) than average. [2]

Procedures. Data were collected from several sources. The files Progress, Inc., kept on each program were primary sources of both quantitative and qualitative information. The quantitative data were taken directly from the operating records. Qualitative data were obtained by coding material in the case files—such as preliminary proposals and organizational analyses; procedural documents and program aids; communication samples and descriptions; tracking reports, memoranda, correspondence, and field notes; and final reports and analyses, including survey results—along the four dimensions suggested by Bullock and Lawler (1984): structure, implementation, situation, and outcome. The structural features included reward characteristics, communications used, administrative procedures and feedback processes, and training plans. Factors affecting implementation included client acceptance, client involvement, and the role of the Progress, Inc., staff. The situational and environmental conditions included the organization's demographics, style of management, work flow interdependency, climate, and market characteristics. The program outcomes included changes in productivity and progress toward any other measured objectives.

To supplement, cross-check, and interpret the archival information, we conducted structured interviews with staff members who had worked intensively on the specific programs. Two staff persons—the project head and operations analyst—were interviewed for each program, except for TSP-1, for which only the project's account manager was still employed by Progress, Inc. Finally, an administrator from each organization was interviewed by telephone several years after the program ended so as to obtain information about possible long-term effects.

Analysis. A detailed report was written for each program. [3] Each report includes a description of the organization, the program's goals and major components, the results, and the factors that influenced the outcome. These reports were submitted to the staff members of Progress, Inc., who had been involved in each case. These staff members were asked to check the reports for accuracy and completion. In all four cases, they judged that the reports needed only minor revisions to be accurate and complete. Abbreviated versions of the revised reports are presented in the section below. Although our major conclusions address implementation, we present a brief summary of the quantitative results for each program.

Results

Case Study: Organization A and PIP-1.

Background. Organization A, a West Coast aerospace manufacturing firm, faced an unstable product market. The firm was nonunion and employed about 700 people. Management reported that it had difficulty attracting and holding experienced workers, and that many employees felt disassociated from the organization. The consultants reported that the employees' training was generally inadequate, people were not used effectively, foremen were inexperienced, and the plant manager was an authoritarian, "semi-tough, hard-nosed guy" who recognized the need to help the foremen improve productivity.

The PIP system was originally sold to Organization A's corporate managers, who decided to conduct the program only three months before its scheduled initiation in 1980. The local management had virtually no involvement in the decision to introduce gainsharing into the plant.

Program Structure and Objectives. PIP-1 was designed to run for 14 months. All employees participated in the program. Twenty-three teams were formed according to job function; 20 were direct measure teams, and 3 were nondirect teams (support service groups). The program's objectives were to improve productivity and quality (i.e., to reduce scrap and "rework"), to increase safety awareness, and to reduce absenteeism. Existing procedures were used to measure productivity and quality. Productivity was measured according to the plant's earned labor hour ratio (ELHR), for which

$$\text{ELHR} = \frac{\text{Allowed hours (standard hours)}}{\text{Actual hours worked}}$$

Quality was measured according to the following ratio:

$$\text{Quality} = \frac{\text{Excess quality cost}}{\text{Standard cost of production}}$$

Safety was measured in terms of days lost because of accidents, and absenteeism in terms of the number of days of work missed.

Award points, which were based on the percentage of improvement over the appropriate base line standard (established during the previous eight-month period), were given monthly for improvements in productivity, safety, and attendance, and quarterly for improvements in plant-wide quality. In addition, awards for five short-term, special "spurt activities" were introduced to emphasize each of the objectives at various times during the program.

Outcome and Evaluation.   Quantitative results. Table 1 reports the measured outcomes. At the end of the program, productivity—as defined by the ELHR—had improved by an average of 9.62 (35.3 percent) over the base period, with a standard error equal to 1.24 for the 23 direct measure teams. A paired comparison test of the improved performance was significant ($t = 7.78$, $p = 0.0001$). Quality had improved by 44.1 percent over the base period, but this figure was not statistically significant. Absenteeism had decreased by 30 percent and lost time from accidents by 36 percent from the historical averages.

The dollar value of the cost savings associated with changes in productivity and quality was calculated by Organization A's chief financial officer based on historical costs from the prior eight-month period. These calculations revealed gross savings from improved productivity of $1.9 million [4] and savings from improved quality of $100,000. The net program savings of $1.3 million were determined by subtracting the program costs (e.g., the costs of awards, program administration, and training) of slightly more than $700,000 from the $2 million total gross savings from productivity and quality changes. [5] These figures represent a 2.1:1 return on investment (ROI) ratio of gross savings to total costs.

Qualitative results.   The archival and inter-

TABLE 1

Gainsharing results for productivity improvement programs

	PIP-1 Organization A	PIP-2 Organization B
Objectives		
Productivity[a]		
Direct measure teams	35.3%	8.5% (nursing) 12.1% (service)
Nondirect teams	N.A.	5.5%
Organization wide	32.0%	11.0%
Quality[a]		
Organization wide	44.1%	N.A.
Supply[a]	N.A.	7.7%
Safety[b]	36.0%	N.A.
Attendance[a]	30.0%	53.0%
Turnover	N.A.	−36.0%
Program's return on investment	2.8:1	2.2:1
Total program costs[c]	$0.7	$1.4
Total program savings[c]	$2.0[d]	$3.1[d]
Total net savings[c]	$1.3	$1.7

[a] Percentage of improvement over base line period.
[b] Reduction in time lost because of accidents.
[c] In millions of dollars.
[d] Productivity and quality savings only; attendance and safety savings not put into dollar terms.

view data indicated that employees perceived the extensive promotion, feedback, communications, and smooth operation of the tracking and payout system as highly positive features of the program. Moreover, all sources agreed that training introduced valuable information and techniques.

The program participants and consultants, however, reported three factors that reduced the program's success. First, the introduction of the program through a direct order from the corporate headquarters and the lack of adequate lead time before it began hindered both the development of positive relationships among the consultants and the firm and the managers' understanding of the project's goals. Second, the consultants reported that the firm's program liaison failed to provide adequate direction. Finally, the support personnel felt left out of the program because they were not included among those whose work was evaluated for changes in productivity and quality. Despite these problems, however, the general consensus was that the program was highly successful.

Follow-up evaluation. Five years after PIP-1 was held, a telephone interview revealed that the training component was still in use. The company's head of production indicated that PIP-1 had helped bring new managers and workers on board during a period of rapid expansion, and that it later aided the management of a reduction in force when sales diminished drastically. The improvements in productivity, safety, and attendance remained stable for at least a year after the program ended (after that time measurement ceased), but the quality ratio was less favorable than it had been during the program's operation. The net long-term effect of the program was considered positive, as major improvements in communication and more efficient management of the business were perceived.

Case Study: Organization B and PIP-2.

Background. Organization B was a 529-bed not-for-profit hospital in the south central United States. In 1980, when PIP-2 was introduced, the hospital employed 1,878 persons and had an avera ge occupancy rate of 95 percent. The Progress, Inc., consultants described the organization's atmosphere as generally friendly and relaxed, with a high level of trust and cooperation among employees and management.

Program Structure and Objectives. The 12-month program, introduced at the CEO's request, was offered organizationwide. A total of 91 teams were formed, 41 direct and 50 nondirect. PIP-2 had the following objectives: Up-

grade and improve management skills, improve hospital-wide and departmental productivity, increase morale and communications among management and employees, and reduce controllable budgetary expenses and turnover. To measure the achievement of these objectives, the following criteria were used: department performance, hospitalwide productivity, conservation of supplies, and attendance.

Monthly award points were granted to the direct teams based on performance improvement over the base period data, for which

$$\text{Performance} = \frac{\text{Hours worked}}{\text{Departmental service units}}$$

Service units were assessed according to criteria appropriate for the task of each department. The productivity earnings for the nondirect teams were based on the average earnings of the direct teams. In addition, bonus award points were granted quarterly for hospitalwide productivity improvements over historic averages. Program participants also earned award points for reducing controllable supply costs, improving attendance, making referrals, and being recognized as a "quality care contributor."

The hospital's existing measures of unit performance, supply costs, and attendance were used. Progress, Inc., did, however, develop a measure of hospitalwide productivity, using as base lines the performance histories for each measured department for the eight months preceding the program's initiation.

In most respects, the program's administrative, communications, and training features adhered to the PIP prototype described above. Because an increase in staff took place one month prior to the start of the program, however, the base for each work group was adjusted to avoid an artificially low base. The quantitative results thus must be interpreted cautiously.

Outcome and Evaluation.   Quantitative results. The data reported in Table 1 reveal that for the

12 months in which the program took place, productivity improved 11 percent over that for the base period. The mean difference in scores for the base period and first 11 months the program was offered [6] was 0.65 performance units. This difference was significant (t = 4.42, p = 0.001, standard error = 0.15). Productivity improved 8.5 percent in nursing, 12.1 percent in the service departments, and 5.5 percent among the support teams. The dollar value of the total productivity improvements (calculated using the method described in Note 4) represented $2.7 million in savings, and the 7.7 percent reduction in supply costs from the historical average represented savings of $256,000. More than 50 percent of the employees earned award points for perfect attendance, and turnover decreased by 36 percent. Based on Organization B's estimates, savings from reduced absenteeism and turnover represented $145,000. Deducting the $1.4 million for program costs from the gross savings of $3.1 million yields a net savings for the hospital of $1.7 million. The ROI (gross savings divided by total costs) was 2.2:1.

Qualitative results. A survey of program participants and department heads, an in-house study by the hospital's accountants, and other archival materials provided additional insights. First, the employees and managers viewed the introduction of a measurement system for hospitalwide performance as valuable. Second, the training was considered successful for changing employee behavior and introducing concepts and methods for improving performance. Other records also indicate that the trainer and consultants thought the program helped employees become more goal oriented and aware of their performance.

Problems stemmed from several sources. First, changes during the program (especially the adjustment of the base intended to accommodate increased staff) and large variations in volume reduced the direct relationship between performance and rewards. Second, some department heads reported that the rule structure was too complicated and that, because of other changes occurring in the organization, too much was happening at one time. Third, the consultants felt that some of the hospital's administrators were not accustomed to accounting for performance savings in a manner consistent with the program's objectives and did not believe that all the results should be attributed to the program. Fourth, people's attention to the program was diverted by other priorities, internal political struggles, and a lack of full commitment to the program. Finally, no one staff member assumed the trainer's role, so that once the trainer left no one remained to institutionalize the behavioral approach. Despite these shortcomings, the participants, trainers, and consultants agreed that the program was successful. The hospital's audit report specifically stated that its general concepts should be retained in future endeavors.

Follow-up evaluation. Five years after PIP-2 ended, the hospital's chief financial officer reaffirmed that the major difficulty with the program had been documenting the resulting savings. [7] He indicated, however, that PIP-2 had educated both the administration and the employees about the significance of productivity measures, and had led to a new productivity measure to complement a major organizational restructuring. The organization has continued the recognition and incentives aspect of PIP-2 by providing merchandise awards for high-quality patient care and to the employee of the month.

Case Study: Organization C and TSP-1.

Background. TSP-1 was implemented in a manufacturing operation (with five divisions) of Organization C. In 1983, when TSP-1 was introduced, the firm had more than 12,000 employees, and the consultants reported that its markets were stable. Twenty-nine plants in the United States, three in Canada, and three in the United Kingdom were included in the program.

Program Structure and Objectives. The executive vice president had requested that TSP-1 be introduced. The firm's major objective for the program was to maintain its position as the lowest-cost producer in its industries. A secondary objective was to increase the individual plants' identification with the parent company. During the four months the program was in operation, 71 percent of the employees participated in it.

Before TSP-1 was initiated, the existing system underwent two changes. First, the suggestion program—which followed a traditional suggestion box format—was suspended. Second, to prevent duplication of effort, the division heads made information from the management cost reduction program already in place available to the project teams.

Outcome and Evaluation.   Quantitative results. Table 2 reveals that 6,365 cost-saving ideas were submitted. The estimated savings from the 2,141 ideas accepted (34 percent) were $12.5 million for the first full year following implementation. When $3.25 million in program costs (for awards, training, and communications) were deducted from the estimated savings, a potential net value of $9.25 million was realized, representing an ROI of 3.8:1.

Qualitative results. The archival sources included a post-program report made by the site managers. The managers felt that TSP-1 had provided an opportunity to consider ideas on a larger scale than normally possible, had alerted management to new ways of saving money, and had increased upward communications, participant involvement, and enthusiasm for the plant's operations. They noted substantial increases in workers' awareness and knowledge of costs and other operating requirements. They also noted that the use of team leaders helped them to identify potential supervisors and managers.

Three factors appeared especially important to the program's success. First, the simplicity of its

TABLE 2

Gainsharing results for team suggestion programs

	TSP-1 Organization C	TSP-2 Organization D
Number of ideas submitted	6,365	3,199
Number of ideas accepted	2,141	936
Acceptance rate	34%	29%
Number of employees	12,034	3,300
Participation rate	71%	93%
Program return on investment	3.8:1	3.5:1
Total program costs*	$ 3.25	$2.60
Total program savings*	$12.50	$9.20
Total net savings*	$ 9.25	$6.60

* In millions of dollars.

structure and concept allowed employees to easily understand the program and increased their willingness to participate in it. Second, the site managers could adapt the concept to local circumstances. Third, the prominent role of the executive vice president and the commitment of all top-level managers aided the program's implementation.

Four shortcomings were recognized. First, the program's length was thought to have hindered the organization's normal operations because it interfered with the regular duties of the managers. Second, unanticipated administrative requirements of the program (e.g., teaching teams to formulate credible ideas) burdened many site managers. Third, members of the evaluation committee were not allowed to participate in the award opportunities, and perceived any awards they did receive to be insufficient. Finally, training in the program's specific operations was not given at all levels, meaning that participants lacked adequate information on assessing costs and managing the rejection of ideas. [8] Despite this, however, the program was judged a major success.

Follow-up evaluation. Three years after the program ended, three developments were reported. First, the organization had successfully introduced a TSP in one of its German plants, which resulted in its adopting ideas that saved approximately $3 million in costs and—even more important, according to the program director—significant improvements in communications and union relations. Second, many ideas from TSP-1 had been implemented, which produced estimated savings of $36 million—three times the initial estimate. Third, although top management continued to view the program positively, the amount of work the program required evoked some negative reaction. The firm had made no commitment to conducting another TSP, although management was considering introducing this system elsewhere in the corporation.

Case Study: Organization D and TSP-2.

Background. Organization D, an East Coast bank, had approximately 3,300 nonunion employees when TSP-2 was introduced in 1983. The consultants reported that the firm had well-defined lines of authority and primarily a top-down system of decision making and information flow. Work units tended to focus on internal matters, to feel protective about their turf, and to have little work flow coordination with other work units.

The bank's CEO fully supported the organizationwide suggestion team concept, but employees remained skeptical because an earlier recommendation by an external consultant had led to the layoff of many persons. The CEO responded by announcing that no ideas accepted would result in anyone's losing her or his job.

Program Structure and Objectives. At the CEO's request, TSP-2 was conducted for 10 weeks. The 377 teams, each having five to seven members, represented a 93 percent participation rate. The program's objectives were to control product costs and to help achieve the CEO's goal of saving $15 million during the next five years.

Outcome and Evaluation.   Quantitative results. Table 2 shows that for TSP-2, 3,199 ideas were submitted. Of these, 936 (29 percent) were accepted, which resulted in $9.2 million in potential cost savings and quality improvements. The cost of implementing the program was $2.6 million; therefore, the potential net value of the cost-saving ideas was $6.6 million (ROI = 3.5:1).

Qualitative results. Interviews and archival materials revealed that increased communication and awareness of important aspects of the firm's operations resulted from TSP-2. The team meetings focused on efficiency and productivity, thereby broadening the perspectives of the participants and increasing their awareness of their relationships with the larger organization. Moreover, communications among units improved because, to satisfactorily determine costs related to their ideas, participants had to discuss their proposals with personnel from other departments.

The consultant noted that the program's success was aided by the visible support of the CEO, the high rate of participation, and extensive preparations for the program. This consultant also, however, identified several shortcomings related to TSP-2's implementation. First, management and team leaders did not receive adequate training on procedures. For example, team leaders complained that they lacked sufficient information for formulating and verifying ideas. Second, the liaison role was not performed effectively, causing the consultant to spend more time giving advice and performing follow-up work for the program than intended. Third, the computerized tracking system had not been completely tested ahead of time and sometimes failed to provide timely feedback. Finally, members of the evaluation committee felt uneasy about making decisions outside their traditional lines of authority.

Follow-up evaluation. Three years after TSP-2 ended, approximately 90–95 percent of the approved ideas had been translated into real savings. Because members of the evaluation team that had approved ideas while the program was conducted were not participating in top management's implementation of the decisions, however, they were responding negatively. Other reported outcomes included the following: increased awareness among top managers as to the value of the firm's workers, greater cost consciousness and understanding of the business by employees, improved management-employee relations, and greater teamwork among interdependent functional units. The effects of these positive outcomes were thought to have diminished with time, however. At least some of this reduced impact was attributed to a combination of high turnover and a rapid increase in business, which together had required approximately 1,000 new employees.

Discussion

Limitations. Several methodological factors must be considered when interpreting the results of this research. First, a great deal of our data came from primary sources. The quantitative information came directly from the program measures, and many of the qualitative findings were derived from archival records. Therefore, much of what we report is likely to have "really happened." Such sources, however, are unlikely to reflect **everything** that happened. For example, clients and Progress, Inc., personnel could have written the records so that these reflected favorably on their work. Similarly, the interviews—which are not primary data sources—may have been influenced by the desire for self-enhancement. The consultants' claims are particularly

likely to have been affected by such intentions, with positive results attributed to an intervention and negative outcomes either ignored or explained as the result of something other than the program.

Second, the quantitative results must be interpreted with caution. In dynamic organizations, many events occur simultaneously. A generic problem is evaluating an intervention in any complex, dynamic organization, for no intervention is truly "representative," even for a specific organization. Nord and Tucker (1987) have noted that the process of innovation in an ongoing organization is strongly affected by other ongoing events (see also Downs & Mohr, 1976). The best means of introducing a particular program into a single organization will seldom be the same from one time to the next. Moreover, for this research no controls for a possible Hawthorne effect were available. The degree to which the improvements resulted from the substance of the programs and/or other concurrent events cannot be determined. Nevertheless, the overall quantitative results are consistent with previous findings and with Lawler's (1988) observation that gainsharing programs work.

The study's external validity is constrained by several factors. First, limitations are related to the method used to select the cases. Only four cases were investigated, and for all four, the programs were offered by a single consulting firm. We selected this firm because its programs matched our interest in the application of incentives. Moreover, the individual programs studied were selected on the basis of the availability of Progress, Inc.'s records and the degree to which they were judged to be representative—not on the basis of random assignment. Second, changes in such areas as personnel and organizational learning probably cause the programs Progress, Inc., offers to vary over time. Finally, these programs represent only two forms of a vast variety of programs called "gainsharing," and—as do most gainsharing programs—they were custom designed to fit particular organizations. Cross-program comparisons are confounded by the various objectives of the particular organizations involved. Moreover, for the PIPs, each unit within the organizations had unique criteria and measures. Still, despite all these sources of uniqueness, the quantitative and qualitative results are congruent with the findings of previous research on gainsharing.

Quantitative Outcomes. The quantitative data provide clear evidence that gainsharing was successful in all four organizations studied. Both PIPs produced significant productivity improvements over the results for the base period and yielded more than $1 million in net savings to their organizations (i.e., ROIs of 2.8 and 2.2). The TSPs yielded $9.25 million and $6.6 million in potential cost savings, and ROIs of 3.8 and 3.5. [9] Moreover, contrary to the findings of earlier studies of gainsharing (Graham-Moore & Ross, 1983), the results suggest that these systems can work in both manufacturing and non-manufacturing settings, at least when assessed against short-term objectives.

The follow-up data, gathered only from informal interviews, provide limited evidence of possible longer-term effects. The PIP follow-up data, based on tracking performance, reveal mixed long-term outcomes. Improvements in productivity, safety, and attendance were sustained for a year after PIP-1 had ended, but the reported improvements in quality (which were not statistically significant to begin with) declined. After PIP-2 ended, the productivity benefits were not altogether believed to result from the program, although the overall merits of a productivity measure were not questioned. Follow-up data for the TSPs focus on the implementation of the cost-saving ideas. For TSP-1, the realized cost savings proved to be three times greater than the estimated savings. For TSP-2, 90–95 percent of the ideas were implemented. Thus, even after the programs ended, evidence indicates that they had lingering benefits. We emphasize, however, that these programs were introduced for a fixed time period. Programs that had been introduced with the expectation that they would be permanent but were later abandoned would likely trigger different recollections.

Finally, the case of PIP-2 indicates that comparisons of program results with historical bases must be scrutinized carefully. Because organizations often change in multiple ways, a given historical base tends to become an inadequate yardstick. If the base is not adjusted to reflect changes in personnel, technology, markets, and the like, it becomes obsolete. Making such adjustments, however, requires judgment and introduces a potential threat to validity. In short, the reported results often understate or overstate the true effects of the intervention.

Qualitative Outcomes. Gainsharing produced several positive changes for the organizations studied, including identifying potential leaders (TSP-1), improving communications between workers and management (TSP-1, TSP-2), reducing mistrust and fostering cooperation (TSP-2), increasing employees' understanding of operations (TSP-1, TSP-2), and increasing workers' awareness of their own performance (PIP-2). Structural benefits also resulted, such as the development of a measurement system (PIP-2). Overall, managers believed that the programs made workers better informed and more aware of the overall goals of the organization. As are the quantitative outcomes, these results are similar to those reported by Hatcher and Ross (1985), O'Dell (1987), and Lawler (1988).

The follow-up information shows that these qualitative results generally lasted longer than did the quantitative ones. Nevertheless, one cannot assume that in dynamic organizations such benefits will endure. For example, constant changes in personnel (such as the turnover after TSP-2 ended) may make an organization's collective memory rather short unless "reminders"—that is, new interventions or repetitions of earlier ones—are introduced.

Factors Influencing Gainsharing. An examination of the implementation of the four gainsharing interventions suggested that several process factors affected the programs' success. Active participation and high levels of involvement by an organization's employees (TSP-1, TSP-2), strong support and commitment to the intervention from the CEO and management (TSP-1, TSP-2), and follow-up work by the Progress, Inc., staff (PIP-1) all played significant roles in producing positive outcomes.

Other important process factors became apparent when the interventions' shortcomings were examined. Contextual factors, such as competing priorities within an organization (PIP-1, PIP-2) or participants' distrust of the program (TSP-2), appear to have compromised the interventions' success. A program's procedures might also cause problems. For example, shortcomings of the programs studied were attributed to objectives not perceived as based on performance (PIP-2), complicated rule structures (PIP-2), uncoordinated motivation and training components (PIP-1, PIP-2), insufficient procedural training (TSP-1, TSP-2), and the programs' being too long or too demanding (TSP-2). Many of these indicate a practical issue easily overlooked when a firm decides to implement gain sharing: Gainsharing programs may require not just management support, but also substantial attention from managers. We argue in greater detail below that the mechanistic focus on formulas often generated by these interventions can increase the chances that what is truly needed for the implementation to succeed will be underestimated or overlooked.

The implementation process itself (both for preparation and actual execution) was also a crucial determinant of a program's success. Problems associated with preparations included proceeding without full management support (PIP-1), changing the bases of measurement immediately prior to implementation (PIP-2), failing to achieve full management ownership of and commitment to the program (PIP-1), and failing to clarify program procedures or to provide all the skills necessary to administer the program (PIP-1, PIP-2, TSP-2). During the course of the programs, problems noted include overburdened program administrators (TSP-1), abnormally high follow-up requirements for consultants (TSP-2), ineffective liaisons (PIP-1, TSP-2), participants' feelings of inequity (PIP-1, TSP-1, TSP-2), misunderstanding related to program results (PIP-2), the evaluation committee's perceiving that it lacked sufficient authority to make decisions on high cost-saving ideas (TSP-2), and some managers' believing that the program interfered with the organization's normal business operations (TSP-1).

Postimplementation factors also proved important, for one could not assume that the programs and their benefits would last indefinitely. Although all of the organizations studied reported lingering benefits, both the quantitative and qualitative benefits tended to diminish once the program ended. Such a decline might not matter as much for a TSP because, at least in the short run, the pool of ideas generally gets drained during the course of the program. For both types of programs, however, if the firm seeks results such as greater employee awareness and enhanced interdepartmental relationships, special efforts to foster these must be made.

The communication elements of the programs, although not commented on explicitly for any of the four cases, may also have important effects on their overall success. The programs demand much communication both before and during implementation, which involves meetings, training, and written documents. During the course of a program, much of the communication involves "spurt" activities (for PIPs), feedback, and promoting rewards (material rewards appear to facilitate promotion better than financial payments do). Thus intensive communication efforts might help motivate employees and maintain the intervention's saliency.

Finally, we note a factor that none of the respondents mentioned, but which is characteristic of gainsharing interventions: Gainsharing tends to work when the interventions act in accordance with at least two principles of human behavior—that is, by introducing "superordinate" (or common) goals among individuals and across departments, and by making rewards contingent upon factors the individual can control or influence (Frederiksen, 1982; Luthans & Kreitner, 1975, 1985; Nord, 1969). Unlike some gainsharing efforts, the interventions we studied had measured and rewarded performance at the work unit level, where people are more likely to perceive a direct relationship between their efforts and the rewards than when rewards are contingent on performance of the entire organization. This may partly explain why these particular interventions were more successful in large organizations than previous research (Lawler, 1981) suggested they would be.

Synergy from Gainsharing and OD.

Shared Goals and Outcomes. The contextual and process issues so important for the cases we studied—and for previously studied efforts to implement gainsharing—are nearly identical to those at the core of contemporary organization development (Beer, 1980). Moreover, the outcomes of enhanced trust, awareness of organizational goals, and commitment, though not explicit goals of the gainsharing interventions, are the stated objectives of most OD initiatives. These results indicate the value of closing the current gap (Hatcher & Ross, 1985) between these two families of interventions.

Complementary Strengths. OD and gainsharing have much to offer each other, because the strengths of each are the lacunae of the other. We note above that gainsharing represents a way of putting into practice some well-established principles of human behavior (e.g., people perform better in response to rewards contingent on performance, to goal setting, and to concrete, timely feedback). Designers of gainsharing plans put these ideas into practice in terms managers value—that is, they generate precise measures and "hard" numbers expressed in dollars. O'Dell (1987) warns, however, that users of these systems can become so involved in formulas and technical matters that they ignore fundamental human resource considerations.

In contrast, OD practitioners emphasize human resource issues, but often lack the interest and/or competence to develop measurement systems for evaluating the contributions of their efforts to an organization's "bottom line." Indeed, students of OD frequently feel repulsed by the control connotations of contingent rewards.

Our results suggest that the successful implementation of gainsharing requires the orientations and skills of the industrial engineer, the accountant, the operations analyst, and the OD specialist. Unfortunately, few change agents are experts in both performance measurement issues (which require knowledge of industrial and engineering operations, accounting, and financial administration) and human resource/process issues.

Implications for Gainsharing Practice and Research. The implications of our research for gainsharing practice are clear: The introduction of gainsharing can be facilitated by incorporating ideas and techniques from OD. Indeed, much could be accomplished if—as suggested previously by Frost, Wakeley, and Ruh (1974) and recently by Hatcher and Ross (1985)—gainsharing were viewed as a major OD intervention, not merely an incentive system.

The benefits of an OD perspective for research on gainsharing are equally great, but less easily explicated. Assessing gainsharing continues to be difficult. The term refers to a diverse set of programs designed according to the core concept of distributing to employees some portion of the benefit of improved performance. The diversity of gainsharing plans and the need to adapt even generally known plans (e.g., the Scanlon plan) to fit local circumstances suggest that the definition of gainsharing may never become truly uniform. Still, much can be done, and the incorporation of organizational and process factors into the research agenda is important.

In-depth longitudinal studies of programs are needed. Such studies must begin early in the design process and continue well into the course of a program. Studies must also provide details of a program's mechanics, the process of implementation, any changes in formulas and historical bases, the organizational context, any changes in structures, personnel, and technology, and what effects a program has on an organization after it ends. This information will help us determine the most salient features of the plans and, more important, will highlight the interaction between a particular intervention and the dynamic system in which it is embedded. Such early associations with organizations implementing such plans would also increase our chances of learning about failures as well as successes. Moreover, long-term, in-depth organizational analysis will also yield information on circumstances affecting both short-run quantitative results and longer-term consequences.

Unfortunately, such comparative, longitudinal, in-depth studies are expensive and rare in this field. More limited research on the use of incentives (e.g., rate of payment, satiation processes, group size, type of rewards, participation in design) could contribute to our knowledge of gainsharing systems. Indeed, those who study behavior modification, incentives, and goals have relevant data—and the technology and conceptual frameworks—for guiding such inquiries.

At a practical level, gainsharing offers managers an orientation and technology they can adapt to specific situations to make rewards contingent on performance. A combined gainsharing-OD perspective could stimulate managers to consider how gainsharing fits the current and desired fabric of their organizations. This would bring process issues to the fore, prompting such questions as the following: Is our culture ready for rewarding performance so explicitly? If not, what intervening steps would be helpful? Do we have the human resources and accounting procedures to develop and administer appropriate standards? What type of training is needed for supervisors and others essential to the program's success? How will we introduce the program to the organization? Is the formula too complicated? Are the rewards related to outcomes that employees directly control? What special circumstances in our history might affect perceptions of the program? Should we consider a short-run program with a fixed time limit (i.e., a "sunset plan") to introduce and test the concept, or should we implement a permanent program? If we choose a sunset plan, how can we sustain the benefits once the program ends? If we choose a permanent program, how will we change its standards to reflect changes in technology, products, the market, and the like? What, if anything, should we do to sustain interest in and visibility of the program, and how should we structure and implement it? What must we do to prepare new employees to work under the program? What will all this cost? Apart from figures related to performance, what other benefits or costs (e.g., trust, employee commitment) should we track to evaluate the program's impact?

Conclusion

Organizations will probably continue to try to improve performance through gainsharing and various pay-for-performance systems. For organizations to become truly performance oriented, they need both cultural change and new systems of measurement and accountability. Although many paths to obtaining this seem available, our study points to one in particular. Change agents who integrate the process skills of traditional organization development with the rewards orientation, measurement systems, and design capabilities associated with gainsharing may serve as a valuable resource to managers seeking to improve the performance of their organizations.

Notes

1. Readers should note, however, that in her survey O'Dell attempted to define gainsharing more narrowly.
2. At the time of this writing, no program facilitated by Progress, Inc., had ever lost money or failed to have an impact on the organization. Conversations with Progress, Inc., managers suggested that the less-successful programs had been adversely affected by external issues (e.g., market "downswings") or were among the first programs conducted, for which insufficient preparations were made for the organization's culture, management, and employees.
3. Copies of these detailed reports may be obtained from the senior author of this article.
4. Organization A's chief financial officer derived this figure using standard cost accounting methods. To illustrate this, consider the case of a particular job. Based on engineering standards, one can estimate that a certain number of hours on the job (e.g., 160) should be required to produce a certain number of units of a product (e.g., 160 widgets, for an ELHR = 1). Historical data might reveal, however, that for some period prior to the intervention (the base period), the ELHR equalled 0.8—that is, 200 hours were required to produce 160 widgets. Suppose an intervention took place and productivity improved so that only 160 hours were required to produce 160 widgets. This would make an

ELHR of 1, indicating a 20 percent savings in labor time. The hourly cost of labor is known; in this case, assume it is $10 per hour. To figure the savings produced by the intervention, calculate the reduction in hours required to produce 160 widgets ($200 \times 0.20 = 40$) and multiply this figure by $10. For this particular job, the gross savings would be $400. The total savings for an entire plant for a given time period would be the sum of all savings for all individual jobs. A similar use of historical costs could be used to calculate savings along many dimensions, such as quality.

5. The net savings determined do not include organizational costs not related to the program (e.g., administrative time). These costs are often insignificant, according to a Progress, Inc., official. Moreover, some less tangible outcomes (e.g., greater camaraderie and better communications among employees, job satisfaction) are not measured systematically.
6. Data for the 12th month were missing from the records for the tests of significance, but not from the overall calculations for program outcomes.
7. This difficulty indicates the general problem of using micro measures in hospitals. Progress, Inc., has since learned the importance of designing productivity measures that reflect both the census and acuity of the patient population.
8. Progress, Inc. now reports that these problems have been evaluated and remedied for all new programs. Specifically, a three-month program is now standard, the administrative processes have been fully computerized, middle managers receive awards consistent with their involvement, and training time has doubled.
9. The larger ROIs for the TSPs are interesting but hard to interpret. First, the customized nature of the individual programs makes cross-organization comparisons difficult. Second, the TSP figures do not represent immediate, tangible gains. The description of these programs indicates that a critical difference between PIPs and TSPs is that whereas net savings from PIPs represent actual cost reductions, the total net savings from TSPs are not realized until the accepted ideas are implemented. Third, with

respect to PIPs, if the organization lacks suitable systems and records, the development of standards can be quite expensive, resulting in lower ROIs.

References

Beer, M. (1980). *Organization Change and Development: A Systems View.* Santa Monica, CA: Goodyear.

Bullock, R. J., & Bullock, P. F. (1982). "Gain Sharing and Rubik's Cube: Solving System Problems." *National Productivity Review, 1,* 396–407.

Bullock, R. J., & Lawler, E. E., III. (1984). "Gain Sharing: A Few Questions and Fewer Answers. *Human Resources Management, 23*(1), 23–40.

Downs, W., Jr., & Mohr, B. (1976). "Conceptual Issues in the Study of Innovation." *Administrative Science Quarterly, 21,* 700–14.

Doyle, R. J. (1982). Gain Sharing—A Total Productivity Approach. *Journal of Contemporary Business, 11*(2), 57–70.

Frederiksen, L. W. (1982). *Handbook of Organizational Behavior Management.* New York: John Wiley & Sons.

Frost, C. F.; Wakeley, J. H.; & Ruh, R. A. (1974). *The Scanlon Plan for Organization Development: Identity, Participation, and Equity.* East Lansing: Michigan State University Press.

Goodman, P. S., & Dean, J. W., Jr. (1983). "Making Productivity Programs Last. In B. E. Graham-Moore & T. L. Ross (eds.), *Productivity Gain Sharing* (pp. 122–140). Englewood Cliffs, NJ: Prentice Hall.

Graham-Moore, B. E., & Ross, T. L. (1983). *Productivity Gain Sharing.* Englewood Cliffs, NJ: Prentice Hall.

Hatcher, L. L., & Ross, T. L. (1985). "Organization Development through Productivity Gain Sharing." *Personnel, 62*(10), 42–50.

Hauck, W. C. (1987). "Productivity Improvement at Branch Banks." *National Productivity Review, 6*(3), 243–49.

Jenkins, G. D., Jr., & Gupta, N. (1982). "Financial Incentives and Productivity Improvement. *Journal of Contemporary Business, 11*(2), 43–56.

Lawler, E. E., III (1981). *Pay and Organization Development.* Reading, MA: Addison-Wesley.

Lawler, E. E., III (1988). "Gain Sharing Theory and Research: Findings and Future Directions. In W. A. Pasmore & R. W. Woodman (eds.), *Research in Organizational Change and Development,* vol. 2, pp. 323–44). Greenwich, CT: JAI Press.

Locke, E. A., & Schweiger, D. M. (1979). "Participation in Decision-Making: One More Look. In B. M. Star (ed.), *Research in Organizational Behavior,* vol. 1, pp. 265–339). Greenwich, CT: JAI Press.

Luthans, F., & Kreitner, R. (1975). *Organizational Behavior Modification.* Glenview, IL: Scott, Foresman.

Luthans, F., & Kreitner, R. (1985). *Organizational Behavior Modification and Beyond: An Operant and Social Learning Approach.* Glenview, IL: Scott, Foresman.

Miller, C. Z., & Schuster, M. H. (1987). Gain Sharing Plans: A Comparative Analysis. *Organizational Dynamics* 16(1), 44–67.

Nord, W. R. (1969). "Beyond the Teaching Machine: The Neglected Area of Operant Conditioning in the Theory and Practice of Management." *Organizational Behavior and Human Performance* 4(4), 375–401.

Nord, W. R., & Tucker, S. (1987). *Implementing Routine and Radical Innovations.* Lexington, MA: Lexington Books.

O'Dell, C. (1987). *People, Performance and Pay.* Houston, TX: American Productivity Center.

Preiwisch, C. F. (1981). "GAO Study of Productivity-Sharing Programs." In V. M. Buehler & Y. K. Shetty (eds.), *Productivity Improvement: Case Studies of Proven Practice* (pp. 177–200). New York: AMACOM.

Ross, T. L. (1983). "Why PG Fails in Some Firms." In B. E. Graham-Moore & T. L. Ross (eds.), *Productivity Gain Sharing* (pp. 141–56). Englewood Cliffs, NJ: Prentice Hall.

Ross, T. L., & Ross, R. A. (1984). "Productivity Gain Sharing: Resolving Some of the Measurement Issues." *National Productivity Review* 3(4), 382–94.

White, J. K. (1979). "The Scanlon Plan: Causes and Correlates of Success." *Academy of Management Journal* 22, 292–312.

READING 31
TEACHING SMART PEOPLE HOW TO LEARN

Chris Argyris

Any company that aspires to succeed in the tougher business environment of the 1990s must first resolve a basic dilemma: success in the marketplace increasingly depends on learning, yet most people don't know how to learn. What's more, those members of the organization that many assume to be the best at learning are, in fact, not very good at it. I am talking about the well-educated, high-powered, high-commitment professionals who occupy key leadership positions in the modern corporation.

Most companies not only have tremendous difficulty addressing this learning dilemma; they aren't even aware that it exists. The reason: they misunderstand what learning is and how to bring it about. As a result, they tend to make two mistakes in their efforts to become a learning organization.

First, most people define learning too narrowly as mere "problem solving," so they focus on identifying and correcting errors in the external environment. Solving problems is important. But if learning is to persist, managers and employees must also look inward. They need to reflect critically on their own behavior, identify the ways they often inadvertently contribute to the organization's problems, and then change how they act. In particular, they must learn how the very way they go about defining and solving problems can be a source of problems in its own right.

I have coined the terms *single loop* and *double loop* learning to capture this crucial distinction.

To give a simple analogy: a thermostat that automatically turns on the heat whenever the temperature in a room drops below 68 degrees is a good example of single-loop learning. A thermostat that could ask, "Why am I set at 68 degrees?" and then explore whether or not some other temperature might more economically achieve the goal of heating the room would be engaging in double-loop learning.

Highly skilled professionals are frequently very good at single-loop learning. After all, they have spent much of their lives acquiring academic credentials, mastering one or a number of intellectual disciplines, and applying those disciplines to solve real-world problems. But ironically, this very fact helps explain why professionals are often so bad at double-loop learning.

Put simply, because many professionals are almost always successful at what they do, they rarely experience failure. And because they have rarely failed, they have never learned how to learn from failure. So whenever their single-loop learning strategies go wrong, they become defensive, screen out criticism, and put the "blame" on anyone and everyone but themselves. In short, their ability to learn shuts down precisely at the moment they need it the most.

The propensity among professionals to behave defensively helps shed light on the second mistake that companies make about learning. The common assumption is that getting people to learn is largely a matter of motivation. When people have the right attitudes and commitment, learning automatically follows. So companies focus on creating new organizational structures—compensation programs, performance reviews, corporate cultures, and the like—that are designed to create motivated and committed employees.

But effective double-loop learning is not simply a function of how people feel. It is a reflection of how they think—that is, the cognitive rules or reasoning they use to design and implement their actions. Think of these rules as a kind of "master program" stored in the brain, governing all behavior. Defensive reasoning can block learning even when the individual commitment to it is high, just as a computer program with hidden bugs can produce results exactly the opposite of what its designers had planned.

Companies can learn how to resolve the learning dilemma. What it takes is to make the ways managers and employees reason about their behavior a focus of organizational learning and continuous improvement programs. Teaching people how to reason about their behavior in new and more effective ways breaks down the defenses that block learning.

All of the examples that follow involve a particular kind of professional: fast-track consultants at major management consulting companies. But the implications of my argument go far beyond this specific occupational group. The fact is, more and more jobs—no matter what the title— are taking on the contours of "knowledge work." People at all levels of the organization must combine the mastery of some highly specialized technical expertise with the ability to work effectively in teams, form productive relationships with clients and customers, and critically reflect on and then change their own organizational practices. And the nuts and bolts of management—whether of high-powered consultants or service representatives, senior managers or factory technicians—increasingly consists of guiding and integrating the autonomous but interconnected work of highly skilled people.

How Professionals Avoid Learning

For 15 years, I have been conducting in-depth studies of management consultants. I decided to study consultants for a few simple reasons. First, they are the epitome of the highly educated professionals who play an increasingly central role in all organizations. Almost all of the consultants I've studied have MBAs from the top three or four U.S. business schools. They are also highly committed to their work. For instance, at one company, more than 90 percent of the consultants responded in a survey that they were "highly satisfied" with their jobs and with the company.

I also assumed that such professional consultants would be good at learning. After all, the essence of their job is to teach others how to do things differently. I found, however, that these consultants embodied the learning dilemma. The most enthusiastic about continuous improvement in their own organizations, they were also often the biggest obstacle to its complete success.

As long as efforts at learning and change focused on external organizational factors—job redesign, compensation programs, performance reviews, and leadership training—the professionals were enthusiastic participants. Indeed, creating new systems and structures was precisely the kind of challenge that well-educated, highly motivated professionals thrived on.

And yet the moment the quest for continuous improvement turned to the professionals' *own* performance, something went wrong. It wasn't a matter of bad attitude. The professionals' commitment to excellence was genuine, and the vision of the company was clear. Nevertheless, continuous improvement did not persist. And the longer the continuous improvement efforts continued, the greater the likelihood that they would produce ever-diminishing returns.

What happened? The professionals began to feel embarrassed. They were threatened by the prospect of critically examining their own role in the organization. Indeed, because they were so well paid and generally believed that their employers were supportive and fair, the idea that their performance might not be at its best made them feel guilty.

Far from being a catalyst for real change, such feelings caused most to react defensively. They projected the blame for any problems away from themselves and onto what they said were unclear goals, insensitive and unfair leaders, and stupid clients.

Consider this example. At a premier management consulting company, the manager of a case team called a meeting to examine the team's performance on a recent consulting project. The client was largely satisfied and had given the team relatively high marks, but the manager believed the team had not created the value added that it was capable of and that the consulting company had promised. In the spirit of continuous improvement, he felt that the team could do better. Indeed, so did some of the team members.

The manager knew how difficult it was for people to reflect critically on their own work performance, especially in the presence of their manager, so he took a number of steps to make possible a frank and open discussion. He invited to the meeting an outside consultant whom team members knew and trusted—"just to keep me honest," he said. He also agreed to have the entire meeting tape-recorded. That way, any subsequent confusions or disagreements about what went on at the meeting could be checked against the transcript. Finally, the manager opened the meeting by emphasizing that no subject was off limits—including his own behavior.

"I realize that you may believe you cannot confront me," the manager said. "But I encourage you to challenge me. You have a responsibility to tell me where you think the leadership made mistakes, just as I have the responsibility to identify any I believe you made. And all of us must acknowledge our own mistakes. If we do not have an open dialogue, we will not learn."

The professionals took the manager up on the first half of his invitation but quietly ignored the second. When asked to pinpoint the key problems in the experience with the client, they looked entirely outside themselves. The clients were uncooperative and arrogant. "They didn't

think we could help them." The team's own managers were unavailable and poorly prepared. "At times, our managers were not up to speed before they walked into the client meetings." In effect, the professionals asserted that they were helpless to act differently—not because of any limitations of their own but because of the limitations of others.

The manager listened carefully to the team members and tried to respond to their criticisms. He talked about the mistakes that he had made during the consulting process. For example, one professional objected to the way the manager had run the project meetings. "I see that the way I asked questions closed down discussions," responded the manager. "I didn't mean to do that, but I can see how you might have believed that I had already made up my mind." Another team member complained that the manager had caved in to pressure from his superior to produce the project report far too quickly, considering the team's heavy work load. "I think that it was my responsibility to have said no," admitted the manager. "It was clear that we all had an immense amount of work."

Finally, after some three hours of discussion about his own behavior, the manager began to ask the team members if there were any errors *they* might have made. "After all," he said, "this client was not different from many others. How can we be more effective in the future?"

The professionals repeated that it was really the clients' and their own managers' fault. As one put it, "They have to be open to change and want to learn." The more the manager tried to get the team to examine its own responsibility for the outcome, the more the professionals bypassed his concerns. The best one team member could suggest was for the case team to "promise less"—implying that there was really no way for the group to improve its performance.

The case team members were reacting defensively to protect themselves, even though their manager was not acting in ways that an outsider would consider threatening. Even if there were some truth to their charges—the clients may well have been arrogant and closed, their own managers distant—the *way* they presented these claims was guaranteed to stop learning. With few exceptions, the professionals made attributions about the behavior of the clients and the managers but never publicly tested their claims. For instance, they said that the clients weren't motivated to learn but never really presented any evidence supporting that assertion. When their lack of concrete evidence was pointed out to them, they simply repeated their criticisms more vehemently.

If the professionals had felt so strongly about these issues, why had they never mentioned them during the project? According to the professionals, even this was the fault of others. "We didn't want to alienate the client," argued one. "We didn't want to be seen as whining," said another.

The professionals were using their criticisms of others to protect themselves from the potential embarrassment of having to admit that perhaps they, too, had contributed to the team's less-than-perfect performance. What's more, the fact that they kept repeating their defensive actions in the face of the manager's efforts to turn the group's attention to its own role shows that this defensiveness had become a reflexive routine. From the professionals' perspective, they weren't resisting; they were focusing on the "real" causes. Indeed, they were to be respected, if not congratulated, for working as well as they did under such difficult conditions.

The end result was an unproductive parallel conversation. Both the manager and the professionals were candid: they expressed their views forcefully. But they talked past each other, never finding a common language to describe what had happened with the client. The professionals kept insisting that the fault lay with others. The manager kept trying, unsuccessfully, to get the professionals to see how they contributed to the state of affairs they were criticizing. The dialogue of this parallel conversation looks like this:

Professionals: "The clients have to be open. They must want to change."

Manager: "It's our task to help them see that change is in their interest."

Professionals: "But the clients didn't agree with our analyses."

Manager: "If they didn't think our ideas were right, how might we have convinced them?"

Professionals: "Maybe we need to have more meetings with the client."

Manager: "If we aren't adequately prepared and if the clients don't think we're credible, how will more meetings help?"

Professionals: "There should be better communication between case team members and management."

Manager: "I agree. But professionals should take the initiative to educate the manager about the problems they are experiencing."

Professionals: "Our leaders are unavailable and distant."

Manager: "How do you expect us to know that if you don't tell us?"

Conversations such as this one dramatically illustrate the learning dilemma. The problem with the professionals' claims is not that they are wrong but that they aren't useful. By constantly turning the focus away from their own behavior to that of others, the professionals bring learning to a grinding halt. The manager understands the trap but does not know how to get out of it. To learn how to do that requires going deeper into the dynamics of defensive reasoning—and into the special causes that make professionals so prone to it.

Defensive Reasoning and the Doom Loop

What explains the professionals' defensiveness? Not their attitudes about change or commitment to continuous improvement; they really wanted to work more effectively. Rather, the key factor is the way they reasoned about their behavior and that of others.

It is impossible to reason anew in every situation. If we had to think through all the possible responses every time someone asked, "How are you?" the world would pass us by. Therefore everyone develops a theory of action—a set of rules that individuals use to design and implement their own behavior as well as to understand the behavior of others. Usually, these theories of actions become so taken for granted that people don't even realize they are using them.

One of the paradoxes of human behavior, however, is that the master program people actually use is rarely the one they think they use. Ask people in an interview or questionnaire to articulate the rules they use to govern their actions, and they will give you what I call their "espoused" theory of action. But observe these same people's behavior, and you will quickly see that this espoused theory has very little to do with how they actually behave. For example, the professionals on the case team said they believed in continuous improvement, and yet they consistently acted in ways that made improvement impossible.

When you observe people's behavior and try to come up with rules that would make sense of it, you discover a very different theory of action—what I call the individual's "theory-in-use." Put simply, people consistently act inconsistently, unaware of the contradiction between their espoused theory and their theory-in-use, between the way they think they are acting and the way they really act.

What's more, most theories-in-use rest on the same set of governing values. There seems to be a universal human tendency to design one's actions consistently, according to four basic values:

1. To remain in unilateral control.
2. To maximize "winning" and minimize "losing."
3. To suppress negative feelings.
4. To be as "rational" as possible—by which people mean defining clear objectives and evaluating their behavior in terms of whether or not they have achieved them.

The purpose of all these values is to avoid embarrassment or threat, feeling vulnerable or incompetent. In this respect, the master program that most people use is profoundly defensive. Defensive reasoning encourages individuals to keep private the premises, inferences, and conclusions that shape their behavior and to avoid testing them in a truly independent, objective fashion.

Because the attributions that go into defensive reasoning are never really tested, it is a closed loop, remarkably impervious to conflicting points of view. The inevitable response to the observation that somebody is reasoning defensively is yet more defensive reasoning. With the case team, for example, whenever anyone pointed out the professionals' defensive behavior to them, their initial reaction was to look for the cause in somebody else—clients who were so sensitive that they would have been alienated if the consultants had criticized them or a manager so weak that he couldn't have taken it had the consultants raised their concerns with him. In other words, the case team members once again denied their own responsibility by externalizing the problem and putting it on someone else.

In such situations, the simple act of encouraging more open inquiry is often attacked by others as "intimidating." Those who do the attacking deal with their feelings about possibly being wrong by blaming the more open individual for arousing these feelings and upsetting them.

Needless to say, such a master program inevitably short-circuits learning. And for a number of reasons unique to their psychology, well-educated professionals are especially susceptible to this.

Nearly all the consultants I have studied have stellar academic records. Ironically, their very success at education helps explain the problems they have with learning. Before they enter the world of work, their lives are primarily full of successes, so they have rarely experienced the embarrassment and sense of threat that comes with failure. As a result, their defensive reasoning has rarely been activated. People who rarely experience failure, however, end up not knowing how to deal with it effectively. And this serves to reinforce the normal human tendency to reason defensively.

In a survey of several hundred young consultants at the organizations I have been studying, these professionals describe themselves as driven internally by an unrealistically high ideal of performance: "Pressure on the job is self-imposed." "I must not only do a good job; I must also be the best." "People around here are very bright and hardworking; they are highly motivated to do an outstanding job." "Most of us want not only to succeed but also to do so at maximum speed."

These consultants are always comparing themselves with the best around them and constantly trying to better their own performance. And yet they do not appreciate being required to compete openly with each other. They feel it is somehow inhuman. They prefer to be the individual contributor—what might be termed a "productive loner."

Behind this high aspiration for success is an equally high fear of failure and a propensity to feel shame and guilt when they do fail to meet their high standards. "You must avoid mistakes," said one. "I hate making them. Many of us fear failure, whether we admit it or not."

To the extent that these consultants have experienced success in their lives, they have not had to be concerned about failure and the attendant feelings of shame and guilt. But to exactly the same extent they also have never developed the tolerance for feelings of failure or the skills to deal with these feelings. This in turn has led them not only to fear failure but also to fear the fear of failure itself. For they know that they will not cope with it superlatively—their usual level of aspiration.

The consultants use two intriguing metaphors to describe this phenomenon. They talk about the "doom loop" and "doom zoom." Often, consultants will perform well on the case team, but, because they don't do the jobs perfectly or receive accolades from their managers, they go into a doom loop of despair. And they don't ease into the doom loop, they zoom into it.

As a result, many professionals have extremely "brittle" personalities. When suddenly faced with a situation they cannot immediately handle, they tend to fall apart. They cover up their distress in front of the client. They talk about it constantly with their fellow case team members. Interestingly, these conversations commonly take the form of bad-mouthing clients.

Such brittleness leads to an inappropriately high sense of despondency or even despair when people don't achieve the high levels of performance they aspire to. Such despondency is rarely psychologically devastating, but, when combined with defensive reasoning, it can result in a formidable predisposition against learning.

There is no better example of how this brittleness can disrupt an organization than performance evaluations. Because it represents the one moment when a professional must measure his or her own behavior against some formal standard, a performance evaluation is almost tailor-made to push a professional into the doom loop. Indeed, a poor evaluation can reverberate far beyond the particular individual involved to spark defensive reasoning throughout an entire organization.

At one consulting company, management established a new performance-evaluation process that was designed to make evaluations both more objective and more useful to those being evaluated. The consultants participated in the design of the new system and, in general, were enthusiastic because it corresponded to their espoused values of objectivity and fairness. A brief two years into the new process, however, it had become the object of dissatisfaction. The catalyst for this about-face was the first unsatisfactory rating.

Senior managers had identified six consultants whose performance they considered below standard. In keeping with the new evaluation process, they did all they could to communicate their concerns to the six and to help them improve. Managers met with each individual separately for as long and as often as the professional requested to explain the reasons behind the rating and to discuss what needed to be done to improve—but to no avail. Performance continued at the same low level and, eventually, the six were let go.

When word of the dismissal spread through the company, people responded with confusion and anxiety. After about a dozen consultants angrily complained to management, the CEO held two lengthy meetings where employees could air their concerns.

At the meetings, the professionals made a variety of claims. Some said the performance-evaluation process was unfair because judgments were subjective and biased and the criteria for minimum performance unclear. Others suspected that the real cause for the dismissals was economic and that the performance-evaluation procedure was just a fig leaf to hide the fact that the company was in trouble. Still others argued that the evaluation process was antilearning. If the company were truly a learning organization, as it claimed, then people performing below the minimum standard should be taught how to reach it. As one professional put it: "We were told that the company did not have an up-or-out policy. Up-or-out is inconsistent with learning. You misled us."

The CEO tried to explain the logic behind management's decision by grounding it in the facts of the case and by asking the professionals for any evidence that might contradict these facts.

Is there subjectivity and bias in the evaluation process? Yes, responded the CEO, but "we strive hard to reduce them. We are constantly trying to improve the process. If you have any ideas, please tell us. If you know of someone treated unfairly, please bring it up. If any of you feel that you have been treated unfairly, let's discuss it now or, if you wish, privately."

Is the level of minimum competence too vague? "We are working to define minimum competence more clearly," he answered. "In the case of the six, however, their performance was so poor that it wasn't difficult to reach a decision." Most of the six had received timely feedback about their problems. And in the two cases where people had not, the reason was that they had never taken the responsibility to seek out evaluations—and, indeed, had actively avoided them. "If you have any data to the contrary," the CEO added, "let's talk about it."

Were the six asked to leave for economic reasons? No, said the CEO. "We have more work than we can do, and letting professionals go is extremely costly for us. Do any of you have any information to the contrary?"

As to the company being antilearning, in fact, the entire evaluation process was designed to encourage learning. When a professional is performing below the minimum level, the CEO explained, "we jointly design remedial experiences with the individual. Then we look for signs of improvement. In these cases, either the professionals were reluctant to take on such assignments or they repeatedly failed when they did. Again, if you have information or evidence to the contrary, I'd like to hear about it."

The CEO concluded: "It's regrettable, but sometimes we make mistakes and hire the wrong people. If individuals don't produce and repeatedly prove themselves unable to improve, we don't know what else to do except dismiss them. It's just not fair to keep poorly performing individuals in the company. They earn an unfair share of the financial rewards."

Instead of responding with data of their own, the professionals simply repeated their accusations but in ways that consistently contradicted their claims. They said that a genuinely fair evaluation process would contain clear and documentable data about performance—but they were unable to provide firsthand examples of the unfairness that they implied colored the evaluation of the six dismissed employees. They argued that people shouldn't be judged by inferences unconnected to their actual performance—but they judged management in precisely this way. They insisted that management define clear, objective, and unambiguous performance standards—but they argued that any humane system would take into account that the performance of a professional cannot be precisely measured. Finally, they presented themselves as champions of learning—but they never proposed any criteria for assessing whether an individual might be unable to learn.

In short, the professionals seemed to hold management to a different level of performance than they held themselves. In their conversation at the meetings, they used many of the features of ineffective evaluation that they condemned—the absence of concrete data, for example, and the dependence on a circular logic of "heads we win, tails you lose." It is as if they were saying, "Here are the features of a fair performance-evaluation system. You should abide by them. But we don't have to when we are evaluating you."

Indeed, if we were to explain the professionals' behavior by articulating rules that would have to be in their heads in order for them to act the way they did, the rules would look something like this:

1. When criticizing the company, state your criticism in ways that you believe are valid—but also in ways that prevent others from deciding for themselves whether your claim to validity is correct.
2. When asked to illustrate your criticisms, don't include any data that others could use to decide for themselves whether the illustrations are valid.
3. State your conclusions in ways that disguise their logical implications. If others point out those implications to you, deny them.

Of course, when such rules were described to the professionals, they found them abhorrent. It was inconceivable that these rules might explain their actions. And yet, in defending themselves against this observation, they almost always inadvertently confirmed the rules.

Learning How to Reason Productively

If defensive reasoning is as widespread as I believe, then focusing on an individual's attitudes or commitment is never enough to produce real change. And as the previous example illustrates, neither is creating new organizational structures or systems. The problem is that, even when people are genuinely committed to improving their performance and management has changed its structures in order to encourage the "right" kind of behavior, people still remain locked in defensive reasoning. Either they remain unaware of this fact, or, if they do become aware of it, they blame others.

There is, however, reason to believe that organizations can break out of this vicious circle. Despite the strength of defensive reasoning, people genuinely strive to produce what they intend. They value acting competently. Their self-esteem is intimately tied up with behaving consistently and performing effectively. Companies can use these universal human tendencies to teach people how to reason in a new way—in effect, to change the master programs in their heads and thus reshape their behavior.

People can be taught how to recognize the reasoning they use when they design and implement their actions. They can begin to identify the inconsistencies between their espoused and actual theories of action. They can face up to the fact that they unconsciously design and implement actions that they do not intend. Finally, people can learn how to identify what individuals and groups do to create organizational defenses and how these defenses contribute to an organization's problems.

Once companies embark on this learning process, they will discover that the kind of reasoning necessary to reduce and overcome organizational defenses is the same kind of "tough reasoning" that underlies the effective use of ideas in strategy, finance, marketing, manufacturing, and other management disciplines. Any sophisticated strategic analysis, for example, depends on collecting valid data, analyzing it carefully, and constantly testing the inferences drawn from the data. The toughest tests are reserved for the conclusions. Good strategies make sure that their conclusions can withstand all kinds of critical questioning.

So, too, with productive reasoning about human behavior. The standard of analysis is just as high. Human resource programs no longer need to be based on "soft" reasoning but should be as analytical and as data-driven as any other management discipline.

Of course, that is not the kind of reasoning the consultants used when they encountered problems that were embarrassing or threatening. The data they collected was hardly objective. The inferences they made rarely became explicit. The conclusions they reached were largely self-serving, impossible for others to test, and as a result, "self-sealing," impervious to change.

How can an organization begin to turn this situation around, to teach its members how to reason productively? The first step is for managers at the top to examine critically and change their own theories-in-use. Until senior managers become aware of how they reason defensively and the counterproductive consequences that result, there will be little real progress. Any change activity is likely to be just a fad.

Change has to start at the top, because otherwise defensive senior managers are likely to dis-

own any transformation in reasoning patterns coming from below. If professionals or middle managers begin to change the way they reason and act, such changes are likely to appear strange—if not actually dangerous—to those at the top. The result is an unstable situation where senior managers still believe that it is a sign of caring and sensitivity to bypass and cover up difficult issues, while their subordinates see the very same actions as defensive.

The key to any educational experience designed to teach senior managers how to reason productively is to connect the program to real business problems. The best demonstration of the usefulness of productive reasoning is for busy managers to see how it can make a direct difference in their own performance and in that of the organization. This will not happen overnight. Managers need plenty of opportunity to practice the new skills. But once they grasp the powerful impact that productive reasoning can have on actual performance, they will have a strong incentive to reason productively not just in a training session but in all their work relationships.

One simple approach I have used to get this process started is to have participants produce a kind of rudimentary case study. The subject is a real business problem that the manager either wants to deal with or has tried unsuccessfully to address in the past. Writing the actual case usually takes less than an hour. But then the case becomes the focal point of an extended analysis.

For example, a CEO at a large organizational-development consulting company was preoccupied with the problems caused by the intense competition among the various business functions represented by his four direct reports. Not only was he tired of having the problems dumped in his lap, but he was also worried about the impact the interfunctional conflicts were having on the organization's flexibility. He had even calculated that the money being spent to iron out disagreements amounted to hundreds of thousands of dollars every year. And the more fights there were, the more defensive people became, which only increased the costs to the organization.

In a paragraph or so, the CEO described a meeting he intended to have with his direct reports to address the problem. Next, he divided the paper in half, and on the right-hand side of the page, he wrote a scenario for the meeting— much like the script for a movie or play— describing what he would say and how his subordinates would likely respond. On the left-hand side of the page, he wrote down any thoughts and feelings that he would be likely to have during the meeting but that he wouldn't express for fear they would derail the discussion.

But instead of holding the meeting, the CEO analyzed this scenario *with* his direct reports. The case became the catalyst for a discussion in which the the CEO learned several things about the way he acted with his management team.

He discovered that his four direct reports often perceived his conversations as counterproductive. In the guise of being "diplomatic," he would pretend that a consensus about the problem existed, when in fact none existed. The unintended result: instead of feeling reassured, his subordinates felt wary and tried to figure out "what is he *really* getting at."

The CEO also realized that the way he dealt with the competitiveness among department heads was completely contradictory. On the one hand, he kept urging them to "think of the organization as a whole." On the other, he kept calling for actions—department budget cuts, for example—that placed them directly in competition with each other.

Finally, the CEO discovered that many of the tacit evaluations and attributions he had listed turned out to be wrong. Since he had never expressed these assumptions, he had never found out just how wrong they were. What's more, he learned that much of what he thought he was hiding came through to his subordinates anyway—but with the added message that the boss was covering up.

The CEO's colleagues also learned about their own ineffective behavior. They learned by examining their own behavior as they tried to help the CEO analyze his case. They also learned by writing and analyzing cases of their own. They began to see that they, too, tended to bypass and cover up the real issues and that the CEO was often aware of it but did not say so. They, too, made inaccurate attributions and evaluations that they did not express. Moreover, the belief that they had to hide important ideas and feelings from the CEO and from each other in order not to upset anyone turned out to be mistaken. In the context of the case discussions, the entire senior management team was quite willing to discuss what had always been undiscussable.

In effect, the case study exercise legitimizes talking about issues that people have never been able to address before. Such a discussion can be emotional—even painful. But for managers with the courage to persist, the payoff is great: management teams and entire organizations work more openly and more effectively and have greater options for behaving flexibly and adapting to particular situations.

When senior managers are trained in new reasoning skills, they can have a big impact on the performance of the entire organization— even when other employees are still reasoning defensively. The CEO who led the meetings on the performance-evaluation procedure was able to defuse dissatisfaction because he didn't respond to professionals' criticisms in kind but, instead, gave a clear presentation of relevant data. Indeed, most participants took the CEO's behavior to be a sign that the company really acted on the values of participation and employee involvement that it espoused.

Of course, the ideal is for all the members of an organization to learn how to reason productively. This has happened at the company where the case team meeting took place. Consultants and their managers are now able to confront some of the most difficult issues of the consultant-client relationship. To get a sense of the difference productive reasoning can make, imagine how the original conversation between the manager and case team might have gone had everyone engaged in effective reasoning. (The following dialogue is based on actual sessions I have attended with other case teams at the same company since the training has been completed.)

First, the consultants would have demonstrated their commitment to continuous improvement by being willing to examine their own role in the difficulties that arose during the consulting project. No doubt they would have identified their managers and the clients as part of the problem, but they would have gone on to admit that they had contributed to it as well. More important, they would have agreed with the manager that as they explored the various roles of clients, managers, and professionals, they would make sure to test any evaluations or attributions they might make against the data. Each individual would have encouraged the others to question his or her reasoning. Indeed, they would have insisted on it. And in turn, everyone would have understood that act of questioning not as a sign of mistrust or an invasion of privacy but as a valuable opportunity for learning.

The conversation about the manager's unwillingness to say no might look something like this:

Professional #1: "One of the biggest problems I had with the way you managed this case was that you seemed to be unable to say no when either the client or your superior made unfair demands." (Gives an example.)
Professional #2: "I have another example to add. (Describes a second example.) But I'd also like to say that we never really told you how we felt about this. Behind your back we were bad-mouthing you—you know, 'he's being such a wimp'—but we never came right out and said it."

Manager: "It certainly would have been helpful if you had said something. Was there anything I said or did that gave you the idea that you had better not raise this with me?"
Professional #3: "Not really. I think we didn't want to sound like we were whining."
Manager: "Well, I certainly don't think you sound like you're whining. But two thoughts come to mind. If I understand you correctly, you *were* complaining, but the complaining about me and my inability to say no was covered up. Second, if we had discussed this, I might have gotten the data I needed to be able to say no."

Notice that, when the second professional describes how the consultants had covered up their complaints, the manager doesn't criticize her. Rather, he rewards her for being open by responding in kind. He focuses on the ways that he, too, may have contributed to the coverup. Reflecting undefensively about his own role in the problem then makes it possible for the professionals to talk about their fears of appearing to be whining. The manager then agrees with the professionals that they shouldn't become complainers. At the same time, he points out the counterproductive consequences of covering up their complaints.

Another unresolved issue in the case team meeting concerned the supposed arrogance of the clients. A more productive conversation about that problem might go like this:

Manager: "You said that the clients were arrogant and uncooperative. What did they say and do?"
Professional #1: "One asked me if I had ever met a payroll. Another asked how long I've been out of school."
Professional #2: "One even asked me how old I was!"
Professional #3: "That's nothing. The worst

is when they say that all we do is interview people, write a report based on what they tell us, and then collect our fees."

Manager: "The fact that we tend to be so young is a real problem for many of our clients. They get very defensive about it. But I'd like to explore whether there is a way for them to freely express their views without our getting defensive.

"What troubled me about your original responses was that you assumed you were right in calling the clients stupid. One thing I've noticed about consultants—in this company and others—is that we tend to defend ourselves by bad-mouthing the client."

Professional #1: "Right. After all, if they are genuinely stupid, then it's obviously not our fault that they aren't getting it!"

Professional #2: "Of course, that stance is antilearning and overprotective. By assuming that they can't learn, we absolve ourselves from having to."

Professional #3: "And the more we all go along with the bad-mouthing, the more we reinforce each other's defensiveness."

Manager: "So what's the alternative? How can we encourage our clients to express their defensiveness and at the same time constructively build on it?"

Professional #1: "We all know that the real issue isn't our age; it's whether or not we are able to add value to the client's organization. They should judge us by what we produce. And if we aren't adding value, they should get rid of us—no matter how young or old we happen to be."

Manager: "Perhaps that is exactly what we should tell them."

In both these examples, the consultants and their manager are doing real work. They are learning about their own group dynamics and addressing some generic problems in client-consultant relationships. The insights they gain will allow them to act more effectively in the future—both as individuals and as a team. They are not just solving problems but developing a far deeper and more textured understanding of their role as members of the organization. They are laying the groundwork for continuous improvement that is truly continuous. They are learning how to learn.

READING 32
ORGANIZATIONAL LEARNING—THE KEY TO MANAGEMENT INNOVATION

Ray Stata

For more than 15 years, Analog Devices grew consistently at a rate of about 25 percent per year. Then for the first time, between 1982 and 1987, we missed our five-year goals—and by a country mile. True enough, like other semiconductor companies we were affected by the malaise in the U.S. electronics industry and by the strong dollar. But the external environment was only part of the problem: something was also wrong internally, and it had to be fixed.

But what was the problem? We had the largest share of our niche market in high-performance linear integrated circuits. We had the best designers and technologists in our business. We had excellent relations with a highly motivated workforce. We were not guilty of underinvestment, nor of managing for short-term profits. The only conclusion was that there was something *about* the way we were managing the company that was not good enough. So I set about to understand what was wrong and how to make it better.

In the 1980s, our plight was not uncommon in corporate America. Companies that for decades enjoyed world leadership in their markets were being brought to their knees. Of course, there are many purported reasons for the loss of U.S. competitiveness. The high cost of capital, an overvalued dollar, a deteriorating education system, overconsumption at the expense of investment, government regulations, misplaced emphasis on military as opposed to economic security, and undisciplined government spending

certainly all contributed to this decline. However, many who have studied the situation believe that the root of the problem is our declining rate of innovation. If this is true, then the challenge lies in better understanding innovation and in determining how to do more of it.

Usually we think of innovation in terms of technologies that give rise to a new class of products or to improvements in the design and manufacture of existing products. But at Analog Devices, and many other U.S. companies, product and process innovation are not the primary bottleneck to progress. The bottleneck is management innovation.

Peter Drucker points out that the rise to industrial dominance of Great Britain, Germany, and the United States was based on technological innovation in engines, electricity, chemistry, aviation, agriculture, optics, and so forth. [1] Japan is the first nation whose rise to industrial power was clearly based on management innovation, not technological innovation in the traditional sense.

Michael Cusumano reinforces this point in analyzing Japan's conquest of the automobile industry. [2] In the early years of the Japanese industry, small Japanese automakers, especially Toyota, beat out their giant U.S. competitors not with product innovation, superior manufacturing technology, or greater capital investment per employee. They did it with management innovations that turned their presumed disadvantage of lower production volume and smaller lot sizes into an advantage: shorter manufacturing cycles, lower inventories, and (eventually) higher quality and lower cost.

Certainly management innovation alone is not enough. As Abernathy and Utterback point

Source: Reprinted from "Organizational Learning—The Key to Management Innovation," by Ray Stata, *Sloan Management Review,* Spring 1989, pp. 63–74, by permission of publisher. Copyright © 1989 by the Sloan Management Review Association. All rights reserved.

out, the optimum blend of product, process, and (I would add) management innovation depends on the circumstances in a particular industry. [3] But I would argue that where many U.S. firms lag most today is in the *management innovation* required to take fullest advantage of their *technology leadership.*

Until very recently management innovation received little serious consideration either from corporations or academic researchers, especially in comparison with the resources invested in product and process innovation. The results of this neglect are evident in the competitive crises facing U.S. industries.

Management innovation, like product and process innovation, depends on new technology. New technology for management, as for engineering, comes in the form of new knowledge, tools, and methods. In my quest to improve the performance of Analog Devices, I began to search for new technologies and ideas that would change, if not revolutionize, the way we were managing our company.

Around that time I had the good fortune to meet MIT's Jay Forrester and Peter Senge and learn of their work in applying system dynamics to the analysis and design of complex social systems. [4] For 30 years Professor Forrester has pioneered the use of feedback theory and systems analysis to examine the behavior of systems not only in management but also in politics, economics, medicine, and the environment. He has created a whole new field of knowledge that is only now finding its way into management practice.

Peter Senge invited me to join eight other organizational leaders in what was called the "New Management Style Project." [5] We have met on a semiannual basis over the past four years, and this collaboration has proven to be fruitful for all of us, practitioners and academics alike. As I shall point out later, this project can serve as a prototype for industry/university partnerships, which are needed to accelerate management innovation.

Organizational Learning

The initial focus of the New Management Style group was on using system dynamics to improve our thinking about complex organizations. But as time progressed, we began to explore systems thinking in a broader context. About this time Arie deGeus, director of group planning for Shell International, joined the group because of his interest in system dynamics as a tool to accelerate organizational learning. As we listened to deGeus's ideas and his experiences at Shell, organizational learning emerged as a fundamental concept; it not only helped us to better appreciate the power of system dynamics but also to integrate a broader range of management tools and methods to facilitate organizational change and improvement.

In an even broader context, as I come to understand this concept more fully, I see organizational learning as the principal process by which management innovation occurs. *In fact, I would argue that the rate at which individuals and organizations learn may become the only sustainable competitive advantage, especially in knowledge-intensive industries.*

What is organizational learning, and how does it differ from individual learning? We tend to think of learning as a process by which individuals gain new knowledge and insights and thereby modify their behavior and actions. Similarly, organizational learning entails new insights and modified behavior. But it differs from individual learning in several respects. First, organizational learning occurs through shared insights, knowledge, and mental models. Thus organizations can learn only as fast as the slowest link learns. Change is blocked unless all of the major decision makers learn together, come to share beliefs and goals, and are committed to take the actions necessary for change. Second, learning builds on past knowledge and experience—that is, on memory. Organizational memory depends on institutional mechanisms (e.g., policies, strategies, and explicit models) used to retain knowledge. Of course, organizations also depend on the memory of individuals. But relying exclusively on individuals risks losing hard-won lessons and experiences as people migrate from one job to another.

The challenge, then, is to discover new management tools and methods to accelerate organizational learning, build consensus for change, and facilitate the change process. Let me share some of the specifics of how organizational learning is serving as an umbrella to unify my approach to systems thinking, planning, quality improvement, organizational behavior, and information systems.

Systems Thinking

Systems thinking, and in particular system dynamics, is a powerful tool to facilitate both individual and organizational learning. One of the early lessons learned from system dynamics is that organizations are like giant networks of interconnected nodes. Changes intended to improve performance in one part of the organization can affect other parts of the organization with surprising, often negative consequences. That is, decisions based solely on information at the local level, which is often the only information available, can be counterproductive to the system as a whole. The undesirable buildup of inventory in distribution channels is a well-known example of what happens when local managers do not understand the conditions of the total environment in which they are operating.

Human cognitive capabilities limit our ability to understand what is actually going on in complex organizations. In fact, recent experimental studies by John Sterman at MIT show that decision makers consistently misjudge complex systems with multiple feedback processes and delays. [6] Fortunately, owing to the work of Forrester and others in system dynamics, tools to analyze and design complex electronic and mechanical systems have been adapted to perform the same functions in complex organization systems. Using these tools and desktop computers, we can simulate organizational behavior and show how the structure and policies of companies may generate undesirable performance that is often blamed on the external environment. We can also demonstrate how decisions that improve performance in the short term sometimes only make it worse in the long term.

Forrester and Senge make the point that the role of organizational leaders is undergoing dramatic change. Historically, leaders were referred to as "captains of the ship" to denote their role in operating the vessel entrusted to their care. But future leaders must be both designers and operators. Their principal contribution will be to shape the design of the organization structure and policies so as to best fulfill the corporate mission. Expertise in organization design will be a critical skill—a skill that will require considerable technical knowledge about how to analyze, modify, and simulate the behavior of complex human systems.

Let us take one of the most elementary concepts of feedback theory as applied to organizational design. That is, when you model organizational behavior, one basic characterization of a system is the delay time between cause and effect—for example, between when an order is received and when it is shipped, when you start manufacturing a product and when you finish, when you start to design a new product and when you introduce it to the market, or when you receive a request for information and when you respond. Using system dynamics to simulate organizational behavior, you find that often one of the highest leverage points for improving performance is the minimization of these system delays. In designing the organization, the leader should focus on optimizing the response time to changes in the external environment, with minimum overshoot and undershoot of output from the desired goals (see Figure 1).

You might argue that this is an obvious conclusion and that you don't need system dynamics

Figure 1

Systems principles: Delays and instabilities

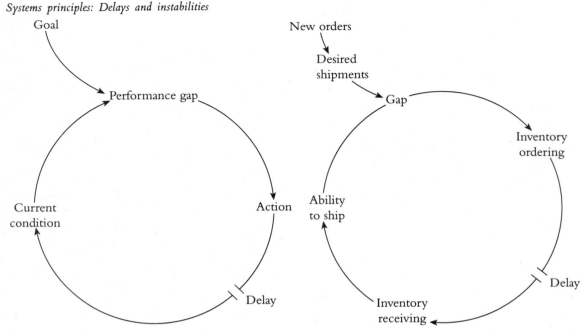

1. Basic Balancing Process with Delay

Balancing or adjustment processes are a universal feature of complex human and social systems. The human body dilates and expands capillaries, opens and closes skin pores, sweats and shivers to maintain body temperature in the face of changing environmental temperatures. Corporations likewise respond to gaps between desired and actual levels of performance.

The purpose of internal adjustment processes is to maintain desired balances in the face of environmental changes. However, adjustment mechanisms can also become the source of unintended and unwanted instabilities, especially when there are long delays between action and consequence (see "1" above). In the presence of delays, an action that persists until a performance gap is eliminated will result in overshoot and oscillation; thus a bather gets scalded by overadjusting a shower that responds slowly to the faucet setting.

2. Balancing Process with Delay in Production Distribution System

The principle of delays and instabilities has many applications in corporate systems. For years, executives and master's students in MIT's introductory System Dynamics courses have done a product-distribution simulation, affectionately known as the "Beer Game." In the simulation, retailers and wholesalers, distributors, and factories interact through ordering and shipping cases of beer to meet changing patterns of customer demand. In the process, the players unintentionally generate uncontrolled cycles in production, inventories, and orders because they fail to take into account the delays that intervene between inventory ordering and inventory receiving (see "2" above).

There are two basic design improvements to reduce instabilities created by delays in adjustment processes: modulate the decision-makers actions or shorten the delays. In the beer game, about 10 percent of the teams achieve stable outputs because they don't overreact in ordering inventory. However, the resulting product-distribution system is still sluggish in response to large changes in customer demands. In real industrial systems, where information systems and means of production and distribution can be redesigned, the leverage often lies in shortening delay times so that the system can be both stable and highly responsive.

to prove it. What is *not* obvious is the magnitude of loss from excessive inventories, excessive lead time, and poor customer service that result from these system delays. Only when the loss is quantified does its critical importance strike home. To put it another way, if these conclusions are so obvious, then why did it take U.S. manufacturers so long to grasp the critical importance of manufacturing cycle time and to focus on reducing time to market? It certainly was not obvious to me five years ago that excessive manufacturing cycle time was the principal cause for our poor delivery performance. And even now that it is obvious, there is considerable debate at Analog Devices about when you reach the point of diminishing returns in driving down cycle time as a means of improving on-time delivery, product quality, and cost.

Another important use of system dynamics is as a training tool. Once we have decided the correct policy on cycle time, for example, how do we help the organization learn how that policy works best and why? By explicitly revealing our mental model of how we believe the organization works or should work—that is, how the "nodes" in the organization are connected and what factors govern their interaction—we create a precise language with which to share our understanding. By comparing our model with others, we provide a mechanism not only to converge on a shared model but also to communicate to younger, less experienced managers the organization's stored experience and knowledge. System dynamics has the same teaching potential in management schools as it does in industry. In fact, MIT recently introduced system dynamics as a teaching tool to augment the case study method. Students use a model developed by John Sterman to learn how flawed business policies led to the dramatic rise and fall of People Express Airlines.

Planning as Learning

My approach to strategic planning for our most recent five-year plan, 1988 to 1992, was strongly influenced by discussions with Arie deGeus in the New Management Style Project. In a recent article, deGeus suggested that the benefits accruing from planning are not just the objectives and strategies that emerge, but the learning that occurs during the planning process. [7] He contends that one form of organizational learning results from understanding the changes occurring in the external environment and then adapting beliefs and behavior to be compatible with those changes. If learning is a goal, then the way you structure the planning process and who you involve in it can make an important difference.

Analog Devices is a highly decentralized company; in the past, top management set the broad corporate objectives and assumptions, but most of the detailed strategic planning was carried out in the divisions. But this time, in order to encourage organizational learning, we formed 15 corporatewide product, market, and technology task forces that drew together 150 professionals from throughout the company. We wanted to better understand the opportunities we faced as a corporation and how we needed to change to fully exploit those opportunities. The result of 12 months of deliberations was a delineation of nine imperatives for change, as well as specific recommendations for how to bring about those changes. An even more important result was that a broad cross-section of our top professionals understood why some basic beliefs and assumptions that had served us well in the past needed modification.

For example, one of our strongest beliefs was that the best way to organize our resources was to use relatively small, autonomous divisions. However, as we worked our way through the planning process, it became clear to all of us that our almost fanatical commitment to decentralization was impeding progress. We concluded that we needed to coordinate technology development across divisions and to centralize certain aspects of manufacturing, especially wafer fabrication. We also had to better coordinate product planning to capitalize on the combined strength of our diverse product and technology base in penetrating new markets. We had to learn to present ourselves as a single vendor to our key accounts instead of as a collection of autonomous divisions, often competing with each other. We all realized that in accepting these conclusions we had unleashed powerful forces that would change the culture, structure, and behavior of the company in ways not yet foreseen.

Another strong belief that melted under scrutiny was that we had to choose between a proprietary, differentiated product strategy and a low-cost producer strategy. This either/or choice has proven to be a false and misleading alternative not only for Analog Devices but for many other U.S. companies, as well. We had always taken pride in technology leadership and focused on opportunities where customers would pay high margins for performance, usually in applications with modest volume requirements. Now some of these applications were developing high-volume potential. Moreover, applications for our products and technology were emerging in computer peripherals, communications networks, and even consumer products like digital audio, and customers were demanding low prices in return for high volume.

We decided that our long-term strategy should be to serve certain selected, high-volume applications where our technology provides unique benefits, lest competitors capture these markets, learn our technology, and eventually use a lower cost structure to penetrate our traditional lower-volume industrial and military markets. This strategy change was drastic. Only through a process of open deliberation, during which the consequences of the alternatives became very clear, did the organization "buy into" this new direction.

Once a decision was made, the organization enthusiastically turned its attention to learning what it would take to win in certain selected high-volume applications that we were well aware of but had long ignored. In less than a year we were selling digital-to-analog converters to compact audio disk player manufacturers in

Japan and Korea, and we had a research effort under way to develop a monolithic analog-to-digital converter for high-definition television.

We now have confidence that we can develop high-volume manufacturing capability to serve these new markets profitably, and we are busy putting these resources in place. We also believe we can and must be both product innovators and lower-cost producers. This change in beliefs has greatly expanded our vision of opportunity and of the types of customers and markets we shall serve in the future.

These examples illustrate just a few of the dramatic changes taking place at Analog Devices. I believe our approach to planning as a learning process has greatly facilitated our ability to forge a consensus for change among those who must make it happen. It has also helped reduce the obstacles and resistance to change—that is, outdated beliefs and assumptions created by past success.

Quality Improvement: A Methodology for Change

Even when there is a strong consensus for change, achieving it is easier said than done. For example, another imperative reinforced by the planning process at Analog Devices was the need to improve customer service, product quality, and yields. Of course, this concern was not new. Since the early 1980s, as our customers have gotten a taste of what Japanese electronic companies could deliver, and as just-in-time (JIT) programs have become more prevalent, pressure has mounted to improve performance. What was new was the realization of just how much we had to improve to meet our customers' expectations, and how little time we had to do it. On-time delivery of products that work has become the major factor in vendor selection and performance evaluation. We can no longer win by the sheer force of being first to market with the latest products and technology.

Quality improvement, or total quality control

as it is often called, is a management methodology for achieving improvement and change. [8] In 1983 we began to introduce quality improvement methods at Analog Devices. We decided to focus our attention on product quality, on-time delivery, lead time, yields, and new-product time to market. We went to seminars, read books, gave speeches, and introduced information systems to measure our performance. But three years into the mission we were not getting very far very fast. I had an uneasy feeling that I did not know what I was supposed to be doing to lead this effort and that there were a lot of other dedicated managers in the same boat.

We knew all about error detection and correction and about doing it right the first time. But we did not have any notion of what rate of improvement was satisfactory or what we could do to accelerate the improvement process. Considering that many Japanese companies had been working the quality improvement game for more than 20 years and that they are not standing still even now, we had a justifiable sense of discomfort.

Because of our "lean and mean" attitude toward staff functions, we had resisted the addition of a quality improvement staff. Line managers were expected to learn on their own. But learn from where, learn from whom? Reading books and going to seminars was not enough. So we finally broke down and recruited a quality improvement professional to teach us how to tap the mainstream of experience and knowledge that is rapidly accumulating in this field and to help our managers become more expert practitioners. Only then did the organization begin to see real progress. One of the early lessons I learned from our quality guru was that there is a rational basis on which to set standards for rates of improvement. From his consulting experience, our director of quality improvement had documented case histories where quality improvement methodology had worked. What these cases showed was that, while the rate of improvement varies from case to case, the rate in each case is remarkably consistent over an extended time period. Figure 2 shows three actual businesses' learning rates.

FIGURE 2A

Examples of quality improvement versus time product defect rate

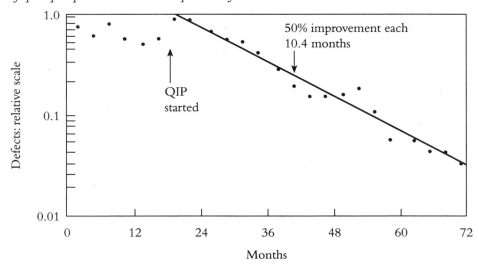

FIGURE 2B

Average defects per unit

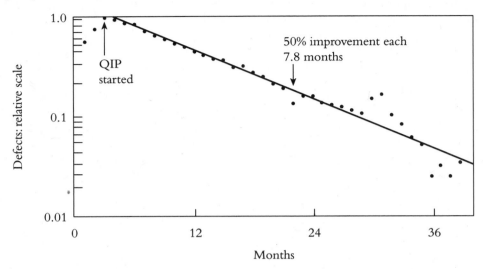

Note that in the first case, performance improved by 50 percent every 10.4 months, in the second case every 7.8 months, and in the third case every 3.6 months. He called this characteristic slope of improvement the *half-life.*

An analysis of a larger number of case studies indicated that the half life for improvement fell within a relatively narrow range, usually 6 to 12 months, across a wide range of applications. [9] The reason for this phenomenon is clear enough when you understand the method by which quality improvement is achieved.

The method is deceptively simple. For example, as I mentioned, one of our goals was to reduce the percentage of orders shipped late. To do this we assembled a team from various organizations involved with customer service to analyze the causes of lateness. For each late shipment we determined the cause, and then we plotted their distribution. We found that a relatively small number of causes was responsible for 50 percent of the problems.

Next we assembled problem-solving teams to attack these major causes of lateness. When the cycle was completed, we repeated the process by prioritizing the causes for 50 percent of the remaining problems and then eliminating those causes. This cycle was repeated again and again; each time the most important remaining problems were identified and resources were focused on solving them.

In this example, as in others using this method, the slope of the learning curve is determined by how long it takes to identify and prioritize the causes of the problem and to eliminate those causes. The skills of the people and the level of resources do have an impact, but surprisingly the time required for each cycle of improvement is largely a function of the complexity and bureaucracy of the organization. Or, to put quality improvement in the larger context of this paper, the slope of the characteristic half-life curve is determined by the rate of organizational learning.

Notice that this theory of learning differs

FIGURE 2C

Failure rate improvement

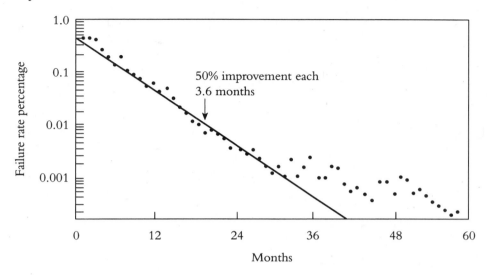

from the Boston Consulting Group (BCG) "experience curve" theory that says learning occurs as a function of cumulative production volume, independent of lapsed time. The quality improvement theory says that learning, properly managed, occurs as a function of time, independent of cumulative volume. How else can we explain the success of the Japanese automobile industry, which learned faster than the U.S. industry with substantially less cumulative volume? If we combine the two ideas, we can say more accurately that the slope of the BCG experience curve is determined by the rate of organizational learning. A steeper experience curve occurring at lower production volume can soon overcome a more shallow experience curve occurring at higher volume.

We know that communication across organizational boundaries is less effective than within organizational boundaries and that many problems accumulate because of poor communication. Quality improvement is a way to create temporary organizational structures, or teams,

that cut horizontally across organizational boundaries and enhance communication and cooperation. It is a way to get people to think about problems and issues objectively and quantitatively instead of subjectively and politically. It is a way to separate the vital few problems from the trivial many—and to focus organizational resources on resolving them. In short, quality improvement is a way to accelerate organizational learning.

Using the half-life concept, at Analog Devices we set very aggressive five-year goals for quality improvement (see Table 1). The results of continuous improvement with 9-to-12-month half-lives over an extended period are awesome. The first reaction of our organization was to recoil from what looked like unrealistic objectives. But we reminded our managers that, if a company really gets its quality improvement act together, there is no fundamental reason why these goals cannot be achieved. There are companies in Japan already operating at these levels on some of these measures.

TABLE 1

Analog devices: Quality improvement program goals

Measurement	1987	Half Life (in months)	1992
External			
On-time delivery	85%	9	>99.8%
Outgoing defect level	500 ppm	9	<10 ppm
Lead time	10 weeks	9	<3 weeks
Internal			
Manufacturing cycle time	15 weeks	9	4–5 weeks
Process defect level	5000 ppm	6	<10 ppm
Yield	20%	9	>50%
Time to market	36 months	24	6 months

Behavioral Influences on the Learning Process

The values and culture of an organization have a significant impact on the learning process and on how effectively a company can adapt and change. In particular, poor communication between people and between organizations can be a major block to learning and quality improvement.

We decided another imperative for change at Analog Devices was to elevate teamwork as a virtue in our culture. We hoped to better balance our historical bias toward divisional autonomy with the recognition that many high-priority changes require interdivisional cooperation. If teamwork was our goal, then other virtues had to be emphasized. We tried to capture the essence of these virtues in the concepts of *openness* and *objectivity*. By openness, we mean a willingness to put all the cards on the table, eliminate hidden agendas, make our motives, feelings, and biases known, and invite other opinions and points of view—thereby engendering trust in relations between people. By objectivity, we mean searching for the best answers

based on reasoned positions and objective criteria, as opposed to political influence and parochial interests. We also mean making judgments based on facts, not on opinions or rumors.

In order to encourage teamwork, openness, and objectivity, we have included these attributes in our performance appraisal process and our criteria for hiring and promotion. Moreover, during performance reviews we solicit feedback from peers and subordinates on these and other competencies. It is only when you tie pay and promotion to these intangible factors that the organization knows you are serious and begins to modify its behavior.

The concept of teamwork has many dimensions. We have found that the best way to introduce knowledge and modify behavior is by working with small teams that have the power and resources to enact change. For example, quality improvement training starts with the division manager and his or her direct reports. The group not only develops a common understanding of new concepts and language, but peer pressure can also help to bring along skeptics who might otherwise block progress. Moreover, the new knowledge can be immediately transformed into action as an integral part of training. This approach, in contrast with sending people individually to centralized training programs, highlights the distinction between individual and organizational learning.

Information Systems: A Help or Hindrance to Learning

Information, of course, is essential to the learning process. It is helpful to think about information *systems* in terms of whether they help or hinder organizational learning. Let me give a few examples to illustrate this point.

Many companies distribute their products through international sales affiliates. Product divisions "sell" their output to sales affiliates at some transfer price. The affiliates, in turn, resell at the highest price the local market will bear. Each group is measured separately on "sales" and "profits," but the company's *real* sales and profits are the combination of the two, with proper accounting eliminations. Analog Devices got started this way because we initially used a network of trading companies and representatives to distribute our products internationally. Over time we replaced these independent agencies with wholly owned sales affiliates, but the original organization and information system remained intact for over 20 years.

The system worked extremely well so long as there were enough profits to satisfy the goals of both organizations. But as competition intensified, more and more time was spent in haggling over the transfer prices between divisions, instead of in figuring out how to retain our market share in a competitive world. The system actually encouraged managers to hide the facts and play games to increase their share of the profit pie. So this year we threw out our old management information system, disbanded transfer prices (except for tax purposes), and went to worldwide product line reporting. Now both affiliates and product divisions operate from the same set of books.

Under the new system, division managers see results on a worldwide basis segmented by territory—with direct visibility, although not complete control, of end-customer sales revenues and distribution costs. By the same token, affiliate managers also see worldwide results with profit and cost visibility segmented by product division.

Under the old system, the only people who saw the worldwide results were the corporate accountants; even then the results were aggregated, rather than segmented by product line. No one in the corporation actually knew the real worldwide sales and profits for any product.

The worldwide product line management system focuses division and affiliate managers on common goals and performance measures that encourage cooperation, rather than conflict. Separate information systems that hide interdependence and give a false sense of control are not realistic. As you might expect, though, our managers ask, "How can we be responsible for what we can't control?" The answer is that we can influence others with information and reason. Control is an illusion—compelling in the short term, but unachievable in the long term. Information systems that hide this dilemma do not get at the problems. Already I can tell you that, since we started using worldwide product line information, a lot of thoughtful discussions have taken place around the company, and some constructive behavior changes have occurred. The new information system is helping managers on both sides to understand their businesses better and to make better decisions.

Another problem with management information systems is that they are strongly biased toward reporting financial information to stockholders and government agencies. Unless quality improvement and other more fundamental performance measures are elevated to the same level of importance as financial measures, when conflicts arise, financial considerations win out. To address this issue, we designed what we call a "division scorecard" that reports only the barest of financial information and places greater emphasis on quality improvement goals. This scorecard is used not only to evaluate division performance but also to structure division bonus plans.

How information is displayed makes an incredible difference. Consider, for example, the format we use to display on-time delivery information (see Figure 3). This simple summary replaces pages of information that used to be circulated to managers. With all these pages, the most crucial information was missing—namely, the half-life trend. Because the information is plotted on a log-linear scale, the trend is readily discernible. For management purposes, displaying all divisions together on a single page has great motivational value. A high level of internal competition exists to generate the fastest learn-

FIGURE 3

Analog Devices on-time customer service performance monthly data (August 1987–July 1988)

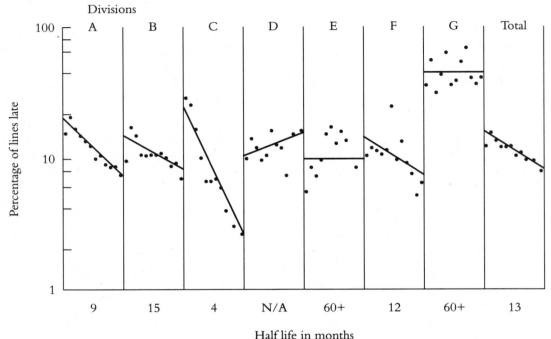

ing curve; it is obvious and embarrassing when you are not performing.

Management information systems transform data into information and then help managers transform information into knowledge and knowledge into action. The challenge is deciding what information and knowledge—in what form—are needed. If we keep organizational learning in mind as a goal of information systems design, then we are more likely to generate the information and knowledge that managers need to take effective action.

We still have only a primitive knowledge of how organizations learn and of how to overcome obstacles to organizational change. Industry and universities need to work together developing tools and concepts that facilitate the process of change.

The Need for Collaborative Research

Among engineers and scientists there is a consensus that collaborative university-industry research promotes innovation and competitiveness. The National Science Foundation's Engineering Research Center (ERC) program, patterned on MIT's interdisciplinary research centers, is an attractive prototype partnership. The criteria for winning ERC grants include cross-disciplinary research, industry participation, new knowledge generation, improvement of the United States competitive position, and linkage to the education system. If we broaden the concepts of innovation and technology to embrace management, then the need for collaborative research in management is no less than it is in engineering. Perhaps it is even greater.

Japanese industry is concentrated in huge, vertically integrated corporations, whereas the United States has a fragmented industry structure, especially in knowledge-intensive industries. In fact, 6 of the world's 10 largest corporations are Japanese; only 3 are American. Because of their size, these mega-corporations can be more self-sufficient in technical and managerial research, education, and training. America's superior research universities could potentially offset this advantage, but only if they work closely with industry.

The New Management Style Project closely follows the ERC model and offers an excellent prototype for the development of collaborative partnerships between business schools and industry. We have learned from this experience that an effective partnership should include the following characteristics.

- *Focus on Critical Management Problems.* Academics and industrialists should work together to identify critical issues of practical significance to practicing managers. They must be issues for which academic research can add to the store of knowledge and tools, codify industry practice into more widely usable and teachable form, or both. In order to do this, universities may need to rethink their research agenda, as well as how faculty contributions and performance are evaluated. It may also require a willingness on the part of universities to set aside their preference for tidy "academic research," and, instead, confront messy, real-life management issues.

- *Develop and Disseminate New Learning Tools and Methods.* One important partnership goal is the broad dissemination of new tools and concepts in both management education and practice, either through academic research or through discovery and documentation of the best industry practices.

- *Test Tools and Methods in Practice.* Some of the companies in the New Management Style Project are testing new concepts by serving as experimental laboratories. The real value of *new* management ideas can be determined only when they are put into practice. Research partnerships provide a unique opportunity to perform controlled experiments in real-world settings.

- *Provide Cross-Organizational Learning.* An important benefit for the industrial partners is the opportunity to share experiences and learn from each other—not superficially, but with the benefit of thoughtful discussion. I certainly learned a great deal from my partners in the New Management Style Project, and so did the academics who heard firsthand about common issues and concerns.

- *Use a Cross-Disciplinary Approach.* Important problems are generally complex; they do not align themselves with a single technology or discipline. Thus a partnership focused on real-world problems should bring together specialists from several related disciplines. MIT has done this very successfully in science and engineering through interdisciplinary research centers. This approach is promising for management schools as well.

- *Provide Cooperative Education Opportunities for Students.* One objective of the partnership is to introduce the most current knowledge and methods into management education, but these partnerships could also provide a unique opportunity for cooperative education.

That is, during the summer months, students could become involved with research projects already being undertaken by the university and the company. These work assignments could lead to a thesis or study project that is part of the academic program. Blending theory and practice in an internship program is perhaps the best approach to professional graduate education.

Conclusions

Five years ago Analog Devices had no conceptual framework for the kind of thinking outlined in this paper and no prayer of making the kind of improvements that are essential to our survival. Now I believe we are on the right track, and we are seeing real progress across a broad front. But the question remains, Are we learning fast enough? Or will one of our competitors, either here or abroad, learn even faster in the future? That unsettling question concerns me most of all.

Management innovation is already an important aspect of industrial competitiveness, and it will surely become even more of a factor in the future. Like any innovation process, management innovation requires new technology and new ideas and then the rapid diffusion of the new knowledge into practice. These results do not come free; they require a major investment of time and resources. We have to ask ourselves, as a company and as a nation, Are we investing enough in management innovation? Do we even know how much or how little we are investing? I suspect we are not investing nearly enough and, as a result, the huge sums we are pouring into product and process development will not produce anywhere nearly their full potential. Clearly, industry has a vested interest in working more closely with universities to advance the state of management technology and practice.

Our research universities must also play a major role in boosting management innovation and restoring competitiveness. One way, as proposed here, is to work with industry to develop better management tools and concepts and to help companies put these ideas into practice. Better understanding of how to accelerate organizational learning and adapt to a changing world environment would be a good place to start.

References

1. P. F. Drucker. "Management and the World's Work." *Harvard Business Review,* September–October 1988, pp. 65–76.
2. M. A. Cusumano. "Manufacturing Innovation: Lessons from the Japanese Auto Industry." *Sloan Management Review,* Fall 1988, pp. 29–39.
3. J. M. Utterback and W. J. Abernathy. "A Dynamic Model of Process and Product Innovation." *OMEGA* 3 (1975), 639–56.
4. J. W. Forrester. "Counterintuitive Behavior of Social Systems." *Technology Review,* January 1971, pp. 52–68.
5. P. M. Senge. "The New Management: Moving from Invention to Innovation." *New Management,* Summer 1986, pp. 7–13.
6. J. Sterman. "Misperceptions of Feedback in Dynamic Decision Making." *Organizational Behavior and Human Decision Processes* 43.
7. A. P. deGeus. "Planning as Learning." *Harvard Business Review,* March–April 1988, pp. 70–74.
8. K. Ishikawa. *What Is Total Quality Control? The Japanese Way,* trans. Lu. Englewood Cliffs, NJ: Prentice Hall, 1985.
9. A. M. Schneiderman. "Setting Quality Goals." *Quality Progress,* April 1988, pp. 51–57.

READING 33
MEETING THE GLOBAL COMPETITIVE CHALLENGE: BUILDING SYSTEMS THAT LEARN ON A LARGE SCALE

Gary E. Jusela

Introduction

Global competition, corporate downsizing, industrial renaissance, economic dislocation, these are the new watchwords of American business. Through the Cold War era the American public viewed the principal external threat to the United States as the military and political force of the Soviet Union and its allies. With the dissolution of the former Soviet Union and the Eastern Bloc this threat has nearly evaporated, while an economic threat from Japan has emerged as the more serious perceived challenge to the future of the United States. [1] Postman (1985, as cited in Mitroff, 1987) argues that the United States is organized to fight the wrong enemy, specifically the Soviet Union, when the more serious enemy, the root of our noncompetitiveness, is contained within our own borders. [2]

While we have shored up our military strength, our economic vitality has atrophied at an alarming rate. The United States world market share has dropped more than 50 percent in 20 years in 20 major industries. [3] Where in 1972 9 of the 10 largest banks in the world, as ranked by total assets, were American, today the top 8 and 15 of the top 25 belong to Japan. [4] Our standard of living has declined significantly in the last two decades; our rate of productivity growth from 1950 to 1985 (2.5 percent) lags far behind that of Japan (8.4 percent), Germany (5.5 percent), Italy (5.5 percent), and France (5.3 percent); and economists estimate that as many as 30 million people within the United States have been dislocated in their working careers by the

Source: Written especially for this volume.

"restructuring" in manufacturing during the last decade. [5] So what has happened, and what is industrial America to do about it?

This paper will examine some of the organizing assumptions and models that have contributed to the competitive decline within U.S. industry and explore one approach to addressing this decline that has been applied within the Ford Motor Company beginning in 1981 and within the Boeing Company beginning in 1988. The approach is called "large-scale systems change" and represents an evolutionary application of many elements of planned change and team development. The large-scale systems change methodology will be described as it has been applied in cultural change and in strategic planning efforts. The paper will further explore some of the outcomes of the large-scale process, internal political prerequisites for applying the methodology, and how the approach may be expected to evolve further.

Organizing Paradigms

While recognizing that industrial competitiveness is rooted in an array of factors broader than within-firm behavior (see, for example, Porter, 1990), the present discussion will be kept principally at the intrafirm level, with some attention given to changes in market expectations and external competitive conditions. The premise of this exploration, and of the intervention work on which it is based, is that many aspects of competitiveness can be addressed and resolved by rethinking and reorienting internal management practices. The chairman of Toyota Motors has been quoted as saying that "competitiveness is a microeconomic issue." [6] While this may be viewed by many as an oversimplification, there are beginning to be enough examples of individual firms turning around declining fortunes to assert that microeconomic factors are, at a minimum, an important dimension of competitive success. [7]

Peters (1988) argues that what is required are new models of industrial organization. Ackoff (1981) has laid out two contrasting organizing paradigms, the machine bureaucracy and the organization as system, that reflect respectively the dominant model for industrial organization for the past hundred years and the evolving model being adopted by the world's most successful firms. The large-scale systems change methodology is aimed at enabling large complex enterprises built around the machine model to adapt to changing external circumstances and move toward the systems model of organization. Before exploring the methodology, we will look first at these contrasting views of the organization.

The Machine Bureaucracy. The machine bureaucracy model of organization evolved out of early industrial engineering and scientific management concepts and Weberian concepts of hierarchical control (see Figure 1). [8] As described by Ackoff (1981), the machine model is based on analysis and reductionism. The underlying assumption is that, for the organization as a whole to work most effectively, each of its parts must be designed and honed to achieve a local optimum of performance. Within the machine bureaucracy, problems are solved by breaking them into their component parts, fixing the parts, and then reaggregating the whole. Authority is clearly defined by organizational level and work is neatly subdivided between functions. As the machine bureaucracy evolves (or devolves), the boundaries between levels and functions may become very severely drawn, limiting local coordination and the flow of people, of ideas, and of resources between units and placing

a large responsibility for regulation and control on senior levels of management. In this case the organization may be characterized as "overbounded" or "arthritic" (see Alderfer, 1976; Dannemiller, 1985). Under conditions in which the owner of the firm has enormous power over his or her employees, the skill requirements of jobs and educational level of employees is low, and the external environment of the organization is relatively stable, this model of industrial organization may be extraordinarily effective. In fact, the rise of the U.S. economy through the first seven decades of this century bears witness to the success of this dominant paradigm.

The Systems Model. Where the machine model is founded on analysis or taking things apart, systems thinking is built on synthesis or putting things together (Ackoff, 1981). Ackoff defines a system as a set of two or more elements that satisfies the following three conditions:

1. The behavior of each element has an effect on the behavior of the whole.
2. The behavior of the elements and their effects on the whole are interdependent.
3. However subgroups of the elements are formed, each has an effect on the behavior of the whole and none has an independent effect on it (p. 15).

Ackoff describes further that:

> The essential properties of a system taken as a whole derive from the interactions of its parts, not their actions taken separately. Therefore, when a system is taken apart it loses its essential properties. Because of this—and this is the critical point—a system is a whole that cannot be understood by analysis (p. 16).

Under the systems way of thinking, problems are solved not by taking things apart but rather by (1) identifying the larger whole containing the element to be explained, (2) explaining the behavior or properties of the containing whole, and then (3) explaining the behavior or charac-

FIGURE 1

The machine bureaucracy

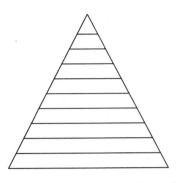

Authority is allocated according to hierarchical level.

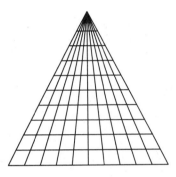

Responsibilities are delineated by clear divisions between functional groups (e.g., engineering, manufacturing, finance, sales, and human resources).

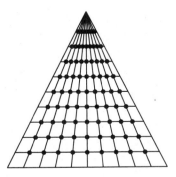

Over time, and with increasing specificity of rules, procedures, and organization charters, the organization becomes overbounded or "arthritic" in its joints and information flow and coordination across subunit boundaries is impeded.

teristics of the element in question in terms of the role or function it serves within the larger context. Perhaps the most significant implication of this paradigm for organizational effectiveness is that, to the extent each part of the system is considered independently and is made to operate as efficiently as possible, the system as a whole will not operate to its potential. The logic of this paradigm suggests that the optimal performance of the system as a whole requires suboptimization at the unit level.

For an organization to function effectively as a whole system, boundary permeability between an organization and its environment and among subunits within the organization must be maintained at an optimal level (Alderfer, 1976). Under conditions of either overboundedness or underboundedness, effective internal regulation or adaptation to a changing external environment breaks down. The extreme form of the machine bureaucracy, where boundaries are hardened to near impermeable states, may be considered, in these terms, a highly overbounded system.

The contrast between the machine and the system paradigms parallels Mitroff's (1987) characterization of old organizing assumptions and new organizing assumptions in the design of jobs and organizations (based on Mills and Lovell, 1985) and Imai's (1986) comparison of Western innovation-oriented management with the Japanese kaizen or continuous improvement philosophy. Two of the core concepts that appear repeatedly in recent discussions of new organizing paradigms are an emphasis on continual learning and the involvement of everyone in the continuous improvement of the system as a whole (see, for example, Hayes, Wheelwright and Clark, 1988; Imai, 1986; Keichel, 1990; Mitroff, 1987; and Stata, 1989). In fact, one of the common targeted objectives of the new paradigm models is that of creating organizations that learn within the context of dynamic boundary relations internally and externally.

Given the objective of moving large complex bureaucracies from old organizing paradigms to new systems perspectives, what are the implications for the practice of organization development and planned change? The answer to this can be found in tracing the roots of organization development and integrating historical group or team-oriented practice with systems-level thinking.

Beyond Teambuilding: Large-Scale Systems Change as a Vehicle for Shifting Culture

Teambuilding.   The practice of organization development has grown in large part out of the early research on group dynamics by Lewin, Lippitt, Bradford and Benne and the experiential learning processes pioneered by the National Training Laboratories beginning in 1947. [9] This origin is reflected in a predominant focus on group behavior and team development by organization development practitioners. Describing characteristics of successful organization development efforts, Beckhard (1969) suggests that they entail a planned program involving the whole system, and that they usually rely on some form of experience-based learning activities. Yet he says they also work primarily with groups. In practice, this has tended to mean relatively small groups.

Today throughout much of industry, one finds cadres of internal facilitators providing consultative support to quality circles and problem-solving teams with 8 to 10 members. Teambuilding has probably been the most common intervention of organization development practitioners in the past 30 years. While the core tenets of early T-group theory parallel systems thinking, the field of organization development seemed to lock onto small-group technology. Teambuilding can have many positive contributions to an organization's vitality or effectiveness. Teams and the individuals within them can develop process skills for handling conflict, making decisions, and setting direction. Yet, when teambuilding is conducted at a subunit level within a complex organization, large system level phenomena, if addressed at all, are typically addressed in only an oblique way (see Figure 2).

Teambuilding, as a vehicle for organization development, can be an instrument for reinforcing the machine bureaucracy and for tightening, rather than opening, the boundaries between groups. Within-group cohesion may be increased at the expense of between-group or systemic integration. Each group being built separately is likely to work with its own unique dataset and shape its objectives in a way that optimizes subunit performance, rather than the performance of the system as a whole. This is a natural consequence not simply of an inherent bias toward self interest but of the fact that the whole system is not present or represented in the room. In the absence of relevant stakeholders influencing the discussion, groups will tend to focus on their own parochial needs.

Getting the Whole System in the Room. Weisbord (1987a) describes an evolution in the practice of management consulting and organization development starting in the early 1900s with Frederick Taylor's scientific management up to the present. The evolution process begins with experts solving problems for others. The second stage, which Weisbord dates from the 1950s to the middle 1960s, has everyone getting involved in the problem-solving process. Stage

FIGURE 2

Teambuilding

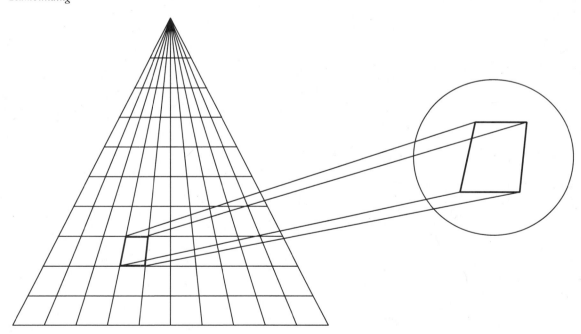

Teambuilding is typically conducted by extracting a single subunit from the larger system, developing the group's skills and capabilities, and then returning the subunit to the larger system, the elements of which often exert pressure to return to the original status quo.

three is characterized by experts working to improve whole systems. The final stage, which Weisbord sees as the next evolution in organization development, entails getting everyone involved in improving whole systems.

Drawing on the community development and futuring the research and practice of Lippitt and Schindler-Rainman (1980), Weisbord (1987a, 1987b) describes four useful practices he feels characterize this next or "third wave" of managing and consulting. The first is an assessment of the potential for action by determining the presence of three prerequisite conditions: committed leadership, a good business opportunity (i.e., a critical business need that must be addressed, such as merger, acquisition, reorganization, business strategy planning, overhead crises, or new technologies), and energized people. Before proceeding, Weisbord advocates a thorough "should we/shouldn't we" discussion with the key stakeholders. The second useful practice is to "get the whole system in the room." The third is to focus on the future, and the fourth is to structure tasks that people can do for themselves. Weisbord's description of these four practices as the next phase of organization development practice matches closely with the large-scale systems change methodology that was initiated within the Ford Motor Company in 1982 and which is the subject of the present discussion.

Large-Scale Systems Change at Ford Motor Company.   Ford Motor Company in 1981 was in the depths of a competitive crisis. The economy was in a cyclical downturn, new and stronger competitors were challenging the market, and customer expectations about automotive quality and performance were shifting dramatically. The company lost nearly 10 percentage points of U.S. market share, and, between 1980 and 1983, recorded losses of $3.3 billion and a North American workforce reduction of approximately 100,000 employees. Chrysler had recently gone to the U.S. government for a bailout, and Ford appeared to be not far behind.

With the company hemorrhaging in the newly competitive global environment, in what Peter Vaill (1986) calls the "permanent whitewater" of present day environmental turbulence, small-scale quick fixes aimed at repairing the boxes of the organization would not produce the required cultural and competitive adjustment or the capacity for continual renewal. Out of these circumstances was born the earliest iteration of the large-scale systems change methodology applied within a large corporate setting.

Ford Motor Company and the United Auto Workers signed an agreement on Employee Involvement as part of their contract negotiations in 1979. This agreement resulted in the initiation of extensive problem solving and quality circle group activities at the shop floor level of the company. As a result of these activities, the company culture in the manufacturing plants began to shift from the highly authoritarian model of the past to a more participative model that engaged the employees' minds as well as their hands. By 1980, as business performance was beginning to collapse severely, the senior management of the company began a process of personal study and education on quality improvement under the tutelage of Dr. W. Edwards Deming. At this time, Ford launched its "Quality is Job #1" campaign, internally as well as externally. The pressure for change within Ford was becoming enormous as the company's competitive position continued to slip, and with these new initiatives, Employee Involvement and "Quality is Job #1," change was beginning nearly simultaneously at the bottom and at the top.

By 1981, the pressure for change had become particularly acute within the Diversified Products Operations (DPO) of the Ford Motor Company. This unit consisted of approximately 70,000 employees within 10 operating divisions, most of which supplied component parts or materials for the automotive business (e.g., steel, castings, climate control, electronics, glass, plastics, paint, and vinyl). These divisions were under especially acute pressure, given that alternative sources for many or most of their products were available outside the company. Their customer divisions were beginning to demand that they meet or beat the external competition in quality, cost, and delivery. This provided the impetus for Tom Page, then executive vice president in charge of DPO, to seek a means to bring about a cultural change rapidly within his entire 70,000 person organization.

Page could see the beginning of positive momentum at the top with the new focus on quality and at the bottom with the emphasis on Employee Involvement. These initiatives, however, left a large gap in the middle, that vast domain containing the roughly 20 layers of hierarchy between his office and the shop floor. Not only had this large bulk of employees not been brought into the fold of the new quality and employee involvement initiatives, but they had been schooled in and continued to practice the best of the old paradigm, machine bureaucracy model of management. Authorities and perquisites were carefully allocated among the vertical layers, and functions were tightly segmented into what were referred to as the "chimneys" (including such organizations as engineering, finance, labor relations, manufacturing, research, and sales). Small-scale initiatives, such as training or team-building with groups of 20 to 25, would not reach a critical mass of people quickly enough, nor would they get at the root of the organizational arthritis that had crept into the organization latticework.

To address the competitive crisis and the necessity for large-scale change, a group of external consultants was invited to collaborate with Page and his management team. [10] The consultants came from Ann Arbor, Michigan, where several of them had each been influenced by the research and practice of Ron Lippitt. Page asked the group to develop a strategy to shift the mass of his organization from an old authoritarian management style to the participative management style he was seeking. The external consultants collaborated with Page's manager for employee involvement and training to develop a methodology they believed could accomplish the needed magnitude and speed of change. [11] What they proposed to Tom Page in 1981 is precisely what Weisbord (1987a, 1987b) describes as the next phase of organization development. The consultants came back to Page with a proposal to work with each of his 10 divisions by developing and conducting what would be division-specific participative management seminars using a large-scale systems change methodology.

The proposed seminars were to be conducted with the division general manager and his top five layers of management as an intact group, which included anywhere from 60 to 150 people (see Figure 3). The intent of the sessions was to create a highly interactive learning environment where participative management would be the medium and a real-time, real-life case analysis of the division's business conducted by the program participants would be the content. Participants were to work together in a series of small group and large group configurations that would bring people together across the hierarchical and functional barriers that had traditionally kept them apart. What the seminar proposed to do, consistent with Weisbord's prescription, was to get the whole system into the room, to focus on the future (and also on the past and present), and to design tasks that people could do for themselves. The participants would provide the vast majority of the content within a context that was designed to promote interactive individual, group, and organizational learning across the whole system. Tom Page was eager to bring about a rapid transformation and saw no better alternative for getting there. Therefore, in an act reflecting what Kanter (1983) describes as the paradox of initiation, Page decreed that each of his general managers should launch the large-scale participative management seminar process within their respective divisions.

The participative management seminar was

FIGURE 3

Large-scale systems change

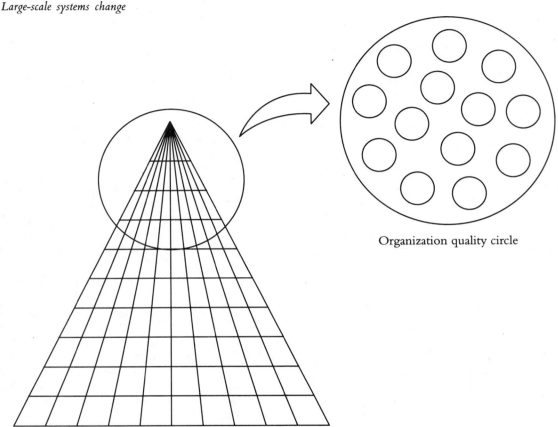

Organization quality circle

The large-scale systems change methodology employed in the Ford participative management seminars took the top five layers of an operating division off-site as an intact group. Participants worked in a variety of small group and large group configurations, beginning with maximum-mix teams that mixed people by level and function into microcosms of the whole.

designed as a five-day event, beginning with an initial three-day meeting followed six to eight weeks later with a two-day follow-up. The sessions were held off-site and brought the top five layers of division management together into what might be called an "organization quality circle." In many cases, this was the first time the entire management group had been in one room at the same time. The seminar was intended to both build participative skills in the management team and to help managers find new ways of working together vertically and horizontally within the system. Managers worked in different teams during the five days; they were grouped variously in maximum-mix teams (microcosm groups consisting of multiple levels and functions), functional teams, natural work teams, Myers-Briggs-personality-type teams, and, finally, as a team of the whole, planning, voting, and coming to consensus around a shared vision for the future.

Within each of the 10 divisions, the seminars were designed using a five-step process:

1. The creation of a consultant/client division collaborative design team to plan the event.
2. The collection of data from key stakeholders within the system.
3. The development of a clear statement of purpose.
4. The development of a detailed process plan for the flow of each day in the five-day design.
5. The continual evaluation of the plan against the purpose and the data and and the evaluation of the events themselves at the end of each day.

Using this approach, each seminar could be custom-tailored to meet the unique and specific requirements of a given division. The design process itself became a vehicle for learning, renewal, and the building of ownership for the large-scale methodology by the microcosm group participating in the planning.

Part of the internal architecture for the seminar was provided by the Gleicher formula for organizational change described by Beckhard and Harris (1977). The formula was adapted for mnemonic purposes as follows:

$$C = D \times V \times F > R$$
$$C = \text{Change}$$
$$D = \text{Dissatisfaction with the status quo}$$
$$V = \text{Vision of the future}$$
$$F = \text{First steps}$$
$$R = \text{Resistance to change}$$

This equation suggests that in order to bring about change in a large system there must be a sufficient degree of dissatisfaction with the status quo (D), a vision of the future that is clear, compelling, and different from the present (V), and practical first steps to move toward the vision (F). Multiplied together these three variables must be greater than the resistance to change, which is assumed to always have a value greater than zero. If any of the three variables D, V, or F is equal to zero the total product will be equal to zero, and resistance to change will win out.

Building from this change formula, the participative management seminar was designed in its various division specific iterations to build a shared systemwide understanding (a common database) of D, V, and F. The participants were invited to identify (through a series of interactive processes working with self-facilitated table teams) what was working and not working within the division and in the division's relationship with key external stakeholders. Second, they were asked to build preferred future visions for the whole system and for their natural work teams. Finally, they were given the opportunity to work together both cross-functionally and in natural teams to begin to develop the first steps and action plans that would move the division toward the shared vision.

One of the significant outcomes of the participative management seminars was that the participants left the sessions better connected with one another across system boundaries (functional and hierarchical) that had historically kept them apart. They left with more understanding of the interdependencies that would determine the future success of the enterprise. The seminars not only addressed Page's concerns about creating the right environment for participative management and quality improvement but, by breaking people out of narrow arthritic boxes, helped move each division from the machine model into the systems age.

While the large-scale change process in each

division was initiated with the top five management layers, there was soon demand to diffuse the process through the rest of the organization in order to expand and accelerate the change process through all of the layers. Diffusion seminars were created to accommodate this need. These diffusion seminars were built in a similar fashion to the original participative management seminar, with the difference that those who were at the lowest levels in the initial event became the senior levels of the next event and so on through the system. This linking pin and cascading process provided an opportunity for many layers of management to demonstrate their leadership capabilities and for the system as a whole to build a broad and shared understanding around the key elements of the change formula. The sense of shared understanding and participation in creating a new vision for quality, participation, and teamwork became refined and enriched by each level as the process moved down through the entirety of the Diversified Products divisions.

The process of large-scale systems change came to be viewed positively within the leadership hierarchy at Ford as a vehicle for effecting cultural change and organization learning. The Diversified Products divisions were able, for the most part, to make significant quantifiable gains in their quality performance and were able to hold onto their business base in a highly competitive environment. The internal manager of employee involvement and training within DPO, with the support of Tom Page and then Ford chairman Donald Petersen, was promoted and given responsibility to create the Ford Executive Development Center for the top managers in the company worldwide. The methodology employed in the large-scale systems change process was integrated as a part of the core technology in the new executive university.

This large-scale change methodology was developed initially to address the need to change management style and build new skills in a management team that was fighting for its competi-

tive life. Thus the initial application was designed to address two (style and skills) of what Pascale and Athos (1980) refer to as the "soft S's" in their seven S model of organization effectiveness. Next we will look at how the large-scale approach has been applied to one of the "hard S's," strategy, within a different context, the Boeing Company in Seattle, Washington. [12]

Large-Scale Strategic Planning

A Vehicle for Building Alignment.   Getting the whole system in the room helps to build an internal community within the organization and to break down barriers between individuals, between groups, and between different functions and hierarchical levels. One potential advantage that was not clearly anticipated at the outset was that of gaining organization alignment around a common strategic direction. In the box-by-box teambuilding approach to organization development there is the opportunity to help subteams within the organization establish clarity of mission, goals, and objectives. Unfortunately this is often conducted without a systems view, and the various subunits aim themselves in different and incompatible directions. Some groups head off to the northeast, while others decide a westerly direction makes more sense. This leads to a lack of coordination internally, confusion for external stakeholders (including customers), and a diminished capacity for a rapid and effective response to a changing business environment. The large-scale systems change process provides a methodology for getting all of the functions and multiple layers of management aligned in one direction simultaneously.

A story from Waterman (1987) based on a consulting project with the Sanwa Bank in Japan illustrates this point nicely. Waterman describes how the broad involvement of multiple layers and functions within the bank led to the successful turnaround of market share losses in record time.

The application of the large-scale systems change methodology to the strategic planning process is a vehicle for creating the type of simultaneity in planning and implementation that Waterman describes. Designed properly, the process of planning can have at least as much influence on organizational outcomes as the specifics of the plan itself. [13] Large-scale strategic planning was launched within Boeing Computer Services in March of 1989 and within Boeing Aerospace and Electronics in September of 1989. The present discussion of the process will focus on the work with the Aerospace and Electronics Division, since this represents the most advanced evolution of the approach. The discussion of outcomes, however, will address observations from each of these Boeing Company divisions.

Boeing Aerospace and Electronics. The circumstances under which large-scale strategic planning was launched at Boeing Aerospace and Electronics Division were not as dire as those confronting the Diversified Products Operations of Ford Motor Company in 1981. However, early warning signs were apparent to the senior division leadership that the organization was headed for trouble. The division was on its way to its first-ever net loss year, with several key programs running behind schedule and over cost and a number of historically loyal customers beginning to question the division's capabilities. The impetus for initiating the process came from Art Hitsman, the executive vice president responsible for the 27,000 person Boeing Aerospace and Electronics organization. Hitsman had initiated a large-scale system change process, patterned after the Ford participative management seminar, in his previous assignment as president of the Boeing Electronics Division. [14] In his new role, Hitsman was seeking to both build bridges among the many units making up his division and to establish a strategic alignment from top to bottom.

One of Hitsman's customer divisions within Boeing had begun experimenting with the Japanese concept of hoshin planning, modeled after Hewlett-Packard's application of the same concept. Under this hoshin planning philosophy, the organization as a whole established clear measurable goals for the year and communicated these to all employees. Each successive layer of the organization from the top on down was responsible for taking the division goals and translating those into unit specific actions that would enable the division to achieve its annual targets. Hitsman was impressed with what he saw in the other division. In his own division, Hitsman hoped to both break down the traditional barriers among functions and hierarchical levels and to achieve a strategic flowdown that would enable each employee to understand how he or she fit into the larger picture. A joint consultant/ client design team was created to develop a process that would address the needs for both cultural change and strategic alignment.

The Strategic Planning Model. Following a development process consistent with that used in creating the participative management seminars at Ford, the design team began its work by conducting diagnostic interviews with key members of the division management team. The data from the interviews were shared openly in the design sessions, as were the views of the design team members on the state of the organization. These data and a simple model for strategic planning (see Figure 4) were used to shape the purpose and process for the intervention.

Applying Ackoff's (1981) concept of systems thinking, the strategic planning model starts by looking at the larger containing whole within which the focal subsystem (in this case Boeing Aerospace and Electronics Division) is contained. Before agreeing on the division level strategic focus, the organization members first develop a clear understanding of their key stakeholders and trends within their industry. Therefore, step one in the strategic planning process is to create the means for bringing the relevant data about the operating environment into the room. This includes information about customers, industry trends, and corporate management expectations,

FIGURE 4

Strategic planning model

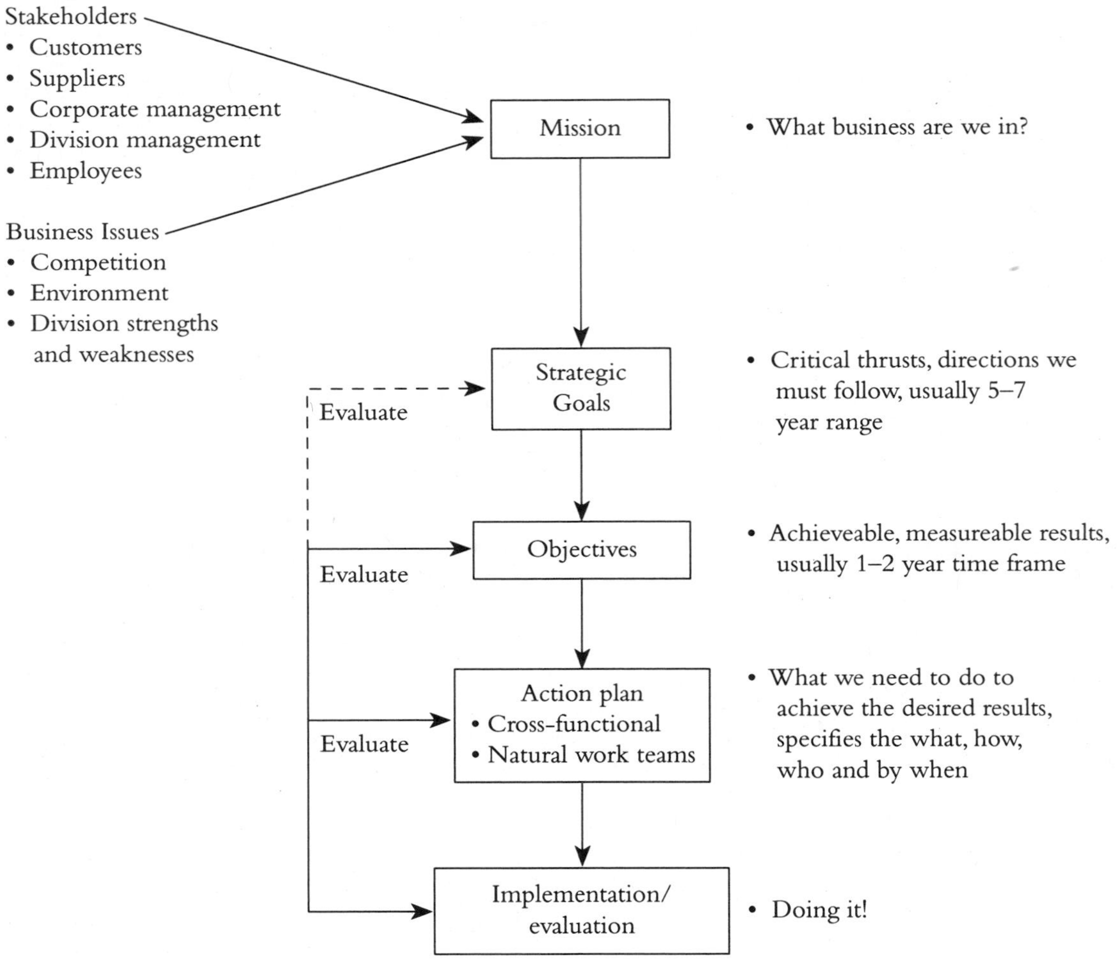

Stakeholders
- Customers
- Suppliers
- Corporate management
- Division management
- Employees

Business Issues
- Competition
- Environment
- Division strengths
  and weaknesses

```
                    ┌──────────────────┐
                    │     Mission      │  • What business are we in?
                    └──────────────────┘
                             │
                             ▼
    ┌ ─ ─ ─ →   ┌──────────────────┐
    Evaluate    │    Strategic     │  • Critical thrusts, directions we
                │      Goals       │    must follow, usually 5–7
                └──────────────────┘    year range
                             │
                             ▼
    ───────→    ┌──────────────────┐
    Evaluate    │    Objectives    │  • Achieveable, measureable results,
                └──────────────────┘    usually 1–2 year time frame
                             │
                             ▼
    ───────→    ┌──────────────────┐
    Evaluate    │   Action plan    │  • What we need to do to
                │ • Cross-functional│    achieve the desired results,
                │ • Natural work teams│  specifies the what, how,
                └──────────────────┘    who and by when
                             │
                             ▼
    ───────→    ┌──────────────────┐
                │ Implementation/  │  • Doing it!
                │   evaluation     │
                └──────────────────┘
```

as well as internal management and employee perceptions of organizational performance and the quality of work life. The next step is to take that understanding of the environment and come to an agreement on the specific business mission of the organization. In this case, "mission" is understood to mean the definition of the division's business or reason for being.

Next, based on the agreed statement of mission, and the opportunities and challenges identified in the environmental assessment, strategic goals are established. Strategic goals are defined as the critical thrusts or directions the organization should pursue or on which it should focus its energies in the next five to seven years if it is to be successful in achieving its mission. [15] By looking five to seven years out, the participants in the process have the opportunity to define a preferred future for the organization; they can create a picture of what they want to see happen, rather than simply planning from where they are and extending themselves inchbug style into the future. In this model, the strategic goals are not developed by building best case and worst case scenarios. Rather, they are built in a manner consistent with what Ackoff (1981) describes as interactive planning. Ackoff's interactive planning begins with what he calls the "formulation of the mess"—that is, understanding the system's threats and opportunities. From that understanding, Ackoff's model moves to the definition of the desirable future state or what he calls "ends planning." The goal planning stage identified in Figure 4 is analogous to this idea of ends planning or to what Lindeman and Lippitt (1979) describe as preferred futuring. Rather than predicting the future and then planning according to the prediction (what Ackoff calls "preactive planning"), the preferred futuring approach works from the premise that the organization members can define a realistic and desirable future state for themselves and then build their plans accordingly. Lippitt (1983), moreover, finds that groups working on preferred futures, as contrasted with those addressing past or present problems, have higher energy and greater ownership for the plans they develop and that their solutions are more creative.

This longer-term goal formation step in the planning process also addresses another common organization dilemma, the activity bias. Often, out of a keen bias for action, organizations, groups, or individuals will jump directly from an environmental squeaky wheel directly to an action to stop the squeak. While this may be effective for addressing near-term problems, this approach can be highly destructive in the long run. In the absence of a coherent set of strategic goals, organization members are left to respond to whatever squeaky wheels they may happen to see and hear, and, as a result, the organization

strategy becomes a random assortment of independent actions. These actions over time can work at cross purposes and lead to the dissipation of the organization's energy. This is an example of the optimization of parts of the system at the expense of the whole. In contrast, the strategic planning process organizes a myriad of internal and external squeaky wheels, first into a coherent environmental analysis, and second, into a clear statement of mission and a preferred set of priority goals. This strategic planning process then can reduce the tyranny of a reactive management style and bring alignment and discipline to near-term actions.

While the strategic goals provide a general sense of direction, the objectives specify achievable and measurable results that must be realized within one to two years if the organization is to make progress toward its desired future state. The objectives are developed with the idea of moving from the abstract to the concrete. The objectives begin to translate the vision implied in the goals to the practical first steps the organization must take to achieve them. The process gets even more specific in the action planning stage. In this phase, action plans—identifying what needs to happen, who needs to be involved, and by when—are developed for each of the organization objectives. This type of action planning is done both on a cross-functional total organization basis and at the natural work team level.

The final element of the strategic planning model is the implementation and continual monitoring and evaluation of the plans. This entails both doing what was planned and the evaluation of what was done. Evaluation of the actions in this case should be done not only in relation to the action plans (did we do what we said we were going to do?) but in relation to the objectives (by doing what we agreed to do, did we achieve the results we expected?) and in relation to the goals (by doing what we agreed to and achieving or not achieving the results we expected, did we move ourselves any closer toward the destination we agreed was desirable?).

This model, together with the Gleicher formula for organization change, provided the framework for the strategic planning process.

Involving the Organization in Three Phases. Using a top-down and bottom-up approach, the strategic planning process was designed in three phases, each phase building towards and being enriched by the next (see Figure 5). Phase I was designed as a two-day working session for the division general manager and 14 of his top executives representing the major functional organizations and the four major product units (Electronics Systems, Missile Systems, Space Systems, and the Huntsville Division) which make up the division. Following the path laid out in the strategic planning model, this executive group spent most of the first day building a common understanding of the corporation's mission, goals, and objectives, and of how the Aerospace and Electronics Division was viewed by several key stakeholders, including senior corporate management, customers, suppliers, and employees. The group also analyzed the strengths

FIGURE 5

Involving the organization in three phases
Boeing Aerospace and Electronics

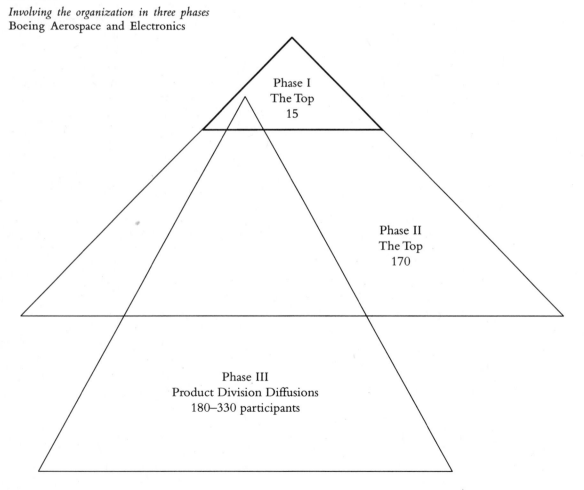

Phase I
The Top
15

Phase II
The Top
170

Phase III
Product Division Diffusions
180–330 participants

and weaknesses of their key competitors, assessed the existing business environment within the defense and space industry, and evaluated the current capabilities of their organization by examining each of their respective organizations against the Malcolm Baldrige National Quality Award criteria.

This environmental analysis provided the basis for the top-management group to develop a first-draft statement of mission, goals, and objectives for the Aerospace and Electronics Division. The objective of this two-day session was to both strengthen the division leadership group (they were referred to as the Division Quality Council) as a team and to develop a preliminary strategic plan that could be used as the basis for further evolution in phase II.

Phase II occurred four weeks after phase I. This phase expanded the planning circle from the top 15 to the top 170 managers in the division. Phase II was designed as a five-day intervention, with the first three days separated from the last two days by a 13-week interim period (see Figure 6). The phase II event began in a similar way to phase I, starting with an assessment of the key stakeholders, several of whom participated in the meeting, and of the existing business environment.

Once they had the opportunity to build a broader understanding of the business environment, the 155 participants below the top 15 were asked to critique and recommend changes to the draft mission, goals, and objectives proposed by the leadership team. The output from phase I thus became input for phase II. The leadership group took all of the feedback from the 155 on the evening of day two and, working late into the night, integrated their comments into a final statement of mission, goals, and objectives. This was reviewed with the 155 the next morning and became the basis for subsequent system-wide and work unit level action planning on day three and in the postinterim session on days four and five. With the overnight turnaround on recommendations for changes to the mission, goals,

and objectives, the ownership for the strategy underwent a major shift from the top 15 to the entire group of 170. Many saw their specific words and concerns incorporated and reflected in the revised document.

Phase III was designed as a series of three-day diffusion events to bring the other 3,000 managers within the division into the strategic planning process. These meetings involved between 180 and 330 managers at a time and each was organized with a focus on one of the four product units. These sessions began with the Corporate and Aerospace and Electronics Division mission, goals, and objectives as givens. The product unit manager and his top leadership team (approximately 15 people in each case) were the principal clients for each of these events. They played the same role that the division general manager and his leadership team had in the phase II events.

As in the phase II process, the product unit leadership team developed a draft statement of mission, goals, and objectives for its organization before the session began. This draft strategy then became the material for debate, critique, and modification by the next tiers of the hierarchy across the functional spectrum in the phase III events. The product units were large organizations in their own right, ranging from 2,000 to 8,000 employees each.

In the product program events, the overall product unit strategy was taken as a given. The results of these sessions included stronger bonds among the participants and an agreed-to set of action priorities and plans at the program level. These priorities and plans were targeted at serving the identified needs of both external and internal customers and at supporting the overall strategic direction of the product unit, the Aerospace and Electronics Division, and ultimately the corporation as a whole.

Phase III was a vehicle for greatly broadening the involvement base in the planning process and for knitting together, through a series of overlapping and interlocking events, the many man-

FIGURE 6

Boeing Aerospace and Electronics
Large-scale systems change, phase II, October 23–25, 1989, and January 16–17, 1990

Purpose: To come together as leaders of Boeing Aerospace and Electronics to:

- Build a shared understanding of our business environment.
- Agree on our BA&E Mission, Goals, and Objectives.
- Identify what we need to do individually and together to lead BA&E successfully into the future with a sense of urgency and strategic intent.

Agenda

Day 1

7:30	Continental Breakfast
8:00	Opening and Welcome—Art Hitsman
8:10	Purpose, Agenda, and Norms
8:30	Telling Your Story
9:15	Break
9:30	View from the Corporate Bridge—Frank Shrontz, Boeing Company Chairman and CEO
10:30	View from the BA&E Bridge—Dan Pinick, President, Boeing Defense and Space Group, and Art Hitsman, Executive Vice President, Boeing Aerospace and Electronics
12:10	Lunch
1:10	Celebrating Diversity (Myers-Briggs)
3:20	Organization Diagnosis: Glads and Sads
4:50	Evaluation
5:00	Adjourn

Day 2

7:30	Continental Breakfast
8:00	Feedback on Evaluations and Agenda for the Day
8:10	Industry Assessment
9:45	Break
10:00	Voice of the Customer
11:40	Lunch
12:30	Interorganization Conflict
3:20	Break
3:35	Revisit Mission, Strategic Goals, and Objectives
3:55	Critique of Mission, Strategic Goals, and Objective
4:40	Feedback to Quality Council
5:10	Evaluation of the Day
5:15	Adjourn
5:20	Quality Council (Leadership Team) and Design Team remain to read evaluations and integrate feedback to achieve new consensus on Mission, Strategic Goals, and Objectives

Day 3

7:30	Continental Breakfast
8:00	Feedback on Evaluations and Agenda for the Day
8:10	Quality Council Response to Critique of Mission, Strategic Goals, and Objectives
9:15	Participants Self-select to Work on Objectives
9:25	BA&E Objective Strategy Groups

FIGURE 6

(concluded)

- Preferred Futuring on Objectives
- Systemwide Action Recommendations

12:00	Lunch
1:00	BA&E Objective Strategy Groups (continued)
1:30	Roomwide Post, Read, and Vote
2:00	Quality Council Summarizes and Reports Voting Results
2:30	Break
2:45	Back Home Groups: Planning for the Interim
3:45	Headline Reports
4:15	Quality Council Commitments for the Interim
4:30	Wrap-up and Next Steps
4:45	Evaluation of the Three Days
5:00	Social Hour

A 13-week interim period separated days three and four.

Day 4

7:30	Continental Breakfast
8:00	Welcome—Art Hitsman
8:10	Purpose, Agenda, and Logistics
8:20	Look Back: Learnings from the Interim
9:50	Break
10:05	Introductions in New Maximum-mix Teams
10:10	Executive Vice President's Commentary on Reports from the Interim
10:15	Motorola Story: What Motorola Learned from Pursuing the Malcolm Baldrige National Quality Award—William Smith, Corporate Senior Executive for Quality, Motorola
11:45	Lunch
12:30	Assessment of BA&E Against the Malcolm Baldrige Criteria
2:45	Break
3:00	View from the BA&E Leadership Bridge—Programs in the News
4:55	Evaluation of the Day
5:00	Adjourn

Day 5

7:30	Continental Breakfast
8:00	Feedback on Evaluations and Agenda for the Day
8:10	Global View—Dr. William J. Taylor, Vice President, International Security Programs, Center for Strategic International Studies
9:45	Strategic Objective Analysis—Assessment of Progress on Objectives Plans Since Day 3 and Identification of Show Stoppers
11:45	Lunch—Show-stopper lists posted in main room for reading and voting for show-stoppers with the most leverage under each objective
1:00	Show-stopper Action Planning
2:45	Break
3:00	Show-stopper Reports
3:35	Back Home Planning
4:35	Headline Reports
5:05	Closing Comments—Art Hitsman
5:15	Evaluation of the Two Days
5:20	Social Hour

agement layers, functional organizations, product units, and program groups that made up the division. Subsequently, the involvement and teambuilding process was cascaded through the nonmanagement ranks of the organization.

Systems Theory in the Context of Planning. Ackoff (1981) outlines three operating principles for carrying out his model of interactive planning: the participative principle, the holistic principle, and the principle of continuity. The participative principle, as Ackoff describes, implies that:

> no one can plan effectively for someone else. It is better to plan for oneself, no matter how badly, than to be planned for by others, no matter how well. The reason for this derives from the meaning of development: an increase in one's desire and ability to satisfy one's own desires and those of others. This ability and desire are not increased by being planned for by others, but by planning for oneself (p. 66).

The three phases of planning outlined here were not designed to simply inform the 3,000 members of management what their leaders had decided, but to involve them actively and simultaneously in both strategy formulation and implementation.

The holistic principle applies Ackoff's systems model of the organization within the planning context and argues for the criticality of building coordination and integration into the process:

> Problems, no matter where they appear, should be attacked simultaneously and cooperatively from as many points of view as possible (p. 73).

and:

> planning done independently at any level of a system cannot be as effective as planning carried out interdependently at all levels (p. 73).

Combining these concepts of coordination and integration, Ackoff maintains that:

the more parts of a system and levels of it that plan simultaneously and interdependently the better. This concept of all-over-at-once planning stands in opposition to sequential planning, either top-down or bottom-up (p. 74).

In his principle of continuity, Ackoff simply cautions that planning should not be done as a discontinuous or static process, but rather should be continuous and dynamic. In the process of moving toward a destination, new information is gained. Plans therefore need to have the flexibility built in to accommodate new data and to allow the setting of new and more appropriate courses.

The process outlined in the present discussion is an attempt to address in particular Ackoff's principles of participation and holism. The effective application of these two principles is likely to build within the organization the adaptive and renewing capabilities addressed by the principle of continuity. While many have argued for the need to address broad participation and holistic thinking in the planning process, little has been written on how to effectively bring this about. What seems to have been missing is a process model for working with large groups. It is in this domain that the work at Ford and Boeing has provided an especially unique opportunity for learning.

Getting the Whole System in the Room Sounds Good in Theory, but What Do You Do When They Actually Show Up?

Conceptually, getting the whole system in the room—what Weisbord (1987) describes as the next phase in the evolution of organization development—makes sense. For all the reasons stated above, about the limitations of the machine model in contrast to the systems perspective, we need to find ways to plan and manage organizations as a whole and not simply on a box by box basis. But in reality, how do you do it? What do you do when the whole system decides to show up?

Large-Scale Application of Small Group Principles. What I have learned, first as a participant observer of the large-scale methodology and subsequently as a process designer, is that the same principles that hold true for managing process effectively at the small group level also apply when larger numbers are brought into the room. Schutz (1984) identifies inclusion, control, and openness as critical elements of effectiveness in a small group's life. When one brings into the room 30 groups of eight people each, the same principles apply. Issues of inclusion, control, and openness must be addressed at the table group level and at the level of the whole room.

In the large-scale systems change methodology, inclusion mechanisms range from the simple—such as having name tags and clear table assignments when people arrive (participants are assigned to cross-level, cross-functional microcosm groups called "maximum-mix teams")—to the more substantial, such as having each participant share his or her personal story about life in the organization with the others at his or her table. Throughout the process of a multiday large group event, the design encourages a maximum of individual involvement and a minimum of passive one-way listening. In each of the series of structured subgroup activities that make up the three days of a phase III event, the subteams are asked to designate members of their group to serve as group facilitator, flipchart recorder, and group spokesperson. Guidelines and coaching for effective performance in these roles are provided by the conference facilitation team. The groups are expected to rotate these roles among their members in successive rounds. This approach is inclusive and places responsibility for control squarely in the groups' hands. In other parts of the design, individuals are given the opportunity to use post-it notes to generate ideas on a roomwide basis under specific strategic issues or to vote with stick-on dots (green for "go for it," red for "don't even think of it") on action plans generated by their own and other subteams. Each element of the design is attentive to both the adult learning principle of active engagement and the individual level needs for inclusion.

Issues of control are also addressed throughout the process, with the objective of keeping the locus of control internal to the participants to the maximum extent possible. Starting with the involvement of the multilevel, cross-functional client/consultant team in the design of each event, participants are involved in shaping the process. The consultants provide an organizing framework for the process, including such concepts as the change formula, the strategic planning model, and the principles of effective group process. The client representatives on the design team and the session participants during the events identify the issues that must be addressed and bring the content specifics to the mission, goals, objectives, and action plans. Both before and during the events, the participants are kept informed of the purpose, agenda, and the underlying theoretical models. Selective prereadings are assigned to prepare the participants to contribute effectively.

Assessment of the process is sought systemically at the end of each day through written participant evaluations. The design team gathers after each session to read the participant evaluations and, based on the feedback, to make any required changes in the subsequent day's agenda. The evaluations are also summarized in extensive detail overnight and fed back to the group as a whole the next morning. The evaluation feedback helps to create a common database of perception on the process and allows the participants to self-correct their behaviors. In this way, the entire process is managed as an open system, with real-time ongoing feedback and adjustment of the design in accordance with the needs of the participants.

Openness is fostered in several ways. Through much of the design, participants are seated in microcosm groups that, by design, exclude their immediate bosses and their direct subordinates.

The sessions themselves are conducted in off-site settings and the participants are asked to dress in casual attire. The elements of the design invite the subgroups to diagnose aspects of system performance that under normal circumstances might be considered undiscussable (Argyris, 1986). However, given that the diagnosis is allowed to be carried out and reported as a group product, no individual is required to risk his or her career or reputation in raising difficult questions or in identifying troublesome problems. Diagnostic data, images of the future, and action plans are generated in teams and shared openly across the room through table team reports, either verbal or written. The sessions are designed to both (1) build a common understanding among the participants of how their management peers view the organization and (2) model an environment of openness that may be continued back in the workplace. The transfer of openness back to the work setting may be expected to be enhanced (when contrasted with learning designs involving only a few individuals or a single unit within the organization) by the fact that a large mass of the system is sharing in the opening process simultaneously.

Designing Simultaneously for the Individual, Group, Intergroup, and the Whole System. The Tavistock model (Bion, 1961; Miller and Rice, 1967) views organization life simultaneously through multiple windows, analyzing behavior at the levels of the individual, the group, intergroup relations, and the organization as a whole system. Similarly, the large-scale systems change methodology is designed to address all four of these levels of behavior.

At the individual level, participants in the large-scale process have the opportunity to simply be students of their own organization and of the organization's stakeholders. The top leader of the subject organization will usually gain insights into how he or she is perceived by others in the system. Each of the participants has the opportunity to gain insights into each's behavioral and leadership style through a self-assessment and group discussion, with like-type peers applying the Myers-Briggs Type Indicator. Each participant is also encouraged throughout to take the learnings from the broad view and apply them to his or her product or functional perspective.

Group level phenomena are addressed in a variety of configurations. During the three days of a phase III event, participants work in several team formats: maximum-mix, Myers-Briggs type, functional, self-select around strategic issues, and back home work group. Many of these are artificially created temporary task teams with a life span limited to a portion of the conference. For the participants, however, these temporary task teams provide opportunities to try out and practice new group roles (e.g., leader, follower, arbitrator, facilitator, recorder, or spokesperson) and to make connections and form relationships with counterparts from other work units. Some of the temporary task teams continue to meet back in the workplace. Natural or back home work teams provide the most obvious transfer device for learnings from the session back into the organization. In some sessions, opportunity is provided for natural work teams to meet for the purpose of assessing, discussing, and improving how they work together. In all of the sessions, the natural work teams serve as the focal points for taking systemwide strategies and action plans and translating them into specific follow-up actions with clear timelines and accountability. The probability of effective follow up is enhanced by virtue of the fact that the entire natural work team experiences the process together.

Intergroup relations are addressed most directly through a process called "organizational valentines." [16] For this activity, participants are seated in functional groups and are asked to work as a team to prepare and send valentines to every other functional group. In this case, a valentine is a response to the statement "these are the things you do as a part of your job that make it more difficult for us to get our job done." Each team receives a blank valentine to send to each of the other functional teams and is asked to work quickly to generate intergroup feedback that is as behaviorally specific as possible. The teams are also asked to sign each valentine with the name of their function. At the conclusion of the writing period, all of the valentines are posted in the main meeting room under headers with the different function names. Again, operating as an open system process, all of the participants are invited to read as many of the valentines as they wish in the time allowed. In this way, individuals can compare the feedback to their own groups with that sent to others.

The functional teams are then sent back to breakout rooms with their valentines and asked to go through a four-step assignment: (1) react and ventilate, (2) listen to and understand what the data are saying, (3) summarize the major themes, and (4) prepare a nondefensive response to the feedback. At the conclusion, the teams return to the main room to report their summaries and responses. All of the participants are asked to hiss softly if they detect defensiveness in a given report. The hissing, humorously and gently, provides feedback on how a group's response to conflict data is perceived by the others in the room. The valentines process not only helps to create part of the database for effective planning but identifies many specific issues on which the functional teams can follow up.

Intergroup relations are also addressed subtly through the relationship building in various subteam configurations and explicitly in the back home action planning where teams are invited to make requests for assistance from other teams.

Systemwide considerations are built into every facet of the design at a large-scale systems change meeting. The organizational valentines process expands intergroup conflict resolution to a whole system level. Each maximum-mix working team provides its members the opportunity to view the organization from other functional or hierarchical perspectives. The mission, goals,

and objectives are the product of hundreds of inputs from the many points of view represented; and action planning is designed with at least two phases—a cross-functional systemwide look and the view from within natural back home work teams. By bringing five layers and all of the functions of the organization together at one time, the large-scale systems change methodology provides the opportunity for creating new circuits of connection within the system as a whole. Systems thinking is at the core of the process.

A Dynamic Environment for Learning. Meetings within Boeing (and many other organizational environments) have historically been designed as a process in which one or a few presenters share information in a show-and-tell format. These sessions usually make use of overhead projectors and are managed in a way that minimizes interaction among members of the audience. The interactions that occur are usually limited to questions or commentary from individuals in the audience to the presenters. In this way, the complexity of group interaction is kept to a minimum, control of meetings is relatively easily maintained, and the audience has relatively little input to the shaping of ideas or decisions and little accountability for follow-on action. Meetings, in many cases, have been conducted in a manner analogous to read only memory in a computer, as a one-way information sharing exercise. This has been a virtually absolute norm for meetings with over 20 participants and fairly typical even of much smaller gatherings.

The large-scale systems change approach represents a major departure from the historical meeting paradigm. At one level, what we are attempting to accomplish is to teach the participants a new process model. We have designed a way of coming together with other organizational members, whether in small groups or large, that encourages openness, dialogue, participation, and complex multilayer and multifunctional communication. By giving the table groups guidelines on facilitation and recording and asking them to select and rotate members to serve in these roles, we are both setting an expectation of and providing practice in effective meeting management. In instances where the agenda calls for presentations by key stakeholders, such as customers, suppliers, senior management, or industry experts, we give the presenters very specific guidelines on the issues we want them to address. Further, we ask that they limit their remarks to a narrow prescribed time, and that they use no slides or viewgraphs. We have found that this approach minimizes audience passivity and maximizes the energy and spontaneity in the presenter's delivery. Such presentations are then immediately followed by time for table discussions, where the participants are asked to share with each other what they heard and their reactions and to generate, as a group, the questions of clarification or understanding they need to ask of the given stakeholder to better comprehend the stakeholder's point of view. The question-generation process then leads to an extended open forum give and take, where table groups are called on to ask their questions of the presenter. In this way, the participants are given the opportunity to shape the agenda with each stakeholder, and important information is shared through a dynamic exchange. Both the presenters and the session participants have responded enthusiastically to this process.

The other elements of the design, as described earlier, involve even more audience participation as subteams are called on to diagnose the effectiveness of existing management systems and practices, critique the draft mission, goals, and objectives, and develop the action plan to move the organization toward the desired future state. So, when the whole system actually does arrive in the room, what we do is provide a framework, including a statement of purpose and process design, that allows the participants maximum opportunity to create their own database, their own vision for the future, and their own plan to get there. The framework, designed effectively, allows a complex array of inputs to be organized into a coherent plan that is both understood and owned by the people responsible for implementation.

Outcomes

Improved organizational performance is the most significant outcome sought through the large-scale systems change methodology. The precise causal linkage between the large-systems approach and performance factors, such as quality, profitability, and customer and employee satisfaction, is difficult to establish, because, in the circumstances in which the methodology has been applied, other management and organization development initiatives have been underway simultaneously. Within the Ford Motor Company, the large-scale systems change methodology was used in concert with a major joint effort between the union and the company to promote employee involvement and an extensive companywide focus on quality improvement and cost-cutting. Each of these interventions is likely to have contributed to the major improvements the company realized in product quality, profitability, and employee satisfaction between the early 1980s and late 1980s. However, one indication of the perceived value of large-scale change process at Ford was the fact that several of the division general managers instituted the methodology as a regular part of their annual business planning activity—bringing together their top 160 managers each year to create a systemwide business plan. Feedback from program participants as well as qualitative assessments within the organization suggested that many of the intervention objectives (e.g., promotion of cross-functional teamwork, increased awareness of the business environment and the need for change, and a shift toward participative management) were achieved. Thompson (1989) documents both business and cultural outcomes associated with the large-scale change applications at Ford.

At Boeing, the large-scale strategic planning methodology was implemented both within the Aerospace and Electronics Division and Boeing Computer Services. Common observations of the organization leaders, as well as other stakeholders, pertain to increased teamwork across functional boundaries and with suppliers and customers, accelerated implementation of major systems and programs, a broader awareness of the needs of customers both internal and external, and much more extensive understanding of business goals and objectives within the organizations. The president of Boeing Computer Services, when asked by the company chairman for his assessment of the process, identified two significant changes. First, he noted that his calendar was much more open than before, because people below him were assuming greater responsibility for running the business, thus freeing him to devote more time to customer relations and strategic issues. Second, he felt his division had achieved unprecedented penetration of awareness even to the nonmanagement ranks regarding the organization's mission, goals, and objectives. One manager within the division remarked that he had accomplished the implementation of an interorganizational network system within six months, which previously would have taken two to three years, given the history of turf battles among the organizations involved. An outside computing hardware vendor noted a significant improvement in internal communications that increased both the efficiency and the effectiveness of his work with the division.

In other cases, organizations within Boeing Computer Services became much more proactive in forming teaming relationships with their customers. Several have created their own large-scale systems change meetings with the customer to focus on their working relationship. In one such meeting, where the historical customer-supplier relationship had been fractious, the principals from the two interfacing organizations enacted their historical conflict by simultaneously dousing one another with lemon meringue pies. As they did so, over 100 of their respective subordinates cheered them on and celebrated the cathartic parody of their past. Then they got down to work and forged a new partnership.

Employees and managers who have participated in the events (both within Boeing Computer Services and Boeing Aerospace and Electronics) have responded in an overwhelmingly positive manner to the experience, based on the data from postsession evaluations and later anecdotal evidence. Several have indicated that the meetings were the most productive they had seen in their careers with the company. Others have been observed explaining, to skeptical nonparticipants from other organizations, the power of seeing their own words incorporated into the substance of the division strategic plan.

In both of the Boeing divisions engaging in this process, significant initiatives were launched to address the strategic goals and objectives developed through the large-scale meetings. However, not all of the goals or objectives received equal attention nor was every subunit within the two organizations equally vigilant in pursuing their actions plans. The long-term impact and implementation depends, as with most organizational initiatives, on the quality of the strategy and plan that is developed as well as on individual responsibility, on division and subunit leadership, on the ongoing measurement and tracking of performance, and on the linkage of performance to pay and other incentives. The preliminary qualitative evidence of positive impact within Boeing is encouraging. The ultimate measure will be based on how much more effectively the organizations are able to serve the needs of their customers as well as their own employees.

Next Steps

Participation in an initial round of large-scale strategic planning does not deliver an organization wholesale from the machine model into the systems age. The intent of the intervention approach described here is to launch and accelerate the cultural transformation process. Much more remains to be done. Most immediately will be a continuation of the large-scale meeting process to encompass the managers and nonmanagers alike who have not yet been involved. At the same time, the development of internal consulting resources to support the substantial demand for follow-on activity within and between subunits is a practical necessity. Some of the internal resources have been developed already through participation in large-scale system change design and implementation teams. Yet, further skill building for these and other resources will be important to equip the organization to extend the process independently. For the leadership teams that have been through one or two rounds of the process, periodic large-scale sessions will help prevent the reinstitution of organizational arthritis and maintain a whole system perspective.

In the longer term, career development philosophies, information systems, and organization structures will need to be adapted to develop and reinforce systemic thinking and behavior. Increased cross-functional career rotation could go a long way toward bridging the differences among disciplines. Information systems designed with broad access can shorten the communication paths among hierarchical layers and among functional organizations. Finally, new organization structures (e.g., Ackoff's, 1981, 1989) circular organization) can bring different organization elements into closer proximity and easier and more fluid relationships. All of these approaches will need to be pursued in assisting old-line corporate hierarchies in the evolution towards whole system integration.

Getting Started: Internal Political Considerations

The approach to cultural and systems change described represents a substantial investment of both financial and human resources. Such an approach can only be undertaken in an environment where the senior leadership is convinced of the necessity for change and has confidence that the large-scale systems change methodology can help. The divisions within Ford and within Boeing where the process was launched were the parts of the respective systems experiencing the most pressure for change. This pressure, coupled in each case with a top leader willing to take a risk, made the large-scale systems change interventions possible. Without a compelling need to change, the intervention would probably appear too complex or too expensive, or both. Without the willingness to take a risk, the leaders would most likely settle for a more conservative and perhaps less demanding approach. The willingness to trust the process at Ford was based both on the criticality of the presenting crisis and pure faith that the consultants were competent. By the time the process was proposed at Boeing, there were already six years of experience with the approach at Ford on which to draw.

I was hired into Boeing in September of 1987 as corporate manager for organization development, with the explicit objective of initiating the type of cultural change approach with which I had been involved at Ford. My position was announced broadly in the organization and came with a good amount of corporate endorsement. The impact of this endorsement and the early footing it provided should not be underestimated. At a minimum, this positioning opened the door to several of what Weisbord (1987) calls "should we/shouldn't we" conversations about the large-scale systems change methodology. Moreover, it may have given the respective leaders confidence that the methodology itself had the blessing and support of corporate management and was thus less of a political risk than it might otherwise have been.

Beyond these considerations, the respective leaders also needed to be convinced purely on their own terms that the approach had merit. In the first year of my tenure with Boeing, I made numerous presentations on the evolution of organization theory from the machine bureaucracy to the systems model and on the experience with large-scale systems change at Ford. The presentations became the basis for planting seeds that might lead to further in-depth conversations with key organization leaders.

In both of the divisions within Boeing, as well as in the Diversified Products Operations within Ford where the process was begun, the senior leader made a decision to proceed with the approach with minimal or no input from his staff. While the approach was greeted initially by the staffs with skepticism, as they became involved their skepticism tended to fade. Symbolically, the large-scale events have sent a message of a willingness to open the company's systems and processes for broad scrutiny. The method has proven valuable for engaging a wide range of employees in the process of change and for taking the first steps toward organizational alignment.

There are also many organizations within Boeing that so far have not been involved. The process is best expanded on a pull basis, drawing on the internal motivation of organization leaders to select themselves for involvement in the approach. Further diffusion of the methodology into Boeing may be easier, because of growing awareness in the organization of the approach and the potential it represents. On the other hand, further diffusion may be more difficult. Other organizations may not experience as much urgency for change as those that went first; or, because of a not-invented-here bias, a general skepticism about the methodology, or an intracompany rivalry, these organizations may opt out.

At the moment, considerable energy and a raft of folklore have been unleashed as a result of the large-scale interventions. How the process continues to unfold within the company as a whole cannot be easily predicted. Boeing has embarked on a significant cultural shift. The large-scale systems change methodology is one vehicle for effecting the shift.

Reprise on Global Competitiveness

The large-scale systems change methodology was developed as a vehicle to accelerate change within overbounded, arthritic corporate hierarchies buffeted by global competition. Building new organizations with effective practices from the ground up certainly presents many unique challenges. Undoing the past and beginning anew with an existing workforce and infrastructure presents quite another set of dilemmas. The large-scale approach was created within this latter context. Neither of the companies described have the luxury of simply shutting down and building afresh with a new workforce and an entirely new set of resources. The challenges they face are not dissimilar to the challenge faced by many other corporations across the United States and throughout the world: that of building their capacity for learning and for adaptation in an increasingly competitive environment.

De Geus (1988) suggests that the only sustainable competitive advantage any firm enjoys is the ability to learn faster than its competitors. Whether one started with a new or an existing workforce, the necessity to build in a continuous learning capability would be the same. None of our large industrial enterprises can afford for long to close themselves off from new learning or to self-righteously cling to a comfortable status quo. There is much renewal to be done in the enterprises that make up our economy, and for many the time available to accomplish this before succumbing to outside competition is growing frightfully short (Dertouzos, Lester, and Solow, 1989; Grayson and O'Dell, 1988). If we are to be successful in turning around our large enterprises and the millions of people they employ, we must find new models of management and people involvement strategies that will greatly accelerate the rate at which these new models are learned and absorbed into the fiber of the organization. Preliminary evidence indicates that the large-scale systems change methodology represents a promising avenue for both accelerated learning and the accelerated involvement of the workforce in the process of change.

Notes

1. "Rethinking Japan." *Business Week,* August 7, 1989, pp. 44–52.
2. Postman argues that the seeds of our national decline may be found in the trivialization of issues and the neutering of substantive debate brought about through the medium of television. While this is not my contention in this paper, I am in agreement with Postman that much of the explanation for our relative decline can be found in factors internal to our society. However, rather than focusing on causality at the macrosocietal level, I will restrict my focus to the firm level.
3. *United Nations International Trade Statistics Yearbook.* New York: United Nations Publications, 1989. The assessment of market share loss was conducted by Colin Fox, managing director, Deltapoint Corporation, Bellevue, Wash.
4. "The 100 Largest Commercial Banking Companies." *Fortune,* August 24, 1992, pp. 213–14.   Grayson, C. J., and O'Dell, C. *American Business: A Two Minute Warning.* New York: Free Press, 1988.   The 1972 banking statistic was provided by Colin Fox, managing director, Deltapoint Corporation, Bellevue, WA.
5. Peters, T. *Thriving on Chaos.* New York: Alfred A. Knopf, 1987, pp. 4–5.
6. Peters, T. "Restoring American Competitiveness: Looking for New Models of Organizations." *The Academy of Management Executive,* May 1988, pp. 103–09.
7. The United States business landscape is dotted with companies having made significant turnarounds in quality, profitability, and customer and employee satisfaction. Some of those most commonly referenced include Ford Motor Company, Harley Davidson, Hewlett-Packard, Milliken, Motorola, and Xerox.
8. Kathleen Dannemiller provided the original illustration of the arthritic organization. See

Jusela, G. E.; Ball, R. A.; Tyson, C. E.; and Dannemiller, D. K. "Work Innovations at Ford Motor." In Shetty, Y. K., and Buehler, V. M. *Quality, Productivity and Innovation.* New York: Elsevier, 1987.
9. See Chin, R., and Benne, K. D. "General Strategies for Effecting Changes in Human Systems." In Bennis, W. G.; Benne, K. D.; and Chin, R. *The Planning of Change.* 2nd ed. New York: Holt, Rinehart & Winston, 1969.
10. The consultants included Kathleen Dannemiller, Alan Davenport, Bruce Gibb, Chuck Tyson, and Jeff Walsh, each of whom had been working independently until they were called together to collaborate on this project.
11. The consulting team was managed and coordinated by Nancy Badore, manager of employee involvement and training for DPO. I joined Ford as an internal organization development consultant in June of 1983 and began to collaborate with the Ann Arbor consultants on further iterations of the large-scale systems change methodology over the next few years.
12. I left the Ford Motor Company in August 1987 to assume the position of corporate manager for organization development with the Boeing Company.
13. See De Geus, A.P. "Planning as Learning." *Harvard Business Review,* March–April 1988, pp. 70–74. See also Stata, R. "Organizational Learning—The Key to Management Innovation." *Sloan Management Review,* Spring 1989, pp. 63–74.
14. The Boeing Electronics Division and its 5,000 employees were subsequently merged with the Aerospace Division, and Hitsman was given responsibility for the entire combined division.
15. The time frame for the look at strategic goals is influenced both by the size of the organization and the magnitude of change required. A smaller organization than Boeing Aerospace and Electronics seeking less substantial changes might use a narrower time horizon.
16. The organizational valentines process was developed by the original large-scale design team at Ford Motor Company as an element of the participative management seminar.

References

Ackoff, R. L. *Creating the Corporate Future.* New York: John Wiley & Sons, 1981.

Ackoff, R. L. "The Circular Organization: An Update." *The Academy of Management Executive,* February 1989, pp. 11–16.

Alderfer, C. P. "Boundary Relations in Organizational Diagnosis." In H. Meltzer, and F. R. Wicker, (eds.), *Humanizing Organizational Behavior.* Springfield, IL: Thomas, 1976.

Argyris, C. "Skilled Incompetence." *Harvard Business Review,* September–October 1986, pp. 74–79.

Beckhard, R. *Organization Development: Strategies and Models.* Reading, MA: Addison-Wesley, 1969.

Beckhard, R., and Harris, R. T. *Organizational Transitions.* Reading, MA: Addison-Wesley, 1977.

Bion, W. R. *Experiences in Groups.* London: Turistock, 1961.

Dannemiller, K. D. "Teambuilding at a Macro Level or Ben Gay for Arthritic Organizations." Arlington, VA: NTL Publications, 1985.

De Geus, A. P. "Planning as Learning." *Harvard Business Review,* March–April 1988, pp. 70–74.

Dertouzos, M. L.; Lester, R. K.; and Solow, R. M. *Made in America: Regaining the Productive Edge.* Cambridge, MA: MIT Press, 1989.

Grayson, C. J., Jr., and O'Dell, C. *American Business: A Two Minute Warning.* New York: Free Press, 1988.

Hayes, R. H.; Wheelwright, S. C.; and Clark, R. B. *Dynamic Manufacturing: Creating the Learning Organization.* New York: Free Press, 1988.

Imai, M. *Kaizen: The Key to Japan's Competitive Success.* New York: Random House, 1986.

Kanter, R. M. *The Change Masters.* New York: Simon & Schuster, 1983.

Keichel, W., III. "The Organization That Learns." *Fortune,* March 12, 1990, pp. 133–36.

Lindaman, E. B., and Lippitt, R. O. *Choosing the Future You Prefer.* Washington, D.C.: Development Publications, 1979.

Lippitt, R. "Future before You Plan." In *NTL Managers' Handbook.* Arlington, VA: NTL Institute, 1983.

Miller, E. J., and Rice, A. K. *Systems of Organization.* London: Tavistock, 1967.

Mills, D. Q., and Lovell, M. R., Jr. "Enhancing Competitiveness: The Contribution of Employee Relations." In B. R. Scott and G. C. Lodge (eds.), *U.S. Competitiveness in the World Economy.* Boston: Harvard Business School Press, 1985, pp. 455–78.

Mitroff, I. I. *Business Not as Usual.* San Francisco: Jossey-Bass Publishers, 1987.

Pascale, R., and Athos, A. *The Art of Japanese Management.* New York: Simon & Schuster, 1980.

Peters, T. *Thriving on Chaos.* New York: Alfred A. Knopf, 1987.

Peters, T. "Restoring American Competitiveness: Looking for New Models of Organizations." *The Academy of Management Executive,* May 1988, pp. 103–09.

Porter, M. E. "The Competitive Advantage of Nations." *Harvard Business Review,* March–April, 1990, pp. 73–93.

Postman, N. *Amusing Ourselves to Death: Public Discourse in the Age of Show Business.* New York: Viking Penguin, 1985.

"Rethinking Japan." *Business Week,* August 7, 1989, pp. 44–52.

Schindler-Rainman, E., and Lippitt, R. O. *Collaborative Community: Mobilizing Citizens for Action.* Riverside: University of California, 1980.

Schutz, W. *The Truth Option.* Berkeley, CA: Ten Speed Press, 1984.

Stata, R. "Organizational Learning—The Key to Management Innovation." *Sloan Management Review,* Spring 1989, pp. 63–74.

Thompson, G. "Large-System Change at the Executive Level in a Traditional Manufacturing Industry." Pepperdine University, unpublished master's thesis, 1989.

United Nations International Trade Statistics Yearbook. New York: United Nations Publication, 1989.

Vaill, P. B. "Seven Process Frontiers for Organization Development." George Washington University, 1986, prepublication draft.

Waterman, R. H., Jr. *The Renewal Factor.* Toronto: Bantam Books, 1987.

Weisbord, M. R. *Productive Workplaces.* San Francisco: Jossey-Bass, 1987a.

Weisbord, M. R. "Toward Third-Wave Managing and Consulting." *Organizational Dynamics,* Winter 1987b, pp. 4–24.

V EFFECTIVE IMPLEMENTATION OF THE OD PROCESS

This section of 11 essays focuses on the organization, implementation, and tracking of the OD process, including organizational transformation. Broadly, it looks at (*a*) effective consultant behavior and (*b*) managing the OD process.

The dimensions covered in Part V are crucial to the effective implementation of an OD effort. OD techniques are important, but they are of no more importance than the kinds of behavior the consultant displays as a person, day in and day out, in contact with clients. Nor is a given technique more important than the context in which it occurs. Techniques, behavior, and context—all are important in an OD effort.

While effective consultant behavior needs to be managed in the sense that consultants who are effective need to be selected, and individual consultants must conscientiously practice the best they know how, the *context* or environment in which the consultant intervenes needs to be carefully shepherded. While the consultant facilitating a team-building session needs to have good group and interpersonal skills, the consultant who is advising (perhaps the same person) on the management of the overall OD effort also needs to have extensive insight into the management of change efforts in complex systems. He or she needs to be aware of the critical "make or break" dimensions involved; for example, the ability of the internal consultant to be a trusted "broker" in bringing together two people or two groups who are in conflict. Knowledge about such make-or-break dimensions is fragmentary, but is evolving. Critical aspects of the consultant's behavior and the context in which that behavior occurs, and suggestions for managing and monitoring the unfolding OD process, are what this part of the book is about.

A. Effective Consultant Behavior

In this section essay topics range widely—from some practical guides for consultants, to the question of how deep interventions should be in terms of the emotional involvement of the client participants, to an early essay on effective team behaviors, and finally, to the concept of "shadow consulting." All of the essays are written by consultants, each of whom has had many years of successful practice.

Some of the themes pertaining to effective consultant behavior that we see in the essays in this section are (1) the need for self-awareness and self-understanding on the part of the consultant, (2) the need for the consultant to have cognitive maps (theories) for analyzing what is going on and what is functional and dysfunctional in the client system, and (3) the need to understand and conceptualize what the individuals in the client system are capable of learning from, in contrast to being hurt by or simply resisting. But a great deal of what these authors are saying has to do with effective and almost intuitive behavior on the part of the consultant as he or she balances, mediates, or modifies any of a myriad countervailing forces in the organization. And these forces can be political, intra-or interpersonal, intra-or intergroup, technological, economic, or having to do with subcultures within the organization.

The first essay, by Herbert Shepard, is an insightful, well-known selection that presents some "rules of thumb" for consultants. Issues of survival, initial entry, and building support are dealt with in this essay. Clearly, Shepard has in mind a model of organizational change, which includes notions about complexity and interdependency in organizations, about the use of power, and about helping relationships (i.e., the need for empathy, participation, and patience).

In the second essay, Marvin Weisbord provides some insights into the nature of the "contract" between consultant and client. He tells us the nature of the explicit agreements he attempts to develop with each client and provides valuable information on how he handles the first meeting. He concludes the essay on when the contract should be ended.

In the third essay, Roger Harrison defines "depth of intervention" and provides some criteria for making professional judgments about this important matter. One issue that is touched on in the Harrison article warrants highlighting. This is the issue of the degree to which a consultant should interpret resistance in a client group and should press for working through the matter. Harrison states the tendency to confront resistance emerged from individual psychoanalysis and psychotherapy, but the conditions are usually so substantially different in the organizational context "that a good many potentially fruitful and mutually satisfying consulting relationships are terminated early because of the consultant's taking the role of overcomer of resistance to change, rather than that of collaborator in the client's attempts at solving his problems."

It may be that psychoanalytic training of the consultant is necessary for constructive use to be made of the interpretation of resistances. In our opinion, most

OD consultants are likely to be more effective if they focus on behaviors and their organizational consequences, in contrast with trying to interpret or hypothesize unconscious motives.

The fourth essay goes all the way back to the early days of the T-group movement. This essay, by Kenneth Benne and Paul Sheats, identifies important group member roles that are associated with group effectiveness, along with a number of "individual roles" that can block effective group functioning. In later years, OD consultants and T-group trainers have been more likely to refer to these roles as behaviors. Training group members to be effective in the use of these behaviors can be very important to constructive team building and other organization development and transformation activities.

Finally in section A, Michael Collins discusses "shadow consulting," in which one OD consultant, dealing with a perplexing client situation, requests confidential assistance from a colleague. The colleague does not meet with the consultant's client organization, but serves as a behind-the-scenes sounding board or mentor to the OD consultant—thus the term *shadow consulting*. In this essay, Collins describes a five-phase shadow consulting process.

READING 34
RULES OF THUMB FOR CHANGE AGENTS

Herbert A. Shepard

The following aphorisms are not so much bits of advice (although they are stated that way) as things to think about when you are being a change agent, a consultant, an organization, or a community development practitioner—or when you are just being yourself trying to bring about something that involves other people.

Rule I: Stay Alive

This rule counsels against self-sacrifice on behalf of a cause that you do not wish to be your last.

Two exceptionally talented doctoral students came to the conclusion that the routines they had to go through to get their degrees were absurd, and decided they would be untrue to themselves to conform to an absurd system. That sort of reasoning is almost always self-destructive. Besides, their noble gesture in quitting would be unlikely to have any impact whatever on the system they were taking a stand against.

This is not to say that one should never take a stand, or a survival risk. But such risks should be taken as part of a purposeful strategy of change, and appropriately timed and targeted. When they are taken under such circumstances, one is very much alive.

But Rule I is much more than a survival rule. The rule means that you should let your whole being be involved in the undertaking. Since most of us have never been in touch with our whole beings, it means a lot of putting together of parts that have been divided, of using internal communications channels that have been closed or were never opened.

Staying alive means loving yourself. Self-disparagement leads to the suppression of potentials, to a win-lose formulation of the world, and to wasting life in defensive maneuvering.

Staying alive means staying in touch with your purpose. It means using your skills, your emotions, your labels and positions, rather than being used by them. It means not being trapped in other people's games. It means turning yourself on and off, rather than being dependent on the situation. It means choosing with a view to the consequences as well as the impulse. It means going with the flow even while swimming against it. It means living in several worlds without being swallowed up in any. It means seeing dilemmas as opportunities for creativity. It means greeting absurdity with laughter while trying to unscramble it. It means capturing the moment in the light of the future. It means seeing the environment through the eyes of your purpose.

Rule II: Start Where the System Is

This is such ancient wisdom that one might expect its meaning had been fully explored and apprehended. Yet in practice, the rule—and the system—are often violated.

The rule implies that one should begin by diagnosing the system. But systems do not necessarily *like* being diagnosed. Even the *term diagnosis* may be offensive. And the system may be even less ready for someone who calls himself or

Source: Herbert A. Shepard, "Rules of Thumb for Change Agents," *Organization Development Practitioner*, November 1975, pp. 1–5. (Publication of the National Organization Development Network, P.O. Box 69329, Portland, OR 97201.)

herself a change agent. It is easy for the practitioner to forget that the use of jargon, which prevents laymen from understanding the professional mysteries, is a hostile act.

Starting where the system is can be called the Empathy Rule. To communicate effectively, to obtain a basis for building sound strategy, the change agent needs to understand how the client sees himself and his situation, and needs to understand the culture of the system. Establishing the required rapport does not mean that the change agent who wants to work in a traditional industrial setting should refrain from growing a beard. It does mean that, if he has a beard, the beard is likely to determine where the client is when they first meet, and the client's curiosity needs to be dealt with. Similarly, the rule does not mean that a female change agent in a male organization should try to act like one of the boys, or that a young change agent should try to act like a senior executive. One thing it does mean is that sometimes where the client is, is wondering where the change agent is.

Rarely is the client in any one place at any one time. That is, she or he may be ready to pursue any of several paths. The task is to walk together on the most promising path.

Even unwitting or accidental violations of that Empathy Rule can destroy the situation. I lost a client through two violations in one morning. The client group spent a consulting day at my home. They arrived early in the morning, before I had my empathy on. The senior member, seeing a picture of my son in the living room, said, "What do you do with boys with long hair?" I replied thoughtlessly, "I think he's handsome that way." The small chasm thus created between my client and me was widened and deepened later that morning when one of the family tortoises walked through the butter dish.

Sometimes starting where the client is, which sounds both ethically and technically virtuous, can lead to some ethically puzzling situations.

Robert Frost[1] described a situation in which a consultant was so empathic with a king who was unfit to rule that the king discovered his own unfitness and had himself shot, whereupon the consultant became king.

Empathy permits the development of a mutual attachment between client and consultant. The resulting relationship may be one in which their creativities are joined, a mutual growth relationship. But it can also become one in which the client becomes dependent and is manipulated by the consultant. The ethical issues are not associated with starting where the system is, but with how one moves with it.

Rule III: Never Work Uphill

This is a comprehensive rule, and a number of other rules are corollaries or examples of it. It is an appeal for an organic, rather than a mechanistic approach to change, for a collaborative approach to change, for building strength and building on strength. It has a number of implications that bear on the choices the change agent makes about how to use him/herself, and it says something about life.

Corollary 1: Don't Build Hills as You Go. This corollary cautions against working in a way that builds resistance to movement in the direction you have chosen as desirable. For example, a program which has a favorable effect on one portion of a population may have the opposite effect on other portions of the population. Perhaps the commonest error of this kind has been in the employment of T-group training in organizations: turning on the participants and turning off the people who didn't attend, in one easy lesson.

---

[1] Robert Frost, "How Hard It Is to Keep from Being King When It's in You and in the Situation," *In The Clearing* (New York: Holt, Rinehart & Winston, 1962), pp. 74–84.

Corollary 2: Work in the Most Promising Arena. The physician-patient relationship is often regarded as analogous to the consultant-client relationship. The results for system change of this analogy can be unfortunate. For example, the organization development consultant is likely to be greeted with delight by executives who see in his specialty the solution to a hopeless situation in an outlying plant. Some organization development consultants have disappeared for years because of the irresistibility of such challenges. Others have whiled away their time trying to counteract the Peter Principle by shoring up incompetent managers.

Corollary 3: Build Resources. Don't do anything alone that could be accomplished more easily or more certainly by a team. Don Quixote is not the only change agent whose effectiveness was handicapped by ignoring this rule. The change agent's task is an heroic one, but the need to be a hero does not facilitate team building. As a result, many change agents lose effectiveness by becoming spread too thin. Effectiveness can be enhanced by investing in the development of partners.

Corollary 4: Don't Overorganize. The democratic ideology and theories of participative management that many change agents possess can sometimes interfere with common sense. A year or two ago I offered a course, to be taught by graduate students. The course was oversubscribed. It seemed that a data-based process for deciding whom to admit would be desirable, and that participation of the graduate students in the decision would also be desirable. So I sought data from the candidates about themselves, and xeroxed their responses for the graduate students. Then the graduate students and I held a series of meetings. Then the candidates were informed of the decision. In this way we wasted a great deal of time and everyone felt a little worse than if we had used an arbitrary decision rule.

Corollary 5: Don't Argue If You Can't Win. Win-lose strategies are to be avoided because they deepen conflict instead of resolving it. But the change agent should build her or his support constituency as large and deep and strong as possible so that she or he can continue to risk.

Corollary 6: Play God a Little. If the change agent doesn't make the critical value decisions, someone else will be happy to do so. Will a given situation contribute to your fulfillment? Are you creating a better world for yourself and others, or are you keeping a system in operation that should be allowed to die? For example, the public education system is a mess. Does that mean that the change agent is morally obligated to try to improve it, destroy it, or develop a substitute for it? No, not even if he or she knows how. But the change agent does need a value perspective for making choices like that.

Rule IV: Innovation Requires a Good Idea, Initiative, and a Few Friends

Little can be accomplished alone, and the effects of social and cultural forces on individual perception are so distorting that the change agent needs a partner, if only to maintain perspective and purpose.

The quality of the partner is as important as the quality of the idea. Like the change agent, partners must be relatively autonomous people. Persons who are authority-oriented—who need to rebel or need to submit—are not reliable partners: the rebels take the wrong risks and the good soldiers don't take any. And rarely do they command the respect and trust from others that is needed if an innovation is to be supported.

The partners need not be numerous. For example, the engineering staff of a chemical company designed a new process plant using edge-of-the-art technology. The design departed radically from the experience of top management, and they were about to reject it. The engineering chief suggested that the design be reviewed by a distinguished engineering professor. The principal designers were in fact former students of the professor. For this reason he accepted the assignment, charged the company a large fee for reviewing the design (which he did not trouble to examine), and told the management that it was brilliantly conceived and executed. By this means the engineers not only implemented their innovations but also grew in the esteem of their management.

A change agent experienced in the Washington environment reports that he knows of only one case of successful interdepartmental collaboration in mutually designing, funding, and managing a joint project. It was accomplished through the collaboration of himself and three similarly minded young men, one from each of four agencies. They were friends and met weekly for lunch. They conceived the project and planned strategies for implementing it. Each person undertook to interest and influence the relevant key people in his own agency. The four served one another as consultants and helpers in influencing opinion and bringing the decision makers together.

An alternative statement of Rule IV is as follows: Find the people who are ready and able to work, introduce them to one another, and work with them. Perhaps because many change agents have been trained in the helping professions, perhaps because we have all been trained to think bureaucratically, concepts like organization position, representativeness, or need are likely to guide the change agent's selection of those he or she works with.

A more powerful beginning can sometimes be made by finding those persons in the system whose values are congruent with those of the change agent, who possess vitality and imagination, who are willing to work overtime, and who are eager to learn. Such people are usually glad to have someone like the change agent join in getting something important accomplished,

and a careful search is likely to turn up quite a few. In fact, there may be enough of them to accomplish general system change, if they can team up in appropriate ways.

In building such teamwork the change agent's abilities will be fully challenged, as he joins them in establishing conditions for trust and creativity; dealing with their anxieties about being seen as subversive; enhancing their leadership, consulting, problem solving, diagnosing, and innovating skills; and developing appropriate group norms and policies.

Rule V: Load Experiments for Success

This sounds like counsel to avoid risk taking. But the decision to experiment always entails risk. After that decision has been made, take all precautions.

The rule also sounds scientifically immoral. But whether an experiment produces the expected results depends upon the experimenter's depth of insight into the conditions and processes involved. Of course, what is experimental is what is new to the system; it may or may not be new to the change agent.

Build an umbrella over the experiment. A chemical process plant, which was to be shut down because of the inefficiency of its operations, undertook a union-management cooperation project to improve efficiency, which involved a modified form of profit sharing. Such plans were contrary to company policy, but the regional vice president was interested in the experiment and successfully concealed it from his associates. The experiment was successful; the plant became profitable. But in this case, the umbrella turned out not to be big enough. The plant was shut down, anyway.

Use the Hawthorne effect. Even poorly conceived experiments are often made to succeed when the participants feel ownership. And conversely, one of the obstacles to the spread of useful innovations is that the groups to which they are offered do not feel ownership of them.

For example, if the change agent hopes to use experience-based learning as part of his or her strategy, the first persons to be invited should be those who consistently turn all their experiences into constructive learning. Similarly, in introducing team development processes into a system, begin with the best-functioning team.

Maintain voluntarism. This is not easy to do in systems where invitations are understood to be commands; but nothing vital can be built on such motives as duty, obedience, security seeking, or responsiveness to social pressure.

Rule VI: Light Many Fires

Not only does a large, monolithic development or change program have high visibility and other qualities of a good target, it also tends to prevent subsystems from feeling ownership of and consequent commitment to the program.

The meaning of this rule is more orderly than the random prescription—light many fires—suggests. And part of a system is the way it is partly because of the way the rest of the system is. To work towards change in one subsystem is to become one more determinant of its performance. Not only is the change agent working uphill but, as soon as he turns his back, other forces in the system will press the subsystem back toward its previous performance mode.

If many interdependent subsystems are catalyzed and the change agent brings them together to facilitate one another's efforts, the entire system can begin to move.

Understanding patterns of interdependency among subsystems can lead to a strategy of fire-setting. For example, in public school systems it requires collaboration among politicians, administrators, teachers, parents, and students to bring about significant innovation, and active opposition on the part of only one of these groups to prevent it. In parochial school systems, on the other hand, collaboration between the adminis-

tration and the church can provide a powerful impetus for change in the other groups.

Rule VII: Keep an Optimistic Bias

Our society grinds along with much polarization and cruelty, and even the helping professions compose their world of grim problems to be "worked through." The change agent is usually flooded with the destructive aspects of the situations he or she enters. People in most systems are impressed by one another's weaknesses, and stereotype each other with such incompetencies as they can discover.

This rule does not advise ignoring destructive forces. But its positive prescription is that the change agent be especially alert to the constructive forces, which are often masked and suppressed in a problem-oriented, envious culture.

People have as great an innate capacity for joy as for resentment, but resentment causes them to overlook opportunities for joy. In a workshop for married couples, a husband and wife were discussing their sexual problem and how hard they were working to solve it. They were not making much progress, since they didn't realize that sex is not a problem but an opportunity.

Individuals and groups locked in destructive kinds of conflict focus on their differences. The change agent's job is to help them discover and build on their commonalities, so that they will have a foundation of respect and trust which will permit them to use their differences as a source of creativity. The unhappy partners focus on past hurts and continue to destroy the present and future with them. The change agent's job is to help them change the present so that they will have a new past on which to create a better future.

Rule VIII: Capture the Moment

A good sense of relevance and timing is often treated as though it were a "gift" or "intuition," rather than something that can be learned, something spontaneous, rather than something planned. The opposite is nearer the truth. One is more likely to "capture the moment" when everything one has learned is readily available.

Some years ago my wife and I were having a very destructive fight. Our nine-year-old daughter decided to intervene. She put her arms around her mother and asked: "What does Daddy do that bugs you?" She was an attentive audience for the next few minutes while my wife told her, ending in tears. She then put her arms around me: "What does Mommy do that bugs you?" and listened attentively to my response, which also ended in tears. She then went to the record player and put on a favorite love song ("If Ever I Should Leave You") and left us alone to make up.

The elements of my daughter's intervention had all been learned. They were available to her, and she combined them in a way that could make the moment better.

Perhaps it's our training in linear cause-and-effect thinking and the neglect of our capacities for imagery that makes us so often unable to see the multiple potential of the moment. Entering the situation "blank" is not the answer. One needs to have as many frameworks for seeing and strategies for acting available as possible. But it's not enough to involve only one's head in the situation: one's heart has to get involved, too. Cornelia Otis Skinner once said that the first law of the stage is to love your audience. You can love your audience only if you love yourself. If you have relatively full access to your organized experience, to yourself, and to the situation, you will capture the moment more often.

READING 35
THE ORGANIZATION DEVELOPMENT CONTRACT

Marvin Weisbord

In OD consulting, the contract is central to success or failure. Most other kinds of contracts—employment, service, research, and the like—focus heavily on content; that is, the nature of the work to be performed, the schedule, and the money to change hands. Generally, these issues are negotiated through a proposal, which one party writes and the other accepts or rejects. The consulting contract most people are familiar with takes two forms: (1) You hire me to study the problem and tell you what to do and (2) You hire me to solve the problem for you. I call these "expert" consulting contracts. In either case the quality of the advice and/or the solution is the focus, and the *consultant* is a central figure, whatever happens.

But in OD consulting, the *client* is the central figure. He hires me to consult with him while he is working on his problem, helping him to achieve a better diagnosis of what has happened and what steps he must take to improve things. This is a form of collaboration which, if successful, helps the client also to achieve better working relationships with others, for example peers, boss, and subordinates.

For that reason, in OD contracting, more so than other kinds, the *process* by which content issues are pinned down is critical. Unless this negotiation is a model of the consultant's values and problem-solving behavior, the contract, when it's tested, probably won't stand up. More about testing later.

What do I mean by contract? I mean an explicit exchange of expectations, part dialogue,

part written document, which clarifies for consultant and client three critical areas:

1. What each expects to get from the relationships.
2. How much time each will invest, when, and at what cost.
3. The ground rules under which the parties will operate.

What Each Expects

Clients expect, and have a right to expect, change for the better in a situation that is making their lives hard. This situation, as my clients experience it, has three main components:

1. Organizational crises (i.e., people leaving; excessive absenteeism; too high costs; too little budget; unmanageable environmental demands; pressure from above; conflict between individuals or work groups).

2. People problems (i.e., one or two or more "significant others" are singled out as particular sore spots).

3. Personal dilemma (i.e., whether this job, or this career, is what I really want).

The third component always grows in magnitude in direct proportion to the first two. Clients in a bind don't get much fun out of their work. They long for something simpler, better suited to their strengths, more consistent with their values. Above all, most clients long for outcomes. They want permanent "change" for the better, with no backsliding. I, on the other hand, see new outcomes as evidence the client is learning a better way of coping. From my point of view the *process*—gathering information, becoming aware of deeper meanings, making

Source: Marvin Weisbord, "The Organization Development Contract," *Organization Development Practitioner* 5, no. 2 (1973), pp. 1–4 (publication of the National Organization Development Network, P.O. Box 69329, Portland, OR 97201).

choices—is my most important product. While the client identifies three kinds of difficult situations he wants to work on, I keep in mind three levels of improvement he might achieve:

1. Solution of the immediate crisis— changing structures, policies, procedures, relationship.
2. Learning something about his own coping style—how he deals with crises, how he might do it better.
3. Learning a process for coping better, continually becoming aware and making choices, about whatever issue presents itself.

From my point of view, the existing problem is a vehicle for learning more about how to manage organizational life better. I have no preferences for the kinds of problems clients have. From my point of view, one issue will do as well as another.

However, clients rarely ask my direct help in cutting costs, reducing absenteeism, raising morale, or improving services. Instead, identifying me mainly with the "people" issue, they nearly always look for guidance in taking swift, painless, self-evidently correct actions toward the significant others who contribute to their misery. I always ask prospective clients to name what outcomes they hope to achieve by working with me.

> Want others to understand our goals better.
> Better communications, fewer misunderstandings.
> _____ will shape up or ship out.
> Better meetings—more excitement, more decisions made.

Notice that each of these statements is somewhat abstract, self-evidently "good," and very hard to measure. I never accept such generalities as adequate statements of a client's expectations. Instead, I push hard on outcomes. What would you see happening that would tell you communications are improving? How will you know when goals are clearer, or morale has gone up? What will people do? Will you be able to watch them do it? When I push at this level, I get more realistic statements:

> Pete will come to me with his gripes directly, instead of going to Fred.
> Deadlines will be taken seriously and met more often.
> In meetings, decisions will be made, actions agreed on, and names and dates put on them.
> I will understand how to set up the _____ unit, and will have agreement on whatever way I decide.
> We will have a new procedure for handling customer complaints.
> I will make a decision whether to keep or fire _____.

These statements are good short-run indicators of change. They are realistic expectations. Are changes like these worth the client's investment of time and money? Is there enough in it for him to go ahead? It's important that he be clear he is choosing to do whatever we do together because it's worth it to him (and not because it's this year's panacea, or somebody else tried it and liked it, or because he thinks his problems will go away). What does he want personally out of this? Easier life? What does *that* mean? etcetera.

I expect some things, too. Clients know I work mainly for money and want to be paid on time. However, I try also to indicate some of my secondary motives for working with them.

For example, I crave variety. I like learning about and using my skills in various "content" areas—manufacturing and service industries, medicine, law enforcement, public education. I like to try new technologies, to break new theoretical ground, to write and publish my experiences. The chance to do something new raises my incentive with any client. So does a client's ready acceptance of some responsibility for the crisis. If clients are well-motivated to work on their problems, so am I—and I tell them so. In doing this, I am trying to say that each of us has a right to some personal benefits from our relationship, apart from any benefits the organization may derive.

Structuring the Relationship: Time and Money

OD, like much of life, is carried forward by a sequence of meetings between people. The central decision in any contract discussion is which people should sit in what room for how long and for what purpose. At some point it is essential to name those people, pick dates, and set a budget. The client has a right to know how much time I will invest in interviewing, or survey sampling, or whatever, and how long our meetings will require. If I need time in between to organize data, I estimate how much. Often the initial contract is diagnostic, to be completed at a face-to-face meeting where the data will be examined, a common diagnosis arrived at, and next steps decided on. Always, I work to clarify the costs, time, and money of each next step. Generally, this information will be written down.

In addition, there are some things I will and won't do, money aside. I know what these things are, and only mention them if the client does, on the premise that there's no point in solving a problem I don't have. For instance, I always turn down opportunities to work weekends. I'll work morning, noon, and night on any scheduled day if necessary. On weekends my contract is with my family. In addition, I have a strong value that *when* you work on your organization indicates how important you consider it. People get themselves into crises during the week. If they don't have time to get out during the week, they're never going to get out by working weekends. That makes me the wrong consultant for them. (Incidentally, I have never lost a client because of this policy.)

Ground Rules

Ground rules speak to the process of our relationship. Sometimes I write them down,

sometimes not. In any case, I try to get an understanding that includes these explicit agreements:

1. I supply methods, techniques, theory, and so on to help you understand and work better on your problems. You supply energy, commitment, and share responsibility for success. I do *not* study your problems and recommend expert solutions.

2. Part of my job is to raise sticky issues and push you on them. You have a right to say no to anything you don't want to deal with. If you feel free to say no, I'll feel free to push.

3. Tell me if I do something puzzling or irritating, and give me permission to tell you the same.

4. I have no special preferences for how you deal with others. Part of my job is to make you aware of what you do, and what possible consequences your actions have for me and for the people around you. My job is also to preserve and encourage your freedom of choice about what, if anything, you should do.

5. My client is the whole organization. That means I intend not to be seen as an advocate for anybody's pet ideas, especially ones requiring your special expertise. However, I do advocate a certain process for problem solving, and recognize that some people oppose my process. I accept that risk.

6. Any information I collect and present will be anonymous. I will never attach names to anything people tell me. However, in certain situations (e.g., team building) I don't *want* confidential information, meaning anything which you are unwilling for other team members to know, even anonymously.

7. All data belongs to the people who supply it. I will never give or show it to anyone without their permission.

8. Either of us can terminate on 24 hours notice, regardless of contract length, so long as we have a face-to-face meeting first.

9. We evaluate all events together, face to face, and make explicit decisions about what to do next.

Contracting, like the seasons, is repetitive and continually renewable. If I have a long-term contract (e.g., four days a month for a year) I also have a separate contract for each meeting, which I present on a flipsheet and discuss at the outset. If I have a contract with a boss to help him build his team, I need to extend it to the team before we go to work. If I succeed with the team, and some members want to work with *their* teams, I need again to negotiate a new deal with the new people. Once, having worked with a team, I found the boss wanting to confront *his* boss. He wanted the whole team to do it with him, with me as consultant. I pointed out that that would require a temporary contract between me, him, and his boss. He set up a dinner meeting—the night before the confrontation—and his boss and I made a one-day contract, which stood up very well next morning.

In short, I'm never finished contracting. Each client meeting requires that I reexamine the contract. Does it cover everybody I'm working with? Is it clear what we're doing now? And why?

Moreover, contracting—while it deals ostensibly and mainly with content issues—has a process side crucial to its success. Consider, in some detail, where and how an OD contract is made.

OD contracts usually begin with a phone call or letter. Somebody has heard about what I did somewhere else. They wonder whether I can do it for (or with, or to) them. If I receive a letter, I respond with a phone call to the writer. If he calls first, I return his call at a time when I can spend 10 minutes or more discussing what he wants and whether or not it makes sense to meet. This initial contact is crucial to any contract. Each of us is trying—over the phone—to decide whether he likes the other well enough to proceed. I try not to prejudge the conversation. I want a face-to-face meeting *if* there's a chance of getting a solid contract. Here are some questions running through my mind:

1. How open is caller with me? Me with him?
2. Is the caller window-shopping, maybe calling several consultants to find the "best deal" (whatever that means)? Does he really want me? Perhaps—as is often the case—he doesn't know what he wants. If that's so, I have a good chance to consult with him on the phone, helping him clarify what he's after.

3. To which of his problems am I the solution? How does he name the issue?

4. What does he see as the solution? Is it a workshop? A meeting? A series of meetings? Magic?

5. Is his mind made up? Has he diagnosed his troubles and prescribed something already, which I'm to administer?

6. Does he have a budget? Is it adequate to his expectations? To mine? Is it likely to be worth my while to invest in a face-to-face meeting? I don't talk price on the phone, but do test whether a budget exists or could be got together. If the answer is no, I decide not to pursue it further.

7. Assume a budget, and a willingness on his part and mine to go forward. We need a meeting. Should anybody else be there? Who? Is the caller in a position to enter into a contract? If not, who is? His boss? Can he make the meeting? Is there another consultant I want to involve? If so, I ask whether I can bring an associate.

I end the phone call by clarifying that each of us intends to explore further whether there is a fit between the kinds of things my potential client needs help on and the skills and experience I have. I am investing up to a day at no fee. (If there are travel expenses involved, I test whether he will pay those.) At the end of that day, each of us will know whether to go further.

First Meeting

I arrive, greet my prospective client, introduce myself and associate to him and his associates. We have coffee and exchange pleasantries. Each of us is deciding, silently, privately, and maybe unconsciously, how much we like the other. We look for cues. We give cues. Early on, we get down to business—or appear to. The content issues might include:

1. Our backgrounds—potential client needs to know enough about me to feel I can help, before he'll put out major problems.

2. Issues bothering client system—are they symptomatic of other things, which are not being discussed? I always ask for examples in terms of observable behavior. "Communications" or "decision making" are not issues you can see, feel, or pin down. Who needs to talk to whom? Why? What do they do now? What do people do when they disagree? What patterns of behavior do the people present see in the organization?

3. What changes would the people I'm talking to like to see? What things would they observe happening that would tell them they are getting desired outcomes? This step in naming outcomes is important in reducing the level of fantasy around OD and what it can do.

4. What first event would be appropriate to moving the system in the desired direction? Nearly always, this event should be diagnostic. It should be an activity which will heighten the awareness of the people I'm meeting with about how the issues they raise are seen by others in the system—colleagues, subordinates, customers, students, peers, etc. If the system is ready, the budget exists, and my reading of the willingness to proceed is good, I may propose a workshop activity, based on interviews. Sometimes I propose that the workshop start with interviews of each person as a first step in agenda building (okay if no more than 10 or 12 attend). Sometimes, it makes more sense to consult to a work group within the framework of their regular weekly or monthly meetings. Sometimes, a survey questionnaire provides a database for a diagnostic meeting.

Whatever the event, we need a schedule, a place to meet, and a division of labor for organizing materials, sending out the agenda, etc. Sometimes these things can be decided in the first meeting. Sometimes I agree to write a formal proposal and proceed from there. Always I try to close on the next step—what I will do, what the client will do, and by what date.

The above considerations focus mainly on content. However, there are several process issues surrounding this meeting which I'm continually working on, too:

1. First among these is, "Do I like this person?" If not a spark of fondness, or warmth, or empathy, then what *am* I feeling? Annoyance? Frustration? Wariness? Can I find *something* to like, respect, or admire about the other person? Usually, I can. Until I do, however, and until the other person finds it in me, I think our work on issues, possible next steps, logistics, etc. is largely fictional. It is a way of using the task at hand to help us get greater clarity about our relationship. Any time I'm uncertain about a relationship I believe my contract is in jeopardy, no matter what fine words are spoken or written on paper. Each time the relationship question is resolved, a little spark jumps. I watch for it.

2. The client's depth of commitment is an issue for me. Does he really want to change things? Does he accept responsibility—at least a little bit—for the way things are? If he says, "I want you to change *them*," and I say, "Okay, but how open are you to changing?", does he pull back, hem and haw? Or does he smile and admit the possibility? How open is he to understanding how what he does affects other people? My value about organizations improving themselves—that is, people learning to do things better with each other—is clear; I try to test how my client feels about that.

3. Part of client commitment is resources. Clients find money to do things they want to do. If money seems to be an insurmountable problem, I look to some other process issue—anxiety about failure, a boss who's negative about OD, fear of opening up "destructive issues," etc. Helping the client get in touch with these possibilities, if I can, is valuable for both of us, whether I work with him again or not. How to do it? By asking such questions as: What is

the risk? What's the worst thing that could happen? How much exposure can you stand? I also ask what good things might happen, and whether the possible outcomes are worth the price.

In some ways OD is like playing the market. Every intervention is a calculated risk. There are no guarantees. The client will have problems no matter what he does. So will I. The question I continually confront is: Which problems would you *rather* have? The ones you have now? Or the ones you *will* have if you try to solve the ones you have now? Once in a while, potential clients decide they would rather live with what they've got. I support this insight. It's better that both of us know it sooner, rather than later.

More often this process leads to greater clarity and commitment on both our parts to make an intervention successful. My value set goes something like this: I want to find out what's real, what the environment will support, what's possible in this relationship, and then learn how to live with it. Of course I want to sell my services. I want to try new interventions. More than that, I want to be successful. I am learning to spot conditions under which I fail. An unclear contract ranks high on the list.

I resist entering untenable contracts, for I know deep down that they are like airplanes without fuel. No matter how beautiful they look, they won't fly. The fuel for an OD contract is (1) client commitment, (2) a good relationship between us, and (3) a clear structure to that relationship, symbolized by our ability to agree on what services I will perform, when, and at what costs in time and money.

Structuring the Relationship

Item 3 brings us to the specific first intervention. It has several criteria:

1. It is responsive to the client's perceived problem. He must see it as helping him gain greater clarity, insight, and control over what-

ever issues are bugging *him*. It is not based on my need to use any particular trick in my bag.

2. It names the people who will come together, when, for how long, and why. "Why" is generally the client's to answer, in his own words, but I help him shape the language if he has trouble. I get clear that *the* boss will tell people why they are there, as he sees it, and *I* will tell them what I see as *my* contract with them. It is never my job to tell people why they are there.

3. It involves some form of diagnosis. That means some systematic information is collected, which will heighten the clients' awareness and enlarge their freedom of choice. Sometimes this information fits some conceptual scheme, which I make explicit. Sometimes I help the client build a scheme from the information, which will make sense to him. Always, data collection, as I see it, must be done in such a way that the people who supply the information will recognize it as critical to their lives together when I collate it and hand it back. The more interpreting or categorizing I do in advance, the less likely this is to happen.

I ensure confidentiality and anonymity. Interpretation, I try to make clear, will result when people who supplied the information meet face to face to assign meaning to it. I try always to specify how much time people must give, what kinds of questions will be asked, and what will become of the answers. This structuring reduces anxiety and sets up reasonable expectations.

4. I establish that part of the contract is mutual feedback. I expect clients to confront me openly on my behavior when it doesn't make sense, to question anything I do, and to point out to me words or behavior that violate their sense of what's appropriate. In return, I expect to be open with them.

It is around this clause, I think, that all contracts are tested sooner or later. In a workshop the test may come in the form of protest that the activities are irrelevant to the agenda and a waste of time. In a one-to-one relationship, the test may be something I did or said that really irritated the client. It takes some risk to let me know. In opening the issue, he is checking to see whether I'm as good at handling deeds as I am at manipulating words.

I define testing the contract as an emotion-provoking exchange between me and the client in some risky situation. As a result our relationship will become more "real," more truly experimental, more like the action research model which I advocate as an appropriate way to live. I don't expect the burden for testing to rest entirely on the client. I test, too, whenever the time seems right, usually around something the client is doing which affects our relationship. Once, I noticed a client would continually express disappointment in others and told him I was worried that one day—if not already—he was going to feel the same way about me. He owned up to the possibility and assured me I would be the first to know, which, when the time came, I was. The confrontation deepened our relationship and strengthened the contract. It might have ended it, too.

I welcome ending a contract explicitly by having it tested and found wanting. Better a clean death than lingering agony. It is time to test (and maybe end) a contract when:

The client keeps putting things off.

Agreements are made and forgotten (by either side).

The consultant appears to have a higher emotional stake in the outcomes than the client does.

The consultant asks for events, or activities, which intensify the feeling of crisis and pressure without much prospect for eventual relief.

The client looks to the consultant to do things which he, as manager of his own organization, should be doing (i.e., arranging meetings, sending out agendas, carrying messages, and getting other people to do everything the client always wanted them to do but was afraid to ask).

The client is doing better and really doesn't need outside help.

For me, a crisp, clean ending remains desirable, but sometimes elusive. Going over 14 major contracts during the last four years, I find 9 ended cleanly with no "unfinished business," 3 ended because the boss lacked commitment to continue, and 2 because organizational changes left a leadership vacuum and me uncertain who the client was.

Where the boss lacked commitment, the intended follow-up meetings never took place; and I let things alone, feeling, I suppose, relatively little commitment myself. In the cases of organizational changes, it became plain the interim leadership lacked either incentive or authority to keep up the contract, and I had other fish to fry.

It seems to me contracts have a natural life. Organizations eventually outgrow or tire of or cease needing a particular consultant, and vice versa. It's better for me and my client that we recognize explicitly when it's time to part.

READING 36
CHOOSING THE DEPTH OF ORGANIZATIONAL INTERVENTION

Roger Harrison

Since World War II there has been a great proliferation of behavioral science-based methods by which consultants seek to facilitate growth and change in individuals, groups, and organizations. The methods range from operations analysis and manipulation of the organization chart, through the use of Grid laboratories, T-groups, and nonverbal techniques. As was true in the development of clinical psychology and psychotherapy, the early stages of this developmental process tend to be accompanied by considerable competition, criticism, and argument about the relative merits of various approaches. It is my conviction that controversy over the relative goodness or badness, effectiveness or ineffectiveness, of various change strategies really accomplishes very little in the way of increased knowledge or unification of behavioral science. As long as we are arguing about what method is better than another, we tend to learn very little about how various approaches fit together or complement one another, and we certainly make more difficult and ambiguous the task of bringing these competing points of view within one overarching system of knowledge about human processes.

As our knowledge increases, it begins to be apparent that these competing change strategies are not really different ways of doing the same thing—some more effective and some less effective—but rather that they are different ways of doing *different* things. They touch the individual, the group, or the organization in different aspects of their functioning. They require differ-

Source: Reprinted with permission from NTL Institute, "Choosing the Depth of Organizational Intervention" by Roger Harrison, pp. 182–202, *Journal of Applied Behavioral Science* 6, no. 2, copyright © 1970.

ing kinds and amounts of commitment on the part of the client for them to be successful, and they demand different varieties and levels of skills and abilities on the part of the practitioner.

I believe that there is a real need for conceptual models which differentiate intervention strategies from one another in a way which permits rational matching of strategies to organizational change problems. The purpose of this paper is to present a modest beginning which I have made toward a conceptualization of strategies, and to derive from this conceptualization some criteria for choosing appropriate methods of intervention in particular applications.

The point of view of this paper is that the depth of individual emotional involvement in the change process can be a central concept for differentiating change strategies. In focusing on this dimension, we are concerned with the extent to which core areas of the personality or self are the focus of the change attempt. Strategies which touch the more deep, personal, private, and central aspects of the individual or his relationships with others fall toward the deeper end of this continuum. Strategies which deal with more external aspects of the individual and which focus on the more formal and public aspects of role behavior tend to fall toward the surface end of the depth dimension. This dimension has the advantage that it is relatively easy to rank change strategies upon it and to get fairly close consensus as to the ranking. It is a widely discussed dimension of difference which has meaning and relevance to practitioners and their clients. I hope in this paper to promote greater flexibility and rationality in choosing appropriate depths of intervention. I shall approach this task by examining the effects of interventions at various depths. I shall also explore the ways in which two important organizational processes tend to make demands and to set limits upon the depth of intervention which can produce effective change in organizational functioning. These two processes are the autonomy of organization members and their own perception of their needs for help.

Before illustrating the concept by ranking five common intervention strategies along the dimension of depth, I should like to define the dimension somewhat more precisely. We are concerned essentially with how private, individual, and hidden are the issues and processes about which the consultant attempts directly to obtain information and which he seeks to influence. If the consultant seeks information about relatively public and observable aspects of behavior and relationships, and if he tries to influence directly only these relatively surface characteristics and processes, we would then categorize his intervention strategy as being closer to the surface. If, on the other hand, the consultant seeks information about very deep and private perceptions, attitudes, or feelings, and if he intervenes in a way which directly affects these processes, then we would classify his intervention strategy as one of considerable depth. To illustrate the surface end of the dimension let us look first at operations research or operations analysis. This strategy is concerned with the roles and functions to be performed within the organization, generally with little regard to the individual characteristics of persons occupying the roles. The change strategy is to manipulate role relationships; in other words, to redistribute the tasks, the resources, and the relative power attached to various roles in the organization. This is essentially a process of rational analysis in which the tasks which need to be performed are determined and specified and then sliced up into role definitions for persons and groups in the organization. The operations analyst does not ordi-narily need to know much about particular people. Indeed, his function is to design the organization in such a way that its successful operation does not depend too heavily upon any uniquely individual skills, abilities, values, or attitudes of persons in various roles. He may perform this function adequately without knowing in advance who the people are who will fill these slots. Persons are assumed to be moderately interchangeable, and in order to make this approach work it is necessary to design the organization so that the capacities, needs, and values of the individual which are relevant to role performance are relatively public and observable, and are possessed by a fairly large proportion of the population from which organization members are drawn. The approach is certainly one of very modest depth.

Somewhat deeper are those strategies which are based upon evaluating individual performance and attempting to manipulate it directly. Included in this approach is much of the industrial psychologist's work in selection, placement, appraisal, and counseling of employees. The intervener is concerned with what the individual is able and likely to do and achieve, rather than with processes internal to the individual. Direct attempts to influence performance may be made through the application of rewards and punishments, such as promotions, salary increases, or transfers within the organization. An excellent illustration of this focus on end results is the practice of management by objectives. The intervention process is focused on establishing mutually agreed-upon goals for performance between the individual and his supervisor. The practice is considered to be particularly advantageous because it permits the supervisor to avoid a focus on personal characteristics of the subordinate, particularly those deeper, more central characteristics which managers generally have difficulty in discussing with those who work under their supervision. The process is designed to limit information exchange to that which is public and observable, such as the setting of performance goals and the success or failure of the individual in attaining them.

Because of its focus on end results, rather than on the process by which those results are achieved, management by objectives must be considered less deep than the broad area of concern with work style which I shall term instrumental process analysis. We are concerned here not only with performance but with the processes by which that performance is achieved. However, we are primarily concerned with styles and processes of work rather than with the processes of interpersonal relationships which I would classify as being deeper on the basic dimension.

In instrumental process analysis we are concerned with how a person likes to organize and conduct his work and with the impact which this style of work has on others in the organization. Principally, we are concerned with how a person perceives his role, what he values and disvalues in it, and what he works hard on and what he chooses to ignore. We are also interested in the instrumental acts which the individual directs toward others: delegating authority or reserving decisions to himself, communicating or withholding information, collaborating or competing with others on work-related issues. The focus on instrumentality means that we are interested in the person primarily as a doer of work or as a performer of functions related to the goals of the organization. We are interested in what facilitates or inhibits his effective task performance.

We are not interested per se in whether his relationships with others are happy or unhappy, whether they perceive him as too warm or too cold, too authoritarian or too laissez-faire, or any other of the many interpersonal relationships which arise as people associate in organizations. However, I do not mean to imply that the line between instrumental relationships and interpersonal ones is an easy one to draw in action and

practice, or even that it is desirable that this be done.

Depth Gauges: Level of Tasks and Feelings

What I am saying is that an intervention strategy can focus on instrumentality or it can focus on interpersonal relationships, and that there are important consequences of this difference in depth of intervention.

When we intervene at the level of instrumentality, it is to change work behavior and working relationships. Frequently this involves the process of bargaining or negotiation between groups and individuals. Diagnoses are made of the satisfactions or dissatisfactions of organization members with one another's work behavior. Reciprocal adjustments, bargains, and trade-offs can then be arranged in which each party gets some modification in the behavior of the other at the cost to him of some reciprocal accommodation. Much of the intervention strategy which has been developed around Blake's concept of the Managerial Grid is at this level and involves bargaining and negotiation of role behavior as an important change process.

At the deeper level of interpersonal relationships the focus is on feelings, attitudes, and perceptions which organization members have about others. At this level we are concerned with the quality of human relationships within the organization, with warmth and coldness of members to one another, and with the experiences of acceptance and rejection, love and hate, trust and suspicion among groups and individuals. At this level the consultant probes for normally hidden feelings, attitudes, and perceptions. He works to create relationships of openness about feelings and to help members to develop mutual understanding of one another as persons. Interventions are directed toward helping organization members to be more comfortable in being authentically themselves with one another, and the degree of mutual caring and concern is expected to increase. Sensitivity training using T-groups is a basic intervention strategy at this level. T-group educators emphasize increased personalization of relationships, the development of trust and openness, and the exchange of feelings. Interventions at this level deal directly and intensively with interpersonal emotionality. This is the first intervention strategy we have examined which is at a depth where the feelings of organization members about one another as persons are a direct focus of the intervention strategy. At the other levels, such feelings certainly exist and may be expressed, but they are not a direct concern of the intervention. The transition from the task orientation of instrumental process analysis to the feeling orientation of interpersonal process analysis seems, as I shall suggest later, to be a critical one for many organization members.

The deepest level of intervention which will be considered in this paper is that of intrapersonal analysis. Here the consultant uses a variety of methods to reveal the individual's deeper attitudes, values, and conflicts regarding his own functioning, identity, and existence. The focus is generally on increasing the range of experiences which the individual can bring into awareness and cope with. The material may be dealt with at the fantasy or symbolic level, and the intervention strategies include many which are noninterpersonal and nonverbal. Some examples of this approach are the use of marathon T-group sessions, the creative risk-taking laboratory approach of Byrd (1967), and some aspects of the task group therapy approach of Clark (1966). These approaches all tend to bring into focus very deep and intense feelings about one's own identity and one's relationships with significant others.

Although I have characterized deeper interventions as dealing increasingly with the individual's affective life, I do not imply that issues at less deep levels may not be emotionally charged. Issues of role differentiation, reward distribution, ability and performance evaluation,

for example, are frequently invested with strong feelings. The concept of depth is concerned more with the *accessibility* and *individuality* of attitudes, values, and perceptions than it is with their strength. This narrowing of the common usage of the term *depth* is necessary to avoid the contradictions which occur when strength and inaccessibility are confused. For instance, passionate value confrontation and bitter conflict have frequently occurred between labor and management over economic issues which are surely toward the surface end of my concept of depth.

In order to understand the importance of the concept of depth for choosing interventions in organizations, let us consider the effects upon organization members of working at different levels.

The first of the important concomitants of depth is the degree of dependence of the client on the special competence of the change agent. At the surface end of the depth dimension, the methods of intervention are easily communicated and made public. The client may reasonably expect to learn something of the change agent's skills to improve his own practice. At the deeper levels, such as interpersonal and intrapersonal process analyses, it is more difficult for the client to understand the methods of intervention. The change agent is more likely to be seen as a person of special and unusual powers not found in ordinary men. Skills of intervention and change are less frequently learned by organization members, and the change process may tend to become personalized around the change agent as leader. Programs of change which are so dependent upon personal relationships and individual expertise are difficult to institutionalize. When the change agent leaves the system, he may not only take his expertise with him but the entire change process as well.

A second aspect of the change process which varies with depth is the extent to which the benefits of an intervention are transferable to members of the organization not originally participating in the change process. At surface levels of operations analysis and performance evaluation, the effects are institutionalized in the form of procedures, policies, and practices of the organization which may have considerable permanence beyond the tenure of individuals. At the level of instrumental behavior, the continuing effects of intervention are more likely to reside in the informal norms of groups within the organization regarding such matters as delegation, communication, decision making, competition and collaboration, and conflict resolution.

At the deepest levels of intervention, the target of change is the individual's inner life; and if the intervention is successful, the permanence of individual change should be greatest. There are indeed dramatic reports of cases in which persons have changed their careers and life goals as a result of such interventions, and the persistence of such change appears to be relatively high.

One consequence, then, of the level of intervention is that with greater depth of focus the individual increasingly becomes both the target and the carrier of change. In the light of this analysis, it is not surprising to observe that deeper levels of intervention are increasingly being used at higher organizational levels and in scientific and service organizations where the contribution of the individual has greatest impact.

An important concomitant of depth is that, as the level of intervention becomes deeper, the information needed to intervene effectively becomes less available. At the less personal level of operations analysis, the information is often a matter of record. At the level of performance evaluation, it is a matter of observation. On the other hand, reactions of others to a person's work style are less likely to be discussed freely, and the more personal responses to his interpersonal style are even less likely to be readily given. At the deepest levels, important information may not be available to the individual himself. Thus as we go deeper the consultant must use more of his time and skill uncovering information which is ordinarily private and hidden.

This is one reason for the greater costs of interventions at deeper levels of focus.

Another aspect of the change process which varies with the depth of intervention is the personal risk and unpredictability of outcome for the individual. At deeper levels we deal with aspects of the individual's view of himself and his relationships with others which are relatively untested by exposure to the evaluations and emotional reactions of others. If in the change process the individual's self-perceptions are strongly disconfirmed, the resulting imbalance in internal forces may produce sudden changes in behavior, attitudes, and personality integration.

Because of the private and hidden nature of the processes into which we intervene at deeper levels, it is difficult to predict the individual impact of the change process in advance. The need for clinical sensitivity and skill on the part of the practitioner thus increases, since he must be prepared to diagnose and deal with developing situations involving considerable stress upon individuals.

The foregoing analysis suggests a criterion by which to match intervention strategies to particular organizational problems. It is *to intervene at a level no deeper than that required to produce enduring solutions to the problems at hand.* This criterion derives directly from the observations above. The cost, skill demands, client dependency, and variability of outcome all increase with depth of intervention. Further, as the depth of intervention increases, the effects tend to locate more in the individual and less in the organization. The danger of losing the organization's investment in the change with the departure of the individual becomes a significant consideration.

Autonomy Increases Depth of Intervention

While this general criterion is simple and straightforward, its application is not. In particular, although the criterion should operate in the direction of less depth of intervention, there is a general trend in modern organizational life which tends to push the intervention level ever deeper. This trend is toward increased self-direction of organization members and increased independence of external pressures and incentives. I believe that there is a direct relationship between the autonomy of individuals and the depth of intervention needed to effect organizational change.

Before going on to discuss this relationship, I shall acknowledge freely that I cannot prove the existence of a trend toward a general increase in freedom of individuals within organizations. I intend only to assert the great importance of the degree of individual autonomy in determining the level of intervention which will be effective.

In order to understand the relationship between autonomy and depth of intervention, it is necessary to conceptualize a dimension which parallels and is implied by the depth dimension we have been discussing. This is the dimension of predictability and variability among persons in their responses to the different kinds of incentives which may be used to influence behavior in the organization. The key assumption in this analysis is that the more unpredictable and unique is the individual's response to the particular kinds of controls and incentives one can bring to bear upon him, the more one must know about that person in order to influence his behavior.

Most predictable and least individual is the response of the person to economic and bureaucratic controls when his needs for economic income and security are high. It is not necessary to delve very deeply into a person's inner processes in order to influence his behavior if we know that he badly needs his income and his position and if we are in a position to control his access to these rewards. Responses to economic and bureaucratic controls tend to be relatively simple and on the surface.

Independence of Economic Incentive. If for any reason organization members become relatively uninfluenceable through the manipulation of their income and economic security, the management of performance becomes strikingly more complex; and the need for more personal information about the individual increases. Except very generally, we do not know automatically or in advance what styles of instrumental or interpersonal interaction will be responded to as negative or positive incentives by the individual. One person may appreciate close supervision and direction; another may value independence of direction. One may prefer to work alone; another may function best when he is in close communication with others. One may thrive in close, intimate, personal interaction; while others are made uncomfortable by any but cool and distant relationships with colleagues.

What I am saying is that, when bureaucratic and economic incentives lose their force for whatever reason, the improvement of performance *must* involve linking organizational goals to the individual's attempts to meet his own needs for satisfying instrumental activities and interpersonal relationships. It is for this reason that I make the assertion that increases in personal autonomy dictate change interventions at deeper and more personal levels. In order to obtain the information necessary to link organizational needs to individual goals, one must probe fairly deeply into the attitudes, values, and emotions of the organization members.

If the need for deeper personal information becomes great when we intervene at the instrumental and interpersonal levels, it becomes even greater when one is dealing with organization members who are motivated less through their transactions with the environment and more in response to internal values and standards. An example is the researcher, engineer, or technical specialist whose work behavior may be influenced more by his own values and standards of creativity or professional excellence than by his relationships with others. The deepest organizational interventions at the intrapersonal level may be required in order to effect change when working with persons who are highly self-directed.

Let me summarize my position about the relationship among autonomy, influence, and level of intervention. As the individual becomes less subject to economic and bureaucratic pressures, he tends to seek more intangible rewards in the organization which come from both the instrumental and interpersonal aspects of the system. I view this as a shift from greater external to more internal control and as an increase in autonomy. Further shifts in this direction may involve increased independence of rewards and punishments mediated by others, in favor of operation in accordance with internal values and standards.

I view organizations as systems of reciprocal influence. Achievement of organization goals is facilitated when individuals can seek their own satisfactions through activity which promotes the goals of the organization. As the satisfactions which are of most value to the individual change, so must the reciprocal influence systems, if the organization goals are to continue to be met.

If the individual changes are in the direction of increased independence of external incentives, then the influence systems must change to provide opportunities for individuals to achieve more intangible, self-determined satisfactions in their work. However, people are more differentiated, complex, and unique in their intangible goals and values than in their economic needs. In order to create systems which offer a wide variety of intangible satisfactions, much more private information about individuals is needed than is required to create and maintain systems based chiefly on economic and bureaucratic controls. For this reason, deeper interventions are called for when the system which they would attempt to change contains a high proportion of relatively autonomous individuals.

There are a number of factors promoting autonomy, all tending to free the individual from dependence upon economic and bureaucratic controls, which I have observed in my work with organizations. Wherever a number of these factors obtain, it is probably an indication that deeper levels of intervention are required to ef-

fect lasting improvements in organizational functioning. I shall simply list these indicators briefly in categories to show what kinds of things might signify to the practitioner that deeper levels of intervention may be appropriate.

The first category includes anything which makes the evaluation of individual performance difficult:

A long time span between the individual's actions and the results by which effectiveness of performance is to be judged.

Nonrepetitive, unique tasks which cannot be evaluated by reference to the performance of others on similar tasks.

Specialized skills and abilities possessed by an individual which cannot be evaluated by a supervisor who does not possess the skills or knowledge himself.

The second category concerns economic conditions:

Arrangements which secure the job tenure and/or income to the individual.

A market permitting easy transfer from one organization to another (e.g., engineers in the United States aerospace industry).

Unique skills and knowledge of the individual which make him difficult to replace.

The third category includes characteristics of the system or its environment which lead to independence of the parts of the organization and decentralization of authority such as:

An organization which works on a project basis instead of producing a standard line of products.

An organization in which subparts must be given latitude to deal rapidly and flexibly with frequent environmental change.

I should like to conclude the discussion of this criterion for depth of intervention with a brief reference to the ethics of intervention, a problem which merits considerably more thorough treatment than I can give it here.

The Ethics of Delving Deeper.   There is considerable concern in the United States about invasion of privacy by behavioral scientists. I would agree that such invasion of privacy is an actual as well as a fantasized concomitant of the use of organizational change strategies of greater depth. The recourse by organizations to such strategies has been widely viewed as an indication of greater organizational control over the most personal and private aspects of the lives of the members. The present analysis suggests, however, that recourse to these deeper interventions actually reflects the greater *freedom* of organization members from traditionally crude and impersonal means of organizational control. There is no reason to be concerned about man's attitudes or values or interpersonal relationships when his job performance can be controlled by brute force, by economic coercion, or by bureaucratic rules and regulations. The "invasion of privacy" becomes worth the cost, bother, and uncertainty of outcome only when the individual has achieved relative independence from control by other means. Put another way, it makes organizational sense to try to get a man to *want* to do something only if you cannot *make* him do it. And regardless of what intervention strategy is used, the individual still retains considerably greater control over his own behavior than he had when he could be manipulated more crudely. As long as we can maintain a high degree of voluntarism regarding the nature and extent of an individual's participation in the deeper organizational change strategies, these strategies can work toward adapting the organization to the individual quite as much as they work the other way around. Only when an individual's participation in one of the deeper change strategies is coerced by economic or bureaucratic pressures, do I feel that the ethics of the intervention clearly run counter to the values of a democratic society.

Role of Client Norms and Values in Determining Depth

So far our attention to the choice of level of intervention has focused upon locating the depth at which the information exists which must be exchanged to facilitate system improvement. Unfortunately, the choice of an intervention strategy cannot practically be made with reference to this criterion alone. Even if a correct diagnosis is made of the level at which the relevant information lies, we may not be able to work effectively at the desired depth because of client norms, values, resistances, and fears.

In an attempt to develop a second criterion for depth of intervention which takes such dispositions on the part of the client into account, I have considered two approaches which represent polarized orientations to the problem. One approach is based upon analyzing and overcoming client resistance; the other is based upon discovering and joining forces with the self-articulated wants or "felt needs" of the client.

There are several ways of characterizing these approaches. To me, the simplest is to point out that when the change agent is resistance-oriented he tends to lead or influence the client to work at a depth greater than that at which the latter feels comfortable. When resistance-oriented, the change agent tends to mistrust the client's statement of his problems and of the areas where he wants help. He suspects the client's presentation of being a smoke screen or defense against admission of his "real" problems and needs. The consultant works to expose the underlying processes and concerns and to influence the client to work at a deeper level. The resistance-oriented approach grows out of the work of clinicians and psychotherapists, and it characterizes much of the work of organizational consultants who specialize in sensitivity training and deeper intervention strategies.

On the other hand, change agents may be oriented to the self-articulated needs of clients. When so oriented, the consultant tends more to follow and facilitate the client in working at whatever level the latter sets for himself. He may assist the client in defining problems and needs and in working on solutions, but he is inclined to try to anchor his work in the norms, values, and accepted standards of behavior of the organization.

I believe that there is a tendency for change agents working at the interpersonal and deeper levels to adopt a rather consistent resistance-oriented approach. Consultants so oriented seem to take a certain quixotic pride in dramatically and self-consciously violating organizational norms. Various techniques have been developed for pressuring or seducing organizations members into departing from organizational norms in the service of change. The "marathon" T-group is a case in point, where the increased irritability and fatigue of prolonged contact and lack of sleep move participants to deal with one another more emotionally, personally, and spontaneously than they would normally be willing to do.

I suspect that unless such norm-violating intervention efforts actually succeed in changing organizational norms, their effects are relatively short-lived, because the social structures and interpersonal linkages have not been created which can utilize for day-to-day problem solving the deeper information produced by the intervention. It is true that the consultant may succeed in producing information, but he is less likely to succeed in creating social structures which can continue to work in his absence. The problem is directly analogous to that of the community developer who succeeds by virtue of his personal influence in getting villagers to build a school or a community center which falls into disuse as soon as he leaves because of the lack of any integration of these achievements into the social structure and day-to-day needs and desires of the community. Community developers have had to learn through bitter failure and frustration that ignoring or subverting the standards and norms of a social system often results in temporary success followed by a reactionary increase in resist-

ance to the influence of the change agent. On the other hand, felt needs embody those problems, issues, and difficulties which have a high conscious priority on the part of community or organization members. We can expect individuals and groups to be ready to invest time, energy, and resources in dealing with their felt needs, while they will be relatively passive or even resistant toward those who attempt to help them with externally defined needs. Community developers have found that attempts to help with felt needs are met with greater receptivity, support, and integration within the structure and life of the community than are intervention attempts which rely primarily upon the developer's value system for setting need priorities.

The emphasis of many organizational change agents on confronting and working through resistances was developed originally in the practice of individual psychoanalysis and psychotherapy, and it is also a central concept in the conduct of therapy groups and sensitivity training laboratories. In all of these situations, the change agent has a high degree of environmental control and is at least temporarily in a high status position with respect to the client. To a degree that is frequently underestimated by practitioners, we manage to create a situation in which it is more unpleasant for the client to leave than it is to stay and submit to the pressure to confront and work through resistances. I believe that the tendency is for behavioral scientists to overplay their hands when they move from the clinical and training situations where they have environmental control to the organizational consulting situation where their control is sharply attenuated.

This attenuation derives only partially from the relative ease with which the client can terminate the relationship. Even if this most drastic step is not taken, the consultant can be tolerated, misled, and deceived in ways which are relatively difficult in the therapeutic or human relations training situations. He can also be openly defied and blocked if he runs afoul of strongly shared group norms; whereas when the consultant is dealing with a group of strangers, he can often utilize differences among the members to overcome this kind of resistance. I suspect that, in general, behavioral scientists underestimate their power in working with individuals and groups of strangers, and overestimate it when working with individuals and groups in organizations. I emphasize this point because I believe that a good many potentially fruitful and mutually satisfying consulting relationships are terminated early because of the consultant's taking the role of overcomer of resistance to change, rather than that of collaborator in the client's attempts at solving his problems. It is these considerations which lead me to suggest my second criterion for the choice of organization intervention strategy: *to intervene at a level no deeper than that at which the energy and resources of the client can be committed to problem solving and to change.* These energies and resources can be mobilized through obtaining legitimation for the intervention in the forms of the organization and through devising intervention strategies which have clear relevance to consciously felt needs on the part of the organization members.

The Consultant's Dilemma: Felt Needs versus Deeper Levels

Unfortunately, it is doubtless true that the forces which influence the conditions we desire to change often exist at deeper levels than can be dealt with by adhering to the criterion of working within organization norms and meeting felt needs. The level at which an individual or group is willing and ready to invest energy and resources is probably always determined partly by a realistic assessment of the problems and partly by a defensive need to avoid confrontation and significant change. It is thus not likely that our two criteria for selection of intervention depth will result in the same decisions when practically applied. It is not the same to intervene at the level where behavior-determining forces are most potent as it is to work on felt needs as they are ar-

ticulated by the client. This, it seems to me, is the consultant's dilemma. It always has been. We are continually faced with the choice between leading the client into areas which are threatening, unfamiliar, and dependency-provoking for him (and where our own expertise shows up to best advantage) or, on the other hand, being guided by the client's own understanding of his problems and his willingness to invest resources in particular kinds of relatively familiar and nonthreatening strategies.

When time permits, this dilemma is ideally dealt with by intervening first at a level where there is good support from the norms, power structure, and felt needs of organizational members. The consultant can then, over a period of time, develop trust, sophistication, and support within the organization to explore deeper levels at which particularly important forces may be operating. This would probably be agreed to, at least in principle, by most organizational consultants. The point at which I feel I differ from a significant number of workers in this field is that I would advocate that interventions should *always* be limited to the depth of the client's felt needs and readiness to legitimize intervention. I believe we should always avoid moving deeper at a pace which outstrips a client system's willingness to subject itself to exposure, dependency, and threat. What I am saying is that, if the dominant response of organization members indicates that an intervention violates system norms regarding exposure, privacy, and confrontation, then one has intervened too deeply and should pull back to a level at which organization members are more ready to invest their own energy in the change process. This point of view is thus in opposition to that which sees negative reactions primarily as indications of resistances which are to be brought out into the open, confronted, and worked through as a central part of the intervention process. I believe that behavioral scientists acting as organizational consultants have tended to place overmuch emphasis on the overcoming of resistance to change and have underemphasized the importance of enlisting in the service of change the energies and resources which the client can consciously direct and willingly devote to problem solving.

What is advocated here is that we in general accept the client's felt needs or the problems he presents as real and that we work on them at a level at which he can serve as a competent and willing collaborator. This position is in opposition to one which sees the presenting problem as more or less a smoke screen or barrier. I am not advocating this point of view because I value the right to privacy of organization members more highly than I value their growth and development or the solution of organizational problems. (This is an issue which concerns me, but it is enormously more complex than the ones with which I am dealing in this paper.) Rather, I place first priority on collaboration with the client, because I do not think we are frequently successful consultants without it.

In my own practice I have observed that the change in client response is frequently quite striking when I move from a resistance-oriented approach to an acceptance of the client's norms and definitions of his own needs. With quite a few organizational clients in the United States, the line of legitimacy seems to lie somewhere between interventions at the instrumental level and those focused on interpersonal relationships. Members who exhibit hostility, passivity, and dependence when I initiate intervention at the interpersonal level may become dramatically more active, collaborative, and involved when I shift the focus to the instrumental level.

If I intervene directly at the level of interpersonal relationships, I can be sure that at least some members, and often the whole group, will react with anxiety, passive resistance, and low or negative commitment to the change process. Furthermore, they express their resistance in terms of norms and values regarding the appropriateness or legitimacy of dealing at this level. They say things like, "It isn't right to force people's feelings about one another out into the open"; "I don't see what this has to do with improving organizational effectiveness"; "People are being encouraged to say things which are better left unsaid."

If I then switch to a strategy which focuses on decision making, delegation of authority, information exchange, and other instrumental questions, these complaints about illegitimacy and the inappropriateness of the intervention are usually sharply reduced. This does not mean that the clients are necessarily comfortable or free from anxiety in the discussions, nor does it mean that strong feelings may not be expressed about one another's behavior. What is different is that the clients are more likely to *work with* instead of *against* me, to feel and express some sense of ownership in the change process, and to see many more possibilities for carrying it on among themselves in the absence of the consultant.

What I have found is that, when I am resistance-oriented in my approach to the client, I am apt to feel rather uncomfortable in "letting sleeping dogs lie." When, on the other hand, I orient myself to the client's own assessment of his needs, I am uncomfortable when I feel I am leading or pushing the client to operate very far outside the shared norms of the organization. I have tried to indicate why I believe the latter orientation is more appropriate. I realize of course that many highly sophisticated and talented practitioners will not agree with me.

In summary, I have tried to show in this paper that the dimension of depth should be central to the conceptualization of intervention strategies. I have presented what I believe are the major consequences of intervening at greater or lesser depths; and from these consequences I have suggested two criteria for choosing the appropriate depth of intervention: first, *to intervene at a level no deeper than that required to produce enduring solutions to the problems at hand;* and second, *to intervene at a level no deeper than that at which the energy and resources of the client can be committed to problem solving and to change.*

I have analyzed the tendency for increases in

individual autonomy in organizations to push the appropriate level of intervention deeper when the first criterion is followed. Opposed to this is the countervailing influence of the second criterion to work closer to the surface in order to enlist the energy and support of organization members in the change process. Arguments have been presented for resolving this dilemma in favor of the second, more conservative, criterion. The dilemma remains, of course; the continuing tension under which the change agent works is between the desire to lead and push, or to collaborate and follow. The middle ground is never very stable, and I suspect we show our values and preferences by which criterion we choose to maximize when we are under the stress of difficult and ambiguous client-consultant relationships.

References

Byrd, R. E. "Training in a Nongroup." *Journal of Humanistic Psychology* 7, no. 1 (1967), pp. 18–27.
Clark, J. V. "Task Group Therapy." Unpublished manuscript, University of California, Los Angeles, 1966.

READING 37
FUNCTIONAL ROLES OF GROUP MEMBERS

Kenneth D. Benne and Paul Sheats

The Relative Neglect of Member Roles in Group Training

Efforts to improve group functioning through training have traditionally emphasized the training of group leadership. And frequently this training has been directed toward the improvement of the skills of the leader in transmitting information and in manipulating groups. Little direct attention seems to have been given to the training of group members in the membership roles required for effective group growth and production. The present discussion is based on the conviction that both effective group training and adequate research into the effectiveness of group training methods must give attention to the identification, analysis, and practice of leader *and* member roles, seen as co-relative aspects of over-all group growth and production.

Certain assumptions have undergirded the tendency to isolate the leadership role from membership roles and to neglect the latter in processes of group training. (1) "Leadership" has been identified with traits and qualities inherent within the "leader" personality. Such traits and qualities can be developed, it is assumed, in isolation from the functioning of members in a group setting. The present treatment sees the leadership role in terms of functions to be performed within a group in helping that group to grow and to work productively. No sharp distinction can be made between leadership and membership functions, between leader and member roles. Groups may operate with various degrees of diffusion of "leadership" functions among group members or of concentration of such functions in one member or a few members. Ideally, of course, the concept of leadership emphasized here is that of a multilaterally shared responsibility. In any event, effectiveness in the leader role is a matter of leader-member relationship. And one side of a relationship cannot be effectively trained in isolation from the retraining of the other side of that relationship. (2) It has been assumed that the "leader" is uniquely responsible for the quality and amount of production by the group. The "leader" must see to it that the "right" group goals are set, that the group jobs get done, that members are "motivated" to participate. On this view, membership roles are of secondary importance. "Membership" is tacitly identified with "followership." The present discussion assumes that the quality and amount of group production is the "responsibility" of the group. The setting of goals and the marshalling of resources to move toward these goals is a group responsibility in which all members of a mature group come variously to share. The functions to be performed both in building and maintaining group-centered activity and in effective production by the group are primarily member roles. Leadership functions can be defined in terms of facilitating identification, acceptance, development, and allocation of these group-required roles by the group. (3) There has frequently been a confusion between the roles which members enact within a group and the individual personalities of the group members. That there are relationships between the personality structures and needs of group members and the range and quality of group membership roles which members can learn to perform is not denied. On the contrary, the importance of studies

Source: Kenneth D. Benne and Paul Sheats. Reprinted with permission of *The Journal of Social Issues*, Spring 1948, pp. 41–49.

designed to describe and explain and to increase our control of these relationships is affirmed. But, at the level of group functioning, member roles, relevant to group growth and accomplishment, must be clearly distinguished from the use of the group environment by individuals to satisfy individual and group-irrelevant needs, if clear diagnosis of member-roles required by the group and adequate training of members to perform group-required roles are to be advanced. Neglect of this distinction has been associated traditionally with the neglect of the analysis of member roles in group growth and production.

A Classification of Member Roles

The following analysis of functional member roles was developed in connection with the First National Training Laboratory in Group Development, 1947. It follows closely the analysis of participation functions used in coding the content of group records for research purposes. A similar analysis operated in faculty efforts to train group members in their functional roles during the course of the laboratory.[1]

The member-roles identified in this analysis are classified into three broad groupings.

1. Group task roles. Participant roles here are related to the task which the group is deciding to undertake or has undertaken. Their purpose is to facilitate and coordinate group effort in the selection and definition of a common problem and in the solution of that problem.

2. Group building and maintenance roles. The roles in this category are oriented toward the functioning of the group as a group. They are designed to alter or maintain the group way of working, to strengthen, regulate, and perpetuate the group as a group.

3. Individual roles. This category does not classify member-roles as such, since the "participations" denoted here are directed toward the satisfaction of the "participant's" individual needs. Their purpose is some individual goal which is not relevant either to the group task or to the functioning of the group as a group. Such participants are, of course, highly relevant to the problem of group training, insofar as such training is directed toward improving group maturity or group task efficiency.

Group Task Roles

The following analysis assumes that the task of the discussion group is to select, define, and solve common problems. The roles are identified in relation to functions of facilitation and coordination of group problem-solving activities. Each member may of course enact more than one role in any given unit of participation and a wide range of roles in successive participations. Any or all of these roles may be played at times by the group "leader" as well as by various members.

a. The *initiator-contributor* suggests or proposes to the group new ideas or a changed way of regarding the group problem or goal. The novelty proposed may take the form of suggestions of a new group goal or a new definition of the problem. It may take the form of a suggested solution or some way of handling a difficulty that the group has encountered. Or it may take the form of a proposed new procedure for the group, a new way of organizing the group for the task ahead.

b. The *information seeker* asks for clarification of suggestions made in terms of their factual adequacy, for authoritative information and facts pertinent to the problem being discussed.

c. The *opinion seeker* asks not primarily for the facts of the case but for a clarification of the values pertinent to what the group is undertaking

[1] A somewhat different analysis of member-participations, in terms of categories used by interaction observers in observation of group processes in the First National Training Laboratory, is described in the *Preliminary Report* of the laboratory, pages 122–32. The number of categories used by interaction observers was "directed primarily by limitations of observer load."

or of values involved in a suggestion made or in alternative suggestions.

d. The *information giver* offers facts or generalizations which are "authoritative" or relates his own experience pertinently to the group problem.

e. The *opinion giver* states his belief or opinion pertinently to a suggestion made or to alternative suggestions. The emphasis is on his proposal of what should become the group's view of pertinent values, not primarily upon relevant facts or information.

f. The *elaborator* spells out suggestions in terms of examples or developed meanings, offers a rationale for suggestions previously made, and tries to deduce how an idea or suggestion would work out if adopted by the group.

g. The *coordinator* shows or clarifies the relationships among various ideas and suggestions, tries to pull ideas and suggestions together, or tries to coordinate the activities of various members or subgroups.

h. The *orienter* defines the position of the group with respect to its goals by summarizing what has occurred, points to departures from agreed-upon directions or goals, or raises questions about the direction which the group discussion is taking.

i. The *evaluator-critic* subjects the accomplishment of the group to some standard or set of standards of group-functioning in the context of the group task. Thus he may evaluate or question the "practicality", the "logic", the "facts," or the "procedure" of a suggestion or of some unit of group discussion.

j. The *energizer* prods the group to action or decision, attempts to stimulate or arouse the group to "greater" or "higher quality" activity.

k. The *procedural technician* expedites group movement by doing things for the group—performing routine tasks (e.g., distributing materials) or manipulating objects for the group (e.g., rearranging the seating or running the recording machine, etc.

l. The *recorder* writes down suggestions, makes a record of group decisions, or writes down the product of discussion. The recorder role is the "group memory."

Group Building and Maintenance Roles

Here the analysis of member-functions is oriented to those participations which have for their purpose the building of group-centered attitudes and orientation among the members of a group or the maintenance and perpetuation of such group-centered behavior. A given contribution may involve several roles and a member of the "leader" may perform various roles in successive contributions.

a. The *encourager* praises, agrees with, and accepts the contribution of others. He indicates warmth and solidarity in his attitude toward other group members, offers commendation and praise, and in various ways indicates understanding and acceptance of other points of view, ideas, and suggestions.

b. The *harmonizer* mediates the differences between other members, attempts to reconcile disagreements, relieves tension in conflict situations through jesting or pouring oil on the troubled waters, etc.

c. The *compromiser* operates from within a conflict in which his idea or position is involved. He may offer compromise by yielding status, admitting his error, by disciplining himself to maintain group harmony, or by "coming halfway" in moving along with the group.

d. The *gate-keeper and expediter* attempts to keep communication channels open by encouraging or facilitating the participation of others ("We haven't got the ideas of Mr. X yet," etc.) or by proposing regulation of the flow of communication ("Why don't we limit the length of our contributions so that everyone will have a chance to contribute?", etc.)

e. The *standard setter* or *ego ideal* expresses standards for the group to attempt to achieve in its functioning or applies standards in evaluating the quality of group processes.

f. The *group-observer* and *commentator* keeps records of various aspects of group process and feeds such data with proposed interpretations into the group's evaluation of its own procedures.

g. The *follower* goes along with the movement of the group, more or less passively accepting the ideas of others, serving as an audience in group discussion and decision.

"Individual" Roles

Attempts by "members" of a group to satisfy individual needs which are irrelevant to the group task and which are nonoriented or negatively oriented to group building and maintenance set problems of group and member training. A high incidence of "individual-centered" as opposed to "group-centered" participation in a group always calls for self-diagnosis of the group. The diagnosis may reveal one or several of a number of conditions—low level of skill-training among members, including the group leader; the prevalence of "authoritarian" and "laissez faire" points of view toward group functioning in the group; a low level of group maturity, discipline, and morale; and inappropriately chosen and inadequately defined group task, etc. Whatever the diagnosis, it is in this setting that the training needs of the group are to be discovered and group training efforts to meet these needs are to be defined. The outright "suppression" of "individual roles" will deprive the group of data needed for really adequate self-diagnosis and therapy.

a. The *aggressor* may work in many ways—deflating the status of others, expressing disapproval of the values, acts, or feelings of others, attacking the group or the problem it is working on, joking aggressively, showing envy toward another's contribution by trying to take credit for it, etc.

b. The *blocker* tends to be negativistic and stubbornly resistant, disagreeing and opposing without or beyond "reason" and attempting to maintain or bring back an issue after the group has rejected or bypassed it.

c. The *recognition-seeker* works in various ways to call attention to himself, whether through boasting, reporting on personal achievements, acting in unusual ways, struggling to prevent his being placed in an "inferior" position, etc.

d. The *self-confessor* uses the audience opportunity which the group setting provides to express personal, nongroup-oriented, "feeling", "insight", "ideology", etc.

e. The *playboy* makes a display of his lack of involvement in the group's processes. This may take the form of cynicism, nonchalance, horseplay, and other more or less studied forms of "out of field" behavior.

f. The *dominator* tries to assert authority or superiority in manipulating the group or certain members of the group. This domination may take the form of flattery, of asserting a superior status or right to attention, giving directions authoritatively, interrupting the contribution of others, etc.

g. The *help-seeker* attempts to call forth "sympathy" response from other group members or from the whole group, whether through expressions of insecurity, personal confusion or depreciation of himself beyond "reason."

h. The *special interest pleader* speaks for the "small business man," the "grass roots" community, the "housewife," "labor," and so forth, usually cloaking his own prejudices or biases in the stereotype which best fits his individual need.

The Problem of Member Role Requiredness

Identification of group task roles and of group building and maintenance roles which do actually function in processes of group discussion raises but does not answer the further question of what roles are required for "optimum" group growth and productivity. Certainly the discovery and validation of answers to this question have a high priority in any advancing science of group training and development. No attempt will be made here to review the bearing of the analyzed data from the First National Training Laboratory in Group Development on this point.

It may be useful in this discussion, however, to comment on two conditions which effective work on the problem of role-requiredness must meet. First, an answer to the problem of optimum task role requirements must be projected against a scheme of the process of group production. Groups in different stages of an act of problem selection and solution will have different role requirements. For example, a group early in the stages of problem selection which is attempting to lay out a range of possible problems to be worked on, will probably have relatively less need for the roles of "evaluator-critic," "energizer," and "coordinator" than a group which has selected and discussed its problem and is shaping a decision. The combination and balance of task role requirements is a function of the group's stage of progress with respect to its task. Second, the group building role requirements of a group are a function of its stage of development—its level of group maturity. For example, a "young" group will probably require less of the role of the "standard setter" than a more mature group. Too high a level of aspiration may frustrate a "young" group where a more mature group will be able to take the same level of aspiration in its stride. Again, the role of "group observer and commentator" must be carefully adapted to the level of maturity of the group. Probably the distinction between "group" and "individual" roles can be drawn much more sharply in a relatively mature than in a "young" group.

Meanwhile, group trainers cannot wait for a fully developed science of group training before they undertake to diagnose the role requirements of the groups with which they work and to help these groups to share in such diagnosis. Each group which is attempting to improve the quality of its functioning as a group must be helped to diagnose its role requirements and must attempt to train members to fill the required roles effectively. This describes one of the principal objectives of training of group members.

The Problem of Role Flexibility

The previous group experience of members, where this experience has included little conscious attention to the variety of roles involved in effective group production and development, has frequently stereotyped the member into a limited range of roles. These he plays in all group discussions whether or not the group situation requires them. Some members see themselves primarily as "evaluator-critics" and play this role in and out of season. Others may play the roles of "encourager" or of "energizer" or of "information giver" with only small sensitivity to the role requirements of a given group situation. The development of skill and insight in diagnosing role requirements has already been mentioned as an objective of group member training. An equally important objective is the development of role flexibility, of skill and security in a wide range of member roles, on the part of all group members.

A science of group training, as it develops, must be concerned with the relationships between the personality structures of group members and the character and range of member roles which various personality structures support and permit. A science of group training must seek to discover and accept the limitations which group training per se encounters in altering personality structures in the service of greater role flexibility on the part of all members of a group. Even though we recognize the importance of this caution, the objective of developing role flexibility remains an important objective of group member training.

Methods of Group Member Training

The objectives in training group members have been identified. Some of the kinds of resistances encountered in training group members to diagnose the role requirements of a group situation and to acquire skill in a variety of member roles have been suggested. Before analyzing briefly the methods used for group member training in the First National Training Laboratory, a few additional comments on resistances to member training may be useful. The problem of group training is actually a problem of retraining. Members of a training group have had other group experiences. They bring to the training experience attitudes toward group work, more or less conscious skills for dealing with leaders and other members, and a more or less highly developed rationale of group processes. These may or may not support processes of democratic operation in the training group. Where they do not, they function as resistances to retraining. Again, trainees are inclined to make little or no distinction between the roles they perform in a group and their personalities. Criticism of the role a group member plays is perceived as criticism of "himself." Methods must be found to reduce ego-defensiveness toward criticism of member roles. Finally, training groups must be helped to make a distinction between group feeling and group productivity. Groups which attain a state of good group feeling often perceive attempts to diagnose and criticize their level of productivity as threats to this feeling of group warmth and solidarity.

1. Each Basic Skill Training group in the Laboratory used self-observation and diagnosis of its own growth and development as a primary means of member training.

a. Sensitization to the variety of roles involved in and required by group functioning began during the introduction of members to the group. In one BST group, this early sensitization to member role variety and role requiredness began with the "leader's" summarizing, as part of his introduction of himself to the group, certain of the member roles in which he was usually cast by groups and other roles which he found it difficult to play, even when needed by the group. He asked the group's help in criticizing and improving his skill in those roles where he felt weakest. Other members followed suit. Various members showed widely different degrees of sensitivity to the operation of member roles in groups and to the degree of their own proficiency in different roles. This introduction procedure gave the group a partial listing of member roles for later use and supplementation, initial self-assessments of member strengths and weaknesses, and diagnostic material concerning the degree of group self-sophistication among the members. The training job had come to be seen by most members as a retraining job.

b. A description of the use of training observers in group self-evaluation sessions is given in the next paper in this issue (David H. Jenkins, "Feedback and Group Self-Evaluation). At this point, only the central importance which self-evaluation sessions played in member training needs to be stressed. Research observers fed observational data concerning group functioning into periodic discussions by the group of its strengths and weaknesses as a group. Much of these data concerned role requirements for the job the group had been attempting, which roles had been present, which roles had probably been needed. "Individual" roles were identified and interpreted in an objective and nonblaming manner. Out of these discussions, group members came to identify various kinds of member roles, to relate role requiredness to stages in group production and in group growth, and to assess the range of roles each was able to play well when required. Out of these discussions came group decisions concerning the supplying of needed roles in the next session. Member commitments concerning behavior in future sessions also came out of these evaluations. These took the form both of silent commitments and of public commitments in which the help of the group was requested.

c. Recordings of segments of the group's discussion were used by most Basic Skill Training groups. Groups listened to themselves, diagnosed the member and leader functions involved, and assessed the adequacy of these.

2. Role-played sessions in each group, although they were pointed content-wise to the skills of the change agent, offered important material for the diagnosis of member roles and of role-requiredness. These sessions offered an important supplement to group self-diagnosis and evaluation. It is easier for members to get perspective on their participation in a role-played episode of group process than it is on their own participation in a "real" group. The former is not perceived as "real." The role is more easily disengaged for purposes of analysis and evaluation from the person playing the role. Ego-defensiveness toward the role as enacted is reduced. Role-playing sessions also provided practice opportunity to members in a variety of roles.

3. Practice by group members of the role of *observer-commentator* is especially valuable in developing skill in diagnosing member roles and in assessing the role requirements of a group situation. In several groups, each member in turn served as observer, supplementing the work of the research observers in evaluation sessions. Such members worked more or less closely with the anecdotal observer for the group on skill-problems encountered. Practice opportunity in the *observer-commentator* role was also provided in clinic group meetings in the afternoon.

Summary

Training in group membership roles requires the identification and analysis of various member roles actually enacted in group processes. It involves further the analysis of group situations in terms of roles required in relation both to a schema of group production and to a conception of group growth and development. A group's self-observation and self-evaluation of its own processes provides useful content and practice opportunity in member training. Practice in enacting a wider range of required roles and in role flexibility can come out of member commitment to such practice with help from the group in evaluating and improving the required skills. Member training is typically retraining and resistances to retraining can be reduced by creating a nonblaming and objective atmosphere in group self-evaluation and by using role-playing of group processes for diagnosis and practice. The training objectives of developing skill in the diagnosis of group role requirements and developing role flexibility among members also indicate important research areas for a science of group training.

SHADOW CONSULTING: WHEN THE CLIENT IS A COLLEAGUE

Michael V. Collins

Contracting for help from a professional colleague presents a unique set of challenges. In addition to dealing with the usual entry issues, each party "knows the business" the other is in (knows how the magician performs the magic, as it were), both are likely to run in the same professional circles, and both may feel their professional reputations are at risk in the relationship. All of this can amplify the usual desire to be seen as knowledgeable and skilled.

The term *shadow consulting* has come into OD jargon usually referring to the situation in which one consultant consults to another who consults to an organizational client. The consultant's consultant doesn't meet with the organizational client He or she is in the shadow—hence the term. The body of literature on shadow consulting is limited. In a recent article, Ritvo and Lippitt (1989) give a working definition, briefly outline the roles and rewards, and discuss the temptations and traps of shadow consulting. The authors invite other practitioners to share their experiences.

As I think about and practice it, shadow consulting has two purposes. One is to help expand the consultant's awareness of what is possible. A second purpose is to help identify blocks, obstacles, and resistances that prevent the consultant from proceeding with energy, enthusiasm, and a sense of meaning. The intent of this article is to describe a model of shadow consulting that has proven effective for me with colleague-clients. I call it Experience-Centered Shadow Consulting. Before detailing the working assumptions and

Source: Michael V. Collins, "Shadow Consulting: When the Client Is a Colleague," *Vision/Action,* December 1991, pp. 16–19. Reprinted with permission.

phases of the model, the next section will present some examples of shadow consulting requests.

Examples of Shadow Consulting Requests

My shadow consulting requests range from specific information/technology requests (e.g., ideas regarding designing an upcoming off-site meeting, managing a particularly difficult consultant-client relationship) to requests for help with multiple, intertwined, "messy" issues. Here are some examples of presenting situations and initial requests:

- An HROD manager of six months was asked by the human resources VP to expand the department's offering of OD services in this Fortune 500 company. The HROD manager had to spend much of his time handling delicate intradepartmental issues, and, though he experienced senior management as supportive, he was not convinced that they were "fully on board" with OD, and he was the only HROD staff person with OD skills and experience. The shadow consulting request: "How can I best respond to the VP's request?"

- An internal consultant was asked to work with a university administrative department following its restructuring. The consultant agreed to a three-month project in which she would collect data and help the department plan and conduct a day-long retreat. The consultant called me because there was unrest in the department. A powerful, informal group was upset with how things were going. The labor union was upset. A newsletter of unknown origin was distributed criticizing management. A week before the retreat was to occur, it was cancelled. Everyone involved was disappointed, frustrated, angry. The shadow consulting request: "What do I do now?"

- An internal consultant was "transitioning" into a four-month-old organizationwide project which had boundaries and processes were originally negotiated by an external consultant. The external consultant (who worked with the task force directing the project) was "transitioned out" when it became clear that the project would take "considerably longer" than was initially planned. Publicly, it was stated that the limited budget would not allow for continuation of the external consultant's services. Privately, it was stated that the external consultant's style was the real issue. The internal consultant assigned to the project had concerns about how it was set up, but was told the major project parameters could not be changed, and felt trapped and resentful. The shadow consulting request: "How best to proceed with the consultation?"

- A consultant who was white was working in a large organization with a department manager who was black. In collecting interview data for the project, it became clear that the department was divided along racial lines both in terms of structure and the staff's experience in the department. With the sole exception of the manager, the people-of-color were in lower grade positions while the whites were in higher grade positions. The white staff members tended to support each other, held stereotypes of, and had issues with the people-of-color individually and

as a group. The same was true of the people-of-color with respect to the whites. The manager denied that there were any racial issues in the department. The shadow consulting request: "How do I get this department to deal with its racial issues?"

Though the specifics of my work with each of the consultants in these situations varied by the nature of the situation and by individual differences with the consultants, the general approach was the same. The approach rested on a set of working assumptions outlined in the next section.

Working Assumptions

Each of us makes assumptions about how the world works. These assumptions guide our actions. Some of our assumptions are more helpful than others. In shadow consulting, I feel most helpful when I act on the following assumptions:

- *It is not easy to ask for help.* Don't make it harder.
- *Even when asking for help, we hope people will see our strengths.* We don't usually ask for this, however.
- *We're all doing the best we can in the moment.* Therefore, as I often wanted to tell my high school basketball coach, "Don't judge. You weren't on the court at the time."
- *We need to make the world make sense.* We develop theories and models to help us—even if we are sometimes unaware of them.
- *Experience is the best teacher—still.* Therefore, help the consultant find answers from his or her experience, share your own relevant experience, including triumphs, trials, and tribulations.

These working assumptions underlie my general approach to shadow consulting. They are the foundation of the shadow consulting model described next.

The Experience-Centered Shadow Consulting Process

The Experience-Centered Shadow Consulting Process has five phases. They are (1) contracting, (2) situation review, (3) framing/reframing, (4) options for action, (5) closure. Each of these phases will now be described.

Contracting.   During this phase, there is information I want to know from the consultant and there is information I want to share. First, I want to know what the consultant wants from our work together. Next, I want to know how the consultant imagines I might be helpful to him or her in this regard. This usually leads to a conversation about confidentiality, how I see shadow consulting, my wants/needs from the consultant, and results in an initial agreement about how we will work together.

Situation Review.

I tend to ask lots of questions. During the "situation review," I ask questions to understand the context in which the consultant is operating. In these background questions, I inquire about:

- Events influencing the organizational client's decision to invite the consultant in (if the consultant hasn't already told me about the events influencing his or her decision to call me, I ask about that, too).
- Why the consultant chose to take on this "project" (hopes, expectations).
- Contracted-for desired outcomes, processes, and so on.
- Structure of the client system (formal and informal).
- The consultant's assessment of where

things now stand (interventions to date, excitements, disappointments, yet-unrealized possibilities).

I try to listen carefully. During the Situation Review, in addition to the content, I listen for the following to attempt to understand what I think of as the consultant's "internal context." It is this latter information that is most useful in the "framing/reframing" phase to follow. Here are five things I listen for and the questions I ask myself:

- *Clarity.* In consulting, as in the rest of life, the clearer we are about intentions, wants, etc., the greater the likelihood of aligning all of our resources and achieving that desired end. Therefore, I ask myself: "How clear is the consultant about what the client wanted/expected? How clear is the consultant about her own vision/wants/needs?"
- *Emotion.* Where there is emotion, there is energy. We infuse with emotion those things we care deeply about. Our emotions, then, are clues to that which we have made important. With this in mind, I ask myself: "How does the consultant seem to feel about what he is relating? What does the consultant's tone of voice say about what is going on for him? How does this "fit" with his description of how he feels?" (A value implicit in Experience-Centered Shadow Consulting is that consulting feels best when conducted with energy, enthusiasm, and a sense of meaning. When it doesn't feel this way, something is wrong. Experience-Centered Shadow Consulting can help identify what "it" is.)
- *Organizing schemes/frameworks/models.* As stated earlier, one of my working assumptions is, "We need to make the world make sense." A key to understanding the consultant's experience

of the situation is understanding how the consultant organizes things. Hence, I ask myself: "What implicit and/or explicit theories does the consultant use to understand events and guide interventions? What evidence does the consultant have that the theories 'fit'?"

- *Language/images/metaphors.* Our choices in this regard reflect our most current understanding of and feeling toward the person, event, or situation we are describing. A key to understanding others is understanding how they use these verbal symbols. For this reason, I ask myself: "What symbols does the consultant use to make sense of and describe things?"

- *Client/consultant connection.* Psychological distance/closeness. In the ideal client-consultant relationship, there is enough closeness for there to be open sharing of sensitive thoughts and feelings. At the same time, there is enough distance for the client to feel "safe" and for the consultant to remain "objective." This can sometimes be a very fine line. "Optimal vulnerability," one might call it. In my shadow consulting role, I ask myself: "Does the consultant seem to be sufficiently connected with the organizational client to bring about the desired outcomes? Too close? Too distant?"

Framing/Reframing. In the "framing" half of this phase, I attempt to organize, integrate, and feed back to the consultant what I've learned thus far. It usually goes something like this:

"So. As I understand it, the desired outcomes for the project you're working on are _____. The context for these outcomes is _____. What you've done to date is (*actions/interventions*) because (*consultant logic/assumptions/theories*). Am I with you thus far?"

[If "yes."]
"It also sounds like you're feeling _____. I can understand that. I remember when (*sharing of a relevant personal experience*). I'm impressed by how you _____."
"So. What you were wanting from our work together is _____."
[If "no."]
"Where did I miss you?"
[Clarify and ask again, "Am I with you?"]

"Reframing" is a cognitive intervention aimed at gaining a new perspective on the consultant's situation by identifying and applying a different set of beliefs, principles, models, theories to the situation. There are a number of methods for doing this. What follows is a description of four methods with a few rough examples of each:

What If. Survey of the situation from a vantage point the consultant has indicated or implied is a more desirable one than the one he or she now occupies:

- "What if you *were* an external consultant, making big bucks and didn't have to report to your consulting manager? How might that affect how you would proceed with this project?"

- "What if you *were* an internal consultant and weren't concerned that the client might think you were only creating work to get another pay check? What would that mean for your work on this project?"

- "Earlier you said you felt like you were 'up the proverbial creek without a paddle.' What if you *did* have a paddle?"

Practice Principle. Explicit application of a particular theory, model, principle that has not yet been applied to the situation:

- "As I recall, Argyris states there are three requirements for a successful intervention: valid data, free choice, and commitment. Let's see if there might be a way to apply that to our thinking here."

- "A principle I've found helpful is 'Don't do for someone what they can do for themselves. To do more is to do less.' If we apply this to your situation, where does that take us?"

Recollection.   Invitation to the consultant to explore a particular set of experiences that seem relevant to the situation at hand:

- "Can you recall a time when you found yourself acting in the 'strange' ways you experience your client as acting in now? What was going on for you at the time? Looking back, what did you want/need then? How might your understanding of yourself then help you to better understand and accept your client now?"
- "Can you recall another time where you 'felt stuck, were afraid that people would think you incompetent,' and you emerged triumphant? What did you do then? What made *that* work? Is there a principle you learned from that experience that we can apply here?"

Thinking Out Loud.   "Monday morning quarter-backing" by request:

- "Frankly, I'm not exactly sure what I'd do, either. However, I'd like to think that I'd _____. I think the principles guiding these actions are _____."
- "I don't know, but, if I was feeling particularly secure in my connection with this client, I'd like to think that I'd _____. Here are the principles behind this _____."

Options for Action.   During this phase, the consultant and I identify and discuss alternative courses of action that follow from the preceding phase. The discussion includes a frank conversation about the political benefits, risks, and costs of the various strategies for all the parties involved, including the consultant. I don't push

for a decision. It is the consultant's choice to act or not. He or she is not responsible to me.

Closure.   There is a statement in the *Tao Te Ching* that goes, "People usually fail just when they are on the verge of success. Therefore, give as much attention to the ending as to the beginning then there will be no failure." I try to remember that as the consultant and I are wrapping-up. Here is some of what I want to do in the "closure" phase:

- Review what the consultant wanted from our work together. (Has this been achieved or not?)
- Discuss follow-up support the consultant might find helpful.
- State what impressed me about the consultant and what *I* learned.
- Say, "Thank you."

Conclusion

Having spent much of this article describing what Experience-Centered Shadow Consulting *is,* here are a few words about what it is *not:*

- It is not supervision. As stated earlier, the consultant is not accountable to me. I have no authority over him or her. The consultant is responsible to the organizational client and, in some instances, to his or her consulting department manager.
- It is not therapy. Though it can be therapeutic. As we've seen, the focus may be on the person in his or her role as consultant, the consulting project, and/or the interaction of the two. Introspection is definitely required. Self-confrontation is sometimes required. Delving into one's psychosocial history, relationship to parents, siblings, significant others, etcetera (often the "stuff" of psychotherapy) is not required, necessary, or appropriate.

So. Enough disclaimers. . . .

A final word: As consultants, we don't always know what to do. Talking about that can help. Assistance (reassurance?) from a colleague can help us in our on-going challenge to bring all of who we are to what we do.

Bibliography

Lao Tsu. *Tao Te Ching* (Gia-Fu Feng and J. English, translators). New York: Vintage Books, 1972.

Ritvo, M., & Lippitt, R. "Shadow Consulting: An Emerging Role." In W. Sikes et al. (eds.), *The Emerging Practice of Organization Development.* Alexandria, VA: NTL Institute, 1989, pp. 219–24.

B. MANAGING MAJOR CHANGE PROCESSES

This part has six selections. In the first essay, Paul S. Goodman and James W. Dean, Jr., look at the factors that affect the institutionalizing of change efforts like quality of work life (QWL) programs. They see five factors—or processes, as they call them—that affect the degree of institutionalization. They define an institutionalized act as "behavior that is performed by two or more individuals, persists over time, and exists as part of the daily functioning of the organization." The selection concludes with recommendations for making change programs last.

The second essay comes from the book, *Power in Organizations,* by Jeffrey Pfeffer. The nature and structure of power situations are described, and an overview of the concepts of power and politics is presented. The reading provides an excellent foundation for understanding the variety of issues inherent in the concept of power.

In the third essay, some practical hints for the OD practioner are provided from Michael Beer's book, *Organization Change and Development: A Systems View.* Specifically, this selection tells how an OD group can gain and maintain the necessary organizational power to conduct its programs by drawing on different sources of power. Political awareness and sophistication, plus attention to political details, spells success when operatiing in a political arena.

The fourth selection, by Don Warrick, was written for this volume. In this essay, Warrick describes three stages of change and what he calls six "basics" of managing change. He believes that paying careful attention to these basics will greatly increase the probability of success in such change efforts as total quality management (TQM) programs.

The fifth essay, by Leonard Goodstein and Warner Burke, examines large-scale and fundamental change, often called "organizational transformation." In this essay, Goodstein and Burke apply Kurt Lewin's model of unfreezing, of movement, and of refreezing to a major change effort at British Airways. They describe how considerable use was made of all of the usual OD "technologies," such as team building, process consultation, and role clarification and negotiations.

Finally, this section includes a "strategy checklist" by Wendell French. This checklist lists many of the dimensions or variables that the author believes must be managed effectively if the OD process is to be successful. Suggestions for the management of each variable are included. The checklist grew out of one of French's experiences as a consultant in a long-range OD effort in a city government situation. This checklist may be particularly useful in highlighting some of the system variables that may "make or break" an OD effort in many settings.

The reader will note that participation by the chief executive officer (CEO) is emphasized in this checklist. This person might be the president of a company, a school superintendent, a city manager, the dean of a relatively autonomous school within a university, or the administrator or chief medical officer of a hospital. It is unrealistic to expect OD efforts to "start at the top" in all instances, but, as a general rule, OD efforts do not flourish unless the CEO of a major unit is involved. Ultimately, even the head of a relatively autonomous unit will at least need support from higher in the organization if the OD effort is to be sustained. Strong CEO involvement and support is crucial, of course, in an organizational transformation effort.

A Note on the Electromation and DuPont Cases

Union involvement, which is mentioned on the checklist, becomes even more important in light of the National Labor Relations Board 1992 decision in the *Electromation* and the *DuPont* cases. In the *Electromation* case, the NLRB ruled that "action committees" established by the Electromation Company were illegal under the Wagner Act. That law, passed in 1935, assumed that labor-management relations were essentially adversarial, and it prohibits companies from establishing, dominating, or interfering with labor organizations. [1]

In the Electromation situation, the NLRB found that the company had dominated the teams in the way they were structured by assigning about five workers and one or two management officials to each. Further, the company had involved the committees in discussing such issues as work rules and wages, areas that the union alleged—and the board agreed—were the province of collective bargaining. [2]

A few months later, in 1993, in a case involving DuPont's Chambers Works plant in New Jersey and the plant's Chemical Workers Association, the NLRB ordered DuPont to disband seven committees that had been formed to deal with recreation and safety issues. A likely consequence will be a major effort in Congress to amend the National Labor Relations Act toward supporting employee involvement efforts, rather than curtailing such efforts. Parenthetically, Labor Secretary Robert Reich has repeatedly stated that he would seek legislation in support of worker-management teams if the actions of the NLRB served to stifle them. [3]

Until the law is further clarified, it would seem that the implications for management and OD consultants include the following. These guidelines, written after the administrative judge ruled and before the full board heard the *Electromation* case, are attributed to Don Zimmerman, a former NLRB member and a Washington lawyer:

> Participation in such groups as action teams, improvement teams, quality circles, and the like should be strictly voluntary.
>
> Committees should focus on such areas as improving productivity, and product/ customer service quality or supplier relations.

Meetings should not be held that appear to be negotiations between management and labor over the terms and conditions of employment.

Committees should not be formed when the company is facing a union organizing campaign. [4]

Notes

1. *New York Times,* December 18, 1992, p. A 15; and *The Wall Street Journal,* December 18, 1992, p. A 12.
2. Ibid.
3. *The Wall Street Journal,* June 7, 1993, pp. A 2 and A 14; *New York Times,* June 8, 1993, p. A 11; and *The Wall Street Journal,* June 9, 1993, p. A 14.
4. Larry Reynolds. "Old NLRB Rule Could Jeopardize Quality Programs." *HR Focus* 68 (December 1991), pp. 1–2.

WHY PRODUCTIVITY EFFORTS FAIL

Paul S. Goodman and James W. Dean, Jr.

In the 1970s we saw a proliferation of new forms of work organization projects conceived by labor and management. These projects were aimed at improving the quality of working life (QWL), the quality of union-management relationships, and organizational effectiveness. In many ways the new forms of work organization were revolutionary in the sense that they represented fundamental changes in how labor and management could work together, how work would be organized, and how organizations might be designed.

Autonomous work groups represent one type of new form of work organization project. Basically, these are self-governing groups organized by process, place, or product. There is a substantial shift in authority and decision making as the group takes over decision making on hiring, discipline, allocation of production tasks, and so on. Matrix business teams represent another new form of work organization. Here line and staff managers are organized around business teams, rather than functions. Attached to each team is a voluntary set of shop floor teams whose task is to improve productivity. Many other organizational changes such as QC circles, Scanlon plans, job enrichment activities, and labor-management problem-solving groups were introduced during this period. They all represent fundamental changes in the organization's communication, decision making, authority, and reward systems. They also create fundamental changes in the relationships among people within the organization.

Source: This paper was partially supported by the Organizational Effectiveness Research Program, Office of Naval Research, Contract N0014-79-C-0167. It was presented at American Psychological Association, August 1981, and Quality of Work Conference, Toronto, Canada, September 1981.

This paper is concerned with whether these programs last. That is, after some initial period of success, do these change programs persist and become institutionalized, or are they just temporary phenomena? Why do some projects decline while others do not? What factors shape whether these QWL projects have some long-term viability?

Significance. The importance of understanding more about the concept of persistence or institutionalization of change should be apparent. If one is interested in bringing about long-term changes in productivity and in the quality of working life, labor-management relationships, and organizational effectiveness, then we must know more about why some change programs remain viable while others decline.

There is some growing evidence (Mirvis & Berg, 1977; Goodman & Dean, 1981) that many of these new forms of work-organization projects do not last. Goodman and Dean recently examined the persistence of change in a heterogeneous sample of new forms of work-organization projects. They selected organizations in which the change program had been *successfully* introduced and where some *positive* benefits had been identified. Goodman and Dean interviewed participants in these organizations four to five years after the projects had been implemented. They wanted to know whether the change activities had persisted. Only *one-third of the change programs* exhibited some reasonable level of persistence. The other change activities were either nonexistent or in decline. Given the huge amount of human and financial resources allocated to programs of change, such a low rate of persistence makes for a disturbing practical problem for managers and practitioners of organizational change.

Institutionalization—A Definition

Our approach is to study the persistence of organizational change via the concept of institutionalization. Institutionalization is examined in terms of specific behaviors or acts. We are assuming here that the persistence of QWL-type change programs can be studied by analyzing the persistence of the specific behaviors associated with each program. An institutionalized act is defined as a behavior that is *performed by two or more individuals, persists over time,* and *exists as a part of the daily functioning of the organization.* It should be clear from our definition of institutionalization that an act is not all-or-nothing. An act may vary in terms of its persistence, the number of people in the organization performing the act, and the degree to which it exists as part of the organization. Most of the organizational cases we have reviewed cannot be described by simple labels of *success* or *failure.* Rather, we find various degrees of institutionalization. The basic questions are, then: What do we mean by degrees of institutionalization? How do we measure these degrees?

We have identified five factors that contribute to the degree of institutionalization:

1. *Knowledge of the behaviors.* Remember that institutionalization is analyzed by looking at the behaviors required by the change program. Here we are interested merely in how many people know about these behaviors, and how much they know. Do they know how to perform the behaviors? Do they know the purposes of the behaviors? For example, team meetings are a part of many QWL programs. In some cases, people know that they are supposed to have team meetings, but don't know what they are supposed to do in the meetings. In other cases, people may not even know that they are supposed to have the meetings. In this type of situation, the change program is not very institutionalized.

This is why knowledge of the behaviors is important.

2. *Performance.* Here we are interested in how many people perform the behaviors, and how often they perform them. This is not quite as simple as it sounds, however. First, some behaviors are supposed to happen more often than others. A labor-management committee may be expected to meet occasionally, say about once a month, while team meetings are held weekly. We would not say that team meetings are more institutionalized than the labor-management committee just because they are more frequent. Second, some behaviors are supposed to be performed by more people than others. Most employees would be involved in team meetings, but only a few would take part in a labor-management committee. Again, we would not want to say that the team meetings were more institutionalized than the labor-management committee. The idea is not merely to count the number of persons or the frequency of behaviors, but rather to compare numbers and frequency to the levels required by the change program. Only then can reasonable comparisons be made.

3. *Preferences for the behaviors.* Here we are interested in how much people either like or dislike performing the behavior. In well-institutionalized change programs, most organizational members will like the critical program behaviors. In change programs on the decline, there generally are negative feelings expressed toward the critical program behaviors.

4. *Normative consensus.* This aspect of institutionalization measures two things: (1) how aware individuals are that other people in the organization are performing the behaviors and (2) how aware people are that other people feel they *should* perform the behaviors. Generally, when we see other people performing a behavior, we assume that they want to perform it, even though this may not be true.

5. *Value.* The final measure of institutionalization is the extent to which people have developed values concerning the behaviors in the

change program. Values are general ideas about how people ought to behave. For example, many change programs include behaviors consistent with the values of freedom and responsibility, as in autonomous work groups. The more people have developed these values, and the more aware they are that others have developed these values, the greater the degree of institutionalization for the change program.

The five aspects above represent measures of the degree of institutionalization. But how do we combine them to get an overall measure? The answer is relatively simple, because the five aspects of institutionalization generally occur in the same order. This is the order in which we presented them. First, people develop beliefs about the behaviors (1), and then they begin to perform them (2). People start to develop feelings about the behaviors (3), and others come to be aware of these feelings (4). Finally, values start to evolve concerning the behaviors (5). The further this sequence has progressed, the more the program has become institutionalized. Thus, in one program, people may know about the behaviors and perform them, but none of the other aspects may be present. In another program, the behaviors may be known, performed, liked, and supported by norms and values. The latter program is obviously more institutionalized.

Factors That Affect Institutionalization

General Framework.   Now that we have a way to represent the degree of institutionalization, we can try to explain how and why it hap-

pens. Why are some QWL programs more institutionalized than others? Our opinion is that there are *five processes that affect the degree of institutionalization*. We believe that these five processes are the major factors in predicting the degree of institutionalization a program will attain. There are, however, other important factors that affect these five processes. They are the *structure of the change* program and *organizational characteristics*. The structure of the change program means such things as the goals of the change, how general it is, the critical roles associated with the change (consultant, facilitator), and so on. Organizational characteristics are arrangements existing in the organization prior to the change program. Organizational characteristics include such things as work force skill level, labor-management relations, and existing values and norms. It should be emphasized that these factors are important only insofar as they affect the five processes (see Figure 1). We will also briefly present in this section some empirical findings of the present authors, as well as others, about the processes and other organizational factors related to institutionalization.

A. Five Processes.

1. Training.   The first process to be discussed is training. Training is providing information to organizational members about the new work behaviors. There are three major situations in which training is important: training as the program is started, retraining after the program has been in place for a while, and training of

FIGURE 1

A simple model of variables related to institutionalization

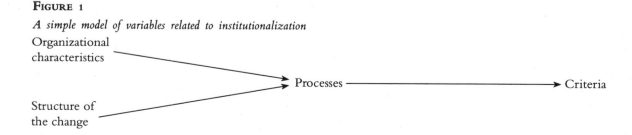

new members of the organization. The importance of training in general has been demonstrated in studies by Golembiewski and Carrigan (1970) and by Ivancevich (1974) in manufacturing firms, and by Goodman (1979) in an underground coal mine. Most organizations do an extensive amount of initial training, but are less consistent in retraining and in the training of new members. Goodman and Dean (1981) found that programs in which attention was paid to these latter types of training were likely to be more institutionalized.

2. Commitment.

Commitment refers to how motivated people are to continue to perform a behavior. Therefore a high degree of commitment should increase the chances that behaviors in a QWL program would continue, or be institutionalized. Commitment toward a behavior is increased when people *voluntarily* select that behavior in some *public context*. A recent study by the present authors (Goodman & Dean, 1981) has demonstrated the importance of commitment for institutionalization. For example, an autonomous work-group program seemed to grow and develop when personal choices were carried out freely. Later in the program, when the organization required others to participate in the program, it began to decline. The same study also found that programs with more frequent commitment opportunities were more institutionalized than those with limited commitment opportunities. Several other studies have noted the impact of commitment on institutionalization. For example, Ivancevich (1972) attributed the failure of a management by objectives (MBO) program to a lack of commitment by top management. Walton (1980), on the other hand, notes high levels of commitment in several successful programs of work innovation. Research on commitment by Kiesler (1971) and his associates suggests that institutionalization can be facilitated by withholding challenges to the new behaviors (e.g., new work group members) until

the workers are firmly committed to the new behaviors.

3. Reward Allocation.

This is the process by which rewards are distributed to employees in connection with the change program. Three aspects of the reward allocation process are important in understanding institutionalization: what types of rewards are available, the links between behaviors and rewards, and problems of inequity in the distribution of the rewards.

Many organizational change programs have been based on the assumption that intrinsic rewards (such as autonomy and responsibility) are sufficient for institutionalization. However, Goodman (1979) and Walton (1980) have questioned this assumption. In the recent study by the present authors, programs that combined both extrinsic (e.g., bonuses) and intrinsic rewards attained the highest degree of institutionalization, while programs with intrinsic rewards alone were less institutionalized.

The second issue in reward allocation concerns the link between the behaviors required by the change program and rewards. It is important that the rewards be linked to the *actual performance* of the behaviors, as opposed to mere participation in the program. We have found that there is a higher degree of institutionalization in programs where the link between performance and rewards is strong. This is consistent with statements by Vroom (1964) and Lawler (1971) concerning reward allocation.

A final issue concerning reward allocation is the potential for problems of inequity. Problems of inequity occur when an employee feels he is not being fairly compensated for the work he is doing. Results of studies have shown that new programs often became complicated by problems of inequity. For example, Goodman describes problems in a program to develop autonomous work groups in a coal mine. Part of the program involved job switching, whereby each new member would eventually learn all the jobs in the crew. The problem was that the entire crew was to be paid at the same (higher) rate, which originally was paid only to certain crew members. Since it had taken years for some of the men to attain this rate, they felt it inequitable that the other crew members should come on it so easily. This contributed to the decline of the change program. Similar problems of inequity have been reported by Locke, Sirota, and Wolfson (1976) in their study of an attempt at job enrichment in a government agency.

4. Diffusion.
Diffusion refers to the spread of the change program from one part of an organization to another. Diffusion is significant because the more the change program becomes diffused, the stronger the levels of institutionalization. As long as the program is restricted to one part of the organization, people may not feel compelled to take it seriously or they may object to it. But as diffusion starts to occur, people in other parts of the organization will begin to consider whether they should participate. As the program spreads, there also are chances for counterattacks on its validity.

The importance of diffusion for institutionalization has been noted by Goodman (1979) in the coal mine study mentioned above. In this study, when the intervention failed to diffuse beyond the original target group, it was perceived as inappropriate and failed to become institutionalized. Similar findings have been reported in a study of work teams in several plants of a large manufacturing company (personal correspondence, 1980). When the innovations continued to be limited to a few parts of the organization, they were not seen as appropriate, and failed to become institutionalized. However, the researchers in this study caution against diffusion that is too rapid, as widespread understanding, acceptance, and resources are necessary to support such an effort. Without these prerequisites, the program will collapse under its own weight. In general then, a medium course must be found between no diffusion and diffusion that is too ambitious for the resources supporting it.

5. Sensing and Recalibration.
Sensing and recalibration are the processes by which the organization finds out how well the program is doing, and takes steps to correct problems that have emerged. One of the common findings in our study (Goodman & Dean, 1981) was that what was actually occurring in the programs was often different from what was intended. That is, the organizations seldom had any formal way of detecting whether the intended change was "in place." Only in the most institutionalized programs in our study did mechanisms exist for feedback and correction. Walton (1980), who has undertaken a number of case studies of organizational change, says that the lack of sensing and recalibration mechanisms is a major cause of the failure of institutionalization. In another study, feedback mechanisms were in place, so information about the progress of the program was available (personal correspondence). However, nothing was done about the problems that were detected. Both sensing and correction mechanisms are important in attaining a high degree of institutionalization.

B. Structure of the Change.
Now that we have discussed the findings about the processes, we can discuss some of the factors that affect the processes. First we will discuss the structure of the change, which refers to the unique aspects of the change program. Specifically, we will talk about the goals of the programs, the formal mechanisms associated with the programs, the level of intervention in the programs, how consultants were used, and sponsorship for the programs.

1. Goals.
Some programs have very specific and limited goals, whereas others have more general, diffuse goals. In our study (Goodman & Dean, 1981), we found that programs with spe-

cific goals became more institutionalized than those with diffuse goals.

2. Formal Mechanisms. Most change programs have some new organizational form and procedures associated with them. These include the hierarchy of groups found in the parallel organization, the self-governing decisions made by autonomous work groups, and so on. Here we are interested in how formal these arrangements are. For example: Are meetings scheduled in advance? Are procedures written down? In general, we have found that programs with more formal mechanisms and procedures attain higher levels of institutionalization.

3. Level of Intervention. Here we are interested in whether the QWL program was introduced in a part of the organization, or in the whole organization. In our study, programs that were introduced throughout the whole organizational unit were more institutionalized than programs limited to a part of the organization. One of the problems with smaller-scale intervention is that people from other parts of the organization sometimes attempt to sabotage the program. This was true in four of the organizations that we studied (Goodman & Dean, 1981), none of which had programs which were very institutionalized.

4. Consultants. Most organizations, when undertaking a change program, will employ a consultant to help them. This was true in the organizations we recently studied. Some organizations use consultants for longer periods than others. We found that firms that rely on consultants for a long time are less able to develop their own capacity for managing the program. Consequently, after the consultant leaves they are less able to institutionalize the program. The greater the dependence on the consultant, the less successful the program.

5. Sponsorship. Another factor that appears to affect the degree of institutionalization is the presence of a sponsor. The sponsor is an organizational member in a position of power who initiates the program, makes sure that resources are devoted to it, and defends it against attacks from others in the organization. If the sponsor leaves the organization, no one will perform these necessary functions, and processes such as commitment and reward allocation will be hampered, thus making it harder for institutionalization to occur. In our study, the initial sponsor was still present in organizations which had more institutionalized programs, but programs whose sponsors had left were low in institutionalization. Problems with withdrawal of sponsorship are well documented in the literature on organizational change, having been reported by Walton (1975, 1978), Miller (1975), Frank and Hackman (1975), Crockett (1977), and Levine (1980).

C. Organizational Characteristics. Organizational characteristics are those aspects of the organization that exist prior to the change program, which will have an effect on the degree of institutionalization that the program will attain. These characteristics are important to the extent that they affect the processes we have discussed (commitment, diffusion, and so on).

1. Congruence with Organizational Values and Structure. Whatever the nature of the change program, one important factor for institutionalization is the extent of congruence or incongruence between the change program and existing organizational properties. In general, the more congruence, the greater will be the likelihood of institutionalization. Various organizational characteristics may be important in understanding congruence. In the cases studied by the present authors, congruence between the change program and preexisting management philosophy led to higher degrees of institutionalization. Other authors have demonstrated the importance of congruence between the organizational change and corporate policies (Fadem,

1976), individual values and motives (Seashore & Bowers, 1978), the authority system (Mohrman et al., 1977), the skills of the employees (Walton, 1980), organizational norms and values (Levine, 1980; Warwick, 1975; Crockett, 1977), and cultural norms and values (Miller, 1975). Of course, if these are already in conflict with one another, it will be difficult for programs to be congruent with all of them.

2. Stability of the Environment. From the evidence reported so far, it should be clear that institutionalizing a change program in an organization is a difficult task, even in the best of situations. Adding instability to the situation only makes things worse. In our study, (Goodman & Dean, 1981) there were only two cases of instability in the environment. In these cases there was a major decline in demand for the organization's products, which led to curtailments in the work force. This in turn changed the composition of many of the groups that were an integral part of the change program. These groups became less effective, which lowered the degree of institutionalization. Similar results were found in another study (personal correspondence) as an economic recession led to layoffs and bumping. Environmental instabilities such as these represent a major obstacle to institutionalization.

3. Union. The role of the union can play a major role in determining the degree of institutionalization. Many of the new forms of work-organization changes run in parallel with other union-management activities related to the traditional collective bargaining process. If there are high levels of labor-management conflict in the collective bargaining area, we expect these to spill over to the productivity and "quality of working life" activities and negatively affect their viability.

Most local unions are part of larger institutional structures. In other studies (c.f., Goodman, 1979) there is evidence that the qual-ity of the relationship between the local union and the international will have a critical impact on the viability of any change program in a given firm.

How to Make Programs Last

Our recommendations for how to make programs last should come as no surprise to the reader, as they are derived from the above findings and theory:

1. Be selective in implementing programs. Organizations or subunits which have labor-management problems or an unstable economic environment are not good locations.

2. Plan for institutionalization in the beginning. Many programs do not persist because all of the resources are directed at initiating the program, rather than maintaining it.

3. Be aware of congruence problems. Programs which are incongruent with organizational norms and values seldom persist. Gradual changes to reduce the incongruence are possible but they require much time and effort (see Goodman & Dean, 1981).

4. Structure of the change. The following characteristics of programs have been shown to facilitate persistence:
   a. Specific, written-out statements on program goals.
   b. Formal procedures to implement the program activities.
   c. Total system intervention, with organizational resources to support it.
   d. Limited, short-term use of consultants.

5. Training over time. Training should not be abandoned after a month or even a year, but must be redone periodically to reinforce the change.

6. Commitment. High commitment comes from (1) voluntary participation in

program activities and (2) opportunities for recommitment over time.

7. Effective reward systems. Reward systems should:
   a. Include both extrinsic and intrinsic rewards.
   b. Link rewards to specific behaviors.
   c. Introduce a mechanism to revise the reward system.
   d. Minimize problems of inequity over compensation.

8. Diffusion. Programs which are linked to one organizational subunit often die in isolation. Attempts must be made to spread the program to other organizational areas.

9. Sensing and recalibration. A direct and accurate feedback mechanism which measures the performance of program activities is necessary if the change program is to adjust, grow, and remain viable over time.

Summary

Many programs of organizational change, while initially successful, do not persist. We have conceived of persistence of institutionalization as occurring by degrees, ranging from knowledge about the behaviors associated with the program to values supporting these behaviors. Five processes which affect the degree of institutionalization have been identified, and aspects of the structure of the change and organizational characteristics which affect the processes were also examined. Finally, recommendations, based on our findings, were enumerated on what managers can do to facilitate persistence of change in their organization.

References

Crockett, W. "Introducing Change to a Government Agency. In P. Mirvis & D. Berg (eds.), *Failures in Organizational Development: Cases and Essays for Learning.* New York: Wiley-Interscience, 1977.

Fadem, J. "Fitting Computer-Aided Technology to Workplace Requirements: An Example." Paper presented at the 13th annual meeting and technical conference of the Numerical Control Society, Cincinnati, March 1976.

Frank, L. L., & Hackman, J. R. "A Failure of Job Enrichment: The Case of the Change That Wasn't." *Journal of Applied Behavioral Science,* 1975, *11* (4), 413–36.

Golembiewski, R. T. & Carrigan, S. B. The Persistence of Laboratory-Induced Changes in Organizational Styles. *Administrative Science Quarterly,* 1970, *15,* 330–40.

Goodman, P. S. *Assessing Organizational Change: The Rushton Quality of Work Experiment.* New York: Wiley-Interscience, 1979.

Goodman, P. S., & Dean, Jr., J. W. "The Process of Institutionalization." Paper prepared for conference on organizational change, Carnegie-Mellon University, May 1981. To be published in a forthcoming volume on organizational change, P. S. Goodman (ed.)

Ivancevich, J. M. "A Longitudinal Assessment of Management by Objectives." *Administrative Science Quarterly,* 1972, *17,* 126–38.

Ivancevich, J. M. "Changes in Performance in a Management by Objectives Program. *Administrative Science Quarterly,* 1974, *19,* 563–74.

Kiesler, C. A. *The Psychology of Commitment: Experiments Linking Behavior to Belief.* New York: Academic Press, 1971.

Lawler, E. E. *Pay and Organizational Effectiveness.* New York: McGraw-Hill, 1971.

Levine, A. *Why Innovation Fails.* Albany: State University of New York Press, 1980.

Locke, E. A.; Sirota, D.; & Wolfson, A. D. "An Experimental Case Study of the Successes and Failures of Job Enrichment in a Government Agency." *Journal of Applied Psychology,* 1976, *61,* 701–11.

Miller, E. J. "Sociotechnical Systems in Weaving, 1953–1970: A Follow-up Study." *Human Relations,* 1975, *28* (4), 349–86.

Mirvis, P. H., & Berg, D. N. (eds.) *Failures in Organization Development and Change.* New York: Wiley-Interscience, 1977.

Mohrman, S. A.; Mohrman, A. M.; Cooke, R. A.; &

Duncan, R. B. "A Survey Feedback and Problem-Solving Intervention in a School District: 'We'll take the survey but you can keep the feedback.'" In P. Mirvis & D. Berg (eds.), *Failures in Organizational Development: Cases and Essays for Learning.* New York: Wiley-Interscience, 1977.

Seashore, S. E., & Bowers, D. G. "Durability of Organizational Change." In W. L. French, C. H. Bell, Jr., & R. A. Zawacki (eds.), *Organization Development: Theory, Practice, and Research.* Plano, TX: Business Publications, 1978.

Vroom, W. H. *Work and Motivation.* New York: John Wiley & Sons, 1964.

Walton, R. E. "The Diffusion of New Work Structures: Explaining Why Success Didn't Take." *Organizational Dynamics,* Winter 1975, pp. 3–21.

Walton, R. E. "Teaching an Old Dog Food New Tricks." *The Wharton Magazine,* Winter 1978, pp. 38–47.

Walton, R. E. "Establishing and Maintaining High Commitment Work Systems." In J. R. Kimberly & R. H. Miles (eds.), *The Organizational Life Cycle,* San Francisco: Jossey-Bass, 1980.

Warwick, D. P. *A Theory of Public Bureaucracy.* Cambridge, Mass.: Harvard University Press, 1975.

READING 40
CONDITIONS FOR THE USE OF POWER

Jeffrey Pfeffer

The following situation was used by Gerald Salancik to illustrate the conditions under which power is employed. Two wounded soldiers are lying in a tent on some distant battlefield. A medical corpsman is with them in the tent. Each man requires precisely one pint of blood to live; if each man does not receive the pint of blood, he will die. The pint of blood, then, is both a necessary and sufficient condition for the survival of each of the two wounded soldiers. In the tent, in addition to some medical supplies, is a single pint of blood. Because of the course of the battle going on around them and the associated logistical difficulties, it would be impossible to get any more supplies in time. A decision will have to be made: one man will live, the other will die. Splitting the blood between the two soldiers will cause them both to die, so compromise is out of the question.

One man is a captain, the other a corporal. Each implores the corpsman to save his life, and each musters arguments to support his position. The captain argues that he is entitled to the blood because of his superior hierarchical rank. If the arguments of rank and formal status are not convincing enough, he further argues that captains are important in the planning and organizational work of fighting. He has many men in his command, and the pint of blood given to him will make his unit a more effective fighting force because it will enable him to recover. While the captain has impact over many men, the corporal has much less influence on the war, being only a single soldier. The corporal, on the other hand, argues that captains are, after all, part of the ad-

ministrative overhead of the war; it is the corporals and the other front line troops that actually do the fighting. The corporal argues that he has killed many more enemy than the captain, and, if he is allowed to live, is likely to have a more direct impact on the fighting in the future. Furthermore, the captain is older, and, other things being equal, the corporal will have a longer life expectancy if he gets the blood. The pint of blood given to him, in other words, will probably result in more years of human life. Each then musters tales of his family—the captain has a wife and two young children back at home; the corporal tells about his poor, aged parents who are depending on him to take over the family business after the war.

How shall the corpsman decide? Each soldier has raised legitimate, relevant, and reasonable criteria which favor him over the other soldier. The captain has rank and organizational impact; the corporal has impact on the direct work of the organization; both have claims based on family and other reasons. The corpsman, who is attempting to provide the maximum benefit to the army, finds it difficult to determine which soldier will really have the greatest potential benefit to the service. After all, there are a lot of desk officers and fighting men are scarce; on the other hand, the ability to lead and organize is important, too.

The corporal reaches into a heap of his possessions, and pulls out a gun. Suddenly, the decision becomes clear. The captain dies and the corporal obtains the blood.

This apocryphal situation is a paradigm of a decision-making setting in which the use of power may be introduced. Furthermore, the situ-

Source: Jeffrey Pfeffer, *Power in Organizations,* Marshfield, Mass.: Pitman Publishing, 1981, pp. 67–94.

ation illustrates well how the introduction of power is both a necessary and sufficient condition for making the choice. The elements that produce conflict and the use of power, or political activity, in organizations are diagrammed in Figure 1. A consideration of that figure along with the example indicates when and why power comes to be employed.

The first condition of the use of power is interdependence, a situation in which what happens to one organization actor affects what happens to others. In the present example, there is competitive interdependence, in the sense that blood which is given to one soldier will not be available to another. Other forms of interdependence exist in organizations, including the interdependence which arises from joint activity on some work product, so what one unit does to the product affects and may be affected by what another unit does. Interdependence is an important condition because it ties the organizational participants together, in the sense that each is now concerned with what the other does and what the other obtains. In the absence of such interde-

pendence, there would be no basis for conflict or for interaction among the participants.

The second condition of the use of power is heterogeneous goals, or goals which are inconsistent with each other. In the present case, the goal of the corporal to stay alive is inconsistent with the goal of the captain to live because of the interdependence. A related condition would be heterogeneous beliefs about technology, or the relationship between decisions and outcomes. In the present example, this was not a problem as there was agreement on the connections between actions and consequences; all parties understood that obtaining the pint of blood was both necessary and sufficient for survival. As we shall explore later, such agreement on technology is not inevitable within organizations.

The third condition producing the use of power is scarcity. If there were two pints of blood, there would be no decision problem. To the extent that resources are insufficient to meet the various demands of organizational participants, choices have to be made concerning the allocation of those resources. The greater the

FIGURE 1

A model of the conditions producing the use of power and politics in organizational decision making

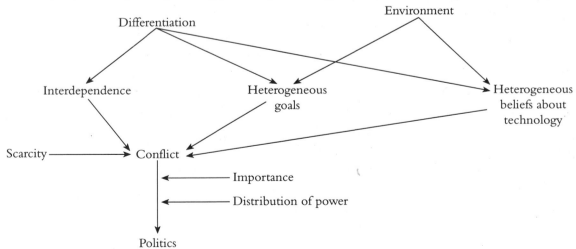

scarcity as compared to the demand, the greater the power and the effort that will be expended in resolving the decision.

As indicated in Figure 1, together the conditions of scarcity, interdependence, and heterogeneous goals and beliefs about technology produce conflict. Whether that conflict eventuates in politics, the use of power in organizational settings depends on two other conditions. The first condition is the importance of the decision issue or the resource. In the case of our example, the resource was very important—necessary for survival. In situations in which the decision may be perceived as less critical, power and politics may not be employed to resolve the decision because the issue is too trivial to merit the investment of political resources and effort. The second condition is the distribution of power. Political activity, bargaining, and coalition formation occur primarily when power is dispersed. When power is highly centralized, the centralized authority makes decisions using its own rules and values. The political contests that sometimes occur in organizations take place only because there is some dispersion of power and authority in the social system.

Before considering each of these conditions in additional detail, one final point should be made about the example. When the conditions which were specified in the figure and present in the example occur, the use of power is virtually inevitable and, furthermore, it is the only way to arrive at a decision. Given conflicting and heterogeneous preferences and goals and beliefs about the relationship between actions and consequences, interdependence among the actors who possess conflicting preferences and beliefs, and a condition of scarcity so that not all participants can get their way, power is virtually the only way (except, perhaps, to use chance) to resolve the decision. There is no rational way to determine whose preferences are to prevail, or whose benefits about technology should guide the decision. There may be norms, social customs, or tradition which dictate the choice, but these may

be all efforts to legitimate the use of power to make its appearance less obtrusive. In situations of conflict, power is the mechanism, the currency by which the conflict gets resolved. Social power almost inevitably accompanies conditions of conflict, for power is the way by which such conflicts becomes resolved. . . .

Some Causes of Goal and Technology Disagreements.   As indicated in Figure 1, differentiation within the organization is one important source of disagreements on goals and beliefs about technology. Differentiation simply refers to the fact that, in most large organizations, there is specialization of the participants and subunits by task—a division of labor which enables the organization to achieve certain economies but which also entails some costs. . . .

Disagreement, Conflict, and the Use of Power

The next part of the model argues that disagreements about cause-effect relations and preferences lead to conflict and, potentially, the use of power to resolve the choice. This position is well supported in the existing literature on the causes of conflict, in which the effects of disagreement are widely recognized. Dahrendorf (1959, p. 135) virtually defined conflict in terms of goal discrepancies:

> All relations between sets of individuals that involve an incompatible difference of objective—i.e., in its most general form, a desire on the part of both contestants to obtain what is available only to one, or only in part—are, in this sense, relations of social conflict.

Schmidt and Kochan (1972, p. 361) noted that "perception of goal incompatibility is a necessary precondition for . . . conflict." Finally, examining the bases of conflict, Walker (1970, p. 18) noted:

> If two members hold divergent goals . . . and if these goals motivate their behavior, then one mem-

ber will be motivated to behave in a way which is inconsistent with the goals of the other.

Because of the potential for goal disagreements to engender conflict and political activity in organizations, goal statements are made frequently at a very general level, so all or at least most of the participants can agree with them. In attempting to explain organizational actions in terms of the stated goals, vaguely stated objectives can cause problems for the analyst. However, the very lack of clarify and specificity in these goal statements makes it possible for the various constituencies within the organization to accept them. This reduces conflict, at least at this level. Of course, as Etzioni (1964) recognized, the operative goals—the bases on which decisions and choices are actually made within the organization—are necessarily more specific. The fact that there may be agreement on general goals will not prevent conflict over the details of what the organization is to do when a specific action is to be taken. At the same time, such overall agreement can serve to potentially moderate the intensity of the conflict and provide some additional integration into the organization for the various participants.

The Role of Profit Maximization. If goal or value dissensus is an important condition leading to the use of power and politics and to a greater effect of power on decision outcomes, then it should be evident why business organizations are, for the most part, less overtly political than organizations in the nonprofit or public sectors such as governmental agencies, hospitals, and universities. The reason is not that businessmen are more rational, more analytical, or less political than administrators in the other organizations. Rather, business organizations have a reasonably agreed-upon goal of profit maximization, and this goal consensus negates much of the need for the use of power that might otherwise exist. In a debate, for instance, over the addition of a piece of medical equipment in a

hospital, the decision turns not just on the return on investment as compared with the hospital's cost of funds. Rather, the hospital may have to go through a certificate-of-need application process, thus exposing itself to regulatory delays and political review. Concerns about cost and return on assets must be balanced against physicians' demands for equipment to improve the quality of patient care. The hospital may have a reputation and self-image as providing state-of-the-art care, and this may influence the decision. A similar type of decision, the addition of equipment, in a business firm is much more likely to turn primarily on economic return considerations. Other issues are less legitimately raised, given the consensus that profit is what business firms are all about.

* * * * *

The objective of profit maximization can serve as an archetype of what a consensually shared goal can accomplish, in terms of legitimating and organizing collective action. Indeed, the development of language that facilitates this process of consensus building is an important administrative activity. It is important to remember, however, that profit is not the only possible objective that could fill such a role of legitimating and organizing behavior. Rather, it fills the role solely because it has come to be shared and believed within this country at a particular period of time.

Scarcity and Power and Conflict

Interdependence among subunits and differences in goals and in perceptions of technology are not sufficient, by themselves, to produce conflict and the resulting use of power and politics to reach decisions. It is only when the conditions are coupled with resource scarcity that conflict and power arise in organizational settings. Schmidt and Kochan (1972, p. 363) note that shared resources are one of the precursors to conflict. But unless these resources are in short supply, there will be little need or incentive for the various organizational actors to engage in a political struggle over them.

Decisions are contested, it is suggested, because choices must be made which will determine who will benefit and how much, from the organization's activities. When benefits and resources allocated within organizations are scarce, the funds allocated to one subunit may make another subunit unable to fulfill its objectives or maintain sufficient support to remain viable, due to its lack of funds. A promotion allocated to one individual forecloses the position to other potential contenders. If there are as many positions as contenders, it will matter much less than if many must contend for a very few promotional opportunities. It is because resources are scarce, because choices have to be made among courses of action, beneficiaries, and others interested in the organization and its activities, that conflict arises and power comes to be used in making decisions.

* * * * *

The fact that resource scarcity produces more power and influence attempts, as well as more conflict over the limited resources to be allocated, is one important reason that formal organizations have a strong preference for growth. As Katz and Kahn (1966), among others, have noted, growth in size provides the organization with more positions, and more budget resources, to allocate each successive year. These positive increments permit all participants to obtain more, to some degree, each year, and limit the intensity and amount of conflict engendered. When the organization faces a constant, or worse yet, shrinking pool of resources, conflict and power struggles become more intense. Because few participants enjoy the conflict and the requirement of making very difficult decisions among numerous worthy contenders for the limited resources, there is a strong preference for growth—a situation in which conflict is reduced

and in which power and political activity are less prominent features in decision making. . . .

The Importance of Decisions

When resource scarcity is coupled with interdependent units and heterogeneous goals and beliefs about technology, conflict is produced within organizations. Two other conditions determine whether or not this conflict will become expressed in political activity organized around the development and use of power in order to obtain the preferred decision. One such condition is that the decision being made or the resource being allocated must be perceived as being important or critical. The use of power requires time and effort. Moreover, power typically is not inexhaustible. Votes or favors called in on one issue may not be available for use in other decisions. Thus the use of the resources that provide power, and power itself, is husbanded. Just as there is no need to use power in the absence of scarcity, there is no desire to use power to affect decisions that are not perceived as being important or critical to the organization's operations. . . .

Centralization and Political Activity

The second condition which determines whether or not political activity will be the method by which choices are made in conditions of conflict is the extent to which power is centralized within the organization. In this dimension, the present analysis departs from the Thompson and Tuden typology, in which the extent to which power was concentrated in the organization was not considered to be a feature which affected the form of decision process that was employed.

This condition is important in explaining why decision making in many organizations appears as it does. Many observers report that most organizational decision making seems to be orderly, systematic, and to employ bureaucratic or rationalistic decision procedures. Yet, it is agreed that few decision situations in complex organizations are characterized by consensus over both goals and technology. Using Thompson and Tuden's argument, one would be left with a paradox—the use of apparently computational decision-making procedures in settings which are not characterized by the requisite amounts of consensus and certainty.

The explanation of this paradox is straightforward. In many organizations, particularly in business organizations, power is relatively highly concentrated at the top of the organization. This concentration of control is sometimes accomplished through concentrated share ownership. In other circumstances the concentration of power may occur because of managerial control over the election of directors, the choosing of auditors, and the consequent release of information. In still other contexts, concentrated power may result from the tremendous rewards and sanctions that may be available to those at the highest executive levels. Furthermore, the socialization accomplished in schools produces an expectation of hierarchical power, so that power which is concentrated at the top of the organization is legitimate and acceptable. When the power is concentrated, potential conflicts in goals and in definitions of technology are resolved by the imposition of a set of preferences and a view of technology which reflects the position of the dominant coalition controlling the organization. The decisions which are made are enforced through various control procedures. The decision-making process appears to be orderly and rational only because technological uncertainty and goal disagreements have been submerged in the organization's choice processes through the use of concentrated power and influence.

Conversely, politics, the less rational-appearing interplay of power and political strategy, occurs when power and control are dispersed. The resolution of conflicting beliefs and goals then occurs on a more equal basis. An analogue can be drawn to make the argument clearer. There is more political activity in democratic countries with relatively equal political parties than there is in countries which are run by strong dictatorships. When power is centralized, decisions are made and imposed by the central authority. When power is dispersed, decisions become worked out through the interplay of various actors with more equal power in a political process. This argument does not mean that power is not critical in determining decision outcomes in either case; regardless of the degree to which power is dispersed, power still affects the extent to which a given social actor's preferences will prevail. The argument, rather, is that when power is highly concentrated, the other participants in the system have little ability or motivation to engage in a contest for control which provokes the visible conflict and political activity observed when power is more equally distributed. . . .

Making Decision Making Less Political

The identification of those factors that tend to lead to the use of power and political activity in decision making also indicates what might be done in organizations to reduce the use of power and politics. It is worth considering the costs of such strategies, to clarify some of the advantages of retaining political decision processes.

Slack Resources.   Slack, or excess resources, in the organization can reduce the use of power and politics in two ways. In the first place, as Galbraith (1973) has noted in his discussion of organization design, slack reduces the amount of interdependence among subunits. Interdependence is an important prerequisite for conflict (e.g., Schmidt and Kochan, 1972). By reducing the amount of interdependence among units in the organization, the potential for conflict is also reduced. Slack reduces interdependence by permitting the activities of the various units to be relatively uncoupled. To illustrate the point, consider one form of slack observed in most organizations: work-in-process inventories. We will consider the copy editing and production departments of a publishing company. If the organization permits large in-process inventories, the two subunits will have little contact and little cause for conflict. The copy editing department will do its work on the manuscript, and then add the book to the inventory of manuscripts ready for production. For its part, the production department will work on the manuscripts as it has time, according to whatever priority rules the organization has set. The existence of the inventory essentially uncouples the two departments. If there were no inventory, then the production department would be arguing with the copy editing department about manuscript preparation, or, the copy editing department would be fighting with the production department about producing finished books. By decoupling the process, interdependence is reduced and so is the potential for conflict.

Slack also reduces conflict by affecting the existence of scarcity of resources. The existence of slack or excess resources implies less scarcity, and less scarcity means that there will be less conflict. With plenty of resources, there is less need to contest for allocations since there will be enough for all subunits to get what they need.

The cost of slack, of course, is the cost of keeping excess resources on hand, a cost that may entail inventory costs and costs of excess capacity. These various costs of slack have led Galbraith (1973) to suggest that this strategy is not very useful in solving coordination problems. By the same token, it may be a rather costly way of reducing the incidence of power and politics in decision making. However, it is clear that slack, or excess resources, is one way of reducing the use of power in organizational choice. As we will argue throughout this book, one of the advantages of organizational growth is its ability to generate excess resources at least in the short run, and this reduces the use of

power and the incidence of conflict within the organization.

One of the more prominent slack-creating tactics used in organizations is the creation of additional administrative positions and titles. Williamson (1975, 120) has argued. "The expansionary biases of internal organization are partly attributable to its dispute-settling characteristics. . . . Persistent conflict . . . results frequently in role proliferation." Instead of choosing among subunits for a new-position incumbent, the vacant position is filled with a person from one subunit *and* additional positions are created to keep at least some of the other subunits moderately happy. If new positions are not created, then titles can be manufactured. In addition to chief executive officers, there can be presidents, chairmen of the board, chief operating officers, chief financial officers, vice chairmen, and so forth. If position creation is a means of producing slack in an attempt to reduce conflict and its consequences for the use of power, then one would expect to see more position creation in systems in which power and conflict might otherwise be endemic. For instance, if resource scarcity produces conflict over the allocation of some kinds of resources, then position creation may proceed apace in order to pay off the subunits that lose in the struggle over those resources. Certainly, the creation of administrative positions in universities has increased as these organizations began to face more and more resource scarcity. Position creation would be expected to increase in situations where there is great interdependence between subunits and great heterogeneity in preferences and beliefs about technology among organizational participants.

Homogeneity and Agreement.   In addition to slack, the use of power can be diminished through the production of a homogeneous set of organizational participants, homogeneous with respect to their goals and preferences and in their beliefs about cause-effect relations. Such homogeneity can be produced through selectively recruiting persons with very similar backgrounds and training, socialization of persons once they have been recruited into the organization, or the use of rewards and sanctions to produce at least outward conformity to the dominant set of beliefs.

The production of homogeneity has its own costs for organizational decision making. Davis (1969), in reviewing the literature on group decision making, noted that groups tended to make better decisions than individuals because of the different information and different points of view that were brought to bear on the situation by the various group members. Homogeneous groups, facing certain kinds of tasks, performed less effectively than more heterogeneous groups. Clearly, the advantages of different sources of information and different perspectives on issues can be lost in an organization in which homogeneity in goals and technological beliefs has been produced.

This problem is likely to be the most troublesome for those organizations that face a changing set of environmental conditions. If the organization faces a stable environment in terms of demands and constraints, then the solutions developed at one point in time will probably suffice long into the future. In this situation, there is less need for change or adaptation, and thus less need for new and diverse informational inputs into decision making. By contrast, an organization facing a more rapidly changing environment may require frequent changes in strategy and direction; such change is less likely to emerge from a homogeneous group. Janis (1972) has illustrated the problems of conformity to a single point of view in his discussion of groupthink and the decision making that occurred in the Kennedy Administration. Janis argued that even in the absence of homogeneity, a crisis situation tends to produce demands for loyalty and conformity within the group that cause the group to make faulty analyses and to miss obvious problems and other alternatives. These problems are certainly going to be worsened if the group is already homogeneous in preferences

and outlook and has been chosen specifically to minimize the potential for conflict.

Reducing the Importance of Decisions. The final strategy to be considered in the reduction of the incidence of power and politics involves reducing the importance, or at least the perceived importance, of the decision being made. This can be accomplished in several ways. In some instances, a decision that is perceived as being critical and about which there is disagreement may simply be avoided. Although this may not seem to be an optimal way of running an organization, the avoidance of conflict is not at all uncommon, and does result at times in the refusal to make a decision. In a firm in California which manufactured and constructed large, highly engineered projects, a conflict arose as to whether or not something should be added to the product line which would involve the use of more standard parts and subassemblies, but which might open up new markets to the firm. The firm, dominated by engineering in the past, wrestled with the decision. Production and marketing favored the addition. Marketing would have more to sell and possibly an easier job in selling. Production would gain substantial power in the firm, because the manufacture of standardized parts and components would not become a more important activity within the firm. At the same time, engineering, which previously had power because of its control over the critical contingencies in the design of the projects, would lose some control. In this particular instance, the decision was simply put off—for additional market research, financial analysis, production facilities feasibility analysis, and so forth. It was clear from observing the key executives that by putting off the decision they were able to avoid a severe conflict. Because of the generally favorable orientation toward analysis and data gathering, the postponements could be made to appear to be a reasonable part of a rational decision-making process.

A second strategy is somewhat more common. Critical decisions are labeled as being relatively unimportant in order to avoid the involvement and concern of organizational participants. This can be accomplished by stating that the decision is relatively unimportant. Relatively little formal analysis can be done and few people, or few people of importance, can be involved in the decision process. Attention can be kept away from the decision and on other matters occurring in the organization. This strategy is somewhat risky and not always successful, in that the criticality of the decision may be so widely known that it is impossible to make it appear otherwise. Nevertheless, power and political activity can be reduced substantially if the choice can be made to seem relatively unimportant.

A related strategy involves taking a decision and breaking it into smaller pieces, each one of which is likely to appear to be less important for the organization. Peters (1978), in describing techniques for implementing change, recommends precisely such a strategy. Its benefit is that change occurs slowly, and in pieces, as part of an ongoing process. Because few may realize the totality of what is occurring, it is less likely that power will organize to contest the decisions.

This strategy is frequently used to change the direction of an organization when the person in charge does not have the direct power to do so. The dean of a school of business which had been primarily research-oriented and firmly grounded in the basic social science disciplines was confronted with the task of changing the orientation and activities of the school. One way to proceed would have been to announce that a decision would be made about the future direction of the school. This would undoubtedly have been perceived as an important decision, and the various constituencies would have organized and mustered their power to affect the choice according to their preferences. There would have been a lot of conflict and a lot of political activity over what would be perceived as a crucial decision. The alternative, and what was done in fact,

was not to make an announcement about a new direction, but rather, to make a series of small and relatively trivial decisions that, in their total effects, resulted in the accomplishment of much of the change that was desired. A decision was made to incorporate a placement center in the school for its master's graduates. This decision was treated as a relatively trivial matter of moving the facility from one part of the campus to the building where the business school was located. Certainly, no one could care much about that. In a similar fashion, alumni relations, corporate fund raising, and external affairs activities were added; the advisory board, comprised of business executives, was involved more heavily in the decision making in the school; and, some changes were made regarding the importance of teaching and in minor aspects of the curriculum. Treated individually, the changes were not worth even thinking about, much less fighting. Taken together, the changes had the effect of moving the school toward a new strategy. Most importantly, the course of action avoided the conflict and exercise of power that would undoubtedly have been engendered, had the total change been announced and effected at once. This strategy, too, has costs. In the case of avoiding important but contested choices, the costs involve failing to act when action may be required, and the possibility of missing opportunities or failing to act in time to avoid threats. In the case of trying to make an important decision appear unimportant, as well as in the strategy of breaking an important decision into a series of small, unimportant ones, the costs include the possibility of discovery, resulting in even more intense conflict. In addition, the disguising of the true consequences of decisions may fail to produce the kind of thorough analysis and discussion that such important actions warrant. Implementation may be achieved, but the wrong action may have been implemented.

In Table 1, we summarize the discussion of strategies for avoiding the use of power and poli-

TABLE 1

Strategies for avoiding the use of power and politics in decision making, and their costs

Strategy	Costs
Slack or excess resources, including additional administrative positions or titles.	Inventory costs, costs of excess capacity, costs of extra personnel and extra salary.
Homogeneity in goals and beliefs about technology produced through: Recruitment practices. Socialization. Use of rewards and sanctions.	Fewer points of view, less diverse information represented in decision making; potentially lower quality decisions.
Make decisions appear less important.	Decision may be avoided; subterfuge may be discovered; analysis and information may not be uncovered.

tics and some of the costs of those strategies. It is clear that it is possible to avoid political decision making, but that the manager must strike a balance between the costs of doing so and the benefits to be obtained through the avoidance of conflict.

References

Dahrendorf, Ralf. *Class and Class Conflict in Industrial Society.* Stanford, CA: Stanford University Press, 1959.

Davis, James H. *Group Performance.* Reading, MA: Addison-Wesley, 1969.

Etzioni, Amitai. *Modern Organizations.* Englewood Cliffs, NJ: Prentice Hall, 1964.

Galbraith, Jay R. *Designing Complex Organizations.* Reading, MA: Addison-Wesley, 1973.

Janis, Irving L. *Victims of Groupthink.* Boston: Houghton Mifflin, 1972.

Katz, Daniel, and Robert L. Kahn. *The Social Psychology of Organizations.* New York: John Wiley, 1966.

Peters, Thomas J. "Symbols, Patterns, and Settings: An Optimistic Case for Getting Things Done." *Organizational Dynamics* 7 (1978), pp. 3–23.

Schmidt, Stuart M., and Thomas A. Kochan. Conflict: Toward Conceptual Clarity. *Administrative Science Quarterly* 17 (1972), pp. 359–70.

Thompson, James D., and Arthur Tuden. "Strategies, Structures and Processes of Organizational Design." In *Comparative Studies in Administration*, eds., J. D. Thompson, P. B. Hammond, R. W. Hawkes, B. H. Junker, and A. Tuden. Pittsburgh: University of Pittsburgh Press, 1959, pp. 195–216.

Walker, Orville C., Jr. *An Experimental Investigation of Conflict and Power in Marketing Channels.* Madison, WI: unpublished doctoral dissertation, 1970.

Williamson, Oliver E. *Markets and Hierarchies: Analysis and Antitrust Implications.* New York: Free Press, 1975.

READING 41
THE POLITICS OF OD

Michael Beer

Staff groups usually develop power in organizations by obtaining the support of top management. This usually means supporting them with services that they require and see as crucial. Often it means avoiding head-on confrontations with their core values and beliefs. The OD group cannot follow this model if it is to be trusted by multiple constituencies and maintain a systems perspective. The problem then is how to achieve neutrality and independence, even with respect to top management, while developing enough power to be effective and survive.

Since it cannot rely on top management or any other constituency for its only source of power, an OD group must develop additional sources of power. This can be done by developing credibility based on competence and ability to provide clients with help that *they* need and request. An OD group can do this by developing a reputation for serving system needs, rather than being self-serving. Research on how specialty staff groups gain influence and power suggests the following six sources of power an OD group can consciously develop:

1. *Competence.* The first and foremost source of influence for the OD group is their own competence and effectiveness. They must be seen by the line organization, the union, or any other group of employees as professionally capable. This means that they are acknowledged experts in organization behavior and in the process and techniques of change agentry. But it also means that they must be interpersonally competent, and model effective ways of managing

conflict—ways which they often encourage in their clients. The OD unit must also demonstrate competence as a group, operating efficiently internally and operating effectively in their relations with various parts of the organization. This means meeting deadlines, achieving goals, following up, keeping people informed, and so on.

2. *Political Access and Sensitivity.* The OD group can increase power by developing multiple relationships in the organization with key power figures (not only management, but union leaders, heads of minority groups, etc.). These relationships are informal and informally developed. They allow the change agents access to key individuals who know what is going on in the organization. Relationships with key power figures allow the change agents to determine what is important to them and gear their services to meet felt needs. Relationships also allow the OD group access to information about their reputation so they can detect early on any political activity aimed at reducing the influence of the group or eliminating it.

3. *Sponsorship.* Substantial research literature supports the general proposition that innovations (technological or managerial) are adopted at least in part because there is a strong and powerful sponsor in the organization who supports the innovation. In the product development area, these people have been called product champions. Organization development groups will gain power to the extent that they have sponsorship, preferably multiple sponsorship, in powerful places. This means vice presidents, presidents, or union leaders, respected elder statesmen, etc. For example, it is likely that Irving Bluestone's sponsor-

Source: Michael Beer, *Organization Change and Development: A Systems View* (Santa Monica, CA: Harper Collins, 1980), pp. 258–61.

ship (he is vice president of the United Auto Workers) of the quality of work projects at General Motors is an important source of power for the OD group. Multiple sponsors can be obtained by successfully completing OD projects in support of powerful people. Thus past clients who are powerful become sponsors and some may even get more powerful as they move up in the organization. The key is not to rely on a single sponsor or power center (e.g., management).

4. *Stature and Credibility.*   Power accrues to people and groups who develop a reputation for success and effectiveness. For the OD group, this stature must come first and foremost from line management's view that OD efforts have paid off. If key line managers spread the word that OD helped their organization to increase profits, reduce turnover, or in some other way improve effectiveness, stature and credibility are assured. Assuming they are capable of providing and delivering successful OD projects, OD groups can help themselves by encouraging their clients to communicate and spread the word. Organization development groups can also enhance their stature by developing a positive reputation in their professional community so that feedback comes back into the organization from other sources. This secondary strategy must be carefully managed so that the group does not become viewed as so "professionally" oriented that they are seen as unconcerned with the organization's primary goals.

5. *Resource Management.*   Power accrues to those who control resources. If OD groups can deliver services to clients when they need to solve problems, they enhance their influence and reinforce interest in OD. Flexibility in assignment of OD specialists is one way to achieve this. A second way is to develop a pool of line and staff people in the organization who are capable of doing OD work, thus freeing the corporate OD group to shift their focus as new requests are made. A third way is for the OD group to bill their services to line managers. In this way the availability of change-agent resources is geared to the demands of clients, rather than to an arbitrary budget of dollars or people. Resources would be added when a client is ready. This stance is also consistent with the idea that change resources are likely to be most effective when the managers are motivated to use them. It is important to recognize, however, that this market strategy has downside risks because it makes the OD group more independent than some managements would like.

6. *Group Support.*   Groups that are cohesive are more powerful. OD units that are able to work out internal differences, agree on common goals and strategies, share a philosophy of OD, and support each other are more likely to be effective. OD work involves a lot of stress and risk taking. It becomes easier when there is an internal atmosphere of supportiveness. Furthermore, internal strife takes up energy that could be spent in task-related activities and in determining future direction. For this reason OD groups, like other specialist groups, need to spend a substantial amount of time in team-building activities. For this they may need an external OD consultant of their own. But this must not be done at the cost of bringing an OD group into conflict with other staff groups whose missions overlap with OD (e.g., personnel). A frequent problem of OD in many corporations has been conflict with the personnel function generated in part by the cohesion and arrogance which OD groups develop.

An OD group that tries to have a systems perspective is constantly balancing two relationships. It must maintain influence with multiple constituencies through the means just described. Unless the OD group can maintain its credibility, its effectiveness in serving the organization as a total system is reduced. When this happens, its capacity to generate enough influence to prevent its own destruction at the hands of a threatened constituency is diminished. On the other hand, the OD group must not allow the process of developing an independent and credible position to become so threatening to the power structure that the group is reduced in size or eliminated. This is likely to happen when top management feels the group has become too independent and systems-oriented and not enough management-oriented. Political access and sensitivity, sponsorship by key members of the power structure, and direct services for members of the power structure are important means of avoiding this outcome.

The essence of this complex political process is simultaneous maintenance of independence from the power structure and the development of dependence by the power structure on the OD group's services. This is a function of both political skill and luck. For example, hard financial times can occur just when the OD group is developing its power base but has not yet attained it. Or sponsorship can be withdrawn for reasons beyond the group's control. However, a combination of competence, political access, and multiple sponsorship can reduce the probability that the occurrence of these events will eliminate the OD group.

WHAT EXECUTIVES, MANAGERS, AND HUMAN RESOURCE PROFESSIONALS NEED TO KNOW ABOUT MANAGING CHANGE

D. D. Warrick

Change management may very well be the most important skill that executives, managers, and human resource professionals will need to master in the 1990s. Change is not the issue. Change is inevitable. We are living in times characterized by accelerated, unpredictable, unprecedented, dynamic, transformational change and by fierce competition. Restructuring, reorganizing, downsizing, and doing more with less have become a way of life. Markets expand and shrink over night in an increasingly global marketplace. New technologies and an explosion of information present a multitude of new opportunities and problems. Paradigm shifts are required of managers and employees alike and often require significant role and skill changes. If managing all of these changes and challenges were not enough, the most competitive organizations must also be committed to being world class learning organizations that excel at performance, people management, internal and external service excellence, and total quality. In sizing up the 90s, one manager said, "I have done so much with so little for so long, I can now do almost anything with nothing!"

Change Management: The Critical Issue in the 90s

The real issue in the 90s is change management. Even the right things done the wrong way are unlikely to succeed. Change mismanagement can have far-reaching ramifications. An executive calls employees together for a one-hour meeting to announce a new reorganization that will solve

Source: Written especially for this book.

most of the organization's problems. A year later, the organization is still in a state of chaos from the one-hour meeting. There was no commitment to the change . . . except by the executive. There was no involvement of the *key stakeholders* (those who are in the best position to influence and contribute to the success of the desired change). Cohesive teams were dissolved and new teams created resulting in confusion about roles and relationships. Employees still do not understand the reasons for the change or have a vision for the future. The list goes on and on. Perhaps most alarming, the executive probably thinks everything is going well! This experience will create an organizational memory about change and how change is managed and will make future changes even more difficult to successfully achieve.

Most of these issues could have been avoided with even a minimal understanding of change management. Sound change management results in better change decisions, accelerates the change process, builds confidence in how change is managed, avoids making cures worse than diseases, and can have a significant impact on bottom line results by improving performance and minimizing wasted time, efforts, and resources.

Who Should Learn Change Management?

The subject of change management is most typically discussed in textbooks on organization development (Cummings & Huse, 1989; French & Bell, 1990) or professional books on changing dynamics in the workplace (Kanter, Stein, & Jick, 1992; Boyett & Conn, 1991; Jamieson & O'Mara, 1991). Organization development

(OD) is a planned, long-range, systems, and primarily behavioral science strategy for understanding, changing, and developing organizations and improving their present and future health and effectiveness (Warrick, 1984).

Change management has primarily been the domain of change agents. Change agents are specialists in managing change and developing high-performance organizations, teams, and individuals. In an age of dynamic change, all organizations, large or small, should have or have access to one or more change agents. However, we have now entered an age of accelerated change where it makes sense to train others in the skills of change management. Foremost, executives need to learn at least the basics of change management. They are in the most strategic position to make and manage or mismanage needed changes. The time needed to successfully implement changes can be significantly reduced when executives understand and champion changes. Since organizations will be increasingly decentralized and managers more empowered, managers as well should learn the basics of change management. It also is imperative for human resource professionals to learn change management. They will play more of a change-agent role in the 90s, and an understanding of change management will effect the way they manage such issues as diversity and delivery training, team building, and other programs. Perhaps the time has arrived when all employees should be trained in the basics of change management, since employees will be increasingly involved in the change process and empowered to make needed changes.

A division of Hewlett-Packard is presently training all of its human resource professionals to be change agents. Executives and managers will then be given a short course on change management so they will know how to orchestrate most of their own changes and link up with change agents when their assistance is needed. Finally, efforts will be made to institutionalize an agreed-on change process so anyone in the organization can refer to the process in making changes.

The Basics of Managing Change

While internal or external change agents or a combination of both may be needed for major or complex changes, such as organization transformation programs (fundamental changes in the whole organization) or major systems changes (structural, technical, or cultural changes, and the like), most changes can be made by following several basics of change management. The basics can make a significant difference in increasing the probability of successful change. Some estimate that, at best, major organization changes like total quality management (TQM) programs have about a 30 percent probability of succeeding (Gallop Poll Survey for the American Society for Quality Control). The 70 percent or more failure rate has little to do with the lack of need for change. It occurs because of poorly managed change. Based on hundreds of programs that I have been involved in as a change agent or trainer of change agents, I am convinced that using sound change management principles can reverse the probability of success to 70 percent or more.

A classic example of the importance of effective change management is the award-winning TQM program at Florida Power and Light (*Training,* February 1991). Millions of dollars and thousands of hours spread over several years was spent on developing a TQM program that eventually won the Deming Prize for quality control. FP&L was the first U.S. company to win this prestigious award bestowed by Japan. Visitors came from all over the world to study this marvelous program. In 1990, James Broadhead, the chairman and CEO of FP&L, dismantled the program. In reality, while some improvements in quality were realized, the program had become a bureaucratic maze complete with three large departments administering the program, an emphasis on documentation, graphs, charts, and reports, and procedures and processes that made it more rather than less difficult for employees to do their jobs and serve customers. Keep in mind that it took top management several years to discover the reality of what was taking place. A few of the basics of change management, such as building in accurate feedback mechanisms, could have saved the company millions and made it possible to make needed corrections.

Basic 1—Clarify Reality and the Need for Change

Changes are sometimes driven by unsubstantiated opinions, assumptions, and information, by selfish ambition, and by pressures from people biased by their own dissatisfaction or agendas. It is very important to conduct a diagnosis that accurately portrays reality and to establish the need for change. Change for the sake of change, change for the wrong reasons, or unneeded change are all counterproductive. A diagnosis to determine reality could be made by evaluating internal information, conducting surveys and interviews, or perhaps benchmarking best practices. The need for change should only be established after reliable information is considered.

Basic 2—Develop a Results-Oriented, Rather than an Activities-Oriented, Strategy for Change

Several recent articles have emphasized the importance of results-oriented change (Beer, Eisenstat, & Spector, 1990; Schaffer & Thomson, 1992). Schaffer and Thomson comment:

> The performance improvement efforts of many companies have as much impact on operational and financial results as a ceremonial rain dance has on the weather. While some companies constantly improve measurable performance, in many others managers continue to dance round and round the campfire—exuding faith and dissipating energy. This "rain dance" is the ardent pursuit of activities that sound good, look good, and allow managers to

feel good—but in fact contribute little or nothing to bottom-line performance.

Activities-driven changes focus on fuzzy and vague outcomes, if they consider outcomes at all, and engage people in endless activities, experiential exercises, and confrontational encounters that do little to make lasting changes or improve bottom-line results. Results-centered changes seek specific and, as much as possible, measurable improvements accomplished during a reasonable time frame. The results focus represents a major and much needed shift in the field of organization development. Some organizations refuse to use the term *organization development* because of their experience with well-intended but ineffective activities-driven change agents who think that OD is a bag of tricks, programs, and experiential exercises that may make people feel good but do little to make lasting changes or impact the bottom line.

Basic 3—Plan and Manage Changes Following the Three Stages of Change and the Seven Steps in the Change Process

Figure 1 shows a model of the *three stages* of change and *seven steps* in the change process. Figure 2 explains what each step consists of. It has been my experience that the concept of change management can be learned quickly by (1) identifying a change, (2) planning the change process by using the checklist as a guide in listing what should be done in each of the three stages of change, and (3) meeting with several informed people to evaluate or involve in planning the change process.

The classic model for managing change is Kurt Lewin's model (Lewin, 1951) that views change as a three-step process: (1) unfreezing; (2) moving; and (3) refreezing. The process includes unfreezing old behaviors, values, and attitudes, making changes, and refreezing new behaviors, values, and attitudes. Unfortunately, this model is too static for an environment of dynamic change. Changes are not always a mat-

466

FIGURE 1

The planned change process

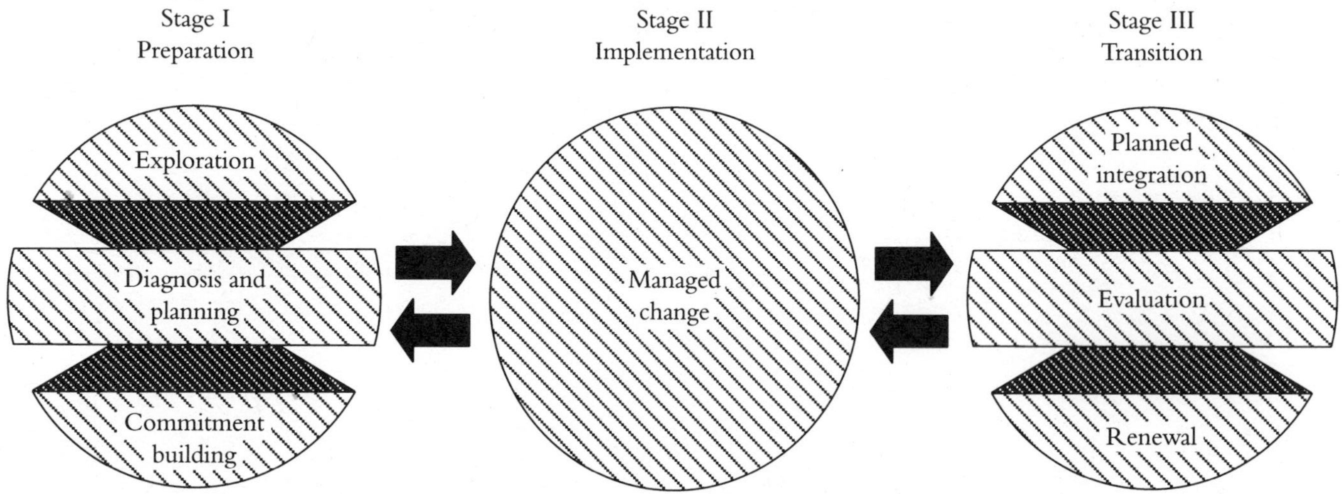

Stage I
Preparation

Stage II
Implementation

Stage III
Transition

Exploration

Diagnosis and planning

Commitment building

Managed change

Planned integration

Evaluation

Renewal

The Six Basics of Managing Change

1. Clarify reality and the need for change.
2. Develop a results-oriented, rather than activities-oriented, strategy for change.
3. Plan and manage the change process by following the three stages of change and the seven steps in the change process.
4. Involve the key stakeholders in planning and managing the change process. Stakeholders include the key people who are in the best position to influence or contribute to the success of desired changes.
5. Build in reliable feedback mechanisms to monitor and manage the change process.
6. Assure that enabling structures (missions, values, goals, resources, organization design, reward and valuing systems, policies, and so on) are aligned to facilitate and reinforce the desired changes.

FIGURE 2

Change management checklist

Stage I—Preparation

Exploration
1. Identification of a need or opportunity for improvement or change.
2. Involvement of one or more Change Champions, Change Agents, a Change Team, or some combination of each in a preliminary needs assessment and consideration of alternatives for change.
3. Clearly identify the key stakeholders and explore ways to involve them in planning and managing the change process.
4. Build support and seed the organization for change (develop advocates, share information and ideas, and so on).
5. Contract for change by involving the appropriate people in designing and negotiating a change strategy that provides a clear vision of what needs to be done.

Diagnosis and Planning
6. Develop a plan for gathering the necessary data and information needed to clarify present realities, future ideals, and how to achieve the ideals.
7. Implement the diagnosis.
8. Utilize the results of the diagnosis for problem solving, action planning, and modifying the change strategy.

Commitment Building
9. Clarify the roles of the key players in the change process (Change Leaders, Change Agents, Change Champions, and Change Teams) and involve each as much as would be appropriate in the design and implementation of the change program.
10. Communicate the change vision to the appropriate people who can impact or will be impacted by the changes, educate them on the change process, involve them when appropriate in the change process, and address their concerns and suggestions.

Stage II—Implementation

Managed Change
11. Educate and train the key players in the paradigms (thinking patterns and models) and in the skills needed to implement the changes.
12. Select and implement the appropriate strategies and changes.
13. Manage resistance to change.
14. Build in reliable feedback mechanisms to monitor and manage the change process and make needed adjustments.
15. Keep people focused on the vision.

Stage III—Transition

Planned Integration
16. Institutionalize the changes by assuring that enabling structures are aligned to facilitate and reinforce the desired changes. A team could be appointed to carry out this important task.
17. Follow through on commitments made in Stage II.
18. Reinforce, reward, and communicate successes, learn from mistakes or failures, make needed adjustments, keep people informed about program progress, and integrate and culturize the changes.

Change Evaluation
19. Conduct a follow-up diagnosis and use the results to evaluate the program, improvements, opportunities for further improvement, and what can be learned from the change process.

Renewal
20. Develop a Renewal Plan for maintaining the gains, planning future actions and improvements, sharing what has been learned with other parts of the organization, monitoring progress, and being prepared to respond quickly to the need for new directions.

ter of unfreezing old behaviors, and refreezing new behaviors is not a desirable goal in a dynamic environment.

The model in Figure 1 identifies the three stages of change as (1) *Preparation,* (2) *Implementation,* and (3) *Transition.* In the Preparation Stage, the organization is prepared for change by *Exploring* the need for change, *Diagnosing* the issues and *Planning* a change strategy, and *Building Commitment* for the change. The Implementation Stage consists of *Managing the Change Process* in a dynamic environment increasingly characterized by uncertainty, unpredictability, and continuously changing circumstances. In this stage, the change is implemented, managed, and monitored by a change agent, change champion (a person responsible for championing the change and the change process), change team, or some combination of each. In most cases a top down/bottom up strategy is used that involves key people at all levels in working as a team to accomplish the desired change. The Transition Stage is essential to successful change. In this stage, the change transitions from one state to another. The change is *Integrated* into existing practices. In addition, structures, processes, and policies are aligned to support the change. The change is *Evaluated* to measure improvements, identify future changes that need to be made, and learn from the change process. When the change appears to be reasonably well integrated into existing practices, a *Renewal Plan* should be developed so gains can be maintained, improvements continued, learnings from the change process shared, and the change can continue to be monitored so problems or the need for new directions can be quickly detected. Without this important stage, few desired changes are realized or sustained. It is a particularly important stage in a dynamic environment when rapidly changing circumstances and priorities may require modifications or totally new directions.

The three stages of change and the seven steps in the change process represent overlapping and interrelated processes that must be adapted to the realities of each unique situation and change. Changes must go through all three stages of change to achieve a high degree of success. Most changes are predominantly Stage II changes. That is why they are so unsuccessful. Someone or some team decides to make a change, the change is announced, and resistance and chaos set in. The initiators are unaware of the change going awry, since reliable feedback mechanisms have not been built into the process and those impacted are afraid to question the wisdom of the initiators. However, unless all three stages are incorporated into the change process, changes have a low probability of succeeding. Even if a change starts in Stage II by mistake, or because pressing circumstances warrant bypassing Stage I, the Preparation Stage should eventually be integrated into the change process to assure commitment to change. Figure 3 shows a model of how to design a change program using the three stages of change. The model is for the Hewlett-Packard program previously mentioned.

Basic 4—Involve the Key Stakeholders in Planning and Managing the Change Process

A manager received word from his boss that, based on an employee survey, performance and morale needed to be improved. Within two days the manager sent a response to his boss and employees outlining 10 changes that would be made immediately. The plan failed! He would have been much better off to involve the key stakeholders in evaluating the survey results and developing a plan to improve performance and morale. The key stakeholders could include higher management, if they can influence the outcome of the changes made. It could also include a cross-section of managers and employees or even union officials. Involvement improves the quality of decisions and increases commitment and buy-in. Expedient changes that bypass the key stakeholders will usually come back to haunt the initiators of change and increase resist-

FIGURE 3

Organization effectiveness program (one-year program)

Goals: (1) develop an organization effectiveness model, change process model, and change agent methodology and instruments by November; (2) change the role of personnel to an organization effectiveness emphasis by January 1; (3) train personnel team members to be operating change agents by January 1; (4) train managers to be change champions and understand how to work with change agents by June; and (5) integrate the change process model into the organization culture by September.

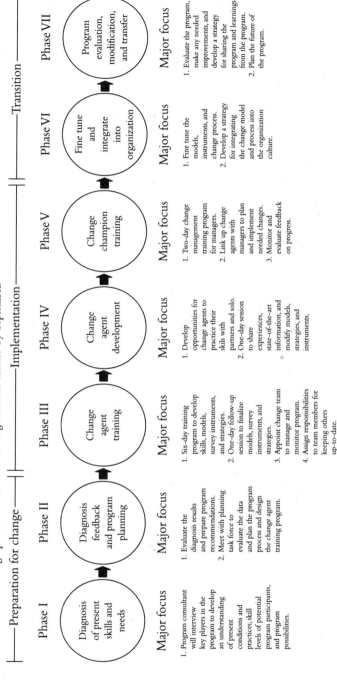

─── Preparation for change ─── │ ─── Implementation ─── │ ─── Transition ───

Phase I — Diagnosis of present skills and needs

Major focus

1. Program consultant will interview key players in the program to develop an understanding of present conditions and practices, skill levels of potential program participants, and program possibilities.

Phase II — Diagnosis feedback and program planning

Major focus

1. Evaluate the diagnosis results and prepare program recommendations.
2. Meet with planning task force to evaluate the data and plan the program process and design the change agent training program.

Phase III — Change agent training

Major focus

1. Six-day training program to develop skills, models, survey instruments, and strategies.
2. One-day follow-up session to finalize models, survey instruments, and strategies.
3. Appoint change team to manage and monitor program.
4. Assign responsibilities to team members for keeping others up-to-date.

Phase IV — Change agent development

Major focus

1. Develop opportunities for change agents to practice their skills with partners and solo.
2. One-day session to share experiences, state-of-the-art information, and modify models, strategies, and instruments.

Phase V — Change champion training

Major focus

1. Two-day change management training program for managers.
2. Link up change agents with managers to plan and implement needed changes.
3. Monitor and evaluate feedback on progress.

Phase VI — Fine tune and integrate into organization

Major focus

1. Fine tune the models, instruments, and change process.
2. Develop a strategy for integrating the change model and process into the organization culture.

Phase VII — Program evaluation, modification, and transfer

Major focus

1. Evaluate the program, make any needed improvements, and develop a strategy for sharing the program and learnings from the program.
2. Plan the future of the program.

ance to change. When the key stakeholders have some level of involvement in the planning and execution of change, the change will have a high probability of success.

Basic 5—Build in Reliable Feedback Mechanisms to Monitor and Manage the Change Process

A company spent millions on consultants, new technology, and training to launch a new software program that affected most of the organization. The new system was designed by consultants and the Information Systems Department with minimal involvement of end users. I might add that it worked magnificently for the consultants and IS people! The new system was launched during the busiest month of the year without a pretest pilot program, with minimal involvement of the primary users of the new system, and without reliable feedback mechanisms built in. The new system was a dismal failure for the end users and customers. End users could not operate the system, files and billings on customers were lost, irate customers began calling in, experienced supervisors no longer had the knowledge and skills to supervise their employees on the new system, problems developed within and between teams, and morale and productivity plummeted. While all this was taking place, top management was being told by the consultants and IS department that the new system was working great except for a few difficulties with employees who were slow learners or who were resisting the changeover to the new system. In fact, top management held a banquet for the consultants and IS Department to celebrate the success of the program. This situation could have been avoided by involving the end users in the design of the system and building in some simple feedback mechanisms to monitor the change process. Feedback can be obtained through questionnaires, interviews, focus groups, and conversations with reliable people who are

involved in the change. The key to feedback is to make it reliable so management can have a true picture of what is happening.

Basic 6—Assure that Enabling Structures are Aligned to Facilitate and Reinforce the Desired Changes

Enabling structures could include mission statements, values, goals, resources, organization designs, reward and valuing systems, policies, training, and anything that would enable or block the change process. For example, an organization may launch a team-building program only to discover there is nothing in the reward system to value teamwork. Innovation, risk taking, and collaboration may be encouraged in a culture that historically has not valued such behaviors. People may be asked to perform tasks or to utilize skills without the training to do what they are expected to do. It is imperative that enabling structures be aligned to support desired changes if the changes are expected to be maintained. This area of change management is often overlooked.

Guidelines for Managing Change

In addition to following the six basics for managing change, several guidelines can be helpful in managing the change process (see Figure 4). Change management, like other management skills, is in many ways state-of-the-art common sense. When changes are planned and implemented in a way that makes sense to both the initiators and recipients of the changes, the motivation to change increases, the change process is accelerated, and confidence in the way change is managed paves the way for future changes. However, common sense is not always common practice. Therefore the guidelines are provided to help manage the change process and improve the probability for successful change.

FIGURE 4

Change management guidelines

1. Staying the same or relying on past successes is a formula for complacency and eventual failure.
2. Quick-fix solutions rarely last. Successful change takes time.
3. The change process (how change is accomplished) is equally as important as the change product (what is targeted for change). Even the right things done the wrong way are not likely to succeed.
4. Always appoint a change agent or change champion and, where appropriate, a change team to manage the change process and make change happen.
5. The focus of change should be on (1) present realities, (2) future ideals, and (3) how to move step by step toward the ideals. Dwelling on the past is energy draining and time wasting. Leave the past behind.
6. All situations are not the same. Change strategies should be tailored to (1) the unique characteristics of the organization and realities of the situation, (2) level of change desired (fine tuning, incremental, transformational), and (3) the desired end results.
7. Involvement in the change process increases understanding, commitment, and ownership. However, involving the wrong people or involvement in overkill will create resistance to change or take change in the wrong direction.
8. Positive change is more effective than negative change. You can motivate people more with honey that vinegar.
9. The incentive to change must be greater than the incentive to stay the same. Perceived incentives (positive or negative) must outweigh the reasons and excuses for not changing.
10. Go where the energy is. Look for windows of opportunity where there is a felt need or an enthusiasm for change.
11. Strike while the iron is hot! Opportunities for change disappear quickly and the momentum for change wanes fast as time elapses.
12. Focus on a "few" high impact changes until they are successfully accomplished. Success builds confidence and momentum for change. Overcommitting builds frustration, resistance, and failure.
13. Think state-of-the-art common sense, simplicity, and balance. The most effective changes are simplified to common sense, rely on trust and judgment, rather than on impersonal and lifeless procedures, and have the feel of balance.
14. Some resistance to change can be expected. However, continued resistance must be dealt with or the change process will be undermined and the leaders sponsoring the changes will lose credibility.
15. The more that is at stake the greater the resistance to change and the need to carefully manage the change.
16. Provide people with the skills needed to successfully adapt to change. Significant changes in thinking, acting, and relating are sometimes required for change to succeed.
17. Think alignment. Systems, processes, values, and reward systems must be aligned to sustain change.
18. You get what you measure and reward, and deserve what you tolerate. People will respond to whatever is measured and rewarded and will continue in inappropriate behaviors that are tolerated.
19. The probability for successful change can be increased by (1) creating a clear and understandable vision of the change and change process, (2) accountability for change, (3) valuing and reinforcing efforts to change, a willingness to innovate and experiment, and successes, (4) removing obstacles, and (5) having reasonable consequences for continued noncompliance.

Change Management Is a High-Payoff Skill

In an age of dynamic change and intense competition, the way that organization's manage change will significantly effect their competitive advantage, the performance and morale of their employees, their ability to adapt with lightning speed to a constantly changing environment, and, in some cases, may be the difference between success and failure. Mismanaged change costs organizations. There are the more obvious costs of wasted time and resources and lost opportunities. However, there are also many hidden costs as well. Frustration, high levels of anxiety and stress, feelings of lack of control and being out of control, breakdowns in trust and communications, a loss of confidence in management, broken or damaged spirits, and internal conflict and strife all accompany mismanaged change.

Of all the actions an organization could take to succeed in the 1990s, the training of executives, managers, and human resource professionals in change management and in developing a change strategy that is used throughout the organization may very well have the highest payoff. Change management is a high payoff skill. However, simply training people in change management is not enough. Organizations need to develop and institutionalize (i.e., integrate into the culture of the organization) a change strategy that is used throughout the organization when anyone considers making a significant change. The strategy could include, for example, a model for change, a change management checklist, and possibly a list of change guidelines similar to those presented in this article. Considerable freedom should be given in applying the strategy, and the strategy should be open game for continuous improvement. Strongly resist any efforts to turn the strategy into a bureaucratic quagmire that would render it counterproductive.

Challenge

What is your organization doing to prepare your executives, managers, human resource professionals, and other key players to manage change? Change management is a critical skill for rapidly changing times, and the time has come when training in change management should be provided throughout the organization. However, even the best-run and best-intended organizations may be overlooking the importance of change management. The road to mediocrity is filled with organizations, including many former excellent organizations, with good intentions and a few important oversights. Make change management a high priority in your organization and increase your probability for success.

Bibliography

Beer, Michael; Russell A. Eisenstat; and Bert Spector. "Why Change Programs Don't Produce Change." *Harvard Business Review,* November–December 1990, pp. 158–67.

Boyett, Joseph H., and Henry P. Conn. *Workplace 2000: The Revolution Reshaping American Business.* New York: Dutton, 1991.

Broadhead, James L. "The Post-Deming Diet: Dismantling A Quality Bureaucracy." *Training,* February 1991, pp. 41–43.

Jamieson, David, and Julie O'Mara. *Managing Workforce 2000: Gaining the Diversity Advantage.* San Francisco: Jossey-Bass, 1991.

Kanter, Rosabeth Moss; Barry A. Stein; and Todd D. Jick. *The Challenge of Organizational Change: How Companies Experience It and Leaders Guide It.* New York: Free Press, 1992.

Lewin, Kurt. *Field Theory in Social Science.* New York: Harper & Row, 1951.

Schaffer, Robert H., and Harvey A. Thomson. "Successful Change Programs Begin with Results." *Harvard Business Review,* January–February 1992, pp. 80–89.

Warrick, D. D. *Managing Organization Change and Development.* New York: Macmillan, 1984.

READING 43
CREATING SUCCESSFUL ORGANIZATION CHANGE

Leonard D. Goodstein and W. Warner Burke

Buffeted at home and abroad by foreign competition that appears to produce higher-quality goods at lower prices, corporate America has now largely forsaken (at least publicly and momentarily) the traditional analogy of the organization as a machine and its organizational members as parts designed to work effectively and efficiently. Instead, many American corporations are accepting the "New Age" view of organizations as "a nested set of open, living systems and subsystems dependent upon the larger environment for survival."

What is surprising about this quote is not its viewpoint, which has been normative in the organizational psychology and behavioral literature for several decades, but its source: *The Wall Street Journal.* And it is typical to find such articles in virtually every issue of most recent American business publications: articles on corporate culture, on the changing attitudes of American workers, on the need for greater employee participation in managerial decision making, and on the place of employees as an important (if not the most important) asset of the corporation.

We are not suggesting that traditionally managed organizations are now extinct in America. Corporate executives, however, have definitely begun to recognize that managing the social psychology of the workplace is a critical element in the success of any organization.

Organizational Change

Organizations tend to change primarily because of external pressure, rather than an internal desire or need to change. Here are a few all-too-familiar examples of the kinds of environmental factors requiring organizations to change:

- A new competitor snares a significant portion of a firm's market share.
- An old customer is acquired by a giant conglomerate that dictates new sales arrangements.
- A new invention offers the possibility of changing the organization's existing production technology.

Other examples include (1) new government regulations on certain health care financing programs and (2) economic and social conditions that create long-term changes in the availability of the labor force. The competent organization will be so alert to early warning signs of such external changes that it can move promptly to make internal changes designed to keep it viable in the changing external world. Competent organizations are those that continue to change and to survive.

Thus it is practically a cliché to state that change in organizations today is a way of life. And clearly it is not saying anything new to comment that executives and managers today are more finely attuned to change or that they more frequently view their role as that of change agent.

But even though we often state the obvious and spout clichés about change, this does not mean that we have an in-depth understanding of what we are talking about. We are only beginning to understand the nature of change and how to manage the process involved, especially with respect to organizations. The purpose of this article is to improve our understanding of organizational change by providing both some conceptual clarification and a case example that illustrates many of the concepts involved.

It is possible to conceptualize organizational change in at least three ways—levels of organizational change, strategies of organizational change, and, more specifically and not mutually exclusive of strategies, models and methods of organizational change. (First we will present the concepts, second the case example, and finally some implications.)

Levels of Organizational Change

A broad distinction can be made between (1) fundamental, large-scale change in the organization's strategy and culture—a transformation, refocus, reorientation, or "bending the frame," as David A. Nadler and Michael L. Tushman have referred to the process—and (2) fine-tuning, fixing problems, making adjustments, modifying procedures, and so on; that is, implementing modest changes that improve the organization's performance yet do not fundamentally change the organization. By far most organizational changes are designed not to transform the organization but to modify it in order to fix its problems.

In this article we address more directly the large-scale, fundamental type of organizational change. (A word of caution: "Organizational transformation," "frame bending," and other expressions indicating fundamental change do not imply wholesale, indiscriminate, and complete change. Thus when we refer to "fundamental change," we do not mean "in any and all respects.")

We are concerned with transformation when an organization faces the need to survive and must do things differently to continue to exist. After polio was licked, for example, the March of Dimes had to change its mission in order to survive as an organization. Although its mission changed from one of attacking polio to one of trying to eradicate birth defects, the organization's core technology—fund raising—remained the same.

A corporate example of transformation is seen in the transition of International Harvester to Navistar. Facing bankruptcy, the company downsized drastically, completely restructured its financial situation, and overhauled its corporate culture. Although many of the company's technologies were sold off, it, too, retained its core technology: producing trucks and engines. Once internally focused, its culture is now significantly market-oriented—and the company is operating far more efficiently than it did in the past.

Although organizational members experience such transformations as a complete change, they rarely if ever are. Theory would suggest that if fundamental—or even significant—change is to occur with any success, some characteristic(s) of the organization must *not* change. The theory to which we refer comes from the world of individual change: psychotherapy. For organizational transformation to be achieved—for the organization to survive and eventually prosper from such change—certain fundamentals need to be retained. Some examples: the organization's ultimate purpose, the previously mentioned core technology, and key people. The principle here is that for people to be able to deal with enormous and complex change—seeming chaos—they need to have *something* to hold on to that is stable.

Conceptually, then, we can distinguish between fundamentally changing the organization and fine-tuning it. This distinction—which is a matter of degree, not necessarily a dichotomy—is useful in determining strategies and methods to be used in the change effort. When fine-tuning, for example, we do not necessarily need to clarify for organizational members what will not change—but in the case of transformation, such clarity is required for its successful achievement.

Strategies of Organizational Change

Organizational change can occur in more than one way. In a 1971 book, Harvey A. Hornstein and colleagues classified six ways: individual change strategies, technostructural strategies, data-based strategies, organization development, violent and coercive strategies, and nonviolent yet direct action strategies. All of these strategies have been used to attempt, if not actually bring about, organizational change. Senior management usually chooses any one or various combinations of the first four and manages them internally. The last two—violent, coercive strategies and nonviolent yet direct-action strategies—are more often than not initiated by actions outside the organization, and the organization's executives typically manage in a reactive mode.

In this article we address some combination of the first four strategies. Yet, as previously indicated, we are assuming that the overwhelming majority of organizational changes are motivated by *external* factors—that executives are responding to the organization's external environment. But even when it is not a reaction to some social movement, organizational change is nevertheless a *response*—a response to changes or anticipated changes in the marketplace, or changes in the way technology will affect the organization's products/services, or changes in the labor market, etc.

This assumption is based on the idea that an organization is a living, open system dependent on its environment for survival. Whether it is merely to survive or eventually to prosper, an organization must monitor its external environment and align itself with changes that occur or will occur in that environment. Practically speaking, the process of alignment requires the organization to change itself.

Models and Methods of Organizational Change

Models of change and methods of change are quite similar in concept and often overlap—so much so that it is not always clear which one is being discussed. Kurt Lewin's three-phase model of change—unfreeze, move (or change), refreeze—also suggests method. Organization development is based on an action-research model that is, at the same time, a method.

More on the model side is the relatively simple and straightforward framework provided by Richard Beckhard and Reuben T. Harris. They have suggested that large-scale complex organizational change can be conceptualized as movement from a present state to a future state. But the most important phase is the in-between one that they label *transition state*. Organizational change, then, is a matter of (1) assessing the current organizational situation (present state), (2) determining the desired future (future state), and (3) both planning ways to reach that desired future and implementing the plans (transition state).

Methods of implementing the change—for example, a new organizational strategy—include the following:

- Setting up a comprehensive training program (individual change strategy).
- Modifying the structure, individuals' jobs, and/or work procedures (technostructural strategy).
- Conducting a companywide survey to assess organizational culture for the purpose of using the data to pinpoint required changes (data-based strategy).
- Collecting information from organizational members about their views regarding what needs to be changed and acting accordingly (organization development strategy).
- Combining two, three, or all of these methods.

The case example we will discuss here illustrates organizational transformation in response to change initiated in the institution's external environment—excluding, however, the violent, coercive strategies and the nonviolent, direct ones. The example, which is analyzed according to Lewin's three-phase model/method, highlights the use of multiple methods for change—in fact, it presents in one form or another a specific method from each of the four other change strategies mentioned earlier.

Case Example

In 1982 Margaret Thatcher's government in Great Britain decided to convert British Airways (BA) from government ownership to private ownership. BA had regularly required large subsidies from the government (almost $900 million in 1982), subsidies that the government felt it could not provide. Even more important, the Conservative government was ideologically opposed to the government's ownership of businesses—a matter they regarded as the appropriate province of private enterprise.

The growing deregulation of international air traffic was another important environmental change. Air fares were no longer fixed, and the resulting price wars placed BA at even greater risk of financial losses.

In order to be able to "privatize"—that is, sell BA shares on the London and New York Stock Exchanges—it was necessary to make BA profitable. The pressures to change thus exerted on BA by the external environment were broad and intense. And the internal organizational changes, driven by these external pressures, have been massive and widespread. They have transformed the BA culture from what BA managers described as "bureaucratic and militaristic" to one that is now described as "service-oriented and market-driven." The success of these efforts over a five-year period (1982–1987) is clearly depicted in the data presented in Figure 1.

This exhibit reflects BA's new mission in its new advertising slogan—"The World's Favorite Airline." Five years after the change effort began, BA had successfully moved from government ownership to private ownership, and both passenger and cargo revenues had dramatically increased, leading to a substantial increase in share price over the offering price, despite the market crash of October 1987. Indeed, in late 1987 BA acquired British Caledonian Airways, its chief domestic competitor. The steps through which this transformation was accomplished clearly fit Lewin's model of the change process.

Lewin's Change Model

According to the open-systems view, organizations—like living creatures—tend to be homeostatic, or continuously working to maintain a steady state. This helps us understand why orga-

FIGURE 1

The British Airways success story: Creating the "World's Favorite Airline"

	1982	1987
Ownership	Government.	Private.
Profit/(loss)	($900 million).	$435 million.
Culture	Bureaucratic and militaristic.	Service-oriented and market-driven.
Passenger load factor	Decreasing.	Increasing—up 16% in 1st quarter 1988.
Cargo load	Stable.	Increasing—up 41% in 1st quarter 1988.
Share price	N/A	Increased 67% (2/11/87–8/11/87).
Acquisitions	N/A	British Caledonian.

nizations require external impetus to initiate change and, indeed, why that change will be resisted even when it is necessary.

Organizational change can occur at three levels—and, since the patterns of resistance to change are different for each, the patterns in each level require different change strategies and techniques. These levels involve:

1. Changing the *individuals* who work in the organization—that is, their skills, values, attitudes, and eventually behavior—but making sure that such individual behavioral change is always regarded as instrumental to organizational change.

2. Changing various organizational *structures and systems*—reward systems, reporting relationships, work design, and so on.

3. Directly changing the organizational *climate or interpersonal style*—how open people are with each other, how conflict is managed, how decisions are made, and so on.

According to Lewin, a pioneer in the field of social psychology of organizations, the first step of any change process is to *unfreeze* the present pattern of behavior as a way of managing resistance to change. Depending on the organizational level of change intended, such unfreezing might involve, on the individual level, selectively promoting or terminating employees; on the structural level, developing highly experiential training programs in such new organization designs as matrix management; or, on the climate level, providing data-based feedback on how employees feel about certain management practices. Whatever the level involved, each of these interventions is intended to make organizational members address that level's need for change, heighten their awareness of their own behavioral patterns, and make them more open to the change process.

The second step, *movement,* involves making the actual changes that will move the organization to another level of response. On the individual level, we would expect to see people behaving differently, perhaps demonstrating new skills or new supervisory practices. On the structural level, we would expect to see changes in actual organizational structures, reporting relationships, and reward systems that affect the way people do their work. Finally, on the climate or interpersonal-style level, we would expect to see behavior patterns that indicate greater interpersonal trust and openness and fewer dysfunctional interactions.

The final stage of the change process, *refreezing,* involves stabilizing or institutionalizing these changes by establishing systems that make these behavioral patterns "relatively secure against change," as Lewin put it. The refreezing stage may involve, for example, redesigning the organization's recruitment process to increase the likelihood of hiring applicants who share the organization's new management style and value system. During the refreezing stage, the organization may also ensure that the new behaviors have become the operating norms at work, that the reward system actually reinforces those behaviors, or that a new, more participative management style predominates.

According to Lewin, the first step to achieving lasting organizational change is to deal with resistance to change by unblocking the present system. This unblocking usually requires some kind of confrontation and a retraining process based on planned behavioral changes in the desired direction. Finally, deliberate steps need to be taken to cement these changes in place—this "institutionalization of change" is designed to make the changes semipermanent until the next cycle of change occurs.

Figure 2 presents an analysis of the BA change effort in terms of Lewin's model. The many and diverse steps involved in the effort are categorized both by stages (unfreezing, movement, and refreezing) and by level (individual, structures and system, and climate/interpersonal style).

Unfreezing. In BA's change effort, the first

FIGURE 2

Applying Lewin's model to the British Airways (BA) change effort

Levels	Unfreezing	Movement	Refreezing
Individual	Downsizing of workforce (59,000 to 37,000); middle management especially hard hit. New top management team. "Putting People First."	Acceptance of concept of "emotional labor". Personal staff as internal consultants. "Managing People First." Peer support groups.	Continued commitment of top management. Promotion of staff with new BA values. "Top Flight Academies." "Open Learning" programs.
Structures and systems	Use of diagonal task forces to plan change. Reduction in levels of hierarchy. Modification of budgeting process.	Profit sharing (3 weeks' pay in 1987). Opening of Terminal 4. Purchase of Chartridge as training center. New, "user-friendly" MIS.	New performance appraisal system based on both behavior and performance. Performance-based compensation system. Continued use of task forces.
Climate/interpersonal style	Redefinition of the business: *service,* not *transportation.* Top-management commitment and involvement.	Greater emphasis on open communications. Data feedback on work-unit climate. Off-site, team-building meetings.	New uniforms. New coat of arms. Development and use of cabin-crew teams. Continued use of data-based feedback on climate and management practices.

step in unfreezing involved a massive reduction in the worldwide BA workforce (from 59,000 to 37,000). It is interesting to note that, within a year after this staff reduction, virtually all BA performance indices had improved—more on-time departures and arrivals, fewer out-of-service aircraft, less time "on hold" for telephone reservations, fewer lost bags, and so on. The consensus view at all levels within BA was that the downsizing had reduced hierarchical levels, thus giving more autonomy to operating people and allowing work to get done more easily.

The downsizing was accomplished with compassion; no one was actually laid off. Early retirement, with substantial financial settlements, was the preferred solution throughout the system. Although there is no question that the process was painful, considerable attention was

paid to minimizing the pain in every possible way.

A second major change occurred in BA's top management. In 1981, Lord John King of Wartinbee, a senior British industrialist, was appointed chairman of the board, and Colin Marshall, now Sir Colin, was appointed CEO. The appointment of Marshall represented a significant departure from BA culture. An outsider to BA, Marshall had a marketing background that was quite different from that of his predecessors, many of whom were retired senior Royal Air Force officers. It was Marshall who decided, shortly after his arrival, that BA's strategy should be to become "the World's Favorite Airline." Without question, critical ingredients in the success of the overall change effort were Marshall's vision, the clarity of his understanding that BA's culture needed to be changed in order to carry out the vision, and his strong leadership of that change effort.

To support the unfreezing process, the first of many training programs was introduced. "Putting People First"—the program in which all BA personnel with direct customer contact participated—was another important part of the unfreezing process. Aimed at helping line workers and managers understand the service nature of the airline industry, it was intended to challenge the prevailing wisdom about how things were to be done at BA.

Movement. Early on, Marshall hired Nicholas Georgiades, a psychologist and former professor and consultant, as director (vice president) of human resources. It was Georgiades who developed the specific tactics and programs required to bring Marshall's vision into reality. Thus Georgiades, along with Marshall, must be regarded as a leader of BA's successful change effort. One of the interventions that Georgiades initiated—a significant activity during the movement phase—was to establish training programs for senior and middle managers. Among these were "Managing People First" and "Leading the Service Business"—experiential programs that involved heavy doses of individual feedback to each participant about his or her behavior regarding management practices on the job.

These training programs all had more or less the same general purpose: to identify the organization's dysfunctional management style and begin the process of developing a new management style that would fit BA's new, competitive environment. If the organization was to be market-driven, service-based, and profit-making, it would require an open, participative management style—one that would produce employee commitment.

On the structures and systems level during the unfreezing stage, extensive use was made of diagonal task forces composed of individuals from different functions and at different levels of responsibility to deal with various aspects of the change process—the need for MIS (management information systems) support, new staffing patterns, new uniforms, and so on. A bottom-up, less centralized budgeting process—one sharply different from its predecessor—was introduced.

Redefining BA's business as service, rather than as transportation, represented a critical shift on the level of climate/interpersonal style. A service business needs an open climate and good interpersonal skills, coupled with outstanding teamwork. Off-site, team-building meetings—the process chosen to deal with these issues during the movement stage—have now been institutionalized.

None of these changes would have occurred without the commitment and involvement of top management. Marshall himself played a central role in both initiating and supporting the change process, even when problems arose. As one index of this commitment, Marshall shared information at question-and-answer sessions at most of the training programs—both "to show the flag" and to provide his own unique perspective on what needed to be done.

An important element of the movement phase was acceptance of the concept of "emotional labor" that Georgiades championed—that is, the high energy levels required to provide the quality of service needed in a somewhat uncertain environment, such as the airline business. Recognition that such service is emotionally draining and often can lead to burnout and permanent psychological damage is critical to developing systems of emotional support for the service workers involved.

Another important support mechanism was the retraining of traditional personnel staff to become internal change agents charged with helping and supporting line and staff managers. So, too, was the development of peer support groups for managers completing the "Managing People First" training program.

To support this movement, a number of internal BA structures and systems were changed. By introducing a new bonus system, for example,

Georgiades demonstrated management's commitment to sharing the financial gains of BA's success. The opening of Terminal 4 at Heathrow Airport provided a more functional work environment for staff. The purchase of Chartridge House as a permanent BA training center permitted an increase in and integration of staff training, and the new, "user-friendly" MIS enabled managers to get the information they needed to do their jobs in a timely fashion.

Refreezing. During the refreezing phase, the continued involvement and commitment of BA's top management ensured that the changes became "fixed" in the system. People who clearly exemplified the new BA values were much more likely to be promoted, especially at higher management levels. Georgiades introduced additional programs for educating the workforce, especially managers. "Open Learning" programs, including orientation programs for new staff, supervisory training for new supervisors, and so on, were augmented by "Top Flight Academies" that included training at the executive, senior management, and management levels. One of the academies now leads to an MBA degree.

A new performance appraisal system, based on both behavior and results, was created to emphasize customer service and subordinate development. A performance-based compensation system is being installed, and task forces continue to be used to solve emerging problems, such as those resulting from the acquisition of British Caledonian Airlines.

Attention was paid to BA's symbols as well—new, upscale uniforms; refurbished aircraft; and a new corporate coat of arms with the motto "We fly to serve." A unique development has been the creation of teams for consistent cabin-crew staffing, rather than the ad hoc process typically used. Finally, there is continued use of data feedback on management practices throughout the system.

Managing change. Unfortunately, the change process is not smooth even if one is attentive to Lewin's model of change. Changing behavior at both individual and organizational levels means inhibiting habitual responses and producing new responses that feel awkward and unfamiliar to those involved. It is all too easy to slip back to the familiar and comfortable.

For example, an organization may intend to manage more participatively. But when a difficult decision arises, it may not be possible to get a consensus decision—not at first, at least. Frustration to "get on with" a decision can lead to the organization's early abandonment of the new management style.

In moving from a known present state to a desired future state, organizations must recognize that (as noted earlier) the intervening *transition* state requires careful management, especially when the planned organizational change is large and complex. An important part of this change management lies in recognizing and accepting the disorganization and temporarily lowered effectiveness that characterize the transition state.

In BA's change effort, the chaos and anger that arose during the transitional phase have abated, and clear signs of success have now emerged. But many times the outcome was not at all clear, and serious questions were raised about the wisdom of the process both inside and outside BA. At such times the commitment and courage of top management are essential.

To heighten involvement, managing such organizational changes may often require using a transition management team composed of a broad cross-section of members of the organization. Other techniques include using multiple interventions, rather than just one—for example, keeping the system open to feedback about the change process and using symbols and rituals to mark significant achievements. The BA program used all of these techniques.

Process consultation. In addition to the various change strategies discussed above, considerable use was made of all the usual organization development (OD) technologies. Structural changes, role clarification and negotiations, team building, and process consultation were all used at British Airways to facilitate change.

In process consultation—the unique OD

intervention—the consultant examines the pattern of a work unit's communications. This is done most often through direct observation of staff meetings and, at opportune times, through raising questions or making observations about what has been happening. The role of the process consultant is to be counternormative—that is, to ask why others never seem to respond to Ruth's questions or why no one ever challenges Fred's remarks when he is clearly off target. Generally speaking, process consultation points out the true quality of the emperor's new clothes even when everyone is pretending that they are quite elegant. By changing the closed communication style of the work teams at British Airways to a more open, candid one, process consultation played an important role in the change process.

The Research Evidence

Granted that the BA intervention appears to have been successful, what do we know generally about the impact of OD interventions on organizations and on their effectiveness? Over the past few years, the research literature has shown a sharp improvement in both research design and methodological rigor, especially in the development of such "hard criteria" as productivity and quality indices. The findings have been surprisingly positive.

For example, Raymond Katzell and Richard Guzzo reviewed more than 200 intervention studies and reported that 87 percent found evidence of significant increases in worker productivity as a result of the intervention. Richard Guzzo, Richard Jette, and Raymond Katzell's meta-analysis of 98 of these same studies revealed productivity increases averaging almost half a standard deviation—impressive enough "to be visible to the naked eye," to use their phrase. Thus it would appear that the success of BA's intervention process was not a single occurrence but one in a series of successful changes based on OD interventions.

The picture with respect to employee satisfaction, however, is not so clear. Another meta-analysis—by Barry Macy, Hiroaki Izumi, Charles Hurts, and Lawrence Norton—on how OD interventions affect performance measures and employee work satisfaction found positive effects on performance but *negative* effects on attitudes, perhaps because of the pressure exerted by new work-group norms on employee productivity. The positive effects on performance, however, are in keeping with the bulk of prior research. A recent comprehensive review of the entire field of OD by Marshall Sashkin and W. Warner Burke concluded, "There is little doubt that, when applied properly, OD has substantial positive effects in terms of performance measures."

Implications and Concluding Remarks

We very much believe that an understanding of the social psychology of the change process gives all of us—managers, rank-and-file employees, and consultants—an important and different perspective for coping with an increasingly competitive environment. Our purpose in writing this article was to share some of this perspective—from an admittedly biased point of view.

The change effort at BA provides a recent example of how this perspective and this understanding have been applied. What should be apparent from this abbreviated overview of a massive project is that the change process at BA was based on open-systems thinking, a phased model of managing change, and multiple levels for implementing the change. Thus both the design and the implementation of this change effort relied heavily on this kind of understanding about the nature of organizations and changing them.

The change involved a multifaceted effort that used many leverage points to initiate and support the changes. The change process, which used transition teams with openness to feedback, was intentionally managed with strong support from top management. Resistance to change was actively managed by using unfreezing strategies at all three levels—individual, structural and systems, and interpersonal. Virtually all of the organizational change issues discussed in this article emerged in some measure during the course of the project.

It is quite reassuring to begin to find empirical support for these efforts in field studies and case reports of change efforts. Moreover, the recent meta-analyses of much of this work are quite supportive of what we have learned from experience. We need to use such reports to help more managers understand the worth of applying the open-systems model to their change efforts. But we also need to remember that only when proof of the intervention strategy's usefulness shows up on the firm's "bottom line" will most line managers be persuaded that open-systems thinking is not necessarily incompatible with the real world. The BA success story is a very useful one for beginning such a dialog.

As we go to press, it seems clear that many of the changes at British Airways have stabilized the company. Perhaps the most important one is that the company's culture today can be described as having a strong customer-service focus—a focus that was decidedly lacking in 1982. The belief that marketing and service with the customer in mind will have significant payoff for the company is now endemic to the corporate culture. Another belief now fundamental to BA's culture is that the way one manages people—especially those, like ticket agents and cabin crews, with direct customer contact—directly impacts the way customers will feel about BA. For example, during 1990, Tony Clarry, then head of worldwide customer service for BA, launched a leadership program for all of his management around the globe to continue to reinforce this belief.

Yet all is not bliss at British Airways, which has its problems. Some examples:

- American Airlines is encroaching upon BA's European territory.
- The high level of customer service slips from time to time.
- Those who can afford to ride on the

Concorde represent a tiny market, so it is tough to maintain a consistently strong customer base.

- Now that BA has developed a cadre of experienced managers in a successful company, these managers are being enticed by search firms to join other companies that often pay more money.

Other problems, too, affect BA's bottom line—the cost of fuel, effectively managing internal costs, and the reactions of the financiers in London and on Wall Street, to name a few. It should be noted that since 1987 and until recently, BA's financials have remained positive with revenues and profits continuing to increase. During 1990 this bright picture began to fade, however. The combination of the continuing rise in fuel costs, the recession, and the war in the Persian Gulf have taken their toll. Constant vigilance is therefore imperative for continued success.

It may be that BA's biggest problem now is not so much to manage further change as it is to manage the change that has already occurred. In other words, the people of BA have achieved significant change and success; now they must maintain what has been achieved while concentrating on continuing to be adaptable to changes in their external environment—the further deregulation of Europe, for example. Managing momentum may be more difficult than managing change.

Selected Bibliography

The Wall Street Journal article referred to at the outset, "Motivate or Alienate? Firms Have Gurus to Change Their 'Cultures,'" was written by Peter Waldbaum and may be found on p. 19 of the July 24, 1987, issue.

With respect to levels of organizational change, see the article by W. Warner Burke and George H. Litwin, "A Causal Model of Organizational Performance," in the 1989 Annual published by University Associates of San Diego. These authors describe the differences between transformational and transactional change. Along the same conceptual lines is the article by David A. Nadler and Michael L. Tushman— "Organizational Frame Bending: Principles for Managing Reorientation" (*The Academy of Management Executive,* August 1988, pp. 194–204).

Regarding strategies of organizational change, see Harvey A. Hornstein, Barbara B. Bunker, W. Warner Burke, Marion Gindes, and Roy J. Lewicki's *Social Intervention: A Behavioral Science Approach* (The Free Press, 1971).

Concerning models and methods of organizational change, the classic piece is Kurt Lewin's chapter "Group Decisions and Social Change," in the 1958 book *Readings in Social Psychology* (Holt, Rinehart & Winston), edited by Eleanor E. Maccobby, Theodore M. Newcomb, and Eugene L. Hartley. For an explanation of organization development as action research, see W. Warner Burke's *Organization Development: Principles and Practices* (Scott, Foresman, 1982). The framework of present state–transition state–future state is explained in *Organization Transitions: Managing Complex Change,* 2nd ed. (Addison-Wesley, 1987), by Richard Beckhard and Reuben T. Harris. A recent article by Donald C. Hambrick and Albert A. Cannella, Jr.—"Strategy Implementation as Substance and Selling" (*The Academy of Management Executive,* November 1989, pp. 278–85)—is quite helpful in understanding how to implement a change in corporate strategy.

A point made in the article is that, for effective organizational change, multiple leverage is required.

For data to support this argument, see W. Warner Burke, Lawrence P. Clark, and Cheryl Koopman's "Improving Your OD Project's Chances of Success" (*Training and Development Journal,* September 1984, pp. 62–68). More on process consultation and team building may be found in two books published by Addison-Wesley: Edgar H. Schein's *Process Consultation, vol. 1: Its Role in Organization Development,* 1988, and W. Gibb Dyer's *Team Building: Issues and Alternatives,* 1987.

References for the research evidence are: Richard A. Guzzo, Richard D. Jette, and Raymond A. Katzell's "The Effects of Psychologically Based Intervention Programs on Worker Productivity: A Meta-Analysis" (*Personnel Psychology* 38, no. 2 (Summer 1985), pp. 275–91); Raymond A. Katzell and Richard A. Guzzo's "Psychological Approaches to Worker Productivity" (*American Psychologist* 38 April 1983, pp. 468–72); Barry A. Macy, Hiroaki Izumi, Charles C. M. Hurts, and Lawrence W. Norton's "Meta-Analysis of United States Empirical Change and Work Innovation Field Experiments," a paper presented at the 1986 annual meeting of the Academy of Management, Chicago; John M. Nicholas's "The Comparative Impact of Organization Development Interventions on Hard Criteria Issues" (*The Academy of Management Review* 7, no. 4 (October 1982), pp. 531–43; John M. Nicholas and Marsha Katz's "Research Methods and Reporting Practices in Organization Development" (*The Academy of Management Review,* October 1985, pp. 737–49); and Marshall Sashkin and W. Warner Burke's "Organization Development in the 1980s" (*Journal of Management,* no. 2 (1987), pp. 205–29).

READING 44
A CHECKLIST FOR ORGANIZING AND IMPLEMENTING AN OD EFFORT

Wendell L. French

We are presenting here a checklist of variables to be considered in the management of an OD effort. We believe that the key players in such an effort must, over time, pay attention to these dimensions if the process is to be optimally effective.

These dimensions are an outgrowth of the author's experience as an external consultant in an OD effort in a city government situation. In that effort, a checklist similar to the one reported here, but without the comment portions, was used several times by the OD steering commit-

Source: Wendell L. French, "A Checklist for Organizing and Implementing an OD Effort." Reprinted with permission from *Organization Development: Theory, Practice, and Research,* 3rd ed., Wendell L. French, Cecil H. Bell, Jr., and Robert A. Zawacki (eds.) (Homewood, IL: BPI/Irwin, 1989), pp. 522–33.

tee over the first three years. The "Comment" column is an amalgamation of experiences across OD efforts in several different kinds of organizations of both the public and private nature.

The various dimensions are listed only very roughly in terms of the sequence with which concerted attention needs to be paid to them. Ideally, team building ordinarily needs to precede attempts at intergroup problem solving for optimum results, and life career planning is not likely to emerge as a high priority area until other things are under way. We say "very roughly" in sequence, however, because most if not all of these dimensions need to be planned and managed in a simultaneous, congruent manner.

Strategy checklist

Dimensions	Imme-diate	3 Months	6 Months	1 Year	18 Months	2 Years	3 Years	Etc.	Comment
Preliminary diagnosis									Some form of preliminary diagnosis needs to occur before the launching of OD efforts, even if it's to be a very tentative start. Shared perceptions of a number of key people that things could be substantially better, that OD might make a significant contribution to the solution of problems, or that OD needs to be a part of a proposed TQM effort, is probably adequate as a starter.
Selection of external consultants									One or more consultants might be interviewed after obtaining recommendations from other clients with whom the consultants have worked, or from NTL Institute for Applied Behavioral Science, university contacts, or other sources. Not infrequently, laboratory (sensitivity) trainers who are experienced in OD are contacted by managers who have had a positive laboratory training experience. However, while group facilitator skills are necessary for OD consulting practice, such skills are not sufficient. The OD practitioner needs a repertory of skills and a perspective which is systemwide.
OD information and knowledge: Briefing sessions									A cognitive understanding of the essential aspects of the process and how it can be linked to continuous improvement efforts is vital to cooperation and support on an OD effort and to the avoidance of confusion about OD vis-à-vis other strategies.
Union involvement									Many organizational participants may cast a baleful eye at any new intervention, having been expected to cooperate with one change program or study after the other over the years. Training workshops are thus important for both diagnostic purposes and surfacing resentments about previously imposed programs. The external consultants should be

Strategy checklist (continued)

Dimensions	Imme-diate	3 Months	6 Months	1 Year	18 Months	2 Years	3 Years	Etc.	Comment
Special seminars									prepared to recommend not going forward if a significant number of key people are not receptive. Union involvement in the early information phase is vital in the unionized situation. Above and beyond these important/discussion sessions for everyone, intensive, specialized seminars in OD for a few selected line managers can be very helpful to the OD effort.
Team-building and team problem-solving workshops: CEO's office and department heads									These activities are at the heart of the OD process, and are likely to constitute the main expenditure of consultant time and off-site workshop time. By CEO we mean the top person in the particular organizational pyramid that is moving in the direction of a comprehensive OD effort.
CEO's immediate office									We include the CEO's immediate office because the culture of the chief's immediate office is frequently overlooked, but the people in it—assistants and secretaries, for example—are significant actors in the system. Incongruency between this subculture
OD steering committee									and others can be highly dysfunctional. Further, we see the top part of the organization modeling behavior for the rest, thus requiring efforts at this level even more intensive an demanding than
Department heads and key people									elsewhere in the organization.
Department A									Follow-up is so important to organizational improvement that this item could well be listed relative to each major OD intervention, such as
Department B									team-building workshops. Follow-up on action plans needs to occur in regular meetings, in special
Department C, etc.									meetings called to review progress, and in subsequent workshops.
Task forces									
Follow-up									
OD steering committee									Our experience suggests that a broad-based steering committee is needed to give overall direction to an
Membership									OD effort. Ideally, membership might look something like this: the CEO, one or two key staff people, such as the human resources director, one
Role in policy, budget, priorities, and the like									major line department head, a representative of

Frequency of meeting	first-line supervision, a rank-and-file employee (or a union officer in the unionized setting if the union is willing to participate in such discussions), the internal OD coordinator, the key external consultant; and one or more internal consultants. Some membership slots might be rotated. Meetings probably ought to occur once a month and should focus on budget, policy, and priorities. We believe that team building for this group is essential and that the group should make a major effort to create a committee culture congruent with the one being fostered through the OD effort.
Internal coordinator Job definition	The percentages of time the person designated as an internal coordinator spends as the coordinator, as consultant, and on other activities, can be a source of tension for that person, for his or her superior, for peers, and for clients. Conflicting demands will inevitably arise and need to be faced openly, sometimes in the steering committee. In addition, unless it is clear what the coordinator's authority is in determining direction, assigning consultants and scheduling off-site sessions, tensions will arise between that person, members of that committee, the consultants, and others. This is an issue that needs to be "worked" periodically in many OD efforts.
Role in policy, budget, priorities, and so on	
Role as a consultant	
Relationship to external and internal consultants	Further, multiple roles will create a number of dilemmas for the internal coordinator. For example, should that person use insights in a team-building session that were derived from some other capacity such as administrative assistant to the CEO? (Probably not.) Should the coordinator report details of a team-building session in X department to the CEO? (Emphatically no.)
Selection and development of internal consultants: Selections	This is a particularly sensitive area. Internal consultants need to be selected for demonstrated potential and interest, but the system needs to be open enough so that it is neither a closed system nor has the appearance of one. Basic competence and continuously enhanced competence in facilitation skills need to be the criteria for
External education	

Strategy checklist (continued)

Dimensions	Imme-diate	3 Months	6 Months	1 Year	18 Months	2 Years	3 Years	Etc.	Comment
Internal progress and development									membership. Those facilitators recognized as having the highest competence need to assume leadership in establishing standards of performance. Competence development also requires that the organization allocates resources for specialized OD training, apprenticeship situations, and interaction with the external consultants.
Process consultation and group effectiveness:									This is a function in which, hopefully, client groups will have high interest and will develop skills. At the outset, consultants can be helpful in modeling this activity and in coaching group members. Ultimately, the client group can routinely rotate this function among group members, and
CEO—department head meetings									
Department meetings									debriefing how things went in a meeting can become a way of life. We see this activity becoming pervasive in the meeting life of the
Other									organization, but, of course, in balance with the tasks to be accomplished. However, we see complacency leading to ignoring this activity to be more likely than overdoing it.
Individual counseling									We suspect that this is insufficiently utilized in most OD efforts, and probably for reasons similar to the following: (1) lack of counseling training for internal consultants and/or (2) lack of stated validation of the worthwhileness of this function by the CEO and other key figures. Counseling, whether by an internal or external consultant, ultimately is a cost item in terms of someone's time. (The costs of not engaging in effective counseling need to be weighed, of course.)
Two-party conflict resolution:									
Sessions with clients									The consultant, whether internal or external, needs high skill and acceptance to be effective in this area. Availability is also critical—he or she needs to be around enough to be in a position to suggest a private meeting between the parties when the

488

Follow-up	moment is right. The consultant and the two clients also need to be available to meet in a subsequent session or sessions to check progress or work on issues still unresolved.
Intergroup team building and problem soliving: Workshops with client groups	Assertiveness by the OD coordinator or other consultants will frequently make the difference on whether or not this actually occurs. People need to know the nature of the process, that top management supports resources being allocated to this function; and consultants need to act in a delicate "broker" role when it becomes evident that two units are expressing difficulty with each other. Follow-up with clients on workshop outcomes is vital.
Follow-up	
Human resources management vis-à-vis OD: Human resources department role in OD	The human resources department needs to be actively involved in the OD process for at least two reasons: (1) unfortunate territorial and status issues have developed in some organizations when personnel people were not involved and (2) many, if not all, personnel practices are potentially critical areas for congruency or incongruency with an OD effort. An autocratic MBO program, for example, occurring simultaneously with an OD effort, which by definition is participative, can have a deleterious effect on either or both processes. The curricula of training and development programs also need to be managed in concert with an OD effort. We are not suggesting a "party line," but we are suggesting that incongruencies between training and OD be surfaced and worked, including the way training needs are assessed. Frequently, many personnel practices become modified as an OD effort proceeds. For example, internal posting of job vacancies tends to occur, group methods may be used in orientation, and so on.
MBO and performance appraisal	
Job enrichment	
Management and employee training and development	
OD applications to and implications for other personnel systems	
Facilitator team (internal plus external consultants): Review of interventions	If a team of consultants is working with a client, clinical review of interventions is obviously best conducted while topics are "hot," and time needs to be allocated for this activity. It also can be highly productive in terms of consultant development to schedule periodic clinics during

Strategy checklist (continued)

Dimensions	Immediate	3 Months	6 Months	1 Year	18 Months	2 Years	3 Years	Etc.	Comment
Team maintenance									which the total consulting staff focuses on their consulting practices and their own relationships. The spin-off of unworked interpersonal and group issues can severely handicap the ability of the facilitator group to help others, because of clients seeing the incongruency between doing and saying, and, more substantively, because of the resulting lack of personal growth.
CEO and line management: Depth of involvement									The team effectiveness and interpersonal effectiveness of the CEO and the top-management group has a profound impact on the climate in the organization and on interpersonal, group, and intergroup effectiveness throughout the organization. We have seen unresolved problems between a CEO and a deputy perpetuating serious problems lower in the organization. Sometimes the spin-off is obvious, sometimes very subtle. Therefore we are strong advocates of the top-management team working longer and harder than anyone else in the organization to get its own house in order.
Internationalization of skills									
Development of external and internal consultants									
Management of the OD process									Ongoing, real involvement by the top team of the organization involved in an OD effort is vital to the success of the OD effort. This includes significant internalization of group dynamics skills. We also see the CEO and top managers playing a vital role in supporting ongoing professional development of the consultants (e.g., supporting regular consultant clinics) and in seeing to it that the overall OD process is managed effectively.
Laboratory (sensitivity) training									The relevance or irrelevance of sensitivity training to an optimally successful OD effort needs to be faced. Our opinion is that positive experience in stranger sensitivity or group dynamics labs may enhance a depth of insight and skill development that will "grease the wheels" of an OD effort. If management and supervisory people are not attending such experiences, we believe the issue should be raised.

Life/career planning	Life/career planning can be a logical offshoot of an OD effort. As the climate becomes more open and trusting, candid discussions between superiors and subordinates and between colleagues about careers becomes natural, and intensive workshops focusing on career development can be very useful. A number of organizations have found that the potential risk in life/career planning workshops of key people gaining so much insight that they leave is far outweighed by the vitality that is unleashed, particularly when the individual attention and concern evidenced in the workshops becomes part of the broader organizational culture.
Key system relationships	In addition to the union, the support and understanding of the board of directors—whether called by that label, or whether called "school board," "city council," or whatever—is necessary for an OD effort to flourish. Ultimately, the board will approve the budget and will set the pattern for what is desirable in the organization. Frequently, boards see the efficacy of the OD effort to their own operation, and, with the help of a facilitator, get involved in the process by looking at their own way of doing things and at their key interfaces with the operating organization or their constituents, or both.

Separate workshops on the nature of the OD process for governing boards—and for union officials in the case of unionized situations, and for members of the press in the case of public agencies under open-meeting laws—can be extremely useful in the early phases of an OD effort to provide a common base of understanding and to avoid the gross distortions that lack of direct information can create. Such workshops can also increase the odds of these groups utilizing OD. |
| Evaluation of OD effort Progress evaluation by department heads and others | A periodic review of the entire OD effort by the steering committee and others is necessary for revitalization of the OD effort and modification in practices and direction. In short, OD needs to be |

Strategy checklist (continued)

Dimensions	Imme-diate	3 Months	6 Months	1 Year	18 Months	2 Years	3 Years	Etc.	Comment
Assessment of dysfunctional aspects of emerging culture									applied to the OD effort routinely to assess climate and progress. In particular, department heads and a cross-section of employees at all levels need to be interviewed to tap their perceptions of the functional and dysfunctional consequences of the OD effort. For example, problems like the formation of in-groups and out-groups sometimes emerge. And, if the OD effort is largely successful, people need to know it.
Review of basic assumptions and purposes									While more painstaking and thorough research would be desirable, including the use of outside researchers, the collection of anecdotal data would seem to be the minimum research needed, both for improvement purposes and for interpreting the effort to the various interested parties. A step closer to more thorough research would be the collection of attitudinal data and "hard" data, such as productivity and quality measures, with an attempt to draw cause and effect conclusions about the impact of various phases of the OD effort.
Review of relationship with external consultants									A review of the relationship between the external consultants and the client system needs to occur periodically. Is there too much dependency on outside help on the part of the client system? Are the consultants being used so infrequently that they are losing interest, feeling alienated? Have internal resources/skills developed to the point that use of external consultants can be reduced greatly or eliminated? What would be the consequences? We are convinced of the efficacy of at least some minimum of external consultant involvement to provide an additional avenue of innovation and to help keep the OD effort "honest" in the sense of helping avoid emerging dysfunctional norms.

Managerial succession:	
Selection	Positive changes in organization culture due to an OD effort can be set back due to turnover in the executive and supervisory ranks. It is important that the board of directors understands this. This has implications relative to the qualifications of replacements, the way they are selected, and the way they are brought aboard. If the momentum of an OD effort is to be sustained, it would seem wise to look for leadership skills and attitudes congruent with the OD effort, and it may be productive to have some subordinate participation in the selection. Further, internal or external consultant help in designing the process of bringing new people aboard—at all levels—may be desirable.
Orientation	

VI   EXAMPLES, ISSUES, AND CHALLENGES OF OD AND OT

As we indicated in the introduction, we believe that organizations and their members are in a decade of continuous/discontinuous change and the challenge for leaders will be to make a paradigm shift to OT and design the dynamically stable organization.[1] This organization of the future is called by many different names. Some of the more popular are the horizontal organization,[2] the knowledge and technology based organization, the STAR organization,[3] the learning organization,[4] and the 1993 Academy of Management Annual Meeting even has the theme of "Managing the Boundaryless Organization."

We believe all of these organizations have more similarities than differences, and, although some authors describe limited successes, these organizations are still in the experimental stages. Figure 1 is an overview of the "old organization" and the "future organization." This model first appeared in *Business Week,* October 23, 1992, and we modified it to include the main patterns from the models listed above. OT is the application of behavioral science theory and practice to help organizations make the paradigm shift to the "future organization."

---

[1] Andrew C. Boynton and Bart Victor, "Beyond Flexibility: Building and Managing the Dynamically Stable Organization," from a paper dated June 27, 1991, and forthcoming in the *California Management Review.*

[2] "The Horizontal Organization," *Information Week,* August 17, 1992, pp. 32–40.

[3] Robert A. Zawacki, "Key Issues in Human Resources Management, *Information Systems Management,*" Winter 1993, pp. 72–75; and Robert A. Zawacki, "Is the Horizontal Organization Already a Dinosaur?", *CASELab Notes* 2:1 (1993), pp. 9–11.

[4] Peter M. Senge, "Transforming the Practice of Management," paper presented at the Systems Thinking Conference, November 14, 1991.

FIGURE 1

The old organization and the Star organization

Current Model	Variable Model	Future Model (Star)
Incremental or rapid	Change	Random
Single loop	Learning	Double loop
Top down	Control	Shared
Hierarchy	Organization	Network and alliances
Leadership sets	Vision	Building shared vision
Security	Expectations	Personal growth
Homogeneous	People	Different vision and values
Individuals	Work design	Self-directed teams
Extrinsic	Motivation	Intrinsic
Domestic	Markets	International
Cost	Strategic advantage	Time
Functional	Structure	Process driven
OK	Quality	Few compromises
Money	Focus	Customer
Quarterly rate of return	Values	People I/E

SOURCE: This is a modification of *Business Week,* October 23, 1992, pp. 62–63.

A. Examples

These readings give examples of OD from several perspectives. The first selection, by Cecil H. Bell, Jr., is a thorough description of a typical long-term OD effort of the 1980s. The U.S. Bureau of Mines sponsored the program at Hecla Mining Company with the objectives of increasing safety and mine productivity. Using team building–problem solving as the principal OD technique, this case study reports significant reductions in injuries (safety) and large increases in average tons of ore per worker (productivity). The Hecla story is rich with the detailed description of the actual intervention, rules for staying alive as a consultant, and a chronology of the stages of the intervention.

The second article, by Larry A. Pace and Dominick R. Argona, is a case history of participatory action research (QWL) at the North American Manufacturing Division of Xerox Corporation. This case is of special interest because it describes their efforts to work with the Amalgamated Clothing and Textile Workers Union in this quality of work life (QWL) experiment. As other organizations in the free world move toward changing control from the top down to a shared vision with the individual contributors, some of these organizations will need to be aware of the union's concerns, and this case is an excellent model of the "give and take" necessary to make QWL programs successful.

The final reading in this section is by Robert M. Frame, Warren R. Nielsen, and Larry E. Pate. It is a description of an organizational transformation (OT) effort at one of the *Chicago Tribune*'s printing facilities. After a strike by 1,000 workers, management made a commitment to create a new culture that emphasized operating beliefs, human resource development, and effective use of capital and resources. The results of this OT effort are very positive, and the authors conclude their descriptive case study with guidelines for organizations of the future.

READING 45
THE HECLA STORY: ORGANIZATION DEVELOPMENT IN THE HARD-ROCK MINING INDUSTRY

Cecil H. Bell, Jr.

In 1979 the U.S. Bureau of Mines sponsored the first organization development (OD) program in the metal–nonmetal mining industry in the United States. The objective was to determine whether OD techniques could improve mine safety and mine productivity. I conducted that program in cooperation with Hecla Mining Company of Coeur d'Alene, Idaho. My purposes in this essay are to describe that project as an example of a long-term OD effort typical of the 1980s and to explore the strategic thinking involved in implementing such a project. First, brief descriptions of the company and the program are presented. Next, the overall program strategy is discussed. Then the program is described in terms of its chronology and stages. Observations about implementing and evaluating OD programs are made, and conclusions are drawn.

Overview of the Hecla Organization Development Project, 1979–1986

The Bureau of Mines proposal called for conducting and evaluating a three-year organization development demonstration project with a cooperating metal–nonmetal mining company to see if organization development techniques could have a positive impact on mine safety and productivity. [1] Metal–nonmetal mining and coal mining are the two major categories of mining in the industry. Several OD programs had been conducted in coal mining, but none had been attempted in metal–nonmetal mining (also called

Source: Written especially for this volume.

"hard-rock" mining). I secured the cooperation of Hecla Mining Company and its president and chief executive officer, William A. Griffith. He agreed to participate because he wanted to improve mine safety at the company's two silver–lead mines located in the "Silver Valley" or Coeur d'Alene region of northeastern Idaho. As I explained to the president, organization development is a process for causing organizational improvements, based on the belief that organization members themselves can identify and solve their major problems if they use a systematic procedure guided by an outside consultant. OD is a generic problem-solving process in which organization members examine how they are doing and look for ways to do better. "Organization development is really not much more than systematic, collaborative, hard work," I said.

Hecla Mining Company was founded in 1891. At the time of the OD program, Hecla was the premier silver producer in the United States. It operated two silver–lead mines in northeastern Idaho (the Lucky Friday Mine and the Star Mine) and several smaller operations in other western states. When the program began, Hecla had about 700 employees, a new president, Mr. Griffith, and a new senior management team. It was, and still is, a healthy and effective organization. "We are proud miners," was the way one of the executives described the company to me.

The Hecla program unfolded as follows: the demonstration project occurred from July 1979 to May 1982. The decision was made to use team building–problem solving meetings as the principal OD intervention. In these meetings boss–subordinate teams identify high priority problems and opportunities and build action plans for solving problems or seizing opportunities. To legitimate team building and to understand what the process entailed, the meetings started with the president and senior management team, then moved down the organizational hierarchy to the vice president of operations and his direct reports, which included all mine managers. Another decision was to make the Lucky Friday Mine the primary target of the OD program; that is where the OD experiment to improve mine safety and productivity would occur. The Lucky Friday Mine manager learned about team building by participating in the sessions with the vice president of operations and was comfortable holding team building meetings with the mine management team and the mine production team (which included first line supervisors called "shift bosses"). After team building meetings were well established with the mine's managerial groups, the sessions were extended to include one-half of the hourly work force and their shift bosses. The intervention strategy thus entailed the following elements: make team building–problem-solving meetings the primary OD technique used; start team building at the top of the company to ensure understanding, support, and buy-in; "cascade" team building meetings down the operations function of the company; target the Lucky Friday management and crews; focus on finding ways to improve mine safety and productivity. 1981 and 1982 witnessed extensive OD activity at the Lucky Friday Mine.

In May 1982, Mr. Griffith asked me to "continue the OD program and train our people to do what you do." That set the stage for the remainder of the program at Hecla. All on-going team building activities were continued. Team building was initiated with the Exploration Department, the Technical Services Department, the Safety and Training Department, the Corpo-

rate Administrative Services Departments, the Corporate Secretaries, the Republic Mine, and the Escalante Mine. Ten company members were trained as OD facilitators. All production managers and first line supervisors were trained to conduct problem-solving meetings. Expanding the program companywide and training company members to conduct it were the main activities of 1982 to 1986.

What were the results of the organization development program? Did the intervention improve safety and productivity at the Lucky Friday Mine? When the project was evaluated in early 1982 for the Bureau of Mines final report, it was found that lost-time injuries had decreased 44 percent at the Lucky Friday Mine and decreased 8 percent at the Star Mine (where no OD activities had taken place) in 1981, compared to 1980. It was concluded that the OD program probably contributed to the significant decrease in mine injuries at the Lucky Friday Mine. Analysis of productivity data showed that productivity had declined about 10 percent at the Lucky Friday Mine and increased about 10 percent at the Star Mine in 1981, compared to 1980. It was concluded that the OD program probably had no effect on productivity at the Lucky Friday Mine. [2]

In 1985 the Bureau of Mines asked me to assess the long-term effects of the organization development program at the Lucky Friday Mine, where team building–problem solving meetings had been held on a quarterly basis since 1981. What long-term effects, if any, did these meetings have on mine safety and productivity? Comparing the first six months of 1985 to the preprogram years 1979 and 1980 yielded the following results:

- The lost-time injury incidence rate was down 78.7 percent.
- Average tons of ore per worker shift for miners breaking the rock was up 54.3 percent.

- Average tons of ore per worker shift for all labor was up 32.6 percent.
- Average ounces of silver per worker shift for all labor was up 47 percent.

The contribution of the OD program to these improvements at the Lucky Friday Mine cannot be known precisely, but these pre-and postprogram comparisons suggest that the OD intervention had beneficial effects on both safety and productivity. Unfortunately, mining operations at the Star Mine were discontinued in 1982, making long-term comparisons between the experimental and control mines unavailable.

With this overview in mind, let's now examine the very important task of developing the program strategy.

Developing Program Strategy

Key decisions need to be made early in the life of an organization development program about which interventions to use, how to sequence interventions, what parts of the organization to target, the specific outcomes that are desired, and so forth. These decisions provide coherence and direction to the program, as well as greatly simplify the consultant's job. They become the major elements of the program strategy and guide decisions and choices throughout the project.

A good game plan or strategy is a necessary ingredient for success in organization development projects. It serves as a roadmap for both the clients and the consultant. Several of the strategic decisions in the Hecla project are obvious from the overview above. This section examines the main elements of the program strategy in greater detail and presents the rationale behind the decisions.

The goal of the Hecla project was to improve mine safety and productivity. Unspecified OD techniques were to be used. The demonstration program would last three years. These "givens" were combined with information about the company's culture and values, with the wants of the president and senior executives, and with my knowledge about organization development to yield the program strategy elements.

Use Team Building–Problem Solving as the Principal OD Technique.   A decision was made early to make team building the foundation of the Hecla project. Team building is one of the most popular and powerful interventions in OD. Getting boss–subordinate teams together to analyze problems and opportunities collaboratively was a natural fit with Hecla's culture. Team building produces tangible results as problems are identified and remedial actions are taken. The president, the senior executives, and I believed team building–problem solving would be an excellent mechanism for implementing the OD program. We added a strong emphasis on problem solving as the reason for the teams to get together and that, too, was viewed as natural, legitimate, and effective. This intervention was defined as follows: Team building–problem solving is a series of meetings facilitated by an OD consultant in which intact work teams analyze high-priority problems and opportunities, analyze and set goals for task accomplishment, and learn and practice skills in problem solving–decision making, and interpersonal communication. Team building was effective for addressing issues of mine safety and productivity at the mines, as well as for working on important issues with corporate staff groups.

Focus on Task Accomplishment—That Is, Getting the Job Done.   The decision to focus on this strategic element was based on my previous experience as an OD practitioner. Team building can be task oriented (getting the job done better) or interpersonal relations oriented (getting people to like each other better), or a combination of both. At Hecla the focus was on task accomplishment, not interpersonal relationships. I have found that a task focus is generally superior to an interpersonal focus when the objective is increased team performance. What happens is that, when task accomplishment is improved, interpersonal relations usually improve as a byproduct. A task focus was also more congruent with Hecla's culture.

Include Hourly Employees and Their Supervisors in the Program.
Mine safety and productivity ultimately occur "where the pick hits the rock." Therefore involving the shift bosses and crews was always where we were headed, even though team building started with the president and worked its way down to the crews. Yes, attitudes and behaviors of shift bosses and miners had to be changed if there was to be a change in accident rates and productivity rates; but miners work within a system of policies, procedures, expectations, assumptions, and beliefs that influences their attitudes and behaviors. Dysfunctional aspects of the system had to be rectified, along with securing changes in individual behavior. That is why we started at the top. We also realized that supervisor–crew relations were important determinants of accidents and work output. Some shift bosses consistently had many injuries on their crews, while others went years without a serious injury. That is why we worked with crews and shift bosses together. The critical role of crews and their supervisors in achieving safe and productive performance was recognized as a key ingredient of program strategy.

Start at the Top of the Organization and Work Downward through the Hierarchy.
This element of strategy was adopted for two reasons: first, top level support is vital for success; and second, upper levels of a company help to establish the system of policies, procedures, expectations, and so forth mentioned above. Successful OD programs are managed from the top. Hecla's president and chief executive officer, William A. Griffith, not only managed the program, he gave it strong support and was an active participant. Starting team building meetings with the presi-

dent sent a strong message to the entire company that the program was valid and worthwhile. Team building meetings with the vice president of operations sent a strong message to the mine managers that the program warranted their support. These were powerful boosts to the credibility of the consultant and the OD program. In addition, the downward progression of team building meetings ensured that each team leader had already been involved in team building at a higher level, knew what to expect from the sessions, and was comfortable with the team-building–problem-solving process.

Address Safety Issues at All Levels of the Hierarchy.
This decision followed from the goals of the OD project and from the belief that safety is a "system" outcome as well as an individual behavioral outcome. Mine safety is a complex, multidetermined phenomenon. The attitudes and behaviors of miners are important, but so are the attitudes and behaviors of management. Incentive systems, working conditions, organizational culture, and managerial practices all influence safety. Each team examined safety-related issues, explored what it could do to improve "the system" related to safety, and implemented specific actions designed to improve safety at Hecla.

Avoid a One-shot, Quick-fix Program.
This guiding principal came from Hecla's president. From the outset he was adamant about the nature of the program. The program was for real—not an academic exercise. It was to instill better ways of managing—not flashy superficial behaviors that would be discarded when the program was completed. President Griffith expected me to deliver valid, useful, results-oriented consulting; he expected his managers (and himself) to become better managers as a result of the program. Recall that in explaining organization development to the president before the program began I said it is "really not much more than systematic, collaborative hard work." He believes

that is a direct path to organizational improvement. So do I.

Be Successful, Don't Get Fired.   This guiding principle was developed by me for me. I did not share it overtly with the company. But this injunction reminded me to give the program my best efforts. This was the first OD program in hard-rock mining. If the program became a failure it could set back OD and management consulting in the mining industry for a long time. It was important to be successful—that is, to improve mine safety. It was also important to avoid failure—that is, not to have the program terminated prematurely. The OD program had to be valuable for the company. The consultant team worked especially hard to ensure that diagnoses were accurate, that interventions were timely and well executed, and that necessary formal and informal communications between clients and consultants occurred.

Establish and Maintain High Program Momentum and Extensive Consultant Involvement.   Successful OD programs have a sense of momentum, excitement, and accomplishment that is established early and maintained throughout. Early successes are sought that will spark a sense of excitement and progress. Continuing successes are sought to instill a sense of achievement, mastery, and competence. High momentum and involvement were central parts of the strategy at Hecla. The consultant team conducted several hundred interviews with company members to get the momentum started. These interviews oriented the consultant team to the company and showed people we were serious about the project. Next I designed a new performance appraisal system for the company, with the active involvement of many employees, and trained everyone how to use it. This was a highly visible "early success." Team building meetings were always launched with a series of meetings held in rapid succession to promote quick, positive results. As soon as team building

was established at one level, it was extended to the next level to promote a sense of urgency and progress. The consultant team made frequent visits to the company throughout the demonstration project.

Conduct a Classic OD Program.   A classic OD program is a long-term effort; it is conducted by an outsider who is trained to understand organizational dynamics and to know how to change them. The intervention plan is developed and implemented based on a thorough diagnosis of the organization. Primary emphasis is placed on examining and changing the culture and processes of work teams to help them function better. Considerable effort is spent working on real, high-priority problems and opportunities. And such programs are deliberately consultant-intensive. In the early 1980s this would be a classic definition of organization development. I decided to accept this model for the Hecla program in the belief it would best serve the company and the Bureau of Mines.

Use Additional OD Techniques as Appropriate.   We had decided that team building–problem-solving meetings would be the primary OD technique in the Hecla program. But classic OD programs "follow the problems wherever they lead" and develop solutions to resolve them. The following OD techniques were used at various stages: individual coaching and counseling; individual and team goal setting; safety experiments and analyses; first line supervisor training; behavior modeling skills training; intergroup problem solving and conflict resolution; role analysis and clarification; performance appraisal training; operations management projects; a goal setting–performance feedback experiment; OD facilitator training; and team problem-solving training for line managers. The rule of thumb was: diagnose the situation, choose an appropriate intervention, apply the intervention, evaluate results. This guideline built flexibility into the program strategy.

Conduct the Program at a "Treatment" Mine and Designate a "Control" Mine to Receive No Treatment. To help assess the effects of the OD program, the Lucky Friday Mine received the program and the Star Mine, located about 10 miles away, did not. Comparisons of safety and productivity data between the two mines would suggest what effects, if any, the OD intervention had. It was a good idea, if not a perfect research design. As it turned out, the Star Mine was shut down in 1982 and long-term comparisons were not possible. My original intention was to give the program to the Lucky Friday Mine and use the Star Mine as a control mine. After about a year or so I would then give the program to the Star Mine and measure program effects there. It was not to be.

These elements formed the foundation of the program strategy at Hecla. Making these decisions early in the program greatly enhanced day-to-day implementation and execution.

Chronology and Stages of the Hecla Program

The purpose of this section is to provide additional details related to planning and implementing this long-term OD program. The Hecla project progressed through a series of identifiable stages:

- Entry, orientation, and diagnosis.
- Designing the action plan and getting it approved.
- Implementing the action plan.
- Consolidating and expanding the program.
- Training company members to conduct and continue the OD activities.
- Terminating the consultant's involvement.

These stages and their corresponding activities are described briefly.

Entry, Orientation, and Diagnosis. Hecla agreed to participate in the demonstration project in July 1979. A memorandum of understanding was signed by the company and the consultant, and the program officially began.

From August through December of that year, the consultant team conducted over 400 interviews with more than 60 salaried employees. The interviews oriented the consultants to the industry, the company, mine safety, and mine productivity, and introduced company members to the consultants, the Bureau of Mines project, and organization development methods and goals. With knowledge gained from the interviews the consultant team designed the intervention program to fit with the organization's culture and values, to build on the organization's strengths, and to address the organization's problem areas.

A fortuitous event occurred in November. President Griffith complained to me about the inadequacies of the performance appraisal system currently in use, and, after some discussion, asked if I would develop a new one for them. I agreed to do so, reckoning that such a project would demonstrate the usefulness of the consultant team to the company and show the company how OD consultants work. First, goals and guidelines for the performance appraisal system were solicited from senior executives. Next actual performance dimensions and performance standards were obtained from three representative groups of employees who would be rated on the new forms. Suggestions for improving the performance appraisal process itself were solicited. Three new appraisal forms were drafted—one for managers, one for professional-technical employees, and one for clerical employees. The forms were submitted to the senior management team and to the representative groups for their reactions and approval. Everyone liked the new forms and the new system that they had helped to create. This "early success" for the OD program had high visibility and widespread approval. In April 1980, when the new system was installed, all persons using it were given a one-half day training session by the consultants on how to use the new system and how to conduct performance appraisals. The training generated another "early success" for the OD program.

Designing the Action Plan and Getting It Approved.   A report summarizing the organizational diagnosis and proposing several alternative ways to proceed was given to the president and senior management team in January 1980. A half-day meeting with them was held in February to discuss the report and decide on implementation strategy and tactics. Most of the strategic elements of the program were decided at this meeting: to use team building–problem solving, to concentrate on the Lucky Friday management and crews, and so forth. Thus developing the program strategy was a collaborative effort between the consultants and senior executives.

The meeting concluded with the president's summary: "We will go with team building, and we will start with me and my team." This was welcome news because a key ingredient for success in OD programs is support by the top executive. It was clear the president intended to be actively involved in the OD project.

The hundreds of interviews we conducted proved to be extremely valuable: they enabled us to present a very accurate diagnosis of the strengths and problems of the company, and they supplied insights into the company's culture and values that we needed to know to be successful and avoid pitfalls.

Implementing the Action Plan.   Team building meetings with the president and senior management team began in June 1980. The procedure for team-building meetings was simple and straightforward: prior to the first meeting everyone on the team was interviewed and asked to identify the strengths and weaknesses of the organization and the team. This confidential information was formulated into themes relating to strengths and problem areas. The themes were reported to the group at the first meeting, and

the problems were prioritized in order of importance. The prioritized list was worked through; each problem was examined and actions were taken to solve it.

Team building with the operations team began in August 1980. Members of this team were the vice president of operations, three mine managers, the project engineer for the Silver Shaft (a new shaft at the Lucky Friday Mine), and the assistant personnel director who had corporate responsibility for mine safety.

Meetings with the Lucky Friday Mine manager and mine management team were begun in October 1980. The mine manager, the mine superintendent, three production foremen, and support personnel from maintenance, safety, geology, engineering, accounting, and warehousing comprised the membership of this team, which had responsibility for overall mine performance.

We struck paydirt in February 1981 when team building meetings with the Lucky Friday production team were started. The mine manager and most of the mine management team attended these meetings, as well as the shift bosses. The shift bosses direct the hourly work force. Mine safety and productivity are a direct result of how well the shift bosses and crews perform. Getting the shift bosses involved in problem solving led to immediate positive results at the mine. Policies were developed and implemented that caused long-standing problems at the mine to disappear. Agreements on goals, procedures, and mutual expectations improved communication, coordination, and cooperation. Another benefit was that the shift bosses realized the company was interested in them, their problems, and their ideas.

A nine-week strike occurred at the Lucky Friday Mine from March 21 to May 23, 1981. The strike was unrelated to the OD program, which at that time involved only salaried employees. The union and the company had serious differences of opinion about wages and benefits, and the strike served to communicate those differences to management.

The strike was settled in May. The miners returned to work. After several months, conditions returned to normal. In August 1981 team building meetings were conducted with about half of the hourly employees and their shift bosses. Seven 45-minute meetings were held during the fall and winter. Prior to the meetings, I explained the program to the union president, secretary-treasurer, and safety committeeman— the top union officials at the mine. They were very supportive of the program and explained and endorsed it to the crews. They particularly liked the idea of a system for constructive dialogue in which management would hear the concerns of the hourly employees. The meetings were generally quite successful, with success depending almost entirely on management's timely response to the suggestions and ideas generated in the meetings.

We had achieved our goal of spreading team building–problem-solving meetings throughout the operations function of Hecla to include top management and a majority of the work force at the target mine, the Lucky Friday Mine. The Bureau of Mines demonstration project was completed in May 1982. A final report to the bureau evaluating the effects of the OD program concluded that the program probably improved mine safety but had no discernible effect on mine productivity.

Consolidating and Expanding the Program. Consolidating the program meant keeping the team building–problem-solving activities going in boss–subordinate teams and institutionalizing them. Operationally, this entailed putting team building meetings on people's calendars. For example, the president and senior management team converted their OD activities into an annual two-day "senior management retreat" that addressed strategic planning matters. The vice president and operations team inagurated semiannual two-day planning and problem-solving meetings. The Lucky Friday Mine management team and mine production

team held one-day meetings quarterly to address priority problems and opportunities at the mine. Problem-solving sessions with the crews became a part of the monthly safety meetings. A new mine manager was appointed at the Lucky Friday Mine in 1983. To orient him to the team building process and to ensure a sound foundation, a new series of diagnostic interviews was conducted, the results of which formed the agenda for the meetings.

Expanding the program meant introducing team building–problem-solving meetings to other major units of the company. As noted above, other mining operations and corporate functional groups adopted the team-building process. The success of team building meetings at the Lucky Friday Mine and the active support of the process by the president and senior management team maximized receptivity to taking the OD program companywide. These consolidation and expansion activities occurred from 1982 through 1984.

Training Company Members to Conduct and Continue the OD Activities. "Work yourself out of a job" is one of the maxims of organization development. Another is, "*Help* the organization members to work successfully on high priority problems and opportunities, then *teach* them to do so without the help of an outside consultant." These guidelines were followed at Hecla. First, the personnel director and director of training were trained to be OD facilitators through an apprenticeship program with me. We would jointly conduct team building–problem-solving meetings and extensively debrief the experience. Soon these two individuals were working on their own as internal facilitators.

Next, all first line supervisors participated in a three-day supervisory and leadership training course conducted by an outside firm specializing in such training. Then the director of training and I developed a team problem-solving (TPS) program for all supervisors and managers in the operations division, showing them how to conduct problem solving meetings. The TPS program upgraded the knowledge and skills of line managers significantly. In addition, the TPS program identified a core group of managers who, because of their natural talent and expressed interest, were trained to become OD facilitators. Ten line managers became fully qualified internal OD consultants.

Organization development techniques—such as coaching and counseling, goal setting, team building–problem solving, intergroup problem solving, and role clarification—are now used routinely at Hecla Mining Company. Teams at all levels periodically meet to discuss two questions: How are we doing? How can we do better? Seeking answers to these two questions is the essence of team building–problem solving, and, in fact, of organization development. The meetings are conducted by the managers themselves or by the managers with assistance from an internal OD consultant.

The president in May 1982 had directed me to "continue the OD program and train our people to do what you do." By 1985–86 I had accomplished that task.

To achieve lasting change in organization development programs, "training and transferring" is probably the most important stage in the entire process.

Terminating the Consultant's Involvement.   Terminating my involvement with the company involved several steps. First my role shifted from "doing" to teaching others to "do." I no longer conducted OD interventions; that was done by internal OD facilitators. Second, and related, I changed the nature of what I did. I trained trainers. I debriefed their experiences with them. I assisted managers with strategic planning. I facilitated the annual senior management retreat. Third, I greatly reduced my presence at the company. Fourth, I looked for a convenient opportunity to bow out gracefully. When William A. Griffith retired in 1986, I

gave a humorous testimonial at his retirement dinner and eased out of the picture. I continue to see Hecla employees on occasion but my involvement in *their* OD program is now minimal.

Observations on The Hecla Story

One theme of this essay is that up-front strategic thinking about the entire project is an important ingredient for success. There should be a strategy or game plan that is jointly developed and mutually agreed to by the clients and the consultant. A game plan tells everybody where they are and where they are going. A game plan is a reference point for evaluating how well the program is progressing. A game plan is really a set of decisions about program targets, goals, interventions, key "leverage points" in the organization, and beliefs about "what works and what doesn't work." The game plan can be revised if conditions warrant, but it is important to have one.

Team building–problem-solving meetings were a powerful and effective intervention at Hecla. I regard them as all-purpose interventions that almost always produce positive outcomes and rarely cause significant harm. Team-building–problem-solving meetings allow a group to focus energy and attention on its most important problems and opportunities—exactly what groups ought to do periodically. Team problem solving increases individual creativity, produces a wealth of ideas, empowers group members, and promotes commitment to decisions. The power of team building stems from the fact that boss–subordinate teams are the basic building blocks of the organization. When teams function better, individuals and the total organization function better.

There is no substitute for top level support. It is vital for success. Hecla's president liked the OD program. But I worked hard to earn his confidence by being timely, relevant, and results-oriented. I kept him apprised of what I was doing and what I was planning to do. Likewise for the two Lucky Friday Mine managers. I worked hard with each of them to establish a good relationship and deliver the best performance I could. Both mine managers strongly supported the OD program because it helped them do their jobs better. The original mine manager was new to the job and he welcomed the program as a means of accomplishing his objectives. The mine manager appointed in 1983 strongly supported the OD effort, expanded the program substantially, spearheaded the institutionalization process, and initiated many managerial improvements. Relations with the key clients are extremely important.

Mine safety and productivity were the dependent variables of interest at the Lucky Friday Mine. Both improved significantly over the course of the project, and it is reasonable to assume the OD program contributed to these results. This suggests that OD techniques and processes constitute a robust, generic organizational improvement strategy that is applicable in a variety of settings to a variety of problems. OD's methods—generating valid public data, which are then used by the organization's members to work on high-priority problems and opportunities—are simple but powerful ways to enhance creativity, problem-solving ability, and effective action taking.

An OD program must be compatible with the organization's culture and values or it will be terminated prematurely. Hecla's culture reinforces straight-talking, action-oriented, get-the-job-done behaviors. We learned this in the orientation/diagnostic interviews, and we tailored the interventions accordingly. Team problem solving fit perfectly with this norm. So did OD facilitator training and training in team problem solving.

Evaluating OD programs is an inherently difficult task. Literally millions of causal events occur in the life space of an organization and its members during the course of a year. It is impossible to specify the effects of selected causal events (say, an OD program) on global changes even though the program may have had an influence. Our solution was to observe a number of productivity and safety-related indicators over time and to designate experimental and control mines. I strongly recommend using the company's ongoing performance indicators on productivity, costs, waste, accident rates, and so forth, to draw tentative conclusions about program effects. The data are valid, reliable, and collected by the company itself. If the OD program has measurable effects, these should show up in pre- and post-intervention comparisons.

The final observation relates to trust between clients and consultant—specifically, how the consultant earns the trust of the company members. I believe there are two primary elements: competence and keeping confidences. Competence means the consultant can plan and execute the program properly. "Deliver what you promise and don't promise anything you cannot deliver." Competence makes you worthy of trust. Keeping confidences also makes you worthy of trust. The consultant possesses an enormous amount of information that should be treated as proprietary to the person who volunteered it. I have a rule never to divulge confidential information gained from one person in the company to another person in the company. I may encourage people to share their information with others, but I don't share it. When the consultant is trustworthy on this dimension, people volunteer more information, sometimes vital information for the success of the OD program. An incident at Hecla showed me how important this dimension is. Arthur Brown became president and chief executive officer when Bill Griffith retired. Art was operations vice president during the OD program. I conducted team building meetings with him; we talked frequently; we worked closely during the entire program. Chatting with Art after he became president, I told him he could use me as a confidential sounding board anytime he wanted to. He thanked me and said he would do so if the need arose. Then he said: "I know I can trust you with confidential information because you have never told me anything Bill Griffith told you in confidence." Being trustworthy means keeping confidential information confidential.

Conclusion

The OD project at Hecla was successful in two ways: it was well received by the organization, running its planned course without disruption; and it produced good results. The second outcome was made possible by the first. My goal in the Hecla Story was to share with you what I believe were some of the critical success factors. If any of these ideas help you in your OD practice, my purpose has been served.

The Hecla project was fun, exciting, and a wonderful learning experience. It was gratifying to see that OD works in the hard-rock mining industry. It was gratifying to be a part of the Hecla Story.

Notes

1. Professor Fred Fiedler of the University of Washington and I were co-principal investigators on the Bureau of Mines project. Professors Fiedler and Martin Chemers of the University of Utah conducted a demonstration project using Leader Match training and behavior modeling training at a trona mine in Wyoming, while I conducted the project at Hecla Mining Company. Members of the research and consulting team at Hecla were John Kohls, Anne Hegarty, and Paul Buller, graduate students at the University of Washington Graduate School of Business. James Peay was the Bureau of Mines technical project officer for the program.
2. Results of the Wyoming project and the Hecla project were reported in F. E. Fiedler, C. H. Bell, Jr., M. M. Chemers, and D. Patrick, "Increasing Mine Productivity and Safety through Management Training and Organization Development: A Comparative Study," *Basic and Applied Social Psychology* 5 (1984), pp. 1–18.

READING 46
PARTICIPATORY ACTION RESEARCH

Larry A. Pace and Dominick R. Argona

A View from Xerox

In 1980, after several years of thought, study, and preparation, and in response to increased foreign and domestic competition, the North American Manufacturing Division (NAMD) of Xerox Corporation and the Amalgamated Clothing and Textile Workers Union (ACTWU, Local 14A) began a joint quality of work life (QWL) experiment that is still in existence eight years later, although in a much different form. In this article we describe the process and its evolution from a highly structured adjunct feature of the work environment to a more integral and flexible approach to solving business problems and enhancing quality of work life. This evolution has not been painless; but our hope is that, by an honest sharing of our successes and diffi-

Authors' note: We are grateful to Bill Whyte, Don Kane, Pete Lazes, Ron Mitchell, Steve Weber, Tony Costanza, Hal Tragash, and the entire Team Xerox/ACTWU QWL team of managers, trainer/coordinators, shop chairpersons, employees, and consultants for their support, encouragement, assistance, and friendship. The names are too numerous to mention, but the contributions of each individual are deeply appreciated. Critical comments by Bill Whyte, Davydd Greenwood, and Peter Lazes resulted in substantial improvements to the manuscript. The views represented herein are the authors' and do not necessarily represent the official position of Xerox Corporation. Please address all correspondence concerning this article and requests for reprints to Larry A. Pace, Department of Management, University of Tennessee, 419 Stokely Management Center, Knoxville, TN 37996-0545.

Source: Larry A. Pace and Dominick R. Argona, "Participatory Action Research: A View from Xerox," *American Behavioral Scientist* 32, no. 5 (May–June 1989), pp. 552–65. Reprinted by permission of Sage Publications, Inc.

culties, we will be able to help other companies and unions struggling with similar issues and problems.

The story of QWL at Xerox is a story of participatory action research (PAR) (Whyte, 1987). Much of what we have learned has been through trial and error, experimentation, and refinement.

What follows are the reflections of two Xerox internal consultants on the evolution of the QWL process at Xerox, a series of major obstacles encountered by the process, the responses to those events, a summary of the organizational learning that occurred, and a listing of current and anticipated issues and concerns faced as the QWL process is merged with the total quality control (TQC) efforts at Xerox. Finally, we reflect on the role of internal consultant itself, giving thought to the various subroles and the social processes involved in being an effective internal consultant to the Xerox QWL process.

The Need for QWL at Xerox

In the mid-to late-1970s, Xerox began to suffer erosion of market share and profits as (a) patents expired, (b) foreign and domestic competition increased in Xerox's mainline copier and duplicator business, and (c) customers began to demand higher value and quality, and greater choice. Worker values were also changing, reflecting changes on the national and international scene. Workers were demanding a greater say over their work and were searching for more than financial rewards for their efforts.

The company was seeking higher productivity and competitiveness. Xerox management believed that worker skills and contributions were not being fully tapped, and that, if this potential could be better utilized, productivity, quality, and worker motivation would increase. The union was not opposed to those goals as long as they did not translate into job loss or speed-up tactics; but more important to the union was the search for an approach that would accord more dignity and respect to its members, increase the quality of their lives at work, and secure their jobs.

The Beginnings of the Xerox/ACTWU QWL Process

In late 1979 management approached the union during contract talks with the idea of establishing a joint employee involvement (EI) experiment. The idea ultimately produced the following joint sponsorship clause, which was ratified into the 1980 collective bargaining agreement (this clause was included verbatim in the 1983 and 1986 contracts):

> A Joint Company-Union Employee Involvement Committee shall be established to investigate and pursue opportunities for enhancing employees' work satisfaction and productivity. To this end, the Joint Committee shall meet regularly to undertake the following responsibilities:

> A. Review and evaluate ongoing programs, projects and experiments, both within and outside the Company, designed to encourage employee involvement.

> B. Develop programs, projects, and experiments that might ultimately be broadly applied.

> C. Establish subcommittees to develop suggested programs for specific areas. Hear and review reports from these subcommittees.

> D. Submit reports and recommendations to the Company and Union regarding the implementation and subsequent progress of specific programs.

To implement this contractual language, in April 1980 the parties founded the Joint Planning and Policy Committee, which consisted of top union officials and company executives. This committee established ground rules for the process and authorized the formation of Joint Plant Advisory Committees (PACs) in each of three major manufacturing facilities covering roughly 5,000 union members. The PACs formed Joint Business Center Steering Committees (BCSCs), which were chartered to guide the EI process in their areas of the plants. EI was conceived as a bottoms-up, grass roots effort to get workers involved in problem solving and decision making at the shop floor level.

Union and management trainer/coordinators (T/Cs) were selected to team teach a 40-hour participative problem-solving and group development curriculum to Problem Solving Team (PST) members. The T/Cs were trained by a third party (first Sidney P. Rubinstein and then Peter Lazes).

The authors were internal consultants who worked closely with the T/Cs, with the external consultants, with line management, with corporate headquarters, and with the union in establishing, maintaining, and expanding the QWL process. Additionally, Argona was appointed manager of the employee involvement function, within the Human Resources Department. The EI function was chartered to develop EI strategy in conjunction with the union, to administer the day-to-day operations of the QWL process, and to report periodically to the Joint Planning and Policy Committee. Argona's union counterpart was Anthony J. Costanza, then General Shop Chairman. Together these two individuals, who later received Xerox's highest honor, the President's Award, were the daily personification of the QWL process.

In the summer of 1980, the T/Cs conducted intensive orientations with the workforce and solicited volunteers for PST membership. The rallying calls for QWL were "Let's work smarter, not harder," "If Japan can, why can't we?" and "The choice is ours." Enthusiasm was high, and at first the supply of volunteers far outstripped the capacity of the organization to train and support PSTs.

PSTs were formed of six or seven union members and a supervisor, all of whom were volunteers from the same work area. (It must be admitted that the union members were far more likely to be true volunteers than were the supervisors.) By the end of 1980, 10 PSTs had graduated and 14 were in training. By mid-1982 there were over 150 active PSTs.

This era of process discovery and diffusion was one of very high excitement among top managers, union officials, and especially PST members. They were given management attention, were allowed time away from their regular jobs to select and solve problems, and were enabled to expand their horizons through participation in decision making.

PST Accomplishments. Problem solving teams, as a form of parallel suggestion involvement (Lawler, 1988), were very successful for Xerox and the ACTWU. Millions of dollars worth of cost savings and productivity improvements were documented. Team accomplishments were mainly in the form of improvements to working conditions, work flow and process, quality, safety, and workmanship. Although the traditionally organized job and work design and organization structure were initially unaltered, worker commitment and productivity were enhanced, especially in areas where the process had middle management support.

1981 to 1983: Four Major Hurdles

Between 1981 and 1983 four difficult and unexpected situations were faced by the QWL process. The responses to those situations challenged and ultimately changed the design of the QWL process.

1. A potential outsourcing situation in the Wire Harness Assembly Plant, part of the Components Manufacturing Operations in Webster, New York. It was determined after a year-long competitive benchmarking study conducted by management that the wire harness assemblies for the new 1075 copier could be purchased on the outside at a saving of over $3 million but a loss of 150 to 180 union jobs.

2. From 1981 through early 1983 Xerox, driven by increasing competitive pressures, went through a substantial "resizing" effort that led to voluntary and involuntary reductions in force in both salaried and hourly ranks. It was very difficult to separate the layoffs from QWL in the minds of those affected.

3. The QWL process reached a plateau. Job movement driven by the rolling production plan disrupted team membership and necessitated the training of replacement members. Additionally, the pool of new volunteers for PSTs evaporated.

4. In 1983, Xerox initiated a TQC process called Leadership Through Quality. This was conceived as a top-down corporate culture change that required managers to learn, use, teach, and inspect the practice of Total Quality Control before cascading the training and application of Leadership Through Quality to the next level. The organizing structure for Leadership Through Quality consisted of a manager and his or her staff. It was hoped that this structure would support the managerial behavior changes that proponents of EI had so often said were lacking. The union had been actively involved in the QWL efforts as a joint partner, but the Leadership Through Quality effort was solely a corporate management initiative.

Overcoming the Obstacles

The Wire Harness Study Team. The union, supported by Lazes, approached management and asked if, in the spirit of QWL, the workers could be given a chance to save their jobs by taking the surplus costs out of the harness plant. This project was given management approval, and a team of six union members and two management employees was selected from a list of 160 volunteers. The team was given six months in which to develop its recommendations, access to all company information, and office, clerical, and travel budget support. The story of the original Wire Harness Study Team has been reported elsewhere (Lazes & Costanza, 1984), but suffice it to say here that the results of the study team were successful beyond either party's initial hopes. The work and the jobs were kept in house, and recommendations were implemented that ultimately saved the company more than $4.2 million annually.

1983 collective bargaining agreement. Because of the success of the Wire Harness Study Team in taking surplus costs out of an internally manufactured commodity, the company was desirous of using the same methodology in all areas of the business in which it was not competitive. Following the layoffs from 1981 to 1983, the union was reluctant to give the company carte blanche to form cost study teams without some measure of employment security. Thus the parties entered the 1983 negotiations with a mix of motives, some complementary, some conflicting. The result was a trailblazing collective bargaining agreement that provided protection against economic layoff for all union members (Local 14A) for the life of the contract (three years). In return for (*a*) stricter absenteeism control measures, (*b*) some deliberalization of benefits, (*c*) containment of wage rate growth, and (*d*) the ability to duplicate the Wire Harness Study Team approach in any area deemed to be uncompetitive, the company was able to provide the employment security union members sought (Costanza & Pace, 1985). This provision was extended in 1986 for another three years. Although the 1983 contract provided job security for union members, the strict no-fault absenteeism measures were not well received by the membership. The problems with the no-fault

absenteeism arrangement were corrected to some extent in the 1986 contract, which provided incentives for good attendance, rather than simply punishment for absence.

Refocusing the involvement process. As the number of teams increased, two phenomena occurred. The pool of volunteers began to evaporate and the ability of the traditionally designed organization to absorb more teams began to diminish. A "balance point" was reached in most of the plant operations at around 15 to 25 percent involvement. (One plant, a continuous process operation, proved to be an exception in achieving the involvement of 60 percent of its employees on PSTs.)

The biggest problem presented by the leveling-out phenomenon was that it created polarized "in-" and "out-" groups. This split into divided camps produced two very different ways of looking at the employee involvement process. To those who were active participants, the process was very meaningful and fulfilling, and tended to be evaluated in terms of its potential to increase member satisfaction and loyalty as well as to lead to superior solutions to organizational problems.

Members of the out-group, however, evaluated the process from an outcome perspective, asking such legitimate questions as how much the process cost, and what was its return on investment.

Moreover, those outside the process often had to work harder to cover the jobs of those who were off at meetings, which often had refreshments served. This led to some frustration and resentment toward the process and its participants. It has often been observed, of course, that participants are more favorable in their evaluations of the participative process than are nonparticipants (see, for example, Nurick, 1985).

The need for a change in approach became obvious. The Quality Circle model would never produce 100 percent involvement in the traditionally organized operations. We made two joint decisions in early 1983. All hourly and salaried employees would be trained in problem solving and group dynamics. Regardless of whether a person volunteered to be on a team, he or she would need to speak the "problem-solving language" in order to operate in the new work system.

The second joint decision concerned the nature of the EI process itself in the plant organizations. The Divisional Planning and Policy Committee instructed each PAC to sponsor off-site strategy sessions with both participants and nonparticipants in the QWL process to answer two basic questions: Why weren't people volunteering to join QWL teams, and how could the process be reorganized so that business and human needs could be simultaneously met?

These joint strategy sessions led to a complete restructuring of the EI process through an interesting application of PAR (Pace & Mitchell, 1985). The plants were encouraged to perform participative, stakeholder evaluations of their EI processes. In the Components Manufacturing Operations, a stakeholder survey was constructed by the PAC with the assistance of Ron Mitchell from Cornell. Pace and Mitchell analyzed the responses to the survey, which was administered to nearly 1,000 employees, and fed the results back to the PAC, which then restructured the EI process. The focus shifted away from Quality Circles and onto problem solving and participative decision making as fundamental ways of organizing work. This led to the formation of Business Area Work Groups as a superior approach to EI (Mitchell and Pace, 1986).

Business Area Work Groups blanket an entire organization with a 100 percent involvement structure. Consisting of from 15 to 50 people, all of whom are connected with a particular product or service, these groups meet regularly on company time (usually for one and one-half hours every other week) to discuss their work area's performance, company business information, and union information, and to recognize individual and group accomplishments. These groups then discuss problems of quality, cost, or delivery

schedules and either solve the problems immediately or commission ad hoc teams to take the problems off-line for resolution. Ad hoc teams usually consist of 3 to 5 people, rather than the usual 8 to 10 in a Quality Circle. After an ad hoc team solves a problem, the team disbands.

The Business Area Work Group strategy solves the in-group versus out-group problem, and enables a traditional work system to migrate toward a high-performing, self-managing work system.

These two decisions resolved the problem of the loss of volunteers for Quality Circle activities and paved the way for integrating the QWL efforts with the Leadership Through Quality strategy.

Creating a desirable future: Horizon Teams. Another effort at refocusing the involvement process was an experiment in participative strategic planning for Xerox Manufacturing (Pace, 1987). The so-called Horizon Teams involved the union and many hourly employees. These teams developed projections and recommendations in the areas of factory automation and robotics, product and process quality, materials management, business scenarios, and human resource management. Pace served as team leader for the Human Resource Management Horizon Team.

1984 to 1986: integrating TQC and QWL. In late 1983, Argona moved to Xerox Corporate headquarters as manager of EI for the entire corporation, and Pace replaced Argona as organizational effectiveness manager for manufacturing. The corporation was developing its Total Quality Control process, which came to be known as Leadership Through Quality, and Argona and Pace were asked to integrate the ongoing EI activities with the corporate-driven Leadership Through Quality approach.

Although the philosophies of TQC and QWL are mutually supportive and highly compatible, a major concern in Webster was the lack of involvement of both the union and the local manufacturing management in the development and rollout of the Leadership Through Quality strategy.

Recognizing the problem, and agreeing that it was a potentially severe one, Xerox corporate management sponsored and supported the following steps:

The union and management T/Cs, who had developed and delivered the initial QWL training, were asked to modify and deliver the TQC curriculum to the industrial workforce. This modification reestablished the concern for human needs at work and also firmly placed the union in an equal status with management in the TQC process wherever bargaining unit employees were involved.

The T/Cs were reclassified as organizational effectiveness specialists (OESs) and given an expanded role as internal consultants to the combined TQC/QWL process. Simultaneous with this development, the OESs were centralized and reported directly to the organizational effectiveness manager. This gave a central focus to the process, which was highly favored by the union.

The Joint Planning and Policy Committee was chartered with overseeing the combined TQC/QWL process in NAMD (which by this time had been renamed the Reprographic Manufacturing Operations—RMO).

These steps provided the organizational base for the TQC training of the entire RMO workforce. Union and management OESs trained management employees and union employees alike, just as had been done with the original QWL training. The implementation of the TQC process following the completion of training was, and is, an issue of joint union/management concern.

1987 to the Present: Current and Anticipated Issues

In 1987, on completion of the TQC training, the OESs were once again returned to the line organization as internal consultants and facilitators for the TQC/QWL process. Simultane-

ously, their ranks were reduced because of the completion of the heavy training schedule. Currently the organization is facing (and dealing jointly with) the following issues:

1. The decentralized OESs, while being more closely tied to the actual deliverables of the business by reporting directly to operations managers, may lose their "organizational effectiveness" and "joint process" perspectives.

2. While the TQC process assumes, and expects to be built upon, a healthy QWL process, this assumption is implicit, rather than explicit. The implicit assumption regarding employee involvement may lead to a reduction in emphasis on the human needs of the members of the organization and too heavy an emphasis on the bottom line (Jacobson, 1988).

3. The role of the production supervisor is undergoing radical change in Xerox's manufacturing operations. One plant in Webster (New Build Operations, the assembly operation) is instituting an improved work system that fully integrates QWL and TQC with the day-to-day operation of the business. In support of this work system, supervisors are being trained in a 360-hour curriculum covering their new role as coach, counselor, resource person, teacher, and facilitator.

4. The next steps for the joint QWL process are not clearly defined at the present. The ACTWU, along with other progressive labor organizations, is seeking a redefined role in the industrial enterprise. What form this role will or should take is not immediately obvious.

Reflections on the Internal Consultant Role

The role of internal consultant in the QWL process at Xerox was a very challenging and exciting one for the authors. At the same time the role was very demanding and often quite frustrating. In the early days of QWL, 60-to 70-hour weeks and even longer were quite common for us.

We lived through eight years of the process, nursing it in its infancy and helping it grow to its current stage of development. In what follows we reflect personally on our experiences by identifying several specific responsibilities (subroles) of the internal consultant and then describing our approach to integrating these various responsibilities.

Human resource strategists. Although case studies abound on the Xerox/ACTWU QWL experiment, few even mention the role of the internal consultant team as strategists. This is a major omission.

In response to the increased foreign and domestic competition, Xerox management had developed a three-phase business effectiveness strategy to lead the company from a position of competitive disparity (Phase I) to a position of parity (Phase II), and finally to a position of competitive leadership (Phase III). This business strategy focused on new product development, technical superiority, strategic planning, competitive benchmarking, and financial control, but was largely silent on human resource issues.

Yet Xerox was aware that the skills and talents of its workforce were being underutilized on the job, and, as early as 1975 for Argona and 1979 for Pace, we began producing and implementing strategies for developing the human potential of Xerox workers and managers. These started with a series of studies by Argona of technical obsolescence in manufacturing engineers and culminated in 1979 in a document coauthored by Argona, Dr. Robert W. Mann, and Pace that laid the groundwork for the QWL process.

In this strategy document titled simply "Project 90," employee involvement was shown to be a necessary ingredient for achieving and maintaining a competitive business advantage. As early as 1979, we had charted a 10-to 15-year course for QWL at Xerox. This human resource strategy provided a blueprint for moving the Xerox Manufacturing organization from a traditionally organized bureaucracy to a high-performing, high-involvement system.

The three phases, each projected to last from three to five years, consisted of a parallel suggestion involvement process for the process entry phase, a job and work group involvement strategy for the competitive parity phase, and a high-involvement work system for the competitive advantage phase. Recognizing the current operating system, and working within the "arc of the possible," the authors initially shared only the first phase of the QWL strategy with Xerox line managers.

While some developments were unexpected, the QWL strategy outlined in Project 90 was amazingly prescient in predicting both the *kinds* of problems that would occur during each phase and the appropriate response to those problems. The actual development of the QWL process is still tracking almost perfectly with the original strategy.

Applied researchers. Based on the approval of the strategic thrust of Project 90, we were given the responsibility to visit our counterparts in other companies and to interact with outside organizations, including consulting firms, universities, governmental agencies, and research organizations.

The purposes of these visits were (*a*) to learn the strengths and weaknesses of various involvement approaches, (*b*) to identify likely problems with process implementation and ways to overcome such problems, (*c*) to learn the strengths and weaknesses of various outside consultants, (*d*) to develop superior approaches to training problem-solving team members, steering committee members, and trainer/coordinators.

The learning that occurred through these visits we developed into a presentation for communicating both internally and externally. For each phase of Project 90, we projected approximately a year of applied research *during the height of success* of the phase, during which the plans could be formulated for the next generation of activity.

We deemed this research necessary because we had adopted a "product life cycle" notion of the involvement approach used in each phase, expecting it to diminish in effectiveness over time.

Salespersons/process champions.   Another of our roles was to "sell" unconvinced line managers and shop representatives on the benefits of the QWL process. In this role, we worked closely with Costanza of the ACTWU and Lazes of Cornell. This activity was most successful when all three parties worked together—for example, by coconducting presentations and training sessions for managers and shop chairpersons. Much of the selling in the early days involved assurances and reassurances to the parties that their own prerogatives would not be undermined by the process, at least not in the initial stages.

A distinct frustration in this role was that, by frequently associating and collaborating with the external consultants and the union, as required and even demanded by the internal consulting role, we lost credibility with many traditionally oriented line managers, especially middle managers.

This highlights one of the key problems of this role. The internal consultant must develop a coproducer/partner relationship with management, with the external consultant, and with the union. All of these relationships must be continually refined and developed, yet, at the same time, none of them can predominate. Juggling and balancing multiple relationships requires a healthy dose of tolerance for ambiguity.

This ambiguity was exacerbated by the fact that we had multiple "bosses." As manager of the EI function, Argona worked for the human resources vice president; but in just as real a sense, he worked for the Joint Planning and Policy Committee, and also for the VP of manufacturing operations.

Simultaneously satisfying the requirements of multiple bosses was difficult at best and sometimes downright impossible. This situation was initially somewhat easier for Pace as an individual contributor since he knew that Argona was his *manager,* while the union, the management, the OESs (T/Cs), and the hourly employees were various *"customers"* who had requirements that should be satisfied as much as possible. Pace, however, later experienced the same role conflict Argona had as the OE manager for manufacturing.

Another aspect of the sales role was that of coach, counselor, and cheerleader for the OESs, who often were at odds with the system as a result of their change agent status, and needed to hear an encouraging word from someone who understood.

Corporate interface.   In addition to our other responsibilities, the authors were given the task of interacting with the corporate office both to keep the headquarters informed of progress and problems with the process and to transfer learning from Webster to other parts of the corporation. This required frequent travel to corporate headquarters and participation on various companywide committees, teams, and task forces.

Integrating the various subroles.   The various roles of the internal consultant—change agent, facilitator, strategist, researcher, and salesperson—were integrated by the authors into a sort of "phantom" role in the process. By this we mean that, to the extent that all the roles were being performed appropriately and at the right intensity, the internal consultant role was largely transparent to management and the union, who were, after all, the joint partners in the process.

When the subroles were out of balance or when crises arose, the overall role became visible; but our approach was to submerge the internal consultant role as soon as we could. If the QWL process worked, we believed the credit should rightfully go to the union and to line management, not to the internal or external consultants.

In addition to requiring a high tolerance for ambiguity, the low profile we took meant that personal career ambition for the internal consultant had to take a back seat to the desire for the QWL process to grow and prosper.

Conclusions

We have shared an insider's view of the evolution of the joint QWL activities at Xerox over an eight-year period. We show that the QWL process has had its share of expected and unexpected events, and that the organizational learning occurring through the PAR approach was quickly internalized within the process.

Over time the QWL process has become a decentralized and contingent involvement structure. While this was desirable from a management perspective, it presents significant problems to the union, which would like to speak with one voice about and to the QWL process.

Some of the words we and others have used in describing the QWL process at Xerox are "robust," "a learning experience," and "evolutionary." The common thread is that the PAR approach has allowed quick although by no means painless adjustments to the process that have helped it to survive, grow, and develop.

Being principal stakeholders, change agents, coproducers, salespersons, researchers, coaches, counselors, and strategists for the QWL process placed multiple demands on the internal consultants. These demands were exacerbated by the ambiguity of multiple and sometimes unclear reporting relationships and customer requirements. On balance, however, we have found the job of internal consultant a fulfilling, challenging, and exciting role.

References

Costanza, A. I., and L. A. Pace. "A Cooperative Approach to Job Security at Xerox." Invited address to the American Productivity Center Employment Security Conference, Washington, DC, July 1985.

Jacobson G. "Employee Relations at Xerox: A Model Worth Copying." *Management Review,* March 1988.

Lawler, E. E. "Choosing an Involvement Strategy." *Academy of Management Executives,* 1988, pp. 197–204.

Lazes, P., and A. J. Costanza. "Xerox Cuts Costs without Layoffs through Labor-Management Collaboration." Labor-Management Cooperation Brief, July 1984. Washington, DC: Department of Labor.

Mitchell, R., and L. A. Pace. "Company-wide Quality Control Programs: Are Quality Circles the Best Vehicle?" Presented at the 40th annual American Society for Quality Control Conference, Anaheim, CA, May 1986.

Nurick, A. J. *Participation in Organizational Change: The TVA Experiment.* New York: Praeger, 1985.

Pace, L. A. "Creative Management through Employee Involvement in Strategic Planning." *J. of Creative Behavior* 21, no. 2 (1987), pp. 127–135.

Pace, L. A., and R. Mitchell. "Participative Evaluation and Organizational Change." Presented at the meeting of the Evaluation Research Society, Toronto, October 1985.

Whyte, W. F. "From human relations to organizational behavior: reflections on a changing scene." *Industrial and Labor Relations Review* 40, no. 4 (1987), pp. 487–500.

READING 47
CREATING EXCELLENCE OUT OF CRISIS: ORGANIZATIONAL TRANSFORMATION AT THE *CHICAGO TRIBUNE*

Robert M. Frame, Warren R. Nielsen, and Larry E. Pate

Recently, popular research-based books—such as *In Search of Excellence, A Passion for Excellence, Reinventing the Corporation, The 100 Best Companies to Work for in America, Creating Excellence, Change Masters, Thriving on Chaos, The Winning Performance, Megatrends,* and *Leaders*—have documented that increasing numbers of corporations have undergone a transformation in both culture and performance. Many of the values, beliefs, and norms that seemed essential in establishing and building the reputations of successful companies are now being challenged, to the extent that many consider a systematic transformation of those variables necessary for companies to remain viable (Bennis & Nanus, 1985; Hickman & Silva, 1986; Peters & Austin, 1985).

Of course, for years the organization development (OD) literature has discussed change processes for creating healthier lives and healthier, more humane work settings (e.g., Beckhard & Harris, 1977; Lippitt, 1982). In the 1980s we

Note: The views expressed in this article are those of the authors and do not necessarily represent the positions or policies of the *Chicago Tribune* or any of its subsidiaries. An earlier draft of this article was presented at the meeting of the Western Academy of Management in Big Sky, Montana, in March 1988. The authors are indebted to Dan Spencer and to the three anonymous *JABS* reviewers for their helpful comments.

have begun to see evidence that the hopes and dreams of many of the "founding fathers" of OD—such as Argyris (1970), Bennis (1969), and Schein (1969)—are becoming realities. Abundant reports indicate that, despite the slow, evolutionary nature of systemwide transformation (which requires changes in behavior, systems, and structures), movement toward excellence in the work place is not only possible but also measurable (Nora & Stramy, 1986).

This article describes one such organizational transformation effort still in progress at the *Chicago Tribune,* one of the largest and most prominent newspapers in the United States. The event that triggered the *Tribune*'s transformation was a 1985 strike involving all five of the production union locals at the newspaper's printing facility in downtown Chicago. We describe below the multiphase transformation effort that took the *Tribune* from crisis to excellence, and some of the results of this effort.[1]

Various conceptual frameworks could readily be applied to aid one's understanding of our research. For example, several organizational (O), change agent (C), and intervention (I) characteristics clearly influenced the results (R) obtained for the *Tribune,* consistent with the OCIR model (Pate, 1979) that postulates that $R = f(O, C, I)$. We speculated, however, that the conceptual framework of the model recently presented by Greiner and Schein (1988) would prove even more useful because (*a*) the transformation effort was intended to move the *Tribune*'s system from a traditional bureaucratic model toward a collegial-consensus model and (*b*) the effort prompted a consideration and transformation of the previously existing power dynamics at the *Tribune*.

We thus found it necessary to consider the essential, albeit subtle, difference between the terms *develop* and *transform*. Organization development efforts should be expected to focus more on improvements building on *previous* learning and behavior (i.e., to seek to develop the organization), whereas organizational transformation efforts should be expected to focus more on the desired *future* state the change effort is intended to create (i.e., to seek to transform the organization). We used 10 transformational factors roughly corresponding to the 10 modules of the 20-week training program as a framework for guiding the research discussed in this article.

Stop the Presses: The Walkout at the *Chicago Tribune*

The production printing plant wherein the organizational transformation occurred received its name of the Freedom Center through an employee contest. The largest offset newspaper printing plant in the United States, it produced a daily edition of the *Tribune, USA Today,* a Sunday insert package, a daily insert package, and a national edition of the *Tribune.* The Freedom Center was built in 1981 to house the equipment for state-of-the-art satellite transmissions, computerized type layout, offset printing, plate making, inserting, and packaging. This plant employed about 1,460 persons, of whom 1,250–1,300 worked in production and the remainder in circulation. The center's newsprint warehouse stored as many as 26,000 rolls of newsprint brought in by rail; its computerized prepress operations did not rely on paste-up and other manual operations; and advertising graphics and data were gathered by operations and composed on computer screens. Approximately 60 percent of the newspaper's volume consisted of advertisements.

In addition to contract matters, the primary issues sparking the strike were control over hiring selection and transfers. The key *Tribune* production managers, who had long believed that these issues were crucial to their ability to combine leading-edge technology with advanced, socially responsible management, responded swiftly to the walkout. They sought to fill all vacant positions without rehiring any of the persons on strike. Within days, they brought in a small core of qualified machine operators and press operators, either by transferring them on temporary assignment from the other *Tribune* operation centers across the country or by hiring them through strategically placed advertisements from other newspapers. For several weeks after the walkout began, management pitched in to help run the presses and the packaging and ancillary equipment to keep the *Tribune* on schedule. During that time, nearly 1,000 new employees—most of them having little or no newspaper experience—had to be screened for hire.

The Freedom Center management, led by a relatively new vice president who had a vision of the production plant's one day being a showcase of technological and managerial leadership, viewed the walkout not as a crisis of survival but as a window of opportunity. In effect, the strike represented a chance to improve the systems of operational and performance management so that they would transcend those characteristic of much of the newspaper industry. Argyris (1974) documents these "restrictive traditions" in describing his own organizational renewal effort for what he calls the *Daily Planet* (which is curiously similar to the *New York Times*). Argyris characterizes the living system of the *Planet* as

competitive and low in trust, and as operating within win-lose dynamics. Evaluation and control are more important than inquiry and innovation; risky issues and innovations tend not to be discussed; additiveness and coherence in problem-solving activities are low; group discussions are ineffective and group meetings are considered a waste of time; and there is a deep pessimism about changing human nature or increasing the effectiveness of the system. (1974, p. 32)

Argyris's description also fit the *Tribune*. Much of the management group prior to the strike had been promoted on the basis of tenure and politics, rather than managerial skill. Unions exercised significant control over operations. The company had avoided some serious issues, but the executives finally decided that management effectiveness had to be improved so as to change the company's performance. Because the *Tribune* had invested $200 million in the Freedom Center, top management determined that one of the key changes should be making the center become what they had intended it to be: a modern, efficient plant. Thus they initiated modifications in management style, measurement methods, and the level of control workers exercised over the measurement system. The powerful unions that had previously been an integral part of the political environment of the *Tribune* prior to the transformation remained in place afterward, but exerted less influence than before.

The Freedom Center's management team, in response to both the walkout and the hiring of nearly 1,000 new employees needing to learn to operate state-of-the art production equipment, wished to minimize the pressures and stress accompanying this transitional period. Within nine months of the strike, the management team administered an employee survey, and felt deeply concerned when the results suggested that low morale permeated the main-line production departments. Further analysis diagnosed poor supervision as a primary cause of low morale, which in retrospect seems understandable. The vice president for production observed:

> once we found ourselves in the situation of having hired a thousand new people, we also found ourselves without a lot of people familiar with the way a newspaper operates. One area in particular is the press area, where our pressroom is a fairly complicated area to work in. There are 10 production machines, each of which today would cost $10–15 million. And you have seven or eight people working each one of those presses. It's fairly compli-

cated work. Presses are fairly unforgiving. You either do the job or the press doesn't run. So we found ourselves there with a need for 19 supervisors at the first level ... supervising groups of 7 people. This in addition to those supervisory jobs filled from outside with experienced people.

Furthermore, the workforce composition had shifted dramatically. The person who was production manager at the time of the walkout noted that supervisors

> went from supervising a group of experienced employees with an average age of 50–55 years to one of 20–25 years old. So ... in some areas we had managers who stayed only accustomed to a highly structured unionized organization, managing new employees talking about quality circles, progressive communication programs, and career path opportunities.

In short, because the former pressroom supervisors were on strike with their employees and all of the other supervisors had learned to supervise according to the traditional model, the entire workforce was ill prepared to carry out a new vision of leadership concerned with "excellence."

Generating Results-Focused Solutions to the Walkout

At this time, the *Tribune* management recognized the immediate need to initiate training for staff and line personnel, both to standardize procedures for the hundreds of newly hired employees with greatly varying habits, and to clarify the standards and requirements expected within the new Freedom Center organization. Top management solicited proposals from qualified organization development and change consultants for designing and implementing a top-down modular management training program for all levels of management. This request for proposals asked for training addressing 12 basic subjects corresponding to the significant deficiencies identified by the survey analysis. In addition, because the production supervisors in the pressroom units were union members who had walked out along with the strikers, the *Tribune* management simultaneously needed to fill 19 positions for new first-level supervisors.

A consulting group that had done work nationwide was hired to conduct both the management training and the assessment of more than 130 self-nominated candidates for the 19 vacant supervisor positions. Because most of these applicants were new to the firm, no one on the pressroom staff knew them. The consulting group therefore followed an Assessment Center approach (which typically relies on the pooled judgments of others) to screen job candidates. Nearly all of the 130 candidates who underwent the Assessment Center process naturally felt concerned about its fairness, as they did not yet have any reason to trust any system of selection or evaluation other than the more traditional one used throughout the industry (Argyris, 1974).[2]

The Assessment Center method, based on a job analysis that identified skills and abilities required or expected for effectively performing the job of supervisor, included the following basic elements:

- Multisituational measures derived from a series of exercises and simulations, each designed to give the candidate an opportunity to demonstrate her or his ability.

- Multiple assessors, all of them knowledgeable pressroom employees familiar with the job's requirements but not with the candidates they assessed.

- Pooled judgments of the assessors comparing individual candidates' attributes to set performance criteria.

Once the training program and Assessment Center were custom designed and initiated, the top management team met away from the job site with a principal of the consulting firm to engage in an activity known as "future state visioning." For years, the company's top executives

had worked off site on operating plans mostly centered around specific projects. This time, however, the off-site experience focused on developing an entirely new management style for the Operating Department. The vice president for operations later commented that instead of talking about "what we were going to do in 1986," top management discussed "where we wanted to be in 1987, 1988, and 1989." All of this activity took place within a four-month period in the spring and summer of 1986.

One of the authors of this article worked on the transformation effort on a daily basis; one was involved on a few occasions; one took no part in designing or conducting the intervention, but afterward helped examine and interpret the resulting data.

The custom-designed management training program condensed coverage of the 12 subjects (as cited in the request for proposals) into 10 eight-hour modules, which were addressed one at a time throughout 20 weeks. These modules were:

1. Overview of management.
2. Interpersonal skills.
3. Leadership.
4. Team building and team-oriented leadership.
5. Situational leadership.
6. Problem solving.
7. Time management and delegation.
8. The performance management system.
9. Coaching.
10. Summary and integration.

Based on the feedback and responses of the groups after they began their training, "downstream" modules were modified and refined to meet the participants' primary needs. The traditional management development approach would be to start such efforts with top management and then follow with a top-down "cascade" training sequence (Pate & Nielsen, 1987). In contrast, the consultants asked that members of the top management team undergo training in the basic program principles only *after* their immediate subordinates had covered at least 7 of the 10 modules. The reason for delaying the top group's training was that this would enable the consultants to provide valuable feedback to managers about the organization based on data generated by their subordinates in response to program content—and thus provide a "real-world" organizational context for many of the program's principles and techniques.

Aware of the underlying values associated with the training program's content, the management team spent an additional four days away from the job site—far away, at a *Tribune*-owned setting in the most northeastern area of Ontario, Canada—refining a new vision for the Freedom Center. The core documents initially drafted by the top group included "mission" and "operating belief" statements, which laid out the team's management philosophy and foundation values, and one providing a cornerstone for a new piece entitled "Performance Management System: Key Result Areas" that discussed performance measures for the overall production plant. In addressing basic transformation questions—such as "Who are we?" and "What do we want to become?"—the management team developed a mission statement incorporating commitment to (*a*) providing "printing . . . for Chicago Tribune Company and others," (*b*) entering into "a partnership with vendors," and (*c*) becoming "customer driven" in philosophy and orientation. All of these goals represented a marked departure from the *Tribune*'s traditional philosophy, direction, and historical definitions for its production plant (e.g., it was not previously "customer driven"). Furthermore, all of these goals are consistent with the focus associated with "excellent" companies (Peters & Austin, 1985; Peters & Waterman, 1982).

The initial drafts of these core organizational transformation documents were refined further by the immediate subordinates of the management team, who also went off-site for several days to do this work. These subordinates refined the mission and philosophy statements and developed Key Result Areas (KRAs) for the 12 major operating production and staff support units of the Freedom Center, which were involved with the following functions:

- Prepress and technical support.
- Newsprint operations.
- Pressroom operations.
- Packaging.
- Plate making.
- Quality/reliability.
- Finance.
- Engineering/maintenance.
- Purchasing/materials management.
- Training.
- Employee communications.
- Administration groups.

Once they had accomplished this transformation work off-site (which included identifying specific KRAs and related performance measures for each one), the consultants began laying the conceptual foundation for a comprehensive process that came to be called the KRA Performance Management System, which they introduced during the later modules of the training program. Developed by Edwin Yager (as outlined by Coonradt, 1985), this system employs sports metaphors understandable by nearly anyone who enjoys some form of sports or recreation, and is based on principles identified in response to the question, "Why, in sports and recreation, will people pay for the privilege of working harder than they will work when they are paid?" The answer—clear goals, unchanging rules, effective score keeping, freedom to choose methods, and immediate feedback based on self-administered measurement systems—provides the keys to a comprehensive performance management system applicable in any work place.

Although the terms *key result area* and *measurement* are used to design and conduct OD programs, the *Game of Work* approach actually represents a departure from OD applications of these concepts. The concepts are similar to those of Deming (1982) and Drucker (1986), and focus explicitly on *results,* rather than on tasks, duties, activities, projects, programs, or methods, which the process interventions of an OD program would more likely address (Schein, 1969). This emphasis distinguishes organizational transformation efforts from OD efforts. The concentration on outcomes and results was outlined in the management development segment of the *Tribune*'s development effort during classroom training, reinforced through written belief statements of a commitment to using measured performance as the basis for rewards, and applied during the OD segment via natural work group interventions at all levels according to the KRA Performance Management System.

Each natural work group developed additional KRAs associated with the mission statements and identified specific performance indicators (e.g., cost per ton), using what were called "results-to-resources" ratios as measures of each KRA. Team building sessions focused upon obstacles and issues associated with sustaining minimum base-line performance standards, and called for charting measured progress for each team's "field of play" and displaying results consistent with effective charting principles.

The team building activities thus were not oriented toward group process—as would be the case in an OD program—but instead dealt with results and measurement, consistent with the philosophy that "if you cannot measure it, you cannot manage it." Furthermore, consistent with a plantwide KRA of customer satisfaction, when issues and obstacles associated with interdepartmental "interfaces" were identified, intergroup team building sessions were designed according to the measured performance orientation.

As soon as charts reflecting results for both the department and work group levels were developed, the consultants strongly recommended that they be posted, believing that the very act of making them visible would help employees focus their efforts on resolving problems related to production, quality, and cost and making improvements that would be reflected in charted results. This expectation was fulfilled. Employees took an immediate interest in the charts, which typically reflected actual performance on a daily or weekly basis, the base-line minimum performance standard, and a rolling average trend line to discourage overreaction to the peaks and valleys normal for most production performance measurement (see Figures 1, 2, 3, and 4 further below).

Finally, three overall plant KRAs were identified at the off-site meetings:

1. Implementation of the operating beliefs (which were outlined and mailed to each employee in a document labeled PACE, which stood for participation-attitude-communication-environment).

2. Human resource development.

3. Effective capital and expense resource utilization.

After some analyses, the measure for the latter KRA was identified as cost per ton, a measure of "through-put" throughout the entire production process. To our knowledge, no other newspaper publisher has used this particular measure as the key to bottom-line productivity and cost improvement.

The implications of developing an entirely new measuring system are far reaching. The key financial managers supported a review of the previous four years so that a history could be developed, which was a significant contribution. More important, the management team's focus shifted from "budget thinking" to "resources thinking" (i.e., capitalizing on and maximizing resources), with dramatic effects. It was determined that *every dollar spent on cost per ton required five to six dollars of advertising expenditures; thus, a cost savings of a million dollars represented five to six million dollars of savings in advertising revenues.*

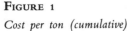

FIGURE 1

Cost per ton (cumulative)

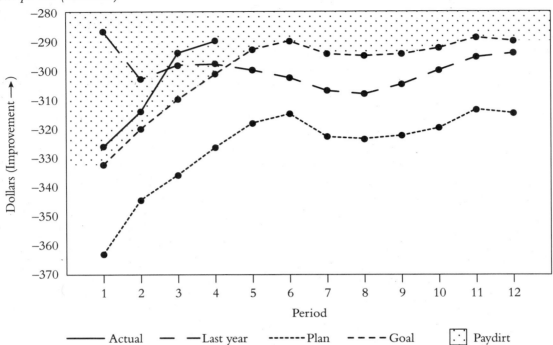

Results

Using numbers projected downward to protect confidential company financial data, Figure 1 shows that a goal for annual metric tons of newsprint was established for 1987 for the *Tribune*'s Freedom Center. This measure was considered the key economic factor in what was considered an "aggressive" budget for the year, as represented by the "plan" line in the figure and the gap between the "goal" and plan lines. Consistent with the *Game of Work* labels associated with Coonradt's (1985) management process, in this chart and in others throughout the plant, savings above the budgeted goal appear in the area called "paydirt."

Figure 1 reflects savings based on an annual average of 200,000 metric tons of newsprint

consumed at $40 per ton ahead of plan through the first four months of the period, representing $8 million in potential "annualized" savings. After applying the *Tribune*'s gross profit margin factor, this represents annualized advertising revenue savings of tens of millions of dollars. For three quarters, performance continued at this record level.

Figures 2, 3, and 4 report other results for the first four months of 1987 or for the period after the organizational transformation effort began. Data are based on production records for previous years.

Figure 2 shows data for the budget plan versus actual productivity in the pressroom in terms of thousands of eight-page papers printed. This unit's performance, when extended through the

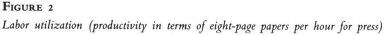

FIGURE 2

Labor utilization (productivity in terms of eight-page papers per hour for press)

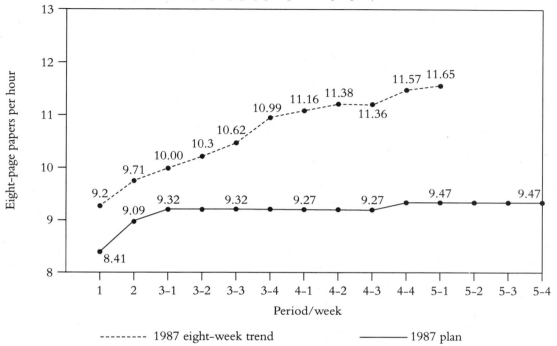

first three quarters of 1987, showed a remarkable 43 percent improvement over the figures for the last quarter of 1986.

Figure 3 reflects improvement in pressroom reliability performance, according to half-hour production targets met for circulation department delivery schedules. The goal for each paper was 90 percent of scheduled target times, a major achievement. The trend continued well beyond the charted 87 weeks.

Figure 4 reflects improvement in pages-per-hour productivity for the composing unit, which was still operating under the union contract work rules during the first five months of 1987. This unit's productivity increased by almost 25 percent during this period, something never before achieved in the unit's history of more than 100 years.

Incentives

Nearly every experienced trainer, change agent, or manager realizes that rewards and consequences are important elements of any performance management system (Lawler, 1981). Merely installing a performance system does not guarantee that people will follow it. For example, Hope and Pate (1988) suggest that individual compliance and self-motivation are influenced by the extent to which one considers a system consistent with one's own sense of integrity. Furthermore, research on the psychology of compensation and its impact on behavior, performance, and results (e.g., Lawler, 1971, 1981, 1983) has consistently demonstrated that effective performance management depends on people's recognizing the importance of individual differences.

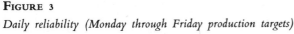

FIGURE 3

Daily reliability (Monday through Friday production targets)

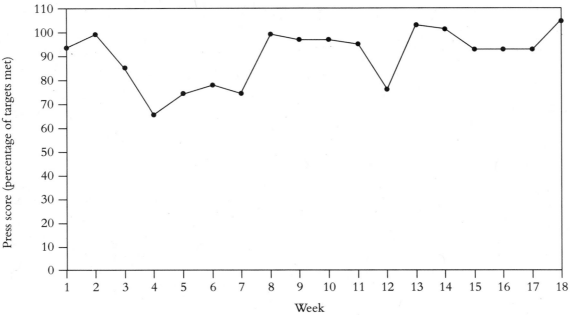

From the beginning of the change effort, the *Tribune*'s management realized the importance of these factors. Their plans evolved into a two-pronged strategy. First, a transitional phase was implemented in which the company's ongoing merit pay and performance appraisal process for salaried employees shifted from evaluating personal qualities and behavior toward rewarding contributions to measured results related to the work group's key result areas. This transition began at the top with "hours-eligible" managers. Before 1987, each manager was informed that her or his bonus would be tied to KRA performance; this represented an attempt to avoid hoping for one behavior while rewarding another (Kerr, 1975).

Second, middle managers and employees alike were invited to get involved in developing self-funding incentive programs to reward hourly employees and their supervisors for performance. The pressroom group was the first to respond to this invitation. With respect to cost-per-ton as the overall plant measure for effective use of resources, the pressroom management team developed an incentive program whose published purpose was to "elevate the pressroom's level of newsprint yield (reduction of waste) and printing quality to the top of the industry as quickly as possible and to compensate you, the pressroom employees, accordingly." This incentive program recognized that waste reduction and quality control were mutually dependent on one another. Therefore, the team set specific goals for the first three years of the plan for controllable waste, with employees to share in the dollar savings resulting from lowering waste costs. Concurrently, a quality component was devised for determining how to distribute the waste award.

FIGURE 4

Composing productivity (in terms of pages per hour)

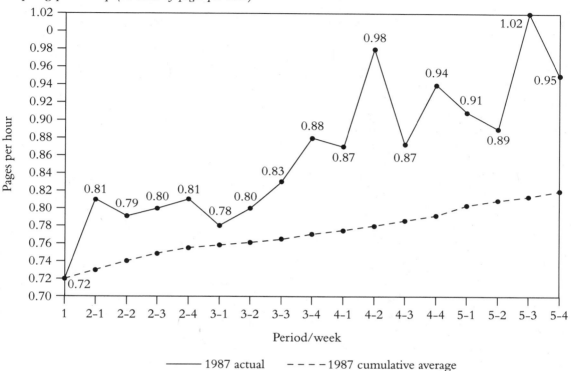

Consistent with the emphasis on internal customer satisfaction, the second department in the production process, packaging, was involved in pulling random copies of newspapers at the start of each production run so that the pressroom management could grade them according to a published quality score sheet. For a given press, a work crew would select a second copy to grade, with these results averaged with those of the pressroom management. This enabled the press crew to work to improve their combined scores. Individual press scores were charted and averaged to determine pressroom-wide weekly press quality scores, which were used to make cumulative quarter-to-date averages that were posted in the pressroom and ultimately used to determine the amount of waste savings to which these employees and their supervisors contributed.

At the time we concluded our analysis, the results of these processes had been encouraging and rewarding for all concerned. Although ratios of productivity gains to wage gains are not available, initial awards for hourly employees represented a 10 percent bonus for the two-month launch period. Just prior to the plan's initiation, when productivity and quality "scorecards" were posted for the first press crew, other crews immediately requested their own—even before monetary rewards were announced. The principle underlying this, as taught during the management development segment of the change effort (and shown during Emery Air Freight's well-publicized experience in obtaining significant performance improvements), is that performance measurement systems indicate to workers what management considers important, and that one can expect performance to increase in response to offering workers appropriate feedback and rewards associated with performance.

As of the completion of our study, the pressroom was continuing to perform well within the "paydirt" parameters for productivity and quality (see Figure 1). If these performance levels persisted—which we have reason to believe they should have—by the year's end the employees would have realized related rewards equivalent to a 15 percent bonus above their base pay. Related contributions to budget plan cost per ton—and hence to the company's bottom line—were significant. Employees in other Freedom Center production departments were completing their own self-funding incentive plans at that time, as expected.

We wish to note that, a week after the first bonus check was cut, quality scores reached 98.5 percent (during some press runs scores of 99.44 percent were obtained). These are significantly better than the industrywide theoretical maximum score of 97 percent, which is based on the assumption that 3 percent waste is normal for a press start-up. Moreover, newsprint utilization scores averaged 90.2 percent.

Discussion

The future of North American organizations continues to be characterized by global competition and a related search for world-class levels of excellence (Peters & Waterman, 1982). Compelling research evidence (e.g., Bennis & Nanus, 1985; Peters & Austin, 1985; Peters & Waterman, 1982) suggests that corporations can increase their odds of competitive success when they develop internal corporate cultures that emphasize human values and human processes and recognize the dignity of individual employees. Such processes promote leadership that provides meaning and inspiration to those expected to be

followers, focus on *measuring results* as a means of directing energies and resources toward both products and customers, and demonstrate that motivation for improving bottom-line results can emerge from development at the individual, group, and organizational levels. Several important factors identified in the recent literature on "excellence" include purpose, vision, alignment, leadership, measured results, system structure, personal power, teamwork, customer needs, and the integration of intuition and reason.

Corporate leaders seem increasingly eager to develop more efficient procedures by using the latest available management techniques (Davis, 1988), such as decision support systems. These, however, will not likely mean much to employees who seek inspiration and respond only to that which affects their personal and financial growth. Peters and Waterman (1982) summed this up in their comment that we should not place too much emphasis on markets, because "Markets don't buy products, people do." For example, most rank-and-file employees would not likely be motivated by management's consideration of democratic capitalism versus return on investment, but would understandably be more stimulated by appeals to their self-esteem, spirit, growth, and survival.

To the extent that a vision without a foundation is only a daydream, we management scholars must ensure that our visions of organizations of the future are well grounded in clear, integrated action steps permitting measurable outcomes. A well-conceived, well-grounded vision of what the organization seeks to become, which we found at the *Chicago Tribune,* is the cornerstone of a fast-tracking transformation effort. Such a vision becomes the "master template" through which participants in the transformation process can—individually and collectively—assess and modify their efforts. The vision's goals, combined with a clear performance management system that links rewards with performance, can foster coordination and the will to achieve the desired future for the organization.

The transformation process described in this

article and illustrated by the *Tribune*'s Freedom Center project is a powerful means of providing such grounding and encouraging its use in other organizations. We wonder, however, about the curious dynamic between crisis and growth. Must crises precede growth—as was the case for the *Tribune*—or can an organization achieve far-reaching, beneficial change without this being externally driven (Greiner, 1972)? Certainly, research is needed to determine how executives and management consultants can encourage dramatic change *without* needing the creative burst of energy generated by dissatisfaction.

Proven OD interventions, such as team building, served the *Tribune* by integrating other segments of the transformation effort as they helped both individuals and work groups work cohesively, systematically, and with a focus on results. This in turn helped align management's internalized philosophy and practices with the pursuit of the vision through performance management.

The *Tribune*'s Freedom Center story constitutes both an ending and a beginning. Thousands of organizations like the Freedom Center need transformation, but, unfortunately, most will never initiate this because their top managers lack the necessary vision. Instead, these organizations are more likely to launch numerous projects with fanfare and enthusiasm, only to see them die for lack of comprehensive, integrated change strategies (Lawler, 1983; Walton, 1985). Dedicated, astute management consultants can provide valuable service to the organizations of the future by primarily helping top managers see and follow their visions of what their organizations are capable of becoming.

Creating excellence by fine-tuning a change and development effort can be difficult (Pate & Greiner, 1989). This task becomes even harder when the issue is that of resurrecting a dead change effort. Integrating transformation techniques, even in organizations such as the *Tribune* that have faced crisis as an antecedent condition, can empower firms to turn crises into opportunities. This article demonstrates that the results in terms of performance and savings can be significant.

Certainly, various organizational, change agent, and intervention variables influence the results of an intervention program (Pate, 1979), and we do not intend to overstate the importance of the consultant or to self-aggrandize the role consultants play. In the case of the *Chicago Tribune*, such factors as the union situation, the status of the 1,000 replacement workers, the elimination of restrictive work practices and featherbedding, changes in equipment and process technology, and new manufacturing structures influenced the results we report. Obviously, changes occurred in the workforce management policies, but we do not know the extent to which the organization altered its production and inventory control systems, cost and other information systems, make/buy decision-making processes, and facilities (i.e., the number, size, location, or capacity). Our point is that we can readily indicate the more significant changes and cost savings that the *Tribune* experienced, but some ambiguity exists as to causality. The paradox is that although much research must be done on the dynamics of the transformation process so as to determine causality or to generalize our findings to other settings, the consultant as artist is the one who will interpret these results as a statement of possibilities, and who will weave the threads within them to create additional tapestries of excellence.

Notes

1. The *Chicago Tribune* is sensitive, as one might understand, about disclosing important financial information. Thus we had to "generalize downward" some of the cost savings reported beyond merely changing the vertical scale numbers. The savings following the change effort were actually *greater* than indicated in the figures in this article. Moreover, as of this writing, arbitration efforts with the unions are still taking place, preventing us from further elaborating on the details of the strike.

2. About 140–150 candidates initially applied for

the supervisor positions, and more than 90 percent of these persons participated throughout the assessment process. When they submitted their applications, candidates were told that the assessment process would be taken quite seriously, that selections would not be based on political considerations, and that the process would necessarily require considerable time and effort. Approximately 12 candidates (fewer than 10 percent) chose to withdraw their applications from consideration, and thus were not included in subsequent assessments.

References

Argyris, C. *Intervention Theory and Method: A Behavioral Science View.* Reading, MA: Addison-Wesley, 1970.

Argyris, C. *Behind the Front Page: Organizational Self-Renewal in a Metropolitan Newspaper.* San Francisco: Jossey-Bass, 1974.

Beckhard, R., & Harris, R. T. *Organizational Transitions: Managing Complex Change.* Reading, MA: Addison-Wesley, 1977.

Bennis, W. G. *Organization Development: Its Nature, Origins and Prospects.* Reading, MA: Addison-Wesley, 1969.

Bennis, W. G., & Nanus, B. *Leaders.* New York: Harper & Row, 1985.

Coonradt, C. A. *The Game of Work.* Salt Lake City: Shadow Mountain Press, 1985.

Davis, M. W. *Applied Decision Support.* Englewood Cliffs, NJ: Prentice Hall, 1988.

Deming, W. E. *Quality, Productivity and Competitive Position.* Boston: MIT Center for Engineering Studies, 1982.

Drucker, P. F. *The New Frontiers of Management.* New York: E. P. Dutton, 1986.

Greiner, L. E. "Evolution and Revolution as Organizations Grow." *Harvard Business Review,* July–August 1972, pp. 37–46.

Greiner, L. E., & Schein, V. E. *Power and Organization development.* Reading, MA: Addison-Wesley, 1988.

Hickman, C. R., & Silva, M. A. *Creating Excellence: Managing Corporate Culture, Strategy and Change in the New Age.* London: Unwin, 1986.

Hope, J. W., & Pate, L. E. "A Cognitive-Expectancy Analysis of Compliance Decisions." *Human Relations* 41 (1988), pp. 739–51.

Kerr, S. (1975). "On the Folly of Rewarding A, While Hoping for B." *Academy of Management Journal,* 18 (1975), pp. 769–83.

Lawler, E. E. *Pay and Organizational Effectiveness: A Psychological View.* New York: McGraw-Hill, 1971.

Lawler, E. E. *Pay and Organization Development.* Reading, MA: Addison-Wesley, 1981.

Lawler, E. E. "Human Resource Productivity in the 80's." *New Management* (1983), pp. 46–49.

Lippitt, G. L. *Organization Renewal: A Holistic Approach to Organization Development* 2nd ed. Englewood Cliffs, NJ: Prentice Hall, 1982.

Nora, J. J., & Stramy, R. J. *Transforming the Workplace.* Princeton Research Press, 1986.

Pate, L. E. (1979). Development of the OCIR Model of the intervention process. *Academy of Management Review,* 4 (1979), pp. 281–86.

Pate, L. E., & Greiner, L. E. (1989). "Invited Commentary: Resolving Dilemmas in Power and OD with the Four ACES Technique." *Consultation: An International Journal,* 8, no. 1 (1989), pp. 58–67.

Pate, L. E., & Nielsen, W. R. (1987). "Integrating Management Development into a Large-Scale System-wide Change Programme." *Journal of Management Development* 6, no. 5 (1987), pp. 16–30.

Peters, T., & Austin, N. *A Passion for Excellence: The Leadership Difference.* New York: Random House, 1985.

Peters, T., & Waterman, R. H. *In Search of Excellence: Lessons from America's Best-run Companies.* New York: Harper & Row, 1982.

Schein, E. H. *Process Consultation: Its Role in Organization Development.* Reading, Mass.: Addison-Wesley, 1969.

Walton, R. E. "From Control to Commitment in the Workplace." *Harvard Business Review,* March–April 1985, pp. 76–84.

B. Issues and Challenges

Organization development and organization transformation are beset with issues and challenges that will greatly challenge practitioners and scholars in the years ahead. This is partly because it is a young field only now approaching the second generation, and undoubtedly partly because of its eclectic nature.

Contemporary OD practice borrows from social psychology, counseling psychology, organization theory, family group therapy, human resources management, group dynamics, management and administration, and other disciplines. Any attempt at an amalgamation of insights from such a spectrum of fields to develop effective interventions for ongoing organizations is bound to create many challenges. For example, how nondirective can the OD consultant afford to be if the client is talking about establishing benefits or privileges in one group without being cognizant of potential perceived inequities by other groups? Counseling psychology has something to say about the utility of a supportive nondirective consultation style, but human resources management and social psychology have something to say about cognitive dissonance and inequity. Reconciling the two conflicting action implications may be difficult in such a situation. What is the optimal mix of the source of authority in a given organization in terms of authority based on expertise, authority based on position, and authority based on group consensus? Organization theory, "principles of management," and group dynamics may have insights about such matters that are not easily reconciled. How does OD relate to various movements or contemporary areas of emphasis like "quality of work life" or the learning organization? Is OD the same thing? Different? How can one articulate the differences or similarities? What are the dangers in not doing so?

But OD and OT practice are also beset with many problems and issues because they inevitably affects people's lives, and sometimes deeply. We would like to think that people are usually affected positively, and we believe this to be so; but questions of ethics, of values, of what is helpful and what is hurtful, must and do arise. How much manipulation is there in the particular OD intervention in the particular context; that is, to what extent is there a hidden agenda in the use of the intervention, or to what extent is the nature of the technique or its consequences kept from the participants? What should be the depth of an intervention in order to be both efficacious and at the same time not harmful? Should the consultant attempt to interpret and surface resistances? Under what circumstances is feedback constructive? How much can, or should, the OD consultant be aligned with the exercise of power in the organization? What should the OD consultant's training be? And how does one know when a consultant is qualified to practice? These are not simple matters.

Other issues have to do with the relationship of OD to culture. For example, what forms of OD bring about a deep change in the culture of an organization and what forms result in only modest changes in organizational functioning?

Some of these issues have been discussed earlier in the book; for example, issues centering on the depth of intervention and the interpretation of resistances. In this section of the book we conclude our overview of OD by presenting seven essays that examine a number of additional key issues about the present and future state of OD and OT.

The first reading is by Warren R. Nielsen, Nick Nykodym, and Don J. Brown, who emphasize that along with the pressures for change in this decade also come critical questions regarding the ethics of change, which must be acknowledged and confronted by those involved in the change process.

The second short article is a concise statement by William Gellermann on the values of OD–HSD professionals. He describes fundamental values, personal and interpersonal values, and systems values.

The third selection, by Robert Golembiewski, Carl Proehl, and David Sink, is a thorough and comprehensive review of the OD research literature. The authors analyzed 574 studies conducted over a 35-year period to determine the types of OD programs in use and the effects of those programs. Their results are promising: a wide variety of programs are in use; OD efforts have been directed toward both public sector and private sector organizations; and positive results were found in the vast majority of programs with very few negative effects reported. Reviews such as this are very useful for taking stock of where OD is as a field and pointing the way toward needed future research efforts.

In the fourth reading, Lawrence M. Baytos addresses perhaps the most important topic in the future organization—the challenges and opportunities associated with managing a culturally diverse workforce.

The fifth selection, by Michael Beer and Elise Walton, is a detailed description of how to develop the competitive organization. The authors take the reader on a journey from changing the old culture (unfreezing) to introducing the new culture, and then on to sustaining the change program with all of the predictable and unpredictable problems.

The sixth article, by Richard W. Beatty and David O. Ulrich, discusses one of the key challenges of this decade—how to re-energize the mature organization. During the past four decades since WWII, many organization's grew, reached maturity, and then began to decline. This article describes the necessary steps to take after downsizing (people) to motivate the remaining people to design an organization for the future that will have a sustained competitive advantage.

The final article, by Henry Mintzberg, continues to build on the theme in the above reading, and he comments on the forces that will shape the organization of the future. He advocates a contingency approach to structure and believes the structure that will be most effective in the future is one that can adopt to changing internal forces and the changing external environment.

READING 48
ETHICS AND ORGANIZATIONAL CHANGE

Warren R. Nielsen, Nick Nykodym, and Don J. Brown

Introduction

Within the United States we are seeing the demise of once large and powerful organizations; the rapid birth, growth and death of many high technologically oriented organizations; large numbers of mergers in an attempt to diversify or generate a stronger financial base; the introduction of, and growth of franchises offering some market stability; and the attack on the once unquestioned military/industrial complexes.

With these changes in society and organizations have come numerous individuals, groups, and fields of study, which offer assistance to organizations in both managing and instigating internal change. The successes, failures, contributions, and inadequacies of management consulting in providing organizations with methodology and technology to improve organizational effectiveness and health and improve the quality of work life for employees have been reviewed in the literature for nearly 20 years.

In any approach there are a number of ethical issues which have been previously considered by Walton and Warwick (1973), Miles (1979), Frame, Hess, and Nielsen (1982), the OD Institute (1985), Nykodym, Nielsen, and Christen (1985), and Nykodym, Ruud, and Liverpool (1986). Unfortunately, many involved in the field of organizational change have been so busy

Note: The authors would like to acknowledge the comments of two anonymous reviewers and those of Larry Pate, Colleen Bement, and Rachel Call on previous drafts of this paper.

Source: Warren R. Nielsen, Nick Nykodym, and Don J. Brown, "Ethics and Organizational Change," *Asia Pacific Journal of Human Resources*, Autumn 1991, pp. 82–93. Reprinted with permission.

collecting data for research, attempting to have a positive impact so consulting operations may continue; or trying to develop and implement new change strategies, that little real attention has been paid to the ethical issues involved in the process of change.

The purpose of this paper is threefold: first, to review the ethical issues which have already been raised; second, to outline some new considerations which have developed over the past few years; and finally, to make some suggestions relative to the ethics of organization change for both the researcher and the practitioner.

In drawing attention to ethical issues already raised, an attempt to not re-invent the wheel will be made by drawing upon Walton and Warwick (1973), Miles (1979), and the OD Institute (1985). The framework used to specify the issues will be to separate them into issues faced before, during, and after the application of any change intervention(s).

Before Intervention

A major ethical issue facing those involved in organizational change is actually engaging in a discussion of the ethics that will provide the overall parameters within which the client, practitioner, or researcher will act. Such action appears to be relatively simple, but experience to date would indicate that it is seldom done. Too often ethical issues are raised during the project, frequently in a conflict situation, when major work must be set aside until differences are resolved. Even whole projects which had great potential for positive impact on organizational effectiveness, health, and quality of work life have been discontinued because of ethical issues between clients, practitioners, and researchers not dealt with before the project began. It may be that some of those involved in organizational change may be reluctant to openly examine the change objectives of the practitioner because of fear that the client would not be willing to proceed if they were known. On the other hand, it may be that the client's ethics regarding change are not examined because of the belief that the change process itself will change them sufficiently so that they will be consistent with the project and/or the underlying values and beliefs of the strategy being applied.

By far the most important ethical issue that should be dealt with before any change strategy is implemented is that of defining the goals, behavioral outcomes, or expected change objectives. Those involved in the field of organizational change are, at times, painfully aware of the vague unspecified goals used to launch an organization change effort. Probably, over the years, most practitioners have been, at one time or another, so anxious to get a major project started and underway that they have deluded themselves and their clients that the work is an 'emerging' process and that the goals will become clear as more and more is learned regarding the organization. Though it would be foolish to imply that all goals could be established before the change process is undertaken, it would be a breach of ethics to not do everything possible to insure that the client and practitioner know where the change process is likely to lead. Too often, attempts at organizational change appear as the proverbial "Christopher Columbus voyage." Kubr (1986) emphasizes the need for the client and consultant to define the problem together. The clients, immersed in the situation, may be too involved to see the problem objectively. Consultants will make greater progress if they work directly with the client on problem definition. From this basis, clients and consultants will be able to effectively work together to clarify what results are desired from the consulting process.

Another critical issue is that of who will be involved in the establishment of the goals and behavioral objectives. Walton and Warwick (1973), Miles (1979), and the OD Institute (1985) all warn of not solely relying on the higher level managers and administrators to establish the goals. They argue that, since most organizational participants could, at some time, be dramatically impacted by the process, those lower in the organization should also have input. Philosophically, it is difficult to argue with such a position, particularly given the underlying values of the field of organizational change. The difficulty with this issue is the ability to get real involvement on the part of all participants, particularly if the change project is in a very large system. When the authors first began working with one large automotive corporation, that organization employed over one million individuals. To even take a sample of what the employees believed should be the goals would have been a major undertaking and would have taken so long that the change effort would never have been undertaken. Also, in some organizations in which unions exist, and where there is a strong adversarial relationship, consultants and researchers may not be permitted to talk to employees at lower levels.

The authors' feeble solution to this issue is to start with overall goals developed primarily by the top, but with an agreement that new, though consistent goals would be established as each new part of the organization becomes involved. Also, in large projects, we have built in provisions for goal review and modification on at least a quarterly basis. As we have struggled with this issue, we found ourselves coming to the position that as many of the participants as possible should be involved in setting goals; however, the value of high involvement must be considered against the possibility of the occurrence of more serious organizational problems developing during the goal-setting process. To move quickly on goals established by only part of the organization and to have positive impact on the organizational variables that will insure a positive position and provide greater flexibility may be more ethical than attempting to involve the entire organization (at least at the beginning) in the goal-setting process.

Another issue that needs to be considered is that of the process utilized to determine the initial targets for intervention. Should top management make the decision or should it be made with input from the rest of the organization? If people have input there is more support; however, given certain information and perspective, the top may, in fact, be in a better position to establish the target area. The size of the organization also affects this dilemma. In a small organization, it may be relatively easy to get input from all potentiall participants; whereas, in a large organization, this is much more difficult. In either case, the issue needs to be discussed and the reasons for how an area is selected should be made very clear.

Prior to the activation of a change process in any organization, the practitioner or researcher should confront some very personal ethical questions such as:

- What are my own personal values, and how will they impact on this project?
- What are my skills and abilities, and are they sufficient to promote the required change?
- Am I willing to accept the responsibility for the consequences of my decisions and acts upon the organization?
- Am I willing to share all "need to know" data with the client?

It is the authors' perception that the whole field of organizational change would be more effective and would have had a greater positive impact on organizations over the past 20 years had these questions been asked and dealt with honestly. It should be noted, however, that clients can also put pressure on change practitioners to accept and direct projects which are beyond their

skill level. The authors are acquainted with a current case where the external consultant does superb team building and has a very positive image with the division management group of a particular manufacturing corporation. This consultant, because of the relationship, was forced upon the management of one of the corporation's assembly plants by division management. The assembly plant, if it is to continue, requires an extensive sociotechnical transformation. Unfortunately, the plant is now involved in a great deal of team building which will likely have little, if any, impact on the real problems of the organization. In addition, the plant has been given a three-year period to move from a negative to a positive position in nearly every measurable organizational performance indicator. If such a turnaround does not occur, the facility is to be sold. The sale of the facility could result in the termination of approximately 4,000 employees.

Another issue that needs to be clarified prior to the initiation of a change project is the projected costs involved. For this issue to be adequately dealt with, the practitioner needs to be very clear with the prospective client regarding fees, travel expenses, material costs, and lost-time cost for participants who will have to be away from their normal work assignments. Currently the authors are involved in a project in Mexico where the travel expenses far exceed the daily fees. Fortunately, the possibility of this situation occurring was openly discussed and agreed to prior to the initiation of the project.

Another crucial issue facing the field of organizational change is that of claims made by practitioners and, to some degree, researchers. Unfortunately, there are few descriptions of failures in the literature, but most practitioners and researchers know of at least several. Too often, those interested in the field, and prospective clients, are faced with the problem of exaggerated claims relative to the viability of organizational change methodologies. If the claims had been more realistic, would the field today have greater credibility in the eyes of prospective clients?

Also, would there be more opportunities of learning how to change organizations had the exaggerated claims not led to the demise of many projects? The authors have found high-level managers and administrators more willing to experiment when they were aware, prior to the beginning of a project, that untested interventions and methods were to be utilized.

Miles (1979) and the OD Institute (1985) raise the issue that all organizational participants should have a choice in launching an organizational change process. They argue that all participants should have full information relative to outcomes and costs prior to committing to a full-scale organizational change project. As with the development of change goals, an ethical statement or position such as this sounds appropriate, but becomes very difficult to accomplish in an organization of any size. Certainly, an attempt to keep everyone up to date through the use of newsletters, group meetings, etc., can and should be made. However, in a large organization the process is likely to be weak at best and may break down and become a deterrent, rather than a help. No doubt, most practitioners and some researchers would question the validity of trying to inform all organization participants prior to intervention and may argue that, to do so, might generate expectations or resistance which could not be dealt with adequately. Many of those involved in change strategies argue for intervening into the organization one part at a time. There may be cases where informing the whole organization could be disruptive to the specific project.

Because change projects can go very well or very poorly, depending on numerous situations, circumstances, and decisions, a specific question needs to be raised for the protection of both the client and practitioner,—"How can the relationship be discontinued?" The authors have very strong feelings that, if a project is going very poorly, due to reasons outside the consultant's control, the consultant should not be forced to continue an effort which is clearly doomed. On the other hand, the client should not have to continue an effort which is seen as harmful to the organization, its employees, and cash flow. Based on the above, the authors always utilize a contract which allows either party to withdraw with a 30-day written notice. The result has been a greater level of trust between the parties and an assurance that both will genuinely try to make the project a success.

During the Activity

As is the case before intervening in a system to produce change, once a project is launched ethical issues arise which need to be recognized and dealt with by both practitioners and researchers.

Relative to issues during a change project, Walton and Warwick (1973), Miles (1979), and the OD Institute (1985) all focus on the collection and use of data which is obtained from organizational participants. They raise such questions as:

- What data are collected?
- What format is utilized?
- What happens to the data?
- Who gets the data?
- Is the autonomy of the providers protected?

There are still pertinent ethical questions that need to be asked and resolved prior to the collection of any data. There is no question that data can be used to punish organizational participants, and steps must be placed in the process to help prevent such behavior. On the other hand, it is possible that the questions above reflect an old bias from the days of sensitivity training and the use of team-building models which were very interpersonal in nature. In today's setting, some slightly different questions need to be asked, such as:

- Will the data be collected and processed in such a manner that the source(s) of problems can be recognized?

- Will the data be given to individuals who can best solve the problems?
- Will the format used facilitate an understanding of the data (allowing those who furnished the data to explain what it means)?
- Will the format facilitate the obtaining of further data which could more specifically define the problems?

Surely practitioners and researchers must be beyond the point of collecting data where anonymity is guaranteed, and the data are processed solely for the review by upper-management personnel who can make little sense of the data and have great difficulty in trying to resolve any issues that may be contained therein.

A few years ago, the authors were involved in a major organizational change project with a large engineering organization. The organization employed nearly 3,000 engineers and support personnel and was part of a multinational corporation. The project was directed by a steering committee made up of individuals from all levels and functions. The steering committee wanted to collect some data utilizing a format which would insure that the data could be acted on. The result was a survey instrument designed to identify data by work group and through which the providers of the data could explain their perceptions and be involved in problem resolution. The survey also provided an opportunity for the respondents to sign the questionnaire if they so desired. All of the employees were brought into a meeting where the purpose of the format of the survey was explained and questions could be asked. The participants were told that problems could only be solved if it was possible to discern the location of the problems, and the individuals in those areas had an opportunity to develop and implement solutions. The survey was given out and each employee was asked to complete the form and mail it to the consultant's office several states away. We have always believed that it was very significant that 100 percent of the questionnaires were returned, and 95 percent were signed.

The point of the above illustration is that the wrong questions relative to data may be being asked. Rather than asking, "Will anonymity be protected?" the question should be, "Will the data make it possible for the organization to act on and solve problems, whether they be technical, social or interpersonal?"

Another issue that is raised, but often ignored, is that of—"Who is the client?" Most change practitioners and researchers are brought in, given access to various aspects of the organization, and paid by the senior management of the organization. Argyris (1970) and Beckhard (1969) take the position that a change effort should, in fact, be directed by the top of the organization. On the other hand, Kubr (1986) realizes that those whose work will be affected by the change process should also be taken into consideration. While guidance from upper-level management is necessary, implementation will require cooperation of the workers. Walton and Warwick (1973) also raise the issue as to the freedom of individuals to participate in the change process. They discuss the necessity of informed consent, lack of coercion, lack of manipulation, and avoiding the misuse of data. Though these issues may be relevant, they again seem to apply more to the highly interpersonal interventions of the past. As change consultants attempt, as they are now, to facilitate large-scale systems change, these issues seem to fade somewhat. In fact, if large-scale systems change is to be accomplished, all organizational participants must participate in the process and cannot have the option of sitting on the sidelines and watching. Also, there simply may not be sufficient time to insure every individual the freedom of choice in the change process.

One model for dealing with some of these issues has been initiated in the General Motors Corporation (GM) where the change teams consist both of salaried employees and employees represented by the United Auto Workers Union

(UAW). Before launching change projects at any particular location, there is an agreement that approval will be given both by GM and the UAW. This model may have great potential in dealing with the issue of freedom of participation; however, it has not been in place a sufficient length of time to determine the real results and impact.

Another issue which has particularly faced practitioners using primarily interpersonal change models has been whether the client system is really interested in change or just the achievement of stability. If the practitioner is restricted to interpersonal models, real change is unlikely to occur (Pate 1979). This being the case, the practitioner could be entrapped into a situation where the real reason for the project is to appease or mollify employees in the organization. Therefore, two factors appear to be critical. First, the practitioner and client must come to a firm agreement that actual change is the goal, and its achievement is to be monitored on a regular basis throughout the project. Second, the project must be so designed that it is not limited to a single organizational variable. Given the interdependencies between organizational variables, work on one area may produce short-run change, but in the long run the organization will most likely return to its prior condition or state.

While working as consultants within a large U.S. insurance firm, the authors became aware of a particular situation which was most troubling and appeared to be a major issue of ethics in organizational change. As change consultants, we were becoming so enthralled with the process of change that we were actually pushing the client system into a position of overplanning and overintervening. The question of how the organizational participants could plan and implement major change and, at the same time, continue the accomplishment of regular tasks and processes, was not asked. As the project continued, it became apparent that pushing the organization to change too many things at one time was lead-

ing to failure. In this situation, organizational participants who genuinely wanted to plan for and initiate change were becoming overloaded to the point where they gave up on change plans and went back to doing only their normally assigned tasks. The ethic then is: *Don't push an organization for more change than that which can be handled within the organization's parameters and constraints.* This is not to say that, in a large transformation effort, normal tasks and duties may not be set aside completely and total attention, time, and skills given to the change effort.

The practitioners must assist those ultimately responsible for the change process to establish specific but attainable goals and priorities within realistic time periods. In addition, these goals, priorities, and time frames need to be carefully monitored to insure that there is consistency between goals and the organization's ability to attain those goals.

The argument has repeatedly been made that an organization is an open system and, therefore, change methodologies and technologies must be based on a systems approach. Unfortunately, an examination of consulting projects (Pate, Nielsen, & Bacon, 1977) shows little evidence that a systems approach to organization change has been utilized. Most projects have focused on one or two variables at the most. In working with client systems, the authors have used a particular descriptive model of organizations to assist those directing the change process in recognizing all the variables which will require anywhere from major change to slight modification. The model is illustrated in Figure 1.

Using the model with clients has helped to insure that a systems approach is taken and that sufficient variables are changed which will, in turn, produce real measurable organizational change.

As a project moves down through an organization, particularly one of any size, another serious question with major ethical implications must be asked and answered. The question is— "How much say will those who are directly or

FIGURE 1

Interaction of organizational variables

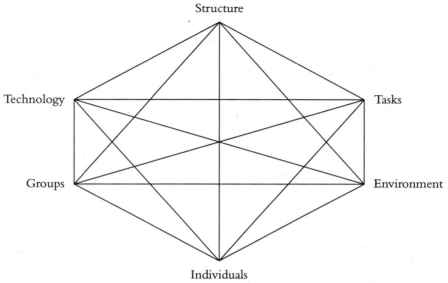

SOURCE: Frame, Hess, and Nielsen. *The OD Source Book,* 1982.

even indirectly affected by the change(s) have in the direction of the change?" It would appear as though this concern is currently being more appropriately dealt with by consultants than in the past. Most current projects with which the authors are familiar, require and have built-in mechanisms to involve organizational participants in planning and directing the required change at their level. Again, the joint GM/UAW consulting team is a good illustration of getting all levels of an organization involved and participating in the process. One of the most significant factors in the design of GM's highly acclaimed Saturn project was the extensive planning involvement of the manufacturing facility system and culture, by individuals from all organizational levels.

The last issue which needs to be mentioned is that of the length of the project itself and how long the organization will need to rely on out-side resources. One of the original purposes of organizational change consulting was to build an organization capable of continually monitoring the need for and initiating appropriate change to respond to changing environments. The ethic of assisting the organization in its attempts to change, but not building dependent relationships, still seems appropriate today. Greiner and Metzger (1983) point out that dependency between the client and the consultant is inherent in long-term relationships. The client depends on the consultant's availability and advice, and the consultant depends on a steady income. But when the consultant begins doing work that could be performed by the client, or when the consultant depends solely on the client for income, the situation is unhealthy and should be discontinued. Kubr (1986) emphasizes that consultants can cause problems by both leaving too early or terminating too late, and that they should discuss withdrawal with the client before intervention and continue discussions periodically throughout the assignment.

After Major Change Interventions

If those who intervene in organizations for the purpose of producing real organizational change have faced and adequately dealt with the ethical issues prior to and during the effort, there are few issues left once the practitioner has left the system. Having said this though, there are some issues that need to be considered by both practitioners and researchers.

One such issue was raised by Miles (1979)— that being possible harm occurring to individuals who have participated in the project. It appears that practitioners who have been in this field for any length of time have made a real effort not to have change strategies primarily utilized for the purpose of reducing headcount, or simply implementing plans which enable fewer people to do more work, thus creating an excess of employees who are subject to employee reductions. Unfortunately, this issue may not be raised prior to intervening in a system and assurances obtained from top management that reduction of employees would not be the primary goal of the change activity. If practitioners are successful in improving the organization, there may well be less employees required, and individuals who lack necessary skills may be identified. In the past, this problem was primarily experienced at the lower levels of organizations; but as practitioners and consultants have become more proficient, the impact of change strategies, as noted by Naisbitt and Aburdene (1985), is being felt by large numbers of middle managers. A conclusion that may be drawn is that, when starting change projects, practitioners and researchers should insist that this issue be brought into the open and that the organizations involved develop and implement effective out-placement programs or changes in retirement programs so that a poten-

tial reduction in force is not a devastating experience for organizational participants.

The second issue noted, which has ethical ramifications, is that of unintended negative results. An illustration may serve to clarify this point. Several years ago the authors were involved in a change effort in a large manufacturing firm with approximately 5,000 employees. The early stages of the project were focused primarily on the production manager and his immediate staff. Through the change activities, the production group became more and more effective and more organizationally powerful. The effect was that other interdependent departments began to interact less and less with the production group. The other departments felt powerless in relation to the production management team and, out of fear, decreased the necessary interaction and supply of services to them. The answer to this problem may be considerably oversimplified, but it appears as though, if potential negative consequences are identified and discussed, plans can be developed to avoid or reduce them.

The problem which has continued to cause the authors the greatest concern over the years is that of working with an organization, seeing great benefits come from the effort, and then, from a distance, watching the organization revert back to previous patterns and outcomes. One such project has been of particular concern. In brief summary: through a great deal of work, the authors, with other outside consultants, were able to bring a major function of one of the world's largest corporations from the position of being the worst to the best on every performance measure and to significantly assist in obtaining a $14 million saving. Unfortunately, today the function has lost at least 50 percent of the gain obtained. The issue that must be dealt with is that of maintenance. Those involved in organizational change could be subject to criticism for not including actions and procedures which adequately maintain and protect gains.

The way in which the authors have attempted

to deal with this dilemma is not to accept contracts which do not include the assurance from top management that an appropriate number of internal resource personnel will be hired or trained to work with the authors and to assure the necessary follow up and maintenance.

One final concern is directed at those involved in research and evaluation. The field of organizational change continues to lack appropriate evaluation and assessment. Data regarding success or failure continues to be primarily anecdotal in nature. Closely controlled, rigorous studies are needed if practitioners are to be able to evaluate their effectiveness, make necessary modifications, and develop new interventions and strategies. Kubr (1986) proposes that evaluation of the consultation process should be a joint effort between client and consultant. He points out that by evaluating specific benefits to the client, such as new capabilities, new systems, and behavior, and new performance, interpretations of the outcome become clearer. Evaluations are also needed which do not stop after one intervention measurement. Evaluations are desperately needed which track the impact of our work with organizations over a significant time.

Current Issues

As mentioned at the beginning of this paper, most companies and industries in the United States are facing the critical need to change quickly. In the last few years, once-strong organizations have disappeared and whole industries have become very weak because of their inability to compete with both domestic and foreign entities. This environmental condition has raised questions for which solutions are required.

First, those involved in changing organizations must focus on more than the human variable. Though few would argue that the human variable is extremely important in the total change process, this is not the only variable which must be changed. Therefore, if practitioners, executives, and researchers are to be successful, they must have skills in dealing with and changing many organizational variables simultaneously. Therefore, three of the current ethical questions that need to be asked by practitioners, consultants, and researchers are:

- Am I ready and do I have the skills to work with numerous variables?
- Am I prepared to obtain and utilize support of other professionals in areas of the change project where I lack the necessary skills?
- If we take on projects without the necessary skills in this new environment, are we being ethical relative to clients, organizational participants, communities, and maybe even societies?

Second, foreign competition has become so fierce that U.S. organizations, if they are to survive, must change and change quickly. This very need for speed in the change process brings current needs into conflict with some of the older ethical statements, such as that everyone in the organization should be informed of the process so they can "have" free choice in terms of participating. A particular ethical issue that may supersede the above mentioned is:

"Am I, as a consultant, researcher, or manager, prepared to do as much as possible in a short time frame to enable organizations and, possibly whole industries to survive?"

Third, whereas ethical concerns of the past have focused primarily upon the organization involved in the change process, growing interdependencies are mandating a broader view. The issue of the potential impact of change interventions on communities, geographical areas, other organizations, and society need to be acknowledged. In addition, as change efforts are initiated which involve multiple organizations and possibly whole industries, the following ethical question needs to be asked: "*Are organizational change practitioners helping to establish new ethics and values in society, and is that their role?"*

Certainly we are bringing about value shifts without getting input from all those impacted upon by our work.

Fourth, organizational change, in the past, has been a relatively slow, deliberate process. Practitioners were facilitators and operated primarily out of a nondirective model. However, the question that can now be raised as the need for fast and extensive change becomes more and more the need of organizations is: *"Is it ethical to hold on to the nondirective philosophy?"*

It may be possible that the ethical question now is whether or not the practitioner has the skills and is ready to provide facilitative content, as well as expert roles. The authors' recent experience would indicate that organizations recognize the need for process consultants, but, because of external pressures for change, need consultants who can also function in the task and expert arenas.

Fifth, current organizational change requirements are pushing those involved in the field to not just talk about systems approaches but to actually use system models in their change activities. No longer can having done team building or conducted experiential training in all parts of the organization be, in any way, considered a systems approach.

Sixth, there is a growing need for consulting teams made up of individuals who are particularly trained to provide options for impacting on specific variables. The question to be asked is: *"Is a change team being utilized which provides for dealing with and impacting on several variables simultaneously?"*

Seventh, overall change strategies with goals, objectives, time frames, change targets, responsibilities, and assessment methods must be developed and utilized. OD practitioners and consultants have had the luxury, in the past, of implementing one phase of a change effort and then determining the next phase or steps. Given the enormous pressure on organizations, a one step at a time process is inconsistent with the needs. This is not to say that flexibility and a commitment to appropriate modification through the change process should be abandoned. However, to enter into a major organizational change effort with a change strategy is, indeed, unethical.

Suggestions and Conclusions

In conclusion, the authors offer a series of suggestions to both the practitioner and the researcher. This is not intended to be an exhaustive list but, rather, a small base upon which others might build.

Relative to practitioners, seven suggestions are offered. First, be aware of and sensitive to the ethical issues in the field of organizational change, as well as the source and strength of these issues. Second, include a discussion and obtain agreement from the client relative to the ethics which will guide the change effort. Third, recognize that the ethics and ethical questions of the past may not fit the current need for rapid and extensive change and that new ethics are emerging. Fourth, discard old variable change models. They may have fit and produced positive results in the past, but are totally inadequate in our current environment. Fifth, insist on more assessment of the impact of interventions. The field of organizational change has once again moved into a time frame where new interventions and approaches are being developed, utilized, and nearly being marketed as the "cure-all" answer to the problems of change. As practitioners and consultants, do not allow a repeat of the past by becoming dependent on anecdotes and continuing to use interventions that have little or no value. Sixth, develop and be able to use the skills necessary to build organizational change strategies. Seventh, stop talking about and begin to truly utilize systems models to produce actual and measurable organizational change.

To the researchers, the authors include some suggestions as well. Again, these are not offered as an exhaustive list but, rather, some areas which need work and which could lead to more and improved assessment. First, produce quality, valid research on organizational change in terms of impact on various variables, intervention effectiveness in accomplishing stated objectives, and identification of real and potential negative consequences as a result of change projects. Second, be willing to provide more than just assessment studies. Assist practitioners by becoming more familiar with organizations in order to provide useful input into the design and implementation of change projects. Third, provide comparison data on the impact of organizational change where different change strategies have been utilized. Fourth, develop longitudinal studies which will provide insights into why particular change projects remain viable and effective over time, while others diminish or die.

In conclusion, the field of organizational change is extremely value-laden. Clients, practitioners, and researchers come into change projects with both individual and organizational values. Interventions come out of values. Interventions in the organization are nearly always based on some value judgment, and the way our results are assessed is often the result of the researchers' value regarding what organizational measures should be assessed.

Those in the field of organizational change are being called upon more than ever to assist organizations to survive and become viable once again. What is done in organizations may have profound impact on society. Those involved in organizational change must acknowledge, deal with, and test the underlying ethics that affect every change project undertaken.

References

Argyris, E. *Intervention Theory and Method.* Reading, MA: Addison-Wesley, 1970.

Beckhard, R. *Organization Development: Strategies and Models.* Reading, Mass.: Addison-Wesley, 1969.

Bermant, G.; Kelman, H. C.; and Warwick, D. P. *The Ethics of Social Intervention.* Washington: Hemisphere, 1978.

Frame, R. M.; Hess, R. H.; and Nielsen, W. R. *The OD Source Book: A Practitioners Guide.* California: University Associates, 1982.

Greiner, L. E., and Metzger, R. O. *Consulting to Management.* Englewood Cliffs, NJ: Prentice Hall, 1983.

Kubr, M. *Management Consulting: A Guide to the Profession.* Geneva: International Labour Office, 1986.

Miles, M. B. "Ethical Issues in OD Interventions." *OD Practitioner* 2, no. 3 (1979).

Naisbett, J., and Aburdene, P. *Reinventing the Corporation.* New York: Warner Books, 1985.

Nykodym, N.; Nielsen, W. R.; & Christen, J. C. (1985) "Can Organizational Development Use Transactional Analysis?" *Transactional Analysis Journal* 15 (1985), pp. 278–84.

Nykodym, N.; Ruud, W. N.; & Liverpool, P. R. (1986) "Quality Circles: Will Transactional Analysis Improve Their Effectiveness?" *Transactional Analysis Journal* 16 (1986), pp. 182–87.

O.D. Institute. "A Statement of Values and Ethics for Professionals in Organization and Human System Development." Organization Development Institute, April 1985.

Pate, L. E. "A Longitudinal Study of the Intervention Process within an Insurance Firm Using Quasi-Experimental Research Designs." Unpublished thesis, University of Illinois, 1979.

Pate, L. E.; Nielsen, W. R.; and Bacon, P. C. "Advances in Research on Organization Development." In *Contemporary Issues in Human Resource Management.* Schuster F. E., Reston Publishing, 1980.

Walton, R. E., Warwick, D. P. "The Ethics of Organization Development." *Journal of Applied Behavioral Science* 9, no. 6 (1973), pp. 681–98.

READING 49
VALUES OF OD-HSD PROFFESIONALS

William Gellermann

Fundamental Values

- *Life and the quest for happiness*—people respecting, appreciating, and loving the experience of their own and others' being, while engaging in the search for and process of co-creating good life.
- *Freedom, responsibility, and self-control*—people experiencing their freedom, exercising it responsibly, and being in charge of themselves.
- *Justice*—people living lives whose results are fair and equitable.

Personal and Interpersonal Values

- *Human potential and empowerment*—people being healthy, aware of the fullness of their potential, realizing their power to bring that potential into being, growing into it, living it, and generally doing the best they can, both individually and collectively.
- *Respect, dignity, integrity, worth, and fundamental rights of individuals and other human systems*—people appreciating one another and their rights as human beings, including life, liberty, and the quest for happiness.
- *Authenticity, congruence, honesty and openness, understanding and acceptance*—people being true to themselves, acting consistently with their feelings, being honest and appropriately open with one another (including expressing feelings and

constructively confronting differences), and both understanding and accepting others who do the same.
- *Flexibility, change, and proaction*—people changing themselves on the one hand and acting assertively on the other in a continuing process whose aim is maintaining or achieving a good fit between themselves and the external reality within which they are living.

System Values

- *Learning, development, growth, and transformation*—people growing in ways that bring into being greater realization of their potential, individually and collectively.
- *Whole-win attitudes, cooperation–collaboration, trust, community, and diversity*—people caring about each other and working together to achieve results that are good for everyone (individually and collectively), experiencing the spirit of community, and honoring the diversity that exists within community.
- *Widespread, meaningful participation in systems affairs, democracy, and appropriate decision making*—people participating as fully as reasonably possible in making the decisions that affect their lives.
- *Effectiveness, efficiency, and alignment*—people achieving desired results with an optimal balance between results and costs, and doing so in ways that coordinate the energies of systems, subsystems, and macrosystems, particularly the energies, needs, and desires of the human beings who comprise those systems.

Source: William Gellermann, "The Core of Professional Identity: Common Purpose, Values, and Ethics," *Organization Development Practitioner,* September 1990, p. 3 (publication of the National Organization Development Network, P.O. Box 69329, Portland, OR 97201). Reprinted with permission.

READING 50
ESTIMATING THE SUCCESS OF OD APPLICATIONS

Robert T. Golembiewski, Carl W. Proehl, Jr., and David Sink

One of the better topics over the years for inspiring argument has involved assessing the state of organization development (OD). In more recent days, however, a curious agreement has developed. Friend and foe alike tend to have real doubts about OD's future. Critics point to a range of problems—theoretical, methodological, and ethical. [1] Many historic supporters see OD at a critical life-stage—as an adolescent, with quite definite signs of lacking those qualities associated with "most likely to succeed." [2] Other supporters see a kind of academic and applied aging, with the memories of early hopes still alive but with a growing sense that the "heydays" are all over. [3] We have in mind a recent academic symposium of OD "afficionados," who had for several hours zestfully played "can you top this" with pronouncements concerning the deficiencies and all-but-inevitable doom facing OD—poor research, inadequate underlying theory, and so on.

Three Base-Line Minima

This article seeks to provide needed perspective for ardent supporters, convinced critics, and zestful flagellants alike, specifically by rooting this argument in three base-line minima about which broad and even universal consensus exists.

First, without doubt, OD still shows many of the signs of a burgeoning area of activity. We will be selective only, but illustrations suffice to make the case. Thus OD texts [4] and books of

readings [5] find a ready market. Professional associations with thousands of members have developed in the last decade. [6] The catalog of public or business organizations having had at least a flirtation with OD is very long and growing. Degree programs in OD have proliferated. It is certainly noteworthy that the largest employers of OD perspectives, designs, and personnel include the U.S. military services, [7] whose base-values provide a very difficult target for penetration by OD perspectives and technologies.

Second, both major interpretations of this business rest on similar bases that are palpably inadequate and may be wrong as well. That is, the business implies to some that OD "works." Others see a kind of "market high" just before an inevitable and formidable sell-off. Commonly, however, neither conclusion rests on satisfactory *and* comprehensive documentation of OD's efficacy, or lack thereof.

Note that this second base-line conclusion refers to satisfactory *and* comprehensive documentation, rather than to the absence of documentation. Documentation exists. Indeed, several comparative studies [8] suggest an appreciable success rate for various OD applications, but such work has two major limitations for present purposes. The databases for such summary studies tend to be small, on the order of scores of cases. For example, the study by Porras deals with 35 cases. [9] Morrison's methodological overview involves 26 cases. [10] In addition, only a small fraction of such databases refers to public sector applications, which are widely regarded as posing unusually difficult problems for OD and, by implication at least, as having low success rates. Perhaps 10–15 percent represents the usual proportion of public applications in available databases, and one-10th of a small database does not provide a very solid foundation for generalizations.

Third, these information gaps have not often deterred enthusiasts or critics. They seem to *know,* absent the required documentation. Artfully, for example, some observers see the OD intervener as a kind of contemporary shaman, [11] while (at least to these authors) also conveying the distinct impression that more rattle-shaking than technology and theory are involved in OD applications. Generally, in addition, the state of affairs is presented as being worse in the public sector. Drawing on his experience as both a designer and a student of OD interventions, for example, Giblin concludes that the "unique constraints imposed on public organizations appear to render them almost immune from conventional OD interventions." [12] Others conclude that public sector OD—if defined as something more than "tinkering with the system"—will be very difficult, if not palpably impossible, for a broad range of reasons.

Burke concludes that: "Most OD consultants find working with bureaucracies, especially public ones, to be difficult at best. . . . Apparently, most OD consultants either become more pragmatic and realistic or they have given up when it comes to working with large, bureaucratic organizations." [13]

The Present Database

What do the data imply about OD applications? Specifically, this article reports an effort to transcend the all-but-universal limitations of the literature, based on a very intensive search for OD applications in both business and government contexts. Five basic sources are used to develop a database of OD applications that could support useful conclusions about effects: [14]

- Seven specialized bibliographies.
- Searches of the several relevant computerized listings (e.g., ERIC) of publications in social science journals over the past 20 years.

- A review of the last 20 years of studies reported in 88 journals, including 10 from overseas.
- More than 100 books surveyed for bibliographic items as well as for reports of interventions.
- Personal letters sent to 50 well-known change agents, especially soliciting unpublished materials, such as internal memos, dissertations or theses, and so on.

Appropriate citations occurred as early as 1945, and the search extended into mid-1980 when it was closed to analyze data. This search-process has two gaps, neither of which is seen as damning, but which all may wish did not exist. First, journals unavailable in English were searched only selectively, but 17 percent of the total batch of interventions were accomplished in non-American settings. This leaves our database with a dominant locus and a distinct cosmopolitan flavor.

Second, the search did not encompass the twice-yearly meetings of the Organization Development Network or of the OD Division of ASTD. Until recently, neither interest group published proceedings. Many interventions reported at these meetings, however, got into our database, either after being published or because they were forwarded by our 50 personal contacts. Through mid-1980, these two gaps notwithstanding, our search uncovered a substantial number of OD applications—574 cases, to be exact. [15]

We make only two claims about this set of cases. First, there seems almost no question that public sector applications get adequate representation. Indeed, the very number of such applications—270—may itself constitute a major finding, since most sources emphasize the paucity of public sector applications. [16] In contrast, public sector cases constitute over 47 percent of the present batch of OD studies.

Second, we propose, a little more tentatively, that the 574 cases provide a reasonable replica of all OD activity. Early published work has some bias toward "successful" applications, but we include a broad range of unpublished sources. Moreover, the 35-year collection period and the large number of cases should substantially compensate for any early but artifactual hopes. Hence we propose that the 574 cases provide a credible source for seeking answers to two major questions concerning OD:

- What is the range and diversity of interventions or applications?
- What is the probability that an intervention will be successful?

Range and Diversity

The range of the 574 interventions is broad, with major representation from all the major classes of interventions associated with OD. Let us build toward this conclusion by providing useful detail.

Most observers see OD as one of the major derivatives of the "laboratory approach"—a major way of learning to learn. Globally, the laboratory approach to OD has at least six distinguishing features: [17]

- Rootedness in a definite set of values, which emphasize openness, trust, and collaborative effort.
- Seeking to simultaneously meet individual needs and the needs of several levels of systems—small groups, large organizations, and so on.
- Grounding in immediate experiences as they occur: this often gets expressed as a here-and-now orientation and is reflected in "process analysis" of the panoply of personal and institutional forces acting on individuals and groups.
- Emphasis on feelings and emotions, as well as on ideas and concepts.
- Preeminence of the individual's

involvement and participation—as subject and object, as generator of data as well as responder to those data—in an "action-research" sense.
- Heavy reliance on group contexts for choice and change; to validate data, to develop and enforce norms, and to provide emotional support and identification.

The laboratory approach had its first major technological expression in the T-group or sensitivity training group. The T-group was typically composed of strangers meeting on a "cultural island" and focused on learning from each other about (for example) "how we are seen by others and how we see them." [18] Such work sparked major attention to interaction-centered OD designs.

In a decade or so, OD became the major extension of such early work. It commonly came to encompass not only interaction-centered designs but those focused on structure and policies/procedures. Basically, the core values and central dynamics of the laboratory approach were built into several classes of learning designs, appropriate for choice or change in large aggregates. Each OD application will be unique to an extent and typically will combine several basic designs. As a first-cut, however, these alternative designs can be classified in terms of eight "activities." The classes are listed here, roughly in order of their complexity and subtlety:

- *Process analysis activities,* or applications of behavioral science perspectives to understand complex and dynamic situations. These perspectives can be simple—for example, as in routine retrospection among task-group members who ask: How do we feel about what we just did? The perspectives also can be complex, as in seeking to understand interpersonal conflict as an expression of differing predispositions.

- *Skill-building activities,* or various designs for gaining facility with behaviors consistent with OD values, as in giving/receiving feedback, listening, resolving conflict, and so on.

- *Diagnostic activities,* which often include process analysis, but which also may employ interviews, psychological instruments, or opinion surveys to generate data from and for members of some social systems. These data get fed back into that system, to serve as the raw material for action-research sequences: diagnosis, prescription of changes, implementation, and evaluation.

- *Coaching/counseling activities,* which seek to apply OD values in intimate situations, as between a pair-in-conflict in an organization via "third-party consultation."

- *Team building activities,* or efforts to increase the efficiency and effectiveness of intact task-groups. Variants may use T-group or sensitivity training modes, as well as one or more of the activities listed here.

- *Intergroup activities,* which seek to build effective and satisfying linkages between two or more task-groups, such as departments in a large organization.

- *Technostructural activities,* which seek to build need-satisfying roles, jobs, and structures. Typically, these activities rest on a "growth psychology," such as that of Maslow, Argyris, or Herzberg. These structural or policy approaches—job enlargement, flexi-time, and so on—often are coupled with other OD activities.

- *System-building or system-renewal activities,* which seek comprehensive changes in a large organization's climate and values, using complex combinations of the seven activities sketched above, and having time spans in the three to five year range.

These eight activities fit with varying precision into three basic OD modes: interaction-centered, structure, and policies or procedures. Process analysis, skill-building, and coaching/counseling are basically interaction-centered. Technostructural and system-building emphasize structure, although not to the exclusion of the other two modes. Team-building and intergroup activities often have dominant interaction emphases, but also deal with structure and especially policies or procedures.

What is the distribution of our 574 cases among these classes of activities? Table 1 implies that our population covers the field of interventions. The most narrow designs—diagnostic activities and process analysis—constitute the dominant intervention mode in *less* than 5 percent of the cases. OD interventions tend to hunt bigger game. To illustrate, nearly 40 percent of the private sector cases can be categorized as emphasizing the most complex intervention modes—system-building or renewal and technostructural activities. Reading the individual case reports in the public sector also reinforces this impression. The applications there seem to give substantial attention to the tough cases, on balance. Hence, the common emphases on racial tension; conflict between individuals, specialties, and organization units; community conflict between police and minorities; and basic reorganization. OD applications seem to respect this difficult prescription: *Intervene where the pain is felt!*

The 574 cases imply similar reliance on dominant OD modes in both public and business settings. In most cases, the probabilities of using the eight classes of activities vary in a very narrow range only. Technostructural activities constitute the most prominent exception, perhaps because public structures/policies/procedures are more likely to be set by distal authorities, especially legislatures. Therefore, these activities would more often be out of convenient reach. Even so, technostructural activities constitute the

TABLE 1

Incidence of eight classes of OD activities in public and private sectors

| | Individual Applications Classified by Dominant Design | | | |
| | Public Sector | | Private Sector | |
Class of OD Design	No.	%	No.	%
Process analysis activities	10	4	6	2
Skill-building activities	65	24	57	19
Diagnostic activities	14	5	18	6
Coaching/counseling activities	19	7	30	10
Team-building activities	51	19	56	18
Intergroup activities	38	14	18	6
System-building or system-renewal activities	29	11	35	11
Technostructural activities	44	16	84	28
	N = 270	100	N = 304	100

dominant OD mode in nearly one of every five public sector cases.

In sum, the 574 cases do not constitute a collection of easy pieces, and the database suggests no huge differences between the reliance on specific modes of OD interventions in public and business sectors. Consequently, the database should provide a real test of the efficacy of OD techniques and perspectives, of how often, and to what degree they tend to "work," within and between the private and public sectors.

The classification of the 574 published OD reports by dominant mode of intervention has a high reliability. Two independent observers classified all cases and had a very high degree of agreement. A 10 percent sample (approximately) places that agreement at nearly 98 percent of the cases. These few differences were reconciled before summation in Table 1.

High interobserver reliability was not crucial in this case. The efficacy of OD interventions was uniform over the full range of dominant modes.

Two Estimates of Success

How can we estimate specifically the efficacy of OD interventions? Do public-sector inter-

ventions have a lower success rate than their counterparts in business organizations? Two approaches to answers will be sketched here and tested against business and government OD applications. The approaches may be labeled "global" and "multiple indicators."

Global Estimate of Efficacy. A few details provide needed perspective on the "global" evaluation of OD interventions. Two independent readers reviewed each of the 574 interventions and assigned each set of effects to one of four categories whose content the observers had discussed and illustrated in detail. The evaluative categories include:

- *Highly positive and intended effects* on the efficacy and effectiveness of some relatively discrete system, as in improving the ability of individuals to hear one another without distortion, or in reducing the degree of hostility between conflicting actors or units.

- *Definite balance of positive and intended effects,* defined in terms of mixed but generally favorable effects—e.g., most but not all intended effects were achieved on a number of variables; or major positive

TABLE 2

Global estimate of the success of 574 OD applications

Rating Categories	Individual Applications Classified by Degree of Effects			
	Public Sector		Private Sector	
	No.	%	No.	%
Highly positive and intended effects	110	41%	122	40%
Definite balance of positive and intended effects	116	43%	148	49
No appreciable effect	18	7	14	5
Negative effects	26	9	20	6
	N = 270	100%	N = 304	100%

effects occurred in one system, while some negative but not counterbalancing effects occurred in another system.

- *No appreciable effect.*
- *Negative effects,* or a case in which substantial reductions occurred in the efficiency and effectiveness of some subsystem or of some broader system of which it was a part.

What did this laborious rating and cross-checking reveal? Four points summarize the major findings. First, by and large, the observers saw the same effects. Specifically, the observers' ratings correlated 0.78, which indicates substantial agreement between raters. Almost all cases of disagreement involved the first two rating categories. Some differences were reconciled after this reliability check, but in all cases, the ratings of one observer are reflected in Table 2. One can then conclude with some confidence that *in this population of studies* more than 80 percent of the interventions had at least a definite balance of positive and intended effects.

Third, global estimates of the efficacy of OD interventions do not vary much between the public and business sectors. Table 2 implies that major point.

Fourth, global estimates of success vary somewhat by dominant mode of intervention. Table 3

summarizes the experience for private sector interventions, which do not differ markedly from public sector experience. Except for two classes of OD activities—process analysis and diagnostic—the efficacy estimates are all 83 percent or greater for at least a definite balance of positive and intended effects.

Multiple Indicators Estimate Efficacy. Another approach to estimating the efficacy of OD interventions relies on numerous multiple indicators which comprise 308 variables. Proehl [19] coded each of the 574 cases in the present batch of studies, in terms of the comprehensive set of indicators developed by Porras and Berg. [20] Proehl describes his procedure in these terms:

> each of the . . . studies in this research's database was searched for the 308 variables developed by Porras and Berg. When one of the variables was found, it was coded according to whether it had improved (0) or not improved (1) during the course of the change project. Once all of the variables present in each study were identified and coded, the "percentage of positive reported change" was calculated for each organizational level (individual, leader, group, or organization) or study. This was accomplished by dividing the number of positive variables by the total number of variables in whch change was desired in each organizational level of each study. For example, a change effort which

Global estimates of efficacy, private sector cases only, N = 304

Class of OD Design	Estimated Effects in Percent*			
	Highly Positive and Intended Effects	Definite Balance of Positive and Intended Effects	No Appreciable Effects	Negative Effects
Process analysis activities	16.7%	50.0%	16.7%	16.7%
Skill-building activities	40.4	52.6	3.5	3.5
Diagnostic activities	33.3	44.4	5.6	16.7
Coaching/counseling activities	40.0	46.7	6.7	6.7
Team-building activities	39.3	51.8	3.6	5.4
Intergroup activities	44.4	39.0	5.6	11.1
System-building or system-renewal activities	45.7	40.0	5.7	8.7
Technostructural activities	40.5	51.2	3.6	4.8

* Due to rounding, totals may accumulate to > 100%.

sought to change five individual-level variables and reported three of them as having changed positively was given a score of 60 percent. Scores ranged from zero percent in a change effort which failed to produce any positive change in process and outcome variables to 100 percent for a case in which positive change was reported in all variables for which change was desired.

The reliability of these assignments was estimated by a limited, if random, process. Three independent observers each rated two randomly selected variables, and agreement existed on 228 of 240 cases. This interobserver reliability of 95 percent is taken to be representative of the record on the other variables, and it seems an acceptable level of reliability of assignments on which to base analysis.

The "percentage of positive reported change" was 70.5 percent, overall, when the 574 cases were scored for all of the 308 Porras/Berg variables applicable in each case. The efficacy of the 574 applications also can be arrayed according to levels of analysis, four of which were distinguished by Porras and Berg. The specific percentages of positive reported change are:

• Individual: 78.1 percent for 243 cases.
• Leader: 68.1 percent for 173 cases.
• Group: 77.9 percent for 161 cases.
• Organization: 72.4 percent for 206 cases.

We conclude that, as the best-informed possible estimate from the standpoint of multiple indicators, at least 7 of 10 variables show a balance of positive effects resulting from OD applications. Because not all of the same variables are considered in the two comparisons above, the success rate at the four levels of analysis surpasses 70 percent by a noticeable margin. In addition, no major differences distinguish public vs. business applications.

Five Perspectives on Success

These results confirm a substantial success rate for a large batch of OD interventions. To be conservative, the two approaches to an estimate imply a success ratio of at least 7 in 10 cases. The more ebullient might choose to give credence to the global bottom-line estimate of efficacy, which approximates an 85 percent success rate.

These data powerfully imply that both critics and previously pessimistic supporters of OD must "sing a different tune" in the future, or at least a more complicated one. Such adaptation must take cognizance of at least five factors. First, these results are reinforced in other studies, although with databases that are small fractions of the size of the present batch. To sample only:

- Eight percent of Morrison's 26 cases deal with "failures." [21]
- In Dunn and Swierczek's 67 cases, 65–70 percent were considered "effective." [22]
- In Porras's 35 cases selected for high degrees of methodological rigor, variables changed in the predicted directions in about 50 percent of the cases. [23]
- Margulies and his associates rated 73 percent of 30 applications as "positive," with 10 percent "mixed," 24 percent "no change," and 3 percent as "negative." [24]

Second, these favorable success rates do not mean that all OD problems have been recognized, let alone solved to such a degree that designs and perspectives can be applied following a cookbook approach. Positively, these results imply that whatever exists in the organizational world can be accommodated, most of the time, by the kind of OD interveners who research and write up their experiences. Diagnosis is critical.

Third, the results do not imply that public sector OD is easier than "in business," more difficult, or the same. To restate the previous point, the results here only imply that the unique constraints existing in various organizations, whether governmental or business, can be accommodated by the written experiences of appropriate OD interventions.

This is no cute conclusion. In fact, we know quite a bit about how to develop such accommodations to the specific characteristics of agencies in the public sector. This is not the place, however, to detail that experience and theory, which has been accomplished elsewhere. [25]

Fourth, greater specificity will be required for finer-tuned analyses than the one attempted here. To illustrate, future comparative analysis will require a more precise typology of interventions, as well as a more complex differentiation of hosts or targets for such interventions. This consciousness has been raised recently, [26] but much remains to be done. In the present case, for example, interventions are distinguished only in gross terms. Targets/hosts are differentiated only as "public" and "business." A more satisfactory typology of OD systems will eventually take into explicit account the full range of differences/similarities usually encapsulated in the short-hand "public vs. private"; and it seems just as clear that this typology also will encompass those equally significant differences/similarities *within* "public" and "business" sectors.

Fifth, and finally, this analysis may be faulted by a major contaminant. As some observers emphasize, [27] published materials may be biased toward reporting "positive results." If this bias characterizes the present database, that would obviously account for some part of the high success rate. Our procedures provide only partial protection against such a bias. Note the effort to solicit unpublished materials—consultant reports, in-house memos, theses, and dissertations; this implies a counterbalance to any bias toward "positive results" in published work. Presumably, unpublished materials would be less contaminated in this regard.

These five concluding points encompass the present analysis, rather than nullify it. The present results may be considered the best available comprehensive estimate of the efficacy of OD efforts.

References

1. Warner Woodworth, Gordon Meyer, and N. Smallwood. "A Critical Assessment of Organization Development Theory and Practice." Unpublished MS, Department of Organizational Behavior, Brigham Young University, 1980.
2. Frank Friedlander. "OD Reaches Adolescence." *Journal of Applied Behavioral Science* 12, no. 7 (January 1976).
3. W. Warner Burke. "Organization Development in Transition," *Journal of Applied Behavioral Science* 12, no. 24 (January 1976); W. Warner Burke, "Organization Development and Bureaucracies in the 1980s." *Journal of Applied Behavioral Science* 16, no. 423 (July 1980).
4. Wendell F. French and Cecil H. Bell, Jr. *Organization Development,* Prentice Hall, Englewood Cliffs, NJ, 1978. Robert T. Golembiewski, *Approaches to Planned Change,* 2 vols., Marcel Dekker, New York, 1979. Edgar F. Huse, *Organization Development and Change,* West Publishing, St. Paul, Minn., 1980.
5. Wendell F. French, Cecil H. Bell, Jr., and Robert A. Zawacki, eds. *Organization Development: Theory, Practice and Research.* Business Publications, Inc., Dallas, TX, 1975. And Robert T. Golembiewski and William Eddy, eds., 2 vols., *Organization Development in Public Administration,* Marcel Dekker, New York, 1978.
6. The Organization Development Network is the most prominent professional association, achieving nearly 5,000 members in less than two decades of existence. Its energy level is reflected in its two yearly meetings, each lasting nearly a week.
7. *Southern Review of Public Administration* 1, no. 406 (March 1978).
8. Peggy Morrison. "Evaluation in OD: A Review and An Assessment." *Group and Organization Studies* 3, no. 42 (March 1978). Jerry Porras, "The Comparative Impact of Different OD Techniques and Intervention Intensities." *Journal of Applied Behavioral Science* 15, no. 156 (April 1979).
9. Porras, note 8.
10. Morrison, note 8.
11. Warner Woodworth and Reed Nelson. "Witch Doctors, Messianics, Sorcerers, and OD Consultants: Parallels and Paradigms." *Organizational Dynamics* 8, no. 16, (Autumn 1979).
12. Edward J. Giblin, "Organization Development: Public Sector Theory and Practice." *Public Personnel Management* 5, no. 108 (March 1, 1976).
13. Burke, "Organization Development and Bureaucracies in the 1980s," p. 429.
14. Carl W. Proehl, Jr. *Planned Organizational Change.* Unpublished doctoral dissertation, Appendix A, University of Georgia, 1980.
15. The full bibliography of 574 cases is reported in ibid., and those interested can obtain copies from the senior author.
16. As an exception, Miller isolates 138 applications that are included in the present batch. See Garald J. Miller, *The Laboratory Approach to Planned Change in the Public Sector.* Unpublished doctoral dissertation, University of Georgia, 1979.
17. Arthur Blumberg and Robert T. Golembiewski. *Learning and Change in Groups.* Penguin, London, 1976, pp. 22–35.
18. Ibid., esp. pp. 57–61.
19. Proehl, note 14.
20. Jerry I. Porras and Per-Olof Berg. "Evaluation Methodology in Organization Development." *Journal of Applied Behavioral Science* 14, no. 151 (April 1978).
21. Morrison, note 8.
22. William N. Dunn and Frederick W. Swierczek. "Planned Organizational Change." *Journal of Applied Behavioral Science* 13, no. 135 (April 1977).
23. Porras, note 20.
24. Newton Margulies, Penny L. Wright, and Richard W. Scholl. "Organization Development Techniques: Their Impact on Change." *Group and Organization Studies* 2, no. 449 (December 1977).
25. A developmental version of guidelines for public sector applications appears in Robert T. Golembiewski, "Managing the Tension between OD Principles and Political Dynamics," pp. 27–46, in W. Warner Burke, ed., *The Cutting Edge: Current Theory and Practice in Organization*

Development, University Associates, La Jolla, Calif., 1978. An expanded version will appear in Golembiewski's *Humanizing Public Organizations* (in preparation).

26. David G. Bowers, Jerome L. Franklin, and Patricia A. Pecorella. "Matching Problems, Precursors, and Interventions in OD: A Systematic Approach." *Journal of Applied Behavioral Science* 11, no. 391 (December 1975).

27. Philip H. Mirvis and David N. Berg, eds. *Failures in Organization Development and Change,* John Wiley & Sons, New York, 1977.

READING 51
LAUNCHING SUCCESSFUL DIVERSITY INITIATIVES

Lawrence M. Baytos

Perhaps no other issue is rising as rapidly to the top of HR priority lists as the challenges and opportunities associated with managing a culturally diverse workforce. For many corporations, the concern is driven by the ethnic, racial, and sexual diversity issues now being encountered. Here are three recent examples:

- To counter a union organizing drive in a mid-sized plant, a successful company-communication campaign had to be delivered in five languages.
- A national services organization was preparing to launch a companywide diversity training program. In their preparations they learned that in a southeastern and a southwestern company office, the workforce was more than 50 percent Hispanic. In other offices they found one that was more than 50 percent black, one 90 percent white, and another had 25 percent foreign-born employees.
- The head of a corporate financial department pondered the staffing implications resulting from 50 percent of his staff now being either pregnant or on maternity leave.

These three examples are cited merely to illustrate to the skeptic that the future (with respect to workforce diversity) does not lie ahead, it is here already.

Many leading-edge companies have aggressively attempted to address diversity issues within their organizations. In the process, there

Source: Lawrence M. Baytos, "Launching Successful Diversity Initiatives," *HRMagazine,* March 1992, pp. 91–97. Reprinted with the permission of *HRMagazine* (formerly *Personnel Administrator*) or *HRNews* (formerly *Resource*) published by the Society for Human Resource Management, Alexandria, VA.

have been some patterns emerging and painful lessons learned. An understanding of these experiences may help others plan their own initiatives.

There is an important caveat to the guidelines described in this article. Though the information and examples that follow describe leading-edge companies with excellent performance in their respective industries, none of the organizations would give themselves high marks for effectively managing workforce diversity. Therefore the guidelines do not claim to represent proven success, but only what appears to be working so far in launching diversity initiatives. Six critical areas that should be covered when planning and executing diversity initiatives are:

1. Establish a clear business rationale for the initiatives.
2. Focus the organization to achieve the changes necessary.
3. Seek employee input broadly on the needs and priorities toward which your efforts are to be targeted.
4. Aggressively convert employee input to action steps.
5. Carefully set the timing/focus/breadth of training.
6. Prepare to maintain momentum over an extended time.

Clarify Business Objectives

Obviously you should have a good business reason for any HR program you want to introduce. However, in the case of diversity initiatives, it is even more important than some other HR areas for several reasons:

- Some changes in organizational culture are often needed to foster an environment that values and capitalizes workforce diversity. Unless a clear business need is established, experience indicates that changes proposed for corporate values and cultural roots will be resisted by the organization.
- On an interpersonal level, attitudes toward people who are different from ourselves are implanted early in our lives and reinforced frequently through the media, family, and acquaintances. The point is that we bring a strong mindset, which has developed over many years, to work situations. Why tinker with our mindset (which creates discomfort) unless there is a strong reason for doing so?
- Historically, issues of workforce diversity have often been handled as a moral issue or from a social responsibility perspective or in some companies from a legal compliance perspective. The first time there are corporate profit pressures or a budget crunch, these well-intentioned programs with "soft" rationale get set aside and the focus is shifted to the "real business" of the company.

The importance of a business rationale can be illustrated with the case of a staff group attempting to create a corporate diversity strategy. Although the CEO had publicly proclaimed that diversity was going to be an important corporate priority, he had not effectively articulated why he thought it should be. Thus the diversity team was unclear in their focus and they were meeting resistance among key managers who had seen the CEO blow hot and cold on other broad programs, such as total quality. Fuzzy objectives will yield action without progress and result in frustration for all concerned.

Figure 1 outlines a conceptual model for managing diversity, developed by Dr. R. Roosevelt Thomas of the American Institute for Managing Diversity, Inc. References to diversity initiatives in this article include three categories—traditional, understanding diversity, and managing diversity—described by Dr. Thomas.

Successful diversity initiatives encompass a wide array of corporate values, programs and practices. Let's examine the role of those professionals who should be involved in the diversity process.

Senior Management

Using the term *senior management* generically, some important roles performed by this group include the following:

- They provide or validate the business rationale and overall objectives for the diversity initiatives and assess the deeper cultural issues.
- Senior managers serve as visible proponents of the initiatives. There will be lots of early skepticism; employees will be waiting for clues to the extent and seriousness of management's interest. One company addressed this issue by starting a broad training effort and scheduling its executive team in the first sessions. The awareness among employees, that senior officers thought the issues important enough to devote two days of their time, provided a credibility that no number of pronouncements could have achieved.

Human Resource Staffs

In most organizations the HR staffs will provide support to the diversity efforts and will be held accountable for the results, or lack thereof. Members of the HR staff will need to accomplish the following:

- **Mobilize resources.** This responsibility includes developing funding and staffing for the initiatives, as well as orchestrating the organizational aspects discussed in

Current approaches to diversity can be categorized as traditional (affirmative action), understanding diversity, and managing diversity.

Traditional. By far the most common approach is still the assimilation/affirmation action/melting-pot model, despite a growing awareness of its shortcomings.

Understanding Diversity (UD). This approach represents a marked departure from the traditional. UD assumes that the difficulty flows from a lack of understanding, so that the objective is to enhance employees' abilities to accept, understand, and appreciate differences among individuals.

Managing Diversity (MD). MD is an emerging supplement to the traditional option. The objective is to create an environment that fully taps the potential of all individuals, in pursuit of corporate objectives, without giving advantage or disadvantage to any person or group of persons. Key features of this pioneering concept, as it has evolved at The American Institute for Managing Diversity, are as follows:

1. MD is a process, not a solution. It is a vehicle for generating company-specific, research-based solutions for moving toward sustainable progress.

2. Because MD defines managing as enabling (or influencing), as opposed to controling, the question becomes, "As a manager goes about enabling his or her workforce, and as it becomes increasingly diverse, do our systems, culture, and management tools work equally well for all employees?" It is a managerial perspective that goes beyond the issues of an individual understanding and appreciating differences in people.

3. MD defines diversity broadly, and it includes white men as well as dimensions other than race, gender and ethnicity.

4. MD relaxes the melting-pot/assimilation assumption and assumes that both the individual and the corporation will have to adjust, that the individual will not bear the burden of adjustment alone.

5. MD focuses on correcting a system so that it works naturally for all employees.

6. MD requires recognition of the business (viability) motive to achieve lasting progress. Employees must understand how MD can enhance the company's competitive posture. Most important, MD calls for cultural and systemic interventions as well as initiatives at the individual and interpersonal levels. Culture is defined as the basic assumptions underlying all activity in a corporation.

other parts of this section. In the early stages, the initiating HR group should involve other HR executives (corporate/division/local).

- **Link diversity initiatives to existing programs.** To avoid a crazy quilt of duplicative or unconnected programs, continuing involvement will be needed at all steps along the way. For example, to implement a high-potential, fast-track program for minorities and women without a tie-in to existing broader programs is to court disaster and confusion.

- **Serve as change agent.** Make no mistake, you will be pioneering an activity within your organization. As an

HR leader, you will become a change agent, driving interventions in policies and programs. This requires that you do the research and introspection needed to confront your own feelings on diversity issues. You must also make sure that a strong power base sufficiently supports this extended process of change.

Using Support Groups

There are two basic types of support groups encountered in diversity initiatives—special focus groups and the diversity task force. Special focus groups are formed to concentrate on the specific needs perceived by their members. Typical special focus groups are composed of either women or minorities. Occasionally minority groups are broken further into African-American, Hispanic, and Asian subgroups. In very large organizations there may be even further delineation; for example, minority engineers.

A philosophically different approach is to establish a diversity task force, made up of individuals representing a cross-section of gender, race, functional disciplines, and organizational levels. Because of its composition, the diversity group is likely to develop a broader perspective than the special focus groups.

In many companies, the groups already existed and were instituted at the grass-roots level. In others, they are formed with active employer support as an affirmative action or a managing diversity initiative. These support groups have been used in several different ways as reported by the organizations in which they reside:

- They can serve as a feedback group (with a facilitator) to provide candid and targeted critique, especially with regard to current issues and priorities.
- A group may aid in the planning and implementing initiatives as a steering committee, or some of its members may sit in on a broader steering committee.
- Some companies start their diversity training with support groups to test the program and to develop the participants for their involvement roles.
- Support groups may serve as test markets for contemplated policy or program changes. Such involvement can be especially important where the process of policy making historically has not incorporated much input from those different from the numerically dominant ethnic or gender group in the organization.

Many companies have found that support groups can enrich the feedback and increase the chances that interventions will be successful. However, such groups also carry some modest risk. One risk is that heavy involvement may be-

come cumbersome and slow the process of change and program introduction. Also, if special focus groups view each other as competing for scarce resources (promotion opportunities, budget dollars) their input may lack objectivity. To eliminate such risks, support groups should be closely linked with the HR team.

Profit-Center Support/Issues

In large, decentralized organizations, profit-center support and involvement will determine the ultimate success. Without a negative word ever being spoken, it is possible for a profit-center head to effectively kill the best-laid plans. To avoid sabotage, follow these steps:

- Get line agreement that there is a solid business rationale for diversity initiatives.
- Work to ensure that efforts across division lines are collaborative, not competitive. Some companies have experienced uncoordinated efforts that lacked an overall theme and thus did not facilitate the profit centers' learning from one another's successes and failures.
- Assure the profit centers and outlying locations that your objective is to meet their needs, not to create a "one-size-fits-all" situation. This approach makes obvious sense from a sales viewpoint and it also fits strategically. When you are developing a training intervention, for example, you may well conclude that some of the materials used with your Minnesota employees should be different from the approach used at your San Antonio facility.

Nontraditional Involvement.

Consider going outside the usual human resource realm and looking for opportunities to bring the best minds of the company into the process. This could include involving a market research staff member in the data gathering and analysis, talking with outside members of the board of directors to identify and make contact with leading companies in the field, convening recruiting sources and community representatives to focus on issues, and so forth.

Seek Employee Input

The addition of focused survey data may help prioritize the dozens of issues you may face. A targeted survey also sends a strong message to your employees that special efforts are underway, and this is not a business-as-usual approach to diversity issues. Furthermore, if properly structured, the survey process can provide both an outlet for potentially volatile feelings and a means to capture the real mood of your workforce.

Of course, written surveys are the most common means of sensing employee attitudes. However, generic attitude surveys often bypass tough questions on sensitive areas. And if a climate of trust does not exist, individuals may be reluctant to provide candid feedback in a process that they may view as threatening or bureaucratic.

As a result, some companies supplement standard survey approaches with targeted one-on-one individual interviews or with feedback groups moderated by facilitators with computer-assisted tools. The services of outside agencies are often used to protect the confidentiality of the data and encourage the participating employees to speak with candor.

Make sure the survey effort is positioned as an integral part of a long-term process and strategy and not as the means to a "quick fix." One company, for example, found that, after it ran its special survey, rumors emerged there was going to be a wave of promotions for women and minorities. Another risk is that your organization may be unwilling or unable to act on the findings.

Convert Data into Action Steps

Every organization has its unique properties that will be reflected in the results of a diversity survey initiative. Even within a given company, the profiles may vary by the nature of the facility (plant versus office), the geographic location, and the quality of management at the local level. Nevertheless, in looking at the data from the perspective of what the participants' concerns may be, some patterns can be anticipated. A conceptual illustration of some typical diversity themes is shown in Figure 2.

Figure 3 gives just a few illustrations of the vast variety of issues that will lead to later interventions. The selection of issues, establishment of connections to current polices and programs, and prioritization for action within a process framework is likely to be the toughest part of your assignment, because you will have to develop an understanding of the meanings behind the raw numbers.

Let's look at several dimensions of a diversity training intervention and raise issues you will want to think through before moving forward. First, what do you hope to achieve with your training. Where is the focus? Some options include the following:

- Education—framework for action, create sense of urgency.
- Training—skill building, dealing with diversity in a job context.
- Training and Education.

Next examine the issue of which employee groups in which company units should be included:

- Targeted—senior managers initially or broad reach?
- Local customizing—emphasize local diversity aspects.
- Organizational—X and Y divisions now, but Z may not be ready.

The issues are so basic that raising them here may seem insulting. However, the issues are raised because the pressure and urgency to find "IT" have resulted in bypassing some of the rigorous needs analysis normally carried out by companies with strong training. Don't overreact

FIGURE 2

The nexus of diversity issues

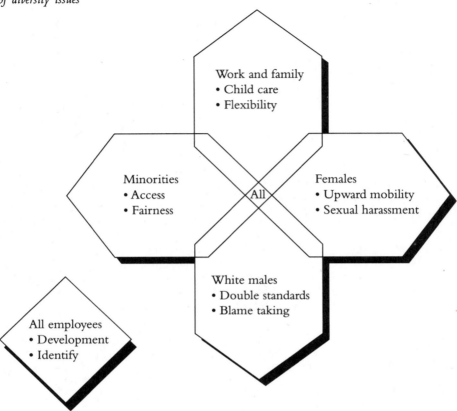

Each of the issues categories shown in the chart requires some amplification.

Minority Issues. ACCESS refers to the ability of minorities to gain entry into the organization but also have access to opportunities beyond the entry level. FAIRNESS is sought in terms of policies and programs that are neutral for all races and sexes both in content and administration (e.g., performance appraisal, job posting, tuition reimbursement).

Work and Family Issues. CHILD CARE concerns focus on the availability, quality, and cost of child care for working parents. FLEXIBILITY is sought in areas that help employees to responsibly balance and fulfill their roles as both employees and parents (e.g., parental leave policies, flexible hours, job sharing).

Women's Issues. UPWARD MOBILITY concerns relate to the absence of the "glass ceiling" and minimal stereotyping of women in job assignments. Women are also looking for an environment that does not condone SEXUAL HARASSMENT and, if it does occur, it is dealt with appropriately.

White Male Employees. Let's not forget that white male employees still form an important part of our diversity fabric! They may worry about the denial of opportunities due to what they may view as a DOUBLE STANDARD of affirmative action. They also do not want to take the BLAME for all the organization's failures, which led to the current status.

All Employees. There is usually widespread concern across all races and genders for future nurturing and DEVELOPMENT leading to growth opportunities. Whether or not employees expect to progress in the organization, they will desire to retain aspects of their personal uniqueness that are critical to their IDENTITY and feelings of self-worth. Having the data is one thing. Knowing what to do with it is another. As stated previously, some companies have gone through extensive special survey efforts, only to have the report gather dust. It is crucial to tie survey results back to specific corporate values, policies, and programs. Otherwise, the exercise will have been wasted.

FIGURE 3

Linking issues to action

Concern	Policy program	Intervention
Upward mobility, "closed programs"	Deelopment and advancement system	Job opportunity posting introduced.
"Unwritten rules"	Policy administration	• Update and broadly distribute manuals. • Audit admin. of current programs.
Ability to compete in the "old boy network"	Management development	Introduce formal mentoring program with diverse mentors and participants.
Discomfort in exclusionary or stereotyping environment	Roots and values	Conscious effort to move from "We are a family" company root to "We are a team."

to the need for activity. Think in terms of designing the total car before you finalize on the windshield wipers.

Maintain Momentum

Most organizations pursuing diversity issues are still relatively early in a multiyear change process. They are pursuing multiple interventions, the efficacy of which have yet to be determined. Nevertheless, we can probably identify some of the issues and challenges that will begin to emerge in your organization.

1. How to avoid unrealistic expectations (among both senior management and women and minorities) about the pace of change?

2. How to prevent intervening crises from continually forcing diversity efforts to the back burner?

3. How to get senior management to address the needed organizational culture changes?

4. How to continually celebrate diversity achievements and send the message throughout the organization?

5. How to minimize potential white male backlash.

6. How to avoid fatigue and loss of interest in a long-term issue?

The challenges represented by workforce diversity are complex and delicate. The process of change requires intensive and time-consuming evaluation of both your personal attitudes and the organization's culture. Some view it as an area where even angels should fear to tread. However, the potential for competitive advantages in the 90s and the next century will make the efforts both necessary and worthwhile in your organization.

READING 52
DEVELOPING THE COMPETITIVE ORGANIZATION: INTERVENTIONS AND STRATEGIES

Michael Beer and Elise Walton

The role of organizations in society is to coordinate the activities of individuals in the accomplishment of a larger purpose, one that individuals cannot achieve alone. The central problem of management, therefore, is to develop the commitment needed to obtain coordinated action and to hire and develop people with the skills needed to work cooperatively. Organization development is concerned with helping managers plan change in organizing and managing people that will develop requisite commitment, coordination, and competence. Its purpose is to enhance both the effectiveness of organizations and the well-being of their members through planned interventions in the organizations' human processes, structures, and systems, using knowledge of behavioral science and its intervention methods (Beckhard, 1969).

The Field of Organization Development

Organization development is primarily a field of practice. It emerged from the consultation of behavioral scientists with managers about problems of group and organizational effectiveness. That consultation led to the invention of many different intervention methods for effecting change in organizations. These methods are rooted in the knowledge and theories of several fields, among them, psychology, sociology, organizational behavior, and management. Thus organization development is not a well-bounded field (Beer &

Source: Michael Beer and Elise Walton, "Developing the Competitive Organization: Interventions and Strategies," *American Psychologist,* February 1990, pp. 154–61. Copyright © 1990 by the American Psychological Association. Reprinted by permission.

Walton, 1987; Sashkin & Burke, 1987). Its practitioners are consultants with varying academic backgrounds and training and, of course, managers who apply its ideas and methods.

Assumptions and Values. Organization development is concerned with improving performance (profits, return on equity, and so on); however, because of an equal concern for the well-being of people, practitioners of organization development assume that the best way to achieve both outcomes is through trust, open confrontation of problems, employee empowerment and participation, the design of meaningful work, cooperation between groups, and full use of human potential. Thus organization development is decidedly normative in its antihierarchical and anti-authoritarian stance. There is considerable evidence, however, that, in stable and predictable business environments and for routine tasks, the approaches advocated may not enhance performance or satisfaction (Lawrence & Lorsch, 1967; Lorsch & Morse, 1974).

Organization development assumes that organizations are multidimensional social systems (Katz & Kahn, 1966). Therefore, intervention in both structure/systems and human processes is necessary for attitude and behavior to change (Beer, 1980). However, consultants have little power to change the whole system. They are dependent on general managers (managers of multifunctional organizations, such as a manufacturing plant, a business unit, or a whole company) who may not share their vision and values.

It is not surprising that in the 1960s and 1970s organization development had limited success in penetrating fundamentally hierarchical and bureaucratic organizations (Mirvis & Berg, 1977). Entry was restricted to organizations led by managers whose values were consonant with those of organization development, and there were not many of them. When these managers were transferred or left, the momentum for change stopped and regression set in. Initiatives at lower levels, in one department or plant of a larger corporation, were often unsupported, even opposed, by top management and corporate staff groups that did not share the values and assumptions of organization development (Crockett, 1977; Walton, 1977).

Two strategies for improving organizational effectiveness and employee well-being dominate organization development theory and practice: the human-process approach and the technostructural approach (Friedlander & Brown, 1974). These strategies need not and should not be mutually exclusive.

The Human-Process Approach. The human process approach involves employees in examining interpersonal, group, and intergroup processes and planning changes in them that will improve effectiveness. By examining openly dysfunctional behavior and practices and developing consensus about desired group and organizational behavior, members can subject to change the very norms that shape their behavior. Bennis, Benne, and Chin (1961) contrasted this participative "normative reeducative" change strategy with more coercive top-down change typically practiced in organizations. Numerous methods for intervening in process were invented (for an in-depth review of different techniques, see Beer, 1976, 1980; Burke, 1982). Three of these interventions are as follows:

Team building. A work group is brought together to discuss conflicts, goals, the decision-making process, leadership, and plan changes (Dyer, 1977).

Intergroup interventions. Representatives from different groups are brought together to surface conflict, diagnose its causes, and plan improvements. Variations have been applied to union—management conflict, mergers, and interdepartmental conflict (Blake, Shepard, & Mouton, 1964).

Organizational diagnosis and feedback. Data from interviews or questionnaires are fed back to a management team. They are used to stimulate a discussion of organizational problems. A diagnosis follows, and plans for change are made (Levinson, 1972; Nadler, 1977).

In pure form, these methods rely on a skilled process consultant (Schein, 1988b) whose role is like that of a therapist's: to collect data, observe, ask questions, reflect back, stimulate dialogue about the data, and help the client organization move to its own diagnosis and plan for change. In theory, at least, the consultant is a neutral third party, not aligned with a particular individual, group, or solution. The focus of consultation ranges from group to organizational effectiveness and usually involves both.

Research has demonstrated that process interventions can change attitudes and behavior (Alderfer, 1977; Beer & Walton, 1987; Friedlander, 1968), at least in the short run. However, more lasting organizational change does not always follow (Beer & Walton, 1987; Boss, 1983; Guzzo, Jette, & Katzell, 1985). This occurs for two reasons. First, these interventions are frequently not imbedded in a larger organizational change process to which higher management is committed. Second, structure and system, which have a substantial influence on attitude and behavior, are often left unaffected by these process interventions.

The Technostructural Approach. This approach assumes that motivation and behavior are powerfully influenced by job design (and its underlying technology), organization structure, and control, and information and reward systems. The following interventions have emerged from research and practice:

Work restructuring. By broadening jobs and

giving individuals or teams responsibility for a whole task, organizations have enabled employees to gain greater experienced meaningfulness, knowledge of results, and a sense of freedom that have led to enhanced motivation and performance (Hackman & Oldham, 1980). Self-managing work teams are increasingly being used in the manufacturing and service sectors with demonstrated improvements in quality and productivity. . . .

Structural change. As the environment becomes more dynamic and uncertain and organizations become more complex, coordination across departments becomes more critical, but cooperation is more difficult to achieve (Lawrence & Lorsh, 1967). Ad hoc teams that cut across departments and hierarchical levels (Zand, 1974) have been used to foster integrated decision making and cooperation. Quality circles and management task forces are examples. Matrix organizations, in which employees report to both their team leader and their functional boss, are also designed to increase coordination (Davis & Lawrence, 1977).

Compensation systems. Lawler (1981) has argued that compensation can be a starting point for organization development. Gainsharing plans (cost savings or profits are typically shared) have been used to develop commitment by workers and cooperation between union and management (Frost, Wakeley, & Ruh, 1974; Hammer, 1988). Skill-based pay systems, which compensate based on the skills employees have, not their assigned job, motivate employees to broaden themselves and promote flexibility.

New information technology. Computers are changing the nature of work and organizations. They can increase top-down control and demotivate employees, or they can empower employees if introduced to provide employees with information needed for decisions. The intention of management and planning determine the result (Zuboff, 1988).

Changes in structures and systems demand new behaviors by individuals and groups, and

that is why they can have long-lasting effects on coordination and effectiveness (Frost et al., 1974; Guzzo et al., 1985; Lawrence & Lorsch, 1969; Macy, Hurts, Izumi, Norton, & Smith, 1986). However, research also suggests that these changes do not always lead workers to develop commitment and competence (Frank & Hackman, 1975; Frost et al., 1974; Lawler & Mohrman, 1987; Macy et al., 1986; Rosen & Quarrey, 1987). To be successful these changes must be accompanied by the development of leadership, human skills, and shared values that are consistent with the purpose of the structures and systems introduced; high commitment; and coordination and cooperation. One reason why this does not always occur is that leaders make structural and systems changes without having culture change objectives clearly in mind. A second related reason has to do with the consultants who are brought in to help with these changes. They rely on their expertise to advise but are often unskilled in designing a participative process for introducing these changes, that is, the human process approach discussed earlier.

The Impact of a Competitive Environment. The competitive environment of the 1980s has dramatically changed many of the conditions that led organization development to have only limited applicability and short-lived success prior to the 1980s. Increased competition is causing more companies to incorporate many of the assumptions of organization development about organizing and managing and to use its interventions to manage change. There are several reasons.

Companies that aim to survive in a turbulent competitive environment must be flexible and adaptable (Burns & Stalker, 1961; Lawrence & Dyer, 1983). They must be able to sense changes in the environment rapidly, transmit that information to relevant departments, and act on that information. To achieve these operating characteristics, such companies require far higher levels of commitment, coordination, and cooperation.

Only organizations that are flatter, less hierarchical, more interested in involving employees in their work, more open, and more concerned about integration across functional departments can be responsive to a changing environment. Of course, these organizational characteristics require managers that are less authoritarian, have a broad business perspective, and possess the skills to work flexibly with others. Thus corporations will have to undergo a paradigmatic transformation in organizing and managing. Economic necessity is the reason.

How Corporations Transform Their Culture

The Pattern of Successful Corporate Transformations.

Successful corporate transformations seem to have a common pattern (Beer, Eisenstat, & Spector, in press). They start with innovations in organizing and managing in outlying manufacturing plants or divisions. If successful, the company has an organizational model and managers skilled in the new way of managing. Early successes convince top management to advocate adoption by other subunits. Thus change that began in a few subunits diffuses to other parts of the corporation, eventually changing the corporation's culture.

This pattern is explained by the fact that top management is usually not ready to lead a corporate transformation until it becomes convinced that innovations in subunits are effective. Even if they were ready to start a corporate transformation from the top, it would meet with massive resistance. It is much easier to make paradigmatic change in a smaller unit, particularly if that unit is new.

Building New Cultures: New Plant Start-Ups.

In recent years the term *high-commitment work system* (Walton, 1987a) has come to describe a new organization in which structure, systems, management process, and employee selection and development are planned to produce

a high "fit" system in which design elements complement each other and support desired values and behavior. Procter & Gamble pioneered in this approach in the 1960s, achieving productivity advantages of 40 percent, according to knowledgeable industry sources. High-commitment organizations share several similar elements. In addition to the newest technology, much of the work design is built around the semiautonomous production team. The team is given responsibility and accountability for producing a whole product or subassembly. Team members are expected to know and do all jobs within the team, including production, maintenance, planning, materials management, financial review, and hiring.

These organizations are flat. Perquisites, such as assigned parking spaces, are absent. Compensation programs are often flatter and simpler, usually based on the skills acquired, rather than on position, thus allowing flexible rotation across jobs within each team. There is high level of participation in decision making, often with special employee voice and governance mechanisms.

Not all of these plants are successful, but when they are it is due to effective implementation (Lawler, 1978). First, each of these plants requires considerable planning by a core group of managers. Widespread participation in implementing the vision developed at the design stage helps establish a solid and robust high-commitment culture. Team-building interventions are often used at the top and at lower levels. Thus both the technostructural and the human process interventions of organization development are applied to create these organizations.

Not surprisingly, shared values are key to getting high commitment. Once agreed to at the top, these values are designed into the work systems and applied in selecting employees. Finding managers who are willing to risk creating a countercultural work environment and who are capable of advocating and implementing a radical vision is essential. Yet, because the ideas are new and managers have limited experience, the assistance of organization development consultants is often sought. When properly designed and implemented, these plants successfully create a context that demands flexible behavior. Through careful selection and orientation of managers and workers, new plants have the powerful advantage of creating a culture from scratch. Despite these advantages, new plants still face socialization and skill problems. Because operating procedures are different from the mainstream work culture, new workers and managers have to learn human and management skills to which they have had little exposure. When these plants recruit labor from local plants where traditional work rules prevail, workers have a particularly difficult time adjusting to the new environment. Although new plant start-ups require even more technical skills than a steady-state operation, they often lack these in their new workforce because of hiring decisions that favored technically unskilled applicants with the desired work orientation over technically skilled applicants from traditional work environments (Walton, 1980). Therefore technical training and support are required, but so is organization development consulting and training to teach team skills.

Changing Old Cultures.   As the competitive environment intensifies, corporations seek to apply new patterns of organizing and managing to older organizations with entrenched cultures and with unions. These changes present predictable obstacles. One obstacle is the inertia of old ways. Entrenched skills, staff, relationships, roles, and structures work together in a high-fit system to reinforce traditional patterns of behavior. Powerful stakeholders, such as unions, management, or customers, may support the status quo. Simultaneous change in all organizational parts and dimensions is impossible. It is therefore inevitable that changes in one part of the organization or in one practice will face difficulty.

Because transformations inevitably restructure power and status in the workforce, they cause resistance. For example, workers of low seniority may benefit more than, and sometimes at the expense of, workers with relatively high seniority (Bocialetti, 1987). In flattening the hierarchy, these changes often eliminate layers of middle management or disseminate power typically held by middle managers. Feeling a loss of power and control, or a threat to job security, middle managers can obstruct changes (Pasmore, 1982; Schlesinger & Oshry, 1984). Unions may also oppose changes that demand modification of contracted work rules. Given the potential for resistance, the central change questions are how to develop motivation for change and a shared understanding of the new approach to organizing and managing, and how to sequence interventions so maximum energy for change is generated and minimum resistance triggered.

Developing motivation.   The first problem for managers who want to stimulate change is to develop dissatisfaction with the status quo among all stakeholders so systemwide change can be made with minimal resistance (Beckhard & Harris, 1977; Beer, 1980; Walton, 1987b). The most effective means is to focus stakeholders on an important business problem, such as lower profits, poor quality, or loss of market share (Beer et al., in press). A competitive crisis makes this task easier, but when a crisis is not visible managers have found that sharing information with employees about competitive threats to the business energizes managers, union, and workers to embrace change. Data about internal problems and barriers are typically gathered using organizational diagnosis and feedback methods described earlier. Such information focuses managers on internal changes that might improve performance. Within the context of heightened awareness of competitive pressures, effective change leaders also set high goals that motivate managers to search for improved management methods (Beer, 1988). Exposing managers to innovative organizations helps to motivate them by presenting a practical ideal (Beckhard & Harris, 1977).

Developing a shared vision. A vision of the new approach to organizing and managing has to be developed (Beer, 1988; Walton, 1986). That vision must define the structure, systems, management process, and skills required in the future. It is often developed by allowing managers to visit leading-edge organizations. Widespread participation in the development of the vision is key to gaining the acceptance of stakeholders (Beer et al., in press; Coch & French, 1948; Walton, 1987b). Participation educates employees about the need for changes and the logic behind new arrangements, puts employees in touch with the realities of the competitive environment, and facilitates the development of trust and human skills that will be needed in the adaptive organization being developed.

Sequencing interventions. How should the technostructural and human-process interventions be sequenced in moving the organization toward the vision? Introducing formal structure and systems too early can cause resistance before the commitment, cooperation, and competence needed to make these new structures and systems work have had a chance to develop. Recent research by Beer et al. (in press) suggests that once energy for change has been developed using the methods described, successful transformations start with reorganizing employees into ad hoc teams aimed at solving problems critical to competitiveness, product development, or quality improvement teams, for example. These arrangements put people into new roles and relationships and give them new responsibilities without causing the resistance that typically accompanies changes in formal structure.

As people work in ad hoc structures, they learn required behaviors and attitudes, particularly if supported with facilitation by organization development consultants. Improved effectiveness brought about by the changes increases commitment to the new approach. Employees who cannot grow into the new responsibilities are replaced. As informal patterns take root, formal changes in systems and structure can be in-troduced (Beer et al., in press). Now they strengthen and further support emergent behavior and attitudes.

This sequence of interventions causes learning to be experiential and to be a conscious by-product of a business-oriented change effort. Rather than being perceived as an irrelevant attempt to introduce participative management, culture change becomes an integral part of a business improvement strategy. The strategy relies on inducing behaviors, not educating people about them. If the new organizational arrangements and behavior are effective in dealing with previously unsolved problems, a growing sense of efficacy leads to changed attitudes about the new ways of managing (Bandura, 1977). A positive reinforcing cycle of behavior and attitude change is under way.

Sustaining Change: Predictable Problems. Both new innovative organizations and redesigned older ones encounter similar difficulties in sustaining the new approaches to management once they take hold.

Mid-course corrections. Changes in the business environment may pressure the innovative organization to make dramatic improvements in performance (e.g., cost, quality, or revenues), forcing it to respond quickly. That response may necessitate the rapid introduction of new manufacturing processes, information technology, or administrative procedures.

Two potential problems are encountered. First, fitting new systems and procedures into the innovative organization without violating the integrity of its original vision and design presents a challenge. Second, unless the means by which new systems or methods are introduced are consistent with the original participative management philosophy, shared values are undermined and so is high commitment. The challenge is for management to respond in a way consistent with the original principles and vision. That is often made more difficult by pressures from the corporation for rapid response to the new problems or by the fact that new managers, less committed to the original values and vision, or less skilled in implementing them, are in charge. This can happen through the natural promotion and transfer process in corporations.

Consider a renowned innovative plant, organized around semiautonomous production teams, that ran into difficulty sustaining its culture (Klein, 1986). Competitive pressures forced the introduction of a "just-in-time" manufacturing system. It undermined the self-management and pacing of semiautonomous production teams by eliminating costly inventory that had allowed each team to set its own pace. Disillusionment and cynicism about the plant's commitment to the original vision followed.

Although some of these difficulties were a function of the new manufacturing system, many problems stemmed from the style with which the new system was introduced by a new plant manager. He did not present employees with the cost problem facing the plant or involve them in designing a just-in-time inventory system that fit with the self-management concept of the plant. Instead, under pressure from corporate headquarters to use a system designed by an outside consulting firm, he limited employee involvement to work station design.

Leadership continuity. The preceding example also illustrates the importance of leadership continuity. A cadre of committed managers who will adhere to original principles under the pressure of changing conditions is critical if innovative organizations are to avoid regression to traditional management practices. Continuity in consulting support can help offset turnover in key management.

Relationship with corporate headquarters. Sustaining change also depends on the innovative unit's relationships with corporate headquarters. There are inevitable conflicts between corporate policies and the innovative unit's unique needs. How well the unit's leaders manage these conflicts influences the reputation and image of the plant and its management. This affects top-

management's perception of the innovative unit's effectiveness and that of its management. Poor relations between General Food's leading-edge Topeka plant and corporate headquarters in the early 1970s caused some of its managers to be transferred and some to resign, resulting in regression (Walton, 1977). Although these outcomes are less likely in corporations committed to change, a condition more prevalent today, even in these companies factions threatened by change often make it difficult for innovative units. It is not surprising, therefore, that the success of unit-level innovations has been found to be a function of the corporate context in which they are imbedded (Beer et al., in press; Walton, 1987b).

The Context for Successful Diffusion of Innovations.   If early innovations are successful, they diffuse to other parts of the company (Beer et al., in press; Walton, 1987b). However, for a company to capitalize on the success of innovative units as efficiently and effectively as possible, a potential competitive advantage, the corporate context, and the broader social and institutional context of the corporation must be managed to support change. The following conditions have been found to be necessary for diffusion to occur (Beer et al., in press; Walton, 1987b).

Champions. Change leaders within both management and union must emerge. They become convinced that change is needed based on a successful personal experience with the new way of managing, or based on observing the success of early innovations (Beer et al., in press).

Symbols. Joint appearances before employees are used by both union and management to illustrate commitment to the change, for example. Public recognition of innovative managers by higher management sends clear signals about what is valued.

Reeducation. Managers and union officials learn through a variety of means. The most powerful involves them directly in the process of change or puts them in touch with successful innovative organizations through visits.

Careful placement, promotion, and transfer. Movement of managers who are skilled in leading change has instrumental and symbolic value. It can do much to spread innovations and sustain them.

Corporate consulting resources. The availability of organization development consultants is associated with successful transformations. They provide expertise about the innovations being contemplated, and they facilitate change through the human-process interventions described earlier.

Social and institutional context. Unions and government affect the success of corporate change efforts. Walton (1987b) found that, in countries with cooperative union, government, and business relations, innovations in the shipping industry that he studied diffused more rapidly. The intergroup interventions mentioned earlier can be used to improve interorganizational relationships.

The Role of Effective Change Leaders

The preceding discussion and research point to the critical importance of leaders, corporate top management, and general managers of subunits in energizing change, envisioning the future state, and enabling organizational members to carry out the change (Beckhard, 1988; Bennis & Nanus, 1985; Schein, 1985). The importance of leadership is supported by findings that paradigmatic change, as compared with incremental change, is almost always associated with the arrival of a new leader (Beer et al., in press; Tushman, Newman, & Nadler, 1988). Effective leaders are able to energize, envision, enable, and model (Tushman et al., 1988). Few executives possess all of these skills; therefore, organization development consultants who possess knowledge, vision, or skills the leader may not possess can play an important supporting role in managing change.

Energize. Effective change leaders cause others to embrace change, to see it in their interest and in the interest of organizational effectiveness, even when a crisis is not apparent. They translate external pressure into practical goals and meaningful themes. Successful change leaders in the 1980s have used quality improvement, a rallying cry at Ford Motor, for example, not improvement in financial performance (Beer et al., in press).

Envision. Imagining and articulating the values, behavior, and organizational arrangements that will be needed in the future is an important leadership task. This requires the ability to translate strategic and task imperatives, dictated by heightened competition, into organizational and behavioral terms. In turn, this requires knowledge about organizational concepts and leading-edge practices (Walton, 1987b). Change leaders also set new and difficult standards of behavior and performance, but without attacking the traditional culture, a source of pride to organizational members (Beckhard, 1988; Tushman et al., 1988).

Enable. Effective change leaders supply resources and rewards. They form an effective management team and a consensus among different stakeholders. They are skilled in advocacy, conflict resolution, and communication (Walton, 1987b).

Model. Change at the subunit level is directly related to leaders' ability to model practices they are asking others to adopt. However, inconsistencies between espoused philosophy and behavior by top managers do not necessarily block a corporate transformation in its early stages, although consistency would obviously be helpful (Beer et al., in press). The finding that inconsistency by top management does not block corporate change is probably due to its greater distance from the changes at the unit level. As the corporate transformation progresses to a later stage, one where changes at headquarters are required, top managers will have to model what they espouse.

The Role of the Consultant

The idealized model of the organization development practitioner is that of a "process consultant." Consultants often describe their role as neutral, as consulting to the entire system, and as the antithesis of the power politics that pervade organizations. They are also supposed to think about organizations systemically and be capable of intervening in all of an organization's facets. However, consultants must mesh this idealized vision of their role with certain realities (Fitzgerald, 1987).

The first reality is that of power. A more pragmatic approach to power may go a long way toward reconciling the schisms between textbook consulting and the reality of how things get done in organizations. Greiner and Schein (1988) advocated that organization development consultants incorporate a power perspective. They argued that organization development has been dominated by a collegial/consensus model of power and needs to integrate elements of a power/pluralist view of power. They suggested that consultants need to turn to expertise, personality, and others' support to establish a stronger power base. They suggested that consultants seek influence by finding a powerful organizational sponsor, gaining access to senior executives, and brokering the recruitment and promotion of senior executives who support change objectives. In view of the fact that line managers, not consultants, lead change (Beer & Walton, 1987; Pettigrew, 1985) and that organization development is becoming more important in developing competitive advantage, consultants will have to learn how to develop influence with powerful executives (Cobb, 1986) without eroding their role in helping executives learn about themselves and their organization. These are opposites that are difficult to mesh.

A second reality that most consultants must deal with is their own relatively narrow base of knowledge, skills, and perspective. Organization development consultants are often skilled in only one intervention, most often a process intervention. Our knowledge of organizational change clearly points to the interdependence and interaction of human processes and the harder elements of structure and systems. Effective consultants are social system diagnosticians and organizational architects. They integrate intervention methods (Beer, 1980; Mendenhall & Oddou, 1983). They mesh the expert advisor role with the process consultation role—again, two opposites that are difficult to integrate.

A third reality is that of task and competition. Concern with human process dominates organization development practice to the exclusion of concern for the organization's business. Yet, we argued earlier that research demonstrates the importance of using the organization's most important task as the means for energizing change and the focus for reorganizing. Consultants who are knowledgeable about the business (strategy, customers, markets, and technology) are in a position to help managers link innovations in organizing with competitive imperatives.

We argue that effective organization development consultants mesh the process consultant's role with the power, systems, and business perspectives. They are opportunistic, take a long-range view, have high tolerance for ambiguity, realize that organizations are messy, and are gratified with small successes (McLean, Sims, Mangan, & Tuffield, 1982). Based on their understanding of organizational dynamics and the change process, they respond flexibly to unfolding events, thereby reducing their reliance on normative models, single interventions, or programmed change strategies (Schein, 1988a).

Conclusion

Organization development's assumptions about effectiveness and its intervention methods and strategies have become more relevant as the competitive environment has intensified. However, to help managers cope with paradigmatic change, particularly as large corporations become the focus, intervention theory and practice are being modified to incorporate the following emergent conclusions.

1. Changes that threaten fundamental assumptions underlying bureaucratic organizations are not possible without competitive pressures.

2. Intervention that aligns roles and responsibilities (the context for behavior) with the organization's most important task, not intervention in relationships or norms, is the most effective starting point for change.

3. Changes in context effect changes in employee behavior first, before attitudes, norms, or skills are well formed. Numerous social psychologists (Bem, 1968; Festinger, 1957; Lieberman, 1956) have found that behavior forced by new roles or circumstances causes people to endorse attitudes consonant with that behavior, even when their original attitudes conflicted with the behavior.

4. Commitment to organizational innovations that employees know will force them to adapt is obtained through involvement in designing the new organization. That involvement must reveal the connection between innovative practices and the organization's competitive challenge in order for managers, workers, and unions to design themselves into an organization that threatens to change traditional behaviors and attitudes.

5. Because commitment to change can be obtained only if all stakeholders see the relevance of innovative management practices to unit competitiveness, corporations with multiple divisions and plants must encourage each unit to follow the process described earlier. Efforts to impose innovations from the top are likely to fail. Moreover, early successes of innovative units can serve as an impetus for change in other units.

These conclusions highlight modifications in organization development theory and practice that are occurring. Competitive pressure must be present for interventions to be relevant and effective. Traditional emphasis on process intervention is being broadened to include organi-zational design, and the two approaches are being integrated more effectively. The participative normative-reeducative strategy for change is being augmented with strategies that focus on the task and business. The therapeutic model of intervention is being enlarged to include a managerial/power perspective.

To remain a viable field organization development faces two challenges. First, it must augment the normative perspective with a more pragmatic and realistic human resource investment perspective. What is being learned about why and how organizations use organization development to become more competitive must be incorporated into a coherent theory of organization development. That theory must specify under what circumstances an investment in organization development is warranted, what improvements in organization effectiveness might be expected from that investment, and the value of these improvements to the organization. The theory must also identify the organizational conditions that must exist for an investment in human resource development to go forward. What kind of managers are needed? What policies and practices will institutionalize a process of organizational renewal, and how should a company organize its change agent resources to manage such a process? Just as important, what corporate business strategies and financial policies make it possible for managers to stick to a long-term organization development strategy, and how do short-term pressures for earnings make this difficult?

Second, the field will be prevented from helping U.S. corporations become more competitive unless educational institutions make it possible for individuals to acquire the complex mix of knowledge and skills required of managers and consultants engaged in the practice of organization development. Until now traditional disciplinary boundaries and the assumption that universities should impart knowledge and not skill has slowed the development of managers competent in leading change and professional practitioners of organization development capable of helping them. An educational enterprise capable of developing such leaders and professionals may be the difference between success and failure of U.S. corporations competing in increasingly global markets.

References

Alderfer, C. A. (1977). "Organization Development." *Annual Review of Psychology,* 28, 197–224.

Bandura, A. (1977). *Social Learning Theory.* Englewood Cliffs, NJ: Prentice Hall.

Beckhard, R. (1969). *Organization development: Strategies and models.* Reading, MA: Addison-Wesley.

Beckhard, R. (1988). "The executive management of transformational leadership." In R. Kilmann & T. J. Covin (eds.), *Corporate Transformation* (pp. 89–101). San Francisco: Jossey-Bass.

Beckhard, R., & Harris, R. T. (1977). *Organizational transitions.* Reading, MA: Addison-Wesley.

Beer, M. (1976). "The technology of organization development." In M. Dunnett (ed.), *Handbook of organizational/industrial psychology* (pp. 937–85). Chicago: Rand McNally.

Beer, M. (1980). *Organization change and development: A systems view,* Glencove, IL: Goodyear/Scott Foresman.

Beer, M. (1988). "The critical path for change: Keys to success and failure in six companies." In R. Kilmann & T. J. Covin (eds.), *Corporate transformation* (pp. 17–45). San Francisco: Jossey-Bass.

Beer, M., Eisenstat, R., & Spector, B. (in press). *Rediscovering Competitiveness: Developing the adaptive organization.* Boston, MA: Harvard Business School Press.

Beer, M., & Walton, E. (1987). "Organizational change and development." In M. Rosenzweig & L. Porter (eds.), *Annual Review of Psychology* (pp. 339–68). Palo Alto, CA: Annual Reviews.

Bem, D. J. (1968). "Attitudes as self-descriptions: Another look at the attitude behavior link." In A. G. Greenwald, T. C. Brock, & T. M. Ostrom (eds.), *Psychological foundations of attitudes* (pp. 197–215). New York: Academic Press.

Bennis, W. G., Benne, K. D., & Chin, R. (1961). *The planning of change.* New York: Holt, Rinehart & Winston.

Bennis, W., & Nanus, B. (1985). *Leaders.* New York: Harper & Row.

Blake, R. R., Shepard, H. A., & Mouton, J. S. (1964). *Managing intergroup conflict in industry.* Houston: Gulf Publishing.

Bocialetti, G. (1987). "Quality of work life: Some unintended effects on the seniority tradition of an industrial union." *Group and Organization Studies,* 12, 386–410.

Boss, W. B. (1983). "Team building and the problem of regression: The personal management interview as an intervention." *Journal of Applied Behavioral Science,* 19, 67–84.

Burke, W. W. (1982). *Organization development: Principles and practices.* Boston: Little, Brown.

Burns, T., & Stalker, G. M. (1961). *The management of innovation.* London: Tavistock.

Cobb, A. T. (1986). "Political diagnosis: Applications in organizational development." *Academy of Management Review,* 11, 482–96.

Coch, L., & French, J. R. P. (1948). Overcoming resistance to change. *Human Relations,* 1, 512–32.

Crockett, W. J. (1977). "Introducing change to a government agency." In P. H. Mirvis & D. N. Berg (eds.), *Failures in organization development and change* (pp. 111–48). New York: Wiley-Interscience.

Davis, S., & Lawrence, P. R. (1977). *Matrix.* Reading, MA: Addison-Wesley.

Dyer, W. G. (1977). *Team building: Alternatives and issues.* Reading, MA: Addison-Wesley.

Festinger, L. (1957). *A theory of cognitive dissonance,* Stanford, CA: Stanford University Press.

Fitzgerald, T. H. (1987). "The OD practitioner in the business world: Theory versus reality." *Organizational Dynamics,* 16, 20–33.

Frank, L. L., & Hackman, J. R. (1975). "A failure of job enrichment: The case of the change that wasn't." *Journal of Applied Behavioral Science,* 11, 413–36.

Friedlander, F. (1968). "A comparative study of consulting process and group development." *Journal of Applied Behavioral Science,* 4, 377–99.

Friedlander, F., & Brown, L. D. (1974). "Organization development." *Annual Review of Psychology,* 25, 313–41.

Frost, C. F., Wakeley, J. H., & Ruh, R. A. (1974). *The Scanlon plan for organization development: Identity, participation, and equity.* East Lansing: Michigan State University Press.

Greiner, L. E., & Schein, V. E. (1988). *Power and organization development: mobilizing power to implement change.* Reading, MA: Addison-Wesley.

Guzzo, R. A., Jette, R. D., & Katzell, R. A. (1985). "The effects of psychologically based intervention programs on worker productivity: A meta-analysis." *Personnel Psychology,* 38, 275–92.

Hackman, J. R., & Oldham, G. R. (1980). *Work redesign.* Reading, MA: Addison-Wesley.

Hammer, T. H. (1988). "New developments in profit sharing, gainsharing, and employee ownership." In J. P. Campbell, R. J. Campbell, & Associates, *Productivity in organizations: New perspectives from industrial and organizational psychology* (pp. 328–66). San Francisco: Jossey-Bass.

Katz, D., & Kahn, R. L. (1966). *The social psychology of organizing.* New York: John Wiley & Sons.

Klein, J. (1986). *Sedelia revisited* (Harvard Business School Case). Boston, MA: President and Fellows of Harvard College.

Lawler, E. E. (1978). "The new plant revolution." *Organizational Dynamics,* 6, 2–12.

Lawler, E. E. (1981). *Pay and organization development.* Reading, MA: Addison-Wesley.

Lawler, E. E., & Mohrman, S. A. (1987). "Quality circles: After the honeymoon." *Organizational Dynamics,* 15, 42–55.

Lawrence, P. R., & Dyer, D. (1983). *Renewing American industry.* New York: Free Press.

Lawrence, P. R., & Lorsch, J. W. (1967). *Organization and environment.* Homewood, IL: Richard D. Irwin.

Lawrence, P. R., & Lorsch, J. W. (1969). *Developing organizations: Diagnosis and actions.* Reading, MA: Addison-Wesley.

Levinson, H. (1972). *Organizational diagnosis.* Cambridge, MA: Harvard University Press.

Lieberman, S. (1956). "The effects of changes in roles on the attitudes of role occupants." *Human Relations,* 9, 385–402.

Lorsch, J. W., & Morse, J. J. (1974). *Organizations and their members: A contingency approach.* New York: Harper & Row.

Macy, B. A., Hurts, C. C. M., Izumi, H., Norton, L. W., & Smith, R. R. (1986, August). *Meta-analysis of United States empirical organizational change and work innovation field experiments: Methodology and preliminary results.* Paper presented at the meeting of the National Academy of Management, Chicago, IL.

McLean, A. J., Sims, D. B., Mangan, I. L., & Tuffield, D. (1982). *Organization development in transition: Evidence of an evolving profession.* New York: John Wiley & Sons.

Mendenhall, M., & Oddou, G. (1983). "The integrative approach to OD: Macgregor revisited." *Group and Organization Studies,* 8, 291–301.

Mirvis, P. H., & Berg, D. N. (1977). *Failures in organization development and change.* New York: Wiley-Interscience.

Nadler, D. A. (1977). *Feedback and organizational development: Using data based methods.* Reading, MA: Addison-Wesley.

Pasmore, W. A. (1982). "Overcoming the roadblocks in work-restructuring efforts." *Organizational Dynamics,* 10, 54–67.

Pettigrew, A. (1985). *The awakening giant: Continuity and change in ICI.* New York: Basil Blackwell.

Rosen, C., & Quarrey, M. (1987). "How well is employee ownership working?" *Harvard Business Review,* 65, 126–128.

Sashkin, M., & Burke, W. W. (1987). "Organization development in the 1980s." *Journal of Management,* 13, 393–417.

Schein, E. (1985). *Organizational culture and leadership.* San Francisco: Jossey-Bass.

Schein, E. H. (1988a). "Back to the future: Recapturing the OD vision." In F. Massarik (ed.), *Advances in OD.* Norwood, NJ: Ablex.

Schein, E. H. (1988b). *Process consultation.* Reading, MA: Addison-Wesley.

Schlesinger, L. A., & Oshry, B. (1984). "Quality of work life and the supervisor: Muddle in the middle." *Organizational Dynamics,* 13, 4–20.

Sundstrom, E.; DeMeuse, K. P.; & Futrell, D. (1990). "Work teams: Applications and effectiveness." *American Psychologist,* 45, 120–33.

Tushman, M. L.; Newman, W. H.; & Nadler, D. A. (1988). "Executive leadership and organizational evolution: Managing incremental and discontinuous change." In R. Kilmann & T. J. Covey (eds.), *Corporate transformation* (pp. 102–30). San Francisco: Jossey-Bass.

Walton, R. E. (1977). "Work innovations at Topeka:

After six years." *Journal of Applied Behavioral Science,* 13, 422–33.

Walton, R. E. (1980). "Establishing and maintaining high commitment work systems." In J. R. Kimberly, R. H. Miles, & Associates (eds.), *The organizational life cycle: Issues in the creation, transformation and decline of organizations* (pp. 208–90). San Francisco: Jossey-Bass.

Walton, R. E. (1986). "A vision-led approach to management restructuring." *Organizational Dynamics,* 14, 4–16.

Walton, R. E. (1987a). "From control to commitment in the work place." *Harvard Business Review,* 63, 76–84.

Walton, R. E. (1987b). *Innovating to compete.* San Francisco: Jossey-Bass.

Zand, D. E. (1974). "Collateral organizations: A new change strategy." *Journal of Applied Behavioral Science,* 10, 63–89.

Zuboff, S. (1988). *The age of the smart machine.* New York: Basic Books.

READING 53
RE-ENERGIZING THE MATURE ORGANIZATION

Richard W. Beatty and David O. Ulrich

Globalization, reduced technology cycles, shifting demographics, changing expectations among workers and customers, and restructuring of capital markets made the 1980s a "white water decade," rapidly introducing changes for both public and private organizations.

The greater the forces for change, the greater the competitive pressure; and the greater the competitive pressure, the greater the demand for change. This seemingly endless cycle of competition-change can become a vicious circle if executives cannot discover novel ways to compete.

Traditional ways of competing have reached a level of parity in which businesses cannot easily distinguish themselves solely on the basis of technology, product, or price. The ability of an organization to conceptualize and manage change—to compete from the inside out by increasing its capacity for change—may represent that novel way to compete. The universal challenge of change is to learn how organizations and employees can change faster than changing business conditions to become more competitive. That is, to change faster on the inside than the organization is changing on the outside.

This need to understand and manage change is salient, particularly for mature firms where the long-established norms of stability and security must be replaced with new values, such as speed, simplicity, unparalleled customer service, and a self-confident, empowered workforce. The purpose of this article is to explore how mature

Source: Richard W. Beatty and David O. Ulrich, "Re-Energizing the Mature Organization." Reprinted, by permission of publisher, from *Organizational Dynamics,* Summer 1991, pp. 16–30.
Copyright © 1991 by American Management Association, New York. All rights reserved.

firms can be re-energized. To do this, we will describe the unique challenges of creating change in mature firms, detail principles that can be used to guide change, and identify the leadership and work activities required to accomplish change.

The Challenge of Change and Organization Life Cycle

Organizations evolve through a life cycle with each evolving stage raising change challenges. We shall use an hourglass to portray the process of organizational life cycles and change challenges.

As illustrated in Figure 1, organizations in their entrepreneurial stage focus on the definition and development of new products and markets. During this life stage, the change challenge is primarily one of defining and learning how to penetrate a market or niche. Managers who translate ideas into customer value overcome this *niche challenge* and proceed to the growth stage.

In the laundry equipment industry, for example, the entrepreneurial stage developed in the early 1900s when over 60 appliance makers entered the market to provide more automated equipment for doing laundry. These autonomous (and often small) appliance makers served local markets with their specialized machines.

During the growth stage, businesses proliferate. This evolutionary stage could become corporate nirvana—if it persists. Unfortunately, as more firms enter a market, meeting the change challenge becomes necessary for survival. Over time, small firms frequently join together to form large firms; firms that cannot compete

FIGURE 1

Organization life cycle and change challenges

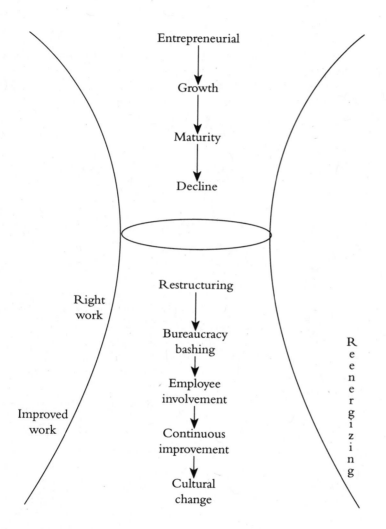

Organization
Life Cycle

Change
Challenges

Entrepreneurial

Niche
identification

Growth

Survival/shakeout

Maturity

Renewal

Decline

Right
work

Restructuring

Bureaucracy
bashing

Employee
involvement

Improved
work

Continuous
improvement

Reenergizing

Cultural
change

either merge or go out of business. Between 1960 and 1985, a major shakeout occurred in the North American appliance market. From over 60 major appliance makers, the market shrank to five major companies that, together, held over 80 percent of the market. Each of these five major appliance makers faced and overcame the shakeout change challenge.

As organizations overcome the niche and shakeout challenges, they develop standard operating procedures. This third evolutionary stage is maturity. Organizations in the mature stage face a significant renewal change challenge. The presence of established norms that once helped accomplish past success may lead to complacency and managers may become too dependent on these for future success. These calcified norms then become irrevocable patterns of behavior that eventually lead to structural inertia as would be evidenced in the way they affect structure, systems, and processes. Not only do they create inertia but the insulation they provide leads to an avoidance of challenges that can lead to success.

In the appliance industry in the late 1980s, renewal became a major agenda. For example, Whirlpool changed its century-old functional organization into business units and formed a joint venture with Phillips to enter markets outside North America. General Electric spent over $1 billion refurbishing plants, technologies, and management systems. These efforts at renewal, still under way, will predict which firms will emerge as winners in the next century. Organizations that fail the renewal change challenge enter a period of decline, during which they slowly lose market share to firms that have renewed.

In many ways, the renewal change challenge is more onerous than the niche identification or shakeout challenges. To overcome the niche and shakeout challenges, managers in successful organizations were able to focus on customers and develop products and technologies to meet customer needs. During the maturity phase, product

and technological parity is likely to emerge. Competitors offer customers similar product features at comparable costs. Given a technological and financial parity, managers facing a renewal challenge must identify additional capabilities to meet customer needs. They must learn to compete through competencies; they must develop the ability to compete from the inside out—to build internal organizational processes that meet external customer requirements.

Organizational Mindsets and Life Cycles

Perhaps the greatest effort involved in overcoming the renewal challenge is to change the mindset of employees at all levels of an organization. The mindset represents a shared way of thinking and behaving within an organization. Mindsets are reflected in "accepted behaviors and attitudes"—customer service at Nordstrom, quality at Ford, and speed, simplicity, and self-confidence at General Electric. Mindsets are often institutionalized in vision, value, and mission.

It takes time for mindsets to be instilled. By the time an organization becomes mature, it has likely established a relatively fixed mindset. Employees self-select into the organization because of its particular set of norms. They are rewarded by promotions, salary increases, and enhanced job responsibility when they embody the mindset. Mindsets become very powerful means of gaining unity and focus. Students of Japanese service organizations have argued that this unity of mindset becomes a means of gaining competitiveness. The mindset provides a common focus and therefore increases the intensity of work done.

In mature organizations, a shared mindset can be a liability and its intensity may hinder the ability to change. Since employees come to accept, adopt, and associate with the mindset of a mature company, the renewal process requires letting go. To accomplish renewal, traditional control measures must be replaced with an empowered workforce that is more self-directed, self-managed, and self-controlled, thus reducing the need not only for strong competencies in managerial control but for large numbers of managers and supervisors as well. Thus a truly empowered workforce is one that acts out of commitment to purpose without the traditional boundaries and narrow mindsets of mature organizations. In Figure 1, the more open end of the hourglass represents the more open and flexible organizations; the closed end of the hourglass represents the constraints of mature organizations. The hourglass analogy shows this movement from more open and flexible (top of hour glass) to closed and inflexible (center). In this model, renewal becomes the change challenge that allows a firm to go through the "neck" of the hourglass and rediscover a vitality and energy that move the mature firm out of the decline trap and into a revived state of activity.

Principles of Renewal

Responding to the renewal challenge is difficult at best, and unlikely in most cases. Few organizations successfully accomplish renewal from within. Rather than renew, organizations that perpetuate outmoded mindsets become prey to consolidations, acquisitions, or mergers—external pressures that *impose* renewal. We propose that the probability of renewal of mature organizations increases if four principles are understood and practiced. If managers recognize these principles, they may be able to help overcome the renewal challenge.

1. *Mature organizations renew by instilling a customer perspective and focusing on customer demands.* To begin to overcome the renewal challenge, a company and all its employees must be completely devoted to gaining a sustained competitive advantage. Competitive advantage comes from understanding and meeting customer needs in unique ways.

One of the most difficult challenges of renewal is the ability to recognize whether existing mindsets and practices are inconsistent with current customer requirements. When the mindset within an organization becomes a way of life, embedded in employee work habits, it is even more difficult to acknowledge or change. By examining the organization from a customer perspective, employees may better understand the internal processes and practices that reinforce existing mindsets. Hewlett-Packard, one of the first organizations to adopt such a practice as a part of its renewal effort, did this by incorporating internal and external customer satisfaction into its performance appraisal system.

A more detailed example of this practice is provided by a company that, in working through the renewal challenge, experienced at first mixed results. While employees enjoyed participating in innovative self-managed work teams and preparing vision statements, over a period of time each new activity that appeared promising fizzled, and employees went back to business as usual. To encourage and advance renewal, a workshop was held in which the employees were asked to examine their organization and four of its major competitors, pretending they were buyers of the product. As customers, they talked about why they would pick one supplier over another. They explored the images each of the five companies communicated and examined reasons why customers picked one competitor over another. After performing this analysis, they were able to articulate, from a customer's perspective, the perceived mindsets residing within each of the five competing organizations.

Having done this customer assessment of the competitors, the employees were able to decipher and enunciate the mindset within their own company and distinguish how their company's mindset differed from those of their competitors.

Becoming devoted to customers comes from employees spending less time thinking about internal company policies and practices and more time interacting with and worrying about their next customers. Companies that compete through service seek creative and extensive ways to involve customers in all activities. Customers may become involved in product design, in reviewing vision statements, in attending and making presentations at training and development sessions, and in doing employee reviews. The more interaction there is between customers and employees, the more a customer perspective is instilled within the organization. By taking an active role in meeting customer needs, employees in mature organizations may begin the conquest of the renewal change challenge. They can in effect change their performance expectations from meeting demands vertically dictated, to focusing horizontally on the process requirements in order to meet internal and external customer requirements. When meeting customer needs becomes more important to the organization than preserving political boundaries, employees will be more willing to renew themselves and their company. There are several reasons for this, including the freedom from autocratic directions by giving autonomy to those whose services are dependent on it.

Mature companies seeking to renew have engaged in a variety of activities to ensure customer commitment. At Hewlett-Packard, engineers who design products spend months meeting with customers in focus groups, in laboratories, and in application settings to ensure that new products meet customer requirements. When the mini-van was first announced at Chrysler, several senior executives were not supportive of the concept. They believed the vehicle was neither a truck nor a passenger car and would have no market. However, after extensive meetings with customers, the executives became convinced that this vehicle created an entire new niche.

At an oil service company, sales personnel were trained to interview and work with customers to identify their needs, rather than to sell products. As these sales personnel spent time with customers and became aware of their current and future needs, the oil service company experienced dramatic market share growth.

The principle of customer-centered activity is consistent with the extensive work on quality done by a number of management researchers over the years. It encourages employees to define their value as a function of customer requirements, rather than of personal gain. It replaces old practices with new ones that add value to customers. It refocuses attention outside to change inside—that is, toward the ultimate and the next customer.

2. *Mature organizations renew by increasing their capacity for change.* Most individuals have internal clocks, or biorhythms, that determine when we wake, when we need to eat, and how quickly we make decisions. Like individuals, most organizations have internal clocks that determine how quickly decisions are made and activities completed. These internal clocks affect how long it takes organizations to move from idea to definition, to action. It has been argued that a major challenge for organizations is to reduce their cycle time, which means to change the internal clock and timing on how decisions are made. For mature organizations to experience renewal, their internal clocks must be adjusted. Cycle lengths must be reduced and the capacity for change increased.

Typically, the internal clocks of mature organizations have not been calibrated for changing erratic and unpredictable business conditions. To enact and increase a capacity for change, managers need to work on alignment, symbiosis, and reflexiveness.

"Alignment" refers to the extent to which different organization activities are focused on common goals. When organizations have a sense of alignment, their strategy, structure, and systems can move more readily toward consistent and shared goals.

Aligned organizations have a greater capacity

for change because less time is spent building commitment, and more energy and time are spent accomplishing work. To calibrate alignment, a number of organizations have sponsored "congruence" workshops where the degree of congruence between organizational activities is assessed.

"Symbiosis" refers to the extent to which organizations are able to remove boundaries inside and outside an organization.

General Electric CEO Jack Welch describes any organizational boundary as a "toll-gate." Any time individuals or products must cross a boundary, an economic, emotional, and time toll is paid. When organizations have extensive boundaries, tolls can be direct and indirect expenses. Direct boundary costs result in higher prices to customers because of extra costs in producing the product. Indirect boundary costs occur from each boundary increasing the time required to accomplish tasks. Boundaries, and the tolls required for crossing, set an organization's internal clock and impair capacity for change. Increasing cycle time and creating symbiosis mean reducing boundaries and increasing capacity for change and action. The Ford Taurus has become a classic example of reducing boundaries and increasing capacity for change. By forming and assigning a cross-functional team responsible for the complete design and delivery of the Taurus, boundaries were removed between departments. The time from concept to production for the Taurus was 50 percent less than established internal clocks.

To ensure that a capacity for change continues over time, individuals must become reflexive and have the ability to continue to learn and adapt over time. "Reflexiveness" is the ability to learn from previous actions. Organizations increase their capacity for change when time is spent reflecting on past activities and learning from them.

The capacity for change principle expedites renewal. When individuals and systems inside an organization can so change their internal clocks that decisions move quicker from concept to action, renewal occurs more frequently. In this way, organizational cycles differ from individual biorhythms: Cycle times are not genetic and intractable but learned and adjustable. By adjusting cycles, the capacity for change increases, which may lead to renewal of mature organizations.

3. *Mature organizations renew by altering both the hardware and software within the organization.* Management activities within an organization may be dissected into *hardware* and *software*. Management hardware represents issues, such as strategy, structure, and systems. These domains of activity are malleable and measurable and can be heralded with high visibility—for example, timely announcements about new strategies, structures, or systems. Also, like computer hardware, unless they are connected to appropriate software they are useless. In the organization, software represents employee behavior and mindset. These less visible domains of organizational activity are difficult to adjust or measure, but they often determine the extent to which renewal occurs.

Most renewal efforts begin by changing hardware—putting in a new strategy, structure, or system. These hardware efforts help mature organizations to turn around or to change economic indicators. They do not, however, assure transformation; this comes only when new hardware is supported by appropriate software. Organizational renewal efforts that focus extensively or exclusively on strategy, structure, and systems engage in numerous discussions and debates. These discussions are necessary but are not sufficient to make any difference. At times, in fact, these discussions consume so much energy and resources that too few resources are left to make sure that employee behavior and mindset match the changes. Just as many companies have storage rooms filled with unused hardware, many organizations have binders of strategy, structure, and system changes that were never implemented.

For renewal in mature organizations, changing strategy and structure is not enough. Adjusting and encouraging individual employee behavior and working on changing the mindset are also critical. In one organization attempting to examine and modify software, the focus was not on strategy, structure, and systems but on work activities. Groups of employees met in audit workshops to identify work activities as done by suppliers for customers, then to examine each set of work activities to eliminate whatever did not add value to customers and to improve whatever did. The key to the success of these work audit workshops was that participants would leave with work inspected and modified in a positive manner. As a result of the workshops, participants have changed some of the existing behaviors and beliefs within the business.

For organizations seeking to increase the probability of renewal, new mindsets must be created that will be shared by all employees, customers, and suppliers. For suppliers, this commonly ᵢs a shared perspective that leverages competitive advantage. Xerox, between 1980 and 1988, reduced its number of suppliers from over 3,000 to 300. By focusing attention and certifying qualified suppliers, Xerox has built a shared mindset among its supplier network. Ford Motor Company has done similar work with suppliers. A team of Ford executives must accredit each Ford supplier on a number of dimensions of quality, delivery, and service. Without passing the accreditation test, the supplier cannot work with Ford. By maintaining this policy, Ford builds its vision and values into its supplier network, and Ford suppliers mesh their vision and values with Ford. These types of activities build the software that reinforces the hardware, or system changes that eventually lead to renewal.

4. *Mature organizations renew by creating empowered employees who act as leaders at all levels of the organization.* Shared leadership implies that individuals have responsibility and accountability for activities within their domain. Individuals become leaders by having influence and control over the factors that affect their work performance.

Organizations that renew have leaders sta-tioned throughout the hierarchy regardless of position or title. Employees are trusted and empowered to act on issues that affect their work performance. Leaders have the obligation of articulating and stating a vision and of ensuring that the vision will be implemented. Leadership can come either from bringing new leaders into the organization or building competencies into existing leadership positions.

When Michael Blumenthal became chairman of Burroughs, he changed 23 of the top 24 managers within his first year. His assessment was that the current leadership team was so weighed down with traditional vision and values that they could not develop a new leadership capability, capacity for change, and competitiveness. Blumenthal could change the top echelon of his organization, but he could not replace the 1,000 secondary leaders throughout the organization. These leaders needed to be developed to induce a renewal within the company.

Primary and secondary leaders must be able to communicate the new mindset, articulating the vision and values in ways that are not only readily understandable and acceptable to all employees but that are inspirational, also. In other words, the employees must believe that it is worth giving extraordinary effort to make the vision a reality.

In addition to communication, leaders are expected to possess the competencies members perceive as necessary to lead the organization to the heights of its vision. Although some of these competencies may be functional, others are clearly the management of human resources, especially the effective use of measures both positive and negative following the actions of all employees. While the use of alternative reward strategies has become extremely popular in the last few years, leaders should be able to confront employees who are unwilling to perform at levels necessary for making a substantive contribution to competitive advantage.

Finally, leaders must be credible. Members must be able to trust in the word of their leaders;

if they cannot, they will be unwilling to accept the vision or the values—and certainly be unwilling to marshall the level of energy necessary to accomplish higher and higher levels of performance. The credibility of leadership cannot be overestimated when trying to energize the organization's human resource.

In brief, we have proposed four principles that can increase the probability of renewal for a mature organization. By understanding these four principles, managers may engage in a series of activities that make this renewal possible.

Leadership and Work Activities

Having identified a need for mature organizations to overcome a renewal challenge, and a set of principles on which renewal is based, we can identify specific leadership and work activities which accomplish this effort. Generally, the process for re-energizing mature organizations follows the five steps shown in Figure 2, although these may not always be in sequence, as some steps may occur simultaneously.

Stage 1: Restructuring. Organizational renewal generally begins with a turnaround effort focused on restructuring by downsizing and/or delayering. Through head-count reduction, organizations attempt to become "lean and mean," recognizing that they had become "fat" by not strategically managing performance at all levels. Organizations continue to improve global measures of productivity (sales or other measures of performance per employee) by reducing the number of employees. At General Electric, staff reductions removed approximately 25 percent of the workforce between 1982 and 1988. This re-

FIGURE 2

A process for reenergizing mature organizations

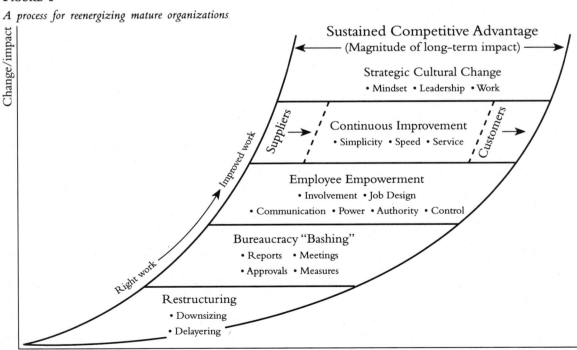

duction came from retirements, reorganizations, consolidations, plant closings, and greater spans of control. Such a head-count reduction can save organizations billions of dollars and initiate renewal. At J. I. Case, the implement manufacturer, well over 90 percent of the top-management group was replaced as the organization faced a substantial change in how it was to do business in a highly competitive global environment.

The leadership requirement during restructuring is clear: Have courage to make difficult decisions fairly and boldly. No one likes to take away jobs. It will not lead to great popularity or emotional attachment of employees. However, leaders who face a renewal change challenge must act. They must implement a process that ensures equity and due cause to employees. By so doing, leaders start the renewal process by turning around an organization through restructuring.

Stage 2: Bureaucracy Bashing. "Bureaucracy bashing" follows restructuring. In this stage, attempts are made to get rid of unnecessary reports, approvals, meetings, measures, policies, procedures, or other work activities that create backlogs. By focusing on bureaucracy reduction, employees throughout the organization experience changes in how they do their work. Often, sources of employee work frustration come from being constrained by bureaucratic procedures and not being able to see or feel the impact of their work. Bureaucratic policies and processes that consume energy and build frustration may have been developed in older work settings, causing more harm than good; these need to be examined and replaced.

In the restructuring stage, mindsets of corporate loyalty are shattered. Employees who believed in lifelong employment and job security may be angered by restructuring activities. Many companies that go through the restructuring phase eliminate corporate loyalty but fail to replace the employee contract with the firm. As a result, employees feel that their contract with the firm is one-way and short-term. They are giving their psychological commitment to the firm, but only for short-term monetary gains. To resolve this imbalance, employees may reduce their commitment. Executives must learn to sustain employee commitment by replacing loyalty with some other means of employee attachment.

In one company, employee contracts based on loyalty were replaced with opportunity. The chief executive of this company was honest with employees. He told them that there were no guarantees. Job loyalty, as known in stable work settings, could no longer be an economically viable alternative. However, he promised each employee that loyalty would be replaced by opportunity. He personally promised each employee that the organization would guarantee that each of them had the opportunity to develop his or her talents, to participate in key management actions, and to feel that they belonged to a part of a winning team. To guarantee this opportunity, bureaucracy had to be removed. Employees were able to identify the bureaucratic blockages in their jobs, to discuss these blockages with their bosses and peers, and to suggest how they could be removed. By so doing, employees could feel and see the value of opportunity in their work.

The bureaucracy bashing stage is necessary because, even though the head count may have reduced costs, the workload still remains, and adjustments must be made to meet the work volume requirements with the reduced head count.

At General Electric, Jack Welch has talked about reducing the workforce by 25 percent but not reducing work. As a result, employees are faced with the burden of doing 25 percent more work, which over a period of time may lead to malaise and lower productivity. Unnecessary, non-value-added work must be removed to gain parity between employees and their work load.

To get rid of bureaucracy requires getting rid of work that adds little value to customers. Continuous improvement programs that focus on meeting needs of internal and external customers may be designed to yield higher quality, speed, and greater simplicity in how all suppliers service the organization.

A process developed by one of the authors and shown in Figure 3 focuses on bureaucracy "busting." A work audit is conducted using two questions: (1) To what extent does this work activity add value to customers? and (2) To what extent are these activities performed as effectively as possible?

The first question is answered by inviting customers to share their views on the value added by work activities performed by the supplier. This dialogue between suppliers and customers may occur exclusively within a company (internal supplier/customer discussions) or between a firm and its external customers. O.1e company began inviting customers to training programs in an effort to understand customer needs and to ensure that work activities proposed within the company met customer requirements. Activities which add little value to customers were removed. This two-step process attempts to determine the "right" of the organization to leverage its competitive advantage and that of its customers.

Activities that add great value to customers become subject to the second question. This question is answered by developing an improved process to perform the work. Auditing work processes encourages specific analysis to ensure that quality in work activities is improved.

However, leaders must first model the bu-

reaucracy busting they advocate. They must be willing to let go of work systems that were implemented but that have added little or no value to the processes' next or ultimate customer. Reports or procedures that may add value to the leader, but that may be seen as bureaucratic blockages to employees, must be identified and leaders must be willing to concede their pet projects for the sake of removing these blockages. Leaders must demonstrate flexibility and listen to all reasonable requests (as long as they add value to customers and fall within legal and ethical boundaries). Finally, leaders need to encourage and reinforce risk taking among employees who initiate bureaucracy busting activities. A single equation predicts the propensity for risk taking. We see risk taking as a function of the will to win, divided by fear of failure. If the numerator is high, by selecting and developing committed employees, then leaders have the responsibility of reducing the fear of failure quotient.

Stage 3: Employee Empowerment Stage. Bureaucracies empower top managers. Bureaucracy busting empowers employees. Removing barriers between employees and managers builds openness and dialogue in ongoing management processes and begins to change the nature of the organization. Self-directed work teams, employee involvement processes, and dialogue should be built into the fabric of the organization. Without employee involvement and a fundamental new approach to management, costs may be reduced, productivity increased, and bureaucracy eliminated—but the results will not be long lasting if employees are now empowered for organizational improvement.

Many work activities encourage employee involvement. In a Japanese firm, newer professional employees have the opportunity and obligation to make the first drafts of important business proposals. By asking new employees to make these first drafts, the employees learn more about the overall business, feel empowered to have an impact on the business, and build rela-

FIGURE 3

Developing a customer focus in bureaucracy bashing

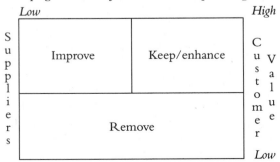

tionships with colleagues in preparing the proposals. Pepsico has involved and empowered all employees by announcing profit sharing for all. Federal Express has institutionalized employee involvement by guaranteeing employees access to the senior management meeting held each Wednesday. Employee complaints may be directed to this forum by employees without fear of any retributions by their immediate bosses. IBM assures employee involvement by allowing employees to work through a corporate ombudsman who can represent the employees' views to management without fear of reprisal or having to undergo subordinate appraisals. Amoco has initiated an extensive employee involvement program where employees are formed into teams to discuss ways to improve work and to get subordinate appraisals of their managers. These examples of employee involvement mark a fundamental change from the traditional work contract of hierarchical mature organizations to a more fluid, flexible, mutual work environment.

Traditional models of power and authority came from position and status. Power and authority in a renewing organization should come from relationships, trust, and expertise. Empowerment is a movement away from leader and expert problem solving to a system where everyone is continuously involved in improving the organization in order to leverage its competitive advantage through speed, simplicity, and service. Leaders must learn that sharing power builds a capacity to change, commitment, and competitiveness.

Stage 4: Continuous Improvement. Employee empowerment builds employee commitment. This initial commitment must be translated into long-term processes so employee involvement is not tied to any one individual but is part of a system.

Continuous improvement efforts began in mature companies by focusing on error detection and error prevention. In these efforts statistical tools—for example, flow charting, Pareto analysis, histograms, studies of variance, and opera-

tional definitions—were used to ensure that errors could be taken out of work procedures.

The continuous improvement required for this stage includes, but also goes beyond, this error focus. Continuous improvement is changing not only the technical tools of management but also the fundamental approaches to management. The continuous improvement philosophy overcomes the practice. The focus on continuous improvement must be upon the "right" work that was identified through restructuring and bureaucracy bashing. The philosophy must be one of service to customers through speed and simplicity in work processes. As this philosophy is understood throughout an organization, it becomes the rallying cry, ensuring an ongoing commitment to improve work processes.

Generating this philosophy becomes the major leadership requirement at this stage. The leader must manage through principles. The leader must articulate and communicate the principles that will govern the organization. These principles must be sensitive to each of the previous stages—restructuring for productivity, bureaucracy busting for flexibility, and employee involvement for empowerment. By instilling a philosophy of management that can then be practiced according to the specific needs of the business, leaders are able to set a direction, motivate, and steer a company through renewal.

Stage 5: Cultural Change. The final stage of renewal is really an outgrowth of the other four. Fundamental cultural change means that employees' mindset—the way they think about their work is shifted. Employees do not feel part of a "mature" company, but they see themselves as having faced and overcome the renewal change challenge. They feel the enthusiasm and commitment of trying new approaches to work and, as a result, they bring more desirable changes into the organization.

We would agree with many others who have studied these issues that accomplishing cultural change takes many years. Our rule of thumb is that, for mature organizations, the cycle time for creating fundamental cultural change is twice the cycle time it takes for introducing a new technology. Some technologies change more rapidly than others—say, for example, genetic engineering as opposed to utilities. In more rapidly changing technologies, there is more receptivity to cultural change. These organizations seem to have a more external focus. In industries with slow changing technologies, the cycle time for cultural change is extended, since these industries probably have a greater structural inertia. The latter are more internally and vertically focused.

In the re-energized organization, every leader would be judged by his ability to persevere, and how strong an advocate he is of the new culture. But it is also necessary that he exhibits tolerance since culture changes require time to take effect.

More importantly a leader must constantly and demonstratively be a model and a cheerleader of the culture he hopes to implement.

At General Electric, Jack Welch has committed the entire company to a cultural change. He constantly talks about his commitment—to financial analysts, to investors, to shareholders, to employees, and to public forums. He has defined a set of principles and has frequently asked managers to spend time implementing these principles. Welch has also asked his managers to provide him with feedback on his personal behavior. At GE he has become the nucleus of encouraging employees to commit energy and time to understanding and adopting the new work culture.

In short, the five stages in Figure 2 indicate a sequence for adopting changes to re-energize a mature organization. By first defining the right work to do, then finding ways to improve that work, companies may make simple, short-term changes that can have major, long-term impact. These five stages are based on the four principles we have identified.

Making It Happen

We have put forward a very simple argument in this paper: Mature organizations must face and overcome the renewal change challenge; they must change; they must redefine how work is done and recreate work cultures consistent with changing customer demands.

How do we anticipate that these changes will occur? It will happen because organizations and leaders at all levels have developed a new vision of strategy and culture. Organizations are becoming far more strategic, far more purposeful, and far more customer oriented. It will happen also because of new tools that are focusing more and more closely upon performance and that are raising difficult questions about the value of work and of the customer requirements within the organization.

Most mature organizations will sooner or later have to face the renewal change challenge. They will then have to find ways to change their culture; their vision will have to actually be translated into specific actions, and managers must be prepared to help employees improve, to observe their progress, and to give them feedback. Employees also must seek responsibilities, strive for continuous improvement, and change the organization's culture by making each effort add value to its customers and investors strategically and continuously.

The role of the leader is to challenge the value of each process for its contribution to customers and investors, encourage a shared vision and values, and enable employees to act by encouraging greater customer and cost consciousness, adaptability, initiative, accountability, and teamwork. To accomplish these goals, managers must model the way and immediately recognize the contributions of employees as they take risks in changing established work habits and attempt to continuously improve and enhance their contributions.

If the renewal change challenge can be overcome, an organization may move through the neck of the hourglass (see Figure 1). At the other side of the hour glass is the ability to become re-energized and meet customer needs through innovative, resourceful, and bold customer-focused initiatives.

Selected Bibliography

Several pieces have appeared recently which explore the broad range of activities and values of interest to us. One is "Why Change Programs Don't Produce Change" by Michael Beer, Russell Eisenstadt, and Burt Spector in *Harvard Business Review,* November–December 1990. It demonstrates how most change programs fail because they are guided by a fundamentally flawed theory of change. The authors claim many change programs assume that change is a conversion experience that requires an attitude change. We agree that real change requires a change in attitude and in the fundamental roles, responsibilities, and relationships that should provide the alignment of the appropriate behaviors. However, our major focus is that change occurs because work and work relationships have been redesigned to leverage the organization's human resource competitive advantage.

Another piece that is consistent with our approach is Randy Myer's "Suppliers Manage Your Customers," in *Harvard Business Review,* November–December 1989. He points out that "customer-back" organizations are successful, because, to satisfy the next and ultimate customers, you must be provided by suppliers who treat you as important customers.

A significant piece on the leader's role appeared in the *Sloan Management Review* in 1990. The article by Peter M. Senge was entitled "The Leader's New Work: Building Learning Organizations." This is a major piece that focuses on the leadership role in transforming organizations. It recognizes that becoming heuristic is essential to successful transformation— that is, an organization must learn and build the internal capability that enables it to return to viability, regardless of the level of environmental turbulence. The article stresses two leadership styles that have emerged over the years: traditional (plan, organize, and control) and transformational (vision, alignment, motivation). But a third type of leader, the leader of the future, is one who is a designer of work, a teacher, and a supporter of change—in essence, the ultimate change agent companies have been alluding to for years but is seldom seen represented.

Finally, a corollary piece appeared in *Harvard Business Review* in January–February 1991 by Robert G. Eccles, entitled "The Performance Measurement Manifesto." It suggests performance measurement is an essential missing element from many organizational change efforts and certainly from discussions on re-energizing mature organizations. Identifying the right work is essential but so is measuring the right work. Clearly, if organizations are to survive, customers need to be prioritized and processes need to be clarified. Both require measures to assess their effectiveness and to test whether they are aligned with organizational goals and objectives.

READING 54
THE EFFECTIVE ORGANIZATION: FORCES AND FORMS

Henry Mintzberg

What makes an organization effective? For a long time we thought we had the answer. Frederick Taylor told us about the "one best way" at the turn of the century, and organizations long pursued this holy grail. First it was Taylor's time and motion studies, later the participative management of the human relations people, in more recent years the wonders of strategic planning. It was as if every manager had to see the world through the same pair of glasses, although the fashion for lenses changed from time to time.

Then along came the so-called contingency theorists, who argued that "it all depends." Effective organizations designed themselves to match their conditions. They used those time and motion studies for mass production, they used strategic planning under conditions of relative stability, and so forth. Trouble was, all this advice never came together: managers were made to feel like diners at a buffet table, urged to take a little bit of this and a little bit of that.

In a way, these two approaches to organizational effectiveness are reflected in the most popular management writings of today. I like to call them "Peterian" and "Porterian." Tom Peters and Robert Waterman implore managers to "stick to their knitting" and to design their structures with "simultaneous loose-tight properties," among other best ways, while Michael Porter insists that they use competitive analysis to choose strategic positions that best match the characteristics of their industries. [1] To Porter, effectiveness resides in strategy, while to Peters it is the operations that count—executing any strategy with excellence.

While I agree that being effective depends on doing the right thing as well as doing things right, as Peter Drucker put it years ago, I believe we have to probe more deeply to find out what really makes an organization effective. We need to understand what gets it to a viable strategy in the first place, what makes it excellent once it's there, and how some organizations are able to sustain viability and excellence in the face of change.

Some years ago I thought I had another answer. I argued that effective organizations "got it all together." By choosing "configuration," they brought their various characteristics of structure, strategy, and context into natural co-alignment. [2] For example, some achieved integration as efficient machines, while others coalesced around product innovation. In a sense, these organizations played jigsaw puzzle, fitting all the pieces of their operations into one neat image.

Recently, however, I have begun to wonder about configuration. There are certainly many effective organizations that seem to fit one image or another—IBM as that "big blue" machine, 3M as the product innovator. But some rather effective organizations do not, and even those that do sometimes confound things. How does that big blue machine come up with critical adaptations when it has to, and why does 3M have those tight financial controls? Thus I have begun to consider another view of organizational effectiveness, in which organizations do not slot themselves into established images so much as

Source: Reprinted from "The Effective Organization: Forces and Forms," by Henry Mintzberg, *Sloan Management Review*, Winter 1991, pp. 54–66., by permission of publisher. Copyright © 1991 by Sloan Management Review Association. All rights reserved.

build their own unique solutions to problems. "Do your own thing" is its motto, LEGO its metaphor.

This article builds a framework around these two approaches. It proposes that the effective organization plays LEGO as well as jigsaw puzzle. The pieces of the game are the forces that organizations experience; the integrating images are the forms that organizations take. Together, they constitute a powerful framework by which to diagnose and deal with the problems organizations face. Below I introduce the forces, as the basic building blocks of all organizations. Then I shall outline the framework that is to follow.

A System of Forces

Much of what happens in organizations can, in my experience, be captured by the interplay of seven basic forces. I array five of these around the outside of a pentagon and put two in the middle, as shown in Figure 1. They are described below.

- First is the force for *direction*; this gives a sense of where the organization must go as an integrated entity. Without such direction—which today is apt to be called strategic vision, years ago grand strategy—the various activities of an

FIGURE 1

A system of forces in organizations

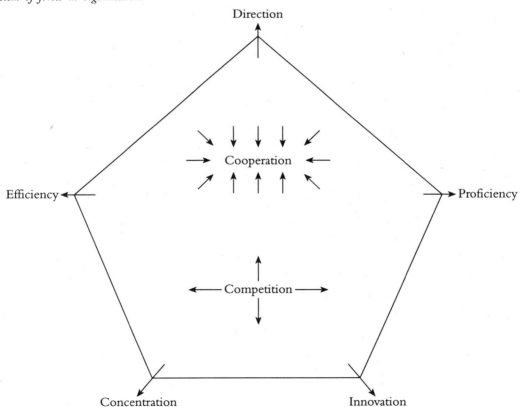

organization cannot easily mesh to achieve common purpose.

- Next is the force for *efficiency,* which attempts to ensure a viable ratio of benefits gained to costs incurred. Without some concern for efficiency, all but the most protected of organizations must eventually falter. Efficiency generally means standardization and formalization; often it reduces to economy. In current practice, it focuses on rationalization and restructuring, among other things.

- Across from the force for efficiency is that for *proficiency*—for carrying out certain tasks with high levels of knowledge and skill. Without proficiency, the difficult work of organizations— whether surgery in the hospital or engineering in the corporation—just could not get done.

- Below efficiency is the force for *concentration*—for particular units to concentrate their efforts on serving particular markets. Without such concentration, it becomes difficult to manage an organization that is diversified.

- At the bottom right is the force for *innovation.* Organizations need central direction and focused concentration, and they need efficiency and proficiency. But they also need to discover new things for their customers and themselves—to adapt and to learn.

- Finally, inside the pentagon are two forces I call catalytic: *cooperation* and *competition.* One describes the pulling together of ideology, the other the pulling apart of politics. By ideology, I mean more than just the culture of an organization; I mean the rich culture of norms, beliefs, and values that knit a disparate set of people into a harmonious, cooperative entity. By politics I mean behaviour that is technically not sanctioned or legitimate.

It acts outside the bounds of legal authority and acknowledged expertise and therefore tends to be conflictive in nature. No serious organization is ever entirely free of politics, few perhaps of at least some vestiges of ideology.

This article's view of organizational effectiveness will be developed as follows. Taking these forces as fundamental and their interplay as key to understanding what goes on in organizations, I shall argue first that when one force dominates an organization, it is drawn toward a coherent, established form, described as *configuration.* That facilitates its management, but also raises the problem of *contamination.* When no single force dominates, the organization must instead function as a balanced *combination* of different forces, including periods of *conversion* from one form to another. But combination raises the problem of *cleavage.* Both contamination and cleavage require the management of *contradiction,* and here the catalytic forces, cooperation and competition, come into play. But these two forces are themselves contradictory, and so the effective organization must balance them as well. Put this all together and you get a fascinating game of jigsaw puzzle-cum-LEGO. This may seem complicated, but bear with me; reading about it here will prove a lot easier than managing it in practice. It may even help!

Configuration

Charles Darwin once wrote about "lumpers" as opposed to "splitters"—synthesizers who think in broad categories and prefer to slot things into well-established pigeonholes, as opposed to analyzers who tend to split things up finely. [3] In a way, of course, we are all lumpers: we all like neat envelopes into which we can put our confusing experiences.

It is ironic, therefore, that in the field of management we do not have established categories by which to distinguish different organizations. Imagine biology without some system of species to consider living things. Biologists might well end up, for example, debating the "one best dwelling" for all mammals—bears as well as beavers. Silly as this example may seem, that is what we do in management all the time.

Configuration refers to any form of organization that is consistent and highly integrated. In the spirit of the jigsaw puzzle, a configuration is an image whose pieces all fit neatly together.

A Portfolio of Forms.   In principle, all kinds of configurations are possible. In practice, however, only a few seem to occur commonly.

Our pentagon contains seven forces. I believe that configuration occurs when any one of these forces dominates an organization, driving it to a corresponding form. That gives us seven basic forms, described below, five of which are shown at the nodes of the pentagon, in Figure 2.

- The *entrepreneurial* form tends to occur when the force for direction dominates an organization, so that the chief executive takes personal control of much of what goes on. This happens especially in startup and turnaround situations, both of which require the imposition of strong vision from the top; it also happens in

FIGURE 2

A system of forces and forms in organizations

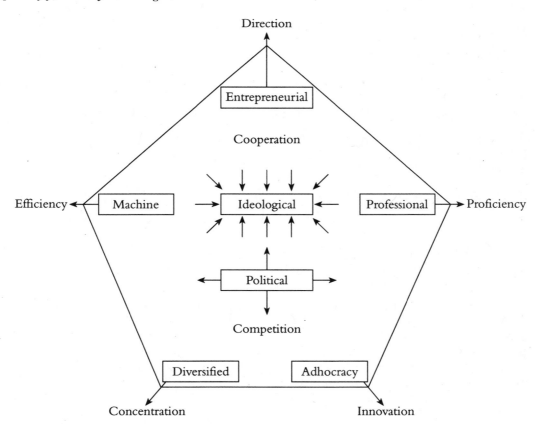

small, owner-managed companies. As a result, there are few middle-management and staff positions, or else they are relatively weak. As a turnaround example, when Jan Carlzon took over the airline SAS in the early 1980s, he established direct links with the operating employees, bypassing much of the established administration and dispensing with many of the standard control systems in order to impose his new vision.

- The *machine* form tends to appear when the force for efficiency becomes paramount; this typically occurs in mass production and mass service organizations (automobile companies, retail banks, etc.) and in ones with an overriding need for control (as in nuclear power plants and many government departments). Here, especially in the larger, more mature organization, middle-management and staff functions are fully developed; they focus on regulating the work of the operating employees by imposing rules, regulations, and standards of various kinds.

- The *professional* form tends to arise when proficiency is the dominant force, as in hospitals, accounting practices, and engineering offices. What matters here is the drive to perfect existing skills and knowledge, rather than to invent new ones. This makes the professional organization a consummate pigeonholer: the hospital, for example, prefers to diagnose entering patients as quickly as possible so it can get on with administering the most appropriate standardized treatment. This characteristic allows for the considerable autonomy found in these organizations: each professional works remarkably free of his or her colleagues, let alone of the managers ostensibly in charge.

- The *adhocracy* form develops in response to an overriding need for innovation. Again we have an organization of skilled experts. But here, because the organization exists to create novelty—such as the unique film or the new engineering prototype—the experts must combine their efforts in multidisciplinary project teams. Doing so requires a good deal of informal communication, with the result that the structure becomes fluid, sometimes called "intrapreneurial." Some adhocracy organizations, such as advertising agencies and think tank consulting firms, innovate directly on behalf of their clients. Others use project work to innovate for themselves, bringing their own new products or facilities on line—for example, some high-technology and chemical firms.

- The *diversified* form tends to arise when the force for concentration, particularly on distinct products and markets, overrides the others. Such organizations first diversify and then divisionalize. Each division is given relative autonomy, subject to the performance controls imposed by a small, central headquarters. The diversified form is, of course, best known in the world of large, conglomerate corporations. But when governments speak of accountability, they have much the same structure in mind.

- The forces for cooperation and for competition can sometimes dominate, too, giving rise to forms I call the *ideological* and the *political*. Examples of both are readily available: the spirited Israeli kibbutz is ideological, and the conflictive regulatory agency in which infighting takes over is political. But I believe these forms are not all that common, at least compared with the others discussed above, and so our discussion will proceed from here mainly on the basis of five forms and seven forces, shown in Figure 2. [4]

Do these forms really exist in practice? In one sense, they do not. After all, they are just words on pieces of paper, caricatures that simplify a complex reality. No serious organization can be labeled a pure machine or a pure adhocracy. On the other hand, we can't carry reality around in our heads; we think in terms of simplifications, called theories or models, of which these forms are examples. We must, therefore, turn to a second question: whether the forms are *useful*. And again I shall answer, yes and no.

While no configuration ever matches a real organization perfectly, some do come remarkably close; examples include the highly regulated Swiss hotel and the free-wheeling Silicon Valley innovator. Just as species exist in nature in response to distinct ecological niches, so, too, do configurations evolve in human society. The hotel guest does not want surprises—no jack-in-the-box popping up when the pillow is lifted, thank you—just the predictability of that wake-up call at 8:00, not 8:07. But in that niche called advertising, the client that gets no surprises may well take its business elsewhere.

My basic point about configuration is simple: when the form fits, the organization may be well advised to wear it, at least for a time. With configuration, an organization achieves a sense of order, of integration. There is internal consistency, synergy among processes, fit with the external context. It is the organization without configuration, much like the individual without personality, that tends to suffer the identity crises.

Outsiders also appreciate configuration; it helps them to understand an organization. We walk into a McDonald's and know immediately what drives it, likewise a 3M. But more important is what configuration does for the managers: it makes the organization more manageable.

With the course set, it is easier to steer, and also to deflect pressures that are peripheral. No configuration is perfect—the professional one, for example, tends to belittle its clients, while the machine one often alienates its workers—but there is something to be said for consistency. Closely controlled workers may not be happier than the autonomous ones of the professional organization, but they are certainly better off than ones confused by quality circles in the morning and time studies in the afternoon. Better to have the definition and discipline of configuration than to dissipate one's energies trying to be all things to all people.

Moreover, much of what we know about organizations in practice applies to specific configurations. There may not be any one best way, but there are certainly preferred ways in particular contexts—for example, time studies in machine organizations and matrix structures in adhocracies.

Thus configuration seems to be effective for classification, for comprehension, for diagnosis, and for design. But only so long as everything holds still. Introduce the dynamics of evolutionary change and, sooner or later, configuration becomes ineffective.

Contamination by Configuration. In harmony, consistency, and fit lies configuration's great strength—and also its debilitating weakness. Experience shows that the dominant force sometimes dominates to the point of undermining all the others. For example, the quest for efficiency in a machine organization can almost totally suppress the capacity for innovation, while in an adhocracy the need for some modicum of efficiency often gets suppressed. I call this phenomenon *contamination*, although we might just as easily rephrase Lord Acton's dictum: among the forces of organizations, too, power tends to corrupt and absolute power corrupts absolutely. For example, the story of medical care in the United States could well be described as the contamination of efficiency by proficiency. No one can deny the primacy of proficiency—who would go to a hospital that favors efficiency?—but few people would defend the extent to which it has been allowed to dominate.

Machine organizations recognize this problem when they locate their research and development facilities far from the head office so that their capacity for innovation will not be contaminated by the technocratic staff. Unfortunately, while lead may block X-rays, there is no known medium to shield the effects of a dominant culture. (The controller drops by, just to have a look: "What, no shoes? Can't they be creative dressed properly?") Of course, the opposite case is also well known. Just ask its members, "Who's the most miserable person in an adhocracy?" as I do in workshops with them. The inevitable reply is a brief silence followed by a few smiles, then growing laughter as everyone turns to some poor person cowering in the corner. Of course, it's the controller. Controllers may wear shoes, but that hardly helps them keep the lid on all the madness.

"Contamination" is another way of saying that a configuration is not merely a structure, not even merely a power system: each is a culture in its own right. Of course, contamination may seem like a small price to pay for being coherently organized. True enough. Until things go out of control.

Configuration out of Control. A configuration is geared not only to a general context but also to specific conditions—for example, a particular leader in an entrepreneurial organization, or a particular product and market in a machine one. Thus, when the need arises for change, the dominating force may act to hold the organization in place. Then other forces must come into play. But because of contamination, the other forces may well be too weak. And so the organization goes out of control. For example, a machine organization in need of a new strategy

may find neither the direction of an entrepreneurial leader nor the innovation of intrapreneurial subordinates. And so its internal consistency is perpetuated while it falls increasingly out of touch with its context.

In addition, each configuration is capable of driving itself out of control. That is to say, each contains the seeds of its own destruction. These reside in its dominating force and come into play through the effects of contamination. With too much proficiency in a professional organization, unconstrained by efficiency and direction, the professionals become overindulged (as in many of today's universities, not to mention medicine); with too much technocratic regulation in a machine organization, free of the force for innovation, an obsession with control arises (as in far too much contemporary industry and government).

My colleagues Danny Miller and Manfred Kets de Vries have published an interesting book about *The Neurotic Organization.* [5] They discuss organizations that become dramatic, paranoid, schizoid, compulsive, and depressive. In each case, a system that may once have been healthy has run out of control. Very roughly, I believe these five organizational neuroses correspond to what tends to happen to each of the five forms. The entrepreneurial organization tends to go out of control by becoming dramatic, as its leader, free of the other forces, takes the system off on a personal ego trip. The machine organization seems predisposed to compulsion once its analysts and their technocratic controls take over. Those who have worked in universities and hospitals understand the collective paranoid tendencies of professionals, especially when free of the constraining forces of administration and innovation. I need not dwell on the depressive effects of obsession with the "bottom line" in the diversified organization; the impact on morale and innovation are now widely appreciated. As for the adhocracy organization, its problem is that, while it must continually innovate, it must also exploit the benefits of that innovation. One requires divergent thinking, the other convergent. Other forces help balance that tension; without them, the organization can easily become schizoid.

In effect, each form goes over the edge in its own particular way, so that behaviours that were once functional become dysfunctional when pursued to excess. Alongside excellence go the "perils of excellence." [6] This is easily seen on our pentagon. Remove all the arrows but one at any node, and the organization, no longer anchored, flies off in that direction.

Containment of Configuration. Thus I conclude that truly effective organizations do not exist in pure form. What keeps a configuration effective is not only the dominance of a single force but also the constraining effects of other forces. I call this *containment*. For example, people inclined to break the rules may feel hard pressed in the machine organization. But without some of them, the organization may be unable to deal with unexpected problems. Similarly, administration may not be powerful in the professional organization; but, if it is allowed to atrophy, anarchy inevitably results. Thus to manage configuration effectively is to exploit one form but also to reconcile different forces. But how does the effective organization deal with this contradiction?

Combination

Configuration is a good thing when you can have it. Unfortunately, some organizations all of the time, and all organizations some of the time, *cannot*. They must instead balance competing forces.

Consider the symphony orchestra. Proficiency is clearly a critical force, but so, too, is direction: such an organization is not conceivable without highly skilled players as well as leadership from a strong conductor. The Russians apparently tried a leaderless orchestra shortly after the revolution, but soon gave it up.

I shall use the word *combination* for the orga-nization that balances different forces. In effect, it does not make it near any one node of the pentagon but instead finds its place somewhere inside.

How common are combinations as compared with configurations? To some extent the answer lies in the eyes of the beholder: what looks like a relatively pure form to one person (a lumper) may look like a combination of forces to another (a splitter). Still, it is interesting to consider how organizations appear to intelligent observers. For several years now, we have sent McGill MBA students out to study organizations in the Montreal area, having first exposed them to, among other things, a book of mine on the five forms of structure. At year end, I have circulated a questionnaire asking them to categorize the organization as one of the forms, a combination of two or more, or neither. In just over half the cases—66 out of 123—the students felt that a single form fit best. They identified 25 entrepreneurial, 13 machine, 11 diversified, nine adhocracy, and eight professional organizations. All the rest were labeled combinations—17 different ones in all. Diversified machines were the most common (nine), followed by innovative professionals (eight), entrepreneurial professionals (six), and entrepreneurial machines (five). [7]

Kinds of Combinations. Combinations themselves may take a variety of forms. They may balance just two forces or several; these forces may meet directly or indirectly; and the balance may be steady over time or oscillate back and forth.

When only two of the five forces meet in rough balance, the organization might be described as a *hybrid*. This is the case with the symphony orchestra, which can be found somewhere along the line between the entrepreneurial and professional forms. Organizations can, of course, combine several forces in rough balance as well.

Consider Apple Computers. It seems to have developed under its founder, Steve Jobs, largely as an adhocracy organization that emphasized new product development. The next CEO, John Sculley, apparently felt the need to temper that innovation; he paid more attention to efficiency in production and distribution. When I presented this framework at an executive program a couple of years ago, an employee of Apple Canada saw other things going on in his operation: he added an entrepreneurial form in sales due to a dynamic leader, professional forms in marketing and training to reflect the skills there, and another adhocracy form in a new venture unit. Organizations that experience such multiple combinations are, of course, the ones that must really play LEGO.

Then there is the question of how the different forces interact with each other. In some cases, they confront each other directly; in others, they can be separated over time or place. The combination in the symphony orchestra must be close and pervasive—leadership and professional skill meet regularly, face to face. In organizations like Apple, however, where different units favor different forces, they can act somewhat independently. And some organizations are lucky enough to buffer the effects of the different forces; in newspapers, the more professional editorial function simply hands over its camera-ready copy to the machinelike plant for production, and there is little need for interaction.

Finally, contrasting with the combinations maintained continuously are those that achieve balance in a dynamic equilibrium over time. In other words, power oscillates between the competing forces. Richard Cyert and James March wrote some years ago about the "sequential attention to goals" in organizations, where conflicting needs are attended to each in their own turn. [8] For example, a period of innovation to emphasize new product development might be followed by one of consolidation to rationalize product lines. (Might Apple Computers simply be in one of these cycles, the innovation of Jobs having been replaced by the consolidation of Sculley? Or will Sculley himself be able to get the organization to balance these two forces?)

Cleavage in Combinations.   Necessary as it may sometimes be, all is not rosy in the world of combination. If configuration encourages contamination, which can drive the organization out of control, then combination encourages *cleavage,* which can have much the same effect. Instead of one force dominating, two or more forces confront each other and eventually paralyze the organization.

In effect, a natural fault line exists between any two opposing forces. Pushed to the limit, fissures begin to open up. In fact, Fellini made a film with exactly this theme. Called "Orchestra Rehearsal," it is about musicians who revolt against their conductor, and so bring on complete anarchy, followed by paralysis. Only then are they prepared to cooperate with their leader, because only then do they realize he is necessary to perform effectively. But one need not turn to allegories to find examples of cleavage. It occurs in most combinations—for example, in the classic battles between the R&D people, who promote new product innovation, and the production people, who want to stabilize manufacturing for operating efficiency. Cleavage can, of course, be avoided when the different forces are naturally buffered, as in the newspaper example. But few combination organizations are so fortunate.

I have discussed combination as if it is unavoidable in certain organizations, but implied that configuration is advantageous where possible, because it is more easily managed. But in reality, combination of one kind or another is necessary in every organization. The nodes of the pentagon, where the pure configurations lie, are only imaginary ideals. Indeed, any organization that reaches one is probably on its way out of control. It is the inside of the pentagon that has the space; that is where the effective organization must find its place. Some may fall close to one of the nodes, as configuration, *more or less,* while others may sit between nodes as combinations. But ultimately, configuration and combination are not so very different: one represents a tilt in favor of one force over others, the other more of a balance between forces. The question thus becomes again: how does the effective organization deal with the contradiction?

Conversion

So far our discussion has suggested that an organization finds its place in the pentagon and then stays there, more or less. But, in fact, few organizations get the chance to spend their entire lives in one place: their needs change, and they must undergo *conversion* from one configuration or combination to another.

Any number of external changes can cause such a conversion. An adhocracy organization may chance upon a great invention and settle down in machine form to exploit it. Or the stable market of a machine organization may suddenly become subject to so much change that it has to become innovative. Some conversions are, of course, temporary; the machine organization in trouble, for example, becomes entrepreneurial for a time to allow a forceful leader to impose new direction (so-called turnaround). This seems to describe Chrysler's experience when Iacocca arrived, as well as SAS's when Carlzon took over.

Cycles of Conversion.   Of particular interest here is another type of conversion, which is somewhat predictable in nature because it is driven by forces intrinsic to the organization. Earlier I discussed the seeds of destruction contained in each configuration. Sometimes they destroy the organization, but sometimes they destroy only the configuration and drive the organization toward a more viable form. For example, the entrepreneurial form is inherently vulnerable, dependent as it is on a single leader. It may work well for the young organization, but with aging and growth the need for direction may be displaced by the need for efficiency. Then conversion to the machine form becomes

necessary—the power of one leader must be replaced by that of numerous administrators.

The implication is that organizations often go through stages as they develop—if they develop—possibly sequenced into life cycles. In fact, I have placed the forces and forms on the pentagon to reflect the most common of these, with the simple, earlier stages near the top and the more complex ones lower down.

What appears to be the most common life cycle, especially in business, occurs around the left side of the figure. Organizations generally begin in the entrepreneurial form, because startup requires clear direction and attracts strong leaders. As these organizations grow, many settle into the machine form to exploit increasingly established markets. But with greater growth, established markets can become saturated, which often drives the successful organization to diversify its markets and then divisionalize its structure, taking it finally to the bottom left of the pentagon.

Those organizations highly dependent on expertise, however, will instead go down the right side of the pentagon, using the professional form if their services are more standardized and the adhocracy form if they are more innovative. (Some adhocracies eventually settle down by converting to the professional form, where they can exploit certain of the skills they have developed; this happens often in the consulting business, for example.)

Ideology is shown above politics on the pentagon because it tends to be associated with the earlier stages of an organization's life, politics with the later ones. Any organization can, of course, have a strong culture, just as any can become politicized. But ideologies develop rather more easily in young organizations, especially with charismatic leadership in the entrepreneurial stage, whereas it is extremely difficult to build a strong and lasting culture in a mature organization. Politics, in contrast, typically spreads as the energy of a youthful organization dissipates and its activities become more diffuse.

Moreover, ideologies tend to dissipate over time, as norms rigidify into procedures and beliefs become rules; then political activity tends to rise in its place. Typically, the old and spent organizations are the most politicized; indeed, it is often their political conflict that finally kills them.

Cleavage in Conversion.   Conversions may be necessary, but that does not make them easy. Some do occur quickly, because a change is long overdue, much as a supersaturated liquid, below the freezing point, solidifies the moment it is disturbed. But most conversions require periods of prolonged and agonizing transition. Two sides battle, usually an old guard committed to the status quo and young "upstarts" in favor of the change. As Apple Computer grew large, for example, a John Sculley intent on settling it down confronted a Steve Jobs who wished to maintain its freewheeling style of innovation.

The organization in transition becomes, of course, a form of combination, and it has the same problem of cleavage. Given that the challenge is to the very base of its power, however, there can be no recourse to higher authority to reconcile the conflict. Once again, then, the question arises: how does the effective organization deal with the contradiction?

Contradiction

The question of how to manage contradiction has concluded each section of this article. I believe the answer lies in the two forces in the middle of the pentagon. Organizations that have to reconcile contradictory forces, especially in dealing with change, often turn to the cooperative force of ideology or to the competitive force of politics. Indeed, I believe that these two forces themselves represent a contradiction that must be managed if an organization is not to run out of control.

I have placed these two forces in the middle of the pentagon for a particular reason. While it is true that each can dominate an organization, and so draw it toward a distinct form (referred to earlier as ideological and political), I believe that these forces more commonly act differently from the other five. While the other forces tend to infiltrate parts of the organization, and so isolate them, these tend instead to *infuse* the entire organization. Thus I refer to them as *catalytic,* noting that one tends to be centripetal, drawing behavior inward toward a common core, and the other centrifugal, driving behavior away from any central tendency. I shall argue that both can promote change and also prevent it, and that either way the organization is sometimes rendered more effective, sometimes less.

Cooperation through Ideology.   Ideology represents the force for cooperation in an organization, for collegiality and consensus. People pull together for the common good—"we" are in this together.

I use the word ideology here to describe a rich culture in an organization, the uniqueness and attractiveness of which binds the members tightly to it. They commit themselves personally to the organization and identify with its needs.

Such an ideology can infuse any form of organization. It is often found in the entrepreneurial form, because, as already noted, organizational ideologies are usually created by charismatic leaders. But after such leaders move on, these ideologies can sustain themselves in other forms, too. Thus we have the ideological machine that is McDonald's and perhaps an ideological adhocracy built by Messrs. Hewlett and Packard. And one study some years ago described colleges such as Swarthmore and Antioch as "distinctive," in other words professional forms infused with powerful ideologies. [9]

Ideology encourages the members of an organization to look inward—to take their lead from the organization's own vision, instead of looking outward to what comparable organizations are doing. (Of course, when ideology is strong, there are no comparable organizations!) A good example of this is Hewlett-Packard's "next bench syndrome": the product designer receives his or her stimulus for innovation, not from the aggregations of marketing research reports but from the needs of a particular colleague at the next bench.

This looking inward is represented on the pentagon by the direction of the arrows of cooperation. They form a circle facing inward, as if to shield the organization from outside influences. Ideology above all draws people to work together to take the organization where all of them believe it must go. In this sense, ideology should be thought of as the spirit of an organization, the life force that infuses the skeleton of its formal structure.

Thus the existence of an ideology would seem to render any particular configuration more effective. People get fired up to pursue efficiency, or proficiency, or whatever else drives the organization. When this happens to a machine organization—as in a McDonald's, which is very responsive to its customers and very sensitive to its employees—I like to call it a "snappy machine." Bureaucratic machines are not supposed to be snappy, but ideology changes the nature of their quest for efficiency. This, of course, is the central message of the Peters and Waterman book, *In Search of Excellence*: effectiveness is achieved, not by opportunism, not even by clever strategic positioning, but by a management that knows exactly what it must do ("sticks to its knitting") and then does it with the fervor of religious missionaries ("hands on, value driven"). [10]

There seems to be another important implication: ideology helps an organization to manage contradiction and so to deal with change. The different forces no longer need conflict in quite the same way. Infused with the common ideology, units used to opposing each other can instead pull together, reducing contamination and cleavage and so facilitating adaptation.

I have always wondered why it is that IBM could come up with the important change when it had to, much like McDonald's, so machine-like, yet rather creative in its advertising and new product development. Likewise, if 3M and Hewlett-Packard really do conform largely to the adhocracy model, why do they have such tight control systems? I suspect we have the answer here. Their strong cultures enable these organizations to reconcile forces that work against each other in ordinary organizations. People develop a grudging respect for one another: when it matters, they cooperate for the common good. "Old Joe, over there, that nut in R&D: we production guys sometimes wonder about him. But we know this place could never function without him." Likewise in the great symphony orchestra, the musicians respect their conductor, without whom they know they could never produce beautiful music.

Such organizations can more easily reconcile opposing forces because what matters to their people is the organization itself, not any of its particular parts. If you believe in IBM more than marketing finesse or technical virtuosity per se, then when things really matter you will suspend your departmental rivalries to enable IBM to adapt.

In *Competitive Strategy*, Michael Porter warns about getting "stuck in the middle" between a strategy of "cost leadership" and one of "differentiation" (one representing the force for efficiency, the other representing quality and innovation). [11] How, then, has Toyota been able to produce such high-quality automobiles at such reasonable cost? Why didn't Toyota get stuck in the middle?

I believe that Porter's admonition stems from the view, prevalent in U.S. management circles throughout this century and reflected equally in my discussion of configuration, that if an organization favors one particular force, then others must suffer. If the efficiency experts have the upper hand, then quality gets slighted; if the designers get their way, productive efficiency must lag; and so on. This may be true so long as an organization is managed as a collection of different parts—a portfolio of products and functions.

But when the spirit of ideology infuses the structure, an organization takes on an integrated life of its own, and contradictions get reconciled.

Thanks to Frederick Taylor and Henry Ford, workers on U.S. assembly lines have long had good reason to consider themselves mere cogs in their bureaucratic machines. Each had a job to do and was not to think about anything else—including quality and innovation. Indeed, even at the highest levels, this separation of functions has had its effect: critics of General Motors continue to bemoan the product development consequences of having had all those financial people in the chief executive's chair. But at Toyota, one has the impression that each individual is made to feel like an embodiment of the entire system—that no matter what job one does, it helps to make Toyota great. Isn't that why the assembly workers are allowed to shut down the line? Each one is treated as a person capable of making decisions for the good of Toyota. Thus the only thing that gets stuck in the middle at Toyota is the conventional management thinking of the West!

So far I have discussed the reconciliation of contradictions between different people and units. But even more powerful can be the effect of reconciling these forces within individuals themselves. Where ideology is strong, not just the researchers are responsible for innovation, nor the accountants for efficiency; everyone internalizes the different forces in carrying out his or her own job. In metaphorical terms, it is easy to change hats if they are all emblazoned with the same insignia.

Limits to Cooperation.   Overall, then, ideology sounds like a wonderful thing. But all is not rosy in the world of culture, either. For one thing, ideologies are difficult to build, especially in established organizations, and difficult to sustain once built. For another thing, established ideologies can sometimes get in the way of organizational effectiveness.

The impression left by a good deal of current writing and consulting notwithstanding, ideology is not there for the taking, to be plucked off the tree of management technology like any other piece of fashionable fruit. As Karl Weick has argued, "A corporation doesn't *have* a culture. A corporation *is* a culture. That's why they're so horribly difficult to change." [12] The fact is that there are no five easy steps to a better culture. At best, those steps lay down a thin veneer of impressions that wash off in the first political storm; at worst, they destroy whatever good remains in the prevailing culture. Effective ideologies are built slowly and patiently by committed leaders who establish compelling missions for their organizations, nurture them carefully, and care deeply about the people who make them work.

But even after an ideology is established, the time can come—and usually does eventually—when its effect is to render the organization ineffective, sometimes to the point of destroying it. This is suggested by Weick's comment that ideologies are "so horribly difficult to change."

I argued above that ideology promotes change by allowing an organization to reconcile contradictory forces. Now I should like to argue exactly the opposite case. Ideology discourages change by forcing everyone to work within the same set of beliefs. In other words, strong cultures are immutable: they may promote change within their own boundaries, but they themselves are not to be changed. Receiving "the word" enables people to ask every question but one: the word itself must never be questioned.

I can explain this by introducing two views of strategy, one as position, the other as perspective. [13] In one case, the organization looks down to specific product-market positions (as depicted in Michael Porter's work), in the other it looks up to a general philosophy of functioning (as in Peter Drucker's earlier writings about the "concept of a business"). I like to ask people in my management seminars whether Egg McMuffin was a strategic change for McDonald's. Some argue yes, of course, because it brought the firm into the breakfast market. Others dismiss this as a variation in product line—pure McDonald's, just different ingredients in a new package. Their disagreement concerns not the change at McDonald's so much as their implicit definition of strategy. To the former, strategy is position (the breakfast market), to the latter it is perspective (the McDonald's way). The important point here is that change of position *within* perspective is easy to accomplish (the McDonald's way, but now for breakfast), whereas change of perspective (a new way, that is, a new ideology) is extremely difficult. (Anyone for McDuckling a l'Orange?) The very ideology that makes an organization so adaptive within its own niche undermines efforts to move it to a different niche.

Thus, when change of a fundamental nature must be made—in strategy, structure, form, whatever—the ideology that may for so long have been the key to the organization's effectiveness suddenly becomes its central problem. Ideology becomes a force for the status quo; indeed, because those who perceive the need for change are forced to challenge it, the ideology begins to breed politics!

To understand this negative effect of ideology, take another look at Figure 2. All those arrows face inward. The halo they form may protect the organization, but at the possible expense of isolating it from the outside world. In other words, ideology can cause the other forces to atrophy: direction comes to be interpreted in terms of an outmoded system of beliefs, forcing efficiency, proficiency, and innovation into ever-narrower corners. As the other arrows of the figure disappear, those of ideology close in on the organization, causing it to *implode*. That is how the organization dominated by the force of ideology goes out of control. It isolates itself and eventually dies. We have no need for the extreme example of a Jonestown to appreciate this negative consequence of ideology. We all know organizations with strong cultures that, like that proverbial bird, flew in ever-diminishing circles until they disappeared up their own rear ends.

Competition through Politics.   If the centripetal force of ideology, ostensibly so constructive, turns out to have a negative consequence, then perhaps the centrifugal force of politics, ostensibly so destructive, has a positive one.

Politics represents the force for competition within an organization—for conflict and confrontation. People pull apart for their own needs. "They" get in "our" way.

Politics can infuse any of the configurations or combinations, exacerbating contamination and cleavage. Indeed, both problems were characterized as intrinsically conflictive in the first place; the presence of politics for other reasons simply enhances them. The people behind the dominant force in a configuration—say, the accountants in a machine organization, or the experts in a professional one—lord their power over everyone else, while those behind each of the opposing forces in a hybrid relish any opportunity to do battle with each other to gain advantage. Thus, in contrast to a machinelike Toyota pulling together is the Chrysler Iaccoca first encountered, pulling apart; the ideology of an innovative Hewlett-Packard stands in contrast to the politics of a NASA during the Challenger tragedy. For every college that is distinctive, there are others that are destructive.

Politics is generally a parochial force in organizations, encouraging people to pursue their own ends. Infusing the parts of an organization with the competitive force of politics thus reinforces their tendency to fly off in different directions. At the limit, the organization dominated by politics goes out of control by *exploding*. Nothing remains at the core—no central direction, no integrating ideology, and, therefore, no directed effort at efficiency or proficiency or innovation.

In this respect, politics may be a more natural force than ideology. That is to say, organizations left alone seem to pull apart rather more easily than they pull together. Getting human beings to cooperate seems to require continual effort on the part of a dedicated management.

Benefits of Competition.   But we cannot dismiss politics as merely divisive. Politics' constructive role in organizations is suggested by the very problems of ideology. If pulling together discourages people from addressing fundamental change, then pulling apart may be the only way to ensure that they do.

Most organizations have a deeply rooted status quo, reinforced especially by the forces of efficiency, proficiency, and ideology, all designed to promote development *within an established perspective.* Thus, to achieve fundamental change in an organization, especially one that has achieved configuration and, moreover, is infused with ideology, the established forces must be challenged, and that means politics. In the absence of entrepreneurial or intrapreneurial capabilities, and sometimes despite them, politics may be the only force capable of stimulating the change. The organization must, in other words, pull apart before it can pull together again. It appears to be inevitable that a great deal of the most significant change is driven, not by managerial insight or specialized expertise or ideological commitment, let alone the procedures of planning, but by political challenge.

I conclude that both politics and ideology can promote organizational effectiveness as well as undermine it. Ideology infused into an organization can be a force for revitalization, energizing the system and making its people more responsive. But that same ideology can also hinder fundamental change. Likewise, politics often impedes necessary change and wastes valuable resources. But political challenge may also be the only means to promote really fundamental change. Thus there remains one last contradiction to reconcile, that between ideology and politics themselves.

Combining Cooperation and Competition.
The two catalytic forces of ideology and politics are themselves contradictory forces that have to be reconciled if an organization is to remain truly effective in the long run. Pulling together

ideologically infuses life into an organization; pulling apart politically challenges the status quo; only by encouraging both can an organization sustain its viability. The centripetal force of ideology must contain and in turn be contained by the centrifugal force of politics. That is how an organization can keep itself from imploding or exploding—from isolating itself, on the one hand, and going off in all directions, on the other. Moreover, maintaining a balance between these two forces—in their own form of combination—can discourage the other forces from going out of control. Ideology helps secondary forces to contain a dominant one; politics encourages them to challenge it. All of this is somewhat reminiscent of that old children's game (with extended rules!): paper (ideology) covers scissors (politics) and can also help cover rocks (the force for efficiency), while scissors cut paper and can even wedge rocks out of their resting places.

Let me turn one last time to the arrows of the pentagon. Imagine first the diverging arrows of competition contained within the converging circle of cooperation. Issues are debated and people are challenged, but only within the existing culture. The two achieve an equilibrium, as in the case of the Talmudic scholars who fight furiously with each other over the interpretation of every word in their ancient books, yet close ranks to present a united front to the outside world. Is that not the very behavior we find in some of our most effective business corporations, IBM among others? Or reverse the relationship and put the arrows pulling apart outside those of the halo pulling together. Outside challenges keep a culture from closing in on itself.

Thus I believe that only through achieving some kind of balance of these two catalytic forces can an organization maintain its effectiveness. That balance need not, however, be steady state. Quite the contrary. It should constitute a dy·amic equilibrium over time, to avoid constant tension between ideology and politics. Most of the time, the cooperative pulling together of ideology, contained by a healthy internal competition, is to be preferred, so the organization can vigorously pursue its established strategic perspective. But occasionally, when fundamental change becomes necessary, the organization has to be able to pull apart through the competitive force of politics. That seems to be the best combination of these two forces.

Conclusion

What is it, then, that makes an organization effective? Of course, were the answer easy—and easily applied—all organizations would be equally effective. Clearly, to be effective means to do the right thing and to do it right—to be both "Porterian" and "Peterian." But I have argued that there is more to organizational effectiveness than this, that the answer must also lie in managing the consistency of form as well as the contradiction of forces. Organizations need focus, but they also need balance. The prescriptions of this article perhaps reduce to the following.

Attain configuration if you can. Getting everything together into a known form, if it all fits, more or less, is not a bad way to organize. One force can dominate just so long as you attend to the other forces, too, to avoid contamination. Otherwise, build a combination if you must, or if you can benefit from the balance of forces. But then be careful about cleavage. And whichever it is, watch out for the occasional need for conversion, during which you must also be careful of cleavage. No matter what, you will still have to manage contradiction. Thus it is critical that you infuse your organization with the cooperative force of ideology, to make it excellent. But beware of that force going out of control, too. Encourage healthy competition, occasionally even outright politics, to ensure needed adaptation. Just be sure to balance ideology and politics in their own dynamic equilibrium.

Of course, this may sound like my own "best

way." But it is not a simple way, nor should it encourage conformity. Playing jigsaw puzzle and LEGO with the same pieces is no easy matter. But that is what effective organizations seem to do.

References

1. See T. S. Peters and R. H. Waterman. *In Search of Excellence.* New York: Harper & Row, 1982. Also, M. E. Porter. *Competitive Strategy: Techniques for Analyzing Industries and Competitors.* New York: Free Press, 1980.

2. See H. Mintzberg. *The Structuring of Organizations.* Englewood Cliffs, NJ: Prentice Hall, 1979. And *Mintzberg on Management.* New York: Free Press, 1989. See also: D. Miller and H. Mintzberg. "The Case for Configuration," in *Organizations: A Quantum View."* eds. D. Miller and P. H. Friesen. Englewood Cliffs, NJ: Prentice Hall, 1984.

3. C. Darwin. *The Life and Letters of Charles Darwin.* ed. F. Darwin. London: John Murray, 1887, p. 105.

4. The first five forms were described in some detail, under slightly different labels, in Mintzberg (1979). The last two forms were developed in H. Mintzberg. *Power In and Around Organizations.* Englewood Cliffs, NJ: Prentice Hall, 1983.

5. D. Miller and M. Kets de Vries. *The Neurotic Organization.* San Francisco: Jossey-Bass, 1984. See also: D. Miller and M. Kets de Vries. *Unstable at the Top.* New York: New American Library, 1987.

6. See D. Miller. *The Icarus Paradox.* New York: Harper & Row, 1990.

7. One might think that the high incidence of entrepreneurial forms reflects the students' bias toward studying small organizations, but I think not. Many more small organizations exist, in business and elsewhere, than large ones, and they are usually entrepreneurial. I would expect the larger ones to be predominantly machine in form in any western society. As for the incidence of combinations, I believe that the diversified and adhocracy forms are the most

difficult to sustain (the former is a conglomerate with no links between the divisions, the latter is a very loose and free-wheeling structure), and so these should be most common in hybrid combinations. Also, some of the combinations reflect common transitions in organizations, especially from the entrepreneurial to the machine form.

8. R. M. Cyert and J. G. March. *A Behavioral Theory of the Firm.* Englewood Cliffs, NJ: Prentice Hall, 1963.

9. B. R. Clark. *The Distinctive College.* Chicago: Aldine, 1970.

10. Peters and Waterman (1982).

11. Porter (1980).

12. Quoted in W. Kiechel III. "Sniping at Strategic Planning (Interview with Himself)." *Planning Review,* May 1984, p. 11.

13. See H. Mintzberg. "Five Ps for Strategy." *California Management Review,* Fall 1987, pp. 11–24.